# DECORATIVE ARTS

# DECORATIVE ARTS

### JUDITH MILLER

A Dorling Kindersley Book

## LONDON, NEW YORK, MELBOURNE, MUNICH AND DELHI

### A joint production from DK and
### THE PRICE GUIDE COMPANY

#### DORLING KINDERSLEY LIMITED
**Senior Editor** Angela Wilkes
**Senior Art Editor** Mandy Earey
**Editors** Anna Fischel, David Tombesi-Walton,
Sylvia Tombesi-Walton, Diana Vowles
**Art Editors** Ian Spick, Simon Murrell, Victoria Short
**Managing Editor** Julie Oughton
**Managing Art Editors** Christine Keilty,
Heather McCarry
**Art Director** Bryn Walls
**Creative Publisher** Jonathan Metcalf
**Publishing Director** Jackie Douglas
**Production** Linda Dare
**DTP Designer** Adam Walker
**Picture Library** Richard Dabb

#### THE PRICE GUIDE COMPANY LIMITED
**Publishing Manager** Julie Brooke
**Editorial Assistants** Jessica Bishop, Sandra Lange,
Carolyn Malarkey, Karen Morden
**Digital Image Co-ordinator** Ellen Sinclair
**Picture Research** Liz Moore

#### CONTRIBUTORS
**Chief Contributor** Daniel Dunlavey
**Contributors** Simon Adams, Theresa Bebbington,
Anna Fischel, Albert Hill, Frankie Leibe, Alycen Mitchell,
Anna Southgate, John Wainwright

First published in Great Britain in 2006 by
Dorling Kindersley Limited
80 Strand, London WC2R 0RL

A Penguin Company

The Price Guide Company (UK) Ltd
info@thepriceguidecompany.com

2 4 6 8 10 9 7 5 3 1

A CIP catalogue record for this book is available
from the British Library.

ISBN-13: 978 1 4053 1290 5
ISBN-10: 1 4053 1290 4

Colour reproduction by Colourscan, Singapore

Printed and bound in China
by Leo Paper Products Ltd

Discover more at
**www.dk.com**

# FOREWORD

The desire to decorate our homes is centuries old. From a prehistoric caveman painting the walls of his cave, to an 18th century aristocrat collecting the new European porcelain, to the late 20th-century desire for individualism and design, the objects we surround ourselves with make our homes our own.

I have always been fascinated by the influences on these decorative arts and their stylistic changes, as well as the stories of the craftsmen and designers who have influenced the course of style through the decades. This book tells those stories and explains the impact they had around the world. This tradition of craftsmanship goes back to ancient Greece and Rome, can be seen in the delicate porcelain figures of Johann Joachim Kändler at Meissen in the 1730s and 40s, the glass of Émile Gallé at the end of the 19th century, the exquisite Rookwood vases painted by Kataro Shirayamadani, and the furniture of Senior and Carmichael, as shown in the desk on the right, in the early years of the 21st century.

As technology developed mass production became possible and many of the decorative arts from the past 200 years reflect this. Factory-made ceramics in the mid-19th century, like the Rococo Revival vase on the left, enabled thousands of newly affluent middle class families to share the decorative possibilities that had, until then, been available only to the wealthy few. The decorative arts became central to all our lives. In the late 20th century even the humble corkscrew gained a design aesthetic which brought it into the realm of decorative art.

I hope that you find the story of the decorative arts as intriguing as I do and that this book will give you a lifelong interest in the styles and history of this fascinating subject.

Judith Miller.

# CONSULTANTS

**Paul Atterbury**
Freelance writer and lecturer specializing in 19th- and 20th-century art and design, particularly ceramics *Age of Excess*

**John Axford**
Director, Woolley & Wallis Fine Art Auctioneers, Salisbury, Wiltshire *Ceramics 1700–1900*

**Keith Baker**
Consultant and valuer *Arts and Crafts, Art Nouveau*

**Lynda Cain**
Vice President American Furniture & Decorative Arts, Samuel T. Freeman and Co., Philadelphia *Folk Art*

**Dudley Browne**
Lamp and Glass Division, James D. Julia Inc., Fairfield, Maine *Age of Excess, Arts and Crafts, Art Nouveau*

**Max Donnelly**
The Fine Art Society, London *The Aesthetic Movement, The Glasgow School, Christopher Dresser*

**Dr Graham Dry**
Jugendstil and Art Deco specialist, Von Zezschwitz Kunst und Design, Munich *Art Nouveau, Birth of Modernism, Art Deco*

**Yves Gastou**
Galerie Yves Gastou, Paris *Art Nouveau, Art Deco, Mid-century Modern, Postmodern and Contemporary*

**Dr Henrietta Graaf**
Furniture historian and lecturer at the Technical University of Munich *Furniture 1700 to the present day*

**Jeanette Hayhurst**
Jeanette Hayhurst Fine Glass, London *Glass 1700 to the present day*

**Mark Hill**
20th-century specialist *Mid-century Modern, Postmodern and Contemporary*

**Liz Klein**
Consultant and collector's agent specializing in 20th-century decorative arts *Mid-century Modern*

**Maître Lefèvre**
Maison de Ventes Beaussant-Lefèvre, Paris *France 1700–1900*

**Nicholas Lowry**
President and Poster Specialist, Swann Auction Galleries, New York *Art Nouveau, Art Deco, Mid-century Modern Posters*

**David Rago**
Expert and Partner, Rago Auction Center, Lambertville, New Jersey *Arts and Crafts, Art Nouveau, Birth of Modernism*

**John Sollo**
Expert and Partner, Sollo:Rago Modern Auctions, Lambertville, New Jersey *Mid-century Modern*

**Hervé de la Verrie**
Head of European Ceramics and Glass department, Christie's, Paris *Ceramics 1700–1900*

**Patrick van der Vorst**
Director and Head of Continental Furniture Department, Sotheby's, London *Furniture 1700–1900*

**Professor Jonathan M. Woodham**
Director, Centre for Research Development (Arts & Architecture), University of Brighton, Sussex *Postmodern and Contemporary*

**Dr Alfred Ziffer**
Art historian and lecturer. Curator of the Nymphenburg Porcelain Bäuml Collection Editor of *Keramos* *Ceramics 1700 to the present day*

---

## PRICE BANDS

Some of the pieces in this book are accompanied by a number that gives an indication of value:

1. £100–500
2. £500–1,000
3. £1,000–2,500
4. £2,500–5,000
5. £5,000–10,000
6. £10,000–20,000
7. £20,000–50,000
8. £50,00–100,000
9. £100,000–250,000
10. £250,000 upwards

**IMAGE ON PAGE 1**
**LOÏE FULLER** Raoul Larche was known for his sculptures of dancer Loïe Fuller. As here, the gilt-bronze forms often doubled as lamps. *H:32cm (12½in)*.

**IMAGES ON PAGES 2–3**
**SWEDISH CONSOLE TABLE** Supporting a marble top, this table's giltwood frame is carved in deep relief, in Louis XV style, with a lion mask, dragons, flowers, and scrolling foliage. *c.1760. W:99cm (39in)*.

**BOHEMIAN OVERLAY GLASS** This lidded goblet made in ruby red over clear overlay glass was wheel-engraved by August Böhm with a forest landscape with a deer on the bowl and grapevines around the lid. *c.1850. H:53cm (21in)*.

**TUDRIC MANTEL CLOCK** Designed by Archibald Knox for Liberty & Co's Tudric range, it has a pewter case with stylized leaf decoration, and an enamelled dial with berry motifs and copper Arabic numerals. *c.1905. H:21cm (8½in)*.

**LORENZL FIGURE** This stylized figure is cast in bronze from a model by Josef Lorenzl and patinated with a silver finish. It has an onyx base. *H:38cm (15in)*.

**HEART CHAIR** Verner Panton's sculptural chair was inspired by the work of Arne Jacobsen. The metal frame and foam construction is fully upholstered in a bright red fabric. *1958. H:101.5cm (40in)*.

**GLASS SCULPTURE** This is made from an opaque orange half-globe and a quarter-globe in clear orange glass by Milos Balgavy. *D:25cm (9¾in)*.

**IMAGES ON PAGES 4–5**
**BALUSTER-SHAPED VASE** The scrolling form is encrusted with applied flowers in the English Rococo Revival style. *1850s. H:27cm (10¾in)*.

**VENUS DESK** Made by Senior and Carmichael for the Marchioness of Bath, the sycamore canopy of this mechanical cylinder yew desk was inspired by the scallop shell in Botticelli's painting *Birth of Venus*. *2005*.

# CONTENTS

# DECORATIVE PAST

FROM THE EARLIEST TIMES MAN HAS FELT THE NEED TO DECORATE HIS HOME. FROM CAVE PAINTINGS TO SILVER CANDELABRA, PORCELAIN FIGURES TO EAMES CHAIRS, THE WAY WE DECORATE OUR HOMES REFLECTS THE AGE WE LIVE IN.

**GREEK POTTERY** The krater was used for mixing wine with water at *symposia*, or drinking parties. The red-on-black decoration shows a figure sitting on an X-framed stool, a Classical furniture form still copied today. The Greek key pattern below the figures is a recurrent Classical motif.

## THE ANCIENT WORLD

From ancient times until fairly recently, only the wealthy could afford the decorative items needed to furnish a home. Furniture, ceramics, silver- and metalware, glass, tapestries and carpets, and sculpture were out of reach of most people.

The items people have used to beautify their homes have changed with fashion and technology – until Johann Friedrich Böttger at Meissen had discovered the formula for hard-paste porcelain in 1709, European potters had to use less refined earthenware. Meanwhile, the popularity of Classical decoration in the 18th century was fuelled by the discovery of Herculaneum (1738) and Pompeii (1748). By the early 19th century Napoleon's campaign in Egypt (1797–98) and the publication in 1802 of Baron Vivant Denon's *Aventures dans la basse et la haute Égypte* (Adventures in Low and High Egypt) inspired the fashion for the Neoclassical and, later, the Empire style.

Nationality also has its bearing on the decorative arts, dictating everything from which woods are used for furniture to the flora and fauna that inspire its decoration. The decorative arts have been with us since cavemen drew pictures of hunting on the walls of caves. But the best

**EGYPTIAN BRONZE** Called a situla, this bucket held holy water for sprinkling at religious ceremonies. It is decorated with images of gods and ancestral rulers.

records of early decoration probably come from the relics of early civilizations that have been found in the Mediterranean countries.

## EGYPTIAN CIVILIZATION

With the rise of the first great civilizations in Mesopotamia, advances such as writing and irrigation spread throughout ancient Egypt, Greece, and Rome. As early as 4,000BCE Egyptian artists had devised a series of rules governing the proper depiction of the human figure, based on a simple grid system. Combined with "frontalism", whereby heads are always shown in profile and torsos from the front, these guidelines marked the beginnings of a formal approach to art.

During the first years of the New Kingdom, from around 1,500BCE, Egypt had become a cosmopolitan place. Its citizens were wealthy enough to support a class of craftsmen. The more affluent members of society enjoyed state-of-the-art creature comforts such as headrests and boxes for cosmetics, made from native woods such as acacia, sidder, and fig, or imported cypress and cedar. The wood might be inlaid with ebony, ivory, semi-precious stones, or painted to look like them. Master craftsmen worked with teams of apprentices, acting as project managers and taking final responsibility for the results of these group efforts. Unlike the uniform style of Egyptian funereal art, decorative pieces for the home were varied, lively, and sometimes even experimental.

**VILLA OF THE MYSTERIES, POMPEII** Pompeii became a Roman colony in 80BCE, and heralded in the so-called Architectural style, which used trompe-l'oeil effects to blur reality and illusion. A screen of painted pillars on a plinth, apparently supporting a cornice, made the wall surface appear set back in space.

## GREEK ORDER

The Greeks, like the Egyptians, valued the look of their homes and possessions. It was the Greeks who first developed a uniform architecture based on "orders". The Doric, Ionic, and Corinthian orders (*see p.54*) dictated the proportions and stylistic features of every part of a building. Decorative artists from almost every historical period since have referred back to them.

Throughout the Greek world, from city-states such as Athens to the Aegean islands and the colonies of southern Italy and Sicily, specialist potters produced a range of decorative homeware. Among the earliest decorative drinking wares was the rhyton, which evolved from the use of ox horns as cups. In time, the horn was replaced with a ceramic replica, moulded or carved with an animal's head at the foot and, often, with a decorative frieze around the rim. The urge to

replicate natural forms has driven decorative artists throughout history. The rhyton was complemented by other vessels, especially the amphora, for storing oil or wine. The krater, used by the Greeks to mix wine with water for parties, was often decorated with images of Dionysus, the god of wine and inebriation. In the Roman world earthenware oil lamps were mould-cast with a variety of decorative subjects ranging from the devotional to the erotic.

## ROMAN GLASS

Evidence for the use of glass in the ancient world is widespread. The Roman historian Pliny attributed the discovery of glass to a troupe of seafaring merchants who used chunks of the saltpetre their ship was carrying to prop up their cooking pots on the beach. The cooking fire fused the sand and ashes with the saltpetre to form the first man-made glass. While this tale is impossible to verify,

archaeologists have unearthed countless examples of refined glassware from ancient times, even leading to speculation that our current mastery of the art has not yet reached the same standard.

**ROMAN GLASS** This tiny honey-coloured container is an *unguentarium*, or ointment bottle. *1st–3rd century CE. H:8.5cm (3¼in).*

## EASTERN INFLUENCE

A separate decorative art tradition evolved in the East. The sophistication of surviving artefacts from Neolithic China (4,000–2,000BCE) is far greater than anything that was produced in the West at the same time.

The ancient Chinese valued jade for its beauty and purity and had been using it for 5,000 years before Confucius said: "When I think of a wise man, his merits appear to be like jade." From the earliest days, Chinese artisans carved jade into exquisite sacrificial vessels, decorative objects, and functional tools and utensils. Even musical instruments such as flutes and chimes were made from blocks of jade. The unparalleled ritual significance of this exalted stone is demonstrated by the existence of jade burial

**ALEXANDER VASE** This rare Chinese vase from the Yuan Dynasty is painted in underglaze cobalt blue with gourd plants, relating the decoration to the double gourd shape. *Mid-14th century. H:47.5cm (18¾in).*

suits, such as that of the prince Liu Sheng, who died in 113BCE. This extraordinary suit was constructed from almost 2,500 pieces of jade sewn together with gold thread.

The next most significant material in early Chinese decorative art was bronze. During the Shang dynasty (1,700–1,027BCE) Chinese metalworkers produced a variety of decorated bronze vessels for ceremonies and banquets. These were cast in ceramic relief moulds and then carved with complex motifs. The fearsome taotie mask often appears, depicted with horns, fangs, and staring eyes.

## CHINESE PORCELAIN

The most outstanding and influential achievement of the Chinese decorative art tradition was porcelain. Fine stoneware was being produced during the Shang dynasty and, by the time of the Eastern Han, around 25CE, Chinese ceramicists had perfected hard-paste porcelain.

During the Tang dynasty (618–907CE) there was already a lively export market with the Middle East. This trade route proved especially beneficial, as it was the cobalt pigment that was imported from the Middle East which enabled Chinese ceramicists to create the first blue and white wares during the Yuan dynasty (1280–1368).

## THE BYZANTINE TRADITION

After Diocletian divided the Roman Empire in two in 286CE, the powerful Emperor Constantine founded a new capital, called Nova Roma or Constantinople, on the site of the ancient

**HAGIA SOPHIA** Embodying the spiritual side of Byzantine art, the temple's many windows allow light to play over the huge dome and columns, polychrome marbles, gold ornaments, exquisite mosaics, and calligraphy.

city of Byzantium in 330CE. This created a bridge from East to West. Byzantine art soon became a force in its own right, spurred on by the Christian zeal and economic prosperity of the new state. Constantine's son and heir, Constantius, began work on the great Christian temple known as the Hagia Sophia, which was eventually completed by Justinian I in 537CE. Considered by many to be the eighth wonder of the world, this building is among the supreme achievements of Byzantine art. The interior is decorated with mosaics and pillars of the local marble.

The decorative arts of Byzantium were often intended to educate or serve a moral purpose. Figures are depicted in stiffly formal poses, and colours tend to be bright and bold so that the

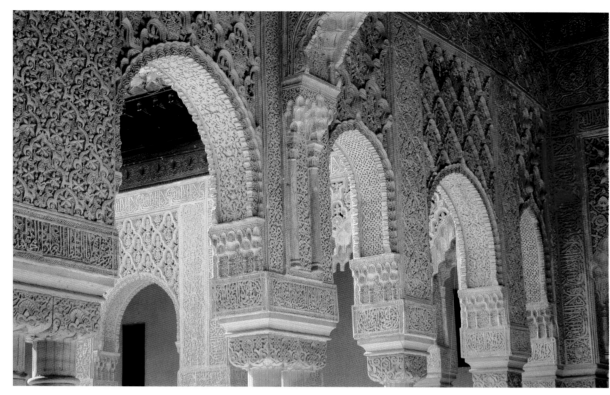

**THE ALHAMBRA** This citadel and palace in Granada, Spain, was built for Moorish kings of the 13th and 14th centuries. Its rich, abstract decoration has influenced designers ever since.

characters and stories represented can be easily recognized and understood. The role of decorative art as an educational medium, capable of bringing about a positive change in the owner or viewer, has since been explored in many historical periods.

## ISLAMIC ART

The Muslim conquest of southern Spain from the 8th century exposed Europe to Islamic art for the first time. Portraiture and any depiction of the human form were forbidden in the Koran, in case they led to idolatry – worshipping a mere likeness instead of God and the prophets. As if to compensate, early Islamic artists excelled in abstract and geometric surface decoration. Complex repeating geometric designs, often based on natural

**IZNIK DISH** The surface is decorated with two saz leaves, carnations, and tulips within a blue ammonite scroll border. *Mid- to late 16th century. D:30.5cm (12in).*

forms, are known as arabesques to this day. The religious aspect of Islamic art, and in particular its veneration of the prophet Allah, centres around the beautification of Arabic calligraphy, especially verses from the Koran. Inscriptions in highly stylized, flowing Arabic script abound in Islamic decorative art and serve the same devotional function as, for example, depictions of the crucifixion in Christian art. The many strands of early Islamic decorative art were drawn together in ambitious projects such as the Alhambra fortress in southern Spain, begun in the 13th century.

## CERAMIC ADVANCES

One of the most significant Islamic contributions to ceramics was the perfection of lustre decoration in the 9th century. This costly and complicated technique makes use of metal oxides to impart a shining metallic surface to pottery.

During the 11th century Islamic potters developed fritware in imitation of Chinese porcelain. This material was a combination of ground quartz, glass frit, and white clay. Ottoman potters produced a particularly fine type of this ware from the late 15th century. Known as Iznik pottery, it was covered in a white slip that acted as an ideal ground for further polychrome decoration.

**ENGLISH FLOOR TILE** This medieval square earthenware tile has a slip decoration of a griffin, a mythical winged creature with an eagle's head and lion's body. *W:12.5cm (5in).*

## THE MIDDLE AGES

While artisans in the Orient and the Islamic world continued to build directly on their ancient decorative traditions, something very different happened in the West. With the fall of the Roman Empire after Rome was sacked in 476CE, Western Europe was abruptly cut off from the Classical past. In its place, the first singularly European decorative style developed, known today as Gothic. Originally a distillation of influences ranging from Burgundian, Byzantine, and Islamic to Norman, the Gothic style flourished from the mid-12th century and dominated European decorative art for around 400 years. The roots of the Gothic style are ecclesiastical, and its greatest legacy is the network of extraordinary cathedrals and abbeys that dominate the landscape of northern Europe.

## GOTHIC ARCHITECTURE

The pointed arch was one of the most important architectural innovations of the period, allowing the construction of larger and more complex buildings with massive interior spaces. Such was its dominance that the pointed arch, together with associated decorative devices such as trefoils, quatrefoils, and tracery, was used extensively not just in the architecture of the Gothic period but throughout the decorative arts.

Using technical devices such as vaulting and immense flying buttresses, the architects of the Gothic cathedrals were able to fit extremely large windows, flooding the interiors with light. Combined with the predominance of primary colours and gold in the decorative scheme, the effect was striking. The Byzantine roots of Christian art are evident in the Catholic Gothic style. Both share the aim of impressing upon a largely illiterate population the glory of God and, along with it, the supreme power of the Church.

## STAINED GLASS

Of all the decorative innovations of the Gothic period, the most awe-inspiring are the great stained glass windows depicting scenes from the Bible and lives of the saints. There is evidence for the manufacture of stained glass dating back to Saxon times, but medieval craftsmen took the art to unscaled heights. Outstanding surviving examples include *Notre Dame de la Belle Verrière* (Our Lady of the Beautiful Window) at Chartres in northern France. The upper sections date from the 12th and 13th centuries and, despite their great age, the colours remain vibrant. The opulence of the church extended beyond the buildings to the sumptuous robes of the clergy and the fine metalware used during mass. These were usually of gold and silver and could even be encrusted with enamels or precious stones. Much of the most exuberant metalware was lost during the

**WINCHESTER CATHEDRAL** The pointed arches of Gothic architecture, with carved and pierced trefoil (three-leaf) and quatrefoil (four-leaf) ornament, were motifs that inspired decorative arts of the Middle Ages and later revivals.

**SILVER SPOON** This elaborately engraved and plated spoon has a stylized motif based on plant forms.

**LADY OF THE UNICORN** The most famous of the *mille-fleurs* (thousand flowers) Tournai tapestries is also the most enigmatic. It depicts an allegory involving a beautifully dressed lady, a unicorn symbolizing chastity, a tame lion, and other animals among the flowers. *Late 15th century.*

Reformation of the 16th century. This attempt to reform the Roman Catholic Church resulted in the start of the Protestant Church.

## ART FOR THE HOME

Secular art of this period was expected to be as pious as religious art, although it was often open to interpretation. A series of tapestries known as the Lady and the Unicorn group, made in Flanders during the late 15th century, represents a high point of medieval decorative art and illustrate the thin line between the sacred and the profane.

The six panels – one representing each of the senses and one entitled *À Mon Seul Désir* (My Only Desire) – can be seen either as a young woman's rejection of worldly pleasures or as a narrative depicting the seduction of a unicorn. Throughout history, designers have defied powerful regimes with similarly sophisticated subtlety and suggestion.

## INTERNATIONAL GOTHIC

Depictions of the human figure in tapestries, manuscripts, stained glass, and paintings during the Middle Ages often exaggerated courtly grace. The proportions of the body were skewed as artists elongated the limbs and necks of their subjects. Called the International Gothic style, it reached its height towards the end of the 14th century. In reaction to the attenuated proportions, many artists started to strive for a less stylized depiction. However, knowledge of anatomy was poor and this frustrated attempts to produce realistic portraits. Even so, the rigidity that characterizes so much early Christian art was slowly giving way to naturalism.

**OUR LADY OF THE BEAUTIFUL WINDOW** In Chartres cathedral in France, the use of strong primary colours made stained glass Biblical stories all the more vivid. The Virgin Mary, with Jesus on her lap, is the largest image in the windows of the nave, surrounded by lives of the saints.

## THE RENAISSANCE

The move away from extreme stylization to observing and recording nature gradually gathered pace. In the wealthy city-states of early 15th-century northern Italy, architects, scientists, philosophers, and artists rediscovered the lost learning of the Classical era and applied it to their work. Reviving the ideas of the Greek philosopher Aristotle, the rich and powerful saw the ownership and display of beautiful works of art as a virtue. The Renaissance began, with far-reaching consequences for the decorative arts, as affluent patrons poured money into commissions to display their prosperity and taste. The pioneers of the Renaissance spirit believed that they were reconnecting themselves with their Classical heritage after a hiatus characterized by barbarism.

## ITALY REDISCOVERS ITS PAST

The term "Gothic" was first coined by Renaissance thinkers to disparage medieval culture by linking it with the rampaging hordes – Goths – who had laid waste to Western Europe after the fall of the Roman Empire. Evidence of past Roman glories was everywhere in Rome, Florence, and Venice – the centres of this new movement. Regular discoveries further reinforced the belief that Classical art was superior to anything produced since. The Laocoon Group, a particularly fine Rhodian marble statue depicting the death of the Trojan priest Laocoon, was escorted to the Vatican by a rejoicing crowd on its rediscovery in 1506. Most discoveries were of architecture, sculpture, and Roman sarcophagi. They inspired sculptors, furniture-makers, and other decorative artists to

**MAIOLICA *ALBARELLO*** Italian maiolica – tin-glazed earthenware – was often used to make drug jars. The waisted gives a secure hold, while the label, sandwiched by coloured decoration, describes the contents. *16th century. H:21.5cm (8½in). RSS*

use motifs from the Classical orders such as acanthus leaves and fluted columns in their own work. Swags and friezes, urns and trophies, sphinxes and putti (naked cherubs) all appeared.

Excavations revealed the *grottes* (underground ruins) of Nero's *Domus Aurea* (Golden House) beneath the Aventine Hill in Rome during the late 15th century, and contributed directly to the grottoesque style of the early Renaissance. The walls of Nero's state apartments were decorated with grotesques – arabesques with animal, human, and mythical figures added. Most early designers used elements from the grotesques. Between 1518 and 1519 Raphael revived them in their original completeness as whole schemes to decorate the walls of the Vatican Loggie.

## ARCHITECTURE AND CRAFTS

Italian architects used the texts of their ancestors as a foundation for their own work – in 1570 Andrea Palladio published *Quattro Libri dell'Architeturra*

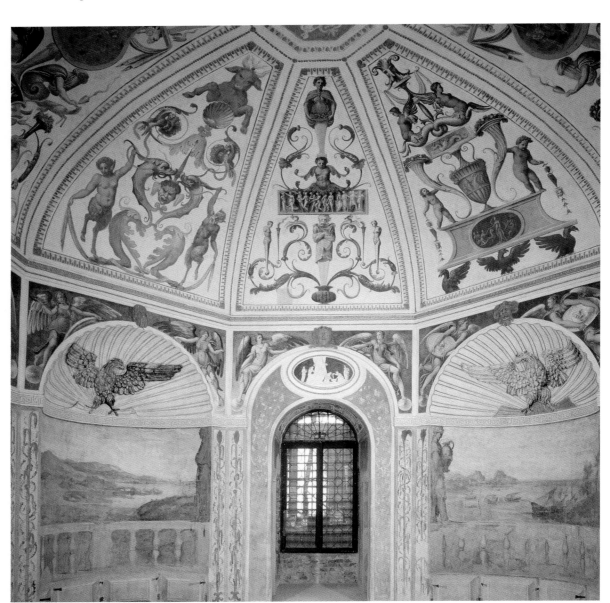

**VILLA CORNARO** Constructed in 1552–53, Andrea Palladio designed the interior to ideal Classical proportions. The spatial harmony is reflected in the balanced decoration, including grotesques in the domed ceiling.

**VENETIAN EWER** Glass has been made on the Venetian island of Murano since the 13th century. This ewer – blown from glass that imitates chalcedony – features an applied handle and spout. *c.1500.*

decoration. One difference was that Venetian glassmakers used soda ash, resulting in a malleable product particularly suited to hot techniques such as blowing and lampwork.

Islamic crafts also informed ceramic art of the period – tin-glazed earthenware from Morocco inspired the creation of Italian maiolica, the name itself born of the misconception that the Moroccan wares came from Majorca.

## MOVING INTO MANNERISM

From Italy, Classical decorative ideals spread north through France and eventually the rest of Europe. In the 1530s two Italian artists, Rosso Fiorentino and Francesco Primaticcio, were commissioned by the French king François I to decorate his palace at Fontainebleau. Fiorentino and Primaticcio brought with them the full repertoire of Classical motifs, but by then the Renaissance style in Italy had developed into Mannerism, which was characterized by sinuous and contorted forms, often within grotesques. This sophisticated style often distorted Classical ideals – elongating the human figure, for instance. Northern European craftsmen discovered the themes and motifs of the Renaissance and Mannerism simultaneously, and the result was a combination of styles their Italian counterparts would never have considered. The strapwork that the Italian artists introduced to Fontainebleau was particularly influential, and became one of the hallmarks of northern European Renaissance and later styles.

One of the quirks of the courtly Mannerist style was a love of precious, bizarre materials or clever use of them. The ceramics of French potter Bernard Palissy were one example. He took casts from real animals such as frogs, snakes, and lizards and applied them to dishes, using translucent coloured glazes that made the reptiles and amphibians look even more realistically slimy and slithery. His wares were widely copied for the grottoesque value that still held great appeal.

**BERNARD PALISSY DISH** The eccentric French potter cast reptiles from nature and applied them, surrounded by leaves, rockwork, and water, to lead-glazed earthenware. *16th century.*

**FRENCH ARMOIRE** This cupboard is decorated with pilaster figures and attributed to Hugues Sambin, who worked in Burgundy. French furniture tended to imitate that of Italy after Italian artists decorated Fontainebleau for the French king. *1550–80. H:200cm (79in).*

(Four Books on Architecture), a direct descendant of *De Architectura* (On Architecture) by Vitruvius, despite the one and a half millennia that separate the two texts. Palladio designed villas and churches in a Classical style that later became highly popular in Britain.

Within the home, wealthy newly wed couples in Italy were given a *cassone*, a richly decorated marriage chest that would be the centrepiece of the interior. Otherwise, furniture was usually simple.

Glass firms on the Venetian island of Murano were at the forefront of the European glass trade – the island's industry was strictly regulated and more than 3,000 glass-blowers were working there by the end of the 15th century. Production at this point was heavily influenced by the prized Islamic glass of the East, particularly in terms of gilding and enamel

# AGE OF
# ORNAMENT
## 1680–1760

# LAVISH OPULENCE

AFTER MORE THAN A CENTURY OF DESTRUCTIVE WARFARE, WHICH
HAD BEEN MOTIVATED AS MUCH BY POLITICAL DIFFERENCES AS
RELIGIOUS ONES, RECOGNIZABLY MODERN NATION STATES BEGAN
TO EMERGE ACROSS EUROPE FROM ABOUT 1650.

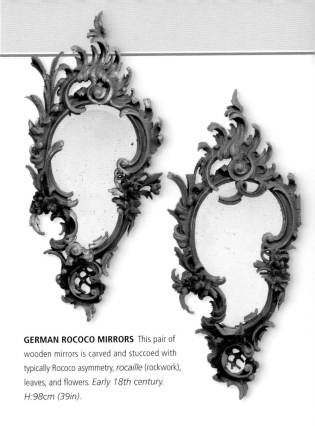

**GERMAN ROCOCO MIRRORS** This pair of
wooden mirrors is carved and stuccoed with
typically Rococo asymmetry, *rocaille* (rockwork),
leaves, and flowers. *Early 18th century.*
*H:98cm (39in).*

## EMERGING STATES OF EUROPE

Power was increasingly centralized under the
monarch, although in Britain and the Low Countries
parliaments were gaining power, and as a result
national identity began to replace
regional or local affiliation.
During the reign of the
autocratic Louis XIV
(1643–1715), France
aggressively extended its
territory and influence
through a series of wars
with its neighbours,

**DUTCH CHAIR** Made of walnut
with floral marquetry, the chair is
carved with shells and has a solid
vase-shaped splat, cabriole legs, and
claw-and-ball feet. *18th century.*

notably Spain and the Low Countries. By the start
of the 18th century it had confirmed its status as
the leading power in Europe. England and the
Low Countries – commercial rivals for much of the
period – were briefly united against the French
threat under the Dutch King William of Orange
from 1688 to 1702.

Both countries grew increasingly rich on
international trade and colonial expansion, while
the union of the English and Scottish parliaments
in 1707, a century after the union of their crowns,
gave birth to a strong and stable United Kingdom.

In central Europe Austria fought off an Ottoman
Turk siege of its capital, Vienna, in 1683, to emerge
as the major power in the region. To its north,
Prussia, under Frederick William I (1713–40) and
his son, Frederick II, "the Great" (1740–86),
became the dominant state in northern Germany.
Both Germany and Italy, however, remained

merely geographical descriptions, as each of them
was a collection of small and disunited kingdoms
and principalities often fought over or controlled
by outside powers.

## THE WIDER WORLD

Outside Europe, the first of the three long-lived
Manchu emperors, Kangxi, reigned from 1662 to
1722, presiding over a lengthy period of stability
and increasing wealth. Trade in tea, porcelain,
spices, and silk between China and Europe
flourished, while European merchants, notably
the British, French, and Dutch, established
commercial bases and small colonies
throughout southern and eastern Asia.
Although in relative decline during this
period, both Spain and Portugal continued
to derive great wealth from their colonial
empires in the Americas.

## THE ENLIGHTENMENT

Intellectually, the leading movement of the
period was the Enlightenment, a Europe-
wide shift in favour of rational thought and
scientific discovery at the expense of religion
and superstition. New ideas in philosophy,
politics, and economics were accompanied

**CHÂTEAU OF VERSAILLES** Louis le Vau, architect to Louis XIV,
remodelled Versailles between 1661 and 1670, turning a small
château into a grand and luxurious Baroque palace. It was the
official residence of the French court from 1682 to 1789.

**HÔTEL DE SOUBISE, PARIS** The four tall windows of the oval salon are reflected in three corresponding mirrors. The white and gold *boiseries* (wood panelling) are decorated with Rococo shells, garlands, and cupids. Above the *boiseries*, under the elaborate cornice, eight paintings by Charles-Joseph Natoire recount the story of Psyche.

by discoveries in astronomy, physics, biology, and botany. One practical result of the Enlightenment was safer navigation at sea and a substantial increase in overseas exploration and trade.

Artistically, the dominant style in Europe and its overseas possessions remained the Baroque. A flamboyant, theatrical style that grew out of the Renaissance, Baroque was used for religious and secular buildings. Its emphasis on order and proportion appealed to monarchs seeking to build capital cities and palaces that glorified their rule. The centres of Rome and Paris were remodelled as Baroque cities. Almost all of St Petersburg and the great palaces of Louis XIV at Versailles, the Habsburg palace of Schönbrunn in Vienna, and

the Royal Palace of the Prussian kings in Berlin, as well as the London skyline after the Great Fire of 1666, owe much to the Baroque style. Towards the end of the period, a lighter, more playful and colourful style known as Rococo predominated, at first in France and then in Germany and Austria.

The new grand palaces and large town houses that sprang up across Europe required furnishing and decorating in the latest style. The first true porcelain in Europe was produced at the Meissen factory in Saxony, Germany, in 1713; the quality of its output was only matched some 40 years later by the French national porcelain factory first at Vincennes and then, after 1756, at Sèvres. Fine silverware was produced in Paris and London,

furniture in many European cities, and large-scale tapestries in French workshops. Such items, although hand-produced at great cost, were bought in large numbers by monarchs, aristocrats, and wealthy merchants anxious to impress with their style and opulence.

**BOHEMIAN GOBLET** Now the Czech Republic, Bohemia was a long-established glassmaking centre in the 18th century. This goblet depicts a battle scene, and has a baluster-shaped stem. *c.1730. H:18cm (7¼in).*

# ELEMENTS OF STYLE

As the 17th century drew to a close, the decorative arts were slowly released from the formal strictures of the heavy Baroque style and began to flourish anew. Artisans enjoyed a new freedom to imbue their work with a more personal aesthetic. The Rococo style was brought to fruition in extravagant commissions for the aristocratic Paris society that flourished during the Régence (1715–23). Oriental influences and the vast natural resources of the New World contributed to the heady atmosphere of the time and also had a direct effect on its decorative art.

RUSSIAN BEAKER
### REPOUSSÉ WORK
The combination of embossing, or hammering, a relief design into metal and then chasing to add further fine detail to the surface is known as repoussé decoration. This design featuring scrolls and birds in high relief is typical of repoussé work of the Rococo period.

FRENCH CARTEL CLOCK
### S-SCROLLS
Frequently seen adorning the corners and aprons of furniture of this period, the S-scroll is derived from the Classical volute that was first used on the capitals of Ionic columns and is thought to be inspired by rams' horns. Cartouches of multiple scrolls were very popular in Baroque and Rococo decorative arts.

MEISSEN FIGURE GROUP
### BRIGHT COLOURS
By the turn of the 18th century a wide range of bright enamel colours was available to painters and decorators of ceramics and glass. Also known by the French name *petit feu*, overglaze enamels changed the face of ceramic design, allowing for brighter and more durable colours.

SCEAUX PLATE
### SPRIGS OF FLOWERS
Rococo designers respected and imitated natural forms. The extensive palette available led to realistic representations of flowers and foliage. European porcelain manufacture was still in its infancy, and decorators frequently used scattered flower sprays to cover small blemishes and firing faults.

ENGLISH CANDLESTAND
### FANTASTICAL BEASTS
A legacy of Classical mythology bearing the influence of the Renaissance grotesque style, fantastical beasts were used frequently in the Baroque and Rococo styles. The naturalistic inclinations of Rococo designers limited them to dragons in the Oriental tradition or sea creatures based on mariners' tales.

AUBUSSON TAPESTRY
### VIBRANT FABRICS
Great tapestry factories in France and the Low Countries continued to flourish during this period. Tapestries were used extensively to adorn walls and cover furniture. Needlework was a popular art form, and many seats were upholstered with petit-point embroidery, particularly in France.

CHANTILLY COOLER
### CHINOISERIE
The increasing fascination with the Orient resulted in a European interpretation of Chinese decoration known as Chinoiserie – an imaginary version of China complete with latticework, fretwork, dragons, Chinese figures, and pagodas. It was used on ceramics and Chinese Chippendale furniture of the period.

LOUIS XV TABLE
### EXOTIC TIMBERS
During the 18th century Europe began to import more and more luxury goods. Along with tea, spices, and fine porcelain, merchants also satisfied a new demand for exotic hardwoods, which were much admired for their rich colours and lent an air of opulence when inlaid into furniture.

SWEDISH BEAKER
### ENAMELLED GLASS
The European glass market was dominated by Bohemia during this period. Among the many specialities of the region was enamel decoration, ranging from the stark monochrome of *Schwarzlot*, or "black lead" enamel, to pastoral themes picked out in multiple colours and gilt.

GERMAN MIRROR
### ASYMMETRY
After the heavy formality of the Baroque period, the Rococo era represented a lighter, more playful style. Asymmetry was an important aspect of this more fluid aesthetic. The more realistic representation of nature that flourished during the period recognized the essential disorder of the natural world.

QUEEN ANNE WALNUT SIDE CHAIR
### SHELL MOTIF
The term "Rococo" is derived from the French word *rocaille* (rockwork) and refers to the irregular rock and shell forms on grotto ornament. Shell motifs – especially scallops, or cockleshells – are found frequently on Rococo silver, ceramics, and furniture. In the late 18th century the conch shell gained popularity.

FRENCH RÉGENCE COMMODE
### METAL MOUNTS
Cast-bronze and gilt-metal mounts were initially used to protect the vulnerable corners of ornate veneered furniture, but they quickly became decorative elements in their own right. The casting of ormolu mounts was a specialist industry in France, and popular motifs included scrolls, masks, and foliate designs.

GEORGE I SECRETAIRE
### JAPANNING
The practice of japanning furniture spread across Europe and the American colonies during this period: shellac varnish was applied to the surface in imitation of Japanese lacquer. A wide range of colours was used, but a white surface provided the most suitable base for further painted decoration, often of Oriental scenes.

ITALIAN TABLE
### CARVING AND GILDING
Furniture made of softer indigenous woods, rather than more expensive tropical hardwoods, was frequently carved with elaborate scrolls and smothered with gesso and gilding to provide a more lavish decorative effect. The carving was often carried out by specialists trained in the art of sculpture.

# FURNITURE

THE DESIRE FOR MORE COMFORTABLE LIVING PROVIDED AN IDEAL CLIMATE

FOR A NEW LOOK IN FURNITURE DESIGN AND A MOVE AWAY FROM THE

RESTRAINTS OF CLASSICISM AND INTO THE REALMS OF FANTASY.

## RÉGENCE TO ROCOCO

The new style had its origins in the refurbishment of the Palais Royal in Paris under Philippe, duc d'Orléans, regent to Louis XV from 1715 to 1723. Architect Gilles-Marie Oppenord introduced a look that was, essentially, curvaceous – a mass of swirling lines incorporating carvings of foliage and flowers in arrangements that were fanciful and deliberately asymmetrical.

A cohesive, unified design was key: chairs were upholstered in elegant silks, satins, and damasks that matched drapery; carved ornament on the furniture echoed motifs in wall panelling and doors; and colours were light and subtle, reflected in elaborately carved gilt-framed mirrors. Much of the design was influenced by women, whose desires to entertain at leisure inspired the creation of the drawing room, or salon. This is evident in the "feminine look" of the period.

### LOUIS XV

The fashion for asymmetry was most extravagant during the reign of Louis XV (1715–74). Natural motifs – shells, flowers, and husks – were

used in abundance, alongside arabesques, C-scrolls, and S-scrolls, in a bid to create the desired effect. This signalled the arrival of the *genre pittoresque*, later named the Rococo style. A derivation of the phrase *rocaille coquille* (rock and shell), the term refers to the rockwork and grotto-like features that became synonymous with the look.

### FASHIONABLE FORMS

Furniture tended to be smaller and more elegant than under Louis XIV, making maximum use of the curve motif in pieces such as tables and commodes with serpentine edges, chairs with undulating top

**SECRÉTAIRE À ABBATANT** This piece has a marble top, ormolu banding with shell and foliate scrolls at the corners, and a tulipwood veneer with floral marquetry. Stamped Joseph. *c.1760. H:114cm (45in).*

*The ornate marquetry-work* **apron** is embellished with carving

**TABLE EN CHIFFONIÈRE** This tulipwood-veneered table has cabriole legs with ormolu mounts and sabots. The top and undershelf marquetry floral cartouches have banded purplewood borders. *c.1755. H:66.5cm (26¼in).*

**LOUIS XIV COMMODE** The top, sides, drawer-fronts, and apron of this piece are decorated with floral, fruit, and foliage marquetry work and augmented with gilding and gilt-bronze mounts. Attributed to Thomas Hache. *1680–90. W:130.5cm (51¼in).*

*Gilt-bronze sabots* take the form of animal hooves under foliage rails, and the ubiquitous S-shaped cabriole leg. The prestigious marble-topped commode existed in a variety of styles, a favourite being the two-drawer version designed by Charles Cressent. The *fauteuil* – an upholstered, open-sided armchair – exemplified the desire for greater comfort, the frame adapted to accommodate fashionable hooped skirts. Close relations were the fully upholstered *bergère* and the fully upholstered sofa, or settee.

The new salons included tea tables, games tables, and sewing tables. Folded away at the edge of the room, such pieces were opened up as the need arose. Writing tables – primarily housed in the bedroom – were also popular. In addition to the men's *bureau plat*, largely unchanged from Baroque forms, there were now smaller, more elegant writing desks for ladies.

## A TASTE FOR THE EXOTIC

Designs were executed in a range of techniques, and exotic woods such as amaranth, purplewood, and kingwood were used to create intricate marquetry inlays that became the height of fashion. Many pieces were finished with ormolu mounts; ostensibly applied to protect vulnerable corners, these were nevertheless exquisite in design.

In France a process for imitating – more economically – Chinese lacquerwork was developed by Martin Frères and called *vernis Martin*. In Venice *lacca povera* (poor man's lacquer) had the same effect. The technique involved pasting coloured images on to furniture and applying several coats of varnish to achieve a glossy finish. In England Thomas Chippendale often used Chinese elements in his furniture designs.

A fashion for carved and painted wood was common in regions of Italy and Scandinavia, where native woods such as pine, beech, and

**GILTWOOD *FAUTEUIL*** One of a pair made by N. Blanchard in the reign of Louis XV, this chair has a characteristically curvaceous frame carved with floral, fruit, and foliate motifs. These are echoed in the petit-point reupholstery. *c.1755. W:71cm (28in).*

**LOUIS XV INTERIOR** The Louis XV Blue Room in Paris's Musée Carnavalet is decorated and furnished in the lighter, airier Rococo style, which supplanted the heavier, more ornate Classicism popular during the reign of Louis XIV.

lime were soft and, therefore, particularly suited to intricate carving. Where the wood was inferior in quality, pieces were also covered in gesso and gilt.

## MASTERS OF THE STYLE

Most of the finest Rococo pieces originated in France – Charles Cressent's two-drawer commode became a seminal design of the period, for example. François Cuvilliés did much to introduce the style to Germany, creating exemplary interiors at the Munich Residenz for the Elector of Bavaria. In Italy the work of Pietro Piffetti epitomized the Rococo style, with intricate marquetry in exotic woods, ivory, and mother-of-pearl.

**LOUIS XV MIRROR** The openwork giltwood frame of this archetypal French Rococo mirror comprises an elaborate concoction of scrolling foliage, trailing and interlaced flowers, and *rocaille. c.1755. H:118cm (46½in).*

**SWEDISH CONSOLE TABLE** Supporting a marble top, this table's gilt-wood frame is carved in deep relief, in Louis XV Rococo style, with a lion mask, dragons, flowers, and scrolling foliage. *c.1760. W:99cm (39in).*

*Ormolu drawer-pulls* are in keeping with other adornments

**LOUIS XV *BUREAU PLAT*** Veneered in tulipwood and purplewood, with elaborate satinwood marquetry of stylized shells and foliate scrolls, this piece is further enriched with similar motifs in the elaborate ormolu mounts. *c.1745. W:193cm (76in).*

## FROM WALNUT TO MAHOGANY

The high-Rococo style that developed in France spread to much of Europe, but in some regions the flamboyance was simply too much. Instead, designers took their lead from developments in the Low Countries and England, where a more restrained version of the style prevailed.

### AN EMPHASIS ON WOOD

At the beginning of the 18th century walnut was the wood of choice throughout much of Europe. It was a good, hard, indigenous wood, and it was suitable for carving. It grew rich in colour over time and had exciting figuring – particularly when selected with burrs or from root timbers. For these reasons, there was a tendency to rely on the wood itself for ornament. Although techniques such as marquetry and lacquerwork existed, these were an exception to the rule and prohibitively expensive to all but the wealthiest of patrons.

From 1725 onwards mahogany began to take the place of walnut, primarily in England, and later across the rest of Europe. Mahogany found favour in the early American colonies, though it was also common to find regional pieces produced in native timbers such as maple in New England, cherry in Connecticut, and walnut in the southern states.

The increased use of mahogany coincided with a blight on walnut trees in Europe, which made their wood rare and expensive, and the removal of import taxes in the 1730s, which significantly reduced the cost of importing mahogany from the West Indies. Because mahogany is a harder wood than walnut, it was a better choice for carving and piercing with intricate decoration. Its darker colour married well with gold, silver, or bronze ornament, and it was not long before the wood became associated with the more elaborate styles of French Rococo, Palladian, and Chippendale furniture.

### STYLE AND ORNAMENT

Although the Rococo style elsewhere was more restrained than in French and Italian furniture, concessions were made, not least the cabriole leg, less exaggerated *bombé* forms, and broken or arched pediments. Ornament was often limited to a

**GEORGE II ARMCHAIR** The mahogany frame is carved in deep relief with shell motifs and acanthus leaves. The legs terminate in claw-and-ball feet. Made in the style of Giles Grendey. *c.1740. H:101cm (39¾in).*

**QUEEN ANNE WALNUT SIDE CHAIR** This piece (one of six) has a vase-shaped splat, cabriole legs with pad feet, and a drop-in seat with period-authentic upholstery. By John York of Warwickshire. *c.1710. H:114cm (45in).*

**GEORGE I SECRETAIRE** This piece is modelled as a walnut-veneered chest-on-chest, and its upper drawers – the fourth of which is a fold-down writing surface – are flanked by carvings of griffins, flowers, and fruit. *c.1725. H:222cm (87½in).*

*The broken pediment* frames a scrolling Rococo cartouche carving

### PALLADIANISM

From the 1720s a style emerged in England that rejected the asymmetrical frivolity of contemporary French design. It was inspired by, and takes its name from, the Italian architect Andrea Palladio, whose own buildings were influenced by the mathematical precision of ancient Classical architecture. The result was a formal style based on symmetry and geometric forms. Such buildings were furnished with massive furniture, often embellished with pediments, pilasters, and fielded panels. Some designers made the occasional concession to the Rococo style by decorating pieces ornately with swirling ribbons and shell motifs, but the overall look remained symmetrical. A leading exponent of the style was William Kent, who designed Holkham Hall in Norfolk.

**GEORGE II CONSOLE TABLE** The *alabastro fiorito* top of this table rests on a gilt-gesso, carved wooden base with a lambrequin-collared female mask and caryatids. Attributed to William Kent. *c.1730. W:143cm (56in).*

*The acanthus-scroll stretcher* has a double scallop shell at the centre

**WILLIAM AND MARY HIGHBOY** Made in New England in flame birch and maple, this two-part highboy – the lower with a scalloped skirt – has ringed ball feet united by cockbeaded stretchers. *c.1700. H:167.5cm (66in).*

**GEORGE II MAHOGANY CARD TABLE** This table has a shaped apron with a carved shell motif and is raised on shell-carved cabriole legs with webbed pad feet. The foldover top hides a baize-lined interior with candle stands. *c.1750. W:86cm (33¾in).*

*The vasiform back splat* is typical of American Queen Anne chairs

*Shell carving* at the top of the chair leg

**QUEEN ANNE DINING CHAIR** With a serpentine-crested top rail terminating in scrolled ears, a vasiform back splat, and shell carvings, this walnut-framed dining chair made in the Delaware Valley is typical of the American Queen Anne style. *c.1760.*

single shell motif on the knee of a cabriole leg or a claw-and-ball foot. The occasional piece may also have been painted in pastel colours and gilt. Although marquetry was not as fashionable in England, it was still popular in the Low Countries, where designers created realistic floral displays. In England, inlaid detail took the form of elegant feather- or crossbanding.

## TYPICAL FURNITURE

The first quarter of the century saw the emergence of the style referred to as Queen Anne. Its most recognizable form was the Queen Anne chair with its rounded back, vase-shaped back splat, and cabriole legs. This design was produced widely in England, the Low Countries, and the American colonies. The chair was most commonly made from solid walnut or oak with a walnut veneer.

Another form particular to these regions, and Germany, during the first half of the 1700s was the bureau cabinet – a two-door cupboard above a chest of drawers. Sometimes the cupboard doors were glazed for displaying ceramics. Some versions also housed a writing surface, a form known as a secretaire cabinet. A close relation, the chest-on-chest, was an architectural piece, often seen with a pediment and fluted pilasters.

Almost exclusive to the early American colonies was the combination of highboy and lowboy,

which rivalled the prestige of the commode in France. Designed en suite for the bedroom, each had a similar form and ornament. With its many drawers, the highboy served as an essential storage piece, while the lowboy functioned both as a dressing table and a writing table.

As in France, the more sociable climate gave rise to the creation of a number of smaller pieces of furniture. These were particularly suited to entertaining and included tea tables, which sometimes took the form of a round tilt-top table on a tripod base, and card tables, which satisfied an increasing fascination with gambling.

## A TOUCH OF FLAIR

Despite the prevailing climate of restraint, Thomas Chippendale's designs stand out as having more exuberance. In his publication *The Gentleman and Cabinet-Maker's Director* (1754), he presented designs for a host of furniture forms elaborately decorated in different styles. Alongside drawings for richly ornamented French pieces with scrolling ribbons and foliage, Chippendale also offered Chinese-inspired designs featuring pagoda surmounts, fretwork galleries, and bamboo-effect carving, as well as Gothic-inspired designs incorporating pointed arches and quatrefoils.

**QUEEN ANNE DRESSING TABLE** The mahogany carcase of this American piece houses four drawers flanked by chamfered and fluted corners. The cabriole legs have claw-and-ball feet. *c.1750. W:87.5cm (34½in).*

# THE HUGUENOTS

FEARING PROSECUTION AFTER THE 1685 REVOCATION OF THE EDICT OF NANTES, LARGE NUMBERS OF THE FRENCH PROTESTANT COMMUNITY, KNOWN AS THE HUGUENOTS, LEFT THE COUNTRY. THEY TOOK WITH THEM THE SKILLS THEY HAD DEVELOPED IN A RANGE OF ARTISTIC DISCIPLINES AND SPREAD THEM ACROSS EUROPE AND THE WORLD.

**Lamerie silver ewer**

**SILVER DISH AND EWER** Made by Paul de Lamerie for Algernon Coote, Sixth Earl of Mountrath, these items display the Earl's coat of arms, as well as delicate scrolling flowers and foliage, intertwined with human figures, typical of Lamerie's designs. *1742–43. Dish: D:76cm (30in); Ewer: H:46.5cm (18¼in).*

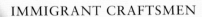

**Lamerie silver dish**

**SILVER SAUCEBOAT** Made by Nicholas Sprimont, this sauceboat in the form of an upturned shell features cast and applied Rococo-style decoration to the body. The foot is in the shape of shells and plant forms, which, combined, take on the appearance of a dolphin – a popular motif of the era. *c.1745.*

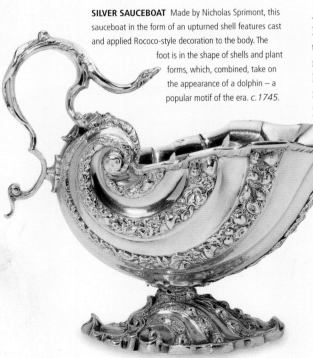

The revocation of the Edict of Nantes by Louis XIV sent shock waves through the Huguenot community of France. Prevented from worshipping freely, at the end of the 1600s Huguenots fled the country in droves. A good number of them were craftsmen, and the host countries – primarily the Protestant Low Countries, Prussia, Switzerland, and Britain – gained from their skills. Many Huguenots also benefited from opportunities further afield: Dutch colonists encouraged travel to the Cape, where several families had success in viticulture; while British colonial interests afforded travel to the early American colonies, where immigrants set up a number of communities.

## IMMIGRANT CRAFTSMEN

In the previous century monarchs had used foreign craftsmen to furnish their palaces in the latest fashions. The concept of using talent from abroad was therefore not a new one. The difference now lay in sheer volume. More than 200,000 Huguenots left France, seeking employment abroad. In a climate of social change, they were not working exclusively for the elite but also contributing to the production of domestic wares for middle-class households.

## A MAN OF INFLUENCE

Daniel Marot had a considerable impact across all the decorative arts. An architect and designer, he made engravings of designs by Jean Bérain before leaving France to work for William of Orange, first in the Low Countries, then in England. He published many designs of his own for ornaments, furniture, and textiles, which were copied and reinterpreted by many contemporary craftsmen. Marot excelled at integrating form and ornament in his designs in a style that was primarily Classical.

## WEAVERS AND SILVERSMITHS

Most of the Huguenots who came to England ended up in London. Spitalfields, an area known for producing silk, attracted weavers on a large scale and soon became the centre of the silk industry, earning the name of "weaver town". Among the immigrants was James Leman, who stood out as an accomplished designer as well as

**HOGARTH ENGRAVING** Entitled *Industry and Idleness – The Fellow Apprentices at Their Looms*, this engraving shows silk weavers working in Spitalfields, London. It is accompanied by proverbs, including: "The hand of the diligent shall maketh rich." *1747.*

a manufacturer, a rarity at the time. His designs were bold, often abstract, incorporating motifs ranging from stylized flowers to accurate botanical drawings, and from Classical architectural forms to elaborate Chinoiserie.

Around Soho, other Huguenots were making a name for themselves in silverware, among them Paul Crespin and Nicholas Sprimont. They produced pieces in unmistakable Rococo style, often with elaborate scrolling ornament and asymmetrical motifs, and created several outstanding items for Frederick, Prince of Wales, among other wealthy patrons. In 1746 Sprimont set up the Chelsea Porcelain factory, where the influence of his work with silver can be seen on early pieces.

But it is Paul de Lamerie who stands out as the genius of the age, becoming the leading exponent of silverware in the Rococo style. Lamerie emigrated to the Low Countries at the end of the 1600s and followed William of Orange to England when he became king. He trained under one of the most accomplished London goldsmiths of the time, Pierre Platel, creating exquisite, well-proportioned pieces in the Régence style. His work reflected the high style that was fashionable in France, and he excelled at producing pieces that combined form with often dense relief ornament. At the peak of his career, Lamerie had an impressive list of clients among London's nobility and wealthy middle classes.

**SILK BROCADE** Made in Spitalfields, London, by Huguenot weavers, this yellow silk fabric is brocaded with naturalistic flowers in polychrome and silver threads. P.A. Ducerceau's publication *Bouquets Propres pour les Étoffes de Tours* provided weavers with a rich sourcebook of floral imagery.

# CERAMICS

AT A TIME WHEN MANY WESTERN POTTERS WERE MIMICKING ORIENTAL
WORKS, AND A SELECT FEW STROVE TO DISCOVER THE SECRET OF PORCELAIN,
OTHERS CONTINUED TO REFINE TRADITIONAL FORMS AND DECORATIONS.

## POTTERY IN EUROPE

First developed by potters in ancient China, by
the Middle Ages stoneware was also produced in
Germany; from here it spread throughout Europe.

The fine, robust body of stoneware is created
by firing clay at about 1,400°C (2,500°F). The
high temperature melts the components of the
clay, forming a non-porous body. Some types
of stoneware are translucent when held to the
light, in a way that is similar to porcelain.

## THE GERMAN LEAD

Germany was at the forefront of the pottery
industry. Soon each region developed its preferred
style of stoneware, embracing the various styles
and properties the material allowed. For example,
many pieces produced in the town of Sieburg
(now Bad Karlshafen), in the northwest of the
country, had a fine, white body. In the Westerwald
stoneware featured a grey body and was used to
make items such as a narrow-necked jug called an
*Enghalskrug* and a globular-shaped tankard known
as a *Kugelbauchkrug*. In Cologne stoneware was
made with a brown body that became synonymous
with the bellarmine jug, a globular bottle with a
mask of a bearded man below the neck.

A large quantity of German stoneware was
imported to Britain in the 17th century, which
inspired British potters to develop their own range.
The London potter John Dwight patented a whitish
stoneware in 1672. In the early 18th century many
potters in Europe, including the German Johann
Friedrich Böttger (*see p.34*), became admirers of
a fine, red stoneware produced in Yixing, China.
Much copied, this Chinese stoneware had a thin
body, making it suitable for tableware, especially
coffee and tea services.

*The Staffordshire
red ware* body was
inspired by Dutch imitations of
Chinese Yixing stoneware

**STAFFORDSHIRE MUG**
The red ware body of this
mug displays delicate applied
cream-coloured decoration in
the form of flora and fauna,
including a lion and a unicorn.
*c.1760. H:12cm (4¾in).*

**RHENISH BELLARMINE** Named
after, and bearing an image of,
Cardinal Roberto Bellarmino
above a lion medallion, this style
of brown, salt-glazed stoneware
vessel originated in Cologne.
*c.1750. H:21cm (8¼in).*

**ANNABERG JUG** A moulded
relief of a Madonna and Child
decorates this bulbous stoneware
jug. They sit among a palm frieze in
bright polychrome against a shiny
brown-black glaze ground. *c.1700.
H:21cm (8¼in).*

**CREUSSEN STEIN** Characteristically squat, the tin-mounted, salt-
glazed stoneware body displays hunting scenes flanked by bands
of stylized flora, all in applied relief and painted with blue, black,
yellow, and white enamels. Other favoured subject matter included
apostles, electors, and the planets. *c.1680. H:21.5cm (8½in).*

**STAFFORDSHIRE CHARGER** In this example of Burslem slipware, the robust, contrasting coloured decoration, in the form of a coat of arms within a spiralling border, is probably by Ralph Simpson. *c.1680. Diam:32cm (12½in).*

## EARTHENWARE

Earthenware is produced by firing coarse clay, often containing impurities, at about 800°C (1,500°F). This is a much lower temperature than is required to produce stoneware, and it endows pottery with a fundamental difference: tiny air spaces remain in the body, resulting in earthenware being porous. An earthenware body is usually reddish brown, as found in British clay, or buff, which can be seen in Delft earthenware when it is chipped. In order to make earthenware waterproof, a glaze must be applied. As well as tin glaze, lead glaze, which is shiny and transparent, was often used on earthenware. Metal oxides were sometimes added to give the glaze a colour.

## DECORATIVE TECHNIQUES

Decorating pottery with an incised pattern – a technique known as sgraffito – had been done for centuries. The technique involves cutting a motif into wet clay. In the 17th and 18th centuries the incised areas were sometimes painted.

Other decorative techniques soon developed. To create a three-dimensional decoration, for example, ornamental elements were formed in a mould and then applied to the body before firing. Slipware was produced – particularly in Staffordshire, Wrotham in Kent, and north Devon, all in Britain – by dipping a red earthenware body into a brown or white slip. The vessel was then decorated by slip-trailing, applying different coloured slips in a trail, not unlike the way a cake is decorated.

Wares were sometimes handpainted with overglaze decoration. In this instance, enamel paints were applied to the glazed surface. They fused together once the piece was returned to the kiln. Underglaze decoration involved a metal oxide being used for a design after an initial firing but before applying the glaze.

*Brickwork pattern* is slip-trailed by hand

**SLIPWARE NIGHTLIGHT** Modelled as an English mansion, this nightlight has architectural fixtures and fittings that are slip-trailed in lead-glazed brown clay on the red clay shell. *c.1760. W:16.5cm (6½in).*

## SALT-GLAZED STONEWARE

A particular type of hard, translucent glaze can be created on stoneware by throwing salt into the kiln while firing the object at a high temperature during the glazing stage. As the salt vaporizes, it leaves behind sodium, which fuses with silicates in the clay forming a thin, glassy surface. Because of iron impurities within the clay, most salt-glazed stoneware has a brown colour, although some is a buff or whitish colour. Red lead was sometimes added to create a more glassy appearance. The glaze may be pitted, with a texture similar to orange peel.

This technique was first employed in Germany, where grey clay was used to produce tankards and bottles, but it spread to Britain in the late 1600s. In Staffordshire in around 1720, a fine, white, salt-glazed stoneware was created that was stronger than other bodies used at the time. It was inexpensive to produce, and large quantities were exported to the rest of Europe and North America, particularly as domestic tableware. A variety of decorative shapes was produced, including teapots modelled as camels and houses. The wares were sometimes decorated with moulded or incised patterns.

Tiny clay chippings were occasionally added to the glaze – for example, to create the appearance of fur on a bear.

**STONEWARE TEAPOT** The English-made, salt-glazed body and cover of this teapot are handpainted with romantic imagery of a courting couple in parkland and with a flautist on the reverse. *c.1760. H:18cm (7in).*

**STAFFORDSHIRE DISH** Made in the form of a leaf with a curled stalk handle, this salt-glazed stoneware dish is moulded with pea flowers in relief, and painted in shades of green, yellow, and pink. *c.1760. W:17.5cm (6¾in).*

**STAFFORDSHIRE JUG** Moulded with the head as a cover, this bear-baiting, salt-glazed stoneware vessel is typically finely wrought and thinly potted. It is covered with tiny clay parings simulating fur. *c.1760. H:25.5cm (10in).*

## TIN-GLAZED EARTHENWARE

In the 9th century, many years before Germany made its mark on the pottery industry, potters in Mesopotamia (now Iraq) were also inspired by Chinese ceramics. To replicate their appearance, they covered their earthenware with a tin glaze that provided an opaque white background for painted decoration. They also developed lustre glazes.

These forms of decoration spread through the Islamic countries and eventually reached Spain, parts of which were still under the rule of the Moors, in the 13th or 14th century. Hispano-Moresque lustreware was produced in the regions of Malaga and Valencia in the 14th and 15th centuries, often in the form of dishes and drug jars known as *albarelli*. These have a cylindrical form with a neck and foot more narrow than the body – a Persian form that spread, along with tin-glazed earthenware, to Italy (*see Maiolica box, right*), France, Germany, the Low Countries, and Britain.

**HANAU EWER** Known as an *Enghalskrug*, this German jug has a typically long-necked and footed, bulbous body. It is decorated with Chinoiserie-style flowers, birds, and insects, rendered in Scharffeuer cobalt blue on white. *c.1725. H:32cm (12½in).*

## FRENCH FAIENCE

French tin-glazed earthenware is known as faience, after the Italian city of Faenza. Its production began in 1512, with the arrival of Italian potters in Lyon. At first wares followed the Italian style, but by the mid-1600s they adopted a native Baroque style, in which ochre and blue were the dominant colours used to depict bold mythological figures. Blue-and-white Oriental motifs, inspired by Chinese exports, became the norm by the end of the century.

An important pottery centre in the 1700s was Rouen, which produced wares with intricate patterns based on lacework, lambrequins, or ironwork. Some French products were left blank or only lightly decorated, in a style known as *faience blanche*. Another style that became popular in the early 18th century was the so-called *grand feu*. This involves painting the decoration on to an unfired glaze with high-temperature enamels – blue, purple, green, yellow, orange-red, and red – before firing. Strasbourg, Lunéville, Marseilles, and Sceaux led the industry.

**MOUSTIERS PLATE** The shape, creamy-grey glaze, and polychrome groups of caricatured figures among flora and fauna are typical of Moustiers faience of the early 1700s. *Diam:25cm (9¾in).*

**ITALIAN SANDER** The tin-glazed, fluted drum-shaped body of this sander is decorated with naturalistic landscape imagery in the Chinese style, rendered in green and black, a favourite Italian palette. *c.1750. D:7cm (2¾in).*

**D'APREY PLAQUE** Made in the factory of Jacques Lallemant de Villehaut, Baron d'Aprey, this plaque has a faience body painted with a landscape characteristic of pastoral French Rococo imagery. *c.1750. W:33.5cm (13¼in).*

Strasbourg also produced wares using the *petit feu* technique, in which colours are painted on to the glaze after it is fired. The pottery is fired again at a lower temperature, which means brighter colours can be used, including crimson, vermilion, and pink.

## GERMAN PRODUCTION

Introduced by Dutch potters in the late 1600s, German Fayence was decorated in a style similar to Delft ware, with blue-and-white Oriental themes. Fayence was occasionally painted with manganese and yellow in addition to blue. *Enghalskrugen* (jugs with a narrow neck) and deep dishes were common forms, as was plain hollow ware. In the 18th century the Chinese themes were replaced by local, native motifs, including figures, landscapes, the double-headed eagle, and coats of arms. Common shapes include the *Walzenkrug* tankard, tureens, plates, dishes, and figures.

## MAIOLICA

Throughout the 18th century, Italian potters continued to make their traditional tin-glazed earthenware, which was inspired by Hispano-Moresque wares imported through a port on the island of Majorca. These wares were named *maiolica*, the Tuscan name for Majorca. One of the most important Italian maiolica centres was the city of Faenza, where pottery production was well established by the mid-15th century. Early wares were decorated in green and purple, depicting figures, animals, and heraldic beasts. A palette dominated by blue followed, and by the 16th century pictorial paintings with episodes from Classical literature or Biblical, mythological, or allegorical scenes covered huge expanses of large dishes, plaques, and other objects – a style known as *istoriato*. The style was particularly popular in the town of Urbino. Other important centres include Castelli, Deruta, and Montelupo, all in central Italy.

**ITALIAN MAIOLICA PLAQUE** Of rectangular form, this plaque has a greyish-cream glazed body decorated with the Madonna and Child in shades of blue, green, yellow, and manganese. *Mid-1700s. W:38cm (15in).*

## DUTCH POTTERY

Dutch potters soon began to imitate the blue-and-white decoration of the Chinese porcelain imported by the Dutch East India Company in the early 17th century. It was known as *kraak* porcelain – after the Portuguese carracks, or merchant ships, which transported the wares from China. Delft became the pre-eminent centre for this product by the mid-1600s, and it even gave its name to the Dutch pottery which is now known as Delft ware.

Dutch potters also painted Dutch landscapes and Biblical subjects on their pieces, which included hollow ware, tiles, plaques, flower holders, and many more forms. By the end of the 17th century they also used a polychrome palette that imitated the Chinese *famille verte* and *famille rose* palettes, as well as Japanese Imari and Kakiemon porcelain.

Tin-glazed earthenware was first produced in Britain in the 1500s, but most of it was made in the 17th and 18th centuries. This British pottery is known as delftware.

In the 17th century Chinese porcelain was a luxury item in Britain. In order to satisfy the appetite of the middle classes for this type of item, British potters created a Chinese-inspired product that was less refined than its Dutch counterpart, with a softer body. Typical decoration included stylized flowers, oak leaves, and the monarch's portrait on such forms as drug jars, dishes, and salts. The blue-dash charger, with a rim decorated with

**DELFT PLATE** This plate is decorated in the cobalt blue and white palette. The design, possibly inspired by a contemporary print, shows cabinet-makers at work within a floral border. *c.1760. D:31.75cm (12½in).*

**DELFT BASIN** Decorated in the Chinese export palette of cobalt blue on white, this basin has a central image of fruit, flowers, and leaves circumscribed by a gently scrolling foliate border. *1720s–40s. D:27.5cm (10¾in).*

broad strokes of blue, was popular in the late 1600s. In the 18th century British delftware became more delicate and was made in a larger range of shapes, including wall pockets, punch bowls, and puzzle jugs, often painted with British figures, landscapes, and buildings, as well as Chinese designs.

**DELFTWARE FLOWER BRICKS** The polychrome Chinoiserie landscape on these flower bricks is rendered in a more open and delicate style than pre-18th-century equivalents. Made in London. *1730–40. H:15cm (6in).*

**DELFTWARE POSSET POT** Made in either London or Bristol (the painting style possibly indicates the latter), this blue-and-white piece features flowering shrubs, birds, and commemorative decoration ("E.I.P."). *1689. D:25cm (9¾in).*

# THE ARCANUM

AMONG EUROPEAN ARISTOCRATS, PORCELAIN WAS
CONSIDERED MORE DESIRABLE THAN GOLD. THIS LED
TO THE RACE FOR THE ARCANUM – THE SECRET TO
MAKING HARD-PASTE PORCELAIN, WHICH THE CHINESE
AND JAPANESE HAD GUARDED FOR CENTURIES.

**MEISSEN MILK JUG** Of octagonal form and characteristically
bulging near the foot, this milk jug has a scroll handle and a
domed cover with a cone knop. It is painted with the Quail
pattern in the Kakiemon palette. *c.1730. H:16.5cm (6½in).*

## JOHANN JOACHIM KÄNDLER

Some of the best Meissen porcelain was produced when
Johann Joachim Kändler was chief modeller (1733–75).
First he created a series of large, naturalistic animals and
birds, some as tall as 1m (3¼ft), for Augustus the Strong's
Japanese Palace. Because these elaborate figures were
expensive to produce, they soon gave way to small figures
and groups, including Commedia dell'Arte actors, exotic
figures, shepherds, aristocrats, street vendors, dogs, and
monkey musicians. Originally modelled in the Baroque
style, the figurines took on the Rococo fashion for light-
heartedness with flowers and scrolls after
Kändler visited Paris in 1747. These
exquisite pieces were the height
of fashion, often displayed on
the dining tables of the rich.

**MEISSEN FIGURE GROUP** Modelled by Kändler, this group shows a
lady with a pug on her lap attended by a Moorish servant. The modeller's
typically vigorous and exotic style is accentuated by a rich polychrome
and gold palette. *c.1740. H:15cm (6in).*

Augustus the Strong, Elector of Saxony and
King of Poland, was a powerful man who had
built up a spectacular – and expensive – collection
of Oriental ceramics. He was keen to find the secret
of the Arcanum, so that he could increase his
collection – and his coffers – by making and selling
the first European hard-paste porcelain. To this
end, Augustus had employed Ehrenfried Walther
von Tschirnhaus, a scientist and mathematician.
However, the work was expensive, and the Elector
was short of funds.

### AN ALCHEMIST'S BOASTS
At the time, one way to gain patronage for
chemical experimentation was to claim the ability
to make gold from base metals. However, this was
a dangerous strategy: a lack of success meant the
possibility of execution.

One man who made such a bold claim was
Johann Friedrich Böttger, a skilled chemist who
had knowledge of both pharmaceutical and
metallurgical techniques. In 1707 Augustus
imprisoned Böttger in Dresden, the capital of
Saxony, both as punishment for failing to
produce gold and to secure the secret of doing
so if he did succeed. Böttger was also forced to
collaborate with von Tschirnhaus on his formula
for making porcelain.

### SUCCESS AT LAST
Von Tschirnhaus was using nearby
deposits of kaolin for his
experiments, but his
porcelain formula lacked
the traces of potash
mica found in its
Chinese counterpart.
Meanwhile, Böttger
began building kilns that
could produce the high
temperatures required.

At first he developed a new
type of red stoneware, known
as *Böttgerporzellan*. This was so
hard that it could be polished on a
lapidary's wheel. Then, after von
Tschirnhaus's death in 1708, Böttger made
refinements to the experiments the two men had
worked on and succeeded in producing Europe's
first hard-paste (or true) porcelain in 1709.

**MEISSEN FIGURE** Made when Johann
Gottlob Kirchner was chief modeller,
this figure depicts an Oriental lady on a
sectioned socle. Her long robe is painted
with polychrome decoration, including some
*Indianische Blumen* (Indian flowers).
*c.1725. H:11.75cm (4½in).*

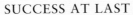

### MEISSEN'S MODEL
The Elector set up a manufactory in Meissen,
a town near Dresden, in 1710. The factory
produced luxury items that differed from the
Oriental wares, based on the shapes and decoration
used for contemporary silverware. However,
demand was slow, and the fashion for all things
Oriental became stronger than ever.

The Meissen factory managed to survive and
became an economic success by 1713. It had
attracted some of Europe's best painters and
modellers, whose work included gold-gilt and
Oriental-inspired decoration, including the
Kakiemon palette. Meissen became, and still is, one
of Europe's most respected porcelain manufacturers.

Meanwhile, Böttger was eventually freed in
1713. He died in 1719, the same year that hard-
paste porcelain was first made in Europe outside of
Meissen, at Claudius Innocentius du Paquier's
factory in Vienna.

**MEISSEN TEAPOT** Made
from early Meissen porcelain
(*Böttgerporzellan*), this teapot
is decorated with gilt-crested oval
reserves showing Chinoiserie scenes
painted in iron red and purple.
*c.1725. H:14cm (5½in).*

**AUGUSTUS THE STRONG'S JAPANESE PALACE** Drawn, painted, and
engraved by Bernardo Bellotto, a nephew of Canaletto, this view includes
Augustus's Japanese Palace (on the left). Begun in 1714 and enlarged in
1722–33 in the late Baroque style, the palace was originally intended to
house Augustus's Oriental porcelain collection. *1748.*

## PORCELAIN

With the help of former Meissen employees, the Vienna factory produced hard-paste porcelain in 1719. At first the shapes were symmetrical Baroque forms with scrollwork decoration. Oriental-inspired floral motifs were used, as well as battle and hunting scenes and Chinoiserie. From around 1750 Vienna began producing Rococo-style wares, as well as figures modelled by Johann Josef Niedermayer. Other 18th-century German factories producing hard-paste porcelain were Höchst, Frankenthal, Nymphenburg, Fürstenberg, and Ludwigsburg.

The Italian firms of Capodimonte and Doccia also worked with hard-paste porcelain. Both companies produced tea and table services and specialized in figures.

### FRENCH SOFT-PASTE PORCELAIN

European firms that could not make hard-paste porcelain or did not have access to kaolin produced soft-paste porcelain. At first the French Saint-Cloud factory decorated its small wares – cutlery handles, snuff boxes, and spice boxes – with underglaze blue borders of *lambrequins*. From about 1730 the body was left white and was sometimes moulded with Chinese-inspired cherry blossoms, wading birds, or overlapping leaves.

Chantilly covered its porcelain with an opaque creamy-white glaze that hid imperfections. The decoration on its plates, teapots, jugs, and jardinières was inspired by Chinese *famille verte* and Japanese Kakiemon style. By the mid-1700s it used a scattering of small sprays of European flowers.

The style of the Vincennes factory (established c.1740) was influenced by Meissen, but used a softer palette and more natural brushstrokes. Early pieces are heavy and decorated with landscapes, sprays of flowers, figures, and scrollwork borders. In 1748 the factory introduced more elegant Rococo-style forms. Vincennes moved in 1756 and became known as Sèvres.

**VINCENNES CUP AND SAUCER** The soft-paste porcelain bodies of these pieces were painted by Pierre Rosset with medallions and flowers in polychrome and gold on white and celestial blue. *1754. Saucer: Diam:9.5cm (3¾in).*

### ELSEWHERE IN EUROPE

In Flanders Tournai made porcelain tableware with basket-weave and spiral borders decorated in underglaze blue with scenes from Aesop's fables

*Floral* and scrolling foliate imagery is contrasted against white and coloured grounds

*By royal order,* gilding on porcelain in France was the exclusive preserve of Sèvres

**SÈVRES FLOWER VASE** Made in soft-paste porcelain in the year after the Vincennes factory moved to – and changed its name to – Sèvres, this Pompadour-pink vase displays the serpentine and scrolling forms and decorative imagery that are quintessential Louis XV Rococo. *1757. W:33.5cm (13¼in).*

*Scrolling foliate feet* are typical Rococo forms

**ANSBACH FIGURE** The young boy with a wine glass and jug represents Autumn. The figure is from a series entitled The Four Seasons, a popular subject matter in the Rococo era. *c.1760. H:18cm (7in).*

*Polychrome painting* is contrasted with gilt edging

**DU PAQUIER VASE** Made at Claudius Innocentius du Paquier's factory in Vienna, this vase is decorated with a polychrome *Indianische Blumen* (Indian flowers) pattern, inspired by Japanese and Chinese porcelain. *c.1725. H:27.5cm (11in).*

*Manganese purple,* yellow, green, and iron red dominate the polychrome palette

**OVAL TOURNAI PLATE** The soft-paste porcelain body is decorated with a large bouquet and smaller sprigs of flowers within a swagged floral border, in a palette dominated by purple, puce, and blue. *1755–65. L:44cm (17¼in).*

and exotic birds. Tournai is also known for figures and groups. The Ansbach factory in Bavaria specialized in figures. The porcelain body was a brilliant white and the painting of good quality.

## BRITISH SOFT-PASTE PORCELAIN

Porcelain production in Britain became established around the mid-1700s. Worcester produced a finely potted body with a thin glaze for tea and coffee wares and decorative tableware. These often had moulded decoration. Early wares had Chinoiserie motifs and flowers, but by the late 1760s strong background colours and Rococo-style panels of exotic birds and flowers became favoured.

Early Chelsea wares copied contemporary Rococo silver forms and were unadorned. By 1749 the decoration was inspired by the Japanese Kakiemon style, which evolved into the rich colours and gilding used between 1756 and 1769, in imitation of Sèvres. Chelsea produced tureens in the shape of animals and vegetables, Meissen-style figures, and plates with botanical designs.

The Bow factory produced wares for a wider market. Some were decorated in underglaze blue with Chinese-inspired patterns, as well as moulded *blanc-de-Chine* cherry blossoms.

Derby began producing porcelain in around 1748. Its *blanc-de-Chine* Chinoiserie figure groups are among the best of its production. The factory was bought by Duesbury & Heath in 1756, and production was soon influenced by Meissen. Derby's Rococo figures have scrolling bases and bocage, a type of tree ornament. Tea services, tureens, dishes, and baskets were painted with birds and flowers.

Lowestoft manufactured wares with underglaze blue decoration that followed Chinese patterns. The Longton Hall factory made domestic wares decorated with delicate multicoloured painting, as well as Meissen-inspired figures.

Richard Chaffers's Liverpool factory mostly used a blue-and-white palette for its soft-paste porcelain. Some wares, however, were decorated in the *famille rose* palette. Lund's Bristol used Cornish soapstone to produce soft-paste porcelain. The heavy glaze used often blurred the underglaze blue decoration.

*Botanical imagery* was a popular subject matter for Chelsea in the 1750s

**CHELSEA CUP AND SAUCER** Their creamy-white porcelain bodies and Meissen-style polychrome floral decoration date these items to Chelsea's Red Anchor period (1752–56). *Saucer: Diam:13.5cm (5¼in).*

**WORCESTER VASE** Of waisted, beaker-like form, this vase is painted in the Kakiemon palette with Chinoiserie imagery, comprising a ho-ho bird on rockwork, flanked by flowering branches. *c.1755. H:14cm (5½in).*

*The Kakiemon palette* includes cerulean blue, iron red, turquoise, brown, yellow, and gold

*Chinese scenes* in well-controlled underglaze blue are typical of Liverpool porcelain

**LIVERPOOL COFFEE POT** Made at Richard Chaffers's factory, this pot has a baluster-shaped body and dome cover. Both are painted in the Chinese style with a Jumping Boy pattern in underglaze blue. *c.1760. H:19.5cm (7¾in).*

**LONGTON HALL TUREEN** Made in the shape of a melon, this soft-paste porcelain tureen is decorated in shades of yellow, green, and puce. Longton Hall was famous for its vegetable and fruit forms. *c.1755. W:24cm (9½in).*

# GLASS

IN THE 17TH AND 18TH CENTURIES SODA AND LEAD GLASS WERE
DECORATED WITH ENAMELS, AND WERE CUT, STIPPLED, ENGRAVED,
AND, WITH THE ADDITION OF VARIOUS OXIDES, COLOURED.

## ENAMELLED GLASS

Coloured enamels were first used on glass by the
Romans, and then by Islamic glassmakers from
the 13th century onwards. Enamelling flourished
in Venice in the 15th century, particularly on
*cristallo* glass, a lightweight, thin, clear glass
developed by Angelo Barovier in around 1450.

Enamels are made of powdered glass mixed with
a coloured oxide and oil. After being painted onto
a surface, they are heated in a furnace to form a
hard material that is bonded onto the glass. Early
decorative patterns tended to be simple, such as
lines and dots, and were restricted to borders.
Later, more complex patterns, including coats of
arms and mythological figures, were
created. German and Bohemian
glassmakers adopted enamelling
in the mid-16th century, and the
technique flourished in central and
northern Europe during the 17th and
18th century. Enamelling was most
commonly applied to drinking
vessels. These included the *Humpen*,
a cylindrical beaker, and the *Römer*,
a heavy footed and stemmed glass
akin to a wine glass.

Patterns were often applied by
*Hausmaler*, enamellers who worked

*The opaque* **Milchglas** *body* is
in imitation of porcelain

**MILCHGLAS** TANKARD Made in either Germany or Bohemia,
this piece has a pewter-mounted *Milchglas* body. It is colourfully
decorated with medallions depicting a cipher and portraits under
a crown and among foliage. *c.1740. H:23cm (9in).*

*Landscape scenes* are a
typical *Schwarzlot* subject

**SCHWARZLOT** GOBLET The funnel bowl is raised on
a cut pedestal stem and embellished with *Schwarzlot*
(black lead) enamelling in the form of a hunting scene.
Made in Saxony. *c.1730. H:22.5cm (8¾in).*

*The naivety* of the
painting, especially in the
lion's almost-human face,
is characteristic of the
style and period

**SWEDISH BEAKER** This cylindrical beaker depicts, in vivid polychrome
enamels, Carolus (Karl) XII of Sweden in military attire, with a lion at his feet.
The reverse is decorated with an equally colourful floral spray and the three
crowns of the Swedish royal coat of arms. *c.1715. H:23.75cm (9¼in).*

at home. In the mid-17th century Johann Schaper, a *Hausmaler* in Nuremburg, developed the use of transparent brown and black enamels. Known as *Schwarzlot* (black lead), this style remained fashionable until the 1750s and was adopted by the Bohemians, whose leading exponent was Ignaz Preissler. Designs were usually based on natural themes, including flowers, landscapes, and hunting and mythological scenes. Political and commemorative themes are also known.

## GILDED GLASS

In the early 18th century *Zwichengoldglas* was developed. Gold or silver leaf was applied to a body, engraved with a design, and then covered with a layer of clear glass. Decorative motifs were similar to those on enamelled glass, and gilding was often used in combination with enamelling.

## COLOURED GLASS

In the late 15th century a "milky" opaque white glass, known as *lattimo*, was developed by the Venetians. It resembled the highly coveted porcelain imported from China and became popular during the 17th and 18th century.

The technique had spread to Bohemia by the 18th century, where it was known as *Milchglas*. Bohemian glassmakers also produced innovative coloured glass, most notably a deep, strong blue glass created by adding cobalt oxide to the glass mix. As with *Milchglas*, this provided a perfect foil for coloured enamels.

At the end of the 17th century Johann Kunckel, a director at the Potsdam Glasshouse, developed a deep pink glass, by adding gold chloride to the mix. It was known as *Rubinglas* or *Goldrubinglas* (gold-ruby glass). As it was expensive to produce, it was often finely engraved or cut. Caspar Wistar, a German glassmaker, emigrated to North America in the early 18th century and founded the first American glass factory, Wistaburgh Glassworks, based in New Jersey.

**BEAKER WITH COVER** On the front of this grey-tinted Bohemian footed beaker are two cooing doves and stylized floral ornaments; the back shows architectural landscapes. *c.1700. H:26cm (10¼in).*

**ALPINE REGION BOTTLE** The semi-opaque brown-glass body is hand-trailed with spirals of opaque white *Milchglas. Mid-1700s. H:11.5cm (4½in).*

## ENGRAVED GLASS

Although engraved glass was made by the Romans and then the Venetians, it was not until the second half of the 16th century that the techniques spread to the rest of Europe.

Diamond-point engraving, in which the design is lightly scratched onto the surface of the glass with a sharp stylus, could be used on thin *cristallo* glass, as the engraved line was so shallow. Stipple engraving is similar, but uses patterns of dots made by tapping the stylus on the glass. Stipple-engraved pieces are less common, as the process was more time-consuming.

Both types of engraving enjoyed a golden age when they were brought to the Low Countries, then Germany and Bohemia, by Venetians during the 17th century. Notable exponents included Willem Mooleyser and Frans Greenwood. Patterns were more complex than many enamelled examples, and included political and mythological figures and portraits, and scrolling fruit and floral motifs. Many were applied to drinking vessels, including the lidded *Pokal* and goblets.

Wheel engraving, in which a spinning wheel is used with abrasive paste to cut a design onto glass, was revived in Europe in about 1600. Germany and Bohemia became centres of production, and the technique was brought to Britain in around 1720. George Ravenscroft's lead crystal glass provided a robust body that was perfect for engraving, ensuring Britain remained an important centre of glass production.

**ENGRAVED COVERED GOBLET** The delicate floral and foliate decoration to the bowl and cover of this glass is by Georg Ernst Kunckel of Thuringia. *1726–30. H:31.25cm (12¼in).*

**FRENCH GOBLET** This glass has a stepped, circular foot and a baluster stem with a heart-shaped knop. The bowl is engraved with stylized heart shapes. *c.1700. H:21.5cm (8½in).*

## *FAÇON DE VENISE*

Glass made in the 15th-century Venetian style, but not produced in Venice, is known by the French term *façon de Venise*. This ornate, delicate glass was made throughout Europe by emigrant Venetian glassmakers, and those they taught, during the 16th and 17th centuries. It was often produced in a grey-toned soda glass and could be elaborately decorated with *filigrana* – thin strands of clear or, more usually, white-coloured glass contained in rods, which were shaped into a pattern.

Serpent-stemmed drinking glasses were a popular form, as were tazze and covered goblets. Ornate curls and geometric shapes were also common. Diamond-point engraving can sometimes be found on the bowls of *façon de Venise* glasses made in the Low Countries.

**FAÇON DE VENISE GOBLET** Made in the southern Low Countries, in the style of 15th-century Venetian glass, this goblet combines clear and coloured (blue) glass and features a typically ornate snake-like pattern in the stem. *1690s. H:31cm (12¼in).*

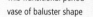

# ORIENTAL INFLUENCE

CHINA DEVELOPED THE FIRST HARD-PASTE PORCELAIN IN THE 10TH CENTURY, AND BY THE 1700S VAST QUANTITIES OF CHINESE WARES WERE SHIPPED TO EUROPE, WHERE, ALONG WITH JAPANESE CERAMICS, THEY HAD A HUGE IMPACT ON EUROPEAN POTTERY.

The strong translucent body of Chinese porcelain, as well as its decoration, was greatly admired by wealthy Europeans. The Portuguese first imported large quantities of Chinese porcelain made specifically for the West, decorated in blue and white, during the Wanli reign (1573–1619). These delicate wares were decorated in a thin, watery blue colour and often featured birds, animals, plants, and landscapes. Peonies, chrysanthemums, and lotuses were commonly used. European potters soon began to copy the designs on their own work.

## CHINESE EXPORTS

During the Transitional period (1620–83), Chinese potters produced new shapes and decoration that catered to European tastes. They used European shapes such as saltcellars, candlesticks, and flasks. They also made technical advances, improving the quality of the porcelain. The cobalt blue glaze on wares from this period has a purplish tone and more naturalistic brushstrokes. Landscape painting became the favourite form of decoration, but narrative scenes were also popular.

Porcelain made during the Kangxi period (1662–1722) is of a higher quality than earlier wares, except pieces made for the

emperor and his court. Flowers and plants among rocks are popular themes on these pieces, as are craggy landscapes, which were replaced by idealized scenes of bending trees and pavilions on islands.

## COLOURFUL CHOICE

Along with the popular, inexpensive blue-and-white, the Chinese also used polychromatic palettes. These include the mid-16th-century *wucai* ("five colour") palette, in which underglaze blue is used as a wash or outline and overglaze iron red, green, yellow, brown, and black provide the pattern. The *famille verte* ("green family") palette, first used during the Qing dynasty (1644–1911), is similar to the *wucai* palette but uses a prominent brilliant green and a duller blue. The 18th-century *famille rose* ("pink family") palette is dominated by rose pink.

Not all wares were coloured: the French term *blanc-de-Chine* refers to the white porcelain exported to Europe from China in the 17th and 18th centuries.

## JAPANESE PORCELAIN

Almost all early Japanese porcelain was produced in Arita, on Kyushu, the main western island close to Korea. Korean potters arrived in this area in the late 16th century and discovered kaolin.

The region is known for three distinct styles. The 17th-century painter and potter Sakaida Kakiemon, thought to have discovered enamelling in Japan, has given his name to Kakiemon ware. Nigoshide, a milky-white porcelain, was used for bowls, vases, and bottles sparsely painted in iron red, blue, turquoise, black, yellow, and occasionally purple enamels. The colourful Imari palette, developed in the late 1600s, saw tableware and large ornaments adorned with textile-inspired patterns, using a dark underglaze blue and iron red, yellow, gold, green, purple, and sometimes turquoise enamelling.

**CHINESE *WUCAI* VASE** This Transitional period vase of baluster shape has a carved and pierced wooden stand and cover. It is painted in the *wucai* palette, with squirrels, grapevines, and rockwork. *c.1650. H:30cm (11¾in).*

**JAPANESE PORCELAIN VASE** Made in Arita, this vase is in the shape of an ancient bronze urn and moulded in shallow relief with chrysanthemums, rocks, and waves, in iron red, blue, and green. *c.1680. H:17cm (6¾in).*

**CHINESE PLATE** Salvaged in 1985 as part of the Nanking Cargo from a Dutch ship sunk in 1752, this Qing dynasty blue-and-white export plate features a Lattice Fence pattern, with a pagoda, willow, and pine. *c.1750. Diam:42cm (16½in).*

## LACQUERING AND JAPANNING

The Orient is the home of lacquering, a technique first used in 4th-century BCE China but perfected in Japan, which involved applying numerous layers of varnish on to wood, leather, or fabric. The varnish came from the sap of the *Rhus vernicifera* tree, and when dried it formed a hard, protective shell that could be carved. Lacquer is often found on furniture, boxes, and *inro*, a type of container with figurative or naturalistic designs highlighted in gold against a typically black or red background. The great demand for the product in Europe led to the development of japanning. For this type of lacquering, the varnish was made from deposits of the *Coccus lacca* (the lac beetle). To create the illusion of depth, sawdust and gum arabic were used to build up areas. Japanning can be found in black, scarlet, or green, often decorated with gilt Chinoiserie.

**QUEEN ANNE KNEEHOLE DESK** Richly japanned on a blue-green ground, this desk features gold Chinoiserie, including elephants, a pavilion, and a warrior on horseback. *c.1710. W:78cm (30¾in).*

**DETAIL FROM A GEORGE I SECRETAIRE** The door is white-japanned all over and decorated with Chinoiserie scenes of dignitaries. The delicately painted figures are rendered in a palette of iron red, yellow, blue, grey, and black. *c.1725.*

# METALWARE

MANY NEW SILVER FORMS APPEARED IN THE LATE 1600S. HOWEVER, DUE TO CHANGES IN FASHION AND THE FACT THAT SILVER WAS OFTEN MELTED DOWN TO FINANCE WAR, FEW ITEMS HAVE SURVIVED FROM BEFORE 1700.

## SILVERWARE

Tea, coffee, and chocolate were first brought to Europe in the late 17th century, to be drunk only by the wealthy few who could afford silverware. The shape of the earliest teapots was based on globular Chinese porcelain teapots, but by the early 1700s the pear-shaped teapot was common in Britain, Germany, the Low Countries, and North America. It had a domed, hinged lid, and the handle and knop on the lid were often made of wood or ivory, which insulated the heat created by the hot liquid. In Britain teapots were occasionally octagonal, imitating the shape of coffee pots.

Early teapots were small (tea was expensive) and decoration was sparse, usually limited to an engraved family crest or coat of arms or cut-card work. By the 1730s teapots were made in a spherical bullet shape and were more ornately

decorated, with chased or engraved flowers, scrolls, and strapwork near the lid. The North Americans preferred an inverted pear-shaped pot on a short stem with a wide foot. A curvaceous body and spout are more symbolic of the Rococo style, as are the double-scroll handle and embossed and chased scroll decoration.

Early 18th-century coffee pots had either a cylindrical or octagonal body, with a straight or curved spout and a wooden handle. Again, decoration was limited to armorials or cut-card work. By the 1740s pots had a flatter lid, a scrolled handle, and a beak-shaped spout. They evolved into a baluster shape, then a pear shape by 1760. Gadrooned rims and decorations of shells, flowers, and scrolls can be found

**ROCOCO CHOCOLATE POT** Fashioned in silver by Charles-Louis Gerard, this waisted pot is raised on four animal feet and decorated with gadroons, shell motifs, and armorials. The handle is of ebonized wood. *1716. H:26.5cm (10½in).*

*Fixed finial,* typical on coffee pots

*The spout is chased* to form a dog's head, neck, and collar

*The carving* of the ebonized wood handle is naturalistic and dynamic

*Gadrooning,* or lobed decoration, was popular in the 16th, 17th, and 18th centuries

**ROCOCO COFFEE POT** Made by William Shaw III, this pot is of footed baluster form, has an ebonized wood handle, and is decorated with fruit, flowers, strings of husks, and scrolling foliage. *c.1760. H:31cm (12¼in).*

**SILVER TEAPOT** The body and cover are selectively gadrooned and engraved. The ebonized wood handle is shaped like an African figure. By Henri Louis Le Gaigneur. *c.1740. H:19cm (7½in).*

on both of these latter forms. The pear shape was originally developed in France, where silversmiths made pots with three feet, a straight handle, and a small pouring lip. The decoration was also more in keeping with the Rococo style.

Chocolate pots were based on the shape of contemporary coffee pots but had a hinged finial where a swizzle stick could be inserted to mix the chocolate. Few were produced after 1750.

### DINING SILVER

Complete dinner services, with plates, tureens, and other serving items became fashionable in France in the late 17th century. Early plates and salvers, used as stands for caudle cups – small, two-handled silver cups – were often plain, decorated with only a family crest or coat of arms. However, by the 1730s, the plain rim was superseded by a wavy one with gadrooning; and by the 1740s the Rococo-style gadrooned borders with shells were common.

Entrée dishes were introduced in the late 17th century, sauceboats first appeared around 1715, and soup tureens around 1720. These were often produced with matching decoration as part of a service, and early examples were plain, decorated with a coat of arms. By the 1730s and 1740s, especially in France, the decoration had become more ornate, with scrollwork and shells, and more extravagant pieces were decorated with vegetables, shellfish, and game.

### OTHER SILVERWARE

The wave of Huguenot immigration to the Low Countries and Britain in the 1690s strongly influenced the style of silverware (*see p.28*). Soon the base, stem, and sconce of a candlestick

**ENGLISH SILVER SALVER** Made by William Justus of London, this has a C-scroll rim with shell clasping around a chased border of scrolling foliage and fish-scale panels, all around a central engraved cartouche. *1747. D:28.5cm (11½in).*

**PAIR OF CANDLESTICKS** These silver candlesticks by John Cafe of London are case cast in a late Rococo style. They have selectively lobed baluster stems and spreading bases with scalloped corners. *1751. H:19.5cm (7¾in).*

were cast separately in solid silver, then soldered together. The stem had a plain baluster shape with knops, which remained popular until the mid-1700s, and the base was round, square, or angled. By the 1730s the previously plain candlestick was ornately decorated with Rococo-style shells and flower-shaped nozzles; some exceptional examples have cast stems in the shape of female figures holding the socket for the candle.

Many other silver items were made in the Rococo style, including tea canisters (later known as tea caddies), sugar bowls, and cream jugs. A variety of items was made for serving wine during dinner – jugs, wine coolers, and monteiths (for cooling wine glasses) – and for condiments. More unusual silver items can be found in the form of andirons, used to hold logs on the hearth of a fireplace.

### METAL MOUNTS

A variety of Chinese porcelain imported into Europe was embellished with ornate metal mounts in the 1500s, but the fashion reached the peak of its popularity in the 1700s, particularly in France. Gilt bronze, silver, and sometimes gold were used to make the mounts, which might be added to protect the piece, to westernize the form by creating handles and bases, or to help adapt the piece into a new form. In the early 18th century French dealers of luxury items purchased Chinese exports from the Dutch East India Company and instructed metalworkers to decorate them. The porcelain was often modified to fit the mounts.

*Chinese celadon glazes* are found in greyish, bluish, and olive green

*Each Buddha* is carved in sandstone and turquoise-enamelled

*Dolphins* are a recurring motif

**FRENCH PERFUME FOUNTAIN** The Chinese celadon-glazed vase of this piece has a gilded rim and is flanked by a pair of Buddhas atop gilded-bronze bases of plant forms and dolphins. *c.1760. H:32cm (12½in).*

**PAIR OF LOUIS XV ANDIRONS** Fashioned in gilded bronze in the style of Jacques Caffieri of Paris, these fire dogs feature reclining male and female Chinese figures raised on volutes. *1760s. L:18cm (7in).*

*The volute* acts as a resting place for the figure

# CLOCKS

THE DAZZLING ACHIEVEMENTS OF BAROQUE AND ROCOCO CLOCK-
MAKERS, ESPECIALLY THOSE WORKING IN FRANCE, REMAIN WITHOUT
PARALLEL IN TERMS OF DECORATIVE IMPACT AND EXUBERANCE.

## THE COURT OF THE SUN KING

That the French should rise to such heights in the field of clock decoration during the reign of Louis XIV, the Sun King, is surely no coincidence. The king himself had a particular interest in time, running his days, and those of his sizable retinue, to a strict timetable. Such was his punctiliousness that he kept no fewer than four clock-makers in his entourage. Their most famous charge – the astronomical clock by Passement – keeps time at Versailles to this day.

The patronage of Louis XIV's court could seal the fortune of any fashion and ensure its replication in elite circles across Europe for many years. The French clock-making industry of the 18th century is, however, more remarkable for the intricate decorative schemes devised by its craftsmen than for the quality or accuracy of its movements. Several horologists owe their long-standing reputation to the efforts of the cabinet-makers and metalworkers who enshrined their machinery in such palatial housings.

Many of the most striking metal mounts take the form of cast figures. Stock Rococo representations of women in pastoral dress, taken straight from popular paintings of the day, can be seen alongside figures drawn from antiquity, including putti and allegorical representations of Father Time.

## ELABORATE CASES

Clock cases of the period were usually made from wood, metal, or a combination. Designs varied from architecturally severe bracket clocks to ethereal cartouche-shaped wall clocks. Decorative embellishments were similarly diverse. Boullework was just as prevalent on clock cases as it was on other furniture at this time. Some cases exhibit brass and tortoiseshell inlays in intricate scrolling designs reminiscent of waves, tongues of flame, or foliate tendrils. Wooden and metal surfaces might be painted or enamelled with convoluted foliate designs or sprays of flowers in a naturalistic style, similar to those found on porcelain of the period.

Background colours include bright greens and deep reds, chosen to complement the gilt-metal mounts that were so prevalent – whether complex openwork scrolls, which were the very epitome of Rococo design, or the more substantial structural additions of bracket or scroll feet, caryatid pillars, and floral finials.

*The numerals* are set on a white-enamelled dial

**CARTEL CLOCK** The open-work case of this Parisian-made, gilded-bronze, cartouche-shaped clock features doves and two quintessential Louis XV Rococo motifs: scrolling foliage and putti. *c.1750. H:58.5cm (23in).*

*The acanthus leaf mounts* are in gilded bronze

**BRACKET CLOCK** Made by Duhamel of Troyes, this clock has a Louis XV Rococo scrolling form, accentuated by gilded-bronze scrolling-foliage mounts and polychrome-painted flowers. *c.1750.*

*French cartel clock cases* are usually cast in gilded bronze, as here, or brass

## EXTENSIVE DECORATION

The clock cases with the strongest association with this fertile period are made entirely from metal. Gilded bronze, or ormolu, was especially prized for its lustre and decorative versatility. The gossamer-thin openwork designs and extensive pierced decoration favoured by some designers were ideally suited to ormolu, and metalworkers were able to manipulate sturdy metals into contortions that would have been impossible in wood. The most unrestrained Rococo clocks lack even a basic form and are delineated by branching leaves, hanging figures, and roaming scrolls around the clock face. This chaos is tempered only by the familiarity of the clock face: most are white-painted or silvered-metal discs, but some are made up of individual numerals picked out in enamel on an engraved metal ground.

## REGULATOR CLOCKS

Regulators, first produced in England and France in the mid-17th century, represented a new breed of timepiece. They tended to be less decorative than other longcase clocks since their function was to keep accurate time: other household clocks and watches would be set by the time shown on the regulator. For ease of reading, regulator dials give greater prominence to the minutes than the hours and often have a subsidiary dial for seconds. Regulator mechanisms, which do not strike, are the most carefully constructed and sophisticated of the period.

**Each numeral** is set within its own white-enamelled plaque

**EBONY BRACKET CLOCK** The caddy top has a carrying handle, and there are embossed pierced panels on the globe finials. The backplate is inscribed "Nicolas Masey A Londres". c.1680. H:38.5cm (15¼in).

**BOULLE BRACKET CLOCK** This clock's tortoiseshell-veneered case has a domed and galleried surmount, with caryatids and corner consoles. These, like all the mounts, are in gilt brass. Made by Jacques Hory of Paris. c.1690. H:70cm (27½in).

## PENDULES RELIGIEUSES

The *pendule religieuse*, or "church clock", is a subcategory of the bracket clock that became prevalent in France in the late 17th century, during the reign of Louis XIV. Of relatively sober design, at least compared with many of the more elaborate excesses of high Rococo horology, these clocks take their name from a supposed similarity to church architecture. The basic form of the *pendule religieuse* is the high arch over the top of the clock face, which can be seen as an imitation of the high, round arches of the ancient Romanesque churches scattered throughout France.

These clocks are usually made from the most opulent materials. Cases are frequently cut from ebony and other rare woods, and feature lavish inlaid decoration, often of Boulle type. Inlays of copper, ivory, and even tortoiseshell add to the understated sumptuousness of these timepieces. Foliate scrolls and asymmetric enamelled floral decoration both help to place the clocks firmly within the Rococo decorative tradition.

**NUMBERING** The hours in the chapter ring are in Roman numerals, in the form of black-on-white enamel cartouches. The minutes are in Arabic numerals and engraved in gilded brass, while the hands are black-enamelled.

**The clock face** is cast in gilded bronze

**The scrolling foliate** and floral decoration beneath the dial is in applied enamel

**BOULLEWORK CLOCK** The wooden body of this clock by Pierre Margotin is decorated with tortoiseshell veneer and brass Boullework. It also has gilded-bronze mounts, including caryatids, scrolling acanthus leaves, and flaming urns. c.1700. H:49cm (19¼in).

**BOULLE PENDULA CLOCK** Made by Voisin of Paris, this piece features gilded brass on brown tortoiseshell Boullework, figural mounts, and an equally elaborate socle with masks and scrolling foliage. c.1730. H:125cm (49¼in).

**SIGNED WORK** The mechanism bears the engraved signature of Pierre Margotin, who is known to have worked in Paris for most of the second half of the 17th century.

# TEXTILES

IN EUROPE THE TRADITION FOR TAPESTRIES CAN BE TRACED AS FAR BACK AS ANCIENT GREECE AND THE WORLD OF HOMER'S *ODYSSEY*, WHILE SILK HAD LIKEWISE BEEN WOVEN IN CHINA FOR MILLENNIA.

## MULTIFUNCTION TAPESTRIES

Weaving cloth has always had both a useful and a decorative purpose. In the Middle Ages in Europe, wall hangings kept out the draughts and blanketed rooms with pictures taken from mythology, morality tales, or nature. In church, tapestries depicting religious scenes helped imprint stories from the Bible on the minds of an illiterate congregation.

Tapestries are made on a loom by weaving coloured weft threads (which run horizontally) between undyed warp threads (which run vertically) to create an image or pattern. Each area of colour is built up separately, following a paper or canvas design known as a cartoon. The coloured threads are wound on to bobbins.

## RISE OF FACTORIES

France and the Low Countries were at the forefront of tapestry-making. Two factories stood out: Gobelins and Aubusson. The former was taken over by Louis XIV's minister of finance, Jean-Baptiste Colbert, in 1662. Under the artistic directorship of court painter Charles Le Brun, Gobelins produced tapestries of unrivalled technical brilliance, the subtle shading of which

increasingly resembled paintings. Le Brun created cartoons for *portières* (tapestries meant for hanging in front of doors) showing a triumphal cart filled with trophies, with Louis XIV's fleur-de-lys coat of arms and his Sun King emblem. The Story of the King ran to 14 large panels and there was also a series of 12 Months, showing a different royal residence for each one.

Le Brun's Baroque style suited the pomp and formality of the Sun King's court. With the advent of the Rococo style, more frivolous designs were introduced, following cartoons by François Boucher, who specialized in erotic mythological scenes. His 1758 series

**AUBUSSON TAPESTRY** Woven in wool and silk for an upholstered settee, this tapestry has picturesque flora and fauna imagery inspired by the fables of 17th-century French poet Jean de La Fontaine. *Early 1700s. W:133cm (52½in).*

**FLEMISH TAPESTRY** Woven in wool, this tapestry displays the overall green colour cast and flora and fauna imagery – a wooded landscape with a castle in the distant background – typical of *verdure* work. *Early 1700s. W:175cm (69in).*

**AUBUSSON TAPESTRY** The scrolling leaf border of this tapestry, woven in wool and silk, frames an exotic Chinoiserie landscape with birds and a pagoda, in the style of French designer Jean Pillement. *Early 1700s. W:228cm (89¾in).*

**AUBUSSON TAPESTRY** The *verdure* silk and wool weave of this tapestry depicts woodland scenes with a *manoir* in the background, all within a ribbon-bound floral border. *c.1865. L:290cm (114in).*

## *VERDURE* TAPESTRIES

From the Middle Ages until the reign of Louis XIV, most factories in northern Europe produced *verdure* tapestry hangings. Revolving around the theme of natural woodlands tamed by man, these showed formal or wild gardens, game preserves, or game parks, sometimes with castles or mansions in the background. Often they included animals and birds as well, and the colour palette focused around greens, browns, and other complementary shades. *Verdure* tapestries were often surrounded by a wide border.

**FLEMISH TAPESTRY** Woven at the Schaerbeck factory in Brussels, this piece was designed in the *verdure* style by M. Chaudoir. It depicts a wild garden made up of numerous independent vignettes. *Early 1700s. W:264cm (104in).*

Loves of the Gods found favour with English as well as French patrons. Today it can be admired at Osterley Park in Middlesex.

After a chequered time during the French Revolution, Gobelins is still in production today, working to designs of artists such as Henri Matisse.

At Aubusson weavers worked at home on low-warp looms rather than at a central location. Unlike Gobelins, this factory catered more for the middle classes, with simpler, coarser tapestries. Motifs were taken from the Bible or mythology, or they depicted *verdures*, or gardens. They also copied designs such as The Hunts of Louis XV

from Gobelins and Beauvais, another royal factory that incorporated Jean Bérain grotesques and scenes from the comedies of playwright Molière.

Like Gobelins, Aubusson continues today, working to cartoons by 20th-century artists such as Raoul Dufy and Graham Sutherland.

### EUROPEAN SILKS

The natural fibre that produces silk comes from the cocoons of a moth native to China, so it is no surprise that the material was first used for textiles here. In 1667 France banned foreign imports of silk textiles, an action that single-handedly put the factories of Lyon on the silk-manufacturing and weaving map. Soon the European silk industry had shifted from Italy and Spain to France. The Lyon factory alone employed more than 3,000 weavers.

In fashion-conscious Europe, designs changed every year. One Lyon range, Bizarre, in gold or silver, with swaying flowers and leaves, jagged lines, and asymmetrical architectural motifs, was a forerunner of the Rococo style. The range existed alongside more formal Baroque patterns, which gave way in about 1730 to naturalistic flowers and fruit, at the instigation of the innovative silk designer Jean Revel.

When the Edict of Nantes was revoked in 1685, many Huguenot weavers fled to London and found work at the Spitalfields silk factories (*see p.28*). In the early 1700s they stuck to Bizarre patterns, then adopted the Rococo style, with designs featuring dainty posies of flowers and ribbons.

Ever capricious, the fashion industry lost interest in patterned silks, and the industry went into terminal decline in the 1770s.

**FLORAL SILK** The floral pattern of this silk, woven in a weight suitable for curtains or wall hangings, was probably inspired by the exotic decoration found on imported Chinese silks and lacquer wares. *Early 1700s. L:104cm (41in).*

**RÉGENCE SILK** A Jacquard-woven silk *lampas* (damask), this displays an all-over pattern of formalized branches, leaves, and blooming flowers in a redcurrant, cream, and green palette. *c.1715. W:125cm (49¼in).*

**AUBUSSON *PORTIÈRE*** Designed to frame a doorway, and woven in wool and silk, this item presents a highly naturalistic woodland imagery in autumnal colours, set against a mountainous backdrop. *Mid-1700s. H:341cm (134¼in).*

# NEOCLASSICISM
## 1760–1840

# A NEW CLASSICISM

IN DIRECT IMITATION OF GREEK AND ROMAN MODELS, NEOCLASSICAL STYLE WAS INSPIRED BY THE EXCAVATIONS OF HERCULANEUM (1738) AND POMPEII (1748), WHERE VILLAS CONTAINING ARTEFACTS WERE UNCOVERED BENEATH THE ASHES OF MOUNT VESUVIUS.

## GRAND TOUR

A steady stream of visitors began to visit the ancient sites around Rome in order to learn more about the Classical world. For a gentleman, such sites were part of the Grand Tour he undertook to complete his education. This renewed interest in ancient Greece and Rome led in turn to the development of a revived Classical style.

## NEOCLASSICAL STYLE

Neoclassicism was a comprehensive style that encompassed painting, architecture, literature, and music, as well as the decorative arts. In furniture, the elaborate decorations and gilding of Rococo gave way to straight lines and geometric motifs. Chairs were modelled on the curule, sat on by the highest civil officials of ancient Rome, and beds on the triclinium, or reclining couch. Bronze acanthus leaf sprays, fan-shaped floral palmettes, and other Classical motifs were applied as decoration. Silverware became more formal and less ornate, while rooms were now decorated in pale-coloured wallpaper with repeating arabesques.

The Neoclassical style varied from country to country, developing into the grand Empire style in France, the Regency style in Britain, the relaxed Biedermeier style in Germany, and the light Gustavian style in Scandinavia. It also spread to the newly independent United States, where it resulted in the elegant Federal style.

Neoclassicism owed its intellectual birth to the Enlightenment, whose philosophers, notably Voltaire and Diderot, believed in the promotion of public morality through art and the social responsibility of the artist and craftsman. Their work should be designed for the collective well-being and education of the community. The noble simplicity and symmetry of antiquity as expressed through Neoclassicism was much better suited to this task than the frivolous decoration of the Rococo. In this respect, Neoclassicism can be seen as the artistic flowering of the Enlightenment.

**FEDERAL MAHOGANY CHAIR** The moulded and rope-carved back encloses an urn and Prince of Wales feathers, draped swags, and leaves, above a serpentine seat on reeded, tapering legs. *1790. H:98cm (38½in).*

## FOUR REVOLUTIONS

The Neoclassical style can also be seen as the artistic response to the four revolutions of the 18th century. The first of these was the agricultural revolution that began in Britain during the early 1700s and spread across the Continent. The enclosure of common land, better crop and animal breeding techniques, and new farm machinery led to a rise in agricultural production. This reduced food prices and created a wealthy land-based middle class and aristocracy that sought an artistic style suited to their rural status.

During the 1760s an industrial revolution in Britain transformed the country and later most of the Continent. New inventions such as the spinning jenny to spin cotton thread, steam engines to power the new weaving machines, and canals and later railways to deliver coal and iron and take away finished goods, made it possible to mass produce cotton and woollen cloth, ceramics, and

**PAVLOVSK PALACE, RUSSIA** Catherine the Great had this imperial residence built from 1777 for her son. Its Classical exterior, influenced by the Italian architect Andrea Palladio, is followed through indoors in Italian and Grecian halls.

**PARIS VASE** One of a pair, the vase is in the resplendent Napoleonic Empire style, painted with a woman in an interior and with caryatid handles. *Early 19th century.*

other household items in purpose-built factories. Workers left their small cottage industries to work in the factories, leading to fast growth in towns and cities at the expense of the countryside. This revolution created new industrial classes of factory owners and workers that transformed the economics and politics of many European nations, while mass production affected design styles and techniques.

## REPUBLIC AND EMPIRE

In the 13 British colonies on the Atlantic coast of North America, discontent with repressive British rule and unrepresentative taxation led to revolt in 1775 and a declaration of independence in 1776. The United States of America that emerged in 1783 was both a political product of the Enlightenment and, in its republican and representative government complete with senate, a positive acknowledgement of Classical political structures.

The final revolution had the most immediate impact. The outbreak of revolution in France in 1789 and the overthrow of the monarchy in favour of a republic in 1792 soon engulfed the whole of Europe in war. The turmoil led in turn to the dictatorship and imperial rule of Napoleon Bonaparte, the leader of the republican armies who crowned himself Emperor of France in 1804. Napoleon consciously used Neoclassical imagery to boost his power and prestige, at the same time introducing an influence based on ancient Egypt, the remains of which he had explored during his expedition to the country in 1798.

**COALPORT TEAPOT**
A spout and handle that terminate in grotesque's heads, together with hand-painted panels and gilt borders and highlights, are typical of the English Neoclassical style. *Early 19th century. H:16cm (6¼in).*

**OSTERLEY PARK, MIDDLESEX** The interior of the house was designed in Neoclassical style by Robert Adam. The wallpaper of the Etruscan Dressing Room was handpainted with arabesques.

# ELEMENTS OF STYLE

Reacting against the excesses of the Baroque and Rococo styles, designers began to look back to antiquity for inspiration, spurred on by the rediscovery of ancient sites. Rather than simply imitate ancient forms, they sought to create a timeless and authentic style using Classical rules of proportion and composition. In time these noble aspirations were swallowed up by the eclectic and disorderly historicism of the 19th century.

GILDED COALPORT VASE
## CLASSICAL URN SHAPE
The urn, or vase, shape was used for glassware, ceramics, and metalware. It became ubiquitous across all disciplines of the decorative arts – carved as a finial atop a longcase clock, surmounting the fluted column of a silver candlestick, or inlaid in an oval panel on a *secrétaire à abattant*.

LION'S MASK DETAIL ON SIDE TABLE
## LION'S HEAD
Used in antiquity to represent majesty and power, the lion's mask was a popular Neoclassical feature. It is found on armrests, friezes, and corners of furniture and is also depicted in prunts (applied glass decoration). Mythological beasts such as the griffin are also widely used Neoclassical motifs.

PARQUETRY DETAIL ON COMMODE
## PARQUETRY
As veneering increased, English and French craftsmen perfected parquetry (geometric patterns) and marquetry (figurative patterns) techniques. The increased availability of exotic woods with rich colours and strong grains encouraged cabinet-makers to make complex parquetry designs on commodes.

BIEDERMEIER GOBLET
## COLOURED GLASS
Pigments developed by Bohemian manufacturers for creating new colours of stained glass were adopted widely across Europe. Transparent tints, often featuring multiple colours or combined with gilding, were used to decorate glass with landscapes and armorial themes.

SCENE ON DERBY COFFEE CAN
## TOPOGRAPHICAL SCENES
In architecture, Neoclassicism brought about a renewed interest in Classical notions of the relation between natural landscape and the built environment. Scenes depicting the integration of buildings, artificial landscaping, and wild nature explored this theme.

ORMOLU SWAG ON CENTRE TABLE
## SWAGS
Originally used to decorate Roman altars, swags are also seen carved into ancient stone architecture. Neoclassical swags often feature bundled laurel leaves – emblematic of honour and victory – tied with ribbons. In the example above, the swag is draped from a rosette stud.

DIAMOND-CUT GLASS
## CUT GLASS
Cut glassware grew far more sophisticated after the development of lead glass in the 1670s. Popular Neoclassical treatments include fluting, diamond cutting, and hobnail, a kind of diamond cutting with stars at the centre of the diamonds. These elaborate designs had not been possible in the past.

DETAIL OF WEDGWOOD BASALT WARE
## NEW CERAMICS
Developments in the ceramics industry included pearl ware – an earthenware with a white finish made by many factories in the Staffordshire area. Inspired by the discovery of ancient ceramics at sites such as Pompeii, Josiah Wedgwood perfected his black basalt ware during the 1760s.

GILT BEADING AND GUILLOCHE
## ARCHITECTURAL MOULDINGS
Many devices used as architectural decoration in the ancient world were adopted by Neoclassical craftsmen. Popular examples include various forms of beading, and shapes like guilloche, a pattern of twisting bands, linked chains, spirals, or double spirals.

BOSTON MAHOGANY CARD TABLE WITH LYRE PEDESTAL
## LYRE SUPPORTS
The ancient Greeks attributed the invention of the lyre to Hermes, messenger of the gods, who gave it to Apollo, the sun god. The motif is frequently seen on Neoclassical chair backs. Apollo's association with the sun means that lyres are often found on clocks, too.

NANTGARW VASE PAINTED BY WILLIAM BILLINGSLEY
## NATURALISTIC FLORAL PAINTING
The development of porcelain in Europe prompted decorators to use the material for fine painting. Floral painting of the Neoclassical period tended to be naturalistic, as exemplified by William Billingsley's work for firms such as Swansea, Derby, Nantgarw, and Coalport.

PLATE WITH GREEK KEY DESIGN
## GREEK KEY
One of the most common variations of the Classical fret motif, the Greek key pattern was revived by Neoclassical craftsmen. It is most often seen as a continuous band. It was used in everything form architectural mouldings to furniture and ceramics in place of the fanciful fretwork popular during the Rococo period.

WEDGWOOD JASPER WARE CANOPIC VASE
## EGYPTIAN MOTIFS
Napoleon installed himself as Emperor of France straight after his conquest of Egypt. His retinue returned to France laden with ancient Egyptian artefacts, sparking an obsession with Egyptian design that spread across Europe. Hieroglyphs, scarabs, obelisks, and lotus leaves permeated the decorative arts.

ROBERT ADAM MARQUETRY DESIGN
## ARABESQUES
One of Robert Adam's favoured motifs, the arabesque is a linear, interlaced pattern based on foliage and tendrils. When human figures are included it is called a grotesque. Arabesques were used across the decorative arts — for vertical wall decoration, marquetry, painting on ceramics, and etching on glass.

# THE ANCIENT WORLD

THE TERM "NEOCLASSICAL", FIRST COINED IN 1861, APTLY DESCRIBES THE STYLE THAT EMERGED IN REACTION TO THE FRIVOLOUS EXUBERANCE OF THE ROCOCO AGE. THE YEARS 1760 TO 1840 SAW A REVIVAL OF CLASSICAL ARCHITECTURE AND DESIGN, WHICH PERVADED ALL AREAS OF THE DECORATIVE ARTS.

**REGENCY MAHOGANY STOOL** The X-frame chair or stool was based on the Roman folding campaign chair. This stool has a subtly shaped seat with scrolled ends and light carving on the surface. c.1810. W:51cm (20in).

## CLASSICAL ORDERS

All public buildings in ancient Greece were built according to the three Orders of Greek architecture – Doric, Ionic, and Corinthian – best represented by the columns of their temples. The Orders were used in various ways throughout the decorative arts.

The Doric column was the simplest, with a plain, circular capital, a fluted shaft, and no base. It tended to be short and wide, and generally massive in form. The Ionic column was taller than the Doric, and also fluted. At the base were a number of graduated rings, while the capital featured two volutes, front and back, which flanked the top of the shaft. Corinthian columns were the most decorative, with flutes and bases similar to those of the Ionic column. They had elaborate capitals carved with acanthus leaves.

Some buildings used all three orders: the simple Doric on the ground floor, Ionic on the first floor, and elaborate Corinthian on the top floor.

**Corinthian capital**

**Ionic capital**

**Doric capital**

The discovery of ancient Roman sites at Herculaneum (1738) and Pompeii (1748) and the Greek site of Paestum (1750s) generated renewed enthusiasm for the Classical age, and a number of scholars published works illustrating the ancient world. Among them was Giovanni Battista Piranesi whose publications *Antichità Romane* (Roman antiquities) and *Vedute di Roma* (Views of Rome) had a lasting impact on artists and architects throughout Europe.

Rome and Naples – home to Herculaneum, Pompeii, and Paestum – became a focus for Grand Tourists. Aristocrats returning home wanted to emulate the Classical architecture and interiors they had seen. Stirred by the antiquities that had been on display during their travels, they returned with a host of ancient-world souvenirs.

### THE DAWN OF NEOCLASSICISM

Inspired by the wall paintings at Herculaneum and Pompeii, early Neoclassical designers introduced similar colour schemes: red, blue, green, and white became popular colours for painted furniture in Italy. German architect Leo von Klenze created fine Pompeian interiors for his clients, and Classical scenes, resembling those of Piranesi, began to appear in European design – from marquetry panels in fine furniture to painted scenes on enamelled *objets de vertu*.

Furniture designers applied the rules of Classical architecture to their pieces, adopting more rectilinear forms, and including architectural

**GRAND TOUR CANDELABRA**
Classical influences are evident in the stylized Corinthian columns of this pair of bronze and gilt candelabra. The orb knop and acanthus pedestal, the tripod base with lion's feet, and the concave marble plinth with leaf cast mouldings all speak of the ancient world. H:73cm (28¾in).

**SPODE STONEWARE VASE** This flared pot pourri vase of Classical form has a flat, pierced cover. It was common for Neoclassical designers to incorporate ancient Greek or Roman scenes in their works, as here with the applied white putti. c.1810. H:16cm (6¼in).

**SNUFF BOX** Many pieces of the time popularized the Grand Tour, embellished with scenes of ancient Rome. This snuff box depicts the Forum in Rome with Trajan's Column and the Colosseum. c.1760. L:7cm (2¾in).

motifs. Fluted columns, volutes, festoons, and paterae were all common. New materials were produced in an attempt to re-create those of the ancient world: Wedgwood developed new ceramics in rosso antico and black basaltes (*see pp.64–65*), and in Germany Count von Buquoy developed black and red-marbled Hyalith glass (*see pp.74–75*).

### INCREASING AUTHENTICITY

As the style developed, so too did a fashion for producing more accurate renditions of ancient forms. Driven by the imperial tendencies of Napoleon, designers began to produce furniture and ornaments that were almost exact copies of original forms, such as the *klismos* chair, the Warwick vase, and the urn shape. Motifs also became more closely associated with the military overtones of a growing empire and included laurel wreaths and fasces (an authority symbol of a bundle of rods bound round an axe). The eagle – emblem of the legions of Rome – appeared in American Classical and Austrian Beidermeier designs, in particular.

**SCHLOSS CHARLOTTENHOF** Designed in 1826, Germany's greatest Neoclassical architect Karl Friedrich Schinkel – also a painter, stage- and interior designer – masterfully integrated the interior, exterior, and landscape setting of this royal pleasure house with his blend of Prussian Hellenism.

# FURNITURE

THE LATE 18TH CENTURY SAW A MOVE AWAY FROM ROCOCO TOWARDS A FURNITURE STYLE THAT WAS STEEPED IN THE CLASSICAL ORDER OF THE ANCIENT WORLD.

## A CLASSICAL STYLE

Buoyed by travel through Europe, and in particular Italy, designers and aristocrats were keen to create interiors inspired by Classical Greece and Rome. They adopted a simpler, more elegant look in furniture: serpentine forms became linear; cabriole legs were replaced with straight, tapering ones; and chair backs progressed from ovals to rectangles.

## EMERGING NEOCLASSICAL

Signs that a new style was emerging were evident in the *Goût grec* furniture that developed in France towards the end of Louis XV's reign. Inspired by architecture, and akin to the British Palladian style, furniture was large, rectilinear, and decorated with Classical motifs such as Vitruvian scrolls, Greek key, and guilloche bands.

The spread of the new style was not instant, however, and furniture design underwent a transitional phase. During the early years of Louis XVI's reign (1774–89) pieces often retained their Rococo form – chests with serpentine fronts and chairs with cabriole legs – but were decorated with typical Neoclassical motifs, including acanthus leaves, palmettes, and lion's masks.

The Neoclassical style that eventually emerged under Louis XVI and spread throughout Europe was one of pure symmetry, arbitrated by skilled cabinet-makers including Martin Carlin and Adam Weisweiler. Forms were rectilinear, light, and well proportioned. Designers abandoned heavy ormolu mounts and turned to carving for decoration. Inspired by English cabinet-makers of the previous half-century, they made much of the wood – usually mahogany – relying on its grain for the success of a piece. Tapering chair and table legs were often fluted, imitating Greek and Roman columns, while Classical ornament included cameos, laurel swags, Greek urns, and anthemia.

Marquetry continued to be popular. Instead of naturalistic floral displays, it was now common to see Classical scenes or motifs – urns, trophies, and stylized fans. French *ébénistes* used trellis marquetry and parquetry to striking effect on large, flat surfaces. Some designers incorporated ceramic plaques by Sèvres or Wedgwood into their pieces, adding a cameo detail.

**SECRÉTAIRE À ABATTANT** The tall fall-front desk became a seminal form of the Neoclassical period. This Parisian version has marquetry panels depicting Classical ruins with figures highlighted in inlaid ivory. *c.1775. H:140cm (55¼in).*

**The table** stands on eight ebonized and ormolu channelled, tapering legs, which terminate in sabots chased with laurel leaves

**Each leg** is headed by ebony blocks outlined in ormolu; the inner ones are each applied with a large foliate rosette

**The laurel swags** appear to run through each block and hang down from each outer leg

**EBONIZED AND ORMOLU CENTRE TABLE** The massive proportions of this table, attributed to Joseph Baumhauer, accentuate the architectural nature of its design. Classical motifs include the moulded guilloche and foliate outer border to the ormolu band that surrounds the writing surface, the use of the Greek key pattern, and the large swags of laurel leaves tied with ribbons suspended from the apron. *c.1760. H:80cm (31½in).*

**Giltwood Adam-style open armchair.** *c.1775.*

**NEWBY HALL, NORTH YORKSHIRE** The interior of the house was redesigned by Robert Adam. In the entrance hall the pale tones of the wall and ceiling are offset by Chippendale furniture. The house also boasts a Gobelins tapestry room and a gallery of Classical statues.

**MAHOGANY ARCHITECT'S TABLE** The rectangular top has a gilt tooled-green leather writing surface and can be raised with a winding mechanism. Stamped A. Weisweiler. *c.1790. H:129.5cm (51in).*

## ADAM STYLE

Robert Adam was the leading Neoclassical architect and designer in Britain. He had studied and travelled in Italy and, although influenced by developments in France, he was also inspired by the work of Piranesi and the Palladian movement in Britain. He designed complete interiors, matching colours, tones, and decoration in furniture, walls, and ornament alike. His designs for furniture, carried out by Sheraton and Hepplewhite among others, tended to use light-coloured woods, including harewood and satinwood, together with delicate painted designs, which incorporated a range of Classical motifs. The refined and elegant result was much sought after and copied – so much so that the Neoclassical look became known generally as Adam style in Britain.

## DESIGN INGENUITY

It was during this era that designers used springs and levers to add novel uses to pieces: sections of a table that could be raised to reveal hidden drawers, or pull-out slides that provided additional useful surfaces. In France Jean-François Oeben developed a *bureau à cylindre*, where the roll top disappeared from view when opened. David Roentgen was particularly adept at creating mechanical pieces, among them architect's and writing tables. Writing desks for ladies continued to be popular. A new form emerged in the *bonheur-du-jour*, a small table with a raised back, almost like a mini-cabinet, containing shelves or pigeonholes and a writing surface above a frieze drawer. First made in the 1760s, they became widespread as the century progressed, and were often used as dressing tables.

The *secrétaire à abattant* was first designed in 1760 by Oeben. This writing desk took the form of a tall fall-front cabinet, housing a writing surface and fitted interior above an arrangement of cupboards or doors. Such was the popularity of the piece that it was made throughout Europe.

**GLAISHER & NASH LTD.**
WORKS OF ART

Telephone:
ELgravia 2285 - 2286
Cables:
NASH LONDON S.W.1

LOWNDES LODGE
CADOGAN PLACE
LONDON, S.W.1

A WELL-DRAWN HEPPLEWHITE MAHOGANY WHEELBACK ARMCHAIR IN THE FRENCH TASTE. CIRCA 1780.

**The chair advertised in** *Country Life Annual*

**UMBRELLA-BACK CHAIR** The wavy back of this mahogany chair has a central floral medallion and carved top rail. The chair stands on cabriole legs. *c.1780. H:90cm (36in).*

**CHIPPENDALE SIDE CHAIR** The serpentine crest rail, carved open splat, cabriole legs, and claw-and-ball feet are typical Chippendale. The style prevailed in the United States until the 1780s. *c.1760.*

## LATE NEOCLASSICAL

Towards the end of the 18th century furniture designs became more austere: linear, geometric forms were even more slender and delicate, and rectangular backs replaced ovals on chairs. The use of ornament declined, and carving made way for inlays of wood imitating carved detail. Lighter woods – satinwood, tulipwood, and ash – were used, often contrasting with darker woods – ebony and mahogany – for decorative effect.

### AMERICAN FEDERAL

American design had remained predominantly Chippendale in style but this changed when the Civil War ended in 1783. In Britain designers George Hepplewhite and Thomas Sheraton had done much to popularize the Neoclassical style with their pattern books, *The Cabinet-Maker and Upholsterer's Guide* (Hepplewhite, 1788) and *The Cabinet-Maker and Upholsterer's Drawing Book* (Sheraton, 1791–94). Their simplified

versions of dominant forms were much copied in Britain and now, with the continued influx of immigrant craftsmen, they were also interpreted in the American Federal style.

New forms included the shield-back chair, the sideboard, and the Pembroke table. Hepplewhite's shield-back chair had a double-carved shield-shaped top rail and tapering uprights. The back was often pierced and decorated with Classical motifs such as urns and wheatsheaves. A typical Sheraton-style sideboard was an elegant *demi-lune* piece, on tall, slender legs. The Pembroke table, which had two drop leaves and two frieze drawers, became a salon addition. Usually raised on casters, it was portable and suited to card games, writing, and dining.

### EUROPEAN INTERPRETATIONS

Much of Europe followed the fashions in France, with a delay in some regions. In Germany David Roentgen produced rectilinear furniture that relied on the grain of the wood – typically mahogany – for decoration, often married with fine gilt-bronze or bronze mounts. He is noted for his outstanding marquetry skills as well as his mechanical pieces.

**The drawers** have simple oval cast-bronze plates with bail handles

**AMERICAN SHERATON SECRETAIRE** The upper case of this mahogany and figured birch Federal secretaire is fitted with a cornice with foliate carved panels below turned and gilded urn finials. The lower section has a hinged fall-front with a banded edge over three drawers with flanking bottle drawers and stands on ring-turned legs. *L:101.5cm (40in).*

**A central flap** lifts to reveal six internal drawers and is flanked by additional graduated drawers

**Ornament** is limited to a simple three-quarter brass gallery and the square drop handles on each of the six external drawers

**The reeded decoration** at the top of each leg is a Sheraton feature

**BRITISH CARLTON HOUSE WRITING TABLE** The simple linear shape of this Sheraton-period desk and slender, turned legs are characteristic of the more refined late Neoclassical style. *c.1800. H:93cm (37in).*

**NEW YORK SIDEBOARD** This Hepplewhite inlaid mahogany sideboard has a subtly bowed front and square, tapering legs. Decoration is minimal, with rope-twist geometric inlay on each of the drawers and diamond-over-oval stringing in the stiles. *L:186cm (73¼in).*

## GUSTAVIAN FURNTIURE

Swedish designers copied the work of their French counterparts but produced a style of their own, with light-coloured painted pieces, ornamented with gold-painted decoration instead of gilt. *Table: H:85cm (33½in).*

*This late-Gustavian table* displays early examples of the use of Egyptian motifs

Roentgen enjoyed commissions from a number of prestigious clients, among them Louis XVI, Catherine the Great of Russia, and Frederick William II of Prussia.

While much of the furniture produced in Italy was larger in scale and less refined that in France, one designer, Giuseppe Maggiolini, produced works to rival any in France. Austere in form, Maggiolini's furniture rarely had mounts or carving. Instead, he decorated pieces in exquisite marquetry, using many different colours to create dazzling displays.

In Sweden cabinet-maker Georg Haupt emulated the Louis XVI style, producing exceptional pieces with exotic veneers, Classical-motif marquetry, and fine ormolu mounts. Gustav III, enamoured with what he had seen on a visit to Versailles before being crowned, invited French craftsmen to Sweden. The result was the the Gustavian style, an elegant interpretation of French taste, painted in light colours – pastel blue, green, and grey – to match the decor of a room.

**GUSTAVIAN ARMCHAIR** One of a pair by J. Lindgren, stamped "ILG".

**HYLINGE, SWEDEN** The Gustavian style emphasized the quality and fitness for purpose of the furniture. In this admiral's house the grouped furniture contributes to the elegant proportions and light colour scheme.

### THE EMPIRE LOOMS

By the turn of the 19th century furniture design in much of Europe was moving in a new direction. With their publication *Recueil des Décorations Intérieures* (Collection of Interior Decorations) in 1801, French architects Charles Percier and Pierre-François-Léonard Fontaine foreshadowed the Empire style that developed under Napoleon. Both men had studied and travelled extensively throughout Italy. Furniture in the Directoire period (1795–99) had been smaller and simpler, while now, during the Consulat period (1799–1804) forms began to copy slavishly ancient Greek and Roman models. Georges Jacob and his sons were leading cabinet-makers of the Consulat period.

*The marquetry design* features flowers and flowing ribbons

*The legs are screwed into place*

**GERMAN MARQUETRY TABLE** This mahogany, rosewood, and maple table would have been used as a writing desk or dressing table. The superb floral marquetry was probably by Johann Michael Rummer, the leading marqueteur in Roentgen's workshop. *c.1770. H:122 (48in).*

**AUSTRIAN LYRE-SHAPED SECRETAIRE** This desk-cabinet is decorated with partial inlay and has an arched pediment flanked by gilded Classical figures. The lyre form is echoed in the string-like decoration. *c.1807. H:139cm (55½in).*

## THE EMPIRE STYLE

Such was Napoleon Bonaparte's personality that, once crowned Emperor in 1804, he dominated social and artistic trends in the whole of Europe, except Britain, cultivating an all-pervasive Empire style. By appointing family members to seats of power as the Empire grew, he vouched that his was the style of choice for Europe's fashionable elite.

Employing the services of architects Percier and Fontaine, and cabinet-makers Jacob-Desmalter (run by Georges Jacob's son), Napoleon moved towards a more masculine form of Neoclassicism, and one that was closely tied in with the sentiments of Roman imperialism. Furniture was more strictly rectangular and symmetrical, often relying on architectural devices – columns, plinths, and pediments – for visual effect. Motifs remained Classical in inspiration, but now included those associated with warfare and victory – fasces and trophies of weapons. Animal motifs were also popular – rams' heads and lions' paws among them – as were all things Egyptian.

Mahogany remained the wood of choice and much was made of its figuring. However, blockades on imports from British colonies made it scarce, so native woods were also used, including bird's-eye maple and walnut. Fabrics were widely used in interiors, bold in colour and striped or with a recurring motif.

### FRENCH EMPIRE FORMS

Empire designers tried to re-create ancient furniture accurately. New forms emerged – the *klismos* chair, a Greek form with sabre legs; the *guéridon*, a small Roman table on tripod legs or a columnar base; and heavy console tables with monopodia legs and a plinth base.

**FRENCH EMPIRE CANDLESTICK** Made of gilt brass, the urn-shaped candleholder rests on a fluted, leaf-decorated column. The column stands on a tripod base with lion's paw feet. *H:29cm (11½in).*

The *fauteuil* (armchair) became more rectangular, with an upholstered back and scrolled top. The open arms had straight supports often carved with sphinx heads. A typical Empire commode was rectangular with flanking columns and a projecting frieze drawer above two or three drawers on a heavy plinth base with gilt-bronze mounts. The *lit en bateau* – essentially a day bed with scrolled ends and raised on a dais – was widely interpreted.

### DEVELOPMENTS IN BRITAIN

As in France, design was driven by one person – the Prince of Wales (later George IV, 1762–1830). With exuberant taste, he commissioned works from a number of designers and architects, resulting in

*The ormolu and black-patinated base is centred by a small pedestal*

*The ormolu has matte and burnished highlights*

**CHÂTEAU DE COMPIÈGNE** Tented areas, particularly in bedrooms, captured the spirit of Napoleon's military campaigns. Here the canopy frames a *lit en bateau*, the focal point of this sumptuous room.

**EMPIRE *GUÉRIDON*** A table of majestic proportions, this is made of ormolu and specimen marbles. The circular inlaid marble table top is edged with an ormolu band and supported on the wings of three sphinx monopodiae, forming a tripod, on a triangular base. *c.1815. H:76cm (30in).*

**AMERICAN CLASSICAL SIDE CHAIR** This mahogany chair was designed by Duncan Phyfe. It has a curved and rolled crest rail above incurved *demi-lune* splats, flanked by reeded stiles. The over-upholstered seat is raised on sabre legs with claw feet.

the Regency style. It had much in common with Empire – clean, symmetrical lines; richly coloured wood veneers; gilt mounts; and ancient motifs such as paterae, laurels, and anthemia – but was a lighter, more elegant, simplified, and feminine version.

While design was dominated by imperial Roman ideals, its designers also sought inspiration from afar. Brighton Pavilion, remodelled for the Prince Regent by John Nash between 1815 and 1823, epitomizes the prevailing fashion for the exotic with Indian-style domes, minarets, Islamic arches, and Chinese-inspired bamboo suites, lacquered panels and furniture, and Indian-style pierced screens.

Popular forms included the side cabinet, or chiffonier, a Regency interpretation of the commode with a pair of doors that had brass grilles backed with coloured silk; the sofa table, with drop ends and designed to stand in front of a sofa for reading or writing; and the chaise longue, a day bed with scrolled ends, similar to the *lit en bateau*.

## STYLE FOR THE BOURGEOISIE

Napoleon's brother, Jérôme, introduced the Empire style to Germany, where it met with approval among the aristocracy. Elsewhere, however, a secondary

style found favour with the middle classes. Originating in Austria, what later became labelled Biedermeier furniture was smaller than its Empire counterparts, strictly geometric, and had architectural features for ornament. Mahogany was the wood of choice, but lighter, local woods were also used, including cherry, birch, and ash. The grain was paramount and many pieces featured large areas of flat veneer. Inlaid borders on pediments or decorative columns made from darker, often ebonized, woods accentuated the grain of the lighter wood.

**AMERICAN EMPIRE SOFA** Upholstered and with outscrolled arms and bolster cushions, the heavy, symmetrical form of this sofa and high-relief-carved seat rail are typical features of the American Empire style. *W:162.5cm (64in).*

## FAR-REACHING INFLUENCES

Around 1800 the elegant American Federal style became more bulky. Heavy, geometric furniture was produced, often with high-relief carving. Typical forms, the *klismos* chair and scroll-end sofa, were Regency inspired, while Duncan Phyfe was a leading Classical exponent, producing a range of fine furniture for New York's elite.

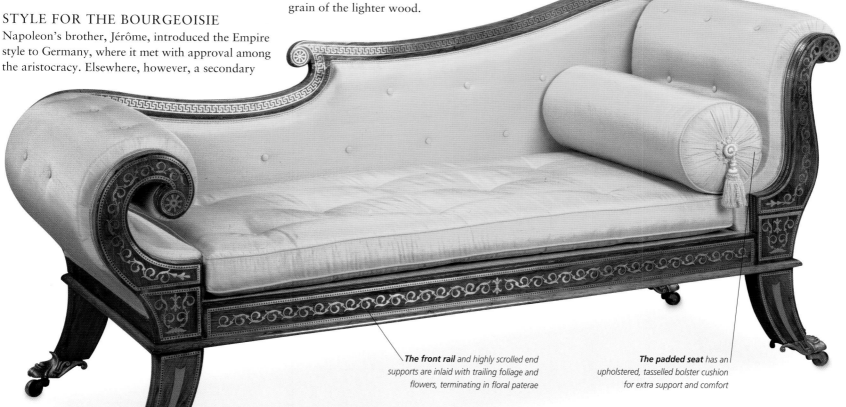

**The front rail** and highly scrolled end supports are inlaid with trailing foliage and flowers, terminating in floral paterae

**The padded seat** has an upholstered, tasselled bolster cushion for extra support and comfort

**ENGLISH REGENCY CHAISE LONGUE** This rosewood chaise longue is inlaid throughout with brass marquetry and supported on outswept sabre legs terminating in lion's paw feet. *c.1810. H:86cm (34in).*

# FURNITURE GALLERY

Neoclassical furniture was characterized by a return to furniture forms of ancient Rome and Greece, and architectural elements such as columns or pediments were common. Shapes became more rectilinear. Ornament included marquetry and rich flame veneers and porcelain insets. Marble was often used to top tables and cabinets. Decorative motifs such as sphinxes and urns were borrowed from Greece, Rome, and Egypt.

## KEY

1. Classical figured mahogany gondola chair. c.1830. ② 2. Gustavian armchair. ② 3. Mahogany sabre leg chair. c.1810. H:86.5cm (34in). ③ 4. Armchair with a white-lacquered beech frame. H:84cm (33in). ③ 5. Rosewood curricule chair by Gillows of Lancaster. c.1811. H:87cm (34¼in). ③ 6. George III mahogany rent table with rotating top by Gillows of Lancaster. c.1790. H:88cm (30¾in). 7. Regency coromandel sofa table with satinwood crossbanding. W:146cm (57½in). ④ 8. Regency rosewood sofa table. c.1820. H:76cm (30in). ⑤ 9. French sycamore, kingwood, and floral marquetry table with porcelain Sèvres-style inset. H:73.5cm (29in). ⑦ 10. Swedish parcel-gilt centre table

**1** Gondola chair

**2** Gustavian armchair

**3** Sabre leg chair

**4** Beech armchair

**5** Rosewood chair

**6** George III rent table

**7** Regency sofa table

**8** Regency sofa table

**9** French table

**10** Swedish centre table

supported on sphinxes. c.1820. H:86.5cm (34in). **11.** Empire mahogany secretaire with marble top. H:140cm (55in). ④ **12.** Dutch mahogany marquetry secrétaire à abattant. Early 19th century. H:163cm (64in). ④ **13.** Louis XVI hardwood parquetry secrétaire à abattant. c.1780. H:124cm (48¾in). **14.** Gustavian chest of drawers by N.P. Stenström. H:83.5cm (33½in). ⑤ **15.** German Empire cherrywood secretaire. c.1805. H:165cm (65in). ⑤ **16.** George III mahogany chest-on-chest. H:194cm (76½in). ⑤ **17.** Louis XVI commode by G. Dester. c.1775. H:93cm (36¾in). **18.** Louis XVI marble-topped mahogany commode. W:136cm (54½in). ⑤ **19.** George III ormolu-mounted, painted, and gilt commode, attributed to George Brookshaw. c.1790. H:89cm (33¾in). **20.** Italian walnut and marquetry commode. c.1800. W:132.5cm (53in). ④ **21.** Mahogany secretaire. c.1800. H:165.5cm (65½in). ⑦

**13** *Secrétaire à abattant*

**11** *Empire secretaire*

**12** *Dutch secrétaire à abattant*

**15** *German secretaire*

**16** *Chest-on-chest*

**14** *Gustavian chest of drawers*

**17** *Louis XVI commode*

**18** *Louis XVI commode*

**19** *George III commode*

**20** *Italian commode*

**21** *Secretaire*

# CERAMICS

THE SECOND HALF OF THE 18TH CENTURY WAS A PERIOD OF DEVELOPMENT IN CERAMICS, AS PORCELAIN-MAKERS HONED THEIR SKILLS AND POTTERY FACTORIES VIED WITH EACH OTHER TO COMPETE WITH THE "WHITE GOLD".

**PEARL WARE PLATE** The Etruscan trophies pattern on this Spode plate reflects an early 19th-century interest in Etruscan style. It is printed in underglaze blue with details picked out in iron red and yellow. *c. 1825. D:21cm (8¼in).*

## BRITISH POTTERY

The Industrial Revolution brought the English pottery industry to prominence. Traditionally the potteries around Staffordshire in the Midlands had made lead-glazed earthenware using brown clays. Now, however, they were experimenting with whiter clays that might be able to compete with porcelain and created creamware, cream-coloured earthenware with a thin, smooth, and transparent lead glaze that made it non-porous.

Josiah Wedgwood perfected the art of creamware, adding cobalt to the earthenware to make it whiter. In the 1770s he found even paler clays. By using a combination of calcium, flints, and cobalt oxide, he changed the light honey tinge of creamware to an ice-blue white, which was called pearl ware.

At first the opportunities for coloured decoration were limited. F.&R. Pratt pioneered the use of colours such as green, yellow ochre, blue, and brown, that could be fired at high temperature,

often over relief decoration. Popular subjects were topical or Classical figures, and Neoclassical motifs such as lion masks and paws, swags, husks, and the Greek key pattern. Similar pieces, called pratt ware, were made by other Staffordshire factories.

Creamware and its variants were used for all kinds of household pieces. Commemorative items were popular, and could be ordered from the local potter. Dinner services, basins, and ewers were all made. By the 1760s creamware was such a success that it was copied on the Continent, leading to the near demise of tin-glazed earthenware by 1800.

### WEDGWOOD

The self-styled "vase maker General to the Universe", Josiah Wedgwood was born in the heart of the Staffordshire potteries, in Burslem, now known as Stoke-on-Trent. Apprenticed at the age of 14, he left the family firm in 1754 and joined forces with Thomas Whieldon, who was known

for making creamware with mottled glazes on marbled light and dark clays. Wedgwood was lame and found it difficult to use a kick-wheel, so he concentrated on making pottery in moulds and improving the quality of the ceramic body. His creamware even found favour with Queen Charlotte, the wife of George III, who allowed him to call his range Queensware.

By the early 1770s Wedgwood was making vases in the Neoclassical style, inspired by archaeological discoveries in Greece. Not content with leading the field in creamware, Wedgwood developed a fine-grained stoneware called basalt ware, or black basaltes. He imitated severe Classical styles for

*Floral decoration is applied where the ribbon-style handle joins the body of the jug*

*The pilasters are headed by lion's masks and end in stylized lion's paw feet*

**Strap handle**

**CREAMWARE JUG** This baluster-shaped jug has simple ribbed decoration around the lower section. Much of the creamware made during this time is unmarked and so difficult to attribute to specific makers. *c. 1780. H:15cm (6in).*

**PRATT WARE JUG** A commemorative naval jug from the turn of the 19th century, one side is moulded with an image of Captain Berry, the other with Admiral Nelson. Each is set between two ships and titled. *c. 1800. H:15cm (6in).*

**JASPER WARE VASE** In this Wedgwood three-colour jasper ware vase the tapering body is decorated with typical Neoclassical motifs including oval paterae and floral swags hung from fluted pilasters. *c. 1794–1800. H:12.5cm (5in).*

this range of black wares, which he made into vases, busts, and tableware. In 1775 he produced a jasper ware range, made from white stoneware that could be tinted different colours. It was often made in blue, the colour most associated with Wedgwood. Decoration – usually white – was applied on top by shaping clay in a mould then applying it to the body of the piece. Although machinery was used, skill was still required, especially for the finer details such as drapery. The decorative motifs were similar to those used by designers such as Robert Adam – lyres, anthemia, toga-clad figures – so the vases would sit comfortably in any Neoclassical interior.

Red stoneware had a history dating back centuries. Wedgwood updated the designs, using engine-turned decoration. Called rosso antico, the unglazed background was decorated in black, in the style of Greek black-figure vases. As well as Classical forms and motifs, Egyptian themes were adopted after Napoleon's invasion of Egypt at the end of the 18th century. Other factories in the area, such as Spode, mimicked Wedgwood's red ware and jasper ware with varying degrees of success.

Wedgwood died in 1795 after a prolific lifetime including 50 years as a potter, during which he paid homage to Classical art. He said he had "endeavoured to preserve...the elegant simplicity of the antique forms". He was also blessed with an astute sense of business.

**RED WARE TEAPOT** This squat, globular Spode teapot is decorated with black hieroglyphs above a meander band. The ribbed cover has a crocodile finial. *1815. H:11.5cm (4½in).*

**DESSERT PLATE** This Mason's Ironstone plate features Neoclassical decoration: a landscape surrounded by a gilt foliate-decorated rim. *c.1820. W:23.5cm (9¼in).*

## TRANSFER-PRINTING

Developments in technology led to the mass production of ceramics, which then became affordable to the expanding middle classes. Transfer-printing was a cheap, quick, and efficient way to decorate homeware. The subject matter could be as complex as a painting, with Classical or topographical scenes. Until the 1820s the colour was usually cobalt blue, the only one that could cope with firing. The design was engraved on a copper plate, using hatching (parallel lines) for shading. The copper was warmed, rubbed with ink, and pressed on to paper, which was placed on the porous, biscuit-fired earthenware. The design was then transferred to the body, ready for glazing and firing.

*The blue of the jasper ware is a byword for Wedgwood*

*The urn shape is ubiquitous, one of the ancient forms Neoclassical designers emulated*

*The vase is raised on a spreading foot, impressed "Wedgwood V"*

**WEDGWOOD VASE** This rare Wedgwood blue jasper ware vase has a lift-out lid and three laurel leaf-bulb holders. The body is decorated with applied figures of Apollo and the nine Muses above a band of trophies. *c.1785–95. H:22.5cm (8¾in).*

**SPODE MEAT DISH** A Caramanian series meat dish of the later indented shape, transfer-printed with the design "Antique Fragments at Limisso". *L:42cm (16½in).*

## TIN-GLAZED EARTHENWARE

"Every man of any status or consequence turned within a week to faience," said Saint-Simon in 1709, after France had melted down silverware to help fund her wars. But by the mid-18th century porcelain was a threat to tin-glazed earthenware. Delft was still being made in Holland, but its popularity was waning. The development of creamware in England posed yet more competition. Some manufacturers on the Continent copied it, while others stuck to tin-glazed earthenware – known as faience in France, fayence in Germany, and maiolica in Spain and Italy – paying lip service to the Neoclassical trend.

### FRENCH RUSTIC FAIENCE

The factory of Moustiers in the south of France rivalled that of Rouen and began a new lease of life in 1738 when Joseph Olerys went into business with Jean-Baptiste Laugier. Olerys had been working at the Spanish factory of Alcora, and brought with him the techniques for polychrome high-temperature decoration. Tableware such as *bouillabaisse* (fish soup) bowls was decorated with garlands and medallions, little figures and flowers, grotesques inspired by the engravings of Callot, and arabesques taken from the designs of Jean Bérain. Complete services were made for the middle classes, copying Sèvres styles. Sometimes the decoration was in a single colour, usually green or yellow, but occasionally mauve.

The factory of Quimper in Brittany, like faience-makers throughout France, followed the Rouen *style rayonnant*, which had been popular under Louis XIV. Its lambrequins, decorative Baroque lacy swags, were the ceramicist's

**PAIR OF EWERS** This pair of Quimper ewers is decorated in the Rouen style with blue and red lambrequins. H:46.5cm (18in).

*Decoration* extends to the handles, where it is complementary but simpler

*Lambrequins* are a deeply scalloped fringe-like ornament

*The base* flares to balance the height of the ewers

**MOUSTIERS PLATE** The plate is decorated in high-temperature green with motifs based on flowers and leaves, centred by a Commedia dell'Arte-style Punch figure. *Late 18th century. D:24cm (9½in).*

**FAIENCE KRUG** The surface of the oval jug is decorated in strong colours, depicting large bunches of grapes and the tools of the viticulturist, surrounded by floral garlands. *1796. H:28cm (11in).*

**SPANISH MAIOLICA FLASK** The ring moulding on the ovoid body defines bands of figures and animals. The handle stretches the full height of the flask and is in the form of a green lizard. *H:26cm (10¼in).*

*Despite the rustic imagery*, the flask displays Neoclassical-style geometry in the coloured banding

**Blue, green, and yellow** were the dominant faience colours in northern Europe

**Geometric bands** of arches and ovals containing flowers at the top and bottom frame the main decoration

**FAIENCE TANKARD** This Austrian pear-shaped tankard has a pewter lid and stand. Geometric borders frame the depiction of a maiden holding a letter. *Late 18th century. H:22cm (8½in).*

equivalent of festoons of drapery. Quimper used more exuberant colours than Moustiers. Nevers, famous for its *bleus de Nevers* solid coloured grounds in the 17th century, kept in business by producing wares with witty inscriptions known as *faiences parlantes* pragmatically switching to political slogans during the French Revolution.

Niderviller near the German border specialized in trompe-l'oeil decoration of a print pinned on to a background that looked like grained wood. It also made beautiful figures in faience. And, using the local Lorraine clay, it produced *faience fine*, which resembled English creamware. Niderviller carried on using original 18th-century moulds into the 19th century and is still in production today.

## GERMAN FAIENCE

Faience factories had sprung up all over Germany after 1700 as the country was divided into numerous principalities, all of which wanted to be self-sufficient. Since Böttger discovered how to make hard-paste porcelain in Meissen around 1709, they had to compete. By the second half of the 18th century they were copying the Neoclassical designs used on porcelain, successfully providing a cheaper alternative. But porcelain did not cause the demise of tin-glazed earthenware. English creamware, which was just as cheap, had a harder body and did not chip as easily.

Bérain's delicate designs were used for *Laub- und Bandelwerk* (leaf- and strapwork) decoration in

Austria and Germany. *Indianische Blumen* (India flowers) from Meissen were the inspiration for naturalistic Strasbourg *deutsche Blumen* (German flowers), whose influence percolated through the states. In Nuremberg a motif of a curling stem with feathery leaves and stylized flowers developed but, partly because Germany was splintered into tiny states, faience decoration varied hugely. It was often the product of an individual potter's fancy.

**PAIR OF *ALBARELLI*** Each of these pharmacy jars has the typically thin waist, to make them easier to lift off a shelf. The geometric banding and blue and white pattern is a late 18th-century style. *H:22cm (8¾in).*

## ITALIAN MAIOLICA

Alongside customary *albarelli* (waisted drug jars), Italian factories adopted Neoclassical forms such as urn-shaped vases. Blue and white borders and Chinoiserie decoration were popular, influenced by Chinese porcelain. The workshops in Savona continued the *istoriato* (narrative) tradition, with lively freehand painting. As in Spain, factories continued to work in earlier styles after 1800.

**MAIOLICA TAZZA** Made in Savona, Italy, the tazza is painted in green, yellow, manganese, and blue and decorated with images of birds, trees, and ruins. *Late 18th century. D:34cm (13½in).*

# NEOCLASSICAL PORCELAIN

In 1764 Madame de Pompadour, Louis XV's mistress and Sèvres' biggest patron, died and the style of Sèvres porcelain began to change. Vases were now made in the Neoclassical urn shape, even though they were still painted with sweet pastoral Rococo subjects including children, lovers, and flowers. The designs became symmetrical and shapes were adorned with applied and moulded Classical decoration such as acanthus leaves, laurel garlands, guilloche, swags, and rosettes. The sides were fluted or reeded, like the ridges on Classical columns. New colours were introduced, such as the overglaze *bleu nouveau*, developed in 1763.

In 1769 Sèvres began to make hard-paste porcelain. Many of its ground colours did not work on the harder porcelain so new ones were developed. Colours became more muted, including purple, brown, and soft green. There was a brief vogue for pearling – applying blobs of enamel over metal foil, which raised the colour like pearls. Rich gilding was used. Medallions (oval or circular panels), often featuring *grisaille* (grey) figures and scenes based on the ancient Roman frescoes at Pompeii, were popular.

## ENGLISH FOLLOWERS

By the 1770s the Neoclassical style was well established in porcelain. English factories such as Worcester and Derby copied Sèvres, using oval panels and straight sides in flat colours enlivened with fluting. Bands of gilding separated areas of decoration, and borders featured Classical patterns such as guilloche, Greek key, Vitruvian scrolls, or Sèvres-style pearling. Chelsea-Derby was founded in 1769 when William Duesbury of Derby bought the Chelsea factory, and continued production until 1784. Its Neoclassical tableware was immensely fashionable. Pale yellow, pink, or green grounds were left plain or were painted with Classical or floral motifs.

**FLARED BEAKER** This Chamberlain's Worcester beaker is decorated in gilt with panels. The central titled oval panel is finely painted in coloured enamels with a portrait of Sappho and Phaon. *1795–1800. H:9cm (3½in).*

**The cover** for the cup has a marigold-shaped finial

**SÈVRES COFFEE CUP AND SAUCER**
The cup and saucer are painted in enamels with birds in landscapes, within gilt oval panels. The rims are painted with bands of birds and laurel garlands. *1793.*

**SÈVRES CHOCOLATE CUP SET**
This set comprises a two-handled cup with cover and stand. It is painted with garlands of flowers and gilt leaf fronds within gilt-decorated blue borders. *1761. Cup: W:18.5cm (7½in).*

**DERBY TEAPOT** This oval fluted, straight-sided teapot has a wishbone handle and loop knop. It has banded decoration, painted in black and grey and picked out in gilt, on a pink ground. *c.1790. H:15cm (6in).*

In Germany Meissen had virtually ceased production during the Seven Years War (1756–63). The French sculptor Michel-Victor Acier was brought in to help it compete with Sèvres, but Meissen had lost its earlier pre-eminence. Factories such as Berlin and Vienna came to the fore, especially at the turn of the century.

### THE NEW CENTURY

After the French Revolution, the Republic took over and Sèvres lost royal privilege, but the factory never stopped production. In 1800 Alexander Brongniart took charge and abandoned soft-paste porcelain. The huge dinner service that Louis XVI had ordered in 1783, the last big soft-paste project, was never finished. Vases became larger and larger as hard paste was less likely to collapse during firing; and elaborate grounds such as agate grey and simulated tortoiseshell were introduced.

**MEISSEN COFFEE POT** The pear-shaped pot has a volute handle and domed lid with a ball knop. The ribbed surface is painted with floral decoration. There is partial gilding. *c.1800. H:24cm (9½in).*

## EMPIRE STYLE

Under Napoleon, porcelain had to be rich and colourful to fit the integrated style of the tent-like draperies and sumptuous furnishings that Percier and Fontaine had designed for Napoleon's palace at Malmaison. The Empire style, similar to Regency in Britain, Biedermeier in Germany, and Empire in Scandinavia, was characterized by massive and more elaborate shapes. As Napoleon modelled himself on a Roman emperor, these were embellished with elaborate ornament in the Classical mode, such as imperial eagles, swans, lions, and caryatid handles. Extensive gilding completed the look of opulence. After Napoleon's Egyptian campaigns, sphinxes, lotus leaves, and other Egyptian imagery were used on porcelain as well as on furniture.

In Britain stoneware was popular in the last quarter of the 18th century, but by 1800 porcelain was once again in demand. The naturalistic flower painting typical of Rococo had remained popular in England. William Billingsley developed a way of making flowers, especially roses, look particularly life-like, by applying pigment and then wiping the colour off, leaving the white porcelain for highlights. He was hired to work in Wales on Nantgarw porcelain bodies, renowned for their whiteness, a perfect foil to his delicate painting.

*The cup has an angular handle, characteristic of the Empire style*

**WELSH PORCELAIN CAMPANA VASE** The form of this vase is a copy of the ancient Greek Borghese vase in the Louvre in Paris. William Billingsley painted the flowers. *1813–23. H:27.5cm (10¾in).*

**BERLIN EMPIRE CUP AND SAUCER** This set has strong geometric patterning and gold details. Diamond panels contain paintings of Classical figures. It is marked KPM. *c.1800. Cup: H:6cm (2¼in).*

# CERAMICS GALLERY

Neoclassical ceramics are more symmetrical and less patterned than Rococo ceramics. Cups and beakers are designed with straighter sides and patterning itself becomes geometric. Bands of decoration are balanced with areas of plain colour. Forms and motifs are taken from the ancient worlds of Rome and Greece, and pieces are based on typical Classical forms such as the urn.

## KEY

**1.** Cozzi figure of a young man, with tricorn hat at his side. c.1770. H:11cm (4¼in). ① **2.** Sèvres porcelain cup and saucer, with tooled gilding and platinum. Late 18th century. ② **3.** Paris coffee can and saucer. c.1810. Coffee can: H:7.5cm (3in). ① **4.** Pair of Sèvres porcelain cups and saucers. Saucer: D:15.5cm (6in). ④ **5.** White-glazed figure of Hygeia, Greek goddess of health. Late 18th century. H:29cm (11½in). ① **6.** Miniature figure by Johann Adam Bauer. H:9cm (3½in). ① **7.** Marcolini Meissen part tea and coffee service, painted with fruit and flowers. ④ **8.** Cozzi group of figures, picking grapes. ② **9.** Pair of figures by John Jacques Louis. c.1775. H:25cm (9½in). ② **10.** Coalport two-handled, enamel-painted sauce tureen and cover, with ball knop. c.1800. ②

1 Cozzi figure

2 Sèvres cup and saucer

3 Paris coffee can and saucer

4 Sèvres cups and saucers

5 Figure of Hygeia

6 Miniature figure

7 Meissen service

8 Cozzi figures

9 Pair of figures

10 Coalport tureen

11. Derby botanical enamel-painted plate, the pink ground border with gilt bands. c.1795. D:23cm (9in). ① 12. Derby plate from the Gosling Service, with gilt initial G. c.1795. D:23cm (9in). ① 13. Paris porcelain plate by Dagoty. D:24cm (9½in). ① 14. Worcester fluted ovoid gilt tea canister and domed cover, with flower knop. c.1772. H:16cm (6¼in). ① 15. Derby plate, painted in Paris style with gilt laurel bands and flowerheads. c.1785. D:23.5cm (9¼in). ① 16. Nymphenburg plate with relief decoration and painted flowers. c.1765. D:23cm (9in). ① 17. Pair of Sèvres-style English porcelain vases and covers. c.1840. H:30cm (11¾in). ③ 18. Pair of Coalport ice pails with gilt handles and feet. 1810. H:28cm (11in). ④ 19. Coalport campana-shaped, two-handled vase, painted with flowers within C-scroll borders. c.1820. H:23.5cm (9¼in). ② 20. Spode porcelain campana-shaped pastel burner. c.1820. H:12cm (4¾in). ③

13 *Paris plate*

11 *Derby plate*

12 *Derby plate*

15 *Derby plate*

14 *Worcester tea canister*

16 *Nymphenburg plate*

20 *Spode pastel burner*

17 *Sèvres-style vases*

18 *Coalport ice pails*

19 *Coalport vase*

# GLASS

THE UNSETTLED POLITICAL SITUATION IN CONTINENTAL EUROPE
DURING THE SECOND HALF OF THE 18TH CENTURY GAVE BRITAIN
AN OPPORTUNITY TO TAKE THE LEAD IN GLASSMAKING.

## CUT AND ENGRAVED GLASS

British designers, looking back to the ancient world, found inspiration in the engravings of Piranesi (*see p.54*) and in the Roman and Greek antiquities they saw on the Grand Tour. The drawings of the architect Robert Adams also inspired designers in many media.

### DOMINANT STYLES

The decoration on earlier Baroque and Rococo glass had tended to be superficial and restrained. Neoclassical glass began to reflect the style in form as well as ornament; claret jugs and decanters, for example, were often fashioned as baluster shapes. A seminal form of the era was the rummer wine glass, with its wide bowl, short, knopped stem,

and square "lemon-squeezer" base, derived from the urn shape. The Neoclassical style of decoration reached its pinnacle in the Regency period. The forms and decoration were evident on decanters, claret jugs, sweatmeat dishes, fruit bowls, and candlesticks. Deep-profile cutting was very popular and various cuts such as pillar, prism, and strawberry diamond dominated. The bases of decanters were often cut with fan shapes or stars.

### MECHANIZATION

A new steam-cutting process was introduced to Britain in 1789, which revolutionized the world of cut glass, making deep-profile cuts possible. This made the most of the lead-based crystal that had been discovered by Ravenscroft in the late 1670s.

**PEDESTAL BOWL** The turnover rim of this cut-glass pedestal bowl is typical of glass made in Ireland around 1800. The rim is cut with three lozenge-fluted bands and the bowl with a central three-strand lozenge band. It is raised on a knopped stem and square lemon-squeezer foot. *c.1800. W:30cm (12in).*

Pieces sparkled as they reflected and refracted the light. Similar techniques were used elsewhere in Europe. In France both the Baccarat Glasshouse, founded in 1764, and the Saint-Louis Glassworks, established in 1767, became well known for their cut-glass tableware from about 1800.

Ireland was given free-trade status in 1780, which reinvigorated its glass industry. The most common decorative techniques were shallow cutting and engraving. Irish cut glass was also popular. Claret decanters with extended spouts, piggin cream bowls with one raised side, and stemmed bowls with deep turnover rims are typical Irish forms.

*The jug is of a large size, which would have made blowing more difficult*

*Hops were usually used to decorate beer jugs*

**LARGE JUG** This baluster-shaped jug has a heavy strap handle and is engraved with sprigs of hops. The base is engraved with initials and dated. *1828. H:21cm (8¼in).*

**MEDICI CUT-GLASS VASES** This pair of glasses have ornate gilt-bronze mounts that display typical Neoclassical motifs: cupids playing cymbals supported on palmettes and vine branches. *c.1820. H:56.5cm (22¼in).*

**REGENCY RUMMERS** These three commemorative dated rummers are inscribed with the monogram "JB" and engraved with shields and paterae suspending swags. The lower section of each bowl is fluted. Each has a lemon-squeezer plinth base. *1823. H:13.5cm (5¼in).*

**INKSTAND** This blue opalescent and clear-pressed glass inkstand with inkwell and sander was made by the Boston and Sandwich Glass Company. *1830–35.*

## ENGRAVING

Engraving glass was still fashionable, especially in early Neoclassical pieces. Engraved ornament was more restrained, leaving large areas of plain glass. However, the popularity of symmetrical, geometric designs was evident in borders of swags and paterae, both common Neoclassical motifs. An engraved medallion might bear an inscription or a client's monogram. Diamond-point engraving was particularly suited to thin-walled glass. Shallow cutting was also popular and included shallow flutes around the base of a decanter, for example, or oval printies on its shoulders.

*The stopper*
*has been bevel-cut to create a flower shape*

*The top of the bowl*
*has a shallow decoration around*

*The pseudo label*
*is a trompe l'oeil effect rather than an actual label*

*The stem*
*is faceted*

**WINE GLASS** The bowl was engraved in the workshop of James Giles, an outside decorator. The engraved motifs include a stag's head and Neoclassical paterae amid interlaced swags and bellflowers. *c.1770. H:11.5cm (4½in).*

**WINE DECANTER** This shape, known as a shoulder decanter, is one of several developed during the early Neoclassical era. It is engraved with a pseudo wine label for white wine. *c.1765. H:29cm (11½in).*

## AMERICAN GLASSMAKING

The early 19th century saw the development of pressed glass in the United States, first made at the New England Glass Company, which was established by Deming Jarves in 1818. The process, which involved pushing molten glass into a plain or patterned brass or cast-iron mould with a plunger, revolutionized glass manufacture. Cheaper than cut glass, it made a greater variety of styles available to more people. It proved an ideal technique for Neoclassical design, allowing easy production of symmetrical shapes for a wide range of domestic glassware.

A number of glass factories was established. The New Bremen Glass Factory in West Maryland was founded in 1787 by German immigrant Johann Friedrich Amelung. A few surviving pieces feature engraved decoration in the Germanic style.

The company Bakewell, Pears & Co. was founded in 1808 by two Englishmen in Pittsburgh, Pennsylvania. It is credited with making the country's first chandelier in 1810. Pressed glass was made here from 1825.

The Boston and Sandwich Glass Company, established in 1825 in Massachusetts by Deming Jarves, also founder of the New England Glass Company, produced sandwich glass and flint glass of exceptional quality – America's answer to British lead-based crystal. From 1828, pressed glass formed most of the company's output.

**LACY COMPOTE** The decoration on this clear, pressed glass compote by the Boston and Sandwich Glass Company was created with a mould to imitate the diamond cutting and fluting often seen on cut glass. *1830–35.*

## COLOURED GLASS

Towards the end of the Neoclassical period, new developments in the field of coloured glass brought French and, in particular, Bohemian glassmakers back to the forefront of glassmaking in Europe.

The creation of opaline glass in France in the mid-1820s heralded a new direction for European glassmaking. The semi-opaque glass looked like fine porcelain and was well suited to the Neoclassical forms and gilded mounts that dominated the French Empire style. The glass was made by adding bone ash to the mix, together with metal oxides for colour, producing a range of soft white, blue, and pink tones. Opaline glass was sometimes referred to as "fire" glass because of its translucent colour when held up to the light. The contemporary German equivalent – principally from Bohemia and Thuringia – was known as *Beinglas* or *Milchglas*.

### MIMICKING THE ANCIENTS

While the French excelled in their production of opaline glass, manufacturers in Germany –

especially Bohemia – were constantly experimenting with new types of coloured glass during this era, primarily in a bid to re-create glass that had been discovered at ancient Roman sites in the first half of the 18th century. Two major pioneers of such glass were Count von Buquoy and Friedrich Egermann.

Inspired by developments in the field of ceramics at the Wedgwood factory in Britain, and in the creation of new materials such as basalt ware and antico rosso, which emulated Roman stoneware (*see pp.64–65*), von Buquoy created red-marbled opaque glass in 1803 and a dark red and sometimes jet-black Hyalith in 1817. This was the first truly successful black opaque glass ever made.

In 1828 Friederich Egermann patented his Lithyalin glass. Also opaque, this marbled glass was the result of staining the surface of coloured – usually red or black – glass with a second colour such as yellow in order to create the desired effect. The idea was to re-create the types of "agate" glass made by the ancient Romans. Agate glass, itself,

**PERFUME BOTTLE** The top section of this turquoise opaline Charles X perfume bottle and its round, fluted stopper have been decorated with gold-painted floral motifs. *c.1825. H:13.5cm (5¼in).*

*This shade of pink* is known as gorge de pigeon (*pigeon's breast*)

*The central panel* is decorated with elegant columns below a Moorish-style frieze

*The heavy bases* are decorated with the laurel leaf motif

**CHARLES X VASES** These rare opaline and bronze vases have several Empire features: their urn shape, the restrained ornament, and the architectural pedestals. *c.1825. H:25.5cm (10in).*

**BLACK HYALITH GLASS TANKARD** This piece has fine gold-painted decoration and a faceted knop. There are bands of decoration and the bulbous section is ornamented with very fine rosettes. *c.1830. H:20cm (8in).*

had been made by combining two or more colours of molten glass, so producing a glass that   such as agate, jaspar, and chalcedony.

Also imitating ancient Roman glass, a third Bohemian glassmaker, Johann Joseph Mildner, revived the *Zwischengoldglas* technique popular in Germany during the 1730s and 1740s (*see p.39*). His designs featured medallion-shaped ovals on the sides and base of a piece – typically beakers and tumblers. Such pieces are now referred to as Mildner glass.

## FLASHED AND CASED GLASS

Additional colouring techniques used at this time included flashing and casing. Flashed glass involved producing a piece in clear glass and dipping it while hot into molten glass of another colour. This was an effective and less costly way of producing glassware that appeared to be one consistent colour. The second, thinner layer of glass was often engraved or cut. Cased glass, particularly popular in Germany, involved producing a clear-glass form and pouring molten glass of another colour into it. The two layers fused when the piece was reheated. Cased glass tended to be heavy, as several colours could be added. Pieces were often deep-cut in order to reveal the different layers for decoration.

## PREVAILING TRENDS

Despite innovations in colour, shapes were still influenced by the designs of the late 18th century.

**ENAMELLED BEAKER** This Viennese drinking glass, decorated by Anton Kothgasser, features a view of Karlsbad within gilded borders. *c.1825. H:11.8cm (4½in).*

**BOHEMIAN GOBLET** The central panel of this Biedermeier cut-glass goblet, made of clear glass flashed with amber, depicts a Persian figure with a horse. *1840. H:16cm (6¼in).*

Popular forms were urn-shaped or taper decanters; short, knop-stemmed goblets; and jewel-like boxes and perfume bottles. The beaker or tumbler with a recessed lip and straight, tapering sides was common throughout Germany. Sometimes the beaker had a slight waist and a domed base; often the sides would be faceted as well. Such pieces might be cased or flashed with engraved or cut decoration. They might also be enamelled (*see below*) or gilded. Common Neoclassical motifs included medallions and recurring geometric designs.

**BOHEMIAN GOBLET WITH COVER** Decoration of this tall, cobalt-blue drinking glass is in the form of faceting to the foot, knops, base of the bowl, cover, and finial. *c.1850. H:19.5cm (8¾in).*

**BIEDERMEIER TANKARD** This Bohemian tankard has a pewter lid with a glass insert and deep-cut ornament. The colourless glass is flashed deep red in parts. *c.1840. H:17cm (6¾in).*

*The D-shaped handle* is clear glass and has been cut to match the decoration on the tankard

*A star motif* has been cut in the base of the tankard

## ENAMELLING

A popular technique during the early 18th century, enamelling continued to find favour with Neoclassical designers, and it was during the early 19th century that the skills of the glass painter reached new heights. With the grandeur of the Empire style, came a fashion for glassware decorated with topographical scenes and Classically inspired portraits. The majority of these were skilfully handpainted in transparent enamels. The best-known exponent of enamelled glass during this period was the Austrian glass and porcelain decorator Anton Kothgasser, who created a number of enamelled city- and landscapes and portraits on beakers and tumblers.

**ENAMELLED BEAKER** This elegant beaker was designed by Friedrich Egermann. The tapering, faceted sides have enamel decoration in red, blue, and black, highlighted with geometric and floral patterning. There are two bands of geometric cut-glass ornament. *c.1837. H:10.5cm (4in).*

# GLASS GALLERY

**N**eoclassical glassware borrowed the urn and goblet shapes from Classical Greece and Rome. Decanters and claret jugs were also popular forms, with mushroom, lozenge, or ball stoppers. Decoration was added by cutting. The diamond-cut pattern, slicing, and star-cut bases were common. Engraving was also used to add decoration, and many pieces featured gilding.

## KEY

**1.** Claret jug with flat-cut flutes, pillar-cut neck rings, and a mushroom stopper. c.1830. H:26.5cm (10½in). ① **2.** Pair of cut-glass piggins, with fan-cut handles and serrated rims above a diamond band. c.1825. D:15cm (6in). ① **3.** Austrian painted glass beaker with a gilt rim. c.1815. H:7.5cm (3in). ④ **4.** Pair of Boulton-style glass and gilt campana wine coolers cut with strawberry diamonds. H:20cm (7¾in). ④ **5.** Sliced and flute-cut claret jug, with a ball stopper. c.1800. H:29cm (11½in). ① **6.** Decanter with cut neck rings, flute-cut base, and la ozenge stopper. c.1800. H:28.5cm (11¼in). ① **7.** Claret jug with a flute-cut body and star-cut base. c.1820. H:23cm (16in). ② **8.** Mallet-shaped decanter and stopper, with gilt inscription "Brandy". H:30cm (12in). ①

1 *Claret jug with mushroom stopper*

2 *Cut-glass piggins*

3 *Austrian painted glass beaker*

4 *Boulton-style wine coolers*

9 *Engraved liqueur glass*

5 *Flute-cut claret jug*

6 *Decanter with lozenge stopper*

7 *Claret jug with star-cut base*

8 *Mallet-shaped decanter*

10 *English airtwist wine glass*

**9.** Engraved liqueur glass with a gilt rim. H:11.5cm (4½in). ① **10.** English wine glass, the stem with an airtwist cable encircled by twin opaque white threads. c.1760. H:15.5cm (6in). ② **11.** Beaker by Friedrich Egermann. H:10cm (3¾in). ① **12.** Biedermeier beaker by Friedrich Egermann. H:13.5cm (5½in). ① **13.** Moulded goblet with an incised twist stem and conical foot. c.1800. H:15.5cm (6in). ③ **14.** Beaker by Anton Kothgasser with a cherub motif within gilding. c.1825. H:11cm (4¼in). ⑤ **15.** Airtwist wine glass, the ogee bowl moulded with broad flutes, the stem with a gauze core within spiral tapes. c.1760. H:18.5cm (7½in). ③ **16.** Bonnet glass, the honeycomb-moulded ogee bowl on a conical foot. c.1790. H:8cm (3¼in). ① **17.** Rummer engraved with a band of swags and stars. c.1830. H:19.5cm (7¾in). ① **18.** Engraved and polished rummer with an egg and tulip band. c.1810. H:14.5cm (5¾in). ①

**12** Biedermeier beaker

**11** Friedrich Egermann beaker

**13** Goblet with twist stem

**14** Anton Kothgasser beaker

**18** Engraved and polished rummer

**15** Airtwist wine glass

**16** Honeycomb-moulded bonnet glass

**17** Rummer with swags and stars

# METALWARE

THE RESTRAINED SURFACE DECORATION OF PLAIN AND
PATTERNED BANDS THAT CHARACTERIZED NEOCLASSICAL SILVERWARE
ACCENTUATED THE REFLECTIVE QUALITIES OF THE METAL.

## FORMAL GRANDEUR

Enormous table services were commissioned at
the end of the 18th century, when dinner for the
aristocracy was a serious, formal, and often public
affair. Centrepieces were as much sculpture as
wrought silver.

To keep up with the latest fashions, many people
had their old silver melted down to make new
pieces or refashioned into the new style and so old
designs have not survived. However, the Orloff
service, made for Catherine the Great's lover by
Jacques-Nicolas Roettiers, shows that some French
silversmiths were working in the massive, Classical
style of Lalive de Jully's furniture, known as *Goût*

**PAIR OF CANDLESTICKS** Made by John Carter of
London, these candlesticks have ornate knopped stems and
bases with swirling flutes. Each stands on a raised, square,
gadrooned plinth. *1779. H:26.5cm (10½in).*

grec (Greek style). Between 1750 and 1770
France was turning away from the Rococo style,
but it lingered on in Scandinavia and Germany
until the 1780s.

### ROBERT ADAM

Although the *Goût grec* was fashionable for a
while in France, Robert Adam was the biggest
influence in Britain. Britain never really took to
Rococo, except in direct copies of the French,
and moved fairly smoothly from the solid,
Classical Palladian style to the lighter Classicism
of the Adam style. Like many designers, Adam
masterminded every aspect of his interiors,
including the main items of silver, which
were often displayed on a table set into a
niche in the dining room. Adam considered

*The finial is in
the shape of a
pine cone*

*The spoons are made of
silver and vermeil*

**CONFITURIER** This silver *confiturier* (jam pot) by Joseph-Gabriel Genu
has 12 spoons. The bowl stands on four uprights with griffin heads and feet,
and the base has a frieze of palmettes. *1798–1809. H:26cm (10¼in).*

**SILVER EWER** Thought to have belonged to Napoleon, this
ewer has a beaded rim and shoulders, a central band of applied
grotesques, a chased acanthus base and stem, and is set on a
square pedestal base. *Early 19th century. H:19cm (7½in).*

## BIEDERMEIER BASKET

This silver basket by Ferdinand Aloysius Hartmann has a boat-shaped, engraved silver body with a cobalt blue glass liner and a domed foot. *W:17cm (6¾in).*

*The twisted silver handle is moveable and can be laid flat*

## SHEFFIELD PLATE

Around 1742 Thomas Boulsover of Sheffield discovered that copper could be sandwiched between sheets of silver and the two metals fused together. The resulting plate was much cheaper than silver and became very popular, displacing pewter. Exported all over Europe and to the United States, its widespread use by the 1780s spread the Neoclassical style. Matthew Boulton used Sheffield plate for coffee- and teapots, applying extra silver at any edges that were likely to wear through to the copper. It is referred to as Old Sheffield plate, which remained popular until the even cheaper method of electroplating was discovered around 1840.

**THREE-LIGHT CANDELABRA** This pair of Sheffield-plated three-light candelabra by Matthew Boulton & Co. has torch finials, reeded scroll branches, and circular bases with gadrooned borders. *1810–20. H:45cm (17¾in).*

*Pierced and galleried rim*

*The front of the urn bears the script monogram "GCC"*

**SUGAR URN** This Philadelphia silver sugar urn by George Drewry has very little ornamentation. The body has a circular lid with a finial and it stands on a circular foot with a square base. *1763. H:26.5cm (10½in).*

**SILVER COFFEE POT** The grandeur of this Eames and Barnard silver coffee pot is characteristic of the British Regency style. The high-relief ornament is balanced with areas of plain silver. *1825. H:22.5cm (9in).*

the ancient world as "a magazine of common property...whence every man has a right to take what material he pleases". Adam led the fashion for forms based on Grecian urns, tripods, and Roman sarcophagi. From 1760 to 1790 favourite motifs were paterae (ovals or circles with a rosette in the middle), ram's heads, often for handles, Vitruvian scrolls (wave patterns), festoons, and husks. Stylized plants in the form of palmettes, anthemion flowers, or trails of leaves abounded, as did spiral fluting and other forms of ridged surface. Bright-cut engraving – cutting an angled groove – made any surface decoration highly reflective. After Napoleon's Egyptian campaigns, sphinxes and eagle heads were added to the Classical repertoire.

This wealth of ornament was limited to bands separated by plain surfaces that formed a contrast to the decoration. Candlesticks were a popular vehicle for banded ornament, especially as they resembled Classical columns in shape. Tea urns, which were ideally suited to the form of the Neoclassical vase, were also popular as they catered to the fashion for drinking hot beverages.

## MASS PRODUCTION

Few people were wealthy enough to commission Robert Adam and other leading architect-designers. Steam-powered machines made it possible to roll out silver objects more thinly and cheaply, so silverware came down in price just as the middle classes became more affluent and wanted to buy it. The patterns of repeated motifs were suited to mass production. By the late 1770s the Adam style was firmly established in Britain. In France the *Goût grec* evolved into the more delicate Louis XVI style.

Matthew Boulton, a Birmingham silversmith, helped to make metalware more affordable for the general public. He teamed up with the architect James Wyatt and manufactured his top-quality designs for thin silver candlesticks, jugs, and snuff boxes. Boulton wrote: "Fashion hath much to do in these things, and as that of the present age, distinguishes itself by adopting the most elegant ornaments of the most refined Grecian artists...I am humbly copying their styles and making new combinations of old ornaments."

British and French styles spread throughout Europe. After an interruption during the American War of Independence, they also reached the United States. Silver imports, pattern books, and catalogues made the styles available to a wider public. Philadelphia and then Baltimore were centres for fashionable silver. In Boston Paul Revere adapted Classical forms for silver tableware, using sparing decoration to emphasize the elegant shapes he used.

# CLOCKS

AS A HIGHLY ARCHITECTURAL STYLE, NEOCLASSICISM WAS EMINENTLY SUITED TO CLOCK CASES. LONGCASE CLOCKS LOOKED PARTICULARLY ELEGANT ADORNED WITH FEATURES INSPIRED BY THE CLASSICAL WORLD.

## LONGCASE CLOCKS

As grand pieces of furniture housing the most important timepiece in the home, longcase clocks enjoyed the attention of some of the best cabinet-makers of the period. The wood of choice through most of Europe was mahogany, and this was frequently inlaid with specimen woods. From simple stringing to complex marquetry and parquetry designs, these decorative embellishments accentuated the fine figure of the dense mahogany case. Some examples feature intarsia panels with depictions of animals or human figures.

### CLASSICAL FEATURES

Wooden longcase clocks typically borrowed a number of features from Classical Greek architecture. Swan-neck pediments, for example, were a variation of the triangular top that adorned ancient temples such as the Greek Parthenon. The pediment might be transformed into a pair of facing S-scrolls, but remained firmly rooted in the Classical world.

The front edges of longcase clocks were often set with pilasters or columns – another basic component of ancient temple architecture. The three main architectural orders developed by the Greeks – Doric, Ionic, and Corinthian (*see p.54*) – can all be seen in the Neoclassical style. Many 18th-century designers regarded the Corinthian order as the most desirable. Its influence on clock design can be seen in the form of columns capped with acanthus leaves.

**REGENCY LONGCASE CLOCK** This mahogany clock is charged with Neoclassical features: the broken arch bonnet; the use of fluted columns either side of the clock face and flanking the door; and the two large inlaid cartouches of Britannia. *c.1800. H:241.5cm (95in).*

**FEDERAL LONGCASE CLOCK** The bonnet has a swan's neck crest with knopped terminals and three brass finials, the centre one with an eagle, above colonettes with contrasting inlaid stringing. *249cm (98in).*

**The broken arch bonnet** *is inlaid with delicate floral rosettes*

**The clock face** *is brass and has a musical works with seven bells and a moon phase*

**MARQUETRY LONGCASE CLOCK** This Austrian clock has a walnut-veneered softwood body inlaid with maple and plumwood. The rectilinear lines of the case are accentuated by those of the marquetry. *H:237cm (93¼in).*

**The dial** *has Arabic numerals within diapering (checks) and floral corner spandrels*

**The clock** *has an original Baroque brass movement*

**The waisted case** *has a shaped door with contrasting inlay*

**An inlaid quarter-column** *lies either side of the door*

*An amphora vase* supporting a large crown tops the clock

*The clock face* has Arabic numerals for both the hours and minutes, and pierced brass hands

*The central panel* is ornamented with fine-carved flaming hearts

*The pendulum* is visible through a small window in the case

**BIEDERMEIER MANTELCLOCK** The enamelled face of this clock has Roman numerals and is housed in a mahogany case with maple inlay and crowned with an eagle. A sun-shaped pendulum hangs from the case, which arches down to a plinth above four bronzed paw feet. *c.1825. H:52cm (20½in).*

A more understated homage to antiquity might take the shape of fluting or a decorated frieze separating the hood from the body of the case.

## NATIONAL VARIATIONS

The American Federal style was as enthusiastic as French Empire and other European Neoclassical movements in its deference to ancient forms. Defining Federal touches include patriotic American emblems – the finial centring a swan-neck pediment might be topped with an eagle,

**GERMAN CARVED AND GILT CLOCK**
When this clock strikes the hour, a musical movement plays a two-minute waltz. It is lavishly decorated with rams' heads, garlands, leaves, and rosettes. *c.1785.*

for example. Clock cases made in the Biedermeier style that originated in Austria tended to be less cluttered than other Neoclassical examples. This lightness of touch was accentuated by the paler woods, including some fruit- and nutwoods, which were popular in northern Europe.

## CLOCK DEVELOPMENTS

More general developments in clock design included the round face. In contrast to the square and then arched clock faces that had previously been preferred, more and more longcase clocks were made with circular faces. From around 1790 many clock faces in France were fitted with gilded brass hands instead of the blued steel that had hitherto been the norm.

Other forms that date from this time include the cartel clock – a highly decorative French wall clock – and the Act of Parliament clock, which is a type of tavern clock made to hang on a wall and popularized by a tax levied on timepieces by the British government in 1797.

## BRACKET CLOCKS

Neoclassical bracket clocks are generally made from mahogany and tend to be larger than their earlier walnut or ebony cousins. Many of them are highly elaborate and feature typically Neoclassical decorative touches such as finials in the shape of flaming urns or pine cones. But these were frequently replaced as fashions changed and so are not a reliable indicator of age.

Balloon bracket clocks, with cases that hug the contours of the round dial, are a less prevalent variation of the typical square-case bracket style; they are often found with satinwood veneers.

Biedermeier designers in particular were drawn to the architectural bracket clock form. French bracket clocks of the period exhibited greater variety and more lavish decoration than those made elsewhere.

## CARRIAGE CLOCKS

The carriage clock was a 19th-century French innovation. As suggested by the name, it was designed as a portable timepiece, suitable for carriage. Most examples have brass cases and are of eight-day duration. To mark the passage of time, many carriage clocks repeat the last hour after striking the quarter-hour – these are known as *grande sonnerie* clocks. Additional features found on the best examples include *cloisonné* decoration, subsidiary dials for seconds, days, or an alarm, repeat buttons, and fine engraving. Carriage clocks remained popular throughout the 19th and 20th centuries. While most were made in France, there are some English examples.

**GRANDE SONNERIE STRIKING CLOCK** This A.L. Breguet clock has spring detent chronometer escapements. *Early 19th century. H:17.5cm (6¾in).*

# OBJETS DE VERTU

THE MAIN REQUIREMENTS FOR AN *OBJET DE VERTU* – A SMALL DECORATIVE
ACCESSORY SUCH AS A SNUFF BOX, PERFUME BOTTLE, OR SEWING KIT – WERE
RARE OR LUXURIOUS MATERIALS AND THE FINEST CRAFTSMANSHIP.

## PRECIOUS GIFTS

At the top end of the market, snuff boxes were
presented as diplomatic gifts. Gold was the obvious
material – Frederick the Great of Prussia had 300
gold snuff boxes. They could be decorated in gold,
most simply by engine turning, or engraved to
reflect the light. Contrasting colours were created
by adding another metal such as silver or iron to the
gold, but pictures were often painted in enamels or
gouache on inset panels. Hunting or mythological
scenes were popular, as were portraits.

Other materials, such as mother-of-pearl,
porcelain, micromosaics, ivory, or Japanese lacquer,
were used as inlays and precious stones might also
feature. Tortoiseshell might be moulded into the
shape of a small box or veneered on to a wooden
box covered in white gesso. Sometimes the gesso
was coloured to create a green or red tinge. Any
decoration was deliberately kept simple so as not
to detract from the striking markings of the shell.

Snuff boxes were not just made for royalty and the
aristocracy. Silver was elegant enough for a Regency
buck to cut a dash, especially
when combined with shell or
quartz, and all the porcelain
manufacturers made snuff boxes
as well as tableware.

Chinoiseries, landscapes, portraits,
or Classical motifs, and sometimes
incorporated Wedgwood cameos.

For wooden boxes, novelty shapes
such as shoes were popular. Boxes
of local hardwoods with ivory inlays
were imported from Vizagapatnam in
India. In England prisoners of the
Napoleonic Wars improved their
lot by making and selling pine
boxes decorated with natural
and dyed pieces
of straw.

### CHANGING STYLES

Robert Adam
drily observed, "To
understand thoroughly
the art of living, it is necessary,
perhaps, to have passed some time
among the French." As always, French high

**SNUFF BOX** The surface of this
circular French two-colour gold
snuff box and cover has engine-
turned decoration and chiselled
foliate borders. *1780–90.
D:6.5cm (2½in).*

**GEORGE III SNUFF BOX** The
rectangular form of this elegant
tortoiseshell and silver snuff box
has serpentine edges and a hinged
lid. *c.1780. W:8.5cm (3½in).*

## EXOTIC INFLUENCES

From 1750 papier-mâché
became increasingly fashionable
as the European alternative to
Oriental lacquer. It was made
by laminating sheets of paper
and varnishing them, but by
the early 1800s factories had
discovered how to pulp paper,
and papier-mâché was often
used to make snuff boxes.
They were painted with

*The painting of the demure
lady has a motto reading* Elle
Attend *(She is Waiting)*

**STOBWASSER SNUFF BOX** The japanner
Johann Heinrich Stobwasser was particularly
renowned for his papier-mâché. Here the lid
of the snuff box is painted with a picture of a
reclining lady. *c.1830. W:9.3cm (3¾in).*

**ANGLO-INDIAN LAP DESK**
This ivory-veneered sandalwood lap desk has
bands of tambour panelling, alternately stained black. The flowerhead- and leaf-
engraved top acts as a writing slope and opens to reveal a partitioned interior. c.1820. W:38cm (15in).

## SNUFF-BOX EROTICA

Snuff boxes were beautifully made and had no fastening
mechanism, but relied on the lid fitting the box perfectly.
They had to fit smoothly so that snuff would not spill out
when the box was opened. This precise workmanship
had another use for boxes that were more for show – or
concealment – than function. Some boxes had hidden
panels that unscrewed to reveal miniature paintings of
erotic boudoir scenes, a lock of hair, musical automata, or
the face of a loved one. One such box in London's Wallace
Collection has a secret panel, only found in 1976, showing
gouache portraits of Voltaire and his mistress.

**TORTOISESHELL SNUFF BOX** This gilt-metal-inlaid snuff box is
decorated with a vase of flowers. The interior unscrews to reveal
a painting on ivory of a boudoir scene. c.1785. D:8cm (3in).

society was the arbiter of taste. So decoration
showing "pagodas and fantastic fripperies" –
the artist William Hogarth's description of
Chinoiserie – Gothic ruins, and pastoral scenes
gave way to Classical ruins and sarcophagus
shapes. The rest of Europe carried on in the
Rococo vein – Chelsea continued making
porcelain toys, as adult accessories were then
called, in imitation of Sèvres' Louis XV style
until it merged with Derby in 1769.

By then, France had moved on towards the
next style. In 1756 the philosopher Denis Diderot
commented on the vogue for the *Goût grec*:
"Everything is now made in the Greek manner.
The taste has passed from
architecture into the
milliners' shops...
our dandies would
think it a disgrace
to be seen with a

snuff box not in the Greek style." Soon the lighter
Louis XVI style was fashionable and after about
1820 shapes became serpentine or *bombé* as the
Rococo style was revived.

## WOMEN'S FANCIES
Women had a wider choice of fashionable
accessories. *Nécessaires* contained miniature kits,
often for sewing. *Étuis* were similarly useful cases
for small items such as writing equipment, sewing
accessories, or tiny sets of cutlery. *Bonbonnières*
were little sweet boxes. Vinaigrettes were silver
boxes, small enough to be tucked into a glove,
that contained smelling salts –
a sponge soaked in
aromatic vinegar. In an
era of unpleasant smells
including open sewerage,
such items were essential
for the fairer sex.

*Gorge de pigeon*
(pigeon's breast) pink
opaline glass

Perfume was another way to ward off body odours.
At the time perfume was not pre-packaged and had
to be decanted into small bottles. Perfume bottles
were usually made of glass, which could be cased,
coloured, and decorated with techniques such as
cutting, pressing, cameo, and frosting. Chelsea,
Sèvres, and Wedgwood also made perfume
bottles out of non-porous ceramics.

**PERFUME BOTTLE** The deep-cut body of this perfume
bottle is in the extremely rare *gorge de pigeon* glass,
which was only made in France between 1815 and 1835. It
has a three-colour gold mount. *1815–25. H:6cm (2¼in).*

**IVORY *NÉCESSAIRE*** This gold-mounted ivory
*nécessaire* contains gold-handled scissors, an
ivory memo, tweezers, a snuff spoon, a thimble,
and a bodkin. H:8.25cm. (3¼in).

**ENAMELLED *ÉTUI*** This gilt-metal mounted case has a
screw cover shaped like a thimble. The case is inscribed
*Sincer en amitie* (Honesty in friendship) and contains a
glass perfume bottle. *Early 19th century. L:8cm (3in).*

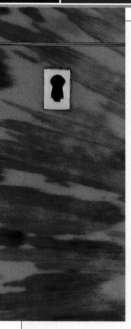

# TEA AND SNUFF

BENEATH THEIR RIGIDLY FORMAL EXTERIORS, OUR
18TH-CENTURY ANCESTORS WERE JUST AS SUSCEPTIBLE
TO VICE AS WE ARE TODAY. THE TWIN TEMPTATIONS
OF TEA AND SNUFF WERE A RICH SEAM FOR THE SINS
OF GREED AND COVETOUSNESS.

Snuff had been known in elite European circles since the 16th century, when the French ambassador to Portugal cured one of Queen Catherine de Medici's interminable headaches with a pinch of powdered tobacco leaf.

## THE POWER OF SNUFF

Snuff was first introduced to the nobility in Britain when large quantities of it were seized from Spanish ships captured at the beginning of the 18th century. As with any addictive substance, the use of snuff soon spawned a range of conventions and peculiar habits. A carved wooden Scottish Highlander was used as a shop sign by many snuff retailers. Many devotees of snuff took to toting

their powdered tobacco around in specially made boxes, although Dr Johnson, one of the most well-documented snuff-takers, carried his loose in his coat pockets. The wide variety of snuff boxes on the market included metal ones decorated with scenes in Staffordshire enamels, engraved silver boxes, boxes studded with precious stones, and countless treen (wooden) examples. Larger snuff mulls, designed to stand on a table for communal use, were often decorated with rams' horns or even fashioned from an entire ram's skull.

## TEA-DRINKING NATION

The popularity of tea in Europe, and especially in Britain, rocketed during the 18th century. In 1685 the British East India Company imported nearly 5,500kg (12,000lbs) of tea – by 1750 it was bringing in about 2,000,000kg (4,500,000lbs) every year. The monopoly enjoyed by the East India Company, combined with an extortionate tax, made tea expensive enough to encourage a thriving smuggler's market. In fact, the value of tea was such, usually 70 per cent of the cargo's worth, that porcelain tea bowls and other ceramics were included with shipments of tea as ballast, just to make up the weight.

The word "caddy" comes from the Chinese for a 1lb weight, which is exactly what the first tea caddies were designed to hold. They were often fitted with locks to safeguard their contents from servants. As with snuff boxes, no expense was spared in the decoration of a tea caddy. The rarest woods and luxury materials such as tortoiseshell, mother-of-pearl, and ivory housed the precious commodity. Elaborate decorative techniques including penwork and painted enamels added an exotic touch. Even the caddy spoons were wrought from silver and decorated immaculately.

## TAX ON TEA

Tea even took on a political importance in the United States. The citizens of Boston, incensed at what they saw as an illegal tax of three pence a pound levied on their supply of tea, refused to let the East India

**ENAMEL TEA CADDY** The sides of this squared caddy are enamelled with Classical myths depicting Pyramus and Thisbe and Perseus and Andromeda and scenes from *The Ladies' Amusement*. c.1760. L:8.5cm (3½in).

**REGENCY TEA CADDY** This tortoiseshell and mother-of-pearl tea caddy is square with canted corners. The case has a geometric lozenge design, the front has a silver escutcheon and initialled mount. W:15cm (6in).

Company dock and unload one fateful day in 1773. The standoff culminated in the Boston Tea Party, when a mass of townspeople dressed as American Indians stormed the boats and threw the cargo of tea into the sea.

Demand for tea reached such an extent in the early 19th century that the East India Company resorted to illegally smuggling opium into China to exchange for huge quantities of the leaf. The result was the loss of an entire Chinese generation to opium addiction and eventually led to war in 1840.

**SOCIAL WHIRL** British cartoonist Thomas Rowlandson parodied the fashionable tea parties of the time.

**ENAMEL SNUFF BOX** The decoration on such items was often inspired by the works of famous Italian and French artists. Here the image is titled *Les Poussins* after Boucher and is on a powder blue ground. c.1770. L:8cm (3in).

**COWRIE SHELL SNUFF BOX** The smooth surface and exotic patterning of the cowrie shell made a luxurious material for a snuff box. The silver cover is engraved with a coat of arms. c.1770. L:8cm (3in).

# AMERICAN FOLK ART

The late 18th century ushered in a golden age of American folk art, perhaps linked to the newly won sovereignty of the 13 original colonies. Although diverse, folk art is characterized by a lack of formal training on the part of the artists and craftsmen. It also tends to follow the artistic traditions of the immigrant communities that forged it, making it the ideal medium through which American citizens could assert their individuality and independence while remaining true to their roots.

## ANONYMOUS CRAFTSMEN

Different areas specialized in different art forms, although Pennsylvania counties have emerged as the most prolific in many spheres. While some folk artists have become famous in their own right, most of the artefacts described as folk art were made by anonymous individuals. Occasionally a body of particularly fine work is attributed to a single unknown craftsman who is given a title such as "The Hannovertown Artist". Folk art takes many forms from the functional to the purely decorative, and examples practised by American communities have encompassed media as diverse

as ceramics, wood, tin, and paper. Popular subjects include animals, often carved in wood. These range from decoy birds with naturalistic painting, used by hunters to lure their prey, to portrait carvings, either of generic animals or favourite pets. Animals such as turkeys, dogs, and horses, important to the livelihoods of early Americans and commonly found on smallholdings, were frequently depicted on painted wood.

## PAINTERLY SKILLS

Painted decoration can transform an ordinary item into an extraordinary piece of folk art. Itinerant painters such as the prodigiously talented Rufus Porter travelled over large areas accepting commissions to decorate anything from walls to boxes. At a local level, a villager known for his skill with a brush would attract the attention of his neighbours and often earn a supplementary income by painting prized possessions.

Certain motifs occur time and again throughout American folk art. The tulip, loaded with significance for early settlers, is particularly prevalent. The flower had associations with contented home life and was also a symbol of

**CARVED AND DECORATED TURKEY** Animal carvings have always been a popular folk art theme. This Pennsylvanian turkey is brightly coloured and has a stylized fantail and beak. *Late 18th century. H:18cm (7in).*

*The decoration* reflects the ebullience of federal America

*Bands and dots* decorate the lid cover

*The moulded base* is painted russet red

*The flowerpots* are decorated with spots

**PAINTED PINE CANDLEBOX** This candlebox from the Lancaster/Lebanon area is incised and has a moulded base. The sliding lid is decorated with *demi-lune* rainbow bands and the sides with stylized potted tulips, chickens, and paisley corners. *c.1800. H:16cm (6½in).*

**PIE PLATE** This earthenware sgraffito pie plate is from Pennsylvania. It is decorated with naive drawings of a horse, two birds, and a tulip, and has green and yellow slip glazing. *c.1800. D:23cm (9in).*

**TOLEWARE COFFEE POT** This gooseneck coffee pot is decorated with fruits and flowers in earthy tones. Most toleware had a black background, so this piece, probably from New England, is rare. *H:26cm (10¼in).*

**RED WARE INKWELL** Most red ware – glazed red earthenware – was made before 1840 by northern European immigrants. This example is a heart-shaped inkwell with pierced sides. *Early 19th century. W:14cm (5½in).*

the Holy Trinity. This religious symbolism is never far from the surface of American folk art of this period. The peacock, another favourite motif, was associated with the resurrection of Christ, while the red rose signified God's love.

## EUROPEAN TRADITION

Folk art ceramics already had a long European history before they were first produced in the United States. Pennsylvania red ware is based on German folk ceramics and other American slip-decorated wares had similar roots in the European tradition. The application of slip is one of the most

straightforward ways of waterproofing and decorating earthenware vessels and was employed extensively by American settlers. More sophisticated potters created sgraffito wares by incising designs into the slip clay. Common themes include the wildflowers and animals of the American landscape as well as the abstract wavy lines of Pennsylvania slipware. These ceramics were instrumental in forging the early American domestic style and continue to exert an important influence on contemporary American ceramics.

Painted tinplate, known as toleware, was decorated using a similar method to the imitation

lacquer technique known as japanning. The base coat is usually made of asphaltum, a naturally occurring tar-like substance that provides a glossy, opaque black ground. Rarer examples have red or even yellow base colours. Oil paints were then stencilled or handpainted on top of the base coat, depicting flowers or abstract patterns. Decorating toleware was difficult and time consuming, so these pieces were often reserved for special occasions and given as wedding gifts. Toleware items such as coffee pots, candlesticks, and trays would probably have been valued as decorative display objects and would only have been used rarely, if at all.

**STORAGE BOX** The heart-shaped motifs on this mahogany-veneered and inlaid storage box are typical of American folk art, while the geometric patterning and shield motifs are characteristic of the Federal era. *c.1820. W:37.5cm (14¾in)*

## FRAKTUR

The German immigrant population in Pennsylvania began to produce *Fraktur* – illuminated manuscripts – in the 18th century. These fall into several distinct categories, the most prevalent of which are the *Taufschein* documents created to record the birth and baptism dates of children born to these early settlers. Local schoolmasters would draw up these records on behalf of the families living within their communities, using goose-quill pens with steel nibs. The most talented artists were in great demand and sometimes even worked in several different counties.

Devotional motifs such as angels, crowns, and the symbolic tulip were drawn from the Lutheran religion of the German settlers. These were combined with astrological and natural symbols such as hearts and stars as well as pictures – images of the family in formal dress are common. English gradually supplanted German as the dominant language for *Taufschein* documents in the 19th century.

Other types of Fraktur include *Vorschriften* – handwriting samplers, bookplates, and house blessings. They are all characterized by extensive use of brightly coloured inks and careful script. Fraktur dwindled in popularity as printing became more common in the United States during the 19th century.

**BIRTH CERTIFICATE** A watercolour and ink on paper birth certificate for Joseph Horner, by Henry Young, Pennsylvania. The two central figures of husband and wife hold hands, while the gentleman presents a bouquet of flowers. *1841. H:26cm (10¼in).*

# TEXTILES

WHETHER THEIR DESIGNS WERE INCORPORATED IN THE WEAVE

OR PRINTED ON TO THE FABRIC, FRENCH TEXTILES WERE THE MOST

INFLUENTIAL OF THE LATE 18TH AND EARLY 19TH CENTURIES.

## THE SILK TRADE

The French city of Lyon has been associated with the silk trade since medieval times. By the start of the 18th century Lyon directed trends and produced luxurious woven silks, which inspired designs all over Europe.

The first 18th-century onwards fashion associated with Lyon was bizarre silks. Used mainly for dresses, these vibrant asymmetrical patterns combined Oriental-style flowers and foliage with jagged lines and architectural motifs. The dominant pattern was usually in gold or silver thread.

From the 18th century onwards the innovative silk weavers of Lyon positioned their products at the top-quality end of the market and attracted leading textile designers to work for them.

**FLORAL LAMPAS SILK** Made by La Maison Grand Frère, this design has a naturalistic flower arrangement within a floral laurel wreath. It is a re-edition of an 18th-century model designed by Gaudin. *1788. L:254cm (100in).*

## KEY DESIGNERS

Jean Revel helped change the look of silk dress fabrics in the 1730s. He developed a special weaving technique – *points rentés* – to create shading and three-dimensional effects. He used this technique to make realistic designs: flowers, fruit, shells, and architectural ruins were among his favourite motifs. The images were woven into the silk entirely by hand. These naturalistic designs dominated silk patterns until the end of the 19th century.

Lyon silk designer Philippe de Lasalle trained under François Boucher, the painter. Like Revel, he, too, was a weaver who improved silk-production techniques. His fabric designs bridge the gap between delicate Rococo and the simpler Neoclassical look. He specialized in furnishing fabric with detailed naturalistic decoration of flowers and motifs of bows, swags, and vases. He sometimes included

**LYON LAMPAS SILK** This length of red silk is decorated with a repeating pattern of eagles, pheasants with their nests, flowers, torches, and flower-filled urns. The pattern was created in 1785. *L:160cm (63¾in).*

animals and birds. Lasalle's textileswere the height of luxury and quality. He supplied fabrics to Louis XVI and European monarchs such as Catherine the Great and Charles III, King of Spain.

The French Revolution was a blow to the Lyon silk trade, which received so much patronage from the monarchy. Fortunately, in the early 1800s, Napoleon took up the role. He commissioned vast quantities of furnishing fabric for his residences. Jean-François Bony designed many of these textiles. His Neoclassical style had the right political connotations, associated with the Roman Empire. Bony used motifs like laurel wreaths, trophies, shields, and Napoleon's personal symbol – the bee.

## TOILES

Indian printed cottons were so popular in the late 17th century that the French government banned them to protect France's wool and silk industry. When the government lifted this law in 1759, Christophe-Philippe Oberkampf founded a cloth printing works in Jouy. As a result this style of printed fabric is called *toiles de Jouy* (cloth from Jouy) even though other cities like Nantes also produced it. The earliest *toiles* were multicoloured floral prints similar to Indian fabrics. The monochrome printing associated with toiles came later. Classic designs feature Chinoiseries, contemporary vignettes, and images from Greek and Roman mythology, printed in red, sepia, mauve, or blue on white or yellow grounds. Immensely influential, *toiles* still inspire fabric designers today.

**COTTON FURNISHING FABRIC** Manufactured by Petitpierre Frères et Cie of Nantes, the design was printed using copper plates. It shows scenes from a comedy by Rabelais. *1785–90. L:181cm (71¼in).*

## WALLPAPERS

Many consider the 18th and early 19th centuries a high point in wallpaper design. At the beginning of the 18th century handpainted wallpapers from China took Europe by storm. Decorated with blossoming trees, long-tailed birds, and exotic scenes, they helped raise wallpaper from a humble substitute for tapestry to something even aristocrats would want. Wallpapers decorated with floral sprays were also popular, while other fashionable designs imitated marble columns or swags of fabric.

French manufacturer Jean Bapiste Réveillon introduced Neoclassical wallpapers in the 1770s. paintings found in Pompeii. He employed leading designers including Jean-Baptiste Huet, also celebrated for his *toiles* designs. Jacquemart and Bénard manufactured papers inspired by Roman wall paintings. During the Revolutionary period they produced designs decorated with republican tricolour ribbons and caps of liberty. In the early 1800s the French firms Zuber and Dufour made wallpaper panels, which formed panoramic views of towns and landscapes such as the Swiss Alps.

**ROYAL LAMPAS SILK** This pattern was created by Michel for Queen Marie Antoinette's games salon at Versailles. The striking yellow-gold ground is decorated with oak boughs and flowers. *1784–86. L:140cm (55in).*

**DIRECTOIRE WALLPAPER** This piece of wallpaper was printed using woodblocks. The central bust of Barras *en grisaille* is framed by wheatsheaves and sprigs of laurel leaves on a blue ground. *c.1798. W:55cm (21½in).*

**WALLPAPER PANEL** This design imitates drapery and is charged with Neoclassical motifs: elaborate columns topped by busts of Classical figures, swags, paterae, and griffin motifs. *c.1800. H:255cm (100in).*

# SAMPLERS

In an age when aristocratic girls' lives were confined to gentle pursuits such as books and music, the embroidered sampler was a testament to their needlework skills and the leisure time available to them. Such skills were important and women produced examples of stitches on cloth scraps for practice and guidance. In the 16th and 17th centuries these samples were worked up into textile samplers. Many bore their maker's name, age, and the date they finished. Some took years to make.

Sampler-making was a social activity that bound the generations together. Mothers helped daughters make these pretty as well as useful guides. Families handed down cherished samplers and proudly displayed them in frames.

The earliest samplers were made by professional needlewomen or well-to-do ladies, who had time to embellish their clothing or beautify their homes.

Samplers were immensely popular in Britain. Pilgrims, the early settlers in the United States, took this custom with them and made them equally popular. The Dutch, Germans, Spanish, and Mexicans also produced samplers in great numbers.

## VERSES ON SAMPLERS

The increased inclusion of text such as the maker's name charts the rise in literacy among the population as a whole in the second half of the 17th century. In the early 18th century samplers were a way of teaching basic reading and mathematical skills as well as giving religious instruction. By the mid-18th century making samplers was a primary educational exercise for girls, and it became rare not to incorporate letters, numerals, or some form of text. Girls began working on a simple sampler with the alphabet and numerals aged five or six. As they grew older, teenage girls aged about 13

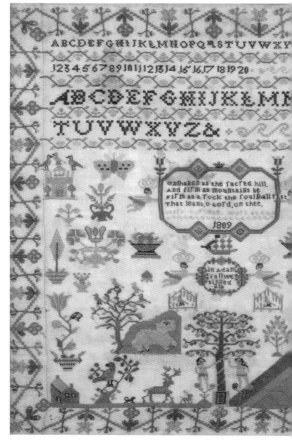

**ALPHABET SAMPLER** Centred beneath the alphabet is a verse within a panel supported by crowned cherubs. Adam and Eve stand beneath the Tree of Life with other home-life designs all within a floral border. *1809. H:56cm (22in).*

produced more sophisticated samplers embroidered at length with motifs and verses that showed off the skills they had acquired. Biblical quotations and pious prose were popular, as were mottoes and rhymes. "*All you my friends who now will see this little piece that has been work'd by me,*" is a typical example.

## PICTORIAL SAMPLERS

Makers carefully and symmetrically arranged images on samplers in the 18th and 19th centuries, unlike the randomly embroidered 17th-century examples. They finished later samplers with decorative borders. The embroidery style on samplers is usually charmingly naive with no attempt at perspective. Typical motifs include fruit, flowers, trees, birds, animals, and geometric designs. Because of their role in religious education, many of these images have Biblical symbolism. Adam and Eve with the snake in the apple tree began regularly appearing as a focal point from the 1740s onwards. The needleworker's own home was another favourite subject. As the anti-slavery movement gathered momentum in the early 19th century, related imagery also appeared on samplers.

**NEEDLEWORK SAMPLER** Within a bold floral border is a panel of pious verse and inscriptions above a hillock with ducks, sheep, rabbits, a horse, and a snake. The sampler was worked by Lydia Ann Beales of Chester County, Pennsylvania, in coloured silk threads on a gauze ground. *1832.*

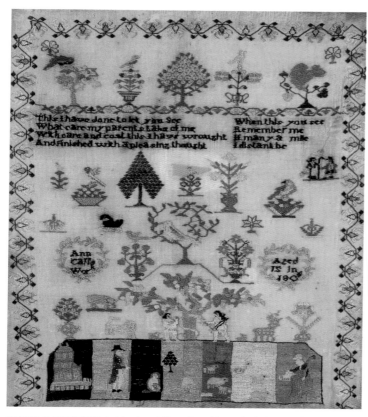

**GEORGE III SAMPLER** Worked in coloured silks on linen, this sampler depicts verse above a Tree of Life with figures, itself above a country landscape. By Ann Carr, aged 15. *1806. H:39cm (15¼in).*

**NEW YORK SAMPLER** This silk-on-linen sampler features a Tree of Life with Adam and Eve by a Federal house, with a strawberry border. By Elizabeth Vermillya, aged 13 years. *1796. H:44.5cm (17½in).*

**WILLIAM IV SAMPLER**
Below an alphabet row, a tree is flanked by plants, figures, birds, and animals, with a strawberry border. Worked in coloured silks by Elizabeth Ambridge, aged 9. *1836. H:34cm (13½in).*

## DARNING SAMPLERS

Before the mid-20th century women mended rather than threw away costly sheets, stockings, and dresses when they became worn or damaged. Learning to darn with near-invisible stitches was a practical skill much in demand. In the late 18th and early 19th centuries women who mastered this skill sometimes turned their fine stitches into art. They created darning samplers, working darning stitches into patterns: usually bold squares, but sometimes floral motifs and trees. A lady's maid looking for work would show her darning samplers as evidence of her ability to care for her mistress's outfits.

After 1850 samplers began to decline in quality and quantity. The sewing machine meant women no longer had to be proficient at basic stitching. Girls' education became more academic so less time was given to needlework. But, most important, colourful, naturalistic images in wool on square meshed canvas were now the height of fashion. This technique, called Berlin wool work, dominated embroidery for the rest of the 19th century.

**TEMPLE OF SOLOMON** This George III sampler is worked in coloured silks. Two jardinières sit amid birds, figures, and trees above the Temple of Solomon and verse, within a strawberry border. *1792. H:31cm (12¼in).*

## MAP SAMPLERS

British women began making map samplers in the 1770s. They usually chose to depict the British Isles and sometimes continental Europe, often in an oval-shaped design. By the late 18th century it had become easier and safer to travel long distances for work or pleasure and geography became an increasingly important part of a young lady's education. British sea power was a source of pride and many women had family and friends in the navy. Map samplers often included naval motifs like compasses and sailing ships. British immigrants to the United States spread the fashion. Map samplers remained a popular embroidery subject until the mid-19th century.

**MAP OF ENGLAND, SCOTLAND, AND WALES** A fascinating record of the contemporary geography of the United Kingdom, this sampler is worked in black silks with the various counties highlighted in reds, greens, ochres, oranges, and blues. *1778. H:50cm (19¾in).*

# SCULPTURE

NEOCLASSICAL SCULPTURE AIMED TO PORTRAY BUSTS AND FIGURES WITH THE "NOBLE SIMPLICITY AND CALM GRANDEUR" THAT THE GERMAN ARCHAEOLOGIST J.J. WINCKELMANN SO ADMIRED IN THE ANCIENT WORLD.

## RETURN TO THE CLASSICAL

The work of Jean-Antoine Houdon and his French peers marked a "return to good taste" after the Rococo "jumble of shells", as a disparaging critic termed it. By the 1750s in Paris – where designers led continental fashion and were quick to change it – there was already nostalgia for the days of Louis XIV and the formality of the palace at Versailles. The imposing medium of marble could be used both for figures from antiquity such as the Olympian gods or Roman emperors, and for prominent people of the day, elevated with a Classical bearing.

Antonio Canova, famous for his Three Graces, standardized the method for working in marble, whether on a large or small scale (only Michelangelo could work straight to marble). From drawings, one or more clay maquettes would be made, then a plaster model would be moulded from wet clay. This could be scaled up to a full-size model by sticking in lead nails, and measuring the distances with callipers, helped by a pointing machine. Successful sculptors had apprentices to hew the marble, working closely to the model. The maestro would then add the finishing touches.

## REINTERPRETING THE ANCIENTS

Marble could end up looking cold in the austere Neoclassical style. In the hands of those who simply made inferior copies of ancient statues, it was lifeless, but the best sculptors such as Houdon and Canova were able to bring marble to life.

The French sculptor Étienne-Maurice

**FOUNTAIN SCULPTURE** The central part of a fountain, this exceptional bronze sculpture depicts the allegories of the hunt, fishing, and gardening. *Early 19th century. H:67cm (26¾in).*

**RECUMBENT FEMALE** This marble sculpture is modelled as a woman reclining on a chaise longue with a sumptuous cushion and raised on a moulded rectangular base. *H:56cm (22in).*

**MINERVA** This bust of the Roman goddess of wisdom and war, known as Athena by the Greeks, was sculpted by Johann Heinrich Dannecker in Rome. Here the goddess is represented in the armoured helmet she is said to have been born with. *1785-86. H:30cm (12in).*

Falconet spent the early part of his career making mildly erotic boudoir-style nymphs that resembled those of the Rococo painter François Boucher. But then he created a massive bronze equestrian statue in a more serious, imposing style for Peter the Great in St Petersburg in 1778.

He shocked his contemporaries by claiming that modern sculptors were better at life-like portrayals than the ancients. He wrote: "In attempting the imitation of the surfaces of the human body, sculpture ought not to be satisfied with a cold likeness, such as man might be before the breath of life animated him...It is living nature, animated, passionate, that the sculptor ought to express." Jean-Antoine Houdon, who was based in Paris but had trained in Rome, came closest to fulfilling Falconet's ideal. His portrait busts of the rich and famous captured the individual personalities, gestures, and expressions of his sitters.

## NEW MATERIALS

Both bronze and marble could be used on any scale, whether for outdoors or inside buildings, but new ceramic materials could also be used for sculpture indoors. Wedgwood's black basalt was hard and imposing, making it the ideal material for a Classical bust. John Flaxman, one of the few English sculptors whose name was known in Europe, started his career designing low-relief plaques and medallions for Wedgwood. Spode, which was known as Copeland and Garrett after 1833, had discovered a recipe for stone china, an extremely hard earthenware, which it started using in 1805. This proved a good material for busts of leading contemporary figures.

As recipes for hard-paste porcelain spread across Europe, this more stable formula enabled factories to make larger examples of ceramics, often as sculptural centrepieces for the dining table. Falconet designed statues for Sèvres that were made in biscuit porcelain and left unglazed to show off the sculptural detail better. His statue of Cupid, with a finger to his lips, was highly popular. By 1780 mythological and Classical subjects had replaced pastoral themes, under Louis-Simon Boizot, who was in charge of the modelling workshop at Sèvres from 1773.

Maurice Falconet's designs were copied by other factory modellers such as Johann Carl Schönheit at Meissen. Meissen adopted the Neoclassical style under the directorship of Count Camillo Marcolini from 1774. He approved of biscuit porcelain for allegorical and Classical figures, as the material resembled the marble sculptures being excavated in Greece and Italy.

**BUST OF THE MARQUIS DE MÉJANES** This marble bust by Jean-Antoine Houdon sits on a pedestal and is of a style predating the French Revolution. *c.1786. H:86cm (34in).*

**DUKE OF WELLINGTON**
This Copeland and Garrat feldspar porcelain bust of the Duke of Wellington gives Wellington the noble bearing of a Roman general. *c.1835. H:44cm (9½in).*

**YOUNG WOMAN** Made of marble and alabaster, this French bust of a young woman wearing a scarf over her hair is signed A. Aurili. *Early 19th century. H:25cm (9¾in).*

*The young woman* has the small facial features characteristic of Classical sculpture

**MEISSEN MARCOLINI BUST**
The bust is a model of Johann Daniel Schöne, sculpted from biscuit porcelain. It is marked "Guttenberg", and has the blue sword mark. *1810. H:12.5cm (5in).*

*The dress*, in a pale red colour, has a square neckline, ornamented with a geometric design

# Age of Excess

## 1840–1900

# 19TH-CENTURY REVIVALS

DURING THE 19TH CENTURY MANY ARTISTS, ARCHITECTS, AND DESIGNERS TURNED THEIR BACKS ON THEIR OWN CENTURY AND BEGAN TO EXPLORE THE STYLES OF EARLIER AGES. IN PARTICULAR THEY TURNED THEIR ATTENTION TO THE MEDIEVAL WORLD.

## THE RISE OF NATIONALISM

The various stylistic revivals of the century can best be understood as an expression of national feeling, for they represented a nostalgic return to long-forgotten or neglected forms of art that gave continuity and substance to newly emerging nations. In seeking inspiration from the past, they were also rejecting the mass production and commercialism of the industrial age in favour of a supposedly purer, more idealistic, Utopian age.

Throughout Europe at this time, nationalism became the dominant theme. Subject peoples – Greeks, Serbs, and Romanians in the Ottoman Empire, Poles in the Russian Empire, Hungarians in the Austrian Empire – struggled for independence and nationhood, while both Italy and Germany emerged as united nations at this time: Italy in 1859–61, and Germany in 1871. Revivalist styles bolstered this nationalist tide.

## THE GOTHIC REVIVAL

The main revivalist style was neo-Gothic, or the Gothic Revival, which took various forms. In Britain, as in Germany, the Gothic style was a continuation rather than a revival, for it had always remained popular. It became closely linked with the revival of Catholicism within the Anglican Church and the renewed strength of Roman Catholicism itself. Many medieval churches were restored in the Gothic style, while Keble College and other buildings in Oxford – the spiritual home of the Anglo-Catholic movement – were built in this style.

In Germany the revival was linked with anti-French sentiments and was heavily nationalistic: one of the major projects of the time was the restoration of Marienburg Castle, the medieval seat of the crusading Teutonic Knights. In Bavaria, an independent kingdom until it joined the German empire in 1871,

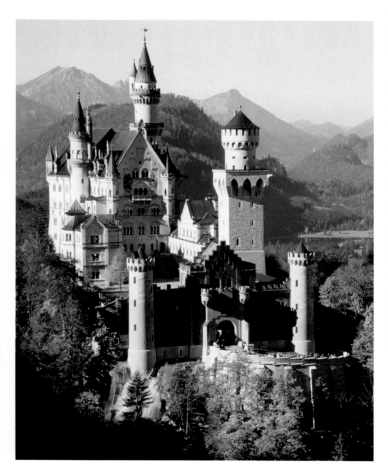

**NEUSCHWANSTEIN CASTLE** The reclusive Ludwig II of Bavaria had this castle built in Gothic style in the 1860s. Inside, the decor illustrated the medieval legends that inspired composer Richard Wagner.

**MEISSEN CLOCK** This porcelain mantel clock has applied decoration of exotic birds and flowers, with a brass dial. *19th century. H:29cm (11½in).*

Ludwig II built fairytale Gothic castles as his personal escape from the modern world. In Italy the return to medievalism was part of the push towards Italian unification, with many Italian cities adopting the style as an echo of their former medieval glory: work was resumed on Milan Cathedral and the façade of Santa Maria del Fiore in Florence, among other projects.

## FRENCH AND OTHER REVIVALS

In France the neo-Gothic style was used to identify the monarchy, which was restored after the defeat of Napoleon in 1815, with its medieval past, and to link national identity with Catholicism: Gothic cathedrals and abbeys were restored and extended in the new revivalist style. Furniture-designers in France, as elsewhere in Europe, also looked back

**DUTCH SILVER BASKET** The undulating Rococo-style shape of the rim is teamed with elaborate decoration including a diamond-cut pattern and Neoclassical swags and medallions. *c.1890. W:26cm (10¼in)*

**CHÂTEAU DE GROUSSAY** This French castle was completed in 1825. The rich, dark interior decor of the library, its heavy furnishings, and eclectic, lavish display of ornaments and pictures is typical of the 19th century.

to the Renaissance, making large, architectural pieces with deep-carved decoration. They also returned to the Baroque styles of Louis XIV's reign, combined with forms and motifs from the Rococo designs of Louis XV's and the Classical styles of Louis XVI's reigns. These influences were seen elsewhere in Europe and the United States and led to increasing clutter: walls were hung with layers of tapestries or numerous paintings; chairs and sofas were richly upholstered and button-backed; rooms were crammed with palms and other exotic plants; and bibelots or knick-knacks were placed on tables, sideboards, and mantelpieces.

The increase in nationalism also brought about a renewed interest in folk motifs and crafts, depicting people in traditional dress or engaged in rural pastimes. Ceramicists revived the rustic folk designs of faience of the late 17th and early 18th centuries. The decorative arts of the Orient continued to influence Western designers. Chinese and Japanese ceramics and furniture, Near and Middle Eastern motifs from Persian carpets, Iznik pottery from Turkey, and ancient Egypt were all inspirations. A final revival took place in the United States, where furniture-makers returned to the colonial styles that had been popular in the 18th century.

**TRIPOD TABLE** Made of papier-mâché and decorated with mother-of-pearl, the central panel on the table top is painted with a mountainous landscape. c.1860. H: 65cm (26in).

# ELEMENTS OF STYLE

A FLURRY OF REVIVAL STYLES dominated 19th-century decorative arts. Designers focused on demonstrating their expertise, sometimes at the expense of decorative cohesion, which resulted in a mix of wildly disparate styles on the same piece. A mania for accumulating and displaying collections of scientific specimens and ornamental trinkets was reflected in a generally cluttered and varied style of interior decoration. Advances in manufacturing technology and the aspirations of the rapidly growing middle class fuelled an unprecedented demand for decorative arts and furniture.

FRENCH PORCELAIN VASE
### EXCESSIVE ORNAMENT
Keen to show off their technical virtuosity, craftsmen cluttered their wares with a wealth of decorative techniques. Ceramics, furniture, and glassware groaned under the weight of enamelling, gilding, and all manner of intricate applied ornament, often obscuring the basic form of the piece.

SILVER GILT GRAPE SCISSORS
### REPRESENTATIONALISM
The 19th-century obsession with natural science had a huge impact on the decorative arts. The study of botany and zoology was boosted by new discoveries in far-flung countries. Depictions of animal and plant life became less stylized and more realistic than ever before in a bid to replicate faithfully even the smallest details.

ENGLISH DINING CHAIR
### GOTHIC
Especially prevalent in Britain, the Gothic Revival was a romanticized reworking of the great church architecture of the Middle Ages. Designers used architectural features such as pointed arches, trefoils, tracery, and pinnacles on heavy-set oak furniture. Stained glass also enjoyed a revival.

PENWORK SIDE CABINET
### NEW TECHNIQUES
Penwork was often applied to furniture that had been covered with faux lacquer, or japanned. The decoration was applied in white shellac, and detail and shading were added with a quill pen. Papier-mâché was used to make everything from trays to furniture. Items were painted black or lacquered, then decorated with paint, gilding, and inlays, including mother-of-pearl and shell.

ENGLISH ROCOCO REVIVAL VASE
### ROCOCO REVIVAL
Alongside the influence of archaic Gothic, Classical, and Renaissance forms, this period also saw renewed interest in 18th-century French design. New technologies paved the way for more economic reproductions of the curled scrolls and intricate foliate applications associated with high Rococo style.

BUTTON-UPHOLSTERED ARMCHAIR
## BUTTONED UPHOLSTERY
Chesterfield sofas and club chairs, with their stuffed and buttoned leather upholstery, became fixtures of exclusive establishments in the 19th century. The increasing importance of comfort prompted upholsterers to use luxurious fabrics such as velvet and damask in the same way.

MICROMOSAIC SNUFF BOX
## REDISCOVERING OLD TECHNIQUES
The rise of nationalism came with a nostalgia for old techniques. Micromosaic – using miniature coloured glass cubes to build up intricate images – became popular for decorating furniture and jewellery. Glassmakers also replicated historic glass, from ancient Venetian soda glass to medieval German glass.

*GRAMMAR OF ORNAMENT* ELIZABETHAN DESIGN
## PATTERN BOOKS
The development of colour printing allowed pattern books to bring historical and modern styles to design studios and factories. As a result, common themes such as Japan, the Celts, and botany developed. The most influential pattern book was Owen Jones's *Grammar of Ornament* (1856).

RENAISSANCE REVIVAL TABLE
## RENAISSANCE REVIVAL
The 16th-century flowering of Italian art and science was first called the Renaissance by 19th-century scholars. Designers began to incorporate details such as caryatid pillars and broken arch pediments into their work as a homage to Renaissance art and architecture.

HUNGARIAN MOON FLASK
## INFLUENCE OF JAPAN
Sir Rutherford Alcock's display at the 1862 London International Exhibition was the first major public showcase of Japanese decorative arts. It sparked a wave of interest in Japanese forms, techniques, and motifs that transformed every sphere of European and North American decorative arts, from ceramic glazes to furniture design.

APPLIQUÉ QUILT
## HANDCRAFTS
Even in the age of industrialization, traditional handcrafting techniques continued to flourish. Examples ranged from Italian master craftsmen producing micromosaic furniture to American homesteaders sewing appliqué textiles. The support of social reformers such as John Ruskin eventually burgeoned into an entire movement in the latter half of the 19th century.

WESTERN PERSIAN RUG
## ORIENTAL INFLUENCE
The decorative arts of the Orient continued to exert an important influence on Western designers. As well as Chinese and Japanese ceramics and furniture, 19th-century designers were inspired by Near and Middle Eastern motifs seen on artefacts like Persian carpets, Iznik pottery, and the art of ancient Egypt.

QUIMPER FAN VASE
## FOLK REVIVAL
An increase in nationalistic feeling in many countries brought about a renewed interest in folk motifs and crafts. Depictions of figures in traditional dress or engaged in customary pastimes became more widespread. Vernacular traditions were practised by cottage industries and also appropriated by industrial manufacturers.

# FURNITURE

FROM THE MID-19TH CENTURY, FURNITURE-MAKERS INCREASINGLY SOUGHT INSPIRATION FROM THE PAST, WHILE THE MECHANIZATION OF MANY PROCESSES INTRODUCED PRODUCTION ON A SCALE NEVER SEEN BEFORE.

## AN AGE OF REVIVALS

The air of nationalism that swept across Europe during this era provoked furniture-makers – in Italy and Germany, in particular – to look back to the former glories of furniture design. The highly skilled craftsmen of the Renaissance were their main source of reference.

### RENAISSANCE REVIVAL

Originating in 14th-century Italy, the Renaissance style had been inspired by the architecture of ancient Greece and Rome. The 19th-century interpretations of the style included large-scale, heavy, architectural pieces laden with deep-carved panels and friezes. Centre tables were of simple construction, with well-proportioned tops raised on legs joined by stretchers. The settle returned as a form, often with galleried

backs or arms incorporating rows of fine spindles, and sometimes raised on short, spiral-turned legs. Renaissance-style court cupboards, with various arrangements of small drawers, niches, and cupboards, were also popular. Broken pediments, moulded cornices, arched doors, and pilasters – all features taken from Classical architecture – were common on such pieces.

Woods of choice were dark, predominantly oak and walnut, both of which lent themselves well to the prolific, deep carving that epitomized the style. Motifs were also inspired by the Classical world

**ITALIAN COURT CUPBOARD** Made in walnut, in the Renaissance Revival style, this cupboard has deeply carved animal-paw feet and corner pilasters incorporating Classical figures and lions. *c.1850. H:205cm (80¾in).*

*The decoration* includes harpies, which were monsters with wings and claws but the head and breasts of a woman

**GERMAN ARMCHAIR** An upholstered leather seat and back are stuffed-over within an oak and walnut frame incorporating bulbous, turned supports and richly carved figures and scrolls. *1890s. H:139cm (54¾in).*

**FRENCH TABLE** Elaborately carved in the Renaissance Revival style, this walnut table features dense figural and foliate imagery in the frieze, feet, and stretcher. This is further enriched with pairs of banded columns, two human figures, and six winged harpies from Classical mythology. *c.1870. L:110cm (43¼in).*

*Dense foliate carving* within a scrolling form on a claw foot and included cherubs, grotesques, and semi-nude figures. In Italy there was a fashion for using blackamoors, which had been popular in the 1700s. In Germany Renaissance Revival pieces often featured elaborate porcelain mounts set into an ebony-veneered or black-painted ground. The finest examples were produced by Meissen and handpainted with Classically inspired or folk scenes taken from 17th-century paintings.

The Renaissance style was also adopted in France, where it was referred to as the Henri II style, and in the United States following the Civil War.

## ROCOCO REVIVAL

Having originally developed in France during the first half of the 18th century, Rococo produced furniture with asymmetrical, curvaceous lines and richly ornamented with naturalistic motifs – shells, rockwork, and elaborate scrolls – as well as gilt-metal mounts, porcelain plaques, and intricate floral marquetry. Furniture-makers operating within the Rococo Revival framework produced furniture that was altogether more feminine than that made under the Renaissance Revival banner.

As well as the return of the Louis XV *fauteuil* – with its shaped back, upholstered seat and arms, and serpentine top and seat rails – this period saw new Rococo-inspired forms in the balloon-back chair and the conversation seat, a sofa with a number of "sections", in which groups of people could talk almost facing each other. Buffets and sideboards had arched tops, asymmetrically carved fielded panels, and shaped aprons.

New techniques introduced innovative materials in laminated and bent woods. The mechanization of a number of processes meant that veneer cutting, carving, and the making of gilt-metal mounts could all be achieved at a fraction of the cost of the previous century. The Rococo style was therefore no longer a style for the wealthy few, but one that was also available to the aspiring middle class.

## INTERPRETATIONS OF ROCOCO

The Rococo Revival style found particular favour in Italy, where slightly larger interpretations of the original version were prominent. Richly carved, often heavily gilt pieces included side tables with pierced and scrolled aprons and marble tops. In Britain a more restrained version emerged, with elaborate decoration in the structure of a piece rather than applied to the surface.

The refurbishment of Palais Lichtenstein in Vienna, by Michael Thonet and Peter Hubert Desvignes between 1837 and 1849, exemplified the style in Austria. In the United States, where serpentine forms began to replace the heavy geometric pieces of the Empire style, John Henry Belter's laminate veneers provided the ideal medium for the florid designs that found favour.

**LOUIS XV-STYLE FAUTEUIL** This walnut chair has a channelled frame; padded back, arm rests, and seat; and carved cabriole legs. W:70cm (27½in).

**FRENCH VITRINE** The Rococo Revival form of this vitrine includes cabriole legs, a serpentine pediment and apron, floral and foliate cresting, gilt-metal mounts, and the romantic *vernis Martin* painting. *1870s. H:187cm (73½in).*

**LOUIS XV-STYLE BOW-FRONT COMMODE** Veneered with palisander wood, rosewood, and violet wood, this commode is decorated with floral marquetry and metal mounts and has a marble top. W:131cm (51½in).

## JOHN HENRY BELTER

A German immigrant who went to the United States in 1833, John Henry Belter had been trained in the art of woodcarving. While in the United States, Belter began experimenting with thin sheets of wood, which he used to make laminate panels. His technique involved gluing one sheet to the next, each time with the grain perpendicular to that of the sheet below. With eight, sometimes 16, sheets of laminate in a single board, the result was a very strong yet pliable material. Belter made furniture from his product in the fashionable Rococo style, using predominantly rosewood, but also oak and mahogany. The nature of the wood enabled Belter to make pieces with intricately carved and pierced ornament incorporating naturalistic flower and vine motifs. He also bent the boards under steam to produce panels with dramatic curves, and these subsequently became a hallmark of his style.

**GILTWOOD CONSOLE TABLE** The serpentine marble top of this Rococo Revival table is raised on a fluted, scrolling frame. *c.1860. W:122cm (48in).*

**AMERICAN SOFA** The Rococo Revival rosewood frame of this Belter sofa is raised on cabriole legs and incorporates serpentine cresting and seat rails with finely carved floral and foliate motifs. *1850s. W:157.5cm (62in).*

## BATTLE OF THE STYLES

The neo-Gothic style that emerged in the 1830s was not a true representation of original medieval Gothic, but rather a pastiche of it. This is true, to some extent, of all the various interpretations of neo-Gothic style in Europe at the time: the work of Pierre Cuypers in the Low Countries; the French Gothic Troubadour, or "cathedral", style of the 1830s and 1840s; and the American interpretation in the second half of the 19th century. All of these styles saw the widespread use of architectural motifs – pointed arches, trefoils, and latticework on otherwise-contemporary forms, typically carved from dark, solid wood such as oak. The style was predominantly masculine in appearance.

As the style developed, however, one exponent in particular was responsible for a movement towards a more accurate rendition of Gothic furniture. A.W.N. Pugin was commissioned to provide furnishings for the refurbishment of the Houses of Parliament in London in the mid-1830s. His designs for furniture were based on existing medieval pieces, and he paid considerable attention to the methods of construction that had been used. This quite often meant that pieces reflected the exposed construction of joints, for example – a concept that was embraced by Arts and Crafts furniture-makers towards the end of the century.

## NEOCLASSICAL REVIVAL

The second half of the 1800s brought renewed interest in Neoclassicism. In France Napoleon III was a driving force behind the style, which advocated a return to the designs of Louis XIV's reign, perhaps combined with forms and motifs from the Classical revivals of Louis XVI's reign. Woods of choice tended to be dark – mahogany and ebony – which contrasted well with the decorative details in gilt-bronze and ivory and mother-of-pearl inlays that were fashionable, as well as new materials such as cast iron and papier-mâché. The revival of Boulle marquetry became a hallmark of this era.

Britain and the Low Countries saw a return to the designs of Adam, Hepplewhite, Sheraton, and Chippendale during the 1870s. Furniture-makers had a host of pattern books at their disposal and were successful in making exceptional copies of a number of pieces. Furniture tended to be small-scale, often made from satinwood, with slim, tapering legs, metal mounts, and stringing made from contrasting wood. Pieces might be decorated

**ENGLISH CABINET** The perpendicular Gothic Revival form of this cabinet is accentuated by parcel-gilt and brass Gothic tracery, including cusps and foils. *c.1870. H:213.5cm (84in).*

*Bands of Gothic* quatrefoil motifs are repeated up the façade

*The multifoil tracery* with plain cusping is framed by the lozenge shapes

*Tudor flower finials* augment brattishing or ornamental crestings of similar form

**ENGLISH DINING CHAIR** The Gothic Revival pitch-pine frame of this "king" carver (one of six) has a floral quatrefoil beneath foliate trefoil carvings on a back with brattishing details. *c.1880. H:141cm (55½in).*

**OAK ENGLISH HALLSTAND** This Gothic Revival hallstand has an angular pediment with stylized floral cut-outs, butterfly fretwork, and a row of tiles by Christopher Dresser. *c.1880. H:246cm (97in).*

with fine marquetry panels or Wedgwood plaques featuring typical Classical motifs: fans, acanthus leaves, and the ubiquitous urns.

The Biedermeier style that had developed in Germany and Austria in the early 1800s continued to be popular for much of the 19th century, both there and in Scandinavia, with pieces featuring architectural elements such as columns and pediments – the only ornament on mostly rectilinear forms – with richly figured veneered surfaces.

## COLONIAL REVIVAL

In the United States, from the late 1870s, a number of furniture-makers returned to furniture styles that had been popular in the 18th century.

Dubbed Colonial Revival, the style reintroduced forms such as the gate-leg table. Dominant forms included large buffets and sideboards for dining rooms – the former a two-tiered piece for displaying all manner of household crockery; the latter used for storing cutlery and wine, perhaps even as a side table for serving food. Buffets tended to be rectangular and architectural in shape, usually made from oak or mahogany and decorated in low relief with Classical motifs such as pilasters, urns, and laurel swags. The Sheraton-style sideboard was also a popular form – *demi-lune* in shape, and with slim, tapering legs. Fixtures and fittings remained simple – typically brass plates with ring pulls.

A number of chair styles returned, including the archetypal "Chippendale" chair, Adam-style chairs, the shieldback, and the chaise longue. Ornament was spare, furniture-makers preferring to rely on the grain of the wood for visual interest. Where motifs did feature, they were subtle renditions of Neoclassical examples and included geometric inlay, parquetry panels, marquetry medallions, and paterae.

## CHARLES LOCKE EASTLAKE

In 1868 the English architect Charles Locke Eastlake published a work entitled *Hints on Household Taste in Furniture, Upholstery and Other Details*, in which designs for furniture included a number with Gothic-inspired examples. Eastlake pioneered the use of authentic materials and methods of construction in representing the Gothic style, but the style that developed as a result of his publication was not truly representative of Gothic forms. Instead, pieces were made with ornate materials, including ebonized cherrywood, and incorporated motifs from a wide range of sources such as Moorish and Arabic.

**HOUSES OF PARLIAMENT, LONDON** The New Palace of Westminster was built between 1840 and 1850. It is the seat of the British government and the finest expression of the 19th-century Gothic Revival "national style".

*The top* features a plum-pudding veneer

**LOUIS XVI-STYLE MAHOGANY TABLE** Designed by Henri Dasson, this table has fluted, octagonal legs with cast mounts. *H:72cm (28¼in)*.

*The turned, tapered legs* are typical of the Sheraton Revival style

**SHERATON REVIVAL SATINWOOD CHAIR** Painted overall with flowers and leaves, this chair bears an ivorine plaque for Edwards & Roberts of London.

**AMERICAN CHIFFONIER** The marble-topped walnut carcase, doors, and drawer-fronts of this chiffonier in the Eastlake Style are carved in shallow relief with floral and foliate motifs. *c.1880. H:207.5cm (81¾in)*.

# FURNITURE GALLERY

In the mid-19th century, a period of revivals, Rococo, Gothic, Neoclassical, and Renaissance design elements were mixed together without restraint, resulting in heavily ornamented pieces of furniture. Decoration was exaggerated and taken to extremes, with large metal mounts and twisted columns. This was also an era that relished comfort, so upholstered furniture was popular, especially overstuffed and button-backed chairs and sofas.

## KEY

1. Miniature mahogany cabinet with a swan-neck crest above two glazed doors. H:38cm (15in).
2. Breakfront armoire with mahogany marquetry and brass inlays. c.1880. W:249cm (98in).
3. Louis XV-style cabinet, the gilt ground with vernis Martin decoration and gilt metal mounts. H:80cm (31½in).
4. Louis XV-style kingwood and cherry marquetry commode with a marble top. W:121cm (47½in).
5. Ebonized credenza with brass stringing and gilt brass mounts. W:190cm (74¾in).
6. Rosewood tea table with a foldover top and cabriole legs. W:91.5cm (36in).
7. Walnut whatnot with a pierced gallery above shelves on spiral supports. W:67cm (26¼in).

1 Miniature mahogany cabinet

2 Breakfront armoire

3 Louis XV-style cabinet

4 Marquetry commode

5 Ebonized credenza

6 Rosewood tea table

7 Walnut whatnot

8 Ebonized settee

**8.** Ebonized settee with buttoned upholstery. W:156cm (62½in). ② **9.** Mahogany-framed easy armchair with a buttoned and upholstered back above moulded supports. ② **10.** One of a pair of mahogany library chairs with a padded and upholstered back. ⑦ **11.** Walnut-framed gentleman's easy chair, with a leather buttoned back and seat. ③ **12.** One of a set of eight oak dining chairs, with foliate carved top rails and leather overstuffed seats. ③ **13.** One of a set of six walnut balloon-back dining chairs with cabriole legs. ① **14.** Walnut and tapestry upholstered prie-dieu, the back flanked by twist columns. H:99cm (39in). ① **15.** Carved walnut nursing chair on cabriole legs. ① **16.** Louis XV-style beech open armchair, with a shieldback and padded woodwork seat, back, and armrests. W:62cm (24½in). ①

11 *Walnut-framed easy chair*

10 *Mahogany library chair*

9 *Mahogany-framed armchair*

12 *Oak dining chair*

13 *Walnut balloon-back dining chair*

14 *Walnut prie-dieu*

15 *Walnut nursing chair*

16 *Beech open armchair*

# CERAMICS

TRADITIONAL POTTERY STYLES OF THE PAST ENJOYED A REVIVAL IN THE LATE 19TH CENTURY, FINDING FAVOUR WITH A MIDDLE CLASS LOOKING FOR DECORATIVE ITEMS WITH WHICH TO FURNISH THE HOME.

**QUIMPER FAN VASE** Decorated in a naive style with a lady and a gentleman in traditional clothing, this fan-shaped vase is marked "Alfred Pourquier". c.1875. H:12cm (4¾in).

## FOLK CERAMIC REVIVAL

Looking back to previous eras for inspiration, European ceramicists revived the vibrant, rustic folk designs of tin-glazed earthenware pottery typical of the late 17th and early 18th centuries. Known as faience in France and Germany, and as maiolica in Italy and Spain, such pieces had been made with tin oxide added to the glaze, which gave a characteristic opaque white finish.

## REPLICATING THE STYLE

Bearing in mind the shapes and styles of the originals that they sought to copy, late 19th-century designers produced pieces that were painted in strong colours derived from natural pigments – yellow, green, orange, purple, and blue. Decorative designs ranged from small-scale repeats of delicate leaves and flowers, to Rococo-style scrolling floral patterns. Animal and bird motifs were also popular, especially domestic fowl, and a number of pieces depicted romantic rural scenes featuring figures in local costume.

## REVIVING FAIENCE

In France the earlier works of Nevers, Rouen, and Moustiers were reinterpreted at factories such as Quimper and Desvres. The former had a long-established history of producing traditional-style faience and, from the late 1800s became renowned for pieces depicting local flora and fauna and decorative figures in customary Breton clothing – typically baggy pantaloons and high lace collars.

The wares emerging from Desvres had a characteristic creamy white background. Designs were applied in the Rouen style, using a vibrant palette of Delft blue, yellow, red, and sage green.

*Exotic flowers,* birds, and figures recall 18th-century imagery

*Rope mouldings* are painted in a floral palette of yellow, blue, manganese, and green

**NEVERS POTTERY URN** This polychrome earthenware urn is decorated with architectural ruins. The tap is in the form of a lion's head. H:55cm (21¾in).

**FRENCH WINE COOLER** One of a pair, this cooler is in a Classical Revival form. Its exotic floral and figural polychrome decoration recalls Moustier's earthenware designs of the late 1700s. c.1870. W:31cm (12¼in).

The 18th-century faience pieces produced in Nuremburg, Magdeburg, and Schrezheim were among the principal sources of inspiration for German potters in the Revival era. In German faience, designs were rendered in more subtle colours than those of France, and fairy tales were popular themes for decoration.

## MAIOLICA'S COMEBACK

At the Cantagalli factory in Italy, pottery-makers were inspired by the maiolica traditions of 14th-, 15th-, and 16th-century Spain and Italy. Among the pieces produced were a number that copied the style of Renaissance della Robbia

ware. High-relief models of fruit and foliage were a common feature of such designs. Copies of the early 16th-century Istoriato style were also popular. In these pieces, usually decorative plates or chargers, the central design represented a Biblical, mythical, or allegorical story.

In Portugal the Caldas da Rainha, a major producer of tin-glazed earthenware, was inspired by the 16th-century French Huguenot glass-painter and potter Bernard Palissy, whose pottery often featured motifs from nature, including snails, foliage, and lizards, in high relief.

## TRADITIONAL SHAPES

Nineteenth-century ceramicists looked to the past for more than just techniques and decorative ideas. They were also instrumental in reviving pottery shapes that had been popular in earlier times. These tended to be simple and peasant-like, especially since they were mostly designed for utilitarian rather than decorative

purposes. Among the most common were pear-shaped jugs, baluster-shaped vases, simple bowls, and, specific to Germany, the traditional beer tankard. Plates were popular for decoration, the edge providing an ideal opportunity for a delicate floral border or for high-relief ornamentation.

Apothecary jars were also in great demand. Largely unchanged since the 16th century, apothecary jars came in two shapes: straight-sided *albarelli* for dry medicines, and more bulbous forms with spouts for wet drugs. In a bid to satisfy the demands and tastes of a growing market, a number of new forms emerged, such as fan-shaped and asymmetrical vases. Other popular forms included candlesticks, ink stands, figures, and jardinières.

**ROCOCO-STYLE ITALIAN MAIOLICA VASE** This moulded vase is decorated with a gentleman and a lady on a country walk. It is marked with a crowned "M". *Late 19th century. W:25cm (10in).*

**GERMAN TANKARD** Made at the Mettlach factory, this tankard has a pewter-mounted stoneware body. The handle is relief-moulded with leaf forms and a dwarf's head thumb rest. *c.1880. H:19cm (7½in).*

## MAJOLICA

Minton's majolica was first seen at London's Great Exhibition of 1851. Developed by Frenchman Leon Arnoux, majolica took inspiration from early faience pieces, and is particularly associated with strong sculpted forms and thick glazes in bright colours. Arnoux was influenced by the work of Palissy, and

early pieces were in the Renaissance style, although more contemporary styles also developed, including those inspired by Chinese, Japanese, and Islamic motifs and forms. Typical themes reflected an interest in horticulture and the countryside, while popular forms included jardinières, umbrella stands, garden seats, pie dishes, and tureens. Majolica became extremely popular in Britain following the Great Exhibition and subsequently in Europe and the United States. By 1860 there were more than 30 major majolica manufacturers throughout the world.

**MINTON MAJOLICA HERON** Modelled by French sculptor Paul Comolera, this piece displays the highly naturalistic style for which he was known. *1876. H:100cm (39½in).*

**ENGLISH GAME PIE DISH** The cover of this pie dish by George Jones & Sons features a woodcock and her chicks amid fern leaves; the sides are decorated with rabbits. *1873. D:36cm (14¼in).*

## ENGLISH CERAMICS

In the course of the 19th century, several favourable circumstances conspired to make England one of the largest and most renowned pottery-producing centres in the world. England was well placed to earn such a reputation. The Industrial Revolution had brought mass production on a scale never seen before; a healthy social climate provided a growing middle class hungry for the latest fashions – whether in tableware or colourful ornamental figures; and Britain benefited from an expanding empire looking for goods to import in considerable quantities.

### STAFFORDSHIRE POTTERIES

Leading England's pottery production on a large scale was the county of Staffordshire. The "Staffordshire potteries" were originally based in and around the six towns – Tunstall, Burslem, Hanley, Stoke, Fenton, and Longton – collectively known as Stoke-on-Trent.

The area owed its success to a number of factors. Primarily, the land was rich in raw materials for the production of pottery – clay for modelling, salt and lead for glazing, and coal for firing

the kilns. As a result of this natural wealth, the area could already boast several well-established, reputable potteries with leading figures at the helm, including Minton, Wedgwood, and Spode.

Already pioneers in the field, the larger companies were ready to embrace industrialization and adapted quickly to mass production. Their switch to mechanization received a further boost in terms of staffing: as a result of the Industrial Revolution, large numbers of agricultural labourers from the surrounding countryside were looking for new employment in the towns.

The final element that contributed to the Staffordshire potteries' prominence in the ceramics industry was that the area had a reliable transport system in place – a network of canals and the ports of Hull and Liverpool, which guaranteed the swift and widespread exportation of goods to the rest of the world.

**BATTLE BETWEEN A BUFFALO AND A TIGER** The transfer-printed underglaze blue pattern is from Spode's Indian Sporting series. This was inspired by Samuel Howitt's illustrations in Captain Thomas Williamson's early 19th-century publication *Oriental Field Sports*. c.1830. L:23.5cm (9¼in).

**TRANSFER-PRINTED DISH** Made by Ralph and James Clews of Cobridge, Staffordshire, this dish features a transfer-printed underglaze blue Romantic Ruins pattern set within a floral border. It portrays Don Quixote- and Sancho Panza-like figures in front of Classical ruins. *1820–30. L:28cm (11in).*

## BLUE-AND-WHITE POTTERY

Particularly successful were the blue-and-white wares mass-produced in Staffordshire using transfer-printing methods developed from the mid-18th century. The middle classes demanded dinner services in the latest styles, and a fascination with Britain's expanding empire promoted designs featuring Classical, mythical, and topographical scenes. Motifs from China and India were also popular, as were those depicting royal events such as the wedding of Queen Victoria to Prince Albert in 1840, and her various jubilees.

A good number of pieces exported to the United States bore designs specifically suited to that market – for example, the Beauties of America series, which featured notable American landmarks. In 1891 the American McKinley Tariff Act saw the introduction of country of origin appearing on wares for exportation, which helps with dating particular pieces today.

## STAFFORDSHIRE FIGURES

Since the late 1700s, Staffordshire potters had been emulating the porcelain figures produced by factories such as Bow, Derby, and Chelsea. As the 19th century

**TRANSFER-PRINTED PITCHER** The Landing of General Lafayette at Castle Garden, New York, is one James & Ralph Clew's patterns intended for export to North America. c.1825. H:43cm (17in).

**TRANSFER-PRINTED TUREEN** The Cambridge College, Massachusetts, pattern is from the Beauties of America series made for export by John and William Ridgway. 1820s. W:39cm (15¼in).

**TRANSFER-PRINTED PLATE** Part of a series of 13 for export to North America, this Thomas Mayer plate has a pattern called Arms of New York. 1825–30. D:25.5cm (10in).

progressed, they started to create their own designs, which could be mass-produced at a fraction of the cost of the earlier figures. The factories made them in vast quantities and in all manner of styles, satisfying the demands and eclectic tastes of their ever-growing market.

These pottery figures tended to be flat-backed, so that they could be displayed with pride on a mantelpiece, and portrayed anything and everything – from domestic animals and pets, such as that perennial favourite, the King Charles spaniel, to portraits of contemporary figures. There was a fashion for renditions of famous people – leading politicians, sports figures, military heroes, and royalty – as well as a huge interest in everyday figures, including soldiers, sailors, courting couples, and country folk in regional costume.

Initially, the figures were relatively well moulded, colourfully painted, and very decorative. Towards the end of the 19th century, however, as demand grew and figures were also made for the working classes, quality tended to deteriorate.

**THE RAILWAY CHILDREN** These spill-holders portray figures dressed in fantasy tartans and sitting above stylized trains. They are mementos of the surge in tourism to Scotland in the second half of the 1800s. c.1860. H:24cm (9½in).

*Flowering trees,* or bocage, are a feature of many Staffordshire figures

**FIGURAL GROUP** Set under bocage, this polychrome-painted pearl ware composition of a performer, tethered bear, and lion displays in the latter a naivety of form characteristic of earlier Staffordshire figures. c.1830. H:23cm (9in).

**STAFFORDSHIRE HEARTH SPANIELS** Also known as "comforters" because of the sense of companionship they gave their owners, this pair may have been inspired by Queen Victoria's pet King Charles Spaniel, Dash. c.1860. H:41cm (16¼in).

## AMERICAN CERAMICS

In the early 1800s the introduction of post-Revolutionary tariffs made it easier for American ceramics to compete with foreign wares. The industry began growing rapidly, but vast quantities of ceramics were still imported to keep up with American needs, especially in the first half of the 19th century. Spatter ware, with sponge-decorated borders, and mocha ware, decorated using liquid clay called slip to resemble mocha stone or moss agate, were two of the most popular products that Staffordshire made for the American market.

### RED WARE

One of the earliest American ceramics was red ware, a form of earthenware made from widely available red clay. During the 18th and 19th centuries in America, this was used for everything from mugs and dishes to chamberpots. Red ware pieces are frequently decorated with creamy-coloured slip, applied like icing. Curly designs and wavy lines were the most popular form of decoration. Some potters produced pieces with names and dates or uplifting messages written in slip, like "Temperance, Health, Wealth" or "A Good Pie". The Pennsylvania Dutch community was renowned for its slip-decorated red ware.

### ROCKINGHAM-STYLE POTTERY

American ceramics manufacturers made a wide variety of mottled brown, glazed earthenware throughout the 1800s. Usually called Rockingham ware after the English ceramics manufacturer that developed it, this glaze was used mainly for everyday items such as teapots and baking dishes, but also for ornamental pieces such as Toby jugs of famous Americans. Though Rockingham ware was made across the country, the Norton & Fenton factory in Bennington, Vermont, was usually associated with its production. In 1849 Norton & Fenton patented flint enamel glaze, a streaked yellow, orange, blue, or brown version of Rockingham glaze.

### STONEWARE

Non-porous stoneware was ideal for jugs, crocks, jars, and other storage vessels for homes and businesses such as breweries. It had been made in North America since colonial times, but production

**PENNSYLVANIA RED WARE LOAF DISH** This rectangular dish is decorated with trailed yellow slip in the form of a series of waves. *W:45.5cm (18in).*

**CANADIAN RED WARE JUG** This Ontario jug has a slightly bulbous form and is covered with a mottled dark red glaze. *c.1875. H:25cm (9¾in).*

**PENNSYLVANIA STONEWARE HARVEST JUG**
Decorated with overall floral patterns in blue on an off-white ground, this jug is impressed "George Renerbel". *H:30.5cm (12in).*

**SPATTER WARE BOWL AND PITCHER** The polychrome stripe-pattern spatter decoration is applied to white earthenware forms copied from mid-18th-century Rococo silverware. *c.1850. Pitcher: H:33cm (13in).*

increased dramatically after the Revolution. This hard ceramic was glazed by throwing salt into the kiln. Stoneware was typically decorated with naive cobalt blue motifs, including birds, flowers, and grapes. Handmade stoneware pieces are sometimes stamped with the maker's name and town.

## CHALKWARE

Many rural homes in 18th- and 19th-century America were brightened up by chalkware ornaments, usually in the shape of an animal. Pieces were sold for pennies at fairs and peddled door to door. Made from moulded, air-dried plaster of Paris rather than fired pottery or porcelain, they were hand-decorated with dashes of oil paint or watercolour, and their name derives from their matte chalky appearance. Chalkware ornaments from the 19th century often imitated pricier Staffordshire dogs or farmyard groups prized by wealthier Americans.

## AMERICAN BELLEEK

In the second half of the 1800s many Americans admired the decorative porcelain designed by the Irish Belleek factory. This firm specialized in eggshell-thin ceramics that looked like shells or woven baskets decorated with life-like flowerheads.

A number of American ceramic firms, such as Ott & Brewer and Ceramic Art Company, began producing their own American Belleek pieces in response to demand. In fact, these delicate ceramics were so popular that some firms even incorporated the name "Belleek" into their trademark or replicated Belleek's designs. Knowles, Taylor & Knowles produced a notable range of American Belleek, called Lotusware, predominantly in cream or white, just like Irish Belleek. This range was often moulded into forms that resembled real leaves, or decorated with raised flowers and beaded ornament. Others were pierced to imitate basketwork. Many Lotusware pieces had a touch of gilding to highlight their naturalistic shapes and relief decoration.

**CHALKWARE DEER** The moulded gypsum body of this Pennsylvania-made deer recalls earlier Staffordshire animal figures. It is similarly handpainted in a simple palette of orange, green, brown, and black. c.1840. H:25.5cm (10in).

**FLINT-ENAMEL LION** Essentially a Classical composition, this lion was made in Bennington, modelled with tiny parings simulating the mane, and decorated with a mottled brown-blue flint-enamel finish. c.1840. H:25.5cm (10in).

## JOHN BENNETT

Originally trained as a ceramics decorator at Coalport, the British porcelain factory celebrated for its tableware, John Bennett emigrated to New York in the 1870s. Here he taught porcelain decoration at his Lexington Avenue studio. Painting decoration on blank porcelain was a fashionable hobby for ladies at the time. They tended to paint realistic fruits and floral designs. Bennett's own work, generally painted on Oriental-shaped vases, often features blossoming branches. Though relatively naturalistic, his simplified motifs show a Japanese influence and can be associated with the Aesthetic Movement that had such an effect on late 19th-century British and American design.

**COVERED JAR** This Bennett jar's ovoid form and cover are handpainted with red roses and branches of yellow dogwood, strongly contrasted against a black ground. 1881. H:39cm (15¼in).

**GOURD-SHAPED PITCHER** Made by Ott & Brewer in exceptionally delicate Belleek-style porcelain, this pitcher features alternate panels handpainted with blossoms in pink and gold, and has a gilded water-lily handle. c.1880. H:23cm (9in).

**LOTUSWARE VASE** Raised on gilded ball feet and handpainted with delicate polychrome flowers, this Belleek-style porcelain vase was made by Knowles, Taylor & Knowles of Liverpool, Ohio. c.1890. H:20cm (7¾in).

**PAIR OF COMFORTS** Imported as white blanks from England, this pair of comforts are handpainted by Bennett with a parrot and a parakeet, in a style that was fashionable at the time. c.1880. H:22.5cm (8¾in).

## MEISSEN

The first European factory to create hard-paste porcelain, Meissen had fallen on hard times when Heinrich Gottlieb Kühn became director in 1833. Lucrative export markets had declined, and the economic situation in Saxony was dire. In an effort to rekindle Meissen's fortunes, Kühn focused on modernizing production techniques and developing new colours.

Ernst August Leuteritz, Meissen's head modeller between 1849 and 1886, was responsible for the factory's finest work. The success of his tenure was favoured by the fact that a prosperous business class was emerging. These wealthy industrialists and merchants were competing in the style stakes with the old aristocracy and wanted to furnish their homes in a similar fashion. Leuteritz reintroduced porcelain figurines in the Rococo style based on 18th-century models by Johann J. Kändler and Peter Reinicke. Neoclassical figures were also put back into production. In response to consumer demand, Meissen ceramics of the mid-19th century became the most flamboyant ever produced by the firm.

### LAVISH DECORATION

At the Great London Exhibition of 1862, the French firm of Sèvres displayed wares decorated with layers of slip clay. At the same exhibition, Worcester exhibited porcelain painted in the style of Limoges enamel work. Both techniques catered to the public demand for lavish decoration, and Meissen was quick to follow suit.

Having recently moved to new, purpose-built premises with larger kilns, the company was able to produce greater quantities of ceramics at a

**MEISSEN STAND AT THE 1851 GREAT EXHIBITION IN LONDON** Like other leading manufacturers of the decorative arts, Meissen exhibited specially made pieces at the large trade exhibitions held in Europe and the United States. The pieces shown were larger and more spectacular versions of their normal range of ceramics.

**The spout** is shaped like a seashell and has a gilded lip

**The main handle** resembles ribbons and vines, grasped at one end by a cherub

**Neptune,** the sea god, watches over his watery domain

**CROSSED-SWORDS MARK** Meissen's crossed-swords mark was frequently copied by unscrupulous manufacturers.

**Sailing ships,** mermaids, and jumping horses decorate the body of the jug

**PORCELAIN WATER JUG** One of a series of Rococo Revival jugs on the theme of the four elements, this jug is glazed, gilded, and painted, and shows Meissen's mastery of scrolling forms and applied detail. The handle and base of the jug are moulded to look like seaweed. c.1850. H:65cm (25½in).

**The base** is almost bell-like

**Applied dolphins** convey a sense of movement typical of the Rococo Revival style better quality than ever before. The *Schneeballen* (snowball) technique, involving the application of dozens of tiny flowers, was particularly well suited to Meissen's new production methods. First developed in the mid-18th century, the *Schneeballen* technique enjoyed a large-scale revival and was widely imitated. Leuteritz also devised theatrical new motifs such as handles in the form of snakes. Gilding became more lavish, and the range of colours available to Meissen's painters was expanded. As the 19th century progressed, Meissen carved out a successful niche supplying Europe's wealthy industrialists with the status symbols that they coveted.

## CROSSED-SWORDS MARK
The famous blue crossed-swords mark found on much Meissen porcelain is based on the coat of arms of the Prince Elector of Saxony. The Electoral Swords, as they are known, were first used on Meissen porcelain in 1723. Meissen's reputation for outstanding quality proved to

be the downfall of the crossed-swords mark as a guarantee of authenticity. It is the most frequently imitated mark in the history of porcelain. Dozens of firms, particularly in the area around Dresden during the 19th century, copied the famous trademark in an attempt to pass off their own inferior wares as Meissen.

## DRESDEN FACTORIES
As the capital of Saxony, situated not far from Meissen, the city of Dresden became a centre of porcelain production in its own right from the second half of the 19th century. A steady trickle of Meissen workers who decided to go into competition with their former employer founded their own factories. More than 40 ateliers were active in Dresden by the end of the 1800s, but many carried on production for only a limited period of time, and most are unknown today.

Decorating ateliers thrived on a steady supply of blanks and seconds. Many of these establishments unscrupulously used the blue crossed-swords mark on their wares in an attempt to pass them off as genuine Meissen products, although a blue crown mark was also in widespread use.

Among the most accomplished ceramicists was Helena Wolfson, who specialized in replicating Meissen's celebrated Watteau figures.

## PALE IMITATION
Although made in the style of Meissen, most of the ceramics made and decorated in Dresden were of inferior quality. The modelling and application of motifs were less refined than on Meissen examples, and the colours and styling more crude. As such, they catered to the aspiring middle classes who coveted the trappings of success but could not afford the high prices commanded by Meissen.

Since styles and marks were copied with impunity for so long, the only way to make sure that a Meissen piece is authentic is to compare it with examples known to be genuine.

**MEISSEN PLATE OF FLOWERS** This mid-19th-century latticework plate has a fluted edge and is covered with naturalistic relief flowers and leaves painted with coloured enamels. It bears the crossed-swords mark. *c.1860. D:27cm (10½in).*

**MEISSEN SNOWBALL VASE** Made of glazed and painted porcelain, this crater-shaped vase has a round base. It is decorated all over with tiny applied snowballs and snowball flowers, overlaid with scrolling branches and a bullfinch. *c.1860. H:35cm (13¾in).*

**DRESDEN POT AND COVER** Based on an 18th-century Meissen model, this baluster-shaped pot with gilded edges by Carl Thieme is painted on both sides with scenes in the style of Watteau. It is covered with applied, naturalistically painted flowers, leaves, and fruit, and the cover is decorated with a bird. *c.1880. H:33cm (13in).*

## EVOLUTION OF STYLE
One of Meissen's great successes was with Johann J. Kändler's charming Rococo figures in the mid-18th century. Flowing robes with realistic folds gave his figures a sense of movement for which they are still celebrated. The painting was also very fine, although areas were often left white to show off the superb quality of the hard-paste porcelain.

Meissen's mid-19th-century Rococo Revival figures had many of the same features as the earlier work but were more lavish. Scrolled bases, more complex poses, and a greater emphasis on applied, painted, and gilded decoration made for a more extravagant product altogether. Improvements and refinements to modelling and production processes helped Meissen preserve its reputation for outstanding quality.

**GARDENER WITH A BASKET** This 18th-century Johann J. Kändler porcelain figure is glazed, painted, and gilded. It stands on a simple round base decorated with flowers. *H:20cm (8in).*

**AUTUMN** Glazed, painted, and gilded, this 19th-century Meissen porcelain figure is elaborately decorated and has an more extravagant Rococo-style base. *H:28cm (11in).*

**DRESDEN SPIRIT BURNER** One of a pair, this gilded spirit burner has a light turquoise ground and a pierced lid. Shaped like a two-handled urn, it is decorated with pastoral scenes in the style of Watteau and has Berlin sceptre marks. *c.1880. H:17cm (6¾in).*

# SÈVRES

From 1800 to 1815 Sèvres created hard-paste porcelain in the Empire style, decorating Classical shapes with elaborate gilding and large painted areas. The factory continued to produce such wares after the Napoleonic Wars and through the reigns of Louis XVIII, Charles X, and Louis-Philippe (the last three French monarchs, who ruled between 1814 and 1850). Although technically brilliant, designs before 1848 could lack originality and included ultra-thin cast porcelain mimicking Chinese eggshell wares and accurate imitations of oil paintings.

## SÈVRES IMITATORS

The large-scale, showy Empire style also prevailed in Russia. During the reign of Tzar Nicholas I, the Imperial Porcelain Manufactory in St Petersburg copied oil paintings in the Hermitage Museum as faithfully as Sèvres reproduced the Old Masters. Military themes were also popular after the Russian

defeat of Napoleon. As at Sèvres, porcelain wares copied other shapes and decorative styles, from Chinese vases to Greek oil jars. Sumptuous gilded wares also featured in Germany and Scandinavia, where Biedermeier was in its golden age.

## BRITISH ROCOCO REVIVAL

Due in part to a reaction against the French Directoire and Empire styles – and their associations with the Revolution and Napoleon – thoughts in Britain returned to Rococo, and a revival was in full swing by 1830. The bone china used was more stable in the kiln, leading to less waste; more durable once fired; and cheaper to make, helping firms such as Minton to emulate early Sèvres.

While the late Neoclassical style promoted majestic sizes and symmetrical forms that left large areas plain for skilled painters to cover, now shapes swirled and surfaces undulated with applied decoration. Painting was swamped by asymmetrical *rocaille* in relief and often gilded, combined with applied flowers. The Great Exhibition of 1851 showed porcelain that wildly embellished the restrained elegance of early Sèvres.

## SÈVRES BACK TO ITS ROOTS

Several French factories followed a similar pattern. Sèvres revived some of its moulds from the 18th century and re-created accurate versions of its original Rococo wares, down to the earlier turquoise and pink grounds decorated with pastoral panels in the style of Watteau and Boucher. In an

*The gilt-bronze mounts* on the cover, neck, and shoulder echo the base

*Areas of white porcelain* remain visible

*The gilt-bronze base* recalls Classical Greco-Roman forms

**PAIR OF CANDELABRA** Renaissance and Rococo forms are evident in this Sèvres composition. Gilt-bronze floral and foliate bouquets and garlands are centred on baluster-shaped blue-porcelain vases. *c.1880. H:73cm (28¾in).*

**COVERED BOWL** Recalling 16th-century Limoges enamels, this Sèvres bowl features polychrome putti musicians on a royal blue-enamelled ground, and gilt-bronze foliate, scrolling leaves, pineapple, and mask mounts. *1845–48.*

**MOUNTED VASE** On a gilt-bronze base with female busts, scrolling leaves, and cloven-hoof feet, this Sèvres vase features romantic-historical imagery. The main scene is of Columbus, attended by a winged cherub, discovering the New World; the other side (*see detail above*) depicts a cherub with the flag of the United States. *Late 19th century. H:56cm (22in).*

earlier financially stricken phase, Sèvres had sold off blank wares to French and German factories that now copied the Rococo Revival decoration. The French factory Samson et Cie sold reproductions of early Sèvres porcelain that looked as genuine as the 18th-century originals – apart from the use of hard instead of soft paste.

## PORCELAIN FIGURES

Sèvres had been making biscuit (unglazed white porcelain) figures since the 1700s. However, the Classical and allegorical subjects that had been popular in the Neoclassical period were replaced by dandies, children, and allegorical groups in sentimentalized Rococo costume, as well as by figures in contemporary dress decorated with C- and S-scrolls. Figures in folk costume were also popular, especially in Russia, where modellers were strong in tradition. As well as the Imperial Porcelain Manufactory, the private company of Gardner, had great success with similar wares.

## PÂTE-SUR-PÂTE

By 1850 a change in fashion and new technology combined to help popularize a revival in Classical style and the porcelain made at Sèvres in the 1750s and 1760s. In the 1860s Sèvres turned its attention to Marc Louis Solon's new method of building decoration *pâte-sur-pâte*, which was ideally suited to Classical figures. The image was built up like a sculpture, by applying several layers of clay slip to produce a relief image. This hand process could take up to 50 days' work before firing, and it achieved great subtlety of texture, from diaphanous drapery to full solidity. Solon came to Stoke-on-Trent and brought the technique to Minton. The Imperial factory in Russia also used *pâte-sur-pâte*, though no one could do it as well as Solon, who retired in 1904.

*Scrolling floral and foliate*
Rococo Revival forms

*The gilded decoration* is over a Limoges enamel-like coloured ground

**ENGLISH VASE** The baluster-shaped body is encrusted with flowers and foliage in relief and polychrome-painted. Along with the scrolling foliate feet, handles, and neck, it displays the English Rococo Revival style at its most extravagant. *1850s. H:27cm (10¾in).*

**REGIMENTAL PLATE** The rim of this Russian plate has an Imperial black eagle and a wreath. The centre depicts His Imperial Highness Grand Duke Nikolai Nikolaievich and His Royal Highness Virtembergsky. *1875. D:24.5cm (9¾in).*

## PARIAN WARE

In the 1840s Britain's answer to Sèvres's biscuit figures was Parian porcelain. This hard, white material, developed by Copeland and Minton by adding feldspar to the mix, had a texture that looked like marble and did not need glazing or dusting. It was the perfect material for small-scale statues and brought sculpture to the masses. A 3m- (10ft-) high sculpture could be reduced to 30cm (12in). Parian statuettes by Copeland and Minton were a runaway success at the 1851 Great Exhibition. Even Queen Victoria had Parian images of all her children made after Thorneycroft marbles. Later in the century, when excitement at its resemblance to marble had worn off, Parian ware was coloured.

**UNA AND THE LION** The subject of this Parian figure modelled for Minton by John Bell was taken from Edmund Spencer's *Faerie Queene*. Una represents Truth and Purity, and the lion, Britain. *c.1850. H:36cm (14¼in).*

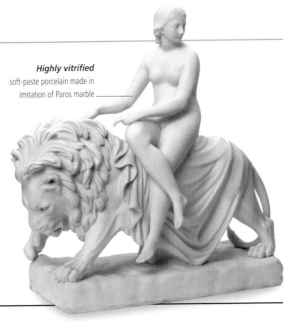

*Highly vitrified* soft-paste porcelain made in imitation of Paros marble

**FRENCH VASE** This Parisian-made piece is essentially Rococo Revival in both form and decoration, but it also incorporates Gothic elements such as the foliate cresting at the rim. *c.1845. H:34cm (13½in).*

# GLASS

THE MID- TO LATE 19TH CENTURY SAW GREAT REFINEMENT AND
EXPERIMENTATION IN GLASS TECHNIQUES. AS WITH ALL THE DECORATIVE
ARTS, THIS WAS ACCOMPANIED BY A REVIVAL OF EARLIER STYLES.

*The scrolling floral imagery* is hand-painted

**CRANBERRY GLASS VASE**
Made in the United States, this transparent Cranberry glass vase, with its distinctive raspberry-pink tint, is further embellished with hand-painted floral, scrolling tendril, and leaf imagery. *c.1850. H:22cm (8¾in).*

## COLOURED GLASS

In the early 1800s, the innovative Bohemian glassmaker Friedrich Egermann had started a trend for coloured glass with his development of Lithyalin, an opaque coloured glass that resembled agate. Other Bohemians soon built on Egermann's discoveries. Josef Riedel found that by adding uranium to the colourless-glass batch, he could produce yellowish-green Annagrün and greenish-yellow Annagelb glass (both hues were named after Riedel's wife). In Britain, in the late 1870s, the Whitefriars Glassworks of James Powell & Sons copied the technique to make vaseline glass, so named because of its slick, smeared appearance. This yellowish-green glass was used for light shades and other household goods.

### CAMEO GLASS

The 1876 British-made replicas of the ancient Roman Portland Vase sparked a revival of cameo glass. In this technique, the top layer of a glass vessel is carved to reveal the underlying layer. To make a good colour contrast, the top layer was often white. Thomas Webb & Sons and Stevens & Williams saw the commercial possibilities of cameo glass and used acid-etching to simplify the difficult technique. Acid-etched motifs were largely naturalistic since figures were too complex and expensive to produce except for exhibitions.

*Naturalistic floral imagery* was fashionable in the mid-19th century

**BACCARAT CAMEO GLASS** This baluster-shaped vase is exquisitely hand-cut and wheel-carved with bands of Moorish stylized flower and leaf imagery and four large medallions of naturalistic bouquets. *1867. H:61cm (24in).*

## FRENCH MASTERS

At this time, the French were also experimenting with bone ash and produced opaline glass, a semi-opaque white glass with a milky appearance that looked red when held up to the light. By using metal oxides, French glassmakers succeeded in making opaline in different colours, including a turquoise similar to Sèvres's porcelain ground, and the pink *gorge de pigeon*, which resembled the iridescent plumage of a pigeon's throat.

Russian, Bohemian, and British factories attempted to make opaline glass but were never as successful as the French. Baccarat was particularly skilled at striking the subtle balance between translucent and opaque.

## STAINED GLASS

Another widely used technique adopted to colour glass was staining. A vessel could have the stain painted on with a brush or be dipped in a vat of it. After firing at a low temperature, the colour looked as though it went right through the glass. Cranberry glass, in an attractive dusky pink, was hugely popular and produced in large numbers in the United States and Britain.

*The applied gilding* contrasts with the turquoise opaline ground

**OPALINE VASE** Probably produced at the Saint-Louis Glassworks in Lorraine, this opaline glass vase has been coloured with metal oxides to produce a turquoise shade, contrasted with gilded flowers of naturalistic composition. *1850–60. H:25.5cm (10in).*

## FLASHED AND CASED GLASS

Bohemians were also at the forefront of reviving Roman cased glass. In this technique, one bubble of coloured glass is blown into shape and then another, differently coloured, bubble is blown into the first. The process can be repeated to create several layers. The whole is then reheated. This is a delicate procedure: each layer has to expand and contract at identical rates, or the glass will crack. The thick glass can then be cut or engraved.

In flashed glass, one layer of coloured glass is laid over another, usually of clear glass. The upper layer can be etched to reveal the underlying one.

**PEACHBLOW VASE** Lined with white opal glass, this long-necked, gourd-shaped vase is in a form of cased glass known as Peachblow, which shades from a buttery yellow at the base to a purplish-red at the top. Made by the Mount Washington Glass Co. *1886–88. H:12.5cm (5in).*

### COLOURS GALORE

The addition of metallic oxides to the mix is what produces coloured glass. In 1878 Stourbridge-based Thomas Webb & Sons showed its Bronze range, which featured a deep, iridescent green, at the Paris *Exposition Universelle*. Meanwhile, glassmakers in the United States were also enjoying a time of great colour experimentation. In 1885, the Mount Washington Glass Co. launched Burmese glass, which graduated from pale yellow at the bottom to pink at the top, with a satin finish. The contribution of Hobbs, Brockunier & Co. in West Virginia was Peachblow, cased glass that went from yellow to red, lined in white opal. The New England Glass Co. also made Peachblow but called it Wild Rose. Amberina glass was another range, tinted pale orange at the base and graduating to red at the top.

Thomas Webb & Sons came up with Burmese, too, also called Queen's Burmese because Queen Victoria liked it, and a Peach range – cased glass that deepened from pink to red. Stevens &

Williams made Rose du Barry (similar to Burmese), Alabaster, and Silveria, which shimmered with the addition of silver foil.

### ENAMELLING

As surface decoration, enamelling became fashionable again in around 1890, often used along with gilding or other techniques. French enamellers were the best and were internationally sought after. For instance, at Stevens & Williams, French glassmaker Oscar Pierre Erard designed Tapestry glass, a range that combined painted flower patterns with machine threading.

**ENAMELLED GLASS VASE** From a series of Islamic-style glass by J. & L. Lobmeyer of Vienna, this yellowish baluster-shaped vase is enamelled and gilded with bands of Moorish stylized floral and foliate motifs. *c.1885. H:24cm (9½in).*

**FOOTED OVERLAY GLASS GOBLET** This goblet was made by F.P. Zach of Munich in red and clear overlay glass engraved with a hunting scene amid scrolling, interlaced foliage. *c.1850. H:22cm (8¾in).*

**The rim** is engraved with the number of the Masonic lodge for which the glass was commissioned

**BOHEMIAN OVERLAY GLASS BEAKER** Made in pale-blue and clear overlay glass, this beaker has a gilded rim and an applied central band engraved with a diaper pattern. *c.1860. H:16cm (6¼in).*

**OPALESCENT GLASS EWER** This glass ewer and matching goblet were made by J. & L. Lobmeyr. They are gilded and engraved with a scrolling foliate ground *en-rocaille. c.1880. H:25cm (9¾in).*

## CUT GLASS

Cut glass, particularly suited to the qualities of lead glass, had been popular in Britain from the early 18th century. The repeal of tax on glass in Britain in 1845 led to a surge in production. The Crystal Palace that housed the Great Exhibition of 1851 was itself made of glass and inside, F.&C. Osler of Birmingham exhibited a huge fountain made entirely out of cut and moulded glass.

Popular cut patterns include Van Dyck points fanning out like lace cuffs at the tops of glasses, as well as diamonds, points, and flutes. Flutes were slender vertical bands in the 1820s, but were cut more broadly in the late 1830s. By 1840 luxury glass was deeply cut with simple, bold designs. One was the Gothic arch; another was the broad hollow,

a circle or oval cut out of a broad flute. By the 1850s relative simplicity had given way to ornate mixed patterns.

John Ruskin disliked cut glass. In *The Stones of Venice*, published in 1853, he wrote: "All cut glass is barbarous, for cutting conceals its ductility and confuses it with crystal." The greatest exponent of this "barbarous" glass was the Waterford Glass factory, but fashions changed and the factory closed in the mid-1850s.

### ENGRAVED AND ACID-ETCHED GLASS

Still popular, engraving had two distinct styles: Neoclassical, with ornamentation derived from ancient Greek pottery, and naturalistic floral decoration. Neoclassical engraving reached its peak between the 1851 Great Exhibition and the Exhibition of 1862, and dominated the luxury end of glassmaking.

Acid etching was patented in 1857 by the English glassmaker Benjamin Richardson. John Northwood developed a template machine in 1861. He devised a similar machine for geometric linear patterns and a technique for frosting the design so that it looked like an engraving. By 1867 Grecian designs were popular again and the published work of the sculptor John Flaxman was used as a source book. Large quantities of acid-etched glass were made at the end of the century by Holmegaard

**BRISTOL BLUE GOBLET** Press-moulded in Britain with stylized floral medallions (front and reverse), this goblet was tinted with cobalt oxide to produce the royal blue colour known generically as Bristol blue. *c.1860. H:20.5cm (8in).*

**PEACHBLOW PITCHER** Produced by the Phoenix Glass Company, this pitcher was press-moulded in relief with a "hobnail" pattern, in warm Peachblow glass. *1880–90. H:11.5cm (4½in).*

of Denmark, Val Saint Lambert in Belgium, Stuart and Sons of Stourbridge, and many other factories.

### ICE GLASS AND ROCK CRYSTAL

Many other techniques were revived, such as the 16th-century Venetian technique of ice, or crackle, glass (called overshot glass in the United States). The hot glass was

*Typically bold* mid-19th-century floral and foliate imagery decorates the body

*American cutting* is typically deep and sharp to the touch

*Swagged forms* acknowledge Classical Greco-Roman ornament

**CUT-GLASS DECANTER** Attributed to Stevens & Williams of Stourbridge, this decanter is cut in green over Cranberry glass with an undulating floral and foliate pattern. It has an applied loop handle in clear glass and a sterling-silver stopper with repoussé floral decoration. *c.1870. H:23cm (9in).*

**CUT-GLASS DECANTER** This ovoid Tiffany decanter is cut with a diamond pattern. The silver stopper is chased with 18th-century-style putti heads, flowers, ribbons, and a trumpet. *1875–91. H:23cm (9in).*

plunged into cold water to craze it. When reheated it retained a finish like cracked ice. In London Apsley Pellatt marketed it as Anglo-Venetian glass.

Thomas Webb & Sons revived the medieval technique of rock crystal – brightly polished cut and engraved glass. From 1879 Stevens & Williams also made it, appealing to sophisticated tastes by engraving the glass with naturalistic Japanese-style designs. The technique was adopted by the Baccarat glass company in France and Thomas G. Hawkes & Co. in the United States.

## PRESSED GLASS

The greatest technical innovation of the century was pressed glass, invented in the United States in the 1820s. Pressing lead glass into metal moulds by machine made production cheap, and factories sprang up, particularly in New England and the

**ROCK CRYSTAL VASE** Made in France, this vase is enamelled and engraved with marine-life imagery, and finely etched to create the subtle mottled appearance of rock crystal. *c.1880. H:22cm (8¾in).*

Midwest. The Boston & Sandwich Glass Co. in Massachusetts was one of the most prolific. Between 1850 and 1900 there were over 70 factories making pressed glass in Pittsburgh alone. To begin with, all-over stippled patterns masked the lines left by the mould. Soon table services were made to look like cut glass. Competition fostered colour production and a wide range of designs. The mould-makers initially used many historical styles but then developed distinctly American designs such as the ubiquitous eagle.

In Britain the success of the cut glass at the Great Exhibition encouraged manufacturers to make pressed glass. Cut glass was expensive but pressed glass, made to imitate it, was cheaper. Several firms made frosted pressed glass, and coloured and marbled glass was made in the 1870s. As moulds were expensive, styles continued with little change into the 1880s and 1890s.

**CRANBERRY GLASS JUG** The distinctive raspberry-pink tint of this Cranberry-glass jug made in Stourbridge, England, is augmented with a crackle pattern and contrasted with a rope-twist handle in clear glass. *c.1880. H:25.5cm (10in).*

**CUT-GLASS WATER JUG** Made by W.H., B.&J. Richardson of Stourbridge, this jug has a clear glass body that is frosted inside, mitre-cut with stylized foliate decoration, and has an applied rope-twist handle. *c.1860. H:24cm (9¼in).*

## BRILLIANT CUT GLASS

The displays by John Gillander & Sons and Christian Dorflinger's factory and others at the influential Philadelphia Centennial Exhibition of 1876, which was visited by ten million people, fascinated the public with a new "rich cut glass". Subsequently known as the Brilliant style, this glass was cut deeply and polished, with a mass of intersections that fractured bold patterns based on stars, diamonds, and scallops into myriad secondary shapes.

The American Brilliant Period lasted from the late 1870s to the early 1900s. Skilled immigrant cutters worked for the American glasshouses, enabling them to develop a product good enough to rival the finest cut glass from England, Ireland, and France.

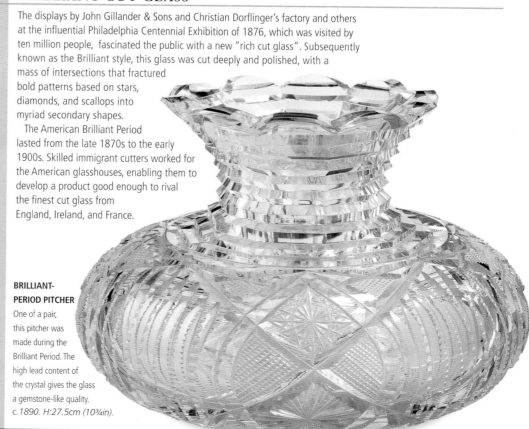

**BRILLIANT-PERIOD PITCHER** One of a pair, this pitcher was made during the Brilliant Period. The high lead content of the crystal gives the glass a gemstone-like quality. *c.1890. H:27.5cm (10¾in).*

## HISTORICAL STYLES

Over 150 glassmaking firms took part in the Great Exhibition of the Works of Industry of All Nations, held in Hyde Park, London, in 1851. Manufacturers from the United States, Germany, Italy, Austria, and Bohemia displayed glass in exciting new colours and a range of extravagant revival styles, whetting the appetite of increasingly prosperous middle-class clients. In particular, the Bohemian exhibitors, the Counts Buquoy and Harrach, were highly praised for their displays of coloured glass. Glassmakers were inspired by the medieval and ancient art on show and started experimenting in an attempt to revive the decorative techniques of the past.

The Great Exhibition was immensely influential and was soon followed by others: New York in 1853, London in 1862, Paris in 1867, Philadelphia in 1876, and Paris in 1878.

### REVIVALS

During this period there was no one coherent style, as glassmakers had access to a wealth of historical styles, forms, and decorative motifs, which they borrowed, mixed, and matched freely. Following the unification of Germany in 1871, German manufacturers tried to forge a sense of national identity by reviving "Old German"-style glass, especially the numerous forms of traditional drinking glass,

including the *Pokal*, a Baroque beaker with a lid. This was often decorated in the colourful Bohemian enamelling tradition with spurious coats of arms or light, playful Renaissance-style motifs.

Alternatively, traditional shapes were made from clear glass cased in two or more colours and skilfully wheel-engraved with romanticized landscapes or hunting scenes by master Bohemian engravers such as August Böhm.

Glassmakers like Salviati & Co. of Murano reinterpreted the hot glass tradition to produce fanciful shapes, such as serpent vases, combined with the strong,

brilliant colours that are characteristic of Venetian glass of this period. Salviati's glass found approval with the influential architect Charles Eastlake in his book *Hints on Household Taste*, published in 1868. Salviati was also commissioned to produce the elaborate glass mosaic tiles for the Albert Memorial in London, which was completed in 1876 – an inescapable mark of Royal approval.

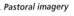

**BOHEMIAN OVERLAY GLASS** This lidded goblet made in ruby red over clear overlay glass was wheel-engraved by August Böhm with a fashionable forest landscape with a deer on the bowl, and featuring grapevines around the lid. *c.1850. H:53cm (21in).*

*Pastoral imagery* was popular in the mid-19th century

*The engraving* cuts through the overlay to reveal clear glass below

*The faceted baluster stem* is in ruby red over clear glass

*Renaissance Revival figures* include Cupid, Bacchus, and Pan

*The polychrome glass rods* are set in clear glass

**RENAISSANCE REVIVAL JUG** Of baluster form with a loop handle, this cobalt-blue jug by J.&L. Lobmeyr is handpainted with Renaissance-style motifs in bright enamels. *c.1870. H:20.5cm (8in).*

**VENETIAN REVIVAL PITCHER** Hand-blown in clear glass with polychrome glass rods, this Salviati & Co. pitcher is in the style of 17th-century Venetian glass. *1880s. H:24cm (9½in).*

**RENAISSANCE REVIVAL CUP** Produced in clear glass by Adolf Meyr of Vienna, this cup is delicately black lead-enamelled by hand with flora, fauna, and images from Classical mythology. *c.1880. H:31cm (12¼in).*

## STAINED GLASS

A renewed interest in stained glass was initiated by A.G.W. Pugin's buildings and studies of Gothic architecture. Many churches had been stripped of their stained glass windows by Henry VIII in the 16th century, but fired with enthusiasm for the 19th-century Gothic Revival, many churches wanted to replace them. William Morris brought stained glass to greater prominence by commissioning the great Pre-Raphaelite painters Dante Gabriel Rossetti and Edward Burne-Jones to design magnificent new church windows. This resurgence of interest in stained glass led to people commissioning stained-glass windows for private homes. Powell of Whitefriars was one of the most prolific producers.

## HISTORICAL TECHNIQUES

Renewed interest in the ancient cameo technique was sparked by the Portland Vase, which was displayed at the British Museum. English glassmakers, such as John Northwood and George Woodall, were masterly exponents of the time-consuming and expensive technique, which was used either on small pieces such as vases and scent bottles or large, dramatic exhibition pieces.

## INFLUENCE OF NATURE

The natural world was a huge influence on Victorian designers. The inspiration for this came from diverse sources: some designers, such as Christopher Dresser, had initially trained as botanists and Owen Jones's seminal pattern book, *Grammar of Ornament* (1856), included detailed plates based on leaves and flowers.

Inspired by books like Moore and Lindley's *The Ferns of Great Britain and Ireland*, published in 1855, and J.K. Colling's *Art Foliage*, published in1865, ferns became one of the main decorative motifs, especially in some of the Scottish glassworks. Firms such as Richardson's of Stourbridge used elaborate, naturalistic enamelling to decorate many glass forms, and Stevens & Williams often used plant imagery to create illusions of the natural world. Many of Webb's less expensive "commercial cameo" pieces, introduced in the 1880s, were decorated with flowers and leaves, as were the wares of many American firms, including Mount Washington and C.F. Monroe's Wave Crest.

**CLARET JUG** Made in clear and green tinted glass by Stevens & Williams, this jug is further embellished with scrolling plants and a similarly fashioned silver mount. *1890s. H:36cm (14¼in).*

**SILVER-MOUNTED BARREL** An example of Mount Washington's Royal Flemish line, this barrel features tinted and enamelled roses outlined with gilt piping. *c.1890. H:18.25cm (7¼in).*

## INSPIRED BY THE EAST

Japan opened its borders to the West in 1853, and in 1862 London hosted the International Exhibition – the first showcase for the arts of that country. The Japanese ceramics, carved ivory, prints, and textiles had a profound influence on European designers and created a passion for all things Oriental that became known as *japonisme*. Motifs such as blossom – notably in the work of the French designer Jules Barbe for Thomas Webb & Sons – chrysanthemums, fish, dragons, and exotic creatures appeared in high-relief enamelling on Oriental-style vases. The fashion for exotic flowers spurred designers into creating a huge number of different styles of vase to hold them.

Nineteenth-century "Islamic" glassware was inspired by the forms and decoration of 13th- and 14th-century Islamic glass mosque lamps. At the 1878 Paris Exhibition, the first prize was awarded to the French glassmaker Philippe-Joseph Brocard for his ewers, individual and pairs of vases, and dishes, all of which were richly decorated with elaborate

symmetrical motifs carried out in a mixture of enamelling, gilding, and jewelling. His fellow countryman, I.J. Imberton, also produced superb "Islamic" glass. The Austrian firm of J.&L. Lobmeyr, established in 1823, won prizes for its magnificent gilded and enamelled jugs and vases, decorated with dense, vividly coloured enamelling and gilding that resembled cloisonné work. The flat, non-representational patterns of Islamic wares were also adapted, less ambitiously, as a motif by English manufacturers such as Stevens & Williams.

*Intricate arabesques* are applied in polychrome enamels

*The body is* in a semi-matte pink crystal

**ARABIAN VASE** J.&L. Lobmeyr's richly enamelled glass vases were inspired by French imitations of 13th- and 14th-century Islamic lamps with their arabesques, scrolls, and stylized floral imagery. *c.1875. H:26cm (10¼in).*

**OVERLAY GLASS JARDINIÈRE** Made in a coppery ruby red glass over smoky brown glass, with golden, ruby, and black powder inclusions, this jardinière has a naturalistic Japanese quince pattern. *c.1880. H:15.75cm (6¼in).*

**DRAGON VASE** This vase's ovoid body is gilded in relief with an Oriental winged dragon, the focal point of a large-scale, Oriental diaper pattern. From Mount Washington's Royal Flemish line. *c.1890. H:19cm (7½in).*

# METALWARE

INCREASINGLY SOPHISTICATED MACHINERY ENABLED MANUFACTURERS
TO REPRODUCE ALMOST ANY FORM OR TYPE OF DECORATION. THIS
TRANSLATED INTO A WEALTH OF CHOICE FOR CONSUMERS.

## SILVERWARE

In the 1840s the increasing refinement of dining
habits and the Victorians' love of ostentatious
display signalled the beginning of a golden age
for silver tableware, which was helped along by
new technological advances. In both Europe and
the United States, machine-produced parts led to
massive production of domestic wares such as
cruets, candlesticks, cutlery, tea and coffee services,
and dining accessories.

## HISTORICAL REVIVAL STYLES

At times, it was a matter of quantity over quality;
however, some manufacturers, including Tiffany
& Co. (est. 1837), successfully combined mass
production with superb quality. German firms
produced luxurious silverware, copying the forms
and decoration of the Baroque and Renaissance
Revival styles. The "plastic" nature of silver
could be shown to full advantage in the swirling,
asymmetric forms typical of the Rococo Revival
(or Louis XV style). Alternatively, designers simply
embellished the plain surfaces of traditional forms
with a plethora of chased decoration.

A growing interest in antiquarianism prompted
the mid-century revival of Italian Renaissance-
style silverware, loosely inspired by sculptor and
goldsmith Benvenuto Cellini. These pieces sat side

by side with Gothic Revival
tea and coffee services;
jugs and flagons inspired
by the austere philosophy of
A.W.N. Pugin; or Neoclassical
amphorae and vases.

From the 1860s, when Japanese
art flowed into Europe, onwards a new
repertoire of motifs became available.
Designers such as Christopher Dresser
reinterpreted Japanese designs to produce a
strikingly modern range of silver domestic wares,
including teapots and toast racks. The Arts and
Crafts movement also revived and reinterpreted
historical styles, decorating items with restrained
naturalistic floral patterns or motifs inspired by
Celtic scrollwork.

**FRUITING VINES** Grapevines have been a popular decorative form in many
vocabularies of ornament, from ancient Egyptian, Classical Roman, early
Christian, Celtic, and Renaissance, to diverse
19th-century revival styles.

*The four-footed base*
is applied in the form of
scrolling branches

**ROCOCO REVIVAL CANDELABRA** Made in the style of Louis XV, each of these
American silver candelabra has seven branches of scrolling foliate form above a
similarly decorated stem and circular base. *c.1850. H:66.5cm (26¼in).*

**GERMAN CENTREPIECE** Cast in silver, this centrepiece combines decorative
motifs such as a guilloche, grapevines, scrolling tendrils and branches, and a
putto in a typically eclectic 19th-century style. *1875. H:32cm (12½in).*

## INSPIRED BY NATURE

By 1851 improved industrial methods made it possible for manufacturers to produce almost any form in silver, including elaborate naturalistic pieces. Large-scale exhibition and presentation pieces featured realistic fruit and flowers, animals, and birds.

Sometimes the form itself imitated nature: shell-shapes made natural containers for food, condiments, or other objects; water lilies became inkwells; and bears became honey pots. Decoration might echo function: fish and shell motifs were often used on sauce boats that accompanied fish dishes; and grapes and foliage, accompanied by idealized putti, became standard decoration on a wide variety of drinking accessories, from bottle and decanter labels to goblets. Natural forms such as shells, flowers, plants, and animals were also liberally added as applied decoration or used as chased, engraved, or repoussé motifs.

## REPOUSSÉ DECORATION

The versatility of the repoussé technique made it an ideal vehicle for elaborate decoration in a wide range of styles. Repoussé could create the fruit and flowers, swags, and garlands of the Baroque, Neoclassical figures, Rococo asymmetric swirls and scrollwork, Celtic motifs, the restrained naturalism of the Arts and Crafts movement, and the grotesques and arabesques of the Renaissance Revival.

Also known as embossing, repoussé creates relief designs on the surface of a metal object. The silversmith works from the back or underside of the sheet of metal, hammering out the motif with plain or decorative punches. The design stands proud of

**SPOON WARMER** In the shape of a large nautilus shell, this spoon warmer made in silver by H. Wilkinson & Co. has a hinged lid and is supported on a *rocaille* base. *1870. H:14cm (5½in).*

**PAIR OF SALTS** Shell forms had been a popular and apt choice for salts from the Middle Ages to the 18th century. This elaborate French example in Continental silver recalls Baroque prototypes. *1880. H:11cm (4¼in).*

the surface, creating a three-dimensional effect that was an essential feature of naturalistic decoration. The resulting surface decoration can then be further embellished with engraving and/or chasing to create more intricate details such as veining on leaves. Engraving, which involves cutting into the surface and removing tiny amounts of metal, was used for delicate details such as monograms. With chasing, the silversmith uses a small hammer and chasing tools to create the design on the outside surface using small indentations but without actually cutting or removing any metal. The American firm of S. Kirk & Son of Baltimore was famous for its skilful chased work.

## ELECTROPLATING

Promoting mass production of plated silverware in fashionable styles at affordable prices, electroplating was pioneered and patented in 1840 by the Birmingham firm of Elkington & Co. (est. 1830s). It involved coating a base-metal object with a thin layer of pure silver, using an electric current to deposit the silver particles. The resulting piece, like the tea kettle on the right, looked like silver but had a whiter, slightly harsher appearance without the soft sheen found on Old Sheffield plate or sterling silver. One of the major advantages of electroplating was that the silversmith could create whole pieces with complex decoration that could then be plated as a whole, covering any seams or joins. The new technique could also be used to gild and replate pieces. By the 1850s and 1860s, electroplate manufacturers were producing a whole range of household wares in fashionable styles, as well as impressive exhibition pieces.

**WATER GOBLETS** The bell-shaped bowls and trumpet feet of these goblets (from a set of six) are embellished with all-over floral repoussé decoration. By S. Kirk & Son of Baltimore. *1835–50. H:17cm (6¾in).*

**SALTCELLAR** Made by Fouquet-Lapar in the Rococo Revival style, this cellar is covered with chased and repoussé scrolling foliate decoration, and has an engraved monogram. *1880. H:15.5cm (6in).*

**TEA KETTLE AND STAND** Made in England, probably in Birmingham, this kettle has a silver-plated body and stand that are essentially Rococo Revival in form and decoration. The latter includes repoussé flowers, scrolls, and cartouches, and an applied bird-of-prey finial. *1850.*

## VICTORIAN INGENUITY

The Industrial Revolution that had begun in England in the 18th century was given a strong technological boost by the inventive Victorians. An era that had initially relied mainly on candlelight and horsepower ended with inventions such as electric lighting, railways, the steamship, and motorcars firmly established.

New artistic styles and materials proved irresistible to craftsmen and designers whose originality swept away the restraint of Georgian design. This was, after all, the period that produced the plant houses at Kew Gardens and the Crystal Palace for the 1851 Great Exhibition.

### BRONZE'S VERSATILITY

In the 19th century, in an attempt to satisfy the wealthier consumers' continued demand for exquisite workmanship, new techniques crept into some aspects of handmade work. Craftsmen took simple, everyday items – the humble andiron (*chenet* in French), for example

*The candelabrum* terminates in a flowering urn finial

*The spool-shaped sockets* are cast with fluting

– and wrought them into veritable works of art. An andiron is a horizontal bar supported on feet, used to hold burning logs above the hearth. It often features an upright decorative frieze at the front. Pairs of andirons are called firedogs. In the 18th century the Sun King, Louis XIV, had *chenets* of silver. Now the utilitarian version was made of iron, although great houses sometimes had bronze or brass firedogs.

An alloy of copper and tin, bronze is a more fusible material than pure copper and eminently suitable for casting. It is also harder than copper, and more durable. In the 18th and 19th century the best work in bronze design and making – much of it from France – was remarkable for its fine hand-finishing and

*The stems are wrapped* in curling laurel leaves

*Shells surmount* the grotesque head

**PAIR OF GILT-BRONZE *CHENETS*** Also known as andirons or firedogs, these *chenets* are modelled in the Louis XVI style in the form of recumbent lions on foliage-decorated bases. They were cast by the Bouhon Frères foundry of Paris. *c.1880. W:32cm (12½in).*

*The ram's head* was a recurring motif in Greco-Roman ornament

**GILT-BRONZE CANDELABRUM** One of a pair made in the Louis XVI style by G. Durand et Fils of Paris, this candelabrum has a three-branch form raised on a tripod marble and ormolu base. It incorporates many Neoclassical motifs, including a flowering urn finial, laurel and stiff leaves, *paterae*, cloven-hoof feet, and, as in the detail above, ram's heads. *c.1890. H:59cm (23¼in).*

**WALL SCONCE** One of a pair made in gilt bronze by the Parisian foundry of Henry Dasson, this wall sconce is cast with a horned grotesque mask issuing forth three scrolling acanthus branches with leafy drip trays. *1887. H:59cm (23¼in).*

**GERMAN GILT-BRONZE TUREEN** Made in the Rococo-Revival style, this tureen is decorated with two monogram medallions flanked by flowers with scrolling tendrils. It has scrolling foliate feet and handles. c.1860. L:108cm (45½in).

gilding. After casting, sculptors and metalworkers decorated the object. They would do this by hammering thin panels or vessels from the back, punching the surface to produce a textured finish, and gilding the surface – a technique that became known as ormolu.

## GOLDEN ORNAMENTS

Ormolu, or gilt decoration, was very popular in Georgian and early Victorian design. The word derives from the French *bronze doré d'or moulu*, meaning "bronze gilded with ground gold". The term is often applied to gilded-bronze objects in general but, in fact, many ormolu pieces were cast in brass, which is rather easier to work with than bronze. Purists usually reserve the term for fire-gilded objects from the 18th century onwards.

Traditionally, craftsmen used an amalgam of gold and mercury to gild an object; they then fired the piece to drive off the mercury, leaving the gold adhering to the metal. By the 19th century they used a gold-coloured alloy of copper, zinc, and sometimes tin – mixed in various proportions but usually containing at least half copper – which gave objects a rich and golden appearance. Craftsmen gilded objects such as clock cases, chandeliers, frames, and candlesticks. They designed ormolu mounts to protect the corners of furniture and to decorate items such as bowls and dishes, aiming to achieve a subtle balance between matte and burnished finishes.

**GILT-BRONZE *CHENETS*** Probably French, these andirons are modelled in the Rococo Revival style in the form of black-painted cherubs – one is painting, the other carving – within scrolling leaf forms. c.1870. H:41cm (16¼in).

## CAST IRON

By the mid-19th century cast iron had almost entirely replaced wrought iron, which requires more time and labour, for practical products. Craftsmen started to use it architecturally for fireplaces and surrounds, hall stands, and garden furniture.

The innovative Shropshire firm of Coalbrookdale used iron for bedsteads, until then traditionally made of wood. Initially, they disguised the iron as brass, by covering it with brass foil and varnish. Coalbrookdale produced garden benches, tables, and chairs, often casting highly ornate pieces decorated in relief with trailing ivy leaves. They also made the quintessential pub table: round with central pedestal supports.

Cast-iron pieces such as stoves, kitchen utensils, coal bins, and stick stands made their way into the home. The English

**GARDEN URNS** Made in painted cast iron by A. Bendroth of New York, these garden urns with *faux-marbre* bases recall Renaissance and Neoclassical models. Decorative motifs include scrolling dragon handles and portrait medallions. 1880s. H:62.5cm (24½in).

designer Christopher Dresser typified the move towards making objects beautiful, championed by the Aesthetic Movement, simplifying their design and integrating form with function. His work included designs for Perry, Son & Co., a Birmingham-based lighting manufacturer.

## WEATHER VANES

The first weather vanes that appeared in the United States were imported from Europe, but American designers soon adapted traditional designs for local consumption. They added new motifs, including arrows and geometric shapes; Native Americans with bows and arrows; and symbols of significance such as the fish – a Christian emblem and New England's main trade. By the middle of the 19th century, thanks to mass production, the market started to offer a plethora of designs. The first commercial manufacturer, Alvin A. Jewell of Waltham, Massachusetts, began in 1852. By the 1880s mass production and marketing meant that every trade had its own specific design – a pig or horse for farmers, for example. Popular motifs that almost every manufacturer made can still be seen today: the cockerel, the horse, an eagle with spread wings perched on a ball, and the goddess of Liberty holding a flag.

**NEOCLASSICAL WEATHER VANE** Made in the United States, this weather vane is modelled in copper as a Native American firing a bow. His feathered headdress is fashioned from sheet copper. c.1880. L:112.5cm (44¼in).

*The Native American's* bow and arrow reflect the traditional arrow indicating the wind direction

*The copper-bodied arrow* has a cast zinc tip

# METALWARE GALLERY

Metalware of this period drew inspiration from the past and mixed various design elements to create a new style. There was an interest in Neoclassical motifs, which in turn were influenced by Classical Greece and Rome, and forms such as urns and vases were popular. Ornamentation was often heavy, incorporating a variety of decorative elements. Natural motifs were common, and many pieces were decorated with flora or fauna.

## KEY

**1.** Louis Jacques Berger silver sugar bowl decorated with blackberries. D:16cm (6¼in). ② **2.** Sterling-silver coffee pot by Dominic & Haff in a Classical urn form with an acorn finial on the hinged top. H:31cm (12¼in). ① **3.** London silver condiment stand by Edward Barnard. 1868. L:21cm (8¼in). ③ **4.** Victorian twin-handled silver desk stand raised on four scroll feet. c.1850. W:31cm (12¼in). ② **5.** Japanese ladle made by Koonoike with the handle modelled as a dragon. c.1860. L:40cm (15¾in). ④ **6.** Japanese silver and enamel vase decorated with irises. c.1890. H:14cm (5½in). ③ **7.** Dutch silver bowl with foliate pierced shaped sides and scroll-cast rim. D:16cm (6¼in). ② **8.** London silver

1 Silver sugar bowl

2 Urn-shaped coffee pot

3 Silver condiment stand

4 Silver desk stand

5 Japanese ladle

6 Japanese vase

7 Dutch silver bowl

8 Silver toast rack

9 Silver-plated biscuit box

10 Silver cup

toast rack by Robert Harper. 1869. H:14cm (5½in). ② 9. Silver-plated biscuit box. c.1860. W:22cm (8¾in). ② 10. Silver cup decorated with floral motifs and flutes. H:22cm (8¾in). ① 11. Pair of silver candelabra in the style of Louis XV. H:54cm (21¼in). ⑥ 12. One of a pair of candelabra on four leaf feet, with a winged putto holding the arms. c.1890. H:29cm (11½in). ② 13. Sheffield silver sweet tray by James Dixon & Sons. c.1900. H:8.5cm (3½in). ① 14. Full-bodied copper cow weather vane with cast head and remnants of gilding. L:66cm (26in). ⑤ 15. American metal eagle-shaped weather vane. H:26cm (10¼in). ① 16. Patchen horse weather vane with gilding, full-bodied copper with cast head, mounted on a metal base. L:105cm (41¼in). ④ 17. Silver pheasant. L:58cm (23in). ⑤ 18. Detail of no. 12.

11 *Silver candelabra*

12 *Candelabrum*

13 *Silver sweet tray*

14 *Copper cow weather vane*

15 *Eagle weather vane*

16 *Patchen horse weather vane*

17 *Silver pheasant*

18 *Winged putto detail*

# PATTERN BOOKS

THE PREDOMINANCE OF SOME DECORATIVE MOTIFS WITHIN CERTAIN PERIODS CAN BE ASCRIBED TO THE POPULARITY OF PATTERN BOOKS. THROUGH TIME, THESE RESOURCES HAVE ACTED AS GUIDES, ESPECIALLY FOR THOSE DESIGNERS WHO HAVE BASED THEIR WORK ON HISTORICAL STYLES.

**GRAMMAR OF ORNAMENT** This plate from Owen Jones's book shows samples of decorative stone carving that might be applied to fretwork, wallpaper, or any number of other media.

## EARLY JAPANESE INFLUENCE

Designs and motifs based on Japanese decorative arts are conspicuous by their absence from many 19th-century pattern books. The reason for this is that it was not until the Meiji period (1868–1912) that Japan opened itself up to the wider world. Japanese artefacts were, however, present in the West – the Netherlands had shared a limited trade agreement with the Tokugawa Shogunate for many years, and discerning European collectors were well aware of the outstanding quality of Japanese art. It is possible to see this influence in Western decorative art even before the great surge in interest in all things Japanese that characterized the Aesthetic Movement.

**IMARI WINE POT** This wine pot has decorative panels featuring lotus flowers and geometric patterns. It is the kind of artefact that Owen Jones used as source material.

The earliest text dealing with ornament is *De Architectura*, written in the 1st century bce by Vitruvius, whose examples of architectural beauty served as templates for generations of builders. During the Renaissance, Andrea Palladio published *Quattro Libri dell'Architettura*, spawning a distinct style of architecture named after the author.

The 18th century saw a proliferation of pattern books by English cabinet-makers. Matthias Lock and Henry Copland published *New Book of Ornaments* in 1746. This was followed by tomes from three greats of English furniture design: Chippendale, Hepplewhite, and Sheraton. In France Percier and Fontaine published *Palais, Maisons et Autres Édifices Modernes Dessinés à Rome* in 1798. These books had a huge influence, even reaching the New World.

### GRAMMAR OF ORNAMENT

The 1851 Great Exhibition held at London's Crystal Palace was, in effect, another manifestation

**COLOUR AND PATTERN** By following his own "propositions" regarding pattern and colour, Owen Jones made the lavish colour plates of his *Grammar of Ornament* into works of art in their own right.

**VICTORIA AND ALBERT MUSEUM** Established in 1852 as a permanent home for objects from the Great Exhibition, the Victoria & Albert Museum acts as a depository for original designs to this day.

of the pattern book. By collecting examples of the "works and industry of all nations" under one roof, the exhibition's organizers were helping to disseminate the vocabulary of ornament.

Owen Jones, superintendent of works for the Great Exhibition, also designed the Egyptian, Greek, Roman, and Alhambra Courts within the Crystal Palace. His 1856 *Grammar of Ornament* was a pictorial guide to the history of design from the ancient world to the 19th century. Jones's remarkable book included more than 3,000 images, arranged in patterns on pages themed by colour and style. The accompanying text comprised a list of 37 "propositions" governing the proper and tasteful application of pattern and colour. It quickly became the most widely used source book in the world.

In France in 1876, Auguste Racinet published an exhaustive study of the history of costume. This book was especially useful for designers working in the historic revival styles that dominated 19th-century decorative art and design. Other works such as M.P. Verneuil's *Étude de la Plante* were more explicitly linked to the representation of natural forms within the decorative arts. The popularity of source books continued unabated throughout the 20th century with the publication of volumes such as Édouard Benedictus's *Relais* and Sonia Delaunay's *Compositions, Couleurs, Idées*.

**GREAT EXHIBITION AT CRYSTAL PALACE** The Medieval Court was one of the focal points of the Great Exhibition. Designed by Augustus Pugin, who also worked on the Palace of Westminster, the court was a celebration of the Gothic Revival that was so popular in Britain at the time. One of the main aims of the exhibition was to raise the public's appreciation of good design.

# CLOCKS

AS CONSUMERS STARTED TO TAKE FOR GRANTED THE ABILITY OF CLOCKS
TO KEEP TIME, THE FOCUS OF CLOCKMAKERS SHIFTED TOWARDS NOVELTY.
REVIVAL STYLES, HOWEVER, STILL INFLUENCED MUCH OF THE PRODUCTION.

**STEEPLE SHELF CLOCK** Housing
an eight-day movement by Birge
& Fuller of Bristol of Connecticut,
the mahogany case has a pointed
gable flanked by pinnacled pillars.
c.1845. H:65cm (25½in).

**FRENCH MANTEL CLOCK** The
red tortoiseshell Boulle marquetry
case of this clock has scrolling
foliate, fruit, and vase mounts of
gilt cast brass in the Rococo Revival
style. c.1840. H:36cm (14¼in).

## REVIVAL-STYLE CLOCKS

The revival styles that monopolized 19th-century
furniture also dominated clock-case design of the
period. This was especially true for the florid Rococo
taste. The association between this style and the
magnificently ornamented French clocks of the 17th
and 18th centuries helped perpetuate its popularity
among horologists and the buying public alike.

### RICH STYLE, CHEAP PRODUCTION

While in the past reliable and accurate clock
movements had been a challenge to engineer, by
this time they were easy to manufacture. As a
result, clockmakers were able to make enormous
quantities of clocks housed in elaborate cases

and at affordable prices. They used intricate
decorative touches, including Boullework and
scrolling brass mounts, to re-create the Rococo
style, often substituting costly handcrafted work
with cheaper machine-production techniques.

Elaborate clock garnitures that combined
a timepiece with a pair of urns, or pairs of
candelabra, obelisks, or vases, became staple
fixtures of mantelpieces in smart 19th-century
homes. They were frequently produced in a
combination of materials, including porcelain,
bronze, wood, and ormolu. Each component often
had an individual base, and vases usually had
removable lids, so that a single garniture might
be made up of a dozen pieces. Makers lavished
attention on the elaborate painted scenes,
foliate decoration, and other adornments –

such as finials – with which they decorated their
creations. The clock face, usually plain white
enamel or painted metal, was invariably the least
decorative component of the entire ensemble.

### AMERICAN CLOCKMAKING

The first American clocks had wooden mechanisms,
but around the 1830s clock factories started
producing sophisticated brass movements.

**LOUIS XVI CLOCK GARNITURE** Neoclassical
elements are revived in this mantel clock with an
urn surmount and two matching ewers. Raised
on giltwood plinths, the porcelain bodies of
the ewers are transfer-printed with Sèvres-style
romantic vignettes. c.1870. H:47cm (18½in).

*The Sèvres-style* enamelled
porcelain dial has black Roman
numerals on white porcelain plaques

*Transfer-printed
vignettes* recall
late 18th-century
Romanticism

**ROCOCO REVIVAL MANTEL CLOCK** The ornate Louis XV-style
case of this clock is cast in gilt bronze and surmounted by a winged
cherub holding a songbird. c.1880. H:53.5cm (21in).

**LOUIS REVIVAL MANTEL CLOCK** Incorporating elements of Louis XV Rococo and Louis XVI Neoclassical ornament, this clock is raised on a marble plinth with gilt-bronze foliate and beaded mounts, and is flanked by a winged cherub and a globe. *c.1880.*

Eli Terry's shelf clock, developed in the 1820s, resembled the hood of a longcase clock and kept time just as accurately, but at a fraction of the cost. Soon other factories all across Connecticut were making shelf clocks in the popular styles of the day.

By the 1860s American makers were also imitating the fashionable French clock styles, but using iron or wood, painted to look like marble, or white metal, painted to look like bronze. Gilt highlights were often used to embellish the decoration.

## MYSTERY MOVEMENTS

The 19th-century predilection for novelty led to the development of the so-called mystery clocks. These timepieces confounded the observer by having no obvious connection between the mechanism and the hands on the clock face. Parisian horologist Robert Houdin devised an ingenious example in which the base, which houses the mechanism, is attached to the face only by a seemingly empty clear-glass cylinder. In actual fact, this cylinder encases a second glass cylinder that rotates slowly, thus transferring the movement up to the clock face via a series of gears. Another variation uses a clear-glass dial with no visible wheels or cogs driving the hands. In this case, the entire dial revolves, driven by a toothed wheel concealed within the bezel and taking the hour with it.

Other novelty clocks relied less on illusion and more on confounding the viewer's expectation of what a clock should look like. Globe clocks, held aloft on a base by putti or naked maidens, sometimes had numerals in a band around the globe and marked the hours with a hand that travelled around the circumference. These were driven entirely from within the globe, with no moving parts in the base.

*The gilt-bronze cherub* berates the world below

*The celestial aspect* is enhanced by the cherub sitting on a cloud

*The face is* white enamel with contrasting black Roman numerals

**LOUIS XV-STYLE MANTEL CLOCK** Made in Paris in gilt bronze, this clock has a case draped in foliage and surmounted by a cherub. It rests above a bronze elephant on a *rocaille* and scrolling foliate base. *1855. H:44.5cm (17½in).*

**LYRE MANTEL CLOCK** This clock incorporates a French movement within a Louis XVI-style green-onyx frame and base elaborately embellished with ormolu garlands, rosettes, and torches. *Late 1800s. H:49cm (19¼in).*

**LOUIS XVI-STYLE GLOBE CLOCK** The spherical case of this clock, with an ormolu cherub surmount, is held aloft by garlanded female nudes in the Classical style. *c.1880. H:61cm (24in).*

# SOUVENIRS

JUST LIKE TODAY, 19TH-CENTURY TRAVELLERS BROUGHT HOME MEMENTOS
AND LITTLE TOKENS AS GIFTS FOR LOVED ONES OR AS REMINDERS FOR
THEMSELVES OF PLACES THEY HAD VISITED.

**MICROMOSAIC SNUFF BOX** Centred in a gilt frame on a granite lid and base, the micromosaic plaque on this snuff box depicts Pliny's Doves, also known as Rome's Capitoline Doves. *Early 19th century. D:6.25cm (2½in).*

## THE RISE OF SOUVENIRS

Throughout the 18th century members of the upper classes rounded off their education with a visit to Europe's cultural capitals – principally Rome. These wealthy young tourists collected souvenirs on a grand scale: marble sculptures, paintings, and rare books by the crateful. Known as the Grand Tour in Britain, the fashion was prevalent throughout Europe. Other European cities such as Paris – as well as the spa towns of Germany – were included in a trip that could take months, or even years, to complete.

By the early 19th century travel had become less hazardous and less expensive. More people began to visit places of interest at home and abroad, including wealthy travellers from the United States. They all took home souvenirs that were less costly than their predecessors' works of art, but no less striking or unusual.

## MICROMOSAICS FROM ITALY

During the first half of the 19th century Italy was a favourite tourist destination. Micromosaic is a version of the ancient technique of mosaic and was developed in the Vatican workshops in the second half of the 18th century. It was soon being copied, to various standards, in private workshops across Italy. Craftsmen placed minute threads of glass about 3mm (¼in) long and a little thicker than a human hair vertically onto a resin-coated copper or glass backing, to form a mosaic picture. The

threads were made in a variety of cross-sections, including rectangular, triangular, circular, and oval, as well as leaf-shaped or S-shaped to mimic animal hair. The finest examples contained up to 5,000 tiny pieces of glass (or microtessarae)

*The rim of the table* is an egg-and-dart ormolu moulding

*Shell and acanthus leaf* ormolu mounts enclose the baluster column

**MICROMOSAIC TABLE TOP** The central cartouche of this micromosaic table top by Michelangelo Barberi depicts St Peter's Square. It is ringed by oval cartouches with views of the Colosseum, the Arch of Constantine, the Pantheon, and the Forum – these set in pink marble between olive branches, wreaths, and Imperial eagles.

**MICROMOSAIC TABLE** The micromosaic table top (*see detail above*) is raised on an ebonized-oak baluster column and triform base with shell, acanthus leaf, winged griffin, and animal-paw ormolu mounts. *c.1845. D:102cm (40¼in).*

**MINIATURE TARTANWARE BOX** Signed by Lamme Cumnock, this box is inked around the sides with a Robertson tartan. The lid is handpainted with a rare view of Balmoral Castle before Prince Albert had it modified. *c.1850. W:3cm (1¼in).*

**TUNBRIDGEWARE WRITING BOX** The sides and lid of this box, housing a pen and inkwells, stamp divisions, and a paper knife, display perspective cube and floral and foliate mosaic work. c.1870. W:32cm (12½in).

**TUNBRIDGEWARE SEWING CLAMP** Particularly ornate, this clamp incorporates various sewing tools – including a waxer, a winder, tape measure, thimble holders, and a needle case – in stickware and painted sycamore "houses". c.1830. L:20.5cm (8in).

per square inch, creating the level of detail seen on a typical computer screen. Tiny micromosaic pictures were often set into jewellery or the lids of snuff boxes, but vases, and even pieces of furniture were also decorated using this delicate technique.

By the mid-19th century micromosaic was being replaced by miniature glass mosiacs, which were cheaper to produce as they often used tesserae containing two or more colours, eliminating the need to arrange several single-colour microtesserae together in order to create a particular colour or effect.

## TUNBRIDGEWARE

In the late 1600s craftsmen in Tunbridge Wells, a spa town in the southeast of England, developed a distinctive form of parquetry that became popular for game boards, tea caddies, writing boxes, and needle cases. They glued together strips and rods of multicoloured wood to create complex geometric and pictorial designs. The solid blocks were cut into thin veneers that could be used to decorate a number of pieces identically. At the height of Tunbridge Wells's popularity as a spa in the early 19th century, Tunbridgeware pieces depicted views and buildings in and around the town.

## SCOTTISH GIFTS

Queen Victoria and her husband, Prince Albert, loved the Highlands so much that in 1848 they bought Balmoral Castle. Royal endorsement and easy travel on the new railways helped make Scottish holidays immensely fashionable in Britain during the second half of the 19th century. The Scottish souvenir industry also benefited from the numbers of visitors to the area. W.&A. Smith, in the Scottish town of Mauchline, had been making snuff boxes since the 1820s. In the 1850s it had a huge success with its tartanware – sycamore wood items covered in "woven" tartan, specially created designs on paper. By the 1860s the firm also made sycamore items decorated with engraved transfer pictures. At first W.&A. Smith concentrated on Scottish souvenirs decorated with images like Robert Burns's Cottage, but it was soon producing pieces with engraved views of other tourist destinations such as the Isle of Wight. By the 1870s the factory had cornered the international market for inexpensive wooden souvenirs, with a varied production that included boxes, book covers, cups, and buttons.

**MAUCHLINEWARE MONEY BOX** The turned sycamore body is transfer-printed with London views: on one side, the New Chelsea Suspension Bridge; on the other, Horseguards from St James's Park. c.1860. H:9.5cm (3¾in).

**MAUCHLINEWARE SPECTACLE CASE** This early Scottish Mauchlineware piece is hand-decorated with flora and fauna imagery in brushed and penned ink. 1820–30. W:12cm (4¾in).

## BOHEMIAN GLASS

Mid-19th-century visitors to middle European spas such as Baden-Baden, Karlsbad, and Marienbad often purchased heavy glass tumblers engraved with views of these resorts. They reminded their owners of the good times they had at these fashionable spa towns and the health-giving benefits of the mineral water that they drank.

Spa glasses were a speciality of the various Bohemian glassworks whose cut and engraved coloured glass was prized throughout Europe at the time. As well as an engraved townscape, these tumblers were also decorated with deep cuts and flashes of brilliant colour such as ruby and amber. These popular souvenirs were made in large quantities for numerous spas. As a result, the engraving and cutting varies enormously in quality and detail. The cheapest examples were decorated with acid-etching rather than wheel-engraving, which is done by hand. Engravers sometimes proudly signed and dated finely crafted spa glasses.

**BOHEMIAN GLASS TUMBLER** Engraved with a view of a French spa town, this tumbler entitled *La Fontaine Elise*, was produced in ruby flashed glass. It has a delicate floral border under the rim. c.1875. H:13cm (5in).

# TEXTILES

DURING THE LATE 19TH CENTURY, A FASHION-CONSCIOUS EUROPEAN MIDDLE CLASS DEVELOPED AN ALMOST-INSATIABLE APPETITE FOR BRIGHT, COLOURFUL RUGS AND CARPETS, FAVOURING THOSE FROM THE "EXOTIC" EAST.

**SOUTHWEST PERSIAN RUG** Woven by the Kashkouli, one of tribes within the Qashqai confederacy, this woollen rug has three diamond-shaped medallions set within a larger hexagonal medallion. *Late 19th century. L:204cm (80¼in).*

## EASTERN APPEAL

Carpets had been imported from the East since the 17th century, but by the mid-1870s, carpet-makers along the now long-established trade routes found themselves producing wares on an unprecedented scale. Interest was further buoyed in 1876, when the Shah of Persia, Nasir al-Din Shah, keen to promote his country's textile industry abroad, made a gift to Queen Victoria of 14 Persian rugs (now in the Victoria & Albert Museum). He also sent several to the Vienna Exhibition in 1891, where they were seen by an eager public.

### PERSIA SETS THE EXAMPLE

Having excelled in rug-weaving in the 16th century, the Persian carpet industry once again dominated the field. Looking back to earlier designs, rug-makers produced carpets that borrowed motifs and colours from Classical examples. Urban workshops in major cities such as Tehran, Kashan, and Tabriz, produced vast numbers of richly patterned carpets, curvilinear in design and featuring floral motifs, arabesques, and palmettes, often arranged around a central medallion and enclosed within ornate borders. Dominant colours were bright, jewel-like reds and blues drawn from natural pigments, sometimes contrasted with ivory.

**The borders** include a sophisticated floral design

**Stylized** floral motifs are scattered over the field

**SHOPPING FOR SOUVENIRS** British soldiers stationed in Egypt in 1882 shop in Cairo's bazaar, buying carpets and other local goods to take home. Souvenirs such as these helped to boost the fashion for Oriental carpets in the west.

**Geometric** animal (or bird) figures commonly appear in Khamseh patterns

**WESTERN PERSIAN RUG** A tribal rug from the Khamseh confederacy, this example is woven in wool with a typically angular Tree of Life design set within characteristic elaborate floral borders. *Late 19th century. L:206cm (81in).*

Rural or tribal communities, such as the Afshar and Khamseh, also made carpets – generally on a smaller scale – where designs tended to be more rectilinear and geometric, though colour schemes were similar.

## MIDDLE-EAST PRODUCTION

The influence of Persian designs was also evident in Turkey and the Caucasus (a region between the Caspian Sea and the Black Sea), where similar carpets were being produced, mainly by village communities and nomadic tribes. Carpets from these areas tend to be more boldly geometric than curvilinear.

Dagestan in the Caucasus and Ghiordes in Turkey became particularly known for the production of prayer mats. Made throughout the Middle East, these rugs often featured a Tree of Life motif and were always directional – the mihrab (an arch pointing to Mecca) on them indicating to the kneeler towards which direction to pray.

## CARPETS FROM CHINA

Hailing from Beijing and Ningxia, in the northwest of the country, Chinese carpets were quite different from Middle Eastern ones. Instead of a design filling the field to capacity, motifs tended to be more sparse, spread out over a single-colour background. Typical designs were neither geometric nor curvilinear, but achieved a balance between the two. Dominant colours were blue and yellow, representing the sky and the earth respectively, and popular motifs included the peony (wealth) and lotus flower (purity). Borders might feature frets, swastikas, and other geometric shapes.

Common layouts included the "four-and-one medallion", in which a cluster of motifs – animals, flowers, or geometric shapes – formed a central "medallion" and each of the four corners featured subsequent medallions. Full-field layouts in which the decorative motifs filled the central space in an apparently random order were also popular.

## FRENCH CARPETS

In keeping with the fashion for revival styles in Europe, French carpet-makers, in particular, looked back to past designs for inspiration. Among

the resulting trends was a revival of the Savonnerie and Aubusson carpets produced under Louis XIV in the 17th century. Typical designs featured floral swags, acanthus leaves, or mythological scenes rendered in rich and luxuriant colours within strong, often-wide, and architectural borders.

**CHINESE CARPET** Chinese rugs incorporate symbolic motifs with specific meanings. Here, the scattered peonies represent nobility and wealth, while the lotus blossoms symbolize purity. *Late 19th century. L:290cm (114½in).*

**CHINESE CARPET** Typical of the Oriental carpets that became popular in the United States in the late 1800s, this has a scattered peony design over and within rectilinear borders. *Late 19th century. L:375cm (150in).*

## PAISLEY SHAWLS

The fashion for paisley shawls in Europe began in the late 1700s, when wealthy merchants first started to return home from their travels in the East with a luxuriously warm material.

The shawls originated in the mountainous region of Kashmir, in northern India, where they had been made from as early as the 1400s using fine, warm wool sourced from the underbelly of the local Kashmir (cashmere) goat. The term "paisley", however, derives from the name of a Scottish company, established in 1805, that went on to become the most prolific producer of such shawls as the century progressed. The woven shawls bore designs

epitomized by a stylized, cone-shaped motif known as the "boteh", which is now recognizable as an elongated curve.

Traditional European designs were woven from silk or wool, which made them heavier than their Kashmir counterparts. Advances in technology, however, soon meant that designs could be printed on to wool/cotton and wool/silk fabrics rather than woven, making the production of lighter versions in a more exciting range of designs and colours a reality. Demand grew in the 19th century, when technologically advanced manufacturing methods meant that paisley shawls could be produced on a large scale for the masses. They proved so popular that millions were printed.

**FRENCH CARPET** This *tapis-ras* carpet (flat-woven using the tapestry technique) is patterned with the elaborate floral bouquets typical of Aubusson weaves of the late 19th century. *L:292.5cm (115¼in).*

**SCOTTISH SHAWL** Inspired by the formalized representations of pine cones found on hand-woven Kashmiri shawls, this paisley pattern is machine-woven in silk and wool. *c.1860. W:320cm (126in).*

**SCOTTISH SHAWL** In addition to the pine-cone motif, paisley patterns also incorporate stylized vegetation based on palms, cypresses, and other plant forms, as on this printed woollen shawl. *c.1880. W:156cm (61½in).*

# NEEDLEWORK

Needlecraft played an important role in women's lives in the 18th and 19th centuries. In bygone eras, sewing was often a communal activity offering women the chance to catch up with friends over some mending or embroidery. Women generally worked on more elaborate items such as quilts, together, each bringing their own design ideas and skills to the piece.

**PENNSYLVANIAN PATCHWORK** This Pennsylvanian German quilt has a bold geometric pattern comprised of blocks of saw-tooth-bordered fans, in white against a red ground. *Mid-19th century. L:202cm (79½in).*

**OHIO APPLIQUÉ** Of immigrant German origin, this appliqué features a bold stylized floral, berry, and foliate pattern. This is geometrically configured in red and near-black dyed calico, sewn to a contrasting ivory-white flat ground. *Mid-19th century. Sq:190cm (74¾in).*

**NEW YORK EMBROIDERED PATCHWORK** The patchwork fans and peacock feathers are embroidered with diverse sprigs of flowers, within a border of embroidered morning-glories, all in silk-on-silk. *c.1880. W:183cm (72in).*

## QUILT DEVELOPMENT

Some of the most intricate and inventive textiles homemade by women are quilts. Early examples from the 18th century were made of three pieces of material: a top; an inner layer of wool, or flock; and a back held together with fancy stitches, usually called "whole-cloth" quilts.

Patchwork quilts – thriftily made from leftover scraps of material – were common by the early 1800s. They were usually made from similar types of material – for example, a combination of cotton patches – pieced together in geometric patterns. There are more than 400 named quilt patterns, the same pattern often having a different moniker in different places. Many have intriguing names such as Tumbling Block, Jacob's Ladder, and Churn Dash. "Crazy quilts" were various types of material like cotton, silk, and velvet all sewn together at random and embellished with embroidery. This popular variety of patchwork quilt was introduced in the 1870s.

Appliqué quilts had a whole cloth base decorated with stitched-on fabric pieces. This technique enabled quilters to create pictorial designs: favourite motifs include flowers, hearts, and pineapples for friendship. Many quilts combine both patchwork and appliqué techniques.

Pioneer women travelling to North America's western frontiers often received quilts as a goodbye present from their friends back east. This form of giving led to a fashion for album, or friendship, quilts, pieced together from separate squares created individually and embroidered with the date and name of their maker.

## NORTH AMERICAN RUG CRAFT

Immigrants from Europe brought their needlework skills – and understanding of the need for thrift – with them. By the mid-1800s hooked rugs were being made throughout North America. They were made from narrow strips of wool or cotton hooked closely together through linen or burlap backing.

Some hooked-rug makers occasionally cut the loops for a more pile-like effect. Hooked-rug designs were often original and highly imaginative: they ranged from simple images – animals, flowers, geometrics, and stripes – to complex scenes such as Fourth of July picnics and sleighing through the snow.

As interest in hooked rugs grew in the 1860s and 1870s, patterns became available. The enterprising Edward Sands Frost from Maine sold designs stencilled on burlap door to door and through mail-order catalogues. He produced 150 patterns, including birds, flowers, and geometric motifs. Hooked-rug making is still a popular craft today.

## NEEDLEWORKED PICTURES
In the early 1800s embroidering pictures was considered a suitable occupation for young women, who had gained proficiency in stitching by producing samplers. In some cases, the embroiderer followed a design sketched by a professional artist or teacher. Prints or pattern books were often used as a source of more elaborate embroidered pictures. Typical subjects included still lifes of fruits and flowers, the girl's home or school, pastoral scenes, and figures in a landscape.

Mourning embroidery, created to commemorate departed loved ones, usually had a figure weeping in a graveyard. They included poignant Classical symbols such as funeral urns and weeping willows, as well as the departed's name and dates. In the United States, many of these were made in memory of George Washington; in Britain, of Nelson.

The production of embroidered pictures declined when girls started receiving a more academic education in the mid-19th century.

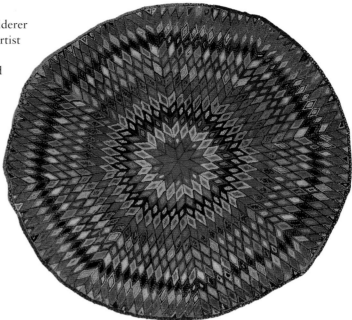

AMERICAN HOOKED RUG The hooked geometric pattern of this rug suggests Shaker origin. It is made up of polychrome diamond forms radiating out from a red eight-pointed star. *Late 19th century. D:197.5cm (77¾in).*

*Woolwork* predates the brighter but cruder colouring of aniline dyes

**AMERICAN BERLIN WOOLWORK**
This framed woolwork still life of a bowl of fruit within a wreath of roses is by Elizabeth Swartz, who was probably from Chester County, Pennsylvania. *1839. W:44cm (17¼in).*

**BRITISH BERLIN WOOLWORK**
Incorporating long and short stitchwork, this maple-framed picture of a first-rate man o' war flying the White Ensign exemplifies the bold, nationalistic imagery popular in Victorian England in the mid-1800s. *W:56.5cm (22¼in).*

## GREENFELL RUGS

British doctor Wilfred Grenfell moved to Newfoundland in 1894 to set up a medical mission. He came up with the idea of supplementing impoverished women's incomes by paying them to make hooked rugs that he would sell. He gave rug-makers kits that included everything they needed – from materials to burlap backing printed with a pattern. Early Grenfell rugs were made of wool and cotton; later examples from donated damaged silk stockings. Designs such as fishing scenes and dog teams reflect Newfoundland's craggy environment. Select stores in North America, such as Eaton's department store in Toronto, sold Grenfell rugs from 1910 to the late 1940s.

GRENFELL HOOKED RUG Typically tightly hooked, thin, and durable, this rug depicts a map of Newfoundland enhanced with a compass and numerous indigenous motifs, including seals, whales, boats, and settlements. *Late 19th century. L:54cm (21¼in).*

# SCULPTURE

IN THE 19TH CENTURY THE POPULARITY OF SMALL BRONZES OF REALISTICALLY PORTRAYED ANIMALS SPREAD SWIFTLY FROM FRANCE TO THE REST OF EUROPE AND THE UNITED STATES. A NEW GENRE OF SCULPTURE WAS BORN.

**EQUESTRIAN BRONZE** This repatinated Coalbrookdale cast is of *Djiin – Cheval à la Barrière*, by French sculptor Pierre-Jules Mêne, widely acknowledged as the leading equine animalier. *c.1890. H:29cm (11½in).*

## FRENCH BRONZES

Bronze sculpture in 19th-century France enjoyed an acclaim that Europe had not seen since the work of Cellini in Renaissance Italy 300 years before. The Industrial Revolution had as great an effect on sculpture as on the other decorative arts. For the first time, it was cheaper to make bronze than marble sculptures; as a result, bronze foundries became more numerous, and more efficient and consistent in quality.

The improvement coincided with the rising wealth of the middle classes, and a new appreciation and study of nature. In Paris there was the thrill of seeing wild animals from the colonies in Africa and the Far East up close at the museum in the *Jardin des Plantes*. Sculptors tapped into this vibrant market by making small, affordable bronzes of animals of all species.

### *LES ANIMALIERS*

As with Impressionism, the term "animalier" was first used by a hostile critic to deride the work of Antoine-Louis Barye and other like-minded sculptors. In previous centuries, animals in art had taken supporting roles to humans or had been presented as allegories. Like people, animals were idealized to conform to Classical notions of

proportion and beauty. Barye flouted all the conventions. He showed nature in the raw, including subjects such as lions attacking and devouring prey, and stags locking horns.

Barye, an artist as well as a sculptor, had worked under painter Baron Goss, who specialized in

**EAGLE BRONZE** Cast by the Barbédienne foundry, Antoine-Louis Barye's *Aigle, les Ailes Déployées* displays the aggression, in this case latent, for which Barye's wild-animal sculptures are known. *Late 1800s. H:14cm (5½in).*

romantic views of battle, with rearing horses and conquering heroes. Captivated by the portrayal of animals in action, and keen to produce anatomically correct replicas, Barye observed the big cats in the *Jardin des Plantes* and drew the skeletons and muscle systems of dead ones. Meanwhile, by working for a goldsmith for eight years, he learned how to model on a small scale.

Barye exhibited his first sculpture, *Tiger Devouring a Gavial*, at the Salon in 1831. Despite mixed reactions from the critics – not all saw natural beauty in instinctive animal behaviour – it was bought for the Luxembourg Gardens. Two years later, Barye exhibited *Lion and Serpent*, which was also purchased by the state. His career as a sculptor had taken off.

## DOMESTIC ANIMALS

Some of Barye's disciples followed in his footsteps and chose to capture moments of predatory violence, but most toned down the subject matter.

*The bronze castings* are finished in a black patina

**BULL BRONZES** Antoine-Louis Barye's *Un Taureau se Défendant* (left) and *Un Taureau Cadre* (right) were modelled in 1841 but not cast in bronze until 1845. These superb black-patinated examples were sand-cast by the Barbédienne foundry in Paris. *c.1870. H:22.25cm (8¾in).*

**EQUESTRIAN BRONZE** French animalier Pierre-Jules Mêne created numerous racing equestrian sculptures. This *Vainqueur du Derby* depicts the winning horse and jockey of the English racing classic. *c.1860. H:25cm (9¾in).*

**HUNTING DOG BRONZE** After horses, Pierre-Jules Mêne's favoured subject was dogs. This *Chien Braque, Anglais Pur-Sang, Gardant du Gibier* depicts a pointer guarding game by a tree stump. *c.1860. H:28cm (11in).*

## VIENNESE BRONZES

In the mid-1800s the trend for small animal bronzes spread to Vienna, where Franz Bergmann started to produce miniature bronze animals and birds.

Over time, bronze acquires a natural patina, which can be chemically induced by the artist. However, Bergmann chose to cold-paint the bronze, a technique usually applied to ceramics or glass. As the name suggests, the paint is not fired to fuse with the body, so it tends to peel or rub off. The tiny naturalistic replicas looked even more realistic with their true colouring. Their size made them affordable, and they were avidly bought. Bergmann's work can be identified by a stamp with his name, sometimes spelled backwards, or a monogrammed "B".

Domestic animals lent themselves to being presented more tamely. Pierre-Jules Mêne specialized in horses and dogs at work and play. By studying animals at the *Jardin des Plantes*, as Barye had done, Mêne managed to create anatomically accurate works that showed animals behaving naturally. He made large editions of his work and was obsessive about quality, making sure that the last in a series was as perfect as the first.

As the middle classes aspired to traditional aristocratic pursuits, sporting art also became a genre, with portrayals of hunting, game shooting, racing, and polo playing. Mêne exhibited at the Great Exhibition of 1851 and was highly popular in Britain. He made some editions specifically for the British market: his *Horse and Jockey*, a portrait of a Derby winner exhibited at the Salon in 1863, was a bestseller.

The work of Isidore-Jules Bonheur was so naturalistic that his Normandy cow was recognized as a standard for the breed. He also made racing bronzes and animal groups, all characterized by sympathetic realism.

**BIRD STUDY** This European jay in cold-painted bronze is highly naturalistic and characteristic of the bronzes produced by the Bergmann factory in Vienna. *Late 1800s. H:11.5cm (4½in).*

**DOG STUDY** Like many of Bergmann's naturalistic, cold-painted figural bronzes, this study of a Great Dane would have originally found a British or an American owner. *Late 1800s. L:14cm (5½in).*

**POLO PLAYER** French animalier Isidore-Jules Bonheur's brown-patinated study of a mounted polo player was cast in bronze by the Hippolyte Peyrol foundry. This is where most of Bonheur's, and his sister Rosa's, casts were made.

*Equestrian studies*, like this one, were partly inspired by Buffalo Bill's travelling Wild West Show

**BULL STUDY** One of a pair by Isidore-Jules Bonheur, *Taureau Beuglant* was cast by Hippolyte Peyrol. Originally retailed by Tiffany & Co. in New York, both studies have a distinguished deep-brown patina. *H:39.5cm (15½in).*

# AMERICAN SCULPTURE

THE OLD WEST PRODUCED A DISTINCT SCHOOL OF ART INFORMED BY THE TOUGH REALITIES OF LIFE BEYOND THE FRONTIER. COWBOY ART WAS BORN OUT OF HARD EXPERIENCE AND KEEN OBSERVATION OF THE ORDINARY PEOPLE AND EVERYDAY EVENTS THAT SHAPED THE AMERICAN WEST.

**THE MEDICINE MAN** This figure was cast in bronze by Roman Bronze Works of New York from an original model by Charles M. Russell. *H:18cm (7in).*

Towards the end of the 19th century – during the years between the end of the Civil War and the closure of the frontier – the American West was a territory of open range and trails, peopled by railroad workers, buffalo hunters, and cowboys, with scant local law enforcement. It was a period of gunfights between gamblers and skirmishes with Native Americans – in short, the era of the Wild West. The romance of these heady days was not lost on the residents of "civilized" America, where news from the frontier was always greeted with excitement.

## CHARLES MARION RUSSELL

Born to wealthy parents in Missouri in 1864, Charles M. Russell found the pull of the West irresistible, and he moved to Montana to work on a sheep ranch at the age of 16. Legend has it that his first successful painting was of an emaciated beef bull being stalked by wolves. It was sent by Russell's employer to a ranch owner in response to an enquiry about the effects of the bitter 1886 winter, and it eventually ended up on display. Russell's ability to capture the spirit of his environment is characteristic of his paintings, which are full of atmosphere

**COUNTING COUP** Documents suggest that this group was the second of Charles M. Russell's sculptures to be cast. From an original model by Russell himself, it was cast in bronze by Roman Bronze Works of New York. *c.1925.*

and charm despite his lack of training. He also exhibited a remarkable ability to portray movement and action, and this influenced his sculptural work. In 1896 Russell married Nancy Cooper, who was responsible for publicizing and creating a market for her reclusive husband's work, notably in the vibrant art market of New York.

## CHARLES SCHREYVOGEL

A struggling painter trying to eke out a living through his art when he first went West in 1893, Charles Schreyvogel quickly became an excellent horseman and learned to communicate with Native American tribes in an effort to persuade them to pose for his paintings and sketches. However, he still had trouble finding patrons. In despair, Schreyvogel sent a painting to the National Academy of Design in 1901 and won the Thomas B. Clarke prize. Interest in his works immediately soared as a result of this accolade, and Schreyvogel joined Russell as a leading exponent of Western art. By the beginning of the 20th century the Old West was already a thing of the past, but this only served to increase public appetite for Western art. The detailed depictions of frontier life in the sculpture and painting of Schreyvogel, Russell, and others helped satisfy a kind of nostalgia.

**THE LAST DROP** Cast in bronze by Roman Bronze Works of New York from an original model by Charles Schreyvogel, this sculpture depicts a cowboy giving his horse water from his hat. *c.1900.*

## 20TH-CENTURY EXAMPLES

The tradition of the original frontier artists has been kept alive, and there exists a vibrant community of cowboy artists to this day. James Nathan Muir worked at ranches in Texas during the 1980s before settling in Arizona and embarking on a career as a sculptor. His militaristic themes show the influence of Frederic Remington, a war correspondent who began sculpting in bronze around the turn of the 20th century. Muir specializes in cavalry subjects – in particular, figures from the Civil War and the Old West. With his attention to detail and his intuitive grasp of movement and action, Muir is the heir of Charles M. Russell.

**SAVING THE FLAG** From a limited edition of 24 cast in bronze from an original model by James Nathan Muir, this group depicts a fallen cavalryman holding a standard up from the ground.

**COWBOY RIDING HIS HORSE UPHILL** Painted in watercolours by Charles M. Russell, this artwork depicts a cowboy in a typical outfit, including hat, neckerchief, holster, chaps, and spurs. Russell's grasp of human and animal anatomy can be seen in this work. The large backdrop of blank sky provides a glimpse of the expansive landscape of the American West.

# ARTS AND CRAFTS
## 1880–1920

# TRADITIONAL VALUES

THE ARTS AND CRAFTS MOVEMENT AIMED TO RECAPTURE THE PURE
DESIGN AND CRAFTSMANSHIP LOST TO MASS PRODUCTION. IT BEGAN
IN BRITAIN BUT GAINED A WIDER AUDIENCE IN THE UNITED STATES,
WHERE EXPONENTS COMBINED HAND AND MACHINE TECHNIQUES.

**TECO VASE** The American firm Teco was known for its green glaze and
architectural forms. This bulbous vase has eight leaf-shaped handles buttressed
to the base and a lobed rim embossed with lotus blossoms. *W:29cm (11½in).*

## REVIVALS GONE MAD

The late 19th century was a powerhouse of
industrial and military might, and wealthy citizens
enjoyed the benefits of unparalleled economic
success. The Great Exhibition of 1851 in London
had shown that no scheme was too elaborate for
British craftsmen; variety and novelty drove
architecture and design.

There were, however, dissenting voices.
A.W.N. Pugin argued that the Gothic architecture
of the Middle Ages had been the product of a
purer, more godly society, and that to replicate it
faithfully it was first necessary to adopt medieval
working practices. John Ruskin took up his plea.
A highly influential figure, Ruskin acted as a sort
of universal conscience for the cultural and artistic
philosophies of Victorian England. Like Pugin, he
held the medieval craftsman in particularly high
regard, believing him to have been free to express
himself through his art. He considered the lives of
Victorian craftsmen wretched by comparison,
maintaining that they were industrial servants,
acolytes of the "Goddess of Getting-on".

## WILLIAM MORRIS

A tireless campaigner, William Morris spread his
romantic vision of a golden age in which artist-
craftsmen found personal fulfilment through their
work. He encapsulated the principles of the Arts
and Crafts movement when he said, "Have nothing
in your houses that you
do not know to be
useful, or believe to be
beautiful." Utility was
fundamental to his
vision, as he rejected
tawdry decoration.
Beauty, it followed,
must be wrought by
other means – including
the careful design of
interiors so that every
element formed part of
a harmonious whole and,
on individual pieces, by
a visible understanding
of and respect for the
raw material.

## HANDMADE VERSUS MACHINE

As the movement spread from London to
provincial cities and, crucially, the countryside,
it acquired stylistic influences from elsewhere.
he Celtic Revival added pagan ornament to the
Catholic medieval tradition, and the pastoral
strain that had always been part of Morris's
vision matured as it absorbed vernacular craft
traditions from all over the country and abroad.

C.R. Ashbee made the most successful shift from
city to country, but even he eventually found that
cheaper manufactured versions of the handcrafted
goods made by his Guild of Handicraft forced him
out of business.

## AMERICAN INTERPRETATIONS

The entrenched interests of large-scale
manufacturing were less of a threat in the United
States, where there was a tradition of skilled
European migrants establishing small workshops.

**THE RED HOUSE** Philip Webb
designed William Morris's home in
Kent with Arts and Crafts principles
in mind. Even the well is unique,
inspired by Gothic architecture.

**GUSTAV STICKLEY TABLE** This luncheon table shows American
Arts and Crafts at its purest: plain and simple, with visible
structure and joinery. *c. 1900. H:69cm (27¼in).*

**RODMARTON MANOR** Ernest Barnsley and the Cotswold Group built and furnished the house to Arts and Crafts ideals for Claud and Margaret Biddulph, beginning in 1909. With local craftsmen, they worked by hand using local stone and timber. Most of the furniture was made in the Rodmarton workshops or by the Barnsleys.

During the second half of the 19th century American society consigned Civil War divisions to the past and took notice of the indigenous community, so long sidelined. Designers developed a national style to define all aspects of America's cultural make-up.

Even before the first Arts and Crafts exhibition was held in London in 1888, the architect Henry Hobson Richardson visited William Morris and began to evangelize on his behalf, recommending Morris & Co. furnishings to his own clients. He was followed by others, notably Elbert Hubbard and Gustav Stickley, whose artistic reconnaissance took them to leading department stores such as Liberty & Co. and Heal & Son. They returned to the United States impressed both by the honest craftsmanship of William Morris and the high volume of sales achieved by the high-street retailers. The American vision of Arts and Crafts combined both factors, and managed to reach a far wider audience than its English antecedent. Despite his revolutionary socialist politics, Morris's detestation of machinery can be seen as an elitist stance that stunted Arts and Crafts in Britain. Only once this bar had been removed could it reach its potential.

**MORRIS AND CO. TAPESTRY**
Designed by John Henry Dearle, the *mille-fleurs* (thousand flowers) tapestry is woven in coloured wools and mohair to show a woodland glade with rabbits, a fox, and fallow deer. *1892. W:460cm (184½in).*

# ELEMENTS OF STYLE

As a reaction against the fussy revivalist styles of the day, Arts and Crafts designers often sought inspiration in the past. They aimed to strip away artifice and return to simple craftsmanship. In Europe designers revered the pre-industrial age as a feudal utopia, while Americans held up the art of the native people as an ideal. Other cultures perceived to have preserved their artisan heritage, such as Japan and Persia, were similarly admired.

DETAIL OF WILLIAM MORRIS TAPESTRY

### MEDIEVAL INFLUENCE

Like John Ruskin, William Morris harboured a romanticized concept of the medieval period as a golden age of honest craftsmanship. The Gothic style provided a starting point for many Arts and Crafts designers. Gothic features such as oak furniture, simple natural forms, and stained glass are prominent in work of the period.

TUDRIC PEWTER VASE

### CELTIC INFLUENCE

Archibald Knox brought the Celtic heritage of his Isle of Man homeland to artistic prominence. Celtic motifs were enthusiastically followed up in Scotland. Entwined knots, Celtic crosses, and complex entrelac (interlaced) designs featured heavily, especially on metalware of this period.

ROOKWOOD VASE

### HANDCRAFTSMANSHIP

The point of Arts and Crafts philosophy was to restore joy in craft. The movement created a rebirth in vernacular handcraft traditions. Artisans invested time and effort handcrafting objects rather than using cheaper and quicker moulds.

ARTIFICER'S GUILD COPPER WALL SCONCE

### STYLIZED NATURE

Nature was a vital source of stylistic inspiration, with plant and animal motifs influenced by medieval stone- and metalwork. Wallpapers and textiles made prominent use of large, repeating flat patterns featuring stylized floral designs. These were coloured with natural plant and vegetable dyes.

DETAIL OF SILVER BOX WITH ENAMEL TOP

### ENAMELLING

The revival of this ancient technique as a popular decorative device was largely the work of London-based painter and silversmith Alexander Fisher. As an affordable alternative to precious stones, enamelling gave a splash of colour to metalware and furniture. Specialists created painterly enamel panels that were inset into jewellery and boxes.

STRAP HINGES
## HANDCRAFTED HARDWARE
To relieve the plain oak finishes of much Arts and Crafts furniture, many manufacturers made features of their applied metal hardware. A number of successful metal workshops was founded to make strap hinges, drop handles, and metal studs used to affix leather upholstery.

DETAIL OF CREWELWORK
## NEEDLEWORK
William Morris sparked a revival of traditional weaving and needlepoint crafts after he was captivated by medieval tapestries in France. His two-dimensional repeating designs featuring stylized foliage and birds were widely imitated. Elsewhere needlework societies kept up their folk traditions by practising the craft.

WILLIAM DE MORGAN TILE PANEL
## ISLAMIC ORNAMENT
The Islamic world was a fund of inspiration, especially after The Arab Hall in Leighton House in London aroused interest in Islamic decoration. Monochrome and lustre glazes owed a debt to Persian ceramics. Complex pierced aprons and galleries on furniture of the period also came from Islamic sources.

ROYCROFT COPPER CHARGER
## HAMMERED METAL
As proof of honest construction, the hand-hammered finish was characteristic of Arts and Crafts metalware, whether on silver, copper, or brass. Some workshops even applied hammer marks to machine-made items purely for their aesthetic appeal.

BRANDED ROHLFS MARK
## CRAFTSMEN'S MARKS
One of the effects of releasing the working man from the tyranny of the factory was to reinstate pride in craftsmanship, and many craftsmen marked their work with prominent initials and ciphers as a way of demonstrating this pride. Shrewd business minds also saw marking as a way of advertising their brands.

DETAIL OF GEORGE OHR GLAZE
## INNOVATIVE GLAZES
An explosion in the range and number of glazes available invigorated the ceramics industry. From Rookwood's high gloss Standard glaze to Grueby's trademark matte green, via a wealth of Chinese-inspired glazes such as *sang-de-boeuf* and flambé, never before had the Western ceramic tradition been so innovative.

EXOTIC INLAY ON A CHAIR BACK
## INLAYS
Although Arts and Crafts craftsmen tended to avoid complicated decorative techniques, some of them used exotic woods, base metals, and leather as ornamental inlays. A labour-intensive technique, using intricate inlays not only lightened dark stained oak, it gave craftsmen a chance to flaunt their considerable skills.

DETAIL OF STAINED-GLASS WINDOW
## STAINED GLASS
The ecclesiastical Gothic roots of the Arts and Crafts philosophy found ideal expression in stained glass. Long-forgotten techniques were revived when new windows were made for church renovations. These techniques were adapted by lighting manufacturers such as Tiffany to stunning effect.

# THE AESTHETIC MOVEMENT

THE AESTHETIC MOVEMENT FLOURISHED IN BRITAIN DURING THE 1870S AND 1880S, INSTIGATING A LIVELY DEBATE ABOUT THE NATURE OF ART. IT HAD A CONSIDERABLE INFLUENCE ON THE EMERGING ARTS AND CRAFTS MOVEMENT.

**JAMES MCNEILL WHISTLER** An expatriate American artist, Whistler was a leading figure of the Aesthetic Movement, rejecting realism in favour of decorative paintings characterized above all by harmony of colour.

At the heart of the Aesthetic Movement was a rejection of the link between art and morality claimed by thinkers such as John Ruskin, and a reaction against the French Revival styles of the high Victorian period. Led by the artists Frederic Leighton and James McNeill Whistler, the Aesthetes firmly believed in the notion of art for art's sake, namely that the form, colour, and decorative features of a work of art were more important than its subject. This pursuit of beauty linked the many strands of the complex movement.

## JAPANESE INFLUENCE

One of the main pillars of the Aesthetic style was the influence of Japan. After years of self-imposed isolation, Japanese ports had reopened for trade in 1859, creating a huge demand for all things Japanese. The first global showcase of Japanese decorative arts was the 1862 International Exhibition in London. Up until then, most people had had very little exposure even to the export lacquer or Kakiemon wares coveted by wealthy collectors. The exhibition created a great clamour, and ceramicists, cabinet-makers, and metalworkers across Europe and North America were soon producing work in the Japonaiserie style. It was characterized by Japanese-influenced glazes and spare, rectilinear construction. The best craftsmen avoided simply applying Japanese motifs to Western forms and tried to fuse the Oriental tradition with their own work.

Meanwhile, Gothic Revival was becoming the English national style in the late 19th century, due partly to the influence of Charles Barry and A.W.N. Pugin's Gothic Revival design for the Houses of Parliament in London. This also strongly influenced the Aesthetic Movement.

## AESTHETIC INTERIORS

The typical Aesthetic interior was decorated in tertiary greens, blues, gold, and white. The furniture was simple in line and ebonized, with

**SATIRICAL TEAPOT** Modelled by James Hadley for Royal Worcester, with Oscar Wilde one side, a fashionable lady the other, the mutual limp wrists form the handle and spout. c.1882. H:15cm (6in).

**JAPANESE VASE** Slender ovoid forms, gilding, and dense polychrome painting, here of Oriental figures in a landscape, characterize Satsuma earthenware of the Meiji period. 1868–1912. H:31cm (12¼in).

spindle legs, often based on the work of E.W. Godwin, one of the most influential designers of the day. Cabinets were made from strips of ebonized wood or sometimes bamboo arranged in a symmetrical, rectilinear form. They were often inlaid with marquetry or ceramic panels and displayed objects, usually Gothic Revival trinkets or Japanese-style porcelain.

Peacock feathers and sunflowers – both archetypal Aesthetic motifs – were displayed alongside handcrafted items and further decoration was provided by Japanese prints, screens, and fans.

A growing distinction between utilitarian and art furniture was reflected in other areas of the decorative arts. The field of ceramics in particular enjoyed an explosion of creativity. Firms such as Doulton championed a revival of interest in the decorative possibilities of earthenware and stoneware, while Worcester and Minton developed glazes and new decorative techniques for porcelain that demonstrated the influence of Japanese ceramic, lacquer, and cloisonné wares.

**Bamboo** is a common Oriental motif

**Exotic plants** echo Oriental blue and white export porcelain

**JAPONAISERIE JARDINIÈRE** Made by Pinder Bourne & Co., the porcelain frame is moulded to look like bamboo, while the underglaze blue-and-white porcelain panels depict Oriental-style plants and birds. c.1880. H:20cm (8in).

**Japanese-style** painted floral panels flank the mirror glass

**Marquetry** in stained red fruitwood contrasts with the ebonized carcase

**The legs** are ring-turned and gilded

**SIDE CABINET** The form, decoration, and colour are inspired by Japan in this dramatic construction of glass and ebonized, inlaid, and painted wood, by Edwards & Roberts. c.1880. H:171cm (68½in).

**PEACOCK ROOM** This room was designed by Thomas Jeckyll and was originally in the London home of Frederick R. Leyland, a wealthy shipowner, where it displayed his collection of blue and white porcelain. Whistler retouched the room in Aesthetic taste as a suitable setting for his painting. The walls bore gilded shelves and huge gold paintings of fighting peacocks and the ceiling was painted with gold leaf and peacock feathers.

# FURNITURE

AFTER THE GREAT EXHIBITION OF 1851, A NEW WAVE OF CRAFTSMEN TOOK
AUGUSTUS PUGIN'S REWORKING OF ENGLISH GOTHIC AS THE STARTING POINT
FOR FURNITURE WITH LESS PAGEANT AND MORE SUBSTANCE.

## MORRIS AND CO.

Inspired by the task of furnishing the Red House –
his new Kent home designed by Philip Webb –
William Morris founded Morris, Marshall,
Faulkner & Co. in 1861 with members of his
inner circle. As a reaction against poor industrial
design, the aim was to coordinate a range of
furniture using local woods such as oak and ash
and other natural materials like rushes for seating.
At first, oak was often ebonized in the Aesthetic
Movement style, easing country-style furniture into
the drawing room. Alternatively it was polished to
a warm brown yellow. Decoration was minimal,
taking nature or medieval legend as inspiration
or emphasizing the structure with large hinges
and exposed dowels securing extended tenons.

Webb gradually took responsibility for the firm's
furniture while William Morris concentrated on
textile design. Chairs and settees

by the company were often upholstered with
fabrics designed by Morris as part of an attempt
to create a harmonious, integrated interior. In
sympathy with influential campaigners such as
Bruce Talbert and Charles Eastlake, Webb had
nothing but scorn for the machine-cut veneers
that covered so much 19th-century furniture and
advocated the use of plain wooden surfaces that
exposed the structural beauty of his designs.

Philip Webb was responsible for much of the firm's
most enduring work, including the redrafting of the
original designs discovered in a Sussex carpenter's
shop that became the celebrated adjustable Morris
Chair. He resigned his full-time position within the
company in 1875 when it was restructured to
become Morris & Co.

Many of the brightest creative lights of the day
became involved with the cabinet-making side of
Morris's company, including W.A.S. Benson and

painter-poet Dante Gabriel
Rossetti. Morris & Co. furniture
was marketed in two distinct tiers, referred to by
Morris as "necessary workaday" tables and chairs
and "state" non-essential items such as sideboards
and cabinets. Unlike the plain furniture, these

**OAK HALL CHAIR** An early
and rare example by C.F.A.
Voysey, this chair has five
vertical back splats, paddle
arms, tapering legs and posts,
and a (new) leather seat.
c.1885. H:21.5cm (55in).

**MORRIS CHAIR** This classic Morris & Co.
design includes original upholstery and
an ebonized walnut frame in which the
elegant parallel curves of the back legs
and arms are characteristically united
by ring-turned spindles. c.1866.
H:101.5cm (40in).

**DRAWING ROOM AT STANDEN** Built 1892–1894 in West Sussex for James Beale by architect Phillip Webb,
Standen was decorated throughout by Morris & Co. Its original furniture, fabrics, and wallpapers were made with the
traditional craftsmanship that underpinned the Arts and Crafts movement.

## THE VERNACULAR TRADITION

As part of the manifesto that celebrated the rustic and the ancient, the Arts and Crafts movement embraced vernacular tradition – conventional practice built up over time and centred around a local area. Furniture-makers in each British region had their own idiosyncracies and expertise.

The Sussex Chair of Morris & Co. was influenced by cottage chairs in the county of its name. There were several versions, including a round-seated one by Rossetti. Ernest Gimson also learned how to manufacture rush-seated chairs, from a Worcestershire rather than Sussex maker. Gimson and Barnsley incorporated vernacular motifs not traditionally associated with furniture, using pitchfork shapes and modelling headboards for beds after wagon backs.

**SUSSEX CHAIR** This chair was designed by Ernest Gimson and made by Edward Gardiner. Curvaceous, horizontal back splats and delicate spindle work make the rush-seated ash frame more sophisticated than its original rustic model. *c.1890. H:85cm (33½in).*

## CRAFTSMEN'S GUILDS

Gimson and the Barnsley brothers moved to the Cotswolds to escape city life and fulfil a rural dream of community involvement, just as Charles Ashbee did some years later. Both moves established rural guilds, set up for a community of craftsmen to work together and learn from each other. Although the foreman of Gimson & Barnsley's furniture workshop was a migrant Dutchman, the labour it employed was drawn overwhelmingly from the area around Sapperton where it was based and it apprenticed a number of local boys. Provincial expertise was crucial to the success of the Cotswold School – Richard Harrison, Sapperton's resident wheelwright, took on the task of sourcing locally available woods such as ash, deal, and oak and supplying them to Gimson's workshop.

Guilds flourished in the capital, too. The Art Worker's Guild, to which Voysey belonged, was founded at the Charing Cross Hotel in London in 1884. It was a forum where designers of anything from buildings to sculpture and furniture met to exchange ideas under the motto "Art is unity".

Whether urban or rural, the concept of the guild – with its connotations of skilled craftsmanship and a respect for the artisan tradition – was very important within the Arts and Crafts movement.

**REVOLVING BOOKCASE** Designed and made in walnut and fruitwood by Cotswold School craftsman Sidney Barnsley, the bookcase is raised on a tri-form base and characteristically incorporates exposed dovetail joints. *1920s. W:38cm (15in).*

"state" pieces could be "as elaborate as we can with carving, inlaying, or painting".

Architect Charles Voysey had little sympathy for such luxury or for decorative baubles. His furniture had elegant, mannered lines that relied on the beauty of oak and minimal pierced decoration. Trademarks of his furniture include tapered square-section legs that continue as uprights and terminate in flat caps.

## REGIONAL VARIATIONS

After leaving London, architect-designers Ernest Gimson and Ernest and Sidney Barnsley moved to the Cotswolds in Gloucestershire in 1892. Sidney Barnsley, in particular, took to cabinet-making and became the archetypal solitary artisan

craftsman. He used oak, with little if any ornament. Any work he could not cope with he referred to his brother Ernest and Ernest Gimson, who created a thriving furniture-making business. They designed for walnut and ebony as well as oak, and used inlays of holly alongside exotic materials such as ivory and abalone shell. Known as the Cotswold School, the work of these craftsmen had a lasting influence.

The vortex of the Arts and Crafts movement in Scotland was in Glasgow. Students at the School of Art received intensive practical training in their craft in on-site studios. The firm of Wylie & Lochhead prospered on the proceeds of Glasgow's shipping industry, fitting the luxury liners built on the Clyde with good-quality furnishings.

**MAHOGANY DINING TABLE** Designed by Philip Webb, made by Morris & Co., and almost identical to a table at Standen, this has an incised-edged oval top above a central support encircled by six ring-turned legs, linked by ring-turned stretchers. *1860s. L:176cm (70¼in).*

**OAK CASKET** The abalone, mother-of-pearl, and coromandel wood inlays in this pigeonholed and multiple-drawer construction are typical of Sidney Barnsley's more elaborate work. *1920s. W:53.5cm (21in).*

## THE STICKLEY DYNASTY

Born to German migrant parents in Wisconsin, the five Stickley brothers – Gustav, Charles, Albert, Leopold, and John George – achieved various degrees of artistic and financial success as manufacturers of Arts and Crafts furniture. When Gustav Stickley dedicated the first issue of his design magazine *The Craftsman* to William Morris, he was consciously allying himself with the father of the British Arts and Crafts movement. Yet, like his brothers, his interpretation of it was distinctly American. The Mission style that came o be associated with the Stickley family had a profound effect on American living, influencing architecture and interiors across the country from New York to Washington state.

Mission became a general term for American Arts and Crafts furniture, but its roots were in Gustav Stickley's statement that "a chair, a table, a bookcase or bed [must] fill its mission of usefulness as well as it possibly can...the only decoration that seems in keeping with structural forms lies in the emphasizing of certain features of the construction, such as the mortise, tenon, key, and dovetail." In keeping with this assertion, Stickley furniture was made from natural materials such as oak with seats and upholstery made of leather or rush. The grain of the quarter-sawn oak was brought out with a finish of fumed ammonia. Forms were mostly

**ILLUSTRATION FROM *THE CRAFTSMAN* MAGAZINE** Gustav Stickley spread Arts and Crafts principles in this influential monthly publication. The notion that design begins with a room is evident in this extract, as is his belief that furniture should suit "the place it had to occupy and the work it had to do". *1910–12. H:28cm (11in).*

rectilinear, based on 17th- and 18th-century settles and trestle tables.

Gustav Stickley, the most prolific of the brothers, originally trained as a stonemason before starting work at his uncle's chair factory in Pennsylvania at the age of 17. During the late 1890s Gustav travelled to England where he met the key players of the Arts and Crafts movement. Already an admirer

of John Ruskin and William Morris, Stickley reaffirmed his own conviction in the beauty of simplicity. A visit to the *1900 Exposition Universelle* in Paris, which featured among other things a full-size replica of a medieval French town, only confirmed his distaste for clumsy reproduction and overwrought decoration. These considerations did not, however, prevent

**Exposed circular dowel ends** are a recurring feature of Stickley joinery

**Square-section posts** exemplify the solid, linear forms used by the Sticklays

**The figuring** of quarter-sawn oak is distinctive, accentuated by the hallmark fumed finish

**Stickley hardware** ranged from copper to pewter to, as with these pulls and strap hinges, wrought iron

**FUMED OAK SIDEBOARD** Gustav Stickley's design is raised on six posts, has four central drawers flanked by cupboards set under a plain, rectangular top with a plate-rack splashback, and wrought-iron hardware. *W:178cm (70in).*

Stickley from using machinery to maintain consistent high quality. Stickley spurned the exclusive use of labour-intensive handcraftsmanship of British Arts and Crafts in favour of a pragmatic American blend of traditional craft and machine technology.

## CRAFTSMANSHIP EXCELLENCE

On returning to the United States, Stickley was flushed with a new enthusiasm for his craftsman ideal. His furniture business was booming and he acquired and refitted Crouse Stables near Syracuse. He christened his new premises the Craftsman Building, using it to house not only his furniture workshops but also a metalwork studio, lecture theatre, and publishing offices for *The Craftsman*, the most important contemporary periodical of the American Arts and Crafts movement.

Ostensibly a marketing tool for Stickley's furniture, *The Craftsman* grew to cover philosophy and architecture, and published house designs by Harvey Ellis. Ellis did much to temper Stickley's austere taste with a more delicate edge. Although their working relationship lasted for little over a year, cut short by Ellis's untimely death in 1904, the influence on Stickley was profound. Craftsman furniture designed by Ellis has decorative touches such as inlaid marquetry that owe much to British designers, including C.R. Mackintosh and Baillie Scott.

**DROP-FRONT DESK** Designed in oak by architect Harvey Ellis, it features floral inlay work, in nickel and stained fruitwood, that characterizes Ellis's lighter touch. *c.1903. W:77cm (30¼in).*

## L. & J.G. STICKLEY

Following the success of their Onondaga shops (*see below*), Leopold and John George renamed their firm L. & J.G. Stickley and unveiled their first line of furniture at a 1905 trade show in Grand Rapids, Michigan. They marketed their product as "simple furniture built along mission lines", clearly influenced by the work of their brother Gustav. Unlike Gustav, however, they had little time for costly handcraftsmanship and opted instead to produce their furniture mechanically. L. & J.G. Stickley were financially successful in a way that Gustav never was, thanks to their better business acumen. In the early 1920s the firm used traditional New England and Pennsylvania furniture designs as inspiration for a new range called the Cherry Valley Collection. They married vernacular American form with Native American wood by using black cherry sourced from the Adirondack Mountains.

**OAK ROCKING CHAIR** L. & J.G. Stickley's version of the Morris Chair is a rocker with flat paddle arms and a leather drop-in seat and back cushion. The back is fixed rather than articulated. *W:80cm (35in).*

## ONONDAGA SHOPS

When Leopold and John George Stickley set up business together in Fayetteville, New York, in 1904, they used the name Onondaga Shops for two years before rebranding themselves as Handcraft. Onondaga was the name of a tribe of Native Americans from the upper New York area. Leopold and John George became successful by producing more economical versions of the Mission furniture made by Gustav Stickley. They took advantage of their brother's relaxed attitude to issues of copyright – Gustav often encouraged architects and designers to customize and so appropriate his plans. Leopold and John George scaled down Gustav's designs, to make them more cost-effective. They also turned out work from designs by Frank Lloyd Wright *(see pp.260–61)*.

**OAK SERVER** Raised on square posts, with an undershelf, a splash-back, and drawers with copper ring pulls, the simple form is typical of the Onondaga Shop. *1904–06. W:110cm (44in).*

## STICKLEY BROTHERS

The first furniture company founded by members of the Stickley family was Stickley Brothers, based in Binghampton, New York, in the 1880s. This early venture involved Charles, Albert, and Gustav, although Charles left to work with John George in Michigan during the early 1890s. After Gustav's departure, Albert was left at the helm of the original family firm. The features that define Stickley Brothers furniture are similar to those used by other members of the family, including plain oak and mahogany surfaces.

Albert's Quaint Furniture trademark was also applied to more decorative items inspired by members of the Scottish School. Albert Stickley's furniture is generally rigidly rectilinear, with conspicuously exposed structural elements including through-tenoned stretchers and rails. He used a variety of stained finishes ranging from rich mahogany red to a yellow-tinged limed oak colour.

**LAMP TABLE** English and Scottish forms are evident in this Stickley Bros. oak table, notably the cut-out spade motifs at the sides, the gently curved stretchers, and the defined feet. *1890s. H:75cm (30in).*

**LARGE CHANDELIER** A hammered and pierced domed iron ring supports nine pendant copper and amber-yellow glass lanterns in this rare Onondaga Metal Shops light fitting. *1904–06. H:80cm (32in).*

## AMERICAN WORKSHOPS

Following in the footsteps of the Stickley brothers, American cabinet-makers began to take a keen interest in the Arts and Crafts style around 1900. Like Gustav Stickley, they often took a pragmatic approach to industrialization, considering it to be liberating rather than constricting if used well. Although anathema to William Morris's ethic, machine production actually enabled American manufacturers to come closer to the ideal of supplying good quality furniture to the masses than Morris ever did. The idealism that spawned the English guild revival was also at work in the United States, and a number of rural craft communities was founded.

### SOLID AND SPARTAN

The city of Grand Rapids in Michigan became something of a centre for the American furniture industry from the 1880s. As well as L.&J.G. Stickley, it was home to Charles Limbert, founder of the Limbert Furniture Co. in 1894. His work owed as much to the early modernity of Charles Rennie Mackintosh as it did to the English and American Arts and Crafts movements. Sparsely

decorated with keyed-through tenons and unobtrusive metalware, Limbert's furniture was mostly made of oak, often stained and sometimes with combinations of contrasting stained finishes. Cut-out patterns relieve the plain oak surfaces on many of his designs, varying from simple squares and circles to half moons and hearts.

### AMERICAN CRAFT COMMUNITIES

The oldest surviving artist's community in the United States, the Byrdcliffe Arts Colony, was established by an Englishman – Ralph Radcliffe Whitehead – and his American wife Jane Byrde McCall. Centred around their home at White Pines near Woodstock in New York, the Byrdcliffe community included craftsmen from many different fields, so ideas flowed between disciplines. Furniture was handmade on the site – often using poplar as a cheaper alternative to oak – and was sometimes painted by artists in the colony. Jane McCall contributed landscapes painted in oils.

The most ambitious and successful American craft community of the period was Elbert Green Hubbard's Roycroft in East Aurora, New York. Inspired by the Kelmscott Press run by William Morris, Hubbard established the Roycroft Print Shop in 1895 as a publishing venture, but cast his brief wider as the years passed. His band of Roycrofters began to attract tourists and a small woodworking operation was set up to create gifts and trinkets to sell them. This part of the business expanded and by 1910 the Roycroft presses were

**OAK CHIFFONIER** Attributed to Jane Byrd Whitehead (née McCall) of the Byrdcliffe Arts colony, it is raised on square corner posts and features a pair of cupboard doors, each with an oil-painted rural landscape. *1904. H:68cm (27¼in). 1904.*

*The top rail* is in a rectilinear style

*The composition* of the drawers and door is symmetrical

**OAK SIDEBOARD** The pronounced linear style promoted by Charles Rennie Mackintosh, the Glasgow School, and the Viennese Secessionists is echoed in this piece by the Michigan-based Limbert Furniture Co. *1900–10. H:146cm (58½in).*

*Slightly tapered legs* and a gently curved apron lighten the composition

**MORRIS CHAIR** The quarter-sawn oak frame with flat-plank arms, legs, and stretchers, and an arched apron, is upholstered in leather. It bears the Limbert Furniture Co.'s branded "Arts & Crafts made in Grand Rapids and Holland" mark. *c.1910. W:72cm (28½in).*

busy producing mail-order catalogues for the huge range of furniture made on site.

The furniture produced by the Roycrofters was made from solid oak to a high standard. Early pioneers of the flat pack, the Roycrofters dispatched furniture in pieces, to be assembled at its destination. For this reason they relied heavily on pegged through-tenon joins, which could be dismantled and reassembled without tools or glue. Every aspect was handcrafted – the on-site metalworking shop produced hand-hammered iron and copper hinges, studs, handles, and locks. Roycroft furniture was stamped with a crossed orb encircling an R, a mark based on that of a medieval monastic scribe. Hubbard died aboard the ocean liner Lusitania when it was torpedoed in 1915, but his community continued to thrive under his son's direction until 1938.

## SHOP OF THE CRAFTERS

After seeing Arts and Crafts furniture at the Louisiana Purchase Exhibition in 1904, retailer Oscar Onken founded the Shop of the Crafters in Cincinnati, Ohio, to give shape to his own vision of the style. In partnership with a Hungarian designer named Paul Horti, Onken imported Austrian woods, which he used to create contrasting coloured panels and marquetry designs. Horti brought a European flavour to the Shop's furniture – like Charles Limbert, he was influenced by Scottish School and Secessionist designs and relied heavily on rectilinear members with cut-outs for decorative effect. The attention given to metalware as part of the integrated design was as close here as at other establishments. Strap hinges and bevelled knobs complemented the rich fumed finishes of the stained oak. Promoted nationally in newspapers and magazines, the Shop of the Crafter's Arts and Crafts furniture remained popular until it was discontinued around 1920.

**INLAID CABINET** Made from quarter-sawn oak with a raised drawer, open shelf, and cupboard, this cabinet displays fruitwood marquetry typical of the Shop of the Crafters. *1905–10. H:129.5cm (51in).*

**OAK ARMCHAIR** Dark stained and of solid, mortise-and-tenon, flat-plank construction, this Shop of the Crafters' piece has a shaped top rail and fruitwood marquetry. *c.1910. H:92.5cm (37in).*

**OAK TABOURET** The plank sides have keyhole cut-outs. One is carved with the primary Roycroft mark: a double-barred cross and orb enclosing an "R", adapted from a 14th-century European monastic manuscript. *1900–10. H:52cm (20½in).*

**PYRAMIDAL BOOKCASE** Cut into graduated shelves, flanked by flared sides scalloped at the base and secured with pegged-through tenons, the oak displays a warm, nut-brown patina often favoured by Roycroft. It is carved with his decorative mark: an oak leaf. *1900–10. W:51cm (20in) at base.*

## GOTHIC REVIVAL STYLE

British and American craftsmen returned time and again to the Gothic roots of the Arts and Crafts style. Scotsman Bruce Talbert had been among the first to praise and popularize the honest construction of Gothic-style furniture in his 1867 book *Gothic Forms Applied to Furniture.*

In the United States Charles Rohlfs made furniture with pierced and decorated Gothic motifs and drew on Moorish and Scandinavian traditions. Gothic arches and metal accessories show Rohlfs's sympathy with Gothic design – he described his own work as having "the spirit of today blended with the poetry of the medieval ages".

Based in Buffalo, New York, Rohlfs established his own studio in 1891, eventually employing a team of craftsmen to execute his designs. He exhibited to great critical acclaim and won many prestigious commissions, including work at Buckingham Palace in England.

**Carved flame finials** emphasize the height of the desk

**Fretwork motifs,** echoed in the carving, include quatrefoils and fleur-de-lys

**Typical intricacies** of construction include a side cabinet with shelving

**DROP-FRONT DESK** This Charles Rohlfs desk is made of dark oak carved with Gothic motifs, and bears his branded shopmark: an "R" set within a fretwork saw. *1900. H:139.5cm (55in).*

# FURNITURE GALLERY

These Arts and Crafts pieces celebrate the vernacular traditions of country and Mission furniture. Typical stylistic features include exposed structural elements such as dowels and mortise-and-tenon joints. Combined with prominent handles and chunky metal hinges, these are often the only forms of decoration on display. Other marks of craftsmanship include inlays of contrasting woods or metals and adzed surfaces.

## KEY

**1.** Hallstand with stylized tubular motifs and a tiled panel by Harris Lebus. c.1905. H:210cm (82½in). ③ **2.** Aesthetic Movement sideboard with Japanese lacquer panels attributed to E.A. Godwin. c.1880. W:127cm (50in). ⑧ **3.** Oak side table with a lattice back by Sidney Barnsley. W:68.5cm (27in). ③ **4.** Display cabinet attributed to E.A. Taylor, with repoussé fenestration and marquetry inlay. c.1905. H:175cm (69in). ② **5.** Glasgow School cabinet with stained glass windows. W:107cm (42¼in). ① **6.** Guild of Handicraft music cabinet on bracket feet, designed by C.R. Ashbee. c.1899. H:124.5cm (49in). ① **7.** Magazine stand with demi-lune cut-outs by Charles Limbert. c.1910. H:94cm (37in). ③

1 | Harris Lebus hallstand

3 | Barnsley side table

7 | Limbert magazine stand

6 | Pine music cabinet

8 | Limbert lamp table

4 | E.A. Taylor display cabinet

5 | Glasgow School cabinet

9 | Shop of the Crafters library table

2 | Aesthetic Movement sideboard

**8.** Lamp table with corbels and cut-out sides, by Charles Limbert. W:112.5cm (45in). ④
**9.** Library table with slatted legs and spade feet by the Shop of the Crafters. c.1910. ③
**10.** Stained oak settee with unusual carving, by Charles Rohlfs. 1900. W:114cm (45in). ①
**11.** Oak hall settle with an arched slat back and a hinged seat. W:122cm (48in). ① **12.** Walnut armchair with a heart cut-out, by E. Punnet. c.1903. H:82cm (32in). ① **13.** Clissett-type elm ladderback chair, designed by Ernest Gimson. ③ **14.** Desk chair with a leather seat by Robert "Mouseman" Thompson. c.1910. H:80cm (31½in). ① **15.** Mahogany elbow chair, the broad back splat with marquetry floral motif. **16.** English oak armchair with a tall carved and panelled back. c.1900. H:130.5cm (51½in). ②

**10** Rohlfs stained oak settee

**11** Oak hall settle

**12** Walnut armchair

**13** Ladder-back armchair

**14** Oak desk chair

**15** Liberty chair

**16** English oak armchair

# CERAMICS

THE LINK BETWEEN MOST SUCCESSFUL ARTS AND CRAFTS CERAMICISTS WAS
A TIRELESS QUEST TO DEVELOP NEW AND BETTER GLAZING TECHNIQUES. IN
THE UNITED STATES ROOKWOOD SET A HIGH STANDARD.

## ROOKWOOD

Despite the Arts and Crafts ideal of the solitary
craftsman, a great deal of pottery was in fact
produced by companies that followed the
principles of Ruskin and Morris. It says much
for the Arts and Crafts ideal of restoring joy to
craftsmanship that perhaps the finest and most
successful American art pottery started as a hobby.
Maria Longworth Nichols Storer was one of many
young women in the Cincinnati area who found
diversion in the popular pastime of painting china
blanks. What made her exceptional was her latent
ambition, combined with the generous backing of
her wealthy family. This enabled her to hire the
best local ceramicists to help her set up her own
pottery, named Rookwood after the family estate.

The early years of the Rookwood Pottery,
established in 1880, were characterized by trial
and error experiments. From the beginning, Storer
was deeply interested in Japanese ceramics and
employed Kataro Shirayamadani
from Japan as one of the
firm's main decorators.

**STANDARD GLAZE VASE** The slender, shouldered
oviform body is designed by Kataro Shiriayamadani and
painted with naturalistic chrysanthemums in shades of
orange, yellow, and green under Rookwood's Standard
brown glaze. *1898. H:30.5cm (12in).*

*The stylized silver
mounts* echo the
painted floral imagery

*The Standard
brown glaze*
imparts its
characteristic
mellow hue

*The naturalistic
painting* by
Shiriayamadani is of
exceptional quality

**LOOP-HANDLED PITCHER** Painted insects and
leaves by Albert Valentien are contrasted on this
pitcher with an incised geometric border around the
shoulder, and enriched with gilt accents. *c.1883.
H:23cm (9in).*

**JAPANESE-STYLE VASE** The cylindrical form
is incised with script and an Oriental peasant
in relief, and these are highlighted in reds,
browns, and greens against a tan ground.
*1882. H:29.25cm (11¼in).*

*The silver mounts*
in elaborate Art
Nouveau style are by
the Gorham Silver Co.

## THE CHEMISTRY OF SUCCESS

When William Watts Taylor was appointed manager in 1883, Rookwood became more commercial. The following year, decorator Laura Fry began to apply coloured slip and, later, background colours with an atomizer, producing the phenomenally smooth finish for which the pottery is renowned. The ceramist Artus van Briggle catered to the continued preoccupation with Asian forms and motifs. During his 13 years with the pottery, he took working holidays in Paris where he studied, among other things, the Oriental collection at the Museé des Arts Décoratifs. In 1889 Rookwood was awarded a gold medal at the *Exposition Universelle* in Paris and the firm recorded a profit for the first time. Maria Storer retired the next year, in 1890.

Among the most celebrated wares produced by Rookwood are the vessels and plaques decorated with underglaze portraits. Leading artists employed by the company, such as Grace Young and Matt Daly, painted a series depicting African Americans and Native Americans. Other designs were drawn from nature, featuring forest and sea landscapes resplendent with flowers, fungi, birds, and fish. The common theme was the beauty and abundance of the American landscape. Some of the more prestigious pieces had sinuous silver overlays.

Rookwood pottery has a whole range of factory marks and features artist's ciphers, process marks, shape numbers, and even clay marks.

**AMERICAN INDIAN SERIES** The Chief High Hawk Standard Glaze plaque (*above*) was painted by Grace Young in 1903, and the red clay charger (*right*) by Henry François Farny in 1881. *H:37.5cm (14¼in).*

**Painted pressed red clay charger** D:28cm (11in)

## ROOKWOOD GLAZES

Two chemists, Karl Lagenbeck and Stanley Burt, ushered in a golden age when the Rookwood Pottery perfected many of the outstanding glazes that made it such a success. The first great accomplishment was the Standard glaze, developed in 1884. A translucent high gloss with a yellow tinge, Standard glaze makes the underlying artwork look darker and heavier. Production of the glaze ceased in 1909 as it was becoming less popular.

Also developed in 1884, Iris is a clear lead-based glaze with a high sheen. It was named after the painted irises that decorate so many of the pots coated with the glaze. A variation known as Black Iris also exists.

Another high gloss glaze, Sea Green gives the underglaze decoration a blue-green colour and an impression of depth. It was particularly suited to seascapes and fish, but also used for flowers.

Noting the success of Grueby's matte glaze, Rookwood devised its own version, simply called Matte, around 1900. Flat and opaque with a relatively coarse texture, it was made and applied in a wide variety of tones.

Vellum, considered to be the link between Rookwood's gloss and matte glazes, was introduced in about 1900. It creates a hazy effect on the underglaze decoration, as if it were viewed through a film. Vellum was generally clear, although it was also available with green and yellow tints. Flowers and landscapes were usual subject matter.

One of Rookwood's later creations, the Jewel Porcelain glaze was first used in 1916. A clear gloss glaze, it is remarkable for its tiny air bubbles that produce a similar effect to the Vellum glaze, but without the same waxiness.

**LIMOGES-STYLE VASE** The French ceramics-inspired imagery of birds in flight and perched on branches was handpainted by N. J. Hirschfeld, and is enriched by a glossy glaze. *1882. H:19cm (7¾in).*

**IRIS GLAZE VASE** Carved in high relief by Matthew A. Daly, hyacinths and leaves are painted in subtle shades of blue and green, set against a mottled and graduated indigo and violet ground. *1901. H:20.5cm (8in).*

**VELLUM GLAZE VASE** The wild mushroom decoration was painted by Carl Schmidt in shades of brown, orange, yellow, green, and grey, against a blue-graduating-into-celadon ground. *1906. H:18cm (7in).*

**MATTE GLAZE VASE** Designed by Kataro Shiriyamadani, this vase is modelled with branches of ginkgo leaves and berries in shallow relief under a typically soft and hazy green and yellow Matte glaze. *1905. H:26.5cm (10½in).*

**JEWEL PORCELAIN GLAZE VASE** Also painted by Carl Schmidt, this vase depicts lavender, irises, and leaves in characteristically soft pastel tones of lavender, white, and green on a shaded blue-green ground. *1925. H:30cm (11¾in).*

**SEA GREEN GLAZE VASE** Designed by Anne Marie Valentin, this vase features an overlaid, languid, verdigris-bronze nude above the typically opalescent Sea Green-glazed ground. *1900. H:13cm (5¼in).*

**GEORGE OHR VASE** This corseted vase is glazed in four panels: brown and green speckled, caramel speckled, gunmetal, and bottle green, all over a marbleized clay body. *1890s. H:21cm (8¼in).*

*The gaping neck* recalls young birds feeding in the nest

*The scrolled handles* suggest tendril-like forms

*Innovative glazing* is a feature of Ohr's earlier pieces

**GEORGE OHR TEAPOT** The large, C-handled vessel with a serpentine spout is finished in one of Ohr's flambé glazes, here dynamically streaked and mottled from blood red to emerald green. *1890s. W:22.75cm (9in).*

## AMERICAN ART POTTERY

The work done at the Biloxi Art Pottery in Mississippi by George Ohr between about 1880 and 1910 remains unique in the world of art pottery. Known to many as the "mad potter of Biloxi", Ohr was an inimitable artisan firmly in the Arts and Crafts mould.

### GEORGE OHR'S MUD BABIES

Not only did Ohr dig his own clay and formulate his own glazes, but he also built his own pottery and throwing wheel – all this with just the occasional help of his son Leo. Complete freedom from organized industry at every level of his operation allowed Ohr to develop a highly personal relationship with his craft. He thought of his prolific stockpile of vessels as his "mud babies". After a fire destroyed his workshop in 1894, he referred to the charred pots rescued from the wreckage as "burnt babies".

**GEORGE OHR POT** With a folded petal rim and a whimsical pinched and applied face, the pot is made of scroddled clay bisque. Like most of Ohr's bisque vessels, it bears his signature in script on the underside. *c.1905. W:14cm (5½in).*

*Scroddled* describes the mottled appearance that comes from scraps of different coloured clays

Ohr's virtuosity at the wheel is evident in the eggshell delicacy of his vessels. It is still unclear how he managed to contort such thin clay into the bizarre twisted, folded, and dented forms that characterize his work – it has certainly never been replicated. Many of Ohr's contemporaries, although exasperated by what they considered his stubborn disdain for the principles of good design, were full of praise for his glazes. Ohr created matte and lustre glazes as well as a wide range of vibrant hues including yellow and pink, but was always more interested in form and left more and more of his work unglazed as time went by.

## ECCENTRIC EXPERIMENTERS

As extravagantly eccentric as he was gifted, Ohr cultivated an enormous waxed moustache and was a consummate self-publicist. Like many a neglected genius, he was firmly convinced that he would one day be revered as a visionary. He put up signs at exhibitions proclaiming himself "the greatest art potter on Earth" and even delivered a selection of his work to the Smithsonian Institution, including an umbrella stand inscribed with a rambling and prophetic dedication ending, "This pot is here, and I am the potter who was." Ohr's legacy – thousands of unsold mud babies packed and crated in his old pottery – was discovered in the late 1960s, some 50 years after his death, and led eventually to a reappraisal of his work.

Another precursor of the studio pottery movement was Theophilus Brouwer. Like Ohr, Brouwer was personally involved in every stage of the production process, from sourcing the clay right through to decorating the finished pots. He was another eccentric with a talent for self-promotion: the entrance to his Middle Lane Pottery in East Hampton was marked with the jawbones of

## CHELSEA KERAMIC ART

The Chelsea Keramic Art Works was established in 1872, one of the first dedicated American art potteries. Early innovations included a fine redware burnished with linseed oil, made for two years from 1876. In 1877 Chelsea began to produce glazed faience pieces, eventually inspiring Rookwood and Grueby. Although the firm sometimes opted for the pick-and-mix approach to historicism so hated by Morris and other Arts and Crafts purists, the quality of its glazes was outstanding.

Chelsea is notable for sacrificing commercial success in favour of artistic experiments and expression. Interesting effects were achieved by hammering the surface before firing, applying real flowers, and exploring the possibilities of slip decoration. Hugh Robertson, son of Chelsea Keramic's founder, spent the 1880s obsessed with replicating the deep red Oriental oxblood glaze. He developed many glaze tones, finally perfecting his Robertson's Blood to great critical acclaim in 1888.

**PILLOW VASE** The bird is painted in barbotine (relief) by Hugh Robertson of the Chelsea Keramic Art Works, and set against a marbleized black and grey ground. *1880s. H:13.5cm (5¼in).*

an enormous whale. Brouwer usually worked on his own, sometimes with the help of Native American assistants.

His most celebrated achievement was the Fire Painting technique, perfected around 1900. This involved applying glaze to a biscuit-fired pot with a brush and then exposing the pot to an open furnace. Once cooled, the process resulted in a high gloss finish with wonderful variegated tones.

## POTTERY AS THERAPY

Arequipa Pottery was steeped in the warm climate of the San Francisco Bay area, where Henry E. Bothin sponsored a sanatorium for the rehabilitation of young women suffering from tuberculosis. The Englishman Frederick Rhead, formerly art director at Roseville, was invited to join the community as ceramicist in 1911, instructing the convalescing women in every aspect of his craft.

Inspired by the lush wooded setting of his new workplace, Rhead began to experiment with the local California clay before Albert Solon succeeded him as director of the pottery in 1913. The rapid turnover of patients meant that new decorators were constantly being trained and then lost, so Arequipa's output was variable in quality. Some of the decorative work is outstanding, including lustre glazes and experiments with squeezebag ornament, in which tubes of slip are applied as though a baker were decorating a cake.

**AREQUIPA VASE** Squeezebag decorated with branches of fruits and leaves, this vase is handpainted in a pale matte blue against a mottled indigo ground. *1911–18. H:15cm (6in).*

**AREQUIPA VASE** The baluster shape of the vase is decorated with a carved pattern of leaves finished with a green and lustrous turquoise glaze. *1913–18. H:34.5cm (13½in).*

**BURNT BABY VASE** Some of Ohr's vases – the burnt babies – survived the fire in his workshop in 1894. The bulbous body and torn neck of this vase emerged covered in shards and extensively charred. *1894. H:11cm (4½in).*

**BROUWER VASE** Bands of dark brown glaze are dripped over a streaked and mottled orange and yellow ground. The lustrous finish was achieved in the kiln by the technique known as Fire Painting. *1890s. H:30.5cm (12in).*

## NEW GLAZES

Towards the close of the 19th century a growing demand for art pottery prompted a number of American ceramics firms to venture into uncharted territory. With the materials, equipment, and skilled staff already in place, many of these companies found new success with their artware, often thanks to innovative approaches to glazing.

The Grueby-Faience Company of Boston, noted for its fine tiles, began to market a range of art pottery in 1897. Designer George Prentiss Kendrick was inspired by the French potter Auguste Delaherche, but found his true muse in the native flora of New England. Grasses, flowers, and above all leaves feature prominently on Grueby pots of this period, often incorporating handles into an overall organic form. The

company blended traditional handcraft with factory production, employing teams of potters – often students from art colleges – to throw pots to specified designs. Decorative elements were then incised, applied, and moulded precisely by hand. The result was a product that was entirely made by hand but to a pre-approved standard.

### THE COLOUR OF NATURE

Proprietor William Henry Grueby was personally responsible for developing his firm's most important asset – its glazes. He concocted a range of matte colours including yellow, blue, and grey, usually used alone but sometimes combined. These were among the first matte glazes available in the United States, after those developed by Chelsea Keramic Art Works and Rookwood (*see p.159*), and they were well received.

It was, however, Grueby's matte green glaze, which he described as being "like the smooth surface of a melon, or the bloom of a leaf", that established the reputation of his firm. The soft variations in leafy green tone are all the more remarkable because they were achieved simply by controlling the kiln environment carefully, without any post-firing treatments.

In 1899 the company was divided into two separate concerns – Grueby Faience (later Grueby Faience and Tile Company), which produced architectural ceramics, and Grueby Pottery, which concentrated on artwares. After enjoying great success with the matte green glaze in particular for several years, the art pottery business began to falter. Despite appointing Karl Lagenbeck from Rookwood superintendent in 1908, the firm stopped production in 1911.

*The glass shade,* in mottled green and yellow, complements the soft green of the base

*The Tiffany shade* is secured above the base with a brass frame

*The flowerheads,* like their trailing stems, are handmoulded

*Grueby's matte glazes* range from pale yellowish green to a rich dark cucumber-skin green

**GRUEBY-TIFFANY LAMP** The colour of the Grueby base is echoed in the glass tiles of the made-to-match Tiffany shade. *c.1905.* *H:55.25cm (21¾in).*

**CUENCA-DECORATED TILE** Mounted in a bronze trivet (not shown), this Grueby tile by Marie Seaman features a red tulip with speckled green leaves against a mottled, darker green matte ground. *c.1905. Sq:15cm (6in).*

**VASEKRAFT VASE** With a pair of long, pierced, buttressed handles, the inverted trumpet shape of this vase is finished with Fulper's Leopard's Skin crystalline glaze in subtle shades of green, brown, and black. *1909–15. H:27.5cm (11in).*

## FROM HOMEWARE TO ARTWARE

Further down the eastern seaboard, the Fulper Pottery Company of New Jersey launched its Vasekraft art pottery after experiments in 1909. Fulper was known for its heavily set homeware and used the same clay mix for this new line, so the art pottery is relatively coarse. Here too the crowning achievement was the glaze, or more accurately the staggering variety of glazes, used to finish the pots. Fulper marketed a range of gloss and lustre glazes, as well as fashionable matte, in colours with evocative names such as Cat's Eye and Elephant's Breath.

Fulper's most prestigious line was named Famille Rose, with a glaze claimed to be an authentic reproduction of the ancient Oriental technique. The glaze was made in six tones, including one called Peach Bloom after the famous antique Chinese vase bought for $18,000 – then a small fortune – by the banker J.P. Morgan.

The Chicago lawyer William Gates had built up a sizeable business manufacturing ceramic pipes and bricks when, in 1901, he began to design art pottery. His trademark, Teco, was derived from Terra Cotta, the name of the Illinois town in which his company was based. Although original and striking, these forms were for the most part moulded rather than thrown, which had the advantage of keeping the prices down. The real craft of the operation was in the mottled earth tone glazes.

Following the phenomenal success of Grueby's matte green glaze, Teco developed a similar product and concentrated on this to the exclusion of all else for almost a decade. This Teco Green can be distinguished from Grueby's matte green by its slight silver lustre.

## A GALAXY OF GLAZES

Other notable achievements were chalked up by Dedham, a Massachusetts firm that formulated a thick, flowing lava glaze and a mysterious crackle glaze achieved by using lamp black. Chemist Cadmon Robertson formulated almost 1,000 distinct recipes for Hampshire Pottery. Marblehead, originally conceived as a therapeutic workshop for convalescing patients, primarily decorated in monochrome but also marketed complex multicoloured pieces.

The Pewabic Pottery was founded by Mary Chase Berry, who was initially interested in decorating ceramics and then started her own business. Nothing if not experimental, Pewabic developed dozens of glazes, among which the iridescent hues are especially prized.

**TECO POTTERY VASE** The organic form is moulded with stylized tulips above a curled leaf base, and finished with a smooth, matte glaze. 1903-10. H:35cm (13¾in).

**MARBLEHEAD POTTERY VASE** The tapering cylindrical body is painted with stylized chestnut trees in muted green and pale pink against a rich, tobacco-brown ground. 1910–15. H:29cm (11½in).

**FLAMBÉ VASE** Its large, squat, ovoid form is streaked and mottled with one of Fulper's Oriental-inspired glazes: a frothy Chinese Blue flambé. 1909–15. W:25.5cm (10in).

**DEDHAM POTTERY VASE** Hugh Robertson's abstract composition comprises a thick, curdled, streaked, and mottled semi-gloss glaze. 1900–10. H:19cm (7½in).

**PEWABIC POTTERY VASE** A slender and elongated baluster form is covered in one of the company's iridescent glazes, in this case a spattered abstract pattern in shades of green indigo. c.1910. H:32cm (12½in).

## CLIFTON

The Clifton Art Pottery, established in 1905, came closer to Morris's Arts and Crafts ideal than most American ceramics firms. Scarcely employing more than a dozen staff, the firm used the local New Jersey red clay in its unglazed state for a range of vessels named Clifton Indian Ware. The shapes and decorative motifs found in this line were directly inspired by Native American pots. Substituting the indigenous American people for Morris' romanticized medieval past, Clifton's craftsmen drew on a vision of a bygone age more in touch with the simple rhythms of nature. The range extended to kitchenware as well as more decorative objects. For these, the porous raw clay was sealed with an application of gloss black glaze to the interior. Other Clifton Art Pottery lines included Crystal Patina, decorated with a pale green glaze and blended tones of other colours including yellow, green, and brown.

**Gourd-shaped Indian Ware vase** W:16.5cm (6½in)

**Tapered oviform Indian Ware vase** H:24.5cm (9½in)

**CLIFTON VASES** Both pieces are modelled in red clay and incised with geometric and eagle (above) motifs inspired by Native American tribal designs. 1905–08.

## BRITISH CERAMICS

The vigorous market for handcrafted ceramics around 1900 was led in Britain by small art potteries. Larger, more established companies followed with artware alongside their existing mass-produced ranges.

### DOULTON

Already a successful producer of architectural stoneware, the Lambeth firm of Doulton & Co. turned to its local art school for its new art pottery venture in the 1870s. Henry Doulton, son of the firm's founder, gave his designers an extraordinarily free reign and the success of his artware can largely be ascribed to individual artists such as George Tinworth and Frank Butler. The firm pioneered the employment of female staff, who enjoyed the same autonomy as their male colleagues. Women such as Emily Edwards and Hannah Barlow produced much of Doulton's most celebrated work in this period.

Hannah Barlow worked for the factory for more than three decades from 1871. Her sgraffito designs featuring horses, goats, and other animals came from the sketches she had made since she was a child. The sgraffito technique itself, involving scratching away at a slip glaze to reveal the contrasting ground beneath, was firmly within the Arts and Crafts tradition. Even after firing, the incised lines retain their original precision, so not only is each pot unique but they all also bear the indelible stamp of the potter's hand.

**The owl's head** forms a push-fit stoneware lid for the jar

**LAMBETHWARE JAR** The footed-owl body is influenced by much earlier 17th-century German examples. The jar is moulded in stoneware and decorated with the greens, blues, browns, and greys typical of Doulton's Lambeth palette. *1883. H:19.5cm (7¾in).*

**LAMBETHWARE VASE** Decorated by Hannah Barlow, a sgraffito band of cows and donkeys lies between grapes on the shoulder and waves on the foot. *1880–1900. H:31cm (12¼in).*

## THE MARTIN BROTHERS

Another famous graduate of Lambeth School of Art, Robert Wallace Martin worked freelance for Doulton before going into business with his brothers in 1873. They were a close-knit team, and each of the Martin brothers specialized in a particular aspect of their craft.

Robert Wallace had the greatest creative input and was responsible for the extraordinarily characterful birds, armadillos, salamanders, and other fantastical creatures that still define the firm's work. Edwin, also trained at Lambeth School of Art, designed seascapes and murky aquatic vistas that, like Robert's models, owed a debt to the Italian grottoesque tradition. Walter Frazer was in charge of throwing pots – work that was carried out entirely by hand, at a wheel. He also contributed glaze recipes and was adept at decorating with incised marks.

Charles was in charge of the administration side of the business. He garnered much favourable press attention as well as prominent clients including Queen Victoria. From 1877 the pottery was based in Southall, where it remained until it closed in 1914.

**BIRD GROUP** Modelled in salt-glazed stoneware by Robert Wallace Martin, each of the three grotesque birds has a detachable head and is glazed in shades of blue, green, and ochre. *1914. H:19.5cm (7¾in).*

**THE BROTHERS** Walter Frazer Martin (*left*), Robert Wallace Martin (*centre*), and Edwin Bruce Martin (*right*), photographed working in the studio of their Southall Pottery in London. *1912.*

**STONEWARE VASE** The oviform body of this Martin Brothers vase is decorated with incised pomegranates and caterpillars in shades of ochre and brown. *1896. H:27cm (10½in).*

## RUSKIN ART POTTERY

William Howson Taylor, founder of the Ruskin art pottery in 1898, was better placed than most to tap the pool of talent nurtured by Britain's art schools. His father, Edward Richard Taylor, was the principal of Birmingham School of Art and a pioneer of craft teaching. William persuaded his father to contribute a number of designs for simple vessels inspired by Chinese forms to the Ruskin Pottery during its early years and Edward had a lasting association with the business.

William Taylor relied almost entirely on local talent to keep his operation afloat, concentrating his own efforts on developing glazes. With superlative results, he joined the vigorous pursuit of the perfect flambé glaze – a challenge that had been occupying the minds of many of Europe's leading ceramicists since the 1870s. First developed in Ming-dynasty China, flambé-glazed wares have a lustrous crimson finish with streaks of turquoise.

The output of the Ruskin Pottery was true to its namesake, avoiding the clutter of so much 19th-century ceramic work. Simple shapes carried little surface adornment, drawing attention to the carefully worked glazes. Taylor's firm found further success supplying ceramic cabochons for department stores such as Liberty & Co. that were looking for a cheaper alternative to precious and semi-precious stones. The cabochons were mounted on mirrors and furniture.

**Different reds**, such as crimson and *sang-de-boeuf*, recur in the high-fired flambé glazes

**Chinese shapes** and forms are echoed in many Ruskin pieces

**Streaks** and graduations of colour, as well as mottling and speckling, are a feature of Ruskin wares

**RUSKIN POTTERY VASE** The elegant, Chinese-inspired shape of the vase is complemented by a high-fired Chinese-style flambé glaze of rich crimson with hints of turquoise. *1910. H:28cm (11in).*

**RUSKIN POTTERY VASE** The shouldered oviform body is finished in a high-fired flambé glaze speckled with crimson, purple, and turquoise. *1912. H:23cm (9in).*

**RUSKIN ONION POT** The squat body of this pot is finished in a high-fired glaze, producing speckled bands of colours ranging from *sang-de-boeuf*, through turquoise and green, to pink. *c.1905. H:24cm (9½in).*

# CERAMICS GALLERY

The inventive use of specialist glazes, both matte and gloss, was a key characteristic of Arts and Crafts ceramics. Underglaze was often used to apply artwork that was then covered in layers of sheer glazes to add depth and texture. Decoration was sometimes added in the form of coloured slips. Flowers and leaves were popular motifs and some pieces depicted whimsical animals.

## KEY

**1.** Adelaide Robineau porcelain tile. W:16.5cm (6½in). ④ **2.** Batchelder tile. H:22cm (8¾in). ①
**3.** W.J. Walley bowl. W:22.5cm (9in). ② **4.** Minton charger decorated by Louis J. Rhead. c.1880. D:41.5cm (16¼in). ⑤ **5.** C.H. Brannam sgraffito jug. 1898. H:30cm (11¾in). ① **6.** C.H. Brannam Puffin jug. H:16.5cm (6½in). ① **7.** Bernard Moore ruby lustre punch bowl. c.1910. D:45.5cm (18in). ③ **8.** Della Robbia ceramic jug. H:19cm (7½in). ② **9.** Salt-glazed stoneware punch bowl by Susan Frackelton. 1902. D:35.5cm (14in). ⑤ **10.** Stoneware charger by Alfred Powell. D:33cm (13in). ②

1 Robineau tile

2 Batchelder tile

3 W.J. Walley bowl

4 Minton charger

5 Sgraffito jug

6 C.H. Brannam jug

7 Bernard Moore punch bowl

8 Della Robbia jug

9 Stoneware punch bowl

10 Stoneware charger

11 Earthenware plate

**11.** Earthenware plate by J. Selwyn Dunn. D:31cm (12in). **12.** Clifton Crystal Patina vase. 1906. W:18cm (7in). ② **13.** Hancock & Sons Morrisware vase by George Cartlidge. H:17.5cm (7in). ③ **14.** Niloak Mission Ware vase. H:19cm (7½in). ① **15.** Elton vase decorated in coloured slips. H:26cm (10¼in). ① **16.** Adelaide Robineau porcelain vase. H:10cm (4in). ③ **17.** Overbeck vase decorated by Elizabeth and Hannah Overbeck. H:21cm (8½in). ⑥ **18.** Walrath vase with a speckled green glaze. H:15cm (6in). ③ **19.** C.H. Brannam vase decorated with sgraffito fish. 1902. H:18cm (7in). ① **20.** Hancock & Sons Morrisware vase by George Cartlidge. H:25cm (9¾in). ③

12 *Clifton vase*

13 *Hancock & Sons vase*

14 *Niloak Mission Ware vase*

16 *Robineau vase*

15 *Elton vase*

17 *Overbeck vase*

18 *Walrath vase*

19 *C.H. Brannam vase*

20 *Hancock & Sons vase*

# EXOTIC INFLUENCES

OUTLINING HIS VISION OF IDEAL INTERIOR DECORATION IN AN 1895 LECTURE, FREDERIC, LORD LEIGHTON SAID: "IT WILL NOT BE FALSE AND PALTRY LUXURY; IT WILL BE OPULENCE, IT WILL BE SINCERITY." THE GREAT CITIES OF THE WEST WERE CERTAINLY CRYING OUT FOR A TOUCH OF TRUE DAZZLE AND SPLENDOUR.

Heavy industry had brought progress and prosperity to the West, but carried soot and dirt in its wake. Those with enough money to travel returned home struck by the riot of colour they had seen in exotic places such as Persia, India, and Morocco.

Owen Jones's *Grammar of Ornament*, written after wide travel in Spain and the Middle East, gave extensive coverage to Moorish and Persian styles. This illustrated guide had a lasting influence and many interior decorators used it as a source book. In the South Kensington Museum, founded to house artefacts from the 1851 Great Exhibition,

the public could see ancient Iznik ceramics at first hand. Designers allied to the Aesthetic Movement looked to Japan for artistic influence, while Eastern architecture had been fashionable since John Nash completed his extraordinary Royal Pavilion at Brighton on the English south coast in the "Hindoo" style.

## EASTERN ALLURE AND LUSTRE

Eager to learn from the craft traditions of other countries, Arts and Crafts designers studied exotic antiques in the hope that they might unearth their secrets. William de Morgan was more successful than most, rediscovering the lost technique of lustre glazing in 1873. Originally used in Persia and spreading as far as Italy before being lost, this technique produced vivid colours. De Morgan used a Persian palette of turquoise, lemon yellow, purple, green, and red enamels over a white ground to create fresh and lively tiles and other ceramic wares after the Eastern tradition.

Glassmaker Thomas Webb introduced a range of cameo glass decorated with intricate repeating tendrils in symmetrical patterns inspired by Moorish designs. George Woodall's finest design for Webb was a cameo plaque entitled "The Moorish Bathers". Department stores, too, responded to demand and soon began to stock exotic furnishings. Liberty & Co., for example, retailed a galleried side table with fretwork panels inspired by Moroccan design.

## LEIGHTON HOUSE

The epitome of exotic style in late Victorian London was Leighton House, the home of Frederic, Lord Leighton. His position as a respected artist had visitors flocking to see the opulence of his Arab Hall, completed in 1881 to designs by George Aitchison.

Modelled closely on the banqueting room at La Zisa, an ancient Saracen palace in Sicily, the Arab Hall's main features include a domed ceiling, numerous carved marble columns, elaborate paintwork, and mosaics. A golden mosaic frieze by Walter Crane encircles the walls and the floor is covered with a mosaic

**WALNUT PLANT STAND** Made for Liberty & Co. in the Anglo-Moorish style, the stand has ebonized Moorish brackets and *mashrabiyya* (bobbin turnings), on angled kickout legs. *c.1890. H:84cm (33in).*

**CAMEO GLASSWARE** English glassmaker Thomas Webb made a range of glasses covered with Moorish-style decoration of semi-abstract patterns. *1890. D:11.5cm (4½in).*

**IZNIK TILE** Potters in Iznik, near Istanbul, made wares with swirling, scrolling designs in blue, turquoise, green, and red. These wares had a huge influence in the late 19th century on designers such as William de Morgan. *c.1570. H:19.5cm (7¾in).*

*Stylized flowers* and leaves are inspired by Islamic pottery

**"IZNIK" VASE AND COVER** The colour scheme and bold, all-over decoration of this William de Morgan vase look directly to Iznik wares. *c.1890. H:27.5cm (10¾in).*

designed by Aitchison. The frieze features exotic creatures, although it was modified from Crane's original design after Leighton told him to "cleave to the sphinx and the eagle, they are delightful. I don't like the duck women." A fountain in the centre of the room is surrounded by a shallow pool, into which guests would apparently inadvertently plunge. Latticework wooden *mashrabiyya* (bobbin-turned) screens line the galleries. Unfortunately, Leighton did not have enough money to commission Edward Burne-Jones to decorate the domed ceiling as originally planned.

**LEIGHTON HOUSE** The Arab Hall is the centrepiece of the house. It was designed to display the vast collection of Islamic tiles that Lord Leighton bought on his travels through Syria, Egypt, and the Greek islands.

# GLASS AND LAMPS

THE ARTS AND CRAFTS GENERATION UNDERSTOOD THE IMPORTANCE OF LIGHT
IN INTERIOR DESIGN. LEADED GLASS FILTERED AND ENHANCED SUNLIGHT,
WHILE LAMPS WERE INCREASINGLY A SOURCE OF ARTIFICIAL LIGHT.

**MEDIEVAL LOOK** Inspiration for much Arts and Crafts stained and leaded
glass came from medieval examples, such as this round window depicting a
horned devil on horseback. *14th century.*

## LEADED GLASS

The use of leaded and stained glass owed much
to William Morris's passion for medieval Gothic
churches, noted for their colourful windows
that provided decoration and stylistic harmony
as well as light. His admiration for Gothic
architecture led him to sites such as York
Minster, the chapel at Merton College in
Oxford, and Chartres Cathedral in northern
France. All boast outstanding decorative leaded
glazing. Taking his lead from A.W.N. Pugin,
father of the Victorian Gothic Revival, Morris
established the early reputation of Morris,
Marshall, Faulkner & Co. for stained glass.

The Pre-Raphaelite painters Edward Burne-
Jones and Dante Gabrielle Rossetti provided
a wealth of designs for the stained glass of
Morris, Marshall, Faulkner & Co. These
men never strayed far from their 14th-century
religious inspiration, drafting designs with

**BIBLICAL IMAGERY** This stained and leaded glass panel
by Morris and Co. depicts St Peter with the keys to heaven,
set against lozenge-shaped lights of British wildflowers
– the latter a favourite Morris motif. *1870s–80s.* .

verdant backgrounds and Biblical subject matter.
So accurate was Morris's re-creation of medieval
stained glass that his competitors accused him of
fraud, arguing that his prize-winning exhibit at the
1862 International Exhibition consisted of restored
glass from the Middle Ages.

### TIMELESS WINDOWS

Morris's company outsourced much of its
manufacturing work to Powell & Sons, experts in
flashed glass, in which the clear body of the glass
is coated with a translucent coloured husk. Other
manufacturers who kept traditional methods alive
included Britten & Gibson, who made glass for
Walter Crane and E.S. Prior. By blowing liquid
glass into flat moulds, they managed to imitate
medieval glass, in which the panes
were thicker at the centre and
distorted the light in an intriguing
way. This bona-fide medievalism was
applauded by Christopher Whall, a
lecturer at the Central School of Arts
and Crafts in London, who was at
the forefront of the stained glass
renaissance in Britain. One of his
principles was that figures in coloured
glass should be drawn from life, not
from paintings.

The British guilds turned to stained
glass as the Arts and Crafts movement
matured. Mackmurdo's Century
Guild was supplied with designs
by clergyman Selwyn Image, while

*Cherish some flower*
*Be it ever so lowly.*

*Work for some end*
*Be it ever so slowly*

**PRE-RAPHAELITE STYLE** Inspired by the
Italian style of painting before the influence of
Raphael, this stained and leaded glass panel
depicts a medieval maiden gathering flowers.
The accompanying romantic verse is by the Pre-
Raphaelite artist and poet, Dante Gabriel Rossetti.
*1860s–80s. H:26.5cm (10½in).*

**AMERICAN FLORAL** Depicting stylized blossoms among a border of small pave-set tiles, around a field of larger tiles with scattered petals, this American window is stained in tones of amber, blue, and pink, and black and white. It survived the 1906 San Francisco earthquake and fire. *1880s. W:145cm (58in).*

**TIFFANY STYLE** Set in oak and iron frames, with protective glass to one side, this pair of leaded glass windows depicts a rural landscape in the style of Louis Comfort Tiffany. They incorporate blown, mottled, striated, and confetti glass in many vivid colours. *c.1905. H:165cm (66in).*

Ashbee's Guild of Handicraft employed the manufacturer Paul Woodroffe. Traditional stained glass workshops were set up all over Britain, with particular success in Scotland and Ireland. Sarah Purser founded Au Túr Gloine (The Tower of Glass) in Dublin in 1903. Like Burne-Jones and Rossetti, she brought her experience as a painter to bear on her new career as a glazier.

## GLASS IN THE HOME

In the mid-19th century glass tax was abolished and domestic glaziers had begun using larger panes of glass, often installed in bay windows. While enjoying the lighter interiors created by larger windows, homeowners could still subscribe to the Arts and Crafts aesthetic by using coloured glass panels as wall hangings or inset into furniture.

There was a reaction against windows with large glass expanses in some circles by those who considered broken, latticed panes more homely. William Purcell and George Elmslie, American architects of the Prairie School, installed over 80 glass panels in Purcell's Minneapolis home. Mostly decorated with simple rectangular and diamond grid geometric motifs, the main virtue of these panes was to harmonize the interior colour scheme.

## FROM LA FARGE TO TIFFANY

The American oil painter and watercolourist John La Farge carefully followed the progress of the Pre-Raphaelite movement and through it was introduced to the leaded glass of Morris, Marshall, Faulkner & Co. Combining these influences with his fascination for two-dimensional Japanese prints, La Farge set about developing his own brand of leaded glass. His church commissions made use of many different types of decorative work within the same window, from cloisonné to confetti glass, a complicated technique that involved embedding tiny flakes of colour within the molten batch of opalescent glass.

La Farge's experiments with opalescent art glass provided a starting point for the most celebrated American designer of leaded glass – Louis Comfort Tiffany. His leaded glass products included screens as well as the widely imitated Tiffany lamps. These ranged in complexity from simple geometric designs to intricate designs of stylized leaves and flowers in many different colours.

Along with leaded glass panes above the front door, leaded glass lampshades became the most common way in which Arts and Crafts principles were applied in the home.

**TABLE SCREEN** This small, tri-fold, leaded glass screen made by the Tiffany Studios depicts stylized trees and leaves in rich autumnal colours. *1905–10. H:21cm (8¼in).*

# LAMPS

Artificial lighting became more efficient towards the end of the 19th century. The messy paraffin lamp was already being phased out in favour of gas lamps when Thomas Edison patented the light bulb in the 1880s. Although not in common use until about 1900, this invention had a huge effect on lighting design, especially in the United States where people were quicker to adopt new technology.

## BEATEN METAL AND GLASS

W.A.S. Benson was an early English pioneer in designs for electric light. He intuitively understood how best to harness the properties of copper and brass – his favoured materials – to create soft lighting. Whereas gas lamps had invariably been directed up towards the ceiling, Benson used reflective metal to deflect electric light back down towards the floor. In his Chelsea home C.R. Ashbee used fittings made from beaten metal and hung with enamel shades to colour and soften his electric lights.

Many American designers such as Dirk van Erp and members of the Roycroft community also favoured beaten metal. Both of them had established reputations for fine hand-hammered copperware in the Arts and Crafts style. Van Erp's signature lamps often have bases converted from milk cans and other everyday items. His conical shades are usually made from stretched mica – a shiny, translucent silicate mineral that mottles the

light source beneath. Roycroft lamps sometimes have hammered copper shades that match their bases, giving them an austere decorative unity. Others have shades made out of stained and leaded glass – an ornamental feature that became very popular in the United States as more households converted to electricity.

*The copper-domed glass shade* terminates in a decorative conical finial

*Pumpkin orange glass* is contrasted around the lower rim with small panels of periwinkle blue glass

*Ring handles* hang from a copper band secured with a typical Arts and Crafts device: exposed rivets

**DIRK VAN ERP LAMP** This early example of Erp's work has a large milkcan-shaped base hand hammered from copper and finished with a warm brown surface patina. Riveted arms from the neck support the shade with its original mica panels secured in a copper frame. *c. 1910. H:61cm (24in).*

**ROYCROFTERS COPPER SHOP LAMP** Designed by Dard Hunter, this lamp has a flared shade and leaded glass. The shade is raised on a hand-hammered, brass-washed, baluster-shaped base with three sockets and a pair of ring handles. *1905–10. H:55cm (22in).*

*The finish* of hand-hammered, patinated copper is highly characteristic of Arts and Crafts metalware

**ROYCROFT LAMP** The hand-hammered shade has a ball finial and is raised above a candlestick-like copper base with ring-shaped knops, a circular foot, and a copper-bead pull. *c. 1910. H:52cm (20½in).*

*The shade* is topped with a vented bronze cap in the form of a lotus flower

*The panels* are made from Tiffany's iridescent Favrile glass

*A lead framework,* as with most Tiffany shades, secures the glass panels

**TIFFANY STUDIOS CHANDELIER** The turtleback shade covers a six-socket fixture and displays two rows of Favrile glass medallions of blue-green lustre. *c.1905. W:56cm (22in).*

lamps incorporate glass turtlebacks into the base or the shade. Made from iridescent Favrile glass, these decorative elements have an uneven finish that diffuses light in an unusual manner and gives the lamps a handcrafted appearance. Tiffany combined his glass shades with exquisitely detailed matching metal bases, making the lamps unique works of art in their own right.

## STURDY WOOD

Gustav Stickley made much plainer lamps than those of Tiffany and his rivals. Combining solid wooden structures with hand-forged matte metal fittings, Stickley's standing Newell post lamps bear a resemblance to his furniture in their simplicity of form and structure as well as their architectural design. At the Roycroft in East Aurora, Elbert Hubbard sold similar simple wooden lamps alongside his hammered-copper creations.

Influential American architects such as the Greene Brothers and Frank Lloyd Wright began to take a keen interest in lighting, recognizing it as a key feature of their building designs. At the Gamble House in Pasadena, the Greenes used light to help define different areas within an interior, and Frank Lloyd Wright experimented with recessed lighting to make it an integral part of his buildings.

Of all the American firms that produced decorated glass lamp shades, Handel was one of the most innovative. Founded in Connecticut in 1885 by Philip J. Handel, the firm is most famous for reviving the old English craft of mirror painting and adapting it to lighting. Handel's reverse-painted and leaded glass designs feature scenes from the natural world. Soft colours and flowing shapes reminiscent of draped fabric give Handel lamps a more feminine look than those of Tiffany, the company's biggest rival.

With a record of success with stained glass, Louis Comfort Tiffany bought a glass furnace at Corona near New York in 1892 and began to manufacture lampshades. Ideal for softening electric light, his coloured leaded glass shades were a huge success and inspired many imitators. Former employees of Tiffany Studios founded both Quezal Art Glass and Steuben Glass Works, and both became successful in their own right. Tiffany's continued experiments with glass resulted in Cypriote, which mimics the pitted finish of ancient Roman glass. Many Tiffany

**HANDEL CO. LAMP** The domed shade has curved panels of marbled, honey-coloured glass. Set under an overlaid lead framework, it is reverse-painted around the rim with an oak leaf border. *c.1910. H:35cm (13¾in).*

*The bronze base* is chemically finished with a rich brown patina

*The urn-shaped base* incorporates a band of iridescent Favrile glass turtlebacks

**TIFFANY STUDIOS LAMP** Its domed leaded-glass shade is composed of graduated panels of marbled green glass, and a border of lozenge-shaped turtlebacks in iridescent green Favrile glass. *c.1905. H:53cm (20¾in).*

**GUSTAV STICKLEY LAMPS** Designed as staircase newel posts, these two lamps have four-sided, hammered-copper lanterns lined with mica glass. These are raised above stained cedar posts with square bases. *1904–15. H:74cm (29½in).*

# METALWARE

INSPIRED BY WILLIAM MORRIS AND THE CELTIC REVIVAL, ARTISAN
METALWORKERS SOUGHT TO MAKE HIGH-QUALITY HANDCRAFTED SILVER
BUT STRUGGLED TO COMPETE WITH CHEAP FACTORY GOODS.

**SILVER VASE** Designed by C.R. Ashbee for the Guild of Handicraft, the vase
is decorated with four embossed stylized trees above a ring of bead moulding.
Each tree is centred with a garnet cabochon. c.1900. H:18cm (7in).

## THE NEW GUILDS

In 1871 John Ruskin had pleaded the importance
of redeveloping rural industry in his *Fors Clavigera*,
a series of letters to the working men of England.
William Morris agreed with his romantic notions
of a benevolent feudal society. Reviving the medieval
guild system saved the skill base of British
metalware. More than just workshops, these guilds
were training grounds for raw talent, where master
craftsmen could pass on their skills to a new
generation. Spreading knowledge was central to
the Arts and Crafts philosophy, undermining the
tyranny of the urban factory by empowering local
communities to keep their traditions going. In
Surrey Godfrey Blount founded The Haslemere
Peasant Industries as part of his proposal to return
England to a pre-industrial economy.

## FROM CITY TO COUNTRY

In 1888 C.R. Ashbee, a London-trained architect
and friend of Blount, founded the Guild of
Handicraft following a series of lectures on Ruskin
he had delivered at Toynbee Hall in London. As
the enterprise grew the Guild moved to larger
premises at Mile End in East London. A smithy
was constructed in the garden. The first metalware
produced by the Guild of Handicraft included
copper and brass dishes decorated with embossed

motifs of foliage and fish.
Ashbee's architectural
commissions kept the smithy busy
producing door furniture and other
fittings. Metalworker John Pearson
worked at the Guild and taught there
until he left in about 1893.

When the lease on the Guild's Mile
End premises expired, Ashbee was
seized by the notion that he and his
band of workers should "leave
Babylon and go home to the land".
The semi-derelict Cotswold market
town of Chipping Campden might
have been custom built for him –
stately but neglected, it was ripe for
an injection of new life.

Around 150 Londoners were
settled in Chipping Campden and
the Guild's workshops installed at
the Old Silk Mill, renamed Essex
House in honour of the Mile End
property they had left behind. The
Guildsmen overcame the initial
hostility of some of the locals by
becoming active in the community,
organizing social events, classes,
and lectures.

**TEAPOT AND MILK JUG** These Birmingham Guild pieces have
a hand-hammered, electroplated silver finish, and were probably
designed by Arthur Dixon. c.1900. W:16cm (6½in).

**Newlyn School charger**

**COPPER BOWL AND CHARGER** The large Newlyn School charger is the work of John Pearson, and is repoussé-hammered with birds set among foliage. *1896. D:63cm (25¼in)*. Also from Newlyn, the bowl is unattributed, but its repoussé fish frieze is inspired by Pearson's use of aquatic imagery. *c.1900. W:29cm (11½in)*.

**Newlyn School bowl**

The move caused quite a stir, and a number of skilled local men were inspired to join. The range of silver- and metalware produced by the Guild of Handicraft developed in scope to include elegant, loop-handled bowls and vases, and boxes set with semi-precious stones and enamel plaques. The outstanding quality of the work – mostly designed by Ashbee himself – was especially remarkable considering many of the Guildsmen were trained entirely on the job. After more than 20 years in business the Guild of Handicraft was dissolved in 1908. Ashbee laid the blame for his project ending on department stores such as Liberty and Heals. They could offer similar products at a much lower cost by using machine production methods.

## REJECTING THE MACHINE
Under the motto "by hammer and hand", the Birmingham Guild of Handicraft avoided the use of machinery as much as its namesake in the Cotswolds. Aside from lathing, every process used to work the metal was done by hand. The Guild was established in 1890 and had close ties with Birmingham Art School. It spread its ideas through *The Quest*, a quarterly, hand-printed magazine. Silverware by the Birmingham Guild was sparsely decorated, inspired by churchware and Celtic design. Pieces often had the hand-hammered finish so typical of Arts and Crafts metalware. They were stamped with the Guild hallmark – individual designers and artists remained largely anonymous.

Montague Fordham, a director of the Birmingham Guild, took over the reins of the London-based Artificer's Guild in 1903 and began to display products by its members at his Maddox Street gallery. His appointment of Edward Spencer as chief designer took the Artificer's Guild in a new direction, producing functional homeware in copper,

brass, and silver, with stylized patterns drawn from natural forms. The hand-hammered finishes, particularly on silverware, are a tribute to the ideals that underpinned the Guild's work.

## GOTHIC AND CELTIC INFLUENCE
Not every metalworker of this period rejected machinery as the new guilds did. Despite his growing belief in Arts and Crafts values, W.A.S. Benson was an unashamed fan of the machine, which helped his commercial success. Benson's work was inspired by the Gothic goblets and lanterns of A.W.N. Pugin and, later, by Christopher Dresser's strikingly geometric metalwork (*see pp.242–243*).

The Celtic influence that had proved such a hit for Liberty & Co. was much in evidence in Scottish metalwork. Alexander Ritchie and others took stylistic cues from the ancient Celtic carvings on Iona, incorporating knots and *entrelac* designs into their work. Phoebe Traquair and Marion Henderson championed this Scottish School style, which found a unique expression among students of the Glasgow School of Art (*see pp.244–245 and 262–263*).

## ENAMELLING
The humility of form implicit in the strictest interpretation of Arts and Crafts style meant that silver- and metalworkers avoided decoration of precious stones. Alongside cabochon and uncut semi-precious stones such as garnets, the use of enamel escalated and became a fine art in its own right. Against a foil of plain or hammered silver, bright polychrome enamel plaques provided fresh and lively embellishment to silver in particular. Galleons in sail and natural landscapes were popular themes. Many silversmiths, such as Omar Ramsden, carried out their own enamel work, although others brought in specialists. One such was Fleetwood Charles Varley, a watercolourist whose landscapes can be seen on silver by the Guild of Handicraft.

**SILVER AND ENAMEL BOX** From the London workshop of Omar Ramsden and Alwyn Carr, its silver carcase is chased with wave-scroll motifs to complement the seascape imagery of the polychrome enamel panel set into the lid. *1907. W:9.5cm (3¾in)*.

**BRASS CANDLE SCONCE** By Agnes Bankier Harvey of the Glasgow School, the backplate is repoussé decorated with a girl's head among poppies. *c.1900. H:30cm (11¾in)*.

**COPPER AND BRASS BOWL** Designed by W.A.S. Benson, the copper, fluted petal bowl is raised on a foliate-form brass base with handle. *c.1900. H:15cm (6in)*.

*A naturalistic leaf shape* creates a handle

*The copper petals* show signs of individual handcrafting

# LIBERTY & CO.

Arthur Lasenby Liberty's store in central London's Regent Street was founded in 1875, selling ornaments, fabrics, and objets d'art from the Far East. The fashionable emporium soon became a favourite source of decorative furnishings and knick-knacks for people who valued good design.

During the 1880s Liberty began to foster commercial ties with those members of his circle involved with the Arts and Crafts movement. In the work of Archibald Knox, Liberty & Co. unearthed a fresh new style and started the Celtic revival.

## HIDDEN TALENT

Liberty & Co. developed a policy of commissioning work from prominent designers and outsourcing production to firms around the country. These products were then sold under the Liberty banner, both designer and manufacturer

remaining uncredited. Such an approach drew scorn from those who struggled to eke out a living while avoiding any concession to the perceived evil of organized mass production – the antithesis of the Arts and Crafts manifesto. C.R. Ashbee was particularly vehement in his criticism, calling Liberty & Co. "Messrs Nobody, Novelty & Co.". Irreconcilable business methods frequently pitted Arthur Liberty and William Morris against one another. When Morris bought a paintworks further down the River Wandle from Liberty's own contractor, Liberty quipped "we send our dirty water downstream to Morris".

The formula was, nonetheless, a successful one, and Liberty found willing collaborators in many of the Arts and Crafts movement's finest talents. In the process, the store also helped buoy the fortunes of many small workshops and individual designers. On the shop floor, furniture by Baillie Scott was sold alongside glass by John Couper & Sons (Glasgow) and James Powell & Sons (Whitefriars), and textiles designed by C.F.A. Voysey and Jessie M. King. The business of printing fabrics was undertaken by Thomas Wardle, an early associate of William Morris.

The Silver Studio, run by Arthur Silver, devised many of Liberty's most popular fabric patterns. Arthur's son, Rex, later became involved with what proved to be Liberty's greatest success.

## SILVER LINING

Unveiled in 1899, the Cymric line of gold- and silverware was an instant hit. The range of jewellery, tea sets, candlesticks, clocks, vases, and other assorted objects was manufactured by the

**CYMRIC VASE** Unattributed but probably by Archibald Knox, this vase incorporates Celtic motifs offset by red and mottled bluish-green enamelling. c.1905. H:24cm (9½in).

Birmingham firm W.H. Haseler using industrial methods, keeping costs within the reach of middle-class families. Rex Silver, Arthur Gaskin, and Jessie M. King contributed designs, but it was Archibald Knox who created most for the Cymric range.

Knox's designs bore the stamp of his Isle of Man background. In the island's capital, where he attended the Douglas School of Art, he carried out extensive research into Celtic ornament. It culminated in published works such as *Ancient Crosses on the Isle of Man*. Knox became friends with Baillie Scott, who first brought him to the attention of Liberty & Co. around 1895. His first drafts for the firm included patterns for fabrics and wallpapers, but it was his metalware that caused a sensation.

**CYMRIC FLOWER VASE** The design is attributed to Archibald Knox. The vase is cast with stylized leaf forms and supported by three curved brackets raised on a dished circular base. 1903. 14cm (5½in).

**TUDRIC ICE BUCKET** An Archibald Knox Liberty Tudric design, the tapering cylindrical form is flanked by angular D-shaped handles, and is embellished in relief with interlaced Celtic flora. c.1903. H:19cm (7½in).

**SILVER PICTURE FRAME** Possibly by Archibald Knox, although more fairytale than Celtic in style, this Liberty & Co. frame is in the form of a canopy of leaves above two tree trunks flanking a pair of copper-hinged, red-enamelled doors with blue-enamelled floral motifs. c.1905. H:16cm (6¼in).

**TUDRIC VASE** This Knox design has a bullet-shaped body with three looped bracket feet, and is embellished with *entrelac* flowers and six cabochon-like bluish-green enamelled plaques. *c.1905. H:29cm (11½in).*

## ARCHIBALD KNOX

Archibald Knox's designs were suffused with Celtic ornament – interwoven knots, intricate *entrelacs*, and stylized foliate motifs feature heavily. Knox never replicated the ancient devices he had studied on standing stones and in illuminated manuscripts, but invented new permutations of their tangled mystery.

Later in his career, Knox took up teaching and eventually returned to the Isle of Man. His work for Liberty & Co., encompassing carpets, ceramics, and garden ornaments as well as metalware and jewellery, was the vanguard of the Celtic revival that became popular in other areas of the Arts and Crafts movement, particularly in Scotland.

**Archibald Knox**

## ANCIENT ORIGINALITY

For the Cymric line and the Tudric range of pewterware that came out in 1900, Knox drew heavily on his Manx heritage and Celtic roots. John Llewellyn, who Liberty employed as manager of the two projects, was entirely sympathetic to Knox's decorative vocabulary and encouraged him to contribute as much to both lines as possible.

Cymric silverware had a hammered finish and was left unpolished to give it a handcrafted look. The plain surface of the silver was tempered through the use of vivid blue, red, and green enamels, and cabochons of semi-precious stones. The Tudric range was cast in pewter to be a more affordable alternative to silver, and had quite distinct designs.

*The overall forms* and decorative details of Tudric wares were die-stamped, then individually hammered for a handmade finish

*Copper numerals,* like enamelling, provide colour contrast with the pewter

*Enamelling* injects vibrant colour into many pewter Tudric wares

**TUDRIC MANTEL CLOCK** Designed by Archibald Knox for Liberty & Co's Tudric range, it has a pewter case with stylized leaf decoration, and a circular, polychrome-enamelled dial with berry motifs and copper Arabic numerals. *c.1905. H:21cm (8¼in).*

**PEWTER AND CLUTHA GLASS BOWL** Designed by Archibald Knox, the mount is pierced and embellished with simple leaf forms. The glass liner is suffused with bubbles and has milky streaks and copper-coloured aventurine inclusions. *H:15.5cm (6in).*

# AMERICAN METALWARE

American craftsmen did not share William Morris's dislike of machinery, but along with salesmen, they enthusiastically adopted the idea of the integrated interior. To preserve the quality of his meticulously handcrafted furniture, Gustav Stickley added a metalwork shop to his Craftsman Workshops rather than resort to the use of machine cut-and-stamped accessories. Other more business-minded producers saw the potential in offering consumers a range of beaten-metal products to complement the Mission-style furniture that was in vogue.

One such entrepreneur was Louis Comfort Tiffany, founder of the interior decorating firm Tiffany Studios. The Studios' metalworking arm was initially set up to make metal bases for the stained glass lamp shades of Tiffany & Co. It grew to encompass desk accessories, candelabra, jugs, and vases. These were mostly brass, with gilt and gold doré finishes on the most expensive pieces. Silver was used only for bespoke commissions.

## STYLISH SIMPLICITY

Dirk van Erp in San Francisco made a similar range of pieces, although they were made of copper. Van Erp was originally from the Netherlands, but settled in California in 1885. He began working in metal as a hobby, hammering hollow ware from the spent artillery shells that littered the naval yard where he worked. He collaborated with Canadian Eleanor D'Arcy Gaw, who had trained at Ashbee's Guild of Handicraft in England. Their working relationship lasted little more than a year but it had a lasting influence on van Erp, who stuck rigidly to the plain look they developed. Surface decoration barely extended beyond a hand-hammered finish or the occasional flash of structural riveting. Lamp shades made from stretched mica integrated style and material in his wide range of lamps. To vary the finish of his metalware, van Erp perfected formulae for patinas in deep green, red, and amber. In his experiments he used materials as diverse as brick dust and driftwood. He was so successful that he inspired imitations, notably the machine-made lamps of Old Mission Kopper Kraft of San José.

Sensing that consumers had developed a taste for hammered copper, Elbert Hubbard opened the Roycrofters Copper Shop in 1903 as part of his growing craft community at East Aurora in New York. Utilitarian wares, including plates and bowls, were supplemented by more decorative pieces such as lamps and bookends.

Karl Kip helped Hubbard's new venture when he moved from the community's bookbinders to the metalwork shop in 1908. The decorative techniques Kip had learned transferred surprisingly well to beaten copper. Relief borders crafted to resemble stitched leather lent a distinctive edge to

**COPPER PLATE** Hand hammered at the Roycrofter's Copper Shop, the plate was also chemically treated to produce an instant aged patina. It bears the distinctive Roycrofters "R" within a cross and orb mark. *1905–15. D:20.25cm (8in).*

the Roycroft's metalware. As with the furniture and printed material produced on the same site, Hubbard promoted and sold his copperware through his popular mail-order catalogue. All his copperware bore the impressed orb and cross stamp of the Roycrofters.

## INNOVATION AND TRADITION

Otto Heintz was another talented entrepreneur who capitalized on the market for Arts and Crafts metalware. Originally a jeweller with the family business in Buffalo, Heintz bought The Arts & Crafts Co. in 1903, renaming it Heintz Art Metal Shop. Foremost among Heintz's achievements was a process he developed to affix silver overlay to a

**COPPER VASE** Made by Dirk van Erp, this broad, baluster-shaped vessel has a slightly planished surface and is finished with one of van Erp's surface patinas: here, a mottled reddish-amber hue. The underside bears van Erp's windmill mark. *c.1910. H:19cm (7½in).*

**COPPER PITCHER** Of bulbous form with a leaded interior, hinged domed cover, riveted loop finial, and an ear-shaped handle, this van Erp vase has a planished surface, finished in a reddish-brown patina. *c.1910. H:30cm (11¾in).*

bronze ground without the use of solder. Like van Erp, Heintz was interested in patina and came up with a wide range of finishes including an iridescent red he called Royal and a silver tone known as French Gray.

## ESOTERIC INFLUENCE

The exoticism that influenced many spheres of Arts and Crafts decoration – notably the early textiles of William Morris and the lustre-glazed ceramics of William de Morgan – also found favour among some metalworkers. Tiffany Studios launched a range of desk accessories with patterns based on the 12 signs of the Zodiac. The exotic roots of this and other ranges produced by Tiffany sets them apart from much of the Arts and Crafts metalware produced by other studios. In contrast to the plain hammered surfaces that dominated this period, Tiffany metalware often has intricate filigree surface decoration and is more opulent.

*The bronze* on many of Heintz's pieces is smooth spun rather than hammered

**SILVER CHALICE** Made as as trophy by the Jarvie Shop, this chalice has a hand-wrought hemispherical bowl raised on a tapering stem above a circular foot. It has a lightly hammered surface, and is chased with floral and leaf decoration by George Grant Elmslie. *1915. H:19.5cm (7¾in).*

**GILT BRONZE INKWELL** This octagonal well made by Tiffany Studios is centred in a square tray, retains its original lead liner, and is chased with a Venetian-inspired pattern of stylized leaf motifs. The gilt finish is also known as gold-doré. *c.1905. W:24cm (9½in).*

**SILVER-ON-BRONZE VASE** Made by the Heintz Art Metal Shop, its elegant baluster form is decorated with a full-height appliqué of sterling-silver flowers, resembling poppies in full bloom with twisting stems, set against a dark bronze patina. *c.1920. H:28cm (11in).*

## KALO SHOP

Taking a cue from the guild revival led by C.R. Ashbee in England, Clara Barck Welles founded a rural craft community in Park Ridge near Chicago in 1900. The great emphasis she placed on apprenticeships certainly paid dividends – the master silversmiths who made the Kalo Shop such a success were drawn largely from a migrant Scandinavian population and trained on the job. The name of the enterprise was taken from the Greek word *kalos*, which translates as beautiful. This sentiment found further expression in the shop's motto – "beautiful, useful and enduring". Offsetting the cost of labour-intensive handcrafting by selling its products direct through its own outlet, the Kalo Shop had a loyal following for its understated, elegant silverware with fluted and hammered decoration.

STERLING HAND WROUGHT AT THE KALO SHOP G152H

**STERLING-SILVER BOWL** This Kalo Shop bowl is raised on a ring foot, has angular D-shape handles, and a lightly hammered surface with four out-pressed, hourglass-shaped lobes. An interlaced "GH" monogram is applied to one side. *1905–14. W:25.5cm (10in).*

**SILVER CANDLESTICKS** This pair of candlesticks is handwrought with broad-flanged, tulip-shaped sockets, rising from slender club-shaped stems, raised on broad, stepped circular feet. The handwrought mark on the underside indicates manufacture after 1914. *1920–25. H:35.5cm (14in).*

# METALWARE GALLERY

Arts and Crafts metalworkers made extensive use of base metals such as copper, brass, and pewter as well as more expensive silver and gold. They avoided precious stones in favour of simpler embellishments such as enamel decoration and uncut or cabochon semi-precious stones. The handcrafted look was fundamental – even machine-made pieces were frequently given a hand-hammered finish. Recurring decorative themes include stylized plants and flowers as well as motifs inspired by ancient Celtic design.

## KEY

**1.** Roycroft brass-washed, hammered copper American Beauty vase. H:47cm (18½in). ③
**2.** Artificer's Guild goblet, the design attributed to Edward Spencer. 1926. H:15cm (6in). ③
**3.** W.A.S. Benson muffin dish. W:25.5cm (10in). ① **4.** Two Scottish School brass vases in the style of Alexander Ritchie. H:31cm (12¼in). ③ **5.** Newlyn Arts & Crafts copper rose bowl. W:40cm (15¾in). ② **6.** Silver vase by C.R. Ashbee. c.1900. H:18cm (7in). ④ **7.** Arts and Crafts plated brass vase, designed by Edward Spencer. H:17.5cm (6¾in). ① **8.** Guild of Handicrafts inkwell, with a foiled enamel boss on the cover. 1906. H:6.5cm (2½in). ③ **9.** Artificer's Guild Edith & Nelson Dawson silver bookmark. 1905. L:12cm (5in). ① **10.** Heintz sterling-on-bronze trophy cup. H:28.5cm (11¼in). ① **11.** Liberty & Co. Tudric pewter candlesticks, designed by Archibald Knox. c.1905.

**3** W.A.S. Benson muffin dish

**2** Artificer's Guild goblet

**4** Pair of brass vases

**7** Plated brass vase

**8** Guild of Handicrafts inkwell

**9** Artificer's Guild bookmark

**1** Roycroft vase

**5** Copper rose bowl

**6** C.R. Ashbee silver vase

**10** Trophy cup

**11** Liberty & Co. Tudric candlesticks

H:23cm (9in). ③ **12.** Artificer's Guild copper wall sconce, design attributed to Edward Spencer. H:27cm (10½in). ③ **13.** Liberty & Co. Tudric pewter and enamel clock designed by Archibald Knox. H:21cm (8¼in). ⑦ **14.** Liberty & Co. Tudric pewter mantle clock. H:20cm (7¾in). ④ **15.** Cotswold School brass fender. W:123cm (49¼in). ④ **16.** Guild of Handicraft silver cigar box with enamel panel, by Fleetwood Varley. c.1904. L:20cm (8in). ⑤ **17.** Guild of Handicraft silver and enamel cigar box. 1903. H:7.5cm (3in). ④ **18.** Artificer's Guild copper and silver box, designed by Edward Spencer. 1931. H:12cm (4¾in). ② **19.** Birmingham Guild copper plate. c.1920. D:21cm (8¼in). ① **20.** Scottish School Arts and Crafts brass planter with repoussé-decorated sides. W:51cm (20in). ① **21.** Artificer's Guild copper tray, the design attributed to Edward Spencer. L:55cm (21½in). ① **22.** Ramsden and Carr silver vase set with agates. 1913. H:28cm (11in). ⑤

14 Liberty & Co. Tudric clock

13 Liberty & Co. Tudric clock

17 Silver and enamel box

18 Copper and silver box and cover

12 Copper wall sconce

16 Silver cigar box

15 Cotswold School brass fender

19 Birmingham Guild copper plate

20 Brass planter

21 Artificer's Guild copper tray

22 Ramsden and Carr silver vase

# CLOCKS

ASSOCIATIONS WITH THE DAILY CYCLE OF LABOUR AND REST RAISED THE STATUS OF THE CLOCK DURING THE ARTS AND CRAFTS PERIOD. CLOCKS WERE DESIGNED AS PART OF AN OVERALL DECORATIVE SCHEME.

## METALWORK CLOCKS

Clocks took on aspects of design appropriate to the materials from which they were made. Consumers began to see the appeal of unified interior furnishings and removed the clutter of the 19th century. In response, clock manufacturers started to model their cases in the dominant styles of the day. At one end of the spectrum individual artist-craftsmen designed and produced clock cases as bespoke commissions, while at the other multinational companies such as the Hamburg American Clock Co. mass-produced fashionable clocks. Bridging the gulf between these two extremes came retailers such as Liberty in London and Tiffany in New York.

### DECORATIVE DEVICES

Decorative elements on clock dials and cases ranged from structural flourishes to labour-intensive embellishments such as repoussé or embossing (hammering on the reverse side to create relief patterns). As well as beautifying the

**MANTEL CLOCK** Made by the Hamburg American Clock Co. for export, this clock has a copper dial set in a wooden carcase. The architectural copper facing has Arts and Crafts style exposed riveting. *c.1900. H:30.5cm (12in).*

clock face while remaining faithful to the material, this technique allowed artisans to display their skill at both embossing and chasing – defining the decoration by impressing outlines from the front. After the Celtic revival peaked around the turn of the 20th century, repoussé decoration frequently took the form of entwined knots and similar devices. Repoussé work was suited to silver and brass, and firms such as Keswick and Newlyn specialized in

*The angular bends* of the entrelac border decoration are characteristically Celtic

*Arabic* numbers rather than Roman numerals were favoured for Arts and Crafts clocks

*Spiral motifs* were much used in Celtic art. These three-lobed examples may represent the Trinity in Christian iconography

**BRASS WALL CLOCK** Made by a metalworker of the Scottish School, the clock's octagonal form incorporates a circular dial with Arabic numbers, within a band of repoussé Celtic interlacing and spiral motifs reserved on a hammered ground. *c.1900. D:36cm (14in).*

**ORIVIT MANTEL CLOCK** Designed by Albin Müller for the German manufacturer Orivit, the chased silvered-pewter case is a stylized plant form raised on tendril-like supports. *c.1900. H:23.5cm (9¼in).*

**ZODIAC DESK CLOCK** Made by Tiffany Studios, the cathedral-shape case has a gold-doré finish. Both the front and sides have polychrome enamelled signs-of-the-zodiac medallions linked by entrelac work. *c.1905. H:13.5cm (5¼in).*

## AESTHETIC CLOCKS

Aesthetic designers were more concerned with the visual impact of individual items than their place as part of a coherent whole. Their clocks therefore had more decorative embellishment than those made by adherents to Arts and Crafts principles. This example displays features typical of Aesthetic Movement trends, the most obvious being the strong Japanese influence. The Satsuma-style ceramic plaques that surround the clock face are drawn indirectly from the Japanese tradition. The intricate turning of the wooden frame serves no structural purpose and would be rejected by an Arts and Crafts designer as frivolous decoration. The wood has been ebonized, whereas Arts and Crafts woodwork was often stained more subtly, allowing the grain to show through.

**MANTEL CLOCK** The turned and carved, ebonized wooden case is in the Anglo-Japanese architectural style of the Aesthetic Movement, and is inset with floral polychrome Satsuma-style tiles. *c.1880. H:40.5cm (16in).*

embossed copper. Exposed rivets on some metal mantel clocks displayed a sympathy with the idea of structural honesty, making a feature out of fixing the component pieces together.

### APPLIED ORNAMENT

As well as features integral to the structure of the clock, many manufacturers applied ornament to achieve the decorative effect they wanted. Enamels, cabochons, and patinas enhanced the metal and wooden ground of the clock case. Popular motifs included galleons and other devices traditionally associated with timepieces.

Of particular note were the many clocks of the period that bear admonitory inscriptions – variations on the theme "Time Flies". These mottoes reflected the work ethic of the Arts and Crafts philosophy, which valued honest toil and frowned upon idle pursuits and wasted time.

The silver and pewter clocks that Archibald Knox designed for Liberty & Co. as part of the store's Cymric and Tudric ranges often had bright enamel dials picked out in primary colours. Across the Atlantic Tiffany & Co. produced bronze desk clocks with scrollwork designs as part of the Zodiac range. Less orthodox materials were used to create timepieces by companies branching out from their traditional areas. Doulton, for example, produced ceramic clocks as part of its art pottery range.

### LONGCASE CLOCKS

Longcase clocks of this period tended to be similar in style to cased furniture. They had plain wooden surfaces, sometimes stained to emphasize the natural grain of the wood. Surface decoration was scarce, and when it was present was usually restricted to subtle use of contrasting inlay.

In keeping with the doctrine of structural honesty, pendulums and weights were often visible, either through a glass door or structural gaps in the case.

**EBONIZED MANTEL CLOCK** Designed by Charles Rennie Mackintosh in characteristically linear style, its ebonized wooden case is inlaid with erinoid (an early type of plastic). *c.1917. H:33cm (13in).*

**LONGCASE CLOCK** The clean, straight lines softened with subtle curves of Richard Riemerschmid's designs are evident in this German clock with a fruitwood frame and a hammered-copper face. *c.1905. H:213.5cm (84in).*

# TEXTILES

FABRICS WERE A KEY ELEMENT OF THE INTEGRATED ARTS AND CRAFTS
INTERIOR. LIKE LEADED GLASS, FABRIC PRINTING, AND WEAVING, THEY
PROVIDED THE CHANCE TO RESURRECT NEGLECTED CRAFTS.

## UNPICKING THE PAST

Before taking rooms at Red Lion Square in London
during the 1850s, William Morris and Edward
Burne-Jones toured northern France's Gothic
cathedrals. This reinforced Morris's admiration
for medieval leaded glass, and the pair were awed
by the Lady and the Unicorn tapestries at Cluny.

Back at home in London, Morris sat at a
traditional wooden embroidery frame for hours and
taught himself stitches by unpicking and reworking
old samples. Later, he had his wife Jane and her
sister Bessie produced a series of appliqué and
embroidery wall hangings that he had designed
for the Red House, his new marital home.

**LINEN PILLOW** American-made and decorated, the pillow is stencilled and
embroidered along three sides with a formalized, dogwood flower and leaf
pattern in shades of blue, green, reddish-brown, and yellow, against an
oatmeal ground. *c.1900. W:49.5cm (19½in).*

## NEEDLECRAFT

Passing the baton to his female relatives proved
prophetic, as Arts and Crafts textiles came to be
dominated by women more than any other area.
Candace Wheeler, a colleague of Louis Comfort
Tiffany and the foremost American practitioner of

Arts and Crafts needlework, ascribed this to the
willingness of polite society to let women create and
even sell handcrafted goods with the proviso that
"she must not supply things of utility – that was
a Brahmanical law". Nonetheless, many women
achieved positions of prominence through
needlework. Morris passed control of his firm's
embroidery production to his daughter May in
1885. The wife of Thomas Wardle, with whom
Morris had collaborated to create many of his early

**BIRD PATTERN** This woollen textile is woven on
a Jacquard loom with one of William Morris's most
popular patterns: Bird. Here seen in a predominantly
red colourway, it was also produced in blue and in
green. *c.1880. L:73.5cm (29in).*

**CREWELWORK SEAT COVER** One of a set of eight,
the William Morris-style pattern of flowering sprays
and foliage was worked in coloured wools by Lady
Phipson Beale on an unbleached linen ground. She
learned her needlework skills from her sister-in-law,
Margaret Beale, who in 1872 helped found the Royal
School of Art Needlework with Princess Helena's
patronage. *1880s. L:44cm (17½in).*

**EMBROIDERED SCREEN** Made by Morris & Co., this
screen has a tri-fold mahogany frame enclosing three
three needlepoint panels with different flower and
foliage patterns. The centre panel displays the Parrot
Tulip pattern, primarily in shades of red and green, and
one of Morris's best-known designs. *c.1900.*

MORRIS & CO. The photograph shows craftsmen hand block-printing chintz patterns in the home crafts workshops of Morris & Co.

STRAWBERRY THIEF PATTERN Presenting thrushes among strawberry plants, this was one of William Morris's most popular designs. This detail is from a pair of printed cotton curtains. *1890s. L:286cm (112½in).*

Needlework was formed in Massachusetts in 1896. Its aim was to preserve the embroidery techniques of the first settler pilgrims.

## AN EMERGING PATTERN

Like the wallpapers for which Morris remains famous, his fabric designs are primarily made up of large, repeating patterns featuring two-dimensional representations of plant and animal life. A master of the mirror-repeat, Morris's best-known works still include block-printed textile patterns such as "Strawberry Thief", "Acanthus", and "Bird".

The Silver Studio became a prolific supplier of fabric patterns to Liberty & Co., which counted them among its best sellers. Established and respected designers such as Walter Crane and Charles Voysey also became involved with fabric design, indicating how far the Arts and Crafts movement had elevated the status of this often dismissed art form.

patterns and dyes, established an embroidery school in Staffordshire. Its members embarked on a re-creation of the Bayeux Tapestry in 1885. The Scottish School produced many skilled female needleworkers – Phoebe Traquair and Jessie Newbery in particular had a huge influence on the direction of textile design with work soaked in Celtic myth. Bessie Burden was head instructor at the Royal School of Art Needlework for a time.

Women up and down the country set themselves to work stitching designs bought from Morris, Marshall, Faulkner & Co. and other companies to decorate their own homes. This was the Arts and Crafts ideal in action, taking work away from the factory and restoring it to the hearthside.

## REINVENTING TRADITION

Printed and embroidered Arts and Crafts textiles were produced by traditional methods. Morris was opposed to the use of artificial or chemical dyes and

experimented with a wide range of plant products to achieve his Aesthetic palette of indigo, sage green, peacock blue, yellow, red, and brown.

Many of the recipes he devised with Thomas Wardle were derived from Elizabethan models. The Hammersmith range of hand-knotted carpets was indebted to ancient Persia in terms of both design and manufacture. Indeed, so labour-intensive was this process that only the wealthiest industrialists and aristocrats could afford them. Textiles presented one of the biggest challenges of making quality crafts affordable.

To make his work more widely available, Morris engaged the Wilton Royal Carpet Factory to produce high-quality machine-made versions that sold at a fraction of the price. This was a significant compromise for Morris, and was a tacit admission that factory production could be put to good use.

Traditional Flemish methods were the basis for much of the tapestry production and leading designers such as John Henry Dearle created some superlative examples. Many firms experimented with Eastern techniques for applying patterns to fabric such as wax resist, also known as batik, and discharge printing. The Society of Blue and White

ESSEX A.17 PATTERN C.F.A. Voysey's stylized floral design was commissioned by Scott Morton & Co. for its Essex range of fabrics and wallpaper. It is shown here as a framed and glazed woodblock proof. *c.1900. L:74.5cm (29¼in).*

# ART NOUVEAU
## 1880–1915

# SINUOUS CONTOURS

FEMININE AND LUXURIOUS, WITH WHIPLASH CURVES AND SEMI-CLAD
MAIDENS, ART NOUVEAU WAS A REACTION TO THE HISTORICAL REVIVALS
THAT HAD DOMINATED FOR DECADES. IT TRANSFORMED THE DECORATIVE
ARTS AS THE 19TH CENTURY CAME TO A CLOSE.

## NATURE AS INSPIRATION

Art Nouveau is one of the most easily recognized
design styles, with its use of exotic materials, rich
colours, curves, asymmetrical lines, and shapes
inspired by nature. A great success in its time, it
inspired architects and designers and continues to
capture the imagination today.

Art Nouveau was the result of intense activity by
visual artists that began in the studios, workshops,
and galleries of the art world but then quickly
moved out across the whole of late 19th-century
culture. It was both elitist and popular, loved and
hated, and occurred not just as architectural
decoration for new museums and official buildings
and in beautiful furniture and jewellery,
but also on biscuit tins, posters, menus,
and children's toys. It was high art, but
also provided the imagery for erotic
theatre and pulp pornography.

## MODERN STYLE

Despite its disparate and often conflicting
nature, Art Nouveau was defined by
modernity. It was the first self-conscious,
internationally based attempt to transform
visual culture according to modernist
ideas. The world was changing fast at the
end of the 19th century, with
technological, economic, and political
developments reshaping the physical
environment. Rapid industrialization, the
growth of cities at the expense of the
countryside, the invention of the
motorcar, the electric light bulb, the
typewriter, and much more besides were
all transforming people's lives across
Europe and in the Americas. A new
aggression in international trade and the
European competition to acquire colonies
in Africa and the Pacific were remodelling
the world on imperialism.

**ALPHONSE MUCHA PLATE** Advertising a mythical product for teaching
purposes, this poster by Mucha has the favoured Art Nouveau subject matter
of an idealized woman with stylized hair and a flowing gown. *c.1902.*
*H:45cm (17¾in).*

These changes did not affect every country in the
same way, which partly explains the differences in
Art Nouveau from place to place. But wherever
they came from, Art Nouveau artists all rejected
the idea of a hierarchy – with fine art at the top
and the decorative arts at the bottom – in favour
of an equality of the arts so that they could all be
made accessible to everyone. When *Les Six* group

**PARIS DOORWAY** The whiplash tendrils
that appear to grow out of the figurehead
and engulf the entrance and first floor
exterior are typical of French Art Nouveau.

**EUGÈNE FEUILLÂTRE CUP**
This silver and enamel cup
and cover is based on an
azalea. The bud terminal tops
the azalea-decorated cover
and body and the stem curls
into roots on the pedestal
foot. *1901. H:25cm (10in).*

**ART NOUVEAU DINING ROOM** Integrated interiors are the epitome of Art Nouveau design. This dining room in the Musée de l'Ecole de Nancy was designed by Eugène Vallin in 1903 and features carved wooden panelling, fireplace, and dresser. The ceiling and leather-upholstered furniture are by V. Proute.

of artists exhibited in Paris in 1898, they stressed that: "It is necessary to make art part of contemporary life, to make the ordinary objects that surround us into works of art."

Art Nouveau designers drew on a wide range of natural, historical, and symbolic references, combining them in surprising ways, sometimes to produce complete interiors. The ideas behind it were formulated in the 1880s but found public expression in 1893, in the drawings of Aubrey Beardsley and the architecture of the Belgian Victor Horta, and in 1895 in the manifesto *Déblaiement d'Art* (A Clean Sweep for Art) written by another Belgian, the polemicist Henry van de Velde.

## UNIVERSAL EXHIBITIONS

After 1895 Art Nouveau quickly spread to the major cities of Europe and North America and, after 1900, around the world. This wide success can be traced to the international exhibitions, those hugely popular world fairs of industry, commerce, and the arts held at regular intervals in the great cities of the world. Art Nouveau made its first appearance at the Brussels exhibition in 1897 and was far more in evidence in Paris in 1900. Two years later, in Turin, almost every pavilion and its contents reflected the new style.

Yet Art Nouveau was little in evidence at the Brussels exhibition in 1910 or the Glasgow and

Turin exhibitions the following year. By then, its role as a modern style had come to an end and its commercial viability was in steep decline. By the time World War I began in August 1914, Art Nouveau had almost disappeared.

**DAUM FRÈRES GLASS VASE** The Daum brothers, Antonin and Auguste, produced blown and cased glass and cameo glass, and used cutting, engraving, painting, and enamelling. This vase is etched with a peacock feather decoration. *c.1905. H:25.5cm (10¼in).*

# ELEMENTS OF STYLE

A RT NOUVEAU ARTISTS AND CRAFTSMEN self-consciously developed their own vocabulary of motifs adapted from nature. Plants, animals, and sensuous women were the main sources of inspiration, often metamorphosing from one to another. In the best examples, form and decoration complement each other to create a unified whole. Although they claimed to have turned their backs on tradition, especially Classical sources, craftsmen also borrowed techniques and ideas from the past but reinterpreted them to create their own, new decorative style.

E. BARRIAS BRONZE FIGURE
### THE FEMALE FORM
The nude was a time-honoured staple of the fine arts, but now sensual female figures, often semi-clad in diaphanous robes or turning into animals or plants, were popular for small-scale sculptures. They also adorned all types of decorative objects from jewellery to furniture and lamps.

EMILE GALLÉ CAMEO GLASS VASE
### CAMEO GLASS
Cameo glass is made by using several layers of coloured glass. Carving or etching away areas of the top layer reveals the underlying glass and creates an image in relief. This technique was adopted enthusiastically by Art Nouveau glassmakers, who used up to five sheets of different coloured glass.

BRASS FIRE SURROUND
### WHIPLASH MOTIF
The key linear motif of Art Nouveau was based on the shapes of swirling plant roots and was similar in look to that of an unfurling whip. As early as 1882, Arthur H. Mackmurdo used the whiplash motif in a distinctive chair back. Hermann Obrist's whiplash embroideries became iconic emblems of the style.

WMF PEWTER CARD TRAY
### ASYMMETRY
A characteristic feature of Art Nouveau, asymmetry owed a debt to the art of Japan. The frothy asymmetry of 18th-century Rococo, which was revived in the 19th century, was also influential. Both shape and decoration could be asymmetrical, often reflecting organic forms found in nature.

DAUM FRÈRES CAMEO GLASS VASE
### DRAGONFLY
The distinctive shape and bright colours of the dragonfly, a familiar sight in the French countryside around Nancy, was used on Art Nouveau glass vases and inspired René Lalique's iconic dragonfly-woman brooch. Émile Gallé even adorned furniture with the dragonfly form, complete with bulbous eyes.

WELLER POTTERY VASE
### INNOVATIVE GLAZES
New, experimental glazes were a striking feature of Art Nouveau ceramics, from Bohemia and France to the United States. Red glazes fired at high temperatures were used on stoneware. Crystalline glazes that produced a speckled finish and lustrous metallic glazes were also commonly used.

TIFFANY LABURNUM LAMP
## LEADED GLASS
Pieces of stained glass enclosed in a metal framework were not only used in window panels but also made into lampshades, so the colours of the glass glowed when the lamps were turned on. Lead was traditionally used for windows, but the more flexible copper was often favoured for lampshades.

LOUIS MAJORELLE CABINET
## MARQUETRY
Elaborate marquetry – making a picture or pattern out of different coloured pieces of wood – was a form of craftsmanship beautifully revived by the furniture-makers of the Nancy School in France. The natural world – from local wildflowers to insects – was the main source of inspiration.

STEUBEN AURENE VASE
## IRIDESCENT GLASS
Contemporary excavations of ancient Roman glass with a pearly sheen inspired Art Nouveau glassmakers to try to re-create the effect themselves, making iridescent glass. They used metal oxides when firing glass to create pieces with gently shimmering, multicoloured surfaces.

ARTUS VAN BRIGGLE VASE
## TULIP DECORATION
The theme of nature unified all aspects of Art Nouveau and was based not only on local flora and fauna, but also on the exotic species often seen in botanical publications. A popular decorative motif, especially for vases, was the tulip, sometimes influencing the shape as well as the decoration of a piece.

SÈVRES PORCELAIN VASE WITH A GILT-BRONZE MOUNT
## GILDED BRONZE
As in many late 17th- and early 18th-century French pieces, bronze was often moulded into mounts and gilded to create a shiny gold surface that framed and complemented a piece of porcelain or glass. Most mounts, such as the one shaped like a frog and lily pad above, were based on natural motifs.

DAUM FRÈRES WINTER LANDSCAPE GLASS VASE
## ETCHED AND ENAMELLED GLASS
Much early French Art Nouveau glass, especially that of Gallé and Daum, was elaborately patterned or bore pictures made by acid-etching, which creates a look similar to that of an etching. The graphic effect of the picture was then strengthened by painting on glowing colours with enamels.

JOHANN VON SCHWARZ PANEL
## *FEMME-FLEUR*
Quintessentially French Art Nouveau, the *femme-fleur* is half-woman and half-flower. The image of a dreamy maiden with flowing hair, much loved by Symbolist poets and artists, was usually entwined with swirling plant tendrils and appeared on metalware, posters, and ceramics.

EDMUND DIOT WALNUT STAND
## HANDCARVED WOOD
As the division between fine and decorative arts became increasingly blurred, sculptors used the forms of furniture to display their skills, and furniture-makers carved wood like sculptors. Motifs included leaves, fruit, flowers, the undulating lines of stems and roots, insects, and the female form.

# FURNITURE

FRENCH FURNITURE-MAKERS WANTED TO BREAK FREE FROM TRADITIONAL CONSTRAINTS, AND NANCY AND PARIS BECAME LEADING CENTRES OF INNOVATION.

## A FRENCH REVOLUTION

The town of Nancy in eastern France was brimming with creativity in the 1890s, and Émile Gallé and his protégé Louis Majorelle were its stars. Many of the style aspects adopted by the school founded by Gallé can be seen in his famous vitrine (*see right*). These include the use of glossy wood, with exotic species for the marquetry (applied small wooden shapes) that covers every flat surface; pierced carvings of Japanese cherry blossoms; and asymmetrical elements.

## NANCY AND NATURE

As a botanist and symbolist, Gallé turned nature into furniture – not just in decoration, but in form, too, with rails shaped like dandelions, headboards resembling moths, frog table feet, and butterfly handles. Dragonflies also abounded, with their bulbous eyes gleaming out of dark, sumptuous woods at the corners of little tables. Marquetry was a traditional technique, but few were as masterful in its use as Gallé, who integrated it into his pieces beautifully, creating delicate plant and animal designs out of different woods for vitrines, table tops, chairs, and bedsteads.

Majorelle was also an exponent of marquetry, but he found its intricacy time-consuming. Familiar with the widespread gilding of

**Detail of marquetry on the top tier**

*Elegant C-scrolls* support the top tier

**TWO-TIER TABLE** The two tops of this rosewood table are inlaid with fine floral marquetry. Designed by Émile Gallé, this rare and important piece was made for the 1900 Paris *Exposition Universelle*. H:83cm (32½in).

*Carved, out-swept legs* are in keeping with contemporary sinuous forms

**WALNUT VITRINE** Designed by Émile Gallé, this vitrine is glazed at the front and sides and has an asymmetrical two-tier interior and exquisite marquetry panels. With a carved, pierced cresting and apron, the piece is raised on carved, out-swept legs. H:148cm (58¼in).

**MARQUETRY TABLE** This two-tier mahogany table was designed by Louis Majorelle. It has bronze foliate handles to the sides and is raised on carved and moulded "W" end supports. W:89.5cm (35¼in).

**GILTWOOD SIDE TABLE** The mottled marble top of this table is set within a carved moulding above a frieze. The tapering, stretchered legs have pierced tops. It was designed by Louis Majorelle. H:78cm (30½in).

18th-century furniture and its 19th-century reproductions, he came to favour gilt-bronze mounts over marquetry. The region of Lorraine, of which Nancy is the capital, was an iron-smelting area, and Majorelle also used wrought iron for decoration.

In order to attract buyers from farther afield than Nancy, Majorelle established *ateliers* (workshops, or studios), in which an assembly line of workers produced multiple identical pieces of furniture to be sold throughout France. Quality and prices were high, and the materials used were deliberately rich to appeal to the luxury market. Dark hardwoods such as mahogany were often incorporated into his pieces.

## COMPLETE INTERIORS
This new generation of designers was not content to design only furniture: they wished to create entire interiors and, since many among them were architects, the exteriors of buildings as well. They believed that everything should go together, as a *Gesamtkunstwerk*, or total work of art. Many of these designers were trained in other artistic disciplines, so they bypassed the traditional French furniture stages of a design being implemented by an *ébéniste*, a

master craftsman who controlled the making of a piece. This idea of a united creative picture governed by a single designer came to fruition with the Art Nouveau designers of Paris.

## ELEGANT AND STYLIZED PARIS
These wishes for autonomy on the part of the designers coincided with the vision of entrepreneur Siegfried (also called Samuel) Bing, who opened his shop La Maison de l'Art Nouveau in Paris in 1895 and gave the style its name. He envisaged whole salons of interior design in the latest fashion and hired leading cabinet-maker Léon Jallot to oversee furniture production. Bing commissioned Georges De Feure, Edward Colonna, and Eugène Gaillard to design the furniture. Colonna and De Feure

designed sitting rooms for Bing's pavilion at the 1900 Paris *Exposition Universelle*, choosing a restrained mode between Louis XV and XVI, with sophisticated carpets, embroidery, and upholstery to complement the furniture. De Feure's – featuring gold-leafed furniture and a butterfly-backed sofa – earned him a gold medal. Colonna's creations incorporated the Parisian stylized use of decoration, suggesting and abstracting nature, rather than proclaiming it. Decoration took a back seat to form, instead of the exuberance of Nancy motifs. Colonna also designed silver mounts for Tiffany glassware, shown at the same Exposition.

Gaillard designed the bedroom and dining room for Bing's pavilion, moulding wood into stem-like forms that took their inspiration from plants. Bends and curves dominated, and one particular armoire featured undulating mirror plates. The native woods used at the beginning of the 19th century were out of favour; Gaillard used exotic woods such as mahogany, amaranth, rosewood, and dark walnut, lightening the panels of the pavilion's bed with figured ash. He sculpted with wood, squeezing it into the required shapes. But while Bing picked the best of the young Parisian designers, another name stands above them all: Hector Guimard.

**The crest of the chair** is pierced and carved with sinuous plant forms

**The frame** features delicate floral scrolling carving

**The plant theme** is echoed in carvings on the chair legs, which terminate in square feet

**CARVED WALNUT CHAIR** The floral, embossed leather upholstery of this chair is original. It sits within a pierced, carved frame with bronze mounts at the tops of the legs. Designed by Eugène Gaillard. H:107.5cm (42in).

**ROSEWOOD-FRAMED FIRESCREEN** This rare piece was designed by Edward Colonna and features distinctive, stylized floral fabric. The frame is raised on dual standard ends. H:80cm (31½in).

## THE STYLE EVOLVES

Visitors who arrived at the 1900 Paris *Exposition Universelle* via the city's underground system would have passed through the still-startling landmark Metro entrances designed by Hector Guimard. Their vegetal, writhing, cast-iron lines gave rise to the alternative name for the Art Nouveau movement: *Le Style Métro*. As an architect-designer in no doubt of his own talents, Guimard put his stamp on every aspect of a commission. His furniture was majestic and architectural, charged with linear swirls, contorting wood as if it were metal. Designers such as Léon Benouville soon followed suit.

### CLEAN, SWEEPING LINES

Like Eugène Gaillard, Guimard owed something to the streamlined forms of the Belgian designer Henry van de Velde. Originally a painter in Antwerp, van de Velde built himself a house in 1894, designing everything, from the exterior to the furniture, plates, knives, and forks – right down to the clothes that his wife was to wear in it.

Passionate about the decorative arts, in 1895 van de Velde published the pamphlet *Déblaiment d'Art* (A Clean Sweep for Art). Like Eugène Emmanuel Viollet-le-Duc in France and John Ruskin and William Morris in Britain, he campaigned for an end to the hierarchy of the fine arts (architecture, sculpture, and painting) above design and the decorative arts. He demanded equality for all – be it building exterior or interior, large or small sculpture, metalware, ceramics, furniture, or graphic art. "Suddenly they were called arts of the second rank, then decorative arts, and then the minor arts... None of [the arts] had been independent; they were held together by a common idea, which was to decorate...We can't allow a split that aims at single-mindedly ranking one art above the others, a separation of the arts into high art and a second-class, low industrial art," wrote Van de Velde in his pamphlet.

Siegfried Bing visited van de Velde's house and commissioned him to design four rooms in his Paris shop. Sweeping forms give van de Velde's furniture a sense of movement that is sympathetic to the natural curves of wood. The extreme distortion of wood

**MIRROR** The gilded plaster frame of this mirror was designed by Hector Guimard, and the curved foliage is reminiscent of his designs for the Paris Metro. *H:137cm (54in).*

that characterized some Parisian examples was not for van de Velde: he chose light-coloured native woods such as beech, walnut, and oak, and his decoration was minimal. Around 1900 he moved away from the organic base of nature as inspiration, towards a Classical, plainer style.

**SIDE TABLE** Léon Benouville designed this mahogany side table with mixed-wood marquetry. Below the inlaid table top is a single drawer above a narrow cupboard. The table has four supports and handmade brass fittings. *c.1900. W:86.5cm (34in).*

### WHIPLASH HORTA

Guimard was quick to acknowledge the influence of another Belgian architect-designer, Victor Horta. Horta also designed his own house from top to bottom, as well as those of several other wealthy Brussels inhabitants. But while van de Velde was influenced by the refined simplicity of the Arts and Crafts style, Horta opted for an airy exuberance

*The central open shelf* is flanked on either side by a small cupboard

*The top of the desk* has a distinctive kidney shape

*The tapering legs* are finished with faceted brass shoes

**Copper key mounts and brass mounts are the only embellishments**

**LADY'S BUREAU** Designed by Henry van de Velde, this mahogany desk has an organic, sweeping shape that is characteristic of his streamlined style. *c.1905. W:123cm (48½in).*

**Detail of pull on cabinet drawer**

**DOUBLE BED** The panelled head- and footboards of this light-brown-stained mahogany bed have profiled edges and are joined by graduated side panels. The bedside cabinets are integral to the design, which is by Victor Horta for the Solvay House in Brussels. *1894. L:200cm (80in).*

**MUSÉE HORTA, BRUSSELS** The Brussels home of Victor Horta has been turned into a museum. The exuberant whiplash motif of this staircase is typical of the Belgian architect's decorative style.

unmatched since Louis XV. The centre of his house – and of others he designed – was an iron cage, with windows at the top so that light flowed down the stairwell. In his hands, a staircase became a place in its own right – somewhere to linger and enjoy rather than a mere passageway from one floor to the next. Horta liked open spaces where people, air, and light could circulate.

He manipulated daylight by using subtly coloured leaded glass in skylights and windows, so that his clients could enjoy the play of light and coloured shadows and reflections to the full. He exploited electric as well as natural light in interesting shapes such as bells, flowers, and showers of stars, always with a particular focus – to illuminate a dining table, or to embellish the colours of a stained-glass window.

The whiplash was Horta's leitmotif – energetic and vital. The sinuous wooden rail of the banisters in his houses was combined with frenetic swirls of

iron that cast shadows on the wall. In many houses he decorated the walls at banister level with a similar whiplash pattern.

Like many Art Nouveau designers, Horta was influenced by the Gothic and Rococo revivals, as well as by the asymmetry and light touch of Japanese art, but he added an individual Brussels flavour to these elements. He played with contrasts of material, juxtaposing cold metal with warm wood and smooth marble with rough stone. He favoured the use of warm colours, reflected in the walls and carpets of his house and the light brown stain of his mahogany furniture. As well as mahogany, Horta used fruitwoods and maple, combined with rich upholstery in materials such as velvet or silk, set on thick carpets or marble floors. Horta's furniture was designed for specific houses, and it often had a dual purpose: the double bed (*see above*), for example, has integrated bedside tables and cupboards.

## CARLO BUGATTI

Like other European designers, the Italian Carlo Bugatti (1856–1940) was looking for a new artistic direction – although his own route was unconventional. He was a craftsman with workshops in Milan, and his furniture was handmade and sometimes handpainted.

Heavily influenced by Middle Eastern and North African architecture and Japanese art, Bugatti incorporated keyhole arches, Egyptian latticework, and decorative inlays based on Arabic writing into his furniture. As well as exotic motifs, he drew on materials such as the silk tassels used on Persian rugs, or used leather and vellum for upholstery and table tops. He often featured inlays of metal, ebony, bone, and mother-of-pearl, too. Bugatti liked to mix wood with brass and pewter, and used quirky decorative devices such as wheel-shaped leg supports and dragonfly handles.

Although his pieces were not particularly comfortable or usable, Bugatti was commissioned to supply the Egyptian royal family with furniture and won first prize for his Moorish interior at the 1902 Turin World Fair.

**CORNER ARMCHAIR** This chair by Bugatti is inlaid with brass and pewter, and the curved arm and back rail is covered with embossed copper and encloses circular totems tied with ropes. The square seat is upholstered with vellum.

*Wheel-segment supports* are characteristic of Bugatti's work

**BUGATTI DESK** This walnut gilt-bronze-mounted desk strung in brass and pewter has two small shelved cupboards above a skiver inset writing surface. *H:92.5cm (36½in).*

## GERMAN JUGENDSTIL

In Germany furniture and other decorative arts had their own renaissance centred around a breakaway band of young designers in Munich. The exhibition in 1897 at the Glaspalast – Munich's answer to London's Crystal Palace – devoted three rooms to the decorative arts. These included glass by Gallé and Tiffany but also showcased the work of Munich designers such as Richard Riemerschmid, Hermann Obrist, and Bernhard Pankok. Designs submitted had to "fulfil the requirements of our modern life", as well as being original, rather than simply new versions of historical styles. However, anything that "overstepped the limits of artistic decorum" or was "exaggerated and misguided through a disregard for materials or through a striving for originality" was to be excluded. So, the excesses of French Art Nouveau were not for the Munich Secessionists. Jugendstil (New Style, derived from the name of the contemporary literary and artistic publication *Jugend*), as Art Nouveau was called in Germany,

was a more sober affair, hovering between British Arts and Crafts and the Wiener Werkstätte, with the occasional continental flourish.

Riemerschmid, among other organizers of the Applied Art Section, consolidated the aims of the exhibition by setting up the *Vereinigte Werkstätten für Kunst im Handwerk* (United Workshops for Art in Handicraft) the same year. Despite the title, handicraft was less important than division of labour, using the latest technology, and bringing modern designs to a wide public, so that everyone involved could make a living.

### RECTILINEAR RESTRAINT

Originally a painter and architect, Riemerschmid first designed furniture in 1895 when he could not find any that she liked for his new marital home. As with his exhibits at the Glaspalast in 1897, he drew on the Arts and Crafts movement for form and Art Nouveau for decorative brasswork and carving; his ornamentation, however, was abstract rather than

**MAHOGANY ELBOW CHAIR** Each arm is carved from a single piece of mahogany, and the tapering legs have block feet. Designed by Richard Riemerschmid. *1897. H:83cm (32½in).*

**Each door panel** has a square inset, echoing the rectilinear form of the piece

**Applied wrought-iron bands** on the top two sections are the only decorative detail

**The rectilinear form** is in keeping with the German Jugendstil movement

**THREE-PIECE PINE CUPBOARD** The top two sections of this cupboard each have two two-part hinged doors, while the lower section has three doors. Designed by Richard Riemerschmid and made by the *Dresdner Werkstätten*, this pine cupboard has a silky, matte polish. *1902. H:211cm (83in).*

**LEMON-MAHOGANY CUPBOARD** Jugendstil references can be seen in the simple, organic relief carving and ornamental copper mountings. The cupboard was designed by Patriz Huber. *1902. H:200cm (80in).*

parts and to designs by Bruno Paul. Riemerschmid fulfilled both elaborate commissions at the top of the market and purely functional furniture designs similar to those of van de Velde, with clean, straight lines softened by slight curves. This "semi mass production" was a huge financial success, and the two workshops amalgamated. Other designers such as Patriz Huber also produced bold, functional designs. Huber carved linear motifs and patterns that offered a more subtle decoration than the continental whiplash. But many German designers ignored all modern styles, and continued producing plain Neoclassical or solid, heavily carved Baroque furniture.

**CHERRY ARMCHAIR** Designed by Bruno Paul for the *Vereinigte Werkstätten für Kunst* in Munich, this elegant chair is polished and upholstered. *1901. H:90cm (36in).*

## AUSTRIAN STYLE

Austria had a similar success story to that of Germany. Thonet's bentwood chairs, first produced in the 1840s, were a household name throughout Europe and even in the United States. The technique of steaming solid or laminated wood so that it could be bent naturally produced the curves characteristic of Art Nouveau. Other Vienna firms, including J.&J. Kohn, built their reputations on bentwood furniture, employing designers such as Marcel Kammerer.

naturalistic. Riemerschmid's furniture was praised by contemporary critics for its spatial awareness and because "its structure is rendered wholly transparent", with simple construction and "modest materials". Emphasizing structure highlighted rather than hid how the furniture was made.

One of Riemerschmid's big commissions was for "The Thieme House" in Munich. Each room had a unified design: formal for the drawing room, with golden motifs and mother-of-pearl inlays repeated

on chairs and cabinets; simpler for family rooms. He also designed carpets, light fittings, and cutlery for the house, and gained a separate commission from Meissen for a porcelain service.

Most of his furniture was made in the Dresden, later German Workshops of Munich, as well as the German Workshops of Dresden-Hellerau. From 1907 the Berlin branch of the United Workshops concentrated on serial production, making *Typenmöbel* (type furniture) from standardized

## ARTS AND CRAFTS CROSSOVER

In Britain and the United States, most new furniture stayed within the Arts and Crafts mould, contemporary with continental Art Nouveau. Many designers worked across two ranges: one simple and plain in local woods, and the other more luxurious, with hardwoods and exotic inlays. Some manufacturers, such as Wylie & Lochhead and Shapland & Petter, used Art Nouveau motifs in their work but their solid architectural forms were more akin to the Glasgow School than the Continental Art designers.

**MAHOGANY HALLSTAND** The rectangular, bevelled mirror sits below a repoussé copper panel with inscription above a pierced frieze of plant motifs. The base incorporates a walking-stick stand and seat. *W:107cm (42in).*

**SALON SUITE** The seating in this suite consists of a settee and two armchairs. The chairs have solid, bentwood beech frames and button-back leather upholstery. Designed by Marcel Kammerer, and produced by J.&J. Kohn, Vienna. *c.1910. Settee: W:75cm (29½in).*

# CERAMICS

WHILE MANY PORCELAIN MANUFACTURERS CONTINUED WITH THEIR TRADITIONAL OUTPUT DURING THE ART NOUVEAU PERIOD, WORKERS IN STONEWARE SET A TREND FOR EXPERIMENTING WITH NEW SCULPTURAL SHAPES, PARTICULARLY IN FRANCE.

**The bud-like shape** reflects the designer's interest in natural forms

**BUD-SHAPED STONEWARE CACHEPOT** Featuring three moulded nymphs around the rim, this Delphin Massier vase has a green, red, and golden lustre glaze. c.1900. H:44cm (17½in).

## INNOVATIVE GLAZES

Non-porous and durable, stoneware had previously been used mostly as a utilitarian medium for containers. It was Théodore Deck who started the movement of French artist pottery when he set up a studio in Paris in 1856 making decorative earthenware. His followers were at the vanguard of the new art, experimenting with innovative, often lustrous glazes that glinted with different colours as they caught the light. Usually fired only once, at *grand feu* (high temperature), stoneware was glazed by adding salt to the kiln. For the first time, potters could call themselves artists. Their status rose, as did that of their materials: stoneware became as popular as porcelain.

In Germany designers such as Richard Riemerschmid and Peter Behrens introduced new colours and decorative motifs – including stylized flowers – to stoneware tankards and flagons. But it was French ceramicists who really brought out the sculptural qualities of the hard material. A sculptor called Jean (Joseph-Marie) Carriès was inspired by the Oriental stoneware at the 1878 Paris *Exposition Universelle*. He started working in stoneware to create figures of Christ, pagan gods, fauns, and other mythical beasts, and waifs and strays on the street. Carriès triggered a reappraisal of stoneware, and other artist-potters started to work with the material, trying out new glazes that emphasized form.

The fact that stoneware was fired only once added uncertainty and meant that each piece was unique. As the painter Paul Gauguin, who worked extensively in unglazed and red-glazed stoneware, said: "Nature is an artist. The colours achieved in the same firing are always in harmony."

## COMBINING ART AND SCIENCE

For many ceramicists, the glaze became more important than the vessel itself. Artists looked to science for new chemicals that would produce new effects. Deck disciple Ernest Chaplet and Auguste Delaherche experimented with iron-red flambé glazes for stoneware, creating rich reds speckled or streaked with other colours such as green, blue, or white. They later applied flambé glazes to porcelain, too. Pierre-Adrien Dalpayrat perfected a glaze of saturated red speckled with green that came to be known as *Rouge Dalpayrat*.

Chaplet, Delaherche, and others also revisited the techniques of Renaissance lustre-glazed Hispano-Moresque wares. They would spray metal oxides into the kiln and cut off the oxygen by blocking the air vents at a key moment. The result was an explosion of gases reacting with the oxides. Once the sooty surface of the vessel was polished, the glaze gleamed like metal. In the past, lead, tin, copper, and iron oxides had been used, but now the repertoire extended to chromium, titanium, and uranium (banned in the 1920s).

In Great Britain these experiments were carried out by the likes of William De Morgan. In 1892 he said of the mystique attached to lustre glazes: "In spite of reproductions, an impression continued to prevail that the process was a secret. I used to hear it talked about among artists, about 25 years ago, as a sort of potters' philosopher's stone."

**TAPERING BELGIAN POTTERY VASE** This circular vase by Henry van de Velde features a twisting, sinuous abstract decoration in green and honey-coloured glazes. H:28.5cm (11¼in).

**STONEWARE VASE** This Pierre-Adrien Dalpayrat stoneware vase with blue and beige glaze is signed "Dalpayrat 1008". c.1905. H:32.5cm (12¾in).

**DELAHERCHE VASE** Glazed in blue on a brown ground, this stoneware vase bears the maker's mark. c.1890. H:36.5cm (14½in).

## SYNERGIZING SHAPE AND GLAZE

If any ceramics can be described as essentially Art Nouveau, it is arguably those produced by the Massier company. This sculptural stoneware decorated with plant forms and semi-clad females typifies the style. Pots were decorated with a lustre glaze developed by Clément Massier, who ran the family factory near Nice in the south of France. His brother, Delphin, who had his own pottery, specialized in sculptural detail, such as owls, applied beneath the overall lustre glaze.

In Belgium Henry van de Velde was as creative as his French counterparts, coming up with organic shapes, sinuous decoration abstracted from nature, and glazes with colours that flowed seamlessly into one another. Adding boric acid to the recipe created streaky glazes with running colours.

## EASTERN EUROPEAN INNOVATIONS

France was not the only country with exciting developments in ceramics. In 1879 Hungarian manufacturer Vilmos Zsolnay came to study ceramics and Oriental art in London and Paris. He had bought his company from his brother in 1865, when it made stoneware in traditional Hungarian peasant style, and built it up to employ 1,000 workers by 1900. He courted ceramic pioneers to come up with new glazes and aesthetics, and in the 1890s one of his chemists, Vince Wartha, invented a new lustre glaze called eosin. It flooded iridescent colour across the ceramic body, which now often took a floral, asymmetrical form. Low-relief moulded detail was a feature of Zsolnay wares. Wartha became artistic director in 1893, and the company specialized in painted decoration created with lustred glazes.

The Zsolnay factory also produced a range of crystalline glazes. Mineral salts added to a coloured glaze formed crystals that looked like frost or ice.

The vase is decorated with a lustrous, iridescent glaze

*LA NUIT* MAJOLICA VASE
The tapering form of this vase by Jean-Baptiste Massier rises to a poppy-seed pod rim, while at the neck of the vase is the figure of an owl. Both elements are associated with and symbolic of the night. H:26cm (10¼in).

The vase is applied with an owl in relief

Original maker's mark clearly visible on the base of the vase

The sinuous outline is modelled with tendrils

The flowers are vividly coloured

RARE VASE WITH STOPPER Produced by the Hungarian manufacturer Zsolnay, this vase has a purple-red and iridescent blue glazed body with a berry-moulded stopper. The pierced body of the vase is decorated with vibrant relief-moulded flowers. H:27cm (10½in).

## ACROSS THE OCEAN

Throughout the history of ceramics, new ideas and techniques have been passed on as experienced workers moved from one factory or country to another, either out of choice or because they had to. Former employees would take their knowledge with them, and new recipes for ceramic bodies and glazes, ideas for shapes, and techniques quickly spread around Europe and to North America. The lustre glazes of the Weller Pottery in Ohio, USA, demonstrate this perfectly. They were very similar to European glazes because their maker, Jacques Sicard, had originally trained as a potter in France under Clément Massier, before going to work at the Weller Pottery in 1901. He eventually returned to France in 1907.

TAPERING VASE With a moulded rim and an iridescent copper ground, this vase is decorated with brightly coloured leaf and branch motifs. It was designed for Weller by the French potter Jacques Sicard. c.1905. H:22.5cm (9in).

## TRADITION AND INNOVATION

While the pottery industry was given a new lease of life by the Art Nouveau movement, traditional porcelain factories hesitated to abandon the successful formula of the previous 100 years and continued making high-quality reproductions of 18th-century designs.

In some cases, however, conventional vases and other objects were manufactured alongside items displaying more contemporary shapes and motifs. The big factories employed new designers for the change in look. The German company Meissen, for example, commissioned Henry van de Velde, among other leading designers, to produce tableware. In France Sèvres, with its royal backing and the inspirational Théodore Deck as director from 1897

until his death in 1901, was also vigorously progressive in strands of its output. The factory commissioned Hector Guimard, who provided Art Nouveau forms in his distinctive fluid sculptural style for stoneware and porcelain.

### REMARKABLE DEVELOPMENTS

Sèvres and Royal Copenhagen in Denmark sparred over their own development of crystalline glazes, using zinc and quartz oxides. The Swedish company Rörstrand produced similar pieces to Royal Copenhagen. Taxile Doat, a disciple of Deck, developed a *pâte-sur-pâte* range for Sèvres, using a technique where he built up a design in relief with layer upon layer of slip. He applied the decoration to porcelain vases and plaques with female figures.

Doat also had his own works, where he experimented with glazes. He wrote in 1903: "The ceramicist does not exist without his kiln any more than a violinist without his violin." With his hands-on approach, taking responsibility for the whole

process rather than handing a design over to a thrower and decorator, Doat was a great influence on American studio pottery.

Meanwhile, as well as its new glazes, Royal Copenhagen developed high-temperature underglaze colours. The soft, hazy blues, greens, and browns, used to paint Danish landscapes influenced by Japanese art, invited a deep look into the glaze.

### FLORAL DECORATION

For many ceramic factories the Art Nouveau style was translated into rich floral motifs, whether applied, incised, or painted. Royal Copenhagen's fellow Danish factory, Bing & Grondahl, also used smoky underglaze colours. It applied naturalistic plant forms to its vases with metal mounts that harmonized with the painted decoration. Both Danish factories were praised for their ceramics at the 1900 Paris *Exposition Universelle*.

The Amphora range of vases made by Riessner, Stellmacher & Kessel (RSK) in Bohemia, in what

**RÖRSTRAND PORCELAIN VASE** The pale grey-blue ground of this urn-shaped vase is decorated with swirling sea currents and stylized red manta rays. The base of the vase bears the factory stamp. *H:23cm (9in).*

*The handles* are shaped like the tails of stylized manta rays

**SILVER-MOUNTED PORCELAIN VASE** The narrow neck and base of this teardrop-shaped vase by Bing & Grondahl of Copenhagen are adorned with pierced silver mounts. The body of the vase is decorated with clover leaves in muted colours. *c.1900. H:17cm (6¾in).*

*The silver mounts* bear poppy motifs

*Thistles* and spiky foliage are moulded in relief

**AMPHORA VASE** The sinuous handles of this ovoid vase are the stems of the thistles and foliage that decorate the vessel. Marked "Amphora, Made in Czechoslovakia". *H:43cm (17in).*

**Brightly coloured** stylized thistle

**Shaped, square-section** body

**EGGSHELL-PORCELAIN VASE** The body of this extremely thin, lightweight vase is decorated with stylized thistles in yellow and orange. The vase is marked "Rozenburg, den Haag". *1902. H:27cm (10½in).*

was to become Czechoslovakia, also received international acclaim. These vases were organic in shape, down to details such as the rim opening out like a flower or handles shaped like stems. Nature also inspired the decoration of the vases, such as embossed water lilies and lily pads, in an exuberant manner similar to the School of Nancy. Flowers and foliage were painted and moulded in relief and highlighted with gilding. As well as adopting the Art Nouveau idiom by fusing naturalistic form and decoration, Bohemian Amphora ware also featured dreamy women with flowing hair and the whiplash motif of curved lines.

In the Netherlands, the Rozenburg and Gouda ceramic factories painted stylized flowers in a unique Dutch manner. Gouda's abstracted plants in strong colours were inspired by the printed cloths, or batiks, typical of their colony, the Dutch East Indies (now Indonesia). By contrast, Rozenburg made exquisite "eggshell porcelain" in flamboyant shapes. Not true porcelain, its fragile thinness was matched by the delicate floral painting floating across the white surface.

Sèvres also painted naturalistic decoration by hand, generally on to traditional shapes, and entwined flowers into patterns in delicate pink, green, blue, and yellow on a white ground.

**This figure** is portrayed playing the tambourine; the other is a dancer

**SÈVRES FIGURINES** This pair of bisque-porcelain figurines was designed by Agathon Léonard for Sèvres. They come from a set of 14 female figures dancing and playing music. *Tallest: H:36cm (14in).*

## FEMALE FIGURES

Many factories capitalized on the vogue for erotic images of women. Sèvres made a stunning table setting of 15 biscuit-porcelain figures designed by Agathon Léonard in 1898. The porcelain was unglazed to focus attention on the sculptural beauty rather than the decoration. The series was based on the flowing scarf dance of the American dancer Loïe Fuller and was exhibited at the 1900 Paris *Exposition Universelle*. Royal Copenhagen also had a fine line of figures. Dancers, children, and satyrs were delicately coloured to bring out the sculptural detail.

In Bohemia Royal Dux specialized in nymphs draped on supports decorated and shaped with rocks, shells, waves, and plants. Naked or semi-clad, the maidens were painted with pale colours and highlighted with gilding. Many German and Austrian ceramicists, such as Ernst Wahliss in Vienna, also produced porcelain female figures. Meissen continued to sell copies of figures from the 18th century, which still sold in huge numbers in 1900, and subsidized new experiments with technique and form.

**The colours are naturalistic**, and have gilded highlights

**A large shell** amid scrolling waves forms the base of the figure

**FIGURE OF A MAIDEN** Reminiscent of 18th-century forms, this voluptuous, semi-clad maiden is modelled leaning against rockwork. The piece bears the impressed pad mark of Royal Dux. *H:42cm (16½in).*

**EARLY NEWCOMB COLLEGE VASE** The elegant yellow and light blue blossoms on this exceptional vase were carved by Leona Nicholson, against a stylized cobalt and deep green ground. *H:32cm (12½in).*

# AMERICAN ART POTTERY

In the United States the tradition of art pottery, which had begun with the Arts and Crafts movement, continued during the Art Nouveau period. Some large commercial works such as S.A. Weller and Roseville rapidly caught on to the international style or copied the originality of firms such as Rookwood. Others such as the Newcomb Pottery developed their own distinctive line of Art Nouveau vases with a regional flavour.

## SOUTHERN FLAIR

The American Civil War of 1861–65 decimated the male population in the United States, and meant that women had to take on jobs formerly held by men, such as pottery-making. In 1895 the New Orleans-based Sophie Newcomb College for Women set up a pottery department. Mary G. Sheerer, a ceramic painter who had trained with Rookwood, taught design. Along with director Ellsworth Woodward, Sheerer led a team of keen students, and together they developed some of the finest American art pottery. Each piece was unique, hand-thrown and handpainted, or modelled.

Woodward's aim was to create "a Southern product, made of Southern clays, by Southern artists, decorated with Southern subjects". The decoration was based on Louisiana flora and fauna, including tobacco and cotton plants, jonquils, lizards, and waterbirds, as well as more abstract motifs indirectly inspired by Japan. Plant drawing was a required course, and many students kept gardens in which to study nature at first hand.

The earliest vases had glossy glazes, with stylized flower patterns incised in outline and painted underglaze. Later wares were covered with matte, muted glazes and soft pastel colours – yellow, blue, green, and black gave way to pale blue, white, and

**OVOID VASE** Thick green stems emerge from the base of this matte blue vase, rising to the delicate narcissus flowers that decorate the vase's neck. They were carved by Henrietta Bailey at Newcomb College. *1918. W:17.25cm (6¾in).*

**LARGE NEWCOMB COLLEGE VASE** This blue, white, and soft-cream vase carved by Sadie Irvine depicts a night-time landscape with palm trees and a full moon. *H:25cm (9¾in).*

**Detail of the star-shaped heads of the narcissus flowers**

*CUERDA SECA* POTTERY These two pieces are typical of the work produced at the Paul Revere Pottery of the Saturday Evening Girls' Club: a simple, brightly coloured bowl depicting a landscape scene with large white geese and green trees; and a bullet-shaped wall pocket with yellow poppies on a white and lime-green ground. The colours and *cuerda seca* technique used for decorating these pieces are reminiscent of early Spanish works. *Bowl: W:29cm (11½in); Wall pocket: H:15cm (6in).*

Artus Van Briggle's mark

VAN BRIGGLE VASE This early vase features embossed leaves under a matte raspberry glaze. *1904. H:25cm (9¾in).*

## VAN BRIGGLE

Uniquely in the United States, the ceramics of Artus Van Briggle were directly influenced by French Art Nouveau.

cream. Decoration became freer. Sadie Irvine, a student who later ran the department, produced one of Newcomb's most famous designs: a dreamy bayou landscape of oaks covered in Spanish moss, with a pale yellow moon half-hidden by the trees.

Students could sign their own work and sell their best pieces to help fund their tuition. As well as Irvine, key names that emerged from Newcomb include Harriet Joor, Anna Frances Simpson, and Henrietta Bailey.

After Ellsworth Woodward's retirement in 1931, quality declined, and Newcomb College's pottery department closed in 1940.

### A NEW SKILL FOR WOMEN

In 1906 James J. Storrow and Edith Brown set up the Saturday Evening Girls' Club in Boston. The aim of this concern was to teach underprivileged girls, often from immigrant families, a craft they could both enjoy and earn money from. The workers learned how to glaze, fire, and decorate thrown pots. The club flourished and soon moved to a bigger site, renaming itself the Paul Revere Pottery after the local silversmith hero of the War of Independence.

The club produced earthenware breakfast bowls, nursery sets, and other useful items. The decoration – flowers, animals, witches on broomsticks, sailing boats, windmills, and landscapes – was often outlined in black, setting off the colourful palette. It was frequently drawn on to the vessel using the *cuerda seca* technique, which involved creating a wax outline to prevent the glaze from running during firing. Instead, the glaze would bead up, subtly flooding the delineated area with colour.

DINNER PLATE The centre of this Paul Revere blue-grey plate features a landscape medallion. The plate also has an "FG" circular stamp on the rim. *D:30.5cm (12in).*

Although the founders set up the club for benevolent rather than commercial reasons, the enterprise flourished and moved again in 1915 to purpose-built premises based on those of Rookwood. Output expanded to include candlesticks, lamps, book ends, and paperweights, but the children's bowls decorated with animals remained a popular line. The Saturday Evening Girls' Club closed in 1942.

BUD VASE This Paul Revere vase is covered in an unusual, thick, green mottled glaze dripping over a blue-grey ground. *H:17.5cm (7in).*

While working at Rookwood, Van Briggle was sent to Paris to study sculpture and painting. Learning to model in clay helped him both at Rookwood and at his own pottery works, which he and his wife Anna set up in Colorado Springs in 1901. Van Briggle's best-known range, Lorelei, displays a typically sculptural feel, with the hair and arms of a languid woman curving around the neck of the vessel, fusing form, function, and decoration. Other decorative motifs include embossed stylized plant patterns or Native American designs. Van Briggle also perfected the use of matte glazes. He often employed an atomizer for spraying on coloured glazes, green being most common, though blue and maroon were also favoured.

Van Briggle died of tuberculosis at 35 in 1904. His wife continued to run the company, only selling it in 1912 and today it is still in production, largely making copies of Van Briggle originals.

SIREN OF THE SEA BOWL The rim of this centre bowl is decorated with a moulded recumbent mermaid figure and has a flower frog in its centre. The bowl is covered in a shaded, matte turquoise glaze. *1920s. H:19cm (7½in).*

# CERAMICS GALLERY

Floral forms are a common theme on these ceramics – the flowers featured tend to be in full bloom, softening the contours of the designs. Young beautiful women, usually portrayed with long, flowing hair, are another popular motif. These curvy lines are typical of the liberated, naturalistic aesthetic that characterized Art Nouveau. Decoration was often moulded in relief to give a greater feeling of depth and texture. Art Nouveau ceramicists favoured a naturalistic palate of greens and browns, although brighter colours and gilding were sometimes added as decorative highlights.

## KEY

**1.** Salvini faience plate with a woman's head in polychrome on a white ground. D:15cm (6in). ①
**2.** Foley Intarsio circular wall plaque depicting two maidens within a band of water lilies. D:38cm (15in). ① **3.** Amphora pottery vase painted with stylized tulips. H:18.5cm (7¼in). ① **4.** Johann von Schwarz vase decorated with sword lilies. H:56cm (22in). ③ **5.** Dutch eggshell-porcelain vase with a single handle. H:15.5cm (6in). ④ **6.** French pottery plate based on a design by Alphonse Mucha. D:31cm (12in). ② **7.** Charlotte Rhead for Bursley Ware bowl with tube-lined Glasgow Rose decoration. D:27.5cm (10¾in). ② **8.** Utzschneider & Co. Sarreguemines vase, with tulip decoration in violet and blue. H:21.5cm (8½in). ① **9.** Eichwald Pottery vase moulded with flowers and with stylized handles. H:25cm (9¾in). ① **10.** A. Stuchly tapering vase, embossed with a lady's

1 Salvini faience plate

2 Foley Intarsio wall plaque

3 Amphora pottery vase

4 Johann von Schwarz vase

6 French pottery plate

5 Dutch porcelain vase

7 Bursley Ware bowl

8 Sarreguemines vase

9 Eichwald Pottery vase

10 A. Stuchly vase

head covered in a brown and green matte glaze. H:30.5cm (12in). ② **11.** Nippon vase decorated in Coralene with yellow and orange lilies on a shaded ground. H:22cm (8¾in). ② **12.** Frainersdorf ceramic vase by P.A. Wranitzki. H:14.5cm (5¾in). ① **13.** Nippon vase decorated in Coralene with pink and russet peonies on a shaded ground. H:21cm (8¼in). ② **14.** Royal Bonn floor vase slip-decorated in matte glazes with thistles and acanthus. H:55.5cm (22¼in). ② **15.** Teren vase embossed with large gold flowers and cabochon hearts on a green ground. H:35.5cm (14in). ① **16.** Moorcroft bulbous vase in the Orchid pattern. H:44.5cm (17½in). ① **17.** Rare Weller Fru Russet vase embossed with flowers under a pale blue-grey and green glaze. H:35.5cm (14in). ③ **18.** Macintyre squat vase painted with stylized poppies and foliage in the Imari palette. H:15.5cm (6¼in). ① **19.** Johann von Schwarz vase with stylized floral imagery. H:9.5cm (3¾in). ② **20.** Two-handled Foley Intarsio vase by Frederick Rhead, decorated with stylized poppies. H:28cm (11in). ①

11 *Nippon lily vase*

12 *Frainersdorf vase*

13 *Nippon peony vase*

14 *Royal Bonn floor vase*

15 *Teren vase*

16 *Moorcroft vase*

17 *Weller vase*

18 *Macintyre vase*

19 *Johann von Schwarz vase*

20 *Foley Intarsio vase*

# ÉMILE GALLÉ

REJECTING THE MID-19TH-CENTURY TASTE FOR HEAVY-CUT CRYSTAL GLASS, GALLÉ EXPLOITED THE TRANSLUCENT AND PLIANT QUALITIES OF THE MEDIUM. HE WAS A PIONEER IN THE FIELDS OF CERAMICS, FURNITURE, AND, ABOVE ALL, GLASS, DISPLAYING ARTISTIC FLAIR AND A WIDE RANGE OF TECHNIQUES.

**AUX LIBELLULES VASE** Made by Gallé, this pale amber vase was designed by Eugène Kremer. It is etched, enamelled, and gilded with dragonflies – a seminal Art Nouveau motif. c.1885. H:13cm (5in).

Born in Nancy, the heartland of French Art Nouveau and a renowned glassmaking area, Émile Gallé (1846–1904) was the son of a glass and faience factory owner. As well as learning the family business, he studied botany, drawing, and landscape painting and travelled throughout Europe. In 1874 Gallé took over his father's factory, and four years later he exhibited at the Paris *Exposition Universelle*. Here, seeing how other avant-garde glassmakers were moulding and treating the material, inspired him to embrace innovative designs. In turn, Gallé's own exhibits, which included enamelled decoration with gracefully stylized plant motifs interpreted from Japanese art, were an inspiration to others.

## LOVE OF NATURE

Gallé saw nature as the underlying force of life. The organic shapes of his designs and decorations found a parallel in the natural world, and his depictions of plants, insects – especially his favourite, dragonflies – and other animals were scientifically accurate.

Gallé chose to depict natural motifs for more than just random aesthetic reasons. He used them symbolically, sometimes including lines of Symbolist poetry by Stéphane Mallarmé or Charles Baudelaire, leading to the tag *verres parlantes* (talking glass). When Gallé helped found the School of Nancy in 1901, he educated his pupils in the theory of symbols. Beetles stood for hard work; thistles for his home region of Lorraine and its separation from Germany; roses for France and love; poppies for sleep; and pine trees he called "a metaphor of energy in repose". Gallé also drew heavily on the swirling asymmetry of Rococo designs – Nancy's central square has a superb example of Louis XV ironwork – and dizzyingly reinterpreted medieval, Islamic, Oriental, and Classical sources.

## TECHNICAL VIRTUOSO

Gallé used a medieval Syrian enamel painting technique to work on glass as freely as if he were using watercolour on paper. He also adopted the internally crackled and coloured glass that fellow glassmakers were using, originally inspired by Chinese carved rock crystal and Japanese lacquerwork. He manipulated light within and without glass using clear, colourless, coloured, and painted glass.

Cameo glass is perhaps Gallé's best-known legacy. In this ancient Roman technique two layers of different coloured glass are fused together. The top layer is then carved, so that the image stands out from its surrounding, lower layer of

glass. Gallé took this basic technique a step further, using up to five similar colours, so that he could shade one into another, creating the illusion of light and shadow. In a lamp, lit from within, the effect was even more subtle and glowing.

Instead of carving the outer layers of glass, acid-etching could be used to eat away the areas around the relief image. Other technical innovations saw Gallé placing metal foil between the glass layers to provide highlights, or pressing small pieces of hot coloured glass into the molten glass body – a glass adaptation of marquetry. Once the glass cooled down, the pieces could be carved.

## THE WORKSHOP

By 1890 Gallé employed more than 300 workers. Only occasionally did he have the time to make the piece himself, so he would usually hand his designs over to trusted glass-blowers and decorators. He also allowed his team of designers artistic freedom, so long as they represented botanical and animal motifs with realistic precision.

After Gallé's death in 1904, a star was added to his signature engraved on glass as a mark of respect. For a time the factory was run by his widow and his lifelong friend Victor Prouvé. After World War I, however, Gallé's son-in-law Paul Perdrizet took over, producing mainly cameo glass with floral designs. The factory closed in 1936.

**GALLÉ AT WORK** Émile Gallé shown in his studio surrounded by botanical specimens and drawings.

**CAMEO GLASS TABLE LAMP** Wild flowers decorate the domed shade and base of this lamp. The organic shape and fascination with nature are typical of Gallé's work. *Early 1900s. H:35cm (13¾in).*

**CHRYSANTHEMUM VASE** Of tapered ovoid form, this cameo vase is etched with chrysanthemum blossoms, buds, and branches in dark ruby-red glass over an amber ground. c.1900. H:31.5cm (12½in).

**OVAL VASE** This vase is decorated in marquetry style with daffodils, each element individually carved. The vase is engraved with Gallé's signature. 1900. H:18cm (7in).

# GLASS

ART NOUVEAU FOUND ITS IDEAL MEDIUM IN GLASS. NOT ONLY COULD IT

BE MOULDED INTO FLUID SHAPES, IT ALSO LENT ITSELF TO THE STYLE'S

RICH COLOURS AND MULTILAYERED DECORATION.

## CAMEO GLASS

Research into ancient techniques combined with innovative industrial methods allowed designers to push the boundaries of glass decoration. At the forefront of the glass revolution was Émile Gallé (*see pp.206–07*), closely followed by the Daum brothers, who in 1887 had taken over their father's glassworks in the French decorative-arts capital of Nancy in the Lorraine region. Cameo glass was a speciality of both factories.

After seeing Gallé's glass at the 1889 Paris *Exposition Universelle*, the Daum brothers were inspired to make their own versions. They also drew on the flora and fauna local to their region for motifs; but while Gallé had invested them with symbolic fervour, the Daum brothers were mostly concerned with the accurate rendition of the natural world.

### INNOVATIVE TECHNIQUES

In order to make plants, animals, and their background setting look even more realistic, the Daum brothers developed a series of complex decorative techniques.

In some instances, the decoration on a vessel would be acid-etched. This process could also be done by a machine, in which case the glass was defined as "faux cameo" to distinguish it from handcarved cameo glass. Once the glass was cold, enamels – powdered coloured glass bound in an oil medium – would be applied over the decoration to give it a natural sense of depth. Enamelled vessels could be sold as they were, without another firing, or reheated to fuse the design to the body and make them more hard-wearing.

**BARREL-SHAPED VASE** Decorated with freshwater plants and dragonflies, this cameo vase is etched and enamelled in subtle shades of blue, green, yellow, and purple. The mottled effect of the glass is characteristic of much glass produced by Daum Frères. Signed "Daum, Nancy". *1904. H:23cm (9in).*

**SPIDER'S-WEB VASE** This rare Daum vase has cameo decoration of green iris blossoms and leaves on a frosted chipped-ice background. A cameo green spider rests on a gold enamel spider's web (*inset, right*). The vase sits in its original embossed silver holder and is signed "Daum Nancy" in gold lettering on the base. *H:23.5cm (9¼in).*

**TWIN-HANDLED VASE** The pink ground of this cameo glass vase is decorated with green trailing-vine motifs. The green of the foliage and swirling tendrils is repeated in the base of the vase and in the handles. It is signed "Daum Nancy". *H:21cm (8¼in).*

Other techniques perfected by the Daum brothers included the *martelé*, or hammered-metal, effect, borrowed from silversmithing to give the surface of a vessel texture and depth; and intercalaire (literally "between the layers") decoration. In this technique, a decorative layer is applied, then covered with a sheet of coloured glass, which acts as the surface for another layer of decoration. Daum Frères also applied high-relief foil-backed decoration and, like Gallé, used *marqueterie-sur-verre* (marquetry on glass), mainly on the Nancy theme of dragonflies over lily ponds.

## THE ELECTRIC REVOLUTION

The advent of electric light meant that the Daum brothers could apply their creativity to a new range of items such as lamps and lampshades. Their collaboration with Louis Majorelle, Gallé's protégé and Nancy's leading metalworker, led to a series of lamps that combined decorated glass shades with metal mounts. Some of the best pieces are those that mirror nature in both form and decoration such as lamps shaped like mushrooms or courgette flowers.

In other instances a glass shade and base would be integrated by using the same decoration for both. The stem of the lamp was sometimes left hollow so that it, too, could be lit from within, creating a stunning effect.

## OTHER CAMEO MAKERS

In other parts of Lorraine the Müller Frères were inspired by Émile Gallé to specialize in cameo glass. Like their mentor, they also illustrated natural themes of flowers, birds, and landscapes, and dark brown and yellow were their favoured colours. Like Gallé and the Daum brothers, the Müller Frères used the technique of fire polishing, which involved melting the surface of the glass a second time to smooth out any imperfections caused by acid-etching.

Another set of brothers, Ernest and Charles Schneider, based in Épinay-sur-Seine, produced an acid-etched cameo range known as *Le Verre Français*, as well as carved, layered, and applied glass. In Paris Auguste Legras simplified the style to appeal to as wide an audience as possible.

Cameo glass had been popular in Britain 100 years earlier, in the Neoclassical era, when its success had been fanned by the Portland

Vase from Roman antiquity. However, in the late 19th century most British designers disregarded Art Nouveau, which they saw as too florid and decadent a style. A handful of artists, though, did embrace the style including Thomas Webb & Sons. This firm made some remarkable ranges of cameo glass, often combining clear glass and a colour, or using white on a coloured ground.

In the United States the Honesdale firm specialized in decorating, and brought in blanks from other companies.

**The bell-shaped shade** resembles a courgette flower

**COURGETTE-FLOWER TABLE LAMP** The arched brass stem and leaves rise from a leaf-shaped base and terminate in a colourless shade decorated with yellow and green matte-etched enamel. *c.1905.*

**The brass base** and stem are likely to be by Louis Majorelle

**NARROW BALUSTER VASE** This ovoid vase with a flared rim and a circular foot has a milky opalescent lustre and is decorated with acid-etched chrysanthemums in coral and green. Designed by Henri Müller, of Croismare, near Nancy. *c.1900. H:27cm (10½in).*

**THOMAS WEBB VASE** Featuring cameo floral decoration of roses and leaves, this three-colour cameo vase (white over red over citron) is signed "Tiffany & Co. Paris Exposition 1889 Thomas Webb & Sons Gem Cameo". *1889. H:19cm (7½in).*

**The opalescent body** is overlaid with amber- and green-coloured glass

**HONESDALE VASE** This cameo-glass vase has a narrow, tapering waist and flared rim and foot. The clear-glass ground is overlaid with acid-etched autumn leaves. There is also gilded decoration at the rim and base. *1915–20. H:25cm (9¾in).*

**FROSTED CAMEO GLASS BOWL** Made by Auguste Legras, this bulbous bowl is decorated with fruiting vines. The narrow neck has a silver band around the top. *H:14cm (5½in).*

## IRIDESCENT GLASS

In the 19th century excavations of ancient Roman sites yielded glass that had turned lustrous from being buried in damp earth. The rebirth of interest in iridescent glass heralded an explosion of creativity in the previously stagnant glassmaking world. Iridescence makes a glass vessel gleam and catch the light with a vast array of colours. Most iridescent glass in existence today was made in the Art Nouveau era. At the same time, the invention of electric light gave rise to new forms and showed off the sparkling colour. Famously associated with Louis Comfort Tiffany (*see pp.212–213*), iridescent glass was widely made in the United States, Europe, and Britain.

### METALLIC FINISHES

Methods and recipes for obtaining iridescent glass varied but, like with ceramic lustre glazes, they all involved metal oxides. Some glassmakers exposed the glass to the fumes of metallic oxides and varied the degree of heat and cooling across the glass; others preferred to spray the glass with a metal-oxide mist. Tiffany developed a complex technique that demanded precise timing. The salts of metal oxides

were dissolved in the molten glass, making the colours luminous. Different metals produced different colours: silver, for example, created a straw colour, and copper a ruby red. The glass was then sprayed with chloride while held in a reducing flame. The chloride left minute lines on the surface that refracted light, making the colours appear to change.

### HOT COMPETITION

Tiffany, however, was not the first to experiment with iridescent glass. The British firm Thomas Webb & Sons in Stourbridge exhibited "bronze glass" at the Paris *Exposition Universelle* back in 1878. Three years later Tiffany took out a patent; then in 1893 he harnessed the Stourbridge expertise by employing Arthur J. Nash, a talented glass-blower who had made iridescent glass at Webb's. The rich lustre that Tiffany and his team perfected would inspire many others.

Among Tiffany's rivals was the Steuben Glassworks, established in 1903 in Corning, New York, by Frederick Carder, another former Stourbridge worker. Carder was the driving force behind some 6,000 shapes and more than 100 finishes. His gold Aurene glass, patented in 1904, usually has a brighter iridescence than Tiffany's, while the Blue Aurene range of 1905 has a bright-blue lustre, and *verre de soie* (silk glass) is clear, with a silvery appearance. Red, brown, green, and other colours followed, used either on their own or in combination, sometimes decorated. Carder was experimenting with *pâte-de-verre* and lost wax techniques when he retired, aged 96.

### THE AUSTRIAN TIFFANY

Bohemia had long been a centre of cut and engraved glass enjoying royal patronage,

**STEUBEN DECORATED VASE** The stylized heart-and-vine decoration on this blue Aurene vase is similar to that seen in European Art Nouveau pieces. The iridescent blue finish has purple highlights. *H:26cm (10¼in).*

*Applied silver trailing* emphasizes the tapering, almost twisted shape of the vase

*The Classical shape* of the vase contrasts with the random heart-and-vine decoration

**LOETZ IRIDESCENT VASE** This glass vase of organic form is decorated with gold and petrol blue bands, as well as applied silver trailings. Signed "Loetz Austria". *H:16.5cm (6½in).*

**STEUBEN VASE** In this Gold Aurene vase with blue and purple highlights, the leaf-and-vine decoration is interspersed with flowers. The piece is signed "Aurene 582". *H:16cm (6¼in).*

but the area's fortunes had waned in the course of the 19th century. Iridescent glass provided Bohemian glassworks such as Loetz with a new lease of life. In the wake of Tiffany's success, in 1897 Loetz launched a spectacular iridescent range with wavy decoration called Phänomen. Another popular pattern was Papillon, which aimed to re-create the delicate patterns of a butterfly's wings in red, gold, or blue.

Loetz director Max Ritter von Spaun experimented with iridescent spots, ribbons, and streaks, and his vessels were sometimes overlaid with open silverwork. Vase shapes were as startling as the colour effects, often with wavy or ruffled rims or swan-necked, like Persian rosewater sprinklers. The factory also employed some of the most progressive designers of the day including Viennese Josef Hoffmann and Koloman Moser, and the Prague glass designer Marie Kirschner.

Loetz's iridescent glass was so similar to that of Tiffany's that the American artist took out a lawsuit against the Bohemian factory, preventing the import of unsigned Loetz pieces to North America.

## THE INSPIRATION OF ROMAN GLASS

In the late 19th century archaeologists excavating ancient Roman sites discovered glass that had been buried for at least 1,700 years. Metal oxides in the soil had reacted on the surface of the glass to make it textured, corroded, and iridescent. With new technology, and a good deal of experimentation, late 19th-century glassmakers managed to speed up the chemical process to create a similar surface sheen in a fraction of the time. While some designers came up with entirely new shapes, many copied not just the surface effects but also the ancient Roman forms.

**OINTMENT BOTTLES** These Roman *unguentaria*, or ointment bottles, exemplify the look that Art Nouveau designers were trying to re-create with their iridescent glass. The aim of the lustre glazes was to achieve the effect of glass that had been worn by years of being buried underground. *1st–3rd century CE. Blue bottle: H:6cm (2½in); Honey-coloured bottle: H:8.5cm (3¼in).*

### A BRIGHT NEW WORLD

In the early days of electricity many light fittings still bore a striking resemblance to traditional oil lamps, shaped as if for an oil-containing base with a domed cover above. Soon, however, it dawned on manufacturers and designers that they were no longer bound to the old shapes and they could exploit their creativity to the full.

Combining glass with metal, and integrating form and decoration, Art Nouveau artists began to flood the market with innovative and colourful lamps in the shapes of plants, flowers, or animals, such as that perennial Art Nouveau favourite, the dragonfly. The peacock, which had appeared in Roman, Persian, Indian, and Byzantine ornament, was also adopted by Art Nouveau glassmakers as the ultimate symbol of beauty and was incorporated into many designs.

*The ruffled rim* is typical of Art Nouveau and appears on much American glass

*The amber shade* is decorated with a feather pattern

**DURAND BOWL** The sides of this iridescent blue art-glass bowl are gently stepped, widening towards the base. *1920s. H:15cm (6in).*

*Light catches* the stepped sides of the bowl, casting shadows on the iridescent surface

*The yellow gold colour* graduates to a foot of green and pinkish red

**PEACOCK LAMP** The bronze base of this lamp is in the shape of a peacock holding the shade ring in its beak. The eyes of the tail feathers are set with iridescent green and blue glass that matches the "pulled" feathers in the art-glass shade made by Loetz. *c.1900. H:49.5cm (19½in).*

*Iridescent* green and blue glass cabochons are used for the eyes of the tail feathers

**FLORIFORM VASE** A ruffled rim and a flared body above a bulbous stem tapering to a splayed round foot characterize this gold-lustre vase produced by the American glassworks Quezal. The base is etched "Quezal". *H:16cm (6¼in).*

# LOUIS COMFORT TIFFANY

ART NOUVEAU FLOURISHED AS THE CAREER OF NEW YORK-BASED TIFFANY MATURED. HE MASTERED A NUMBER OF DISCIPLINES – NOTABLY SILVERWARE, JEWELLERY, AND GLASSWORK – AND HIS PIECES ARE BYWORDS FOR AMERICAN ART NOUVEAU, OFTEN CALLED THE "TIFFANY STYLE".

America's answer to Émile Gallé (*see pp.206–207*), Louis Comfort Tiffany (1848–1933) had all the credentials to become a superb designer – and the zeal to match. His father owned a successful jewellery company in New York called Tiffany & Co. The firm's art director, Edward C. Moore, was an important formative influence on the young Tiffany: he had a huge collection of Classical, medieval, Oriental, and Islamic decorative arts, and an extensive library including Owen Jones's *Grammar of Ornament*. Tiffany studied glass-blowing in Venice, met William Morris in London, and travelled to North Africa and Spain, where he painted watercolours of Moorish architecture.

## SOURCES OF INSPIRATION
At the beginning of his career, Tiffany set up an interior-design business called Louis C. Tiffany & Associated Artists, starting an unprecedented collaboration with furniture and textile designers. Like many designers of the time, Tiffany's inspirations were wide-ranging: he was interested in Celtic and Native American art, as well as the exotic. He looked to nature and to historic sources, and his glass, jewellery, ceramics, enamelled copper, furniture, wallpaper, fabrics, and mosaics were frequently decorated with natural motifs such as dragonflies, flowers, and grapes.

Form and decoration were often more important than function – a vase, for example, could become an excuse for a glass sculpture of a single flower and its stem, dispensing with the purpose of holding fresh flowers. Among such floriform vases, the most distinctive is arguably the Jack-in-the-Pulpit vase, shaped like the North American wild flower of that name. Other pieces were swan-necked, inspired by the slender, undulating shape of Persian rosewater sprinklers.

## EXPERIMENTAL TECHNIQUES
In 1894 Tiffany launched his Favrile (from "fabrile", Old English for "handcrafted") range of iridescent glass, which was an instant success. Another bestseller was the Lava range, with trails of molten glass oozing like lava down the iridescent surface of a vessel.

Tiffany also made vases in the so-called paperweight-glass style, with a magnifying dome of clear, faceted, or cased glass often enriched with a lampwork

**PEACOCK LAMP** Twenty peacock eyes decorate the orange, amethyst, and teal green shade of this table lamp. The scalloped base is decorated with a raised peacock-feather design in bronze relief, each feather with a single peacock eye made of mosaic glass. *H:63.5cm (25in).*

design or *millefiori* decoration. In this technique brightly coloured canes (tiny glass rods) are arranged in patterns and embedded in clear glass. Such glass was difficult to make into vases, and few pieces were ever produced.

## METAL AND GLASS
When art dealer Siegfried Bing opened his prestigious Paris shop La Maison de l'Art Nouveau in 1895, he bought many Favrile pieces. Then he commissioned Edward Colonna to design mounts for Tiffany vases, so that light would play over the gleaming surfaces of both the glass and the silver bases.

In 1900 Tiffany set up Tiffany Studios to make the lamps that would become his best-known legacy, embodying the marriage of metal and glass. Where the stand was an integral part of the lamp, the two elements always worked in harmony, so a flower lamp would have a base in the shape of a stem, for instance. Tiffany also made a positive feature of the metal linking the pieces of glass in the shade – it might be used, for example, to create the outlines of a dragonfly's wings or the petals of a flower.

Despite the name "leaded glass", Tiffany actually used copper rather than lead, as it was more flexible, enclosing small pieces of sheet glass coloured with some possible 5,000 variations.

**PAPERWEIGHT VASE** This rare Tiffany carved cameo vase is inlaid with different colours and engraved. *c.1910. H:18cm (7in).*

**LILY LAMP** Produced by Tiffany Studios, this three-light lily lamp has one Tiffany-style shade and two Quezal shades. Each is shaped like a blooming lily and has an iridescent finish. The piece is signed, and the base is impressed "Tiffany Studios New York 313". *H:30cm (12in).*

**MAXIM'S, PARIS** Once dubbed "the Museum of Art Nouveau", Maxim's was the place to be seen during the Belle Époque. Tiffany's luxurious interiors epitomized his talent for creating a harmonious, integral look. The stained-glass ceiling and organic-framed mirrors create a magnificent, jewel-like atmosphere.

# GLASS GALLERY

The organic forms that feature so prominently as decorative designs on Art Nouveau glassware are often echoed on the rims of vases and other vessels. Moulded or pinched rims and handles with whiplash curves extend the floral motifs. Decorative themes are overwhelmingly botanical – vistas of trees or parts of plants such as petals, tendrils and leaves predominate. Iridescent finishes, wrought by exposing the glass to metal oxide fumes, were also in vogue.

1 Carved glass vase

2 English vases

3 Auguste Jean vase

4 Footed vase

5 Harrach decanter and glasses

6 Metal-mounted vase

7 Austrian vase

8 Steuben vase

(10½in). ③ **9.** Wilhelm Kralik Sohn glass bowl with etched decoration. 1900. H:9.5cm (3¾in). ①
**10.** Amédée de Caranza vase decorated with cherries and leaves on a mustard ground. H:16cm
(6¼in). ③ **11.** Loetz vase of organic form, with trailed iridescent decoration. H:20.25cm (8in). ①
**12.** Pallme-König glass vase. c.1905. H:21cm (8¼in). ① **13.** English glass light shade with short neck
and rim and ruffled base. c.1900. H:18.5cm (7¼in). ① **14.** Elisabeth Glass Factory vase of pinched
form with threaded iridescent decoration. H:11.5cm (4½in). ① **15.** Josef Rindkopfs Söhne vase with
a trefoil lip and lappet decoration on a red ground. H:17cm (6¾in). ③ **16.** Handel Teroma covered
jar painted with birds flying in a bamboo thicket, in polychrome on dark green. H:19cm (7½in). ③
**17.** Cameo glass vase by De Vez, acid-etched with red poppies on a lemon yellow ground. H:16cm
(6¼in). ① **18.** Villeroy & Boch cameo glass vase by Edmund Rigot. c.1930. H:31cm (12¼in). ③

9 *Etched bowl*

10 *Caranza vase*

11 *Iridescent Loetz vase*

12 *Pallme-König vase*

13 *English light shade*

14 *Pinched-form vase*

15 *Trefoil-lip vase*

16 *Handel Teroma jar*

17 *De Vez cameo vase*

18 *Cameo vase*

# LAMPS

DOMESTIC ELECTRICITY REVOLUTIONIZED LAMP DESIGN. IT WAS AMERICAN
GLASSMAKERS WHO LED THE FIELD, EXPERIMENTING WITH FINISHES AND
THE OPPORTUNITY OF COMBINING GLASS WITH METAL.

## BEAUTY AND FUNCTIONALITY

While many creative disciplines of Art Nouveau
followed the Aesthetic Movement's credo of "art
for art's sake", electric lamps proved that it was
possible to be useful as well as beautiful. Lamps
could be a pleasure to look at and touch, as well
as supremely useful items, providing light at the
mere flick of a switch.

### REVERSE-PAINTING

As electricity became more commonplace
in homes throughout the United States, glass
manufacturers came up with shades designed
to enhance the beauty and effects of lamplight.
  One of the most popular techniques used to
decorate the shades was reverse-painting, in
which artists painted the inside of the lamp,
where the design would be better
protected and therefore less
subject to wear and tear.
  Transferring a design on to
a lampshade was not as
simple as transferring it
on to a flat surface,
and it involved several
laborious stages. The
starting point was a
watercolour design
with precise notes
on what colours to
use where. First
the image was
transferred to steel-
engraving plates. A thin, transparent piece of
paper was then put over the plates, and the image
was traced by piercing holes with a fine metal
point. The paper tracing was then fixed to the
inside of the shade, where it was wiped over with
a swab dipped in charcoal to reproduce the dotted
lines of the original image. The decorator filled
in the outline dot to dot and applied the
colour following the instructions given
with the original master design.

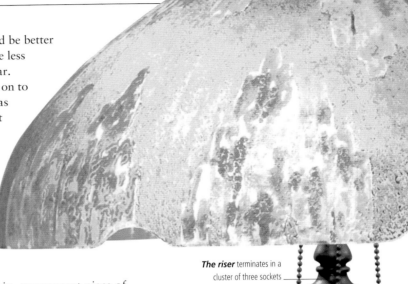

*The riser* terminates in a
cluster of three sockets

*A lava-glass
ball* supports
the riser

**LAVA GLASS TABLE
LAMP** The shade of this
rare Handel lamp has an
amber-coloured textured
background over which
white and turquoise "lava"
flows. The three-legged
bronzed-spelter base
supports a matching lava
glass ball. Signed "Handel
Lamps". *H:63.5cm (25in)*.

*The lamp stands* on
a grey-white marble foot

*Reverse-painting*
looks dramatic when
the lamp is lit

**HANDEL TABLE LAMP**
The autumnal landscape
on the lamp's hemispherical
glass shade has been reverse-
painted. The painted shade
is marked as model number
"Handel 7039", and the rim
is stamped "Handel Lamps
Patent". *H:59.5cm (23½in)*.

*The bronzed base*
is embossed with trees

*A Japanese
theme* reflects the
Oriental influence
on Art Nouveau

*The metal
base* is ribbed

**REVERSE-PAINTED LAMP**
The design of this Handel lamp
features a Japanese scene of
pine trees, mountains, and a
pagoda. The bronzed metal
base stands on a moulded
foot. *H:59.5cm (23½in)*.

**HANDEL HYDRANGEA TABLE LAMP** The shade of this lamp is painted with large pink and white clusters of flowering hydrangeas on a light green background. The lamp stands on a bronzed metal, pear-shaped base in an unusual acid-finished patina. *H:59cm (23¼in).*

*The shade* has a frosted, chipped ice finish

*The base* has two flying scroll handles and a circular foot

**HANDEL DESK LAMP** The yellow-orange, reverse-painted shade of this desk lamp is held within a metal overlay frame. The curved, sinuous lamp stem rises from a deep, rounded foot.

*Exquisite detail* is shown in the metal overlay

*The rich colours* give the lamp an almost tropical feel

## HANDEL LAMPS

One of the biggest makers of reverse-painted lamps was the Connecticut-based company Handel, which bought in ready-moulded shades of various shapes – domed, hemispherical, or cylindrical, for example. These shades were then decorated with a vast range of subjects: floral patterns, colourful butterflies and birds like macaws and flamingos, and landscapes and seascapes, whether local or exotic, the latter often inspired by the Orient. Sunset scenes looked particularly effective when the light was turned on. The curve of the shade also gave the opportunity to show depth and the effects of perspective, as objects grew paler, hazier, and smaller in the distance. In typical Art Nouveau fashion, the bases were designed to integrate perfectly with the shades, reflecting the theme of the lamp with unusual designs or figures.

## TEXTURED FINISHES

As well as painting the lamps, manufacturers textured the outer surface of the shade to diffuse the light. Ribbing was one such common effect. The more unusual finish known as frosted glass was created by a technique called chipped ice, in which glue was applied to the surface and heated. When the glue dried, it flaked off, leaving a textured finish.

## LEADED GLASS

Instead of painting or texturing a lampshade, some glassmakers preferred to use coloured glass. Inspired by the richness of medieval stained glass, Tiffany and other American manufacturers created mosaics out of glass and metal that came

to life and changed colour when the light was turned on. The subject matter, as with reverse-painted lamps, was taken from nature and included stylized flowers, insects, landscapes, and sunset scenes.

The success of the final product lay in the hands of the glassmaker, who graduated the colour even within a single tessera of glass and textured it to suit its subject matter. Glass was fibrillated and striated for the sky, rippled for the sheen of an insect wing, and fractured for a sunset or a flower. The purpose was to re-create nature in its subtle infinity of colour, light and shade, and texture.

Each piece of glass had to be cut with minute precision to slot into its allotted space in the metal framework. The base, as always, was crucial to the success of the lamp's aesthetics. The shape was naturally reminiscent of a tree trunk, and decoration on this theme was particularly apt when the lampshade was patterned with flowers or a woodland landscape.

## PUFFY LAMPS AT PAIRPOINT

The Pairpoint Corporation in New Bedford, Massachusetts, had an interesting line in top-quality lampshades. Whereas most shades were cast in a mould, this company produced blown ones, called Puffy table lampshades. Some were decorated with high-relief flowers and foliage, with naturalistic details taken to such an extent that there might be bees and butterflies alighting on the blooms. Puffy lamps were painted in pastel tints of pink, yellow, blue, and green. Pairpoint also made bases in copper, bronze, brass, silver plate, and wood. The base was designed to go with the shade, although buyers could choose from other, interchangeable styles – plain, patterned, or "tree trunk" – if they wished.

The company used a full repertoire of other decorative techniques for their lampshades including reverse painting, acid-etching, ribbing, and frosting for texture, and scenic pictures, sometimes signed by the artist. Scenes included rural local landscapes, Roman temples, and follies in landscaped parkland, sometimes combined with Neoclassical shapes on the base, and seascapes. Like Handel, Pairpoint produced other items as well as lampshades, made with cut, etched, moulded, and blown glass and quadruple-plated metal.

**PUFFY BOUDOIR LAMP** The design of this lamp is characteristic of the Pairpoint brand, with puffy roses in pink and yellow decorating the shade. The lamp has its original tree-trunk base in a silver finish. Signed "PAIRPOINT". *H:26.5cm (10½in).*

# METALWARE

METALWORK PLAYED A KEY ROLE IN SPREADING ART NOUVEAU WORLDWIDE.
FRENCH DESIGNERS TARGETED THE ELITE, WHILE GERMANY, THE UNITED
STATES, AND BRITAIN MADE PIECES FOR MIDDLE-CLASS HOUSEHOLDS.

## FRENCH LUXURY

Even more so than other craftsmen, silversmiths and metalworkers had spent the 19th century working in historical styles. Mass production gave little scope for individuality or change. Architect-designer Hector Guimard was a keen proponent of iron, and he created his own prefabricated range, writing: "Why condemn architects for using outmoded decorative devices, when component manufacturers can only supply Louis XVI models?" The same applied to domestic wares.

## TECHNIQUES AND MATERIALS

Designers at the cutting edge despised factory methods such as die-stamping and pressing; instead, they aimed to raise standards by reviving traditional techniques and using them in the modern style. Planishing – smoothing out the surface with a hammer – left a surface that could be polished and made shiny. Decoration could be raised by embossing (called *repoussé* in French). For this effect, the piece would be hammered from the inside – or the back for something flat like a tray – to push out the decoration. Chasing sharpened up the design from the front, without removing any of the silver, unlike engraving, which cut into the surface.

**SILVER WATER JUG** Simple in form and decoration, this rare piece by Maurice Dufrêne has a leaf-shaped cover and a sinuous thumbpiece. The leaf motif is repeated in other places. Stamped "Leverrier". H:20cm (7¾in).

Like many Parisian designers, Guimard and the jeweller Lucien Gaillard worked in an organic Rococo manner that was tauter and less frilly than the original style. They simplified Rococo's organic naturalism, appealing to the wealthy with extravagant materials kept simple. Guimard also let the metal speak for itself in his sculptural bronze vases. He would have agreed with artist Paul Gauguin, who asked: "Why repaint iron so it looks like butter?" However, gilding still appealed to many designers and their buyers. Although metal acquires a natural patina over time, the process can be sped up with chemicals.

Many metalware designers crossed disciplines and mixed media with confidence. Materials combined

**RARE BRONZE VASE** The sides of this tapering vase by Hector Guimard are decorated with vertical sinuous bands that culminate in high-relief whiplash curves and leafy fronds around the shoulders and neck. H:28cm (11in).

**TEA AND COFFEE SERVICE** This Paul Follot silvered-metal service comprises a tray, coffee pot, teapot, sucrier, and cream jug. Each piece features arcing, fluted decoration. Signed "Follot". c.1900. Coffee pot: H:20cm (7¾in).

with gold and silver included ivory from the Belgian Congo colony, horn, and enamels. Lucien Gaillard made exquisite Art Nouveau horn combs. Paul Follot was also an interior designer; Maurice Dufrêne, later a key Art Deco figure, was chief designer for the German art critic and dealer Julius Meier-Graefe. Dufrêne's porcelain tableware, similar in style to his silverware, sold at La Maison Moderne, Meier-Graefe's gallery outlet in Paris.

## DECORATIVE SOURCES

It was nature, the root of Art Nouveau, that inspired the shapes and decoration of silverware. With spare restraint, Dufrêne could link the handle of a jug to its body with a leaf, and more foliage would decorate the cover. Other motifs might include shells, their linear emphasis matched by whiplash curves, leafy fronds, and vertical sinewy bands. By contrast, other makers were producing works with a veritable forest of foliage, poppy flowers, and plant tendrils.

Gaillard also drew inspiration from ancient Egypt, with a scarab beetle, the symbol of sun, life, and regeneration. Taken up in the 19th

century, the scarab was a good-luck charm on necklaces, bracelets, and belts. René Lalique (*see pp.286–87*) had a similar penchant for beetles. He created hybrid creatures with the colouring of European beetles and the distinctive shape of a North Indian species. Their distinctive, life-size appearance raised questions as to whether he cast them from nature, like the French 16th-century ceramicist Bernard Palissy. Some of his hybrids were more obvious fantasy figures, such as his iconic dragonfly-woman brooch.

Gaillard had a passion for all things Japanese, even bringing craftsmen from Japan to teach him their techniques, such as painting metal. Many of the Art Nouveau motifs filtered through to the West from Japan after the country reopened for trade in the 1880s. Insects, birds, flowers (including cherry blossoms and chrysanthemums), bamboos, and fans all found their way on to silver- and metalware. The asymmetry of Japanese designs fused with that of Rococo to inspire Art Nouveau designers.

*Dense foliate decoration* covers the entire surface of the vase

*Stems of poppy flowers* rise up to form twin handles at the shoulders

**GILT-BRONZE VASE** The bulbous, tapering body of this vase by Alexandre Vibert is decorated all over with poppy motifs in high relief. The piece is signed "A. Vibert". *H:24cm (9½in).*

*Each handle is created* from a scarab proboscis

**CAST-BRONZE VASES** Made by François-Raoul Larche, each of these exceptional vases is finely cast with four allegorical female figures standing among relief-moulded lilies. The vases are inscribed with Larche's signature and the foundry mark "Siot Fondeur Paris". *H:41cm (16in).*

### SCARABÉES VASE

This striking vase designed and signed by Lucien Gaillard has a thin, tapering neck above a shaped, bulbous body. The base is cast with four applied scarab beetles, each with an exaggerated proboscis that extends to form a loop handle. *H:24cm (9½in).*

*The scarab beetles* are life-size and highly detailed

## PLIQUE-À-JOUR ENAMEL

Some of the best luxury pieces of French metalware were small items and jewellery using enamel. Technically challenging, enamelling involves fusing vitreous paste to metal at extremely high temperatures, uniting materials that expand and contract differently. The most skilled practitioners revived the ancient technique of *plique-à-jour* – enclosing translucent enamel within a fragile unbacked metal frame so that the light can shine through. It was just right for the representation of dragonflies, peacock feathers, and other such colourful but delicate motifs. Eugène Feuillâtre was chief enameller in Lalique's studio until 1897. His work proved hugely popular when he exhibited enamelled objects in his own name in 1898, as did the stunning Norwegian *plique-à-jour* enamelwork shown at the 1900 Paris *Exposition Universelle*.

**EUGÈNE FEUILLÂTRE VASE** This exquisite, silver-and-enamel twin-handled small vase, or *coupe*, takes the form of an artichoke. It has a green petal pattern around the ribbed base and *plique-à-jour* foliage handles. *W:7.5cm (3in).*

## NORTHERN EUROPE

Handmade silver- and metalware at the top end of the market was extremely expensive. Most silversmiths carried on making pieces in the traditional styles on which their reputations had been based throughout the 19th century. Other manufacturers, however, saw an opening for mass-produced ranges, using less precious metals such as pewter and electroplated brass, and working with a new look. WMF (*Württembergische Metallwaren-Fabrik*) in Germany was at the forefront of this less luxurious but still quintessentially Art Nouveau style of metalware.

### AFFORDABLE QUALITY

The designers at WMF might have been working with less precious metals, but they still adopted the florid, luxuriant forms typical of the Art Nouveau style. Some of the items they created became true icons of the French decorative style. Metal (usually pewter) vases might be decorated in relief with long-haired maidens wearing flowing robes or intricate floral and foliate patterns. The decoration was not limited to the body of the vessel but extended to the handle. Some examples have handles that mirrored the whiplash motif, while others represented female figures, such as mermaids or *femmes-fleur*.

The sinuous French and Belgian idiom was not to everyone's taste. Germany, Austria, and Britain preferred a more restrained and geometric style

(*see* The Birth of Modernism, *pp.236–63*). WMF also made wares to suit this taste. The German firm created every type of household object, from toast racks to candlesticks, mirrors to trays, and cigar boxes to fruit stands. Small wonder that its workforce escalated from 16 workers in 1853, when it first opened, to 6,000 by 1914, with factories in Germany, Poland, Austria, and outlets in London, Paris, Hamburg, and Berlin. Other manufacturers of boxes and biscuit tins distributed the style to an even wider public, making metalware second only to posters in terms of disseminating Art Nouveau.

**SILVER-PLATED WMF VASE** Made from Britannia pewter alloy and green glass, this baluster-form vase has high relief decoration of a boy emerging from flowers and reaching a rose out to a draped nude. The base has stamped marks. *H:51cm (20½in).*

**Naked boy** emerging from iris flowers

**WMF PEWTER CENTREPIECE VASE** The elongated baluster-shaped body of this vase with glass liner is decorated with a pair of *femmes-fleur*, their flowing robes forming the splayed foot of the vase. A floral pattern adorns the neck of the item, which is flanked by two whiplash handles. *c.1900. H:35cm (13¾in).*

**Toga-like robes** flow to the base of the vase, creating a splayed foot

### JEWELLERY

René Lalique (*see pp.286–287*) set a lasting trend for making the craftsmanship of jewellery more important than the value of the gold and precious gems used. Firms such as Unger Brothers in the United States specialized in mass-producing small items and affordable jewellery. They used sterling silver a lot, sometimes finished with matte gold plating. Much of their jewellery depicted the ubiquitous beautiful, languid maiden with whiplash hair. Their Floradora and Gibson Girl lines were made into brooches, bracelets, necklaces, pendants, and even earrings.

**BELT PIN** This Unger Brothers belt pin features a classic Art Nouveau motif of a girl with billowing hair. The brooch is sterling silver with selected matte ("French") finish gold plating. *1904–05. W:4.5cm (1¾in).*

## BRITISH OUTPUT

A handful of British designers made metalware in the Art Nouveau style, but their treatment of form and motif differed from the lavish continental look. Avant-garde silver designers such as C.R. Ashbee and Archibald Knox had an allegiance to the Arts and Crafts movement and found inspiration in the Middle Ages rather than in whiplashes and dreamy maidens. However, Ashbee's Guild of Handicraft became more flamboyant in its output around 1900, with exaggerated loop handles and swooping lines.

Each country was influenced by its own past, and Celtic devices – which Owen Jones described in his book *The Grammar of Ornament* as "strange, monstrous animals and birds with long top-knots, tongues, and tails, intertwining in almost endless knots" – were the dominant inspiration in Britain and Ireland. This knotty work, also known as *entrelac* (interlaced), was used in metalwork with great technical skill. The whole surface was often covered with curvilinear designs, achieved by applying spirals of gold wire. The Celtic wheel cross, the Christian cross on a circle, was another frequent motif.

## INDIVIDUALS AND ORGANIZATIONS

Architect W.A.S. Benson was the leading metalworker of the Arts and Crafts movement, excelling in brass and copper. He designed in the Art Nouveau idiom, making great use of asymmetry and motifs from nature. His domestic wares were on sale in London and in Siegfried Bing's shop in Paris.

Alexander Fisher was a sculptor turned enamellist who trained in France. His silver and enamel plaques with Celtic decoration made his name and influenced the next generation of silversmiths, such as Nelson and Edith Dawson, who set up the Artificers' Guild in 1901.

Companies such as William Hutton & Sons and Hukin & Heath were the exceptions to the Arts and Crafts dominance. They created Art Nouveau silverware with sweeping lines and entwined tendrils, mixing them with the peacock feathers beloved of the Aesthetic Movement and other Japanese-inspired decoration. Christopher Dresser (*see pp.242–243*) designed restrained silverware for Hukin & Heath that reflected the influence of Japan, while Omar Ramsden, in partnership with Alwyn C.E. Carr, blended Art Nouveau with medieval ornament and forms.

## AMERICAN SILVERWARE

The Gorham Silver Company in Providence, Rhode Island, was the largest American silver factory and one of the first to use machinery. It adopted Japanese motifs such as dragons, butterflies, bamboo, fans, fish, and Oriental bird for wares in silver and copper in the 1870s and 1880s. In the 1890s British director William Colman allocated a workshop to make Art Nouveau silver by hand. In fact, its output was only a hair's breadth away from the mainstream Rococo revival style that most American manufacturers continued to produce.

Gorham used the trade name of Martelé, meaning hand-hammered, for its new range influenced by the attention to craftsmanship of the Arts and Crafts movement as much as by Art Nouveau. The Martelé range was made to the Britannia standard, containing more silver than sterling. Launched at the 1900 Paris *Exposition Universelle*, it was phased out after 1910 as sales dropped.

Another American company, Roycroft, based in East Aurora, New York, also deliberately kept the hammer marks naturally left by planishing – hand-raising a piece from a flat sheet. In a twist of irony, the company even enhanced the marks of the hammer mechanically – using a machine to make their wares look more handmade. Unger Brothers and William B. Kerr in New Jersey both worked in the French Art Nouveau style, incorporating *femmes-fleur* and leaf patterns into their silver.

**PHOTOGRAPH FRAME** Produced by William Hutton & Sons Ltd., this silver easel-back frame is embossed with stylized peacock feathers and trailing tendrils. There is some blue and green enamelling to the arched cresting of the piece. *1904. H:22.5cm (8¾in).*

**GORHAM VASE** The spiralling sides of this vase of slender baluster form are embossed with a lily-of-the-valley decoration. The everted rim of the vase and its lobed base are composed of overlapping leaf petals. Monogrammed beneath the base. *1902. H:39cm (14½in).*

*The lily-of-the-valley* gives an Art Nouveau slant to Gorham's standard design

*Overlapping leaves* on the base and rim were central to the range

*Leaves* were a common Art Nouveau theme. Benson also used them to refract the light

**W.A.S. BENSON CANDLESTICKS** In these English counterweighted candlesticks, the candle holder sits on a copper, leaf-shaped base, which is joined by a curved stem to a copper leaf and brass fruit-shaped weight. *1890–1900. L:30cm (11¾in).*

*The addition* of weighted fruit was novel and practical

# GEORG JENSEN

Self-styled as an *orfèvre sculpteur* (goldsmith-sculptor), the Danish designer Georg Jensen (1866–1935) worked briefly but brilliantly in a unique Art Nouveau style. He intended to pursue a career as a sculptor but was apprenticed at the age of 14 to a goldsmith. While an apprentice, he went to art classes and, once qualified, he studied sculpture at the Royal Danish Academy of Fine Arts. In 1897 Jensen's wife died, leaving him with two small children (his son, Soren Georg Jensen, eventually became chief designer for the firm from 1962 to 1974). After working briefly as a modeller for Bing & Grondahl, Jensen set up a porcelain firm, which went bankrupt. His chequered career as a porcelain-maker was mitigated by two years travelling around Europe on a grant from the Danish Academy, during which Jensen witnessed the growth of Art Nouveau.

## STYLE DEVELOPMENT

Jensen also worked with Mogens Ballin, a Danish painter and silversmith who made jewellery with simple curved shapes and abstract patterns. Jensen was 37 by the time he started his own silver firm in Copenhagen. He began by making jewellery rather than silver because the materials were cheaper. By 1906 he embarked on designs for coffee and tea services, bowls, tureens, candlesticks, and cutlery. In the early stages of his career Jensen kept his majestic rounded shapes free of any distracting ornament. He gradually introduced bunches of fruit and bouquets of flowers to finials, stems, and bases, tendril-shaped handles, and paw feet. The ornament, however, never distracted from the cleanness of the shape but contributed to its elegant formality.

## A TYPICALLY DANISH LOOK

Jensen was quoted as saying: "Do not follow fashion, but be guided by the present if you want to stay young in the struggle." Following his own

**GEORG JENSEN CUTLERY** Jensen's decoration was often inspired by nature, as in these servers (*right*) and fish knife and fork (*near left and far left*). Note the shell and fish motifs on the knife and fork – a play on the function of the cutlery. *c.1920. Servers: L:20cm (7¾in); Fish knife: L:22cm (8¾in).*

**Spiralling stems** and grapes decorate the tall pedestal

**TRAINING AND SUPPORT** This picture, taken in Georg Jensen's silversmithy in 1908, portrays Jensen next to his female trainee Alba Lykke Andersen. Kay Bojesen, who was also a trainee, is shown on the left.

**SILVER TAZZA** The shallow, flared bowl of this elegant tazza is raised on a slender twisted stem that terminates in a spreading circular foot. Design No. 263. *c.1920. H:19cm (7½in).*

advice, he created designs that looked contemporary but were distinctive, original, and Danish. Their simple lines drew on both recent Danish trends and the 18th-century French traditions. The naturalistic motifs that characterized Art Nouveau and Arts and Crafts (called *skonvirke*, meaning "aesthetic work" in Danish) inspired the decoration. Jensen's statuesque shapes came from his training as a sculptor, combined with his instinctive feel for the malleable medium of silver.

As well as for the uncluttered look and pleasing proportions of his pieces, Jensen became renowned for his satin finish. He created the shiny look by annealing the piece (heating it to remove stresses and make it workable), submerging it in sulphuric acid, and then buffing it, leaving slight oxidization on the surface.

When it came to designing cutlery, Jensen produced forks with more widely spaced prongs and knives with shorter blades than usual. As in his hollow ware, the functional areas are plain and the handles decorated with motifs such as grapes, spiralling stems and tendrils, berries, and blossoms. The handles of tea and coffee services were often in ivory, contrasting with the satin surface of the silver. Occasionally he incorporated semi-precious stones such as amber.

## GROWING SUCCESS

The popularity of Jensen's wares spread to the rest of Scandinavia and Europe. His work was also successful in the United States, where the publishing billionaire William Randolph Hearst bought a whole exhibition of Jensen silver. Still in operation today, Jensen's empire now has 85 outlets worldwide. His studio is still famed for its dedication to traditional techniques, with handmade pieces. After his death in 1935, the *New York Herald* described Jensen as "the greatest silversmith of the last 300 years".

## JEWELLERY DESIGNS

Jensen's first jewellery range under his own name was created in the Danish Arts and Crafts style and exhibited in the Danish Museum of Decorative Art. It won him international recognition and gave him the freedom to expand his output.

Like other Danish jewellers of the time, Jensen worked mainly in silver. He usually left the surface unplanished, with a visible patterning of hammer marks. Sculptural like his tableware, his jewellery pieces had high-relief decoration on themes taken from Nature such as plump birds and stylized soft, round berries, foliage, flowers, and fruit. For colour, he embellished his jewellery with cabochons of semi-precious stones such as amber, amethyst, agate, and lapis lazuli, rather than the enamelwork so exquisitely executed by his fellow Scandinavians in Norway. All Jensen's work has an exceptionally high standard of craftsmanship.

**SILVER BROOCH** Acorns were a popular motif for Jensen. Here an amber acorn is central to the design of this drop-pendant brooch. *c.1905. L:11.5cm (4½in).*

## JENSEN AND HIS COLLEAGUES

Georg Jensen designed many pieces himself, but as his reputation and business grew, he also employed other designers. Mindful of his own humble beginnings and difficult youthful career, \]and with a sociable, generous nature, he encouraged creativity in his employees and allowed them artistic freedom. Jensen also acknowledged the individual contributions of his

**BALL *BONBONNIÈRE*** Designed by Johan Rohde, this *bonbonnière* has a bowl and lid with the unornamented, satin-like patina of many of Jensen's designs. Design No. 43. *1920s. H:15.5cm (6in).*

**FIVE-LIGHT CANDELABRUM** Designed by Johan Rohde, this candelabrum is raised on a baluster-form stem and faceted foot. Design No. 472. *c.1925. H:43cm (17in).*

designers, so it is usually possible to tell the exact provenance of a piece. Most pieces are marked with a design number or the initials of the designer.

Painter Johan Rohde was a key member of the silverware team. Way ahead of their time, Rohde's designs typically had streamlined shapes even simpler than Jensen's, with the emphasis on form rather than decoration. In 1906 Rohde asked Jensen for help putting his designs into practice and in 1913 agreed to an exclusive design contract with the company. So began a creative collaboration that lasted until their deaths, in the same year. Both Jensen and Rohde went on to become leading Art Deco figures.

Other prominent designers who helped ensure the longevity of the Jensen studio were Harald Nielsen, a pioneer of Art Deco and, later on, Henning Koppel and Vivianna Torun Bulow-Hube.

**GRAPE GOBLET** The stem of this simple drinking goblet of clean, rounded form is ornamented with grapes and vines – recurring motifs in Jensen's work. Design No. 296. *c.1920. H:9.5cm (3¾in).*

# METALWARE GALLERY

ART NOUVEAU DESIGNERS favoured curves, with an emphasis on sensual vitality and fertility. The whiplash curve, suggestive of plant tendrils, is often seen on metalware of the period. The same curve is generally used to depict the   is another common design feature, giving metalware an intricate complexity that again represents a stylized vision of nature.

## KEY

**1.** WMF champagne bucket designed by Albert Mayer. c.1900. H:33cm (13in). ④ **2.** Elkington & Co. set of four silver candlesticks. 1906. H:32cm (12½in). ⑦ **3.** Kayserzinn pewter candelabrum designed by Hugo Leven. c.1900. H:49.5cm (19½in). ⑤ **4.** WMF visiting card tray. c.1900. W:19cm (7½in). ② **5.** Kayserzinn bonbonnière, with a bud finial. H:11cm (4¼in). ② **6.** French silver-plated mermaid dish. c.1900. L:19.5cm (7¾in). ① **7.** Weighted silver vase of organic design with tendrils. 1906. H:23cm (9in). ① **8.** WMF electroplate photograph frame. H:25.5cm (10in). ② **9.** Orivit

**2** Silver candlesticks

**3** Pewter candelabrum

**1** WMF champagne bucket

**4** WMF visiting card tray

**8** WMF photograph frame

**5** Kayserzinn bonbonnière

**6** Silver-plated mermaid dish

**9** Gilded centrepiece

**7** Silver vase

**10** Silver-plated picture frame

centrepiece, with original gilding and liner. c.1900. L:27.5cm (10¾in). ② **10.** WMF silver-plated picture frame. c.1905. H:19.5cm (7¾in). ② **11.** G.A. Scheid silver cigarette case, the enamelled lid with a picture of a young woman. 1901. H:8cm (3¼in). ② **12.** WMF double-handled silver-plated tazza. W:24cm (9½in). ① **13.** WMF silver-plated claret jug. c.1900. H:41cm (16in). ② **14.** Albert Edward Jones two-handled silver comport. 1910. L:32cm (12½in). ④ **15.** Albert Edward Jones silver tea and coffee service. 1928–30. Coffee pot: H:19cm (7½in). ⑤ **16.** Kayserzinn pewter liquor set designed by Hugo Leven. c.1905. H:21.5cm (8½in). ① **17.** WMF silver-plated and glass claret jug. c.1905. H:43cm (17in). ③ **18.** Repoussé vase with foliate decoration. ①

**13** WMF claret jug

**11** Cigarette case

**11** Silver-plated tazza

**14** Silver comport

**15** Silver tea and coffee service

**17** WMF claret jug

**16** Pewter liquor set

**18** Repoussé vase

# CLOCKS

IN THE ART NOUVEAU ERA, EVERY FUNCTIONAL OBJECT WAS RESTYLED.

THE HUMBLE CLOCK WAS TREATED LIKE A SCULPTURE: STRAIGHT LINES

AND GEOMETRIC SHAPES WERE REPLACED BY CURVES AND ASYMMETRY.

## THE NEW METAL

The response to public demand for cheaper metalware led to the revival of pewter, an alloy of tin and lead, putting well-designed household objects within the reach of the many. Pewter had a slight softness that made it suitable for decoration. Firms such as WMF in Germany produced machine-made clocks in silver-plate of a high quality. Instead of angular contours, the sides of the clock were often gently curved, reflected in the decoration, and a female bust might grace the top. In some extreme examples the form and decoration were wildly asymmetrical. London's Liberty & Co. also sold pewter clocks in its Tudric range designed by Archibald Knox, often with an enamelled dial in contrasting bright colours.

The tall proportions of a longcase clock lingered on even in a small mantel clock. But instead of a slender rectangle, the framework softened to curves, without one single straight line. Silverwork was often embossed with Art Nouveau organic decoration such as interlaced tendrils and flowers.

## SHAPES AND FINISH

Designers created ingenious shapes such as oval hollows that made use of negative space as well as positive form. Often the purpose was to introduce a female figure, whether a nymph or fairy, either semi-clad or with artfully arranged diaphanous robes. Sometimes the figurative element extended to a couple. Mottoes on the theme of time often featured somewhere on the clock and were usually relevant to the decoration. French sculptors draped beautiful maidens over clocks in which both the shape and decoration used the organic motifs of nature.

Metal could be patinated to give it an attractive surface sheen and the appearance of age. The large ceramics firm of Goldscheider in Vienna specialized in making earthenware look like metal by enamelling it with a bronze patination. The voluminous robes of its terracotta women were used to conceal light fittings in lamps as well as to adorn clocks.

Ceramics could mimic other materials, too (*see Foley Intarsio ware box, opposite*). But one designer who had no wish to disguise the material he was using – nor, indeed, to opt for figural representation – was the Belgian Victor Horta.

## METAL TOUR DE FORCE

Horta gloried in metal. In his architecture as well as in his interiors, he exploited both the structural and ornamental potential of iron in particular. Even in delicate forms, metal could imply its strength and power. The asymmetrical whiplash that supports and decorates Horta's bronze clocks has the same verve that he brought to his ironwork banisters and balustrades.

**MANTEL CLOCK** The silvered dial of this clock sits within a broadly tapering, patinated bronze case, cast with tendrils above a shaped opening. The opening encloses a seated fairy in diaphanous robes. *H:28cm (11in).*

**SILVER-PLATED CLOCK** This WMF-style clock combines the rectilinear lines associated with the Jugendstil movement with the Art Nouveau motifs of the female figure and flowing drapery, here rendered with more restraint. *c.1900. H:33cm (13in).*

**SILVER-FACED CLOCK** The wooden frame of this clock has a sinuous outline and a silver panel to the front. In keeping with the shape of the piece, the silver is embossed with interwoven tendrils and florets. The clock has Birmingham date marks. *1910. H:36cm (14in).*

*The enamel dial is painted with flowers*

**MANTEL CLOCK** This patinated mantel clock has a circular enamel dial painted with flowers. The case, of flowering organic form, is moulded with leaves and dragonflies and surmounted by the figure of a young girl in diaphanous robes. The base is signed by Aristide de Ranieri. *H:58cm (22¾in).*

While fellow Belgian Henry van de Velde leant towards the abstract, Nature's life force is always visible in Horta's designs. His clocks look as though they have legs and feet, which give them a firm foundation but seem as though they want to spring into action like a caged animal – quivering yet controlled energy. The whiplash motif was plant rather than animal in origin, inspired by roots, leaves, and shoots, and Horta's clocks seem to grow up towards the sun, with tendrils of bronze escaping from the framework. Horta uses the clock form to translate the whiplash into three dimensions and his treatment of metal differs from Italian sculptor Aristide de Ranieri's use of curve.

**Foliate stems** and sinuous tendrils are hallmarks of Victor Horta's work

## THE LINEAR LOOK

Critical opinion at the time, even within Belgium and France, was divided as to whether the whiplash was a mishmash of freeform curves or an artistic expression of nature's beauty. Whichever, the whiplash was typical of early Art Nouveau before about 1900 and pervaded all possible decorative art forms. Like its fellow ornament of the time, the arabesque, the success of the whiplash relied on the designer's sensitivity of line. The English designer Walter Crane, while disparaging of Art Nouveau's excesses, understood the importance of line. He wrote: "Line is all important. Let the

**FRIENDSHIP CONQUERS TIME** In this brown-coloured stoneware clock by Friedrich Goldscheider of Vienna, two young lovers stand either side of the curved, out-swept case. Below the dial is the Latin inscription: *Amicitia vincit horas* (Friendship Conquers Time). 1900–1902. H:40cm (15¾in).

designer, therefore, in the adaptation of this art, lean upon the staff of line – line determinative, line emphatic, line delicate, line expressive, line controlling and uniting." Belgian Art Nouveau designers followed this creed, although Horta's frenzy of line might not be quite what Crane had in mind. Van de Velde summed up the key to design strength, saying: "Line is a force."

## FOLEY INTARSIO WARE

The British ceramics manufacturer Foley made a range of Intarsio wares, with areas of flat colour that looked like marquetry in wood. The clock below may have been wittily designed to look like a house, complete with pitched roofs and canted sides. Foley also used pretty girls for decoration, often with stylized patterns of flowers and countryside scenes. As well as clocks, Foley made vases and table services in Intarsio, and the range was featured in Liberty & Co.'s catalogues. Trading as Shelley from 1925, the company had even greater success with Art Deco tableware.

**VICTOR HORTA BRONZE CLOCK** The elegant dial is suspended amid a mass of wildly sinuous bronze foliate stems that extend as supports. The clock is reminiscent of much of Horta's work at Hotel Tassel. c.1895. H:46cm (18in).

**INTARSIO MANTEL CLOCK** The circular, enamel dial of this Foley clock has Arabic chapters and sits within a rectangular case with a pitched roof and canted sides. The case is printed and painted in bright colours, features Art Nouveau maidens, lilies, and boats sailing on a river, and bears the inscriptions *Carpe Diem* (Seize the Day), *Dies* (Day), and *Nox* (Night). H:29.5cm (11½in).

# TEXTILES

THE SOFT FURNISHINGS, CURTAINS, AND RUGS PRODUCED IN THE
LATE 19TH CENTURY WERE DECORATED WITH THE STYLIZED FLOWERS,
FOLIAGE, ANIMALS, AND BIRDS TYPICAL OF THE ART NOUVEAU STYLE.

**WILTON RUG** This large rug, with a luxuriant, all-over flowering design within a deep scrolling foliate border, was designed by C.F.A. Voysey and woven by Tomkinson and Adam for Liberty & Co. *L:271cm (106½in).*

## THE TEXTILE REVOLUTION

In the last decade of the 19th century, the eclectic mass of unrelated knick-knacks that cluttered the typical Victorian room gave way to a lighter, more streamlined interior where each element worked in conjunction with the next to create an overall harmonious effect. Textile furnishings played a fundamental role in these interiors. As in other Art Nouveau disciplines, France and Belgium soon took a place at the forefront of textile design, but in each country traditional textile crafts were reinterpreted and brought up to date.

### ARTS AND CRAFTS INFLUENCE

The British Arts and Crafts movement, active at the same time as continental Art Nouveau, was heavily influential. An 1896 Arts and Crafts exhibition in London was a showcase for the latest developments in textiles. By this time William Morris had stopped designing textiles, but his influence remained strong. He had shown Britain, Europe, and the United States how textiles brought colour and texture into the interior, and raised the profile of tapestry, embroidery, carpets, and printed material.

C.F.A. Voysey, one of the leading lights of the band of Arts and Crafts designers a generation younger than Morris, is credited with the first repeating pattern. Some of his nature-inspired patterns were humorous, such as the punningly titled *Let Us Prey*, showing the food chain as rows of cats looking up at birds looking up at tulip flowers.

### "CONTINENTAL EXCESS"

The Belgian artist Henry van de Velde said of Voysey's fabrics: "It was as if spring had come all of a sudden." The compliment was not returned, however. Voysey disapproved of the florid Art Nouveau style and was quoted in *The Studio* magazine as saying: "It is not necessary for artists to...be crammed to overflowing with the knowledge of the products of foreign nations," and, later, that the Continental trends had "brought into our midst foreign styles of decoration totally out of harmony with our national character and climate". Such xenophobia was typical of many Arts and

**PEACOCK PRINT** Typical of so many Art Nouveau textiles, this cotton print bears a formalized repeat pattern of natural forms: a peacock sitting among a field of sunflowers. *1890–1900. L:86.5cm (34in).*

Crafts designers, for Art Nouveau had neither their socialist ideals nor any trace of British understatement, even though it shared the same concept of the integrated room. However, many designers in France such as Georges de Feure and Edward Colonna used British textiles in rooms created for Siegfried Bing, as did Victor Horta and van de Velde himself.

## INFLUENCED BY PAINTING

Textiles had the same two-dimensional quality as a picture, so it was a logical conclusion that textile designers would follow current trends in painting. One of van de Velde's celebrated wall panels, *La Veillée des Anges*, displays complete confidence with embroidery skills and a painter's eye for composition and colour. It shows the influence of Gauguin in its flat areas of colour, which are used expressively rather than realistically. The patches of colour are darkly outlined in the cloisonné enamelling technique that Gauguin himself had translated into paint. The Nabis ("prophets" in Hebrew) group of artists who worshipped Gauguin used colour for its own sake and for symbolic purposes, emphasizing rather than disguising the flatness of the painting surface.

## REPEATING PATTERNS

Flat, repeated patterns were the order of the day. Foliage and flowers became so stylized in the flattening process as to be unrecognizable, abstract, and increasingly geometric. So textiles, of all the decorative arts, paved the way for the emergence of Art Deco and Modernism.

**PRINTED COTTON** The poppy-flower pattern of this printed cotton was available as both upholstery and curtain fabric, in keeping with the prevailing desire for integrated design. It was also printed on either a red or pink ground. *L:166.5cm (65½in)*.

## THE SILVER STUDIO

Not all British designers were as insular as Voysey in their outlook. The Silver Studio, run from 1880 until 1963, commissioned designers to come up with patterns for textiles and wallpapers in Art Nouveau and Arts and Crafts styles, which it supplied to shops such as Liberty & Co. In total, including designs for other decorative arts, the company produced some 30,000 designs. Open to the commercial opportunities of continental art, the Silver Studio created designs that featured seed pods, thistles and teasels, bindweed, and hemlock. This acknowledgment of French floral motifs was acceptable to the cautious British taste and also sold well abroad. By 1906 40 per cent of the Silver Studio's designs were sold on the Continent, mostly to weaving firms in the French town of Lille. The company had excellent artists on its books such as Celtic-inspired Archibald Knox and Harry Napper. Napper was comfortable with the exuberance of French and Belgian textiles and designed in a distinctly continental style himself.

**POPPY PRINT** This Silver Studio printed cotton bears a repeat flower-and-scrolling-leaf pattern in red and pink on a black ground. *L:228.5cm (90in)*.

## THE WHIPLASH MOTIF

After it was exhibited at the 1896 Arts and Crafts exhibition, Swiss-born Hermann Obrist's (1862–1927) whiplash embroidery was described by *The Studio* magazine as "the lightning-like flick of a whip...the endless continuity of line and spring of curve of some fascinating monster orchid". Its stylized stems, lashing back and forth on themselves, and flower-heads ending in a tangle of roots broke all the rules of artistic depiction of nature.

Obrist's embroidery was the blueprint for a mass of textile patterns. In all, he exhibited six embroideries and one hearth rug, part of a much larger collection of his work that toured Munich, Berlin, and London. Each of the panels was embroidered by Berthe Ruchet, who managed Obrist's workshop. She serrated the stems and shaded them with the utmost delicacy. Her use of gold and brightly coloured thread on dark lustred backgrounds made the patterns of the embroideries stand out all the more richly.

In Germany Obrist's work was hailed as "the birth of a new applied art". A multidisciplinary man of the age, he designed furniture and ceramics as well as textiles and won gold medals at the 1889 Paris *Exposition Universelle*.

Other important textile designers of the era included the Czech Alphonse Mucha, better known for his posters, and Gerhard Munthe of Norway. Like van de Velde, Munthe was influenced by the Nabis and his group of artists; his compositions illustrate the folklore of his native country. The judging panel at the 1900 Paris *Exposition Universelle*

**PEITCHENHIEB** This exquisite and iconic embroidery, the name of which means "whiplash", is stitched in gold-coloured silk on a woollen panel. Made by Berthe Ruchet, it depicts flowers, stalks, and roots in an organic, swirling pattern. *c.1895. W:183cm (72in)*.

credited him with triggering "a truly national style in the modern art of Norway".

Other countries took textile art in their own national directions: the Netherlands learned the batik technique used in the Dutch East Indies colonies (now Indonesia), while Hungary used its traditional lace-making industry to make startlingly modern patterns.

# SCULPTURE

FOR A VISUAL DEFINITION OF ART NOUVEAU, ONE NEED

LOOK NO FURTHER THAN THE SMALL SCULPTURES

MADE IN PARIS BETWEEN ABOUT 1890 AND 1910.

## A NEW MARKET

In mid-19th-century France sculpture was very much run by the state, which commissioned clichéd, Classical-style works that were considered the acceptable model. Auguste Rodin, however, revived the moribund Salon, opening the door for other avant-garde sculptors. The invention of the pantograph in 1838 had made it possible to scale sculpture down to a domestic size and reproduce it in series. Now an artistically aware public was eager to buy sculpture in the form of statuettes. Foundries capitalized on the new market and commissioned sculptors to work in the Art Nouveau style. France, especially Paris, was the acknowledged centre of sculpture, and Siegfried Bing put together an international array of sculptures in the modern style in 1895.

## FEMALE SENSUALITY

Nature, symbolism, and, above all, erotic women were uppermost in the fin-de-siècle French mind. For sculpture, figures and female curves gave the perfect opportunity for myriad poses – from a straightforward bust, to a dancing woman, or a more pensive mood. Women were depicted nude or with clinging drapery, often metamorphosing into plants as the Art Nouveau *femme-fleur*, who draws strength from nature. The dancer Loïe Fuller was an inspiration (*see box, opposite*), ingeniously depicted by Raoul Larche in the form of a lamp. Her diaphanous dress swirled into the lampshade above her head, and rippled around her body to hide all the fittings and the bulb. Her hair, typically of Art Nouveau women, trailed into plant-like forms.

## EXOTIC MATERIALS

Ivory was often combined with the more traditionally used metals for dramatic contrast, and Belgian designers in particular incorporated ivory because their king promoted trade in the material with its African colony, the Congo. Both exotic and ancient, ivory paid homage to the traditional craft process and advertised the wealth of

**LOÏE FULLER** Designer Raoul Larche was particularly well known for his sculptures of contemporary dancer Loïe Fuller. As here the gilt-bronze forms often doubled as lamps and light fittings. The piece bears the mark "Siot, Paris". *H:32cm (12½in).*

**DANCER** With her dress caught by her movement, this cast-bronze dancer in the style of Loïe Fuller is a perfect snapshot. Made by Rudolf Küchler, it has both light and dark patination and stands on an oval base. *c.1900. H:58.5cm (23in).*

**REVERIE BY PODANY** Dreamy, pensive maidens were a popular motif for Art Nouveau designers. Here the bronze figure is seated on a rocky outcrop with legs pulled up and looking down to see her reflection. The piece is signed and marked "1869". *H:60cm (23½in).*

**GILT-BRONZE FEMALE BUST** The smiling face of this maiden, turned slightly to the right, is surrounded by her long, boldly modelled flowing hair. The bust is signed by the maker, Léopold Savine. *H:32cm (12½in).*

the Belgian empire. Nautilus shells were another wonder of nature that was used in sculpture, such as in the ingenious bronze table lamp produced by the Austrian Gustav Gurshner (*see right*).

Sculptors also worked in biscuit porcelain, which, as an unglazed medium, was perfect for showing off the intricacy of their handiwork. The sculptural possibilities of stoneware and earthenware were explored, too, as the hierarchy of sculpture over ceramics was questioned.

In the hands of Rupert Carabin, furniture became a vehicle for bound and otherwise subjugated women carved from wood. Sadistic overtones aside, when he submitted a bookcase carved with female figures to the *Société des Indépendantes* in 1890, it was refused on the grounds that it was not a sculpture. The outcry over the snobbery of even this supposedly independent body – let alone that of the official Salon – forced a rethink of the artistic hierarchy, and unity was called for within the art world.

## CYCLE OF FASHION

After a decade of must-have popularity, the French appetite for sensual female figurines was shifting. What had once been fresh now seemed as stale as the hackneyed sculpture that it had replaced. But the female form as sculptural subject matter was unlikely to go away. Indeed, it found itself back in vogue in a new decorative style in the years following World War I.

## LOÏE FULLER

The greatest inspiration for Art Nouveau dancing figurines was an American dancer called Loïe Fuller, who came to Paris in 1892. In her unique dances, performed at the Folies-Bergère, she used electric light to illuminate the swirls of her billowing drapery; at one point she seemingly transformed into a bat. In 1897 there were no fewer than nine bronze sculptures of the idolized dancer at a single exhibition, including studies by Raoul Larche and Rupert Carabin. At the 1900 Paris *Exposition Universelle* there was a Loïe Fuller Theatre, the entrance topped by a sculpture of her by Pierre Roche. Loïe Fuller figures and lamps epitomize French Art Nouveau.

**FOLIES-BERGÈRE POSTER** Designed by Jules Chéret, this striking poster captures Loïe Fuller in full flight. The rich colours and play on light and dark convey the pure drama of her performances. *1893.*

## HOUSEHOLD OBJECTS

Part of the French Art Nouveau policy was expressed in the tenet *l'art dans tout* (art in everything). Household objects – whether bowls, inkwells, vases, candlesticks, or mirrors – had to be functional, but they could still be beautiful. Raoul Larche subscribed to the philosophy with his table lamps, as did his fellow sculptor Maurice Bouval, whose pewter planter (*below*) is entwined with leaves. In contrast to the dark metal, the gilt-bronze nude female perched on the edge gleams brightly. Bouval is said to have given his maidens enigmatic and even sad expressions that reflected the soul-searching visions of Symbolist painters and poets and the beautiful but serious women depicted by Pre-Raphaelite painters such as Dante Gabriel Rossetti and Edward Burne-Jones.

Lamps were the ideal art form for sculptors – a new type of object for a new look. The figure of a woman or her trailing robes could easily conceal the mechanics of the light fitting. She often held the lampshade in her hands

as in the bronze table lamp with a nautilus-shell shade (*below*) by the Austrian Gustav Gurschner. When the light was turned on, the glow picked out the delicacy of modelling on her face and body. Gurschner's mermaid figure is much more spare, abstracted, and elongated than the curvaceous, idealized sensuality of the French models. Public taste was turning in favour of the lean, geometric look coming out of Vienna and Glasgow (*see pp.236–263*) and ultimately it became a more lasting style than French Art Nouveau.

**BRONZE TABLE LAMP** The form of this lamp is fashioned as a sinuous mermaid, supported on her tail. She clutches a pale nautilus shell, which acts as a pearlized shade. The lamp was designed by Gustav Gurschner for K.K. Kunst-Erzgiesserei, Vienna. *c.1900. H:28cm (11in).*

**ART NOUVEAU PLANTER** Maurice Bouval's pewter open planter has a leaf-moulded handle and foot. To one side sits a gilt-bronze reclining nude. Signed by the maker. *W:33cm (13in).*

**BRONZE VASE** This bulbous vase is decorated in relief with a female face set among scrolling waves. The piece is signed "F. Madurelli". *H:14cm (5½in).*

# POSTERS

AS NEW PRODUCTS CAME ON TO THE MARKET, MASS ADVERTISING CASHED IN. ADVANCES IN PRINTING TECHNOLOGY LED TO A DELUGE OF POSTERS, MAGAZINES, AND PRINTS, QUICKLY SPREADING THE STYLE OF ART NOUVEAU.

## FRENCH STREET ART

Alphonse Mucha, who was born in South Moravia but spent most of his career in Paris, used all the Art Nouveau ingredients to perfection in his poster work. His sophisticated use of beautiful women, selling a way of life rather than a product, launched a trend that is still a mainstay of the marketing world today. Women, doyennes of consumerism, could appreciate the pleasure principle as much as men. The woman in Mucha's *Les Arts* panels has whiplash hair and elaborate Art Nouveau jewellery and is reverently haloed by a zodiac. Mucha often used Eastern symbolic forms in his posters.

*LES ARTS* One of four decorative panels by Alphonse Mucha (*below*), each of which depicts one of the four seasons with a Muse as the central motif. Each Muse is inscribed within a highly decorative circle with seasonal floral ornamentation above and wears a light, flowing gown. *1898. H:56cm (22in).*

Mucha had a meteoric rise in 1895 when he designed a poster for the play *Gismonda*, with legendary actress Sarah Bernhardt. With its attenuated figure in a format to match, soft colours, and integral decorative motifs, Mucha's poster was an overnight success. He collaborated with Bernhardt on her next 13 plays, designing costumes, jewellery, and posters. The imagery he used worked up an insatiable appetite for his posters, which sold out the moment they were printed.

Mucha's printed designs included postcards, stamps, biscuit barrels, bank notes, menus, fabric, and magazine covers. He also designed the interior of Georges Fouquet's Paris jewellery shop, using carved wood, glass, and metal in peacock motifs and foliate whiplashes; the Bosnia-Herzegovina Pavilion for the 1900 Paris *Exposition Universelle*; and murals and stained-glass windows in Prague.

The posters of Jules Chéret featured more blatantly sexy women. Throughout his career he designed almost a thousand posters, which advertised everything from coffee to cough sweets, cigarettes

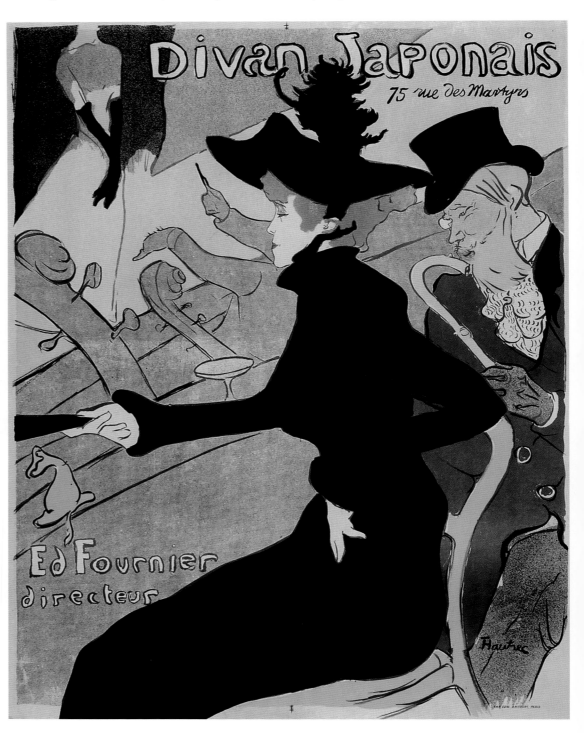

*DIVAN JAPONAIS* One of Henri de Toulouse-Lautrec's best-known posters (*right*), in the style of Japanese woodblock prints, this shows the dancer Jane Avril seated next to the literary critic Edouard Dujardin. *1893. H:81cm (32in).*

**ELDORADO** The bright colours and lively imagery of this rare poster are hallmarks of its creator, Jules Chéret. It is an advertisement for the king of Parisian music halls, Eldorado, and the allegory of dance and music perfectly sums up this mecca of performing arts. c.1895. H:118cm (46½in).

**LE CHAT NOIR** This rare poster by Théophile Steinlen was designed for the cabaret club Le Chat Noir. The clever positioning of the huge, wide-eyed black cat allows for a lot of text. It is a simple, powerful image rendered in only a few colours; many text versions exist. c.1895. H:61.5cm (24¼in).

to cabaret, and were also available to buy commercially. The Parisian music hall Eldorado inspired one of Chéret's classic posters (*above*), which incorporates the use of a powerful perspective gleaned from sources such as the ceiling allegories of Old Master painter Giovanni Battista Tiepolo.

## THE JAPANESE INFLUENCE
Henri de Toulouse-Lautrec was captivated by the Japanese prints coming into the West. A contemporary critic described the blueprint: "Take any representative Japanese print...and it will be

found to embody all that a good poster should. One dominant idea is presented graphically, beautifully. The detail does not weaken, but actually enforces the motif. There is not a superfluous line. The colour scheme...is fresh and striking, but always harmonious. The composition gives an idea of balance and breadth, but affords no hint as to how these qualities have been obtained...The general effect is decorative in the highest degree, may be humorous, and is certainly pervaded by the 'hidden soul of harmony'." Toulouse-Lautrec's flat silhouettes, asymmetrical composition, elongated figures, and firm outline all recall Japanese art. However, for his neutral portrayals of hedonistic modern life, he set his figures in real places, rather than in the symbolic, decorative settings that were so beloved of core Art Nouveau artists.

Eugène Grasset was mainly influenced by William Morris and the Pre-Raphaelites, but his thick, black outlines are reminiscent of the woodcuts that were coming from Japan, as well as of Paul Gauguin's cloisonné painting technique. Grasset's portrayal of the feminine form, linked closely with nature, was more delicate than the provocative Chéret women, idealized Mucha maidens, or worldly Toulouse-Lautrec sophisticates.

Théophile Steinlen's well-known poster for the Symbolist cabaret Le Chat Noir (*above left*) fused Art Nouveau's symbolic and decorative motifs. A contemporary critic wrote: "The walls of Paris have been dignified by the presence of this haloed cat, hieratic, Byzantine, of enormous size, whose thin fantastic silhouette hangs high above the crowd in the streets."

### LE STYLE MUCHA
The French poster style spread to Belgium, where designers such as Privat-Livemont and Fernand Toussaint took up the baton. Following Mucha's lead, they used decorative women to imply the beauty of a product.

**SALON DES CENT** Depicting a woman with red hair holding flowers, a pen, and a pad, this is considered one of the best images by Eugène Grasset. A 100-copies limited edition without lettering. 1899. H:63cm (24¾in).

## LITHOGRAPHY AND TYPOGRAPHY

Advances in colour lithography allowed artists to work directly on the lithographic stone, which was then inked for transfer to paper. Jules Chéret's technical refinements made it possible to produce a rainbow of colours. His designs, brighter than Mucha's muted palette, were sometimes produced in several different colour combinations.

Words were a key element of posters, magazine covers, and advertisements, and they were treated increasingly as an integral part of the design. Paul Berthon, a pupil of Eugène Grasset, made a frame for his Folies Bergère poster (*right*) out of the name of both the cabaret and the dancer, lessening the severity of the tall, thin format. He used a fleshy, flowing typeface that suited the floral motifs and female figure, haloed with a spider's web. Austrian Secession artists (*see pp.236–63*) went much further, designing typefaces that were more stylized than legible – an abstracted element that dominated the decorative surface.

**FOLIES BERGÈRE** A rare masterpiece of the French Art Nouveau movement, this poster was designed by Paul Berthon for Liane de Pougy's first appearance at the famed Folies Bergère cabaret. The image of the performer is flanked, top and bottom, by the typography. c.1895. H:148.5cm (58½in).

## EUROPE AND BEYOND

The craze for posters spread from France to the rest of Europe and the United States. With it went the Art Nouveau style, which, as with all the decorative arts, each country adapted in its own way.

### GERMAN FLAVOUR

All over Europe artistic magazines were springing up, due partly to more efficient printing and distribution. Britain's *The Studio* journal had its German equivalent in the Munich-based magazine *Die Jugend*, launched in 1896. It gave the name Jugendstil (New Style) to Art Nouveau in Germany. On the whole, German Art Nouveau was more geometric, closer to the styles of the Austrian

Secession and the Glasgow School. Multidiscipline designer Peter Behrens turned his hand to posters in the 1890s, with stylized entwined couples, flowers, and butterflies. His industrial designs for AEG electricity, however, were more severe and geometric, suited to the 20th century's machine age.

The Low Countries made fascinating contributions to the poster industry. In Belgium, Privat Livemont returned from painting stage sets in Paris and began producing posters. He made 30 between 1896 and 1900, all with dreamy Belle Époque flower-strewn maidens. They were as popular in Belgium as in France. The Dutch Symbolist artist Jan Toorop also made posters, with attenuated women with skeletal fingers,

rhythmic coils of hair, and billowing dresses. He had made several visits to England during the 1880s, and his work bears similarities to that of Aubrey Beardsley.

### BRITISH CONTRIBUTIONS

Apart from the Glasgow School and Aubrey Beardsley, both with their own unique twists and interpretations, British designers made few forays into Art Nouveau graphic design. In John

**DELFTSCHE SLAOLIE** Characteristic of the work of its designer, Jan Toorop, this Dutch advertisement for salad oil combines a symbolic mixing of the Javanese puppet influence with frantic arabesques. *1895. H:86cm (34in).*

***JUGEND*** A lithograph in pink, yellow, turquoise, and black, this poster was designed by Josef Rudolf Witzel for the Munich-based illustrated magazine *Jugend*. The image is of a young maiden draped in a garland of flowers and sitting beneath a tree surrounded by butterflies. *1896–97. H:113cm (44½in).*

***THE GIRL & THE GODS*** This poster by British designer John Hassall draws on imagery from the Classical period, rendered in the Art Nouveau style. *H:76cm (30in).*

PARIS Beautifully rendered in shades of pale green, blue, red, and pale brown, this image of peacocks in Paris was designed by Louis J. Rhead. The scene depicted shows a male peacock wooing a female, with a full display of his tail feathers. *1897. W:153.5cm (60½in).*

L. PRANG & CO.'S HOLIDAY PUBLICATIONS Designed by Louis J. Rhead, this advertisement shows a woman in lavender seated at a green desk, holding up Christmas books. It features red and green lettering against a yellow background. *1895. H:56cm (22in).*

WOMEN'S EDITION COURIER Here the depiction of the "Art Nouveau woman" is less rigid than in many other American images of the time. One of only two posters designed by Alice Russell Glenny. *1895. H:68.5cm (27in).*

Hassall's poster (*opposite*), all the elements are Classical, but the swirl of steam emanating from the teapot and linking the various parts of the composition is distinctly Art Nouveau in style.

## AMERICAN POSTER PARTIES

Louis John Rhead was born in Britain and trained in London and Paris before moving to New York. Most of his work was on posters for New York newspapers such as *The Herald* and *The Sun*, but he also created advertisements for scent, soap, and cigarettes. He favoured a bold palette and contrasting colour schemes. His poster for Prang Holiday Publications shows the influence of the Pre-Raphaelite painters, and his portrayals of demure women with striking looks and manes of hair suited the American market. Rhead was also in thrall to the work of Eugène Grasset, whose images had inspired him to become a poster designer himself. Like Grasset, he used a thick, dark outline to make the clear statement needed in a graphic image. Grasset's work in stained glass and his knowledge of Japanese woodcuts both influenced his own style.

Edward Penfield used strong outlines in his 1897 poster calendar, made bolder by the contrast of complementary colours. However, Rhead was versatile and could work in a more intricate style, as in his Parisian peacock scene (*above left*).

## A NEW SCHOOL

Female designers, such as Alice Russell Glenny, also played a part in the poster movement. Another key American graphic designer was Will Bradley, who worked in a more dynamic, organic, and linear style than Rhead. He wrote: "I think the American poster has opened a new school whose aim is simplicity and good composition. One can see its effect in all directions, especially the daily papers." Bradley's greatest inspiration was Aubrey Beardsley, who had a keen Japanese asymmetry, even if simplicity was not always his aim.

POSTER CALENDAR 1897 This image was designed by Edward Penfield and featured as the cover for this deluxe-edition calendar. It depicts an artist setting to work, accompanied by his cat. Male figures were a relatively rare feature in Art Nouveau design. *1896. H:35cm (14in).*

## AUBREY BEARDSLEY

In 1893 *The Studio* journal was launched with a feature on Aubrey Beardsley, which catapulted the illustrator to fame. Notoriety followed when he illustrated Oscar Wilde's play *Salome* with a predatory elongated femme fatale hawkishly clutching the head of John the Baptist, complete with arabesques of blood. The combination of decorative and grotesque, especially pronounced with his graphic use of black and white, both in flat areas and linear ornament, sparked accusations of depravity. Beardsley died of tuberculosis in 1898, at the age of 25.

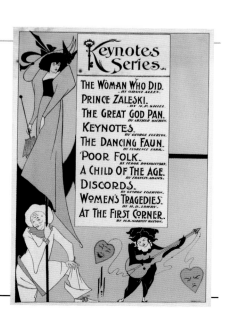

KEYNOTES SERIES Designed by Aubrey Beardsley, this poster depicts various figures promoting a series of books. Bold and simple images, rather than florid, elaborate designs are characteristic of Beardsley's work. *1896. H:47.5cm (18¾in).*

# BIRTH OF MODERNISM

## 1860–1920

# DYNAMIC DESIGNERS

IT IS DIFFICULT TO DATE THE BIRTH OF MODERNISM WITH ANY
PRECISION BUT, FROM THE 1860S ONWARDS, THERE WERE CERTAIN
DESIGNERS WHOSE WORK STOOD OUT FROM THE PREDOMINANT
TRENDS OF THE DAY AND LOOKED FORWARD IN STYLE AND CONCEPT.

**STIRRUP VESSEL** Christopher Dresser's design for Ault Pottery
is decorated with a distinctive streaked and dribbled glaze, which is
far removed from the historical revival trends of the time. *c.1890*.

## EARLY MODERN THINKERS

In Vienna the German designer Michael Thonet
designed a bentwood chair in 1859 that, when
mass-produced, sold 50 million copies by 1930.
It was included by architect Le Corbusier as a
prime example of modernist design in his 1925 Paris
exhibit *Pavillon de L'Esprit Nouveau*. In England
Christopher Dresser set out a theory of aestheticism
that combined nature with designs from disparate
cultures and periods into a new, harmonious whole
in *The Art of Decorative Design* (1862).

The Scottish designer Charles Rennie Mackintosh
developed a new rectilinear style with gentle curves
and geometric decoration to produce elegantly
attenuated furniture, as well as interiors and whole
buildings. Three Viennese designers – the painter
and book illustrator Koloman Moser, the architect
Josef Hoffmann, and the painter Carl Otto Czeschka
– set up the Wiener Werkstätte (Viennese Workshops)
in 1903 to produce simple, functional and well-
designed furniture, textiles, metalwork, and other
items. Like Mackintosh, they rejected the sweeping
curves and floral motifs of Art Nouveau in favour
of straight lines and geometric shapes.

What these and other designers had in common
was that, while they were often placed within
existing stylistic movements, their work displayed
a more modernist approach. Modernism was never
conceived as a single style but was more a loose
collection of related ideas covering a range of styles
and movements in different countries. In rejecting
history and tradition, modernism embraced the
new, having an almost utopian desire to create
a better world, sometimes from scratch. It rejected
decoration and embraced abstraction. Most important,
it believed in the power and potential of the machine
and industrial technology to change the world.
Modernism was often allied with left-wing social
and political beliefs, as both held that art and
design could transform society.

## CONTINUING THE TREND

Such radical design continued in Europe,
flourishing alongside Art Deco and motivated by
the belief that the world needed to be rethought
and reshaped after the carnage of the trenches.
The Russian Revolution of 1917 offered a model
of how that new society might look. In the
Netherlands a group of designers and artists
led by Piet Mondrian founded the De Stijl group,
which promoted a rigorous, abstract approach
to art and design. In 1918 one of their members,
Gerrit Rietveld, designed a red and blue chair that
was not only a three-dimensional equivalent of

**SCHRÖDER HOUSE**
Gerrit Rietveld designed
this house in Utrecht
in the Netherlands as a
series of abstract planes,
with projecting roofs
and balconies but no
historical ornament.

**EBONIZED
SYCAMORE CHAIR**
Designed by Charles
Rennie Mackintosh,
the emphasis is on
verticals softened by
a slightly curved back.
Crosspieces form a
panel of squares like
a stylized tree. *1904*.
*H:72cm (28½in)*.

**BEDROOM BY WALTER GROPIUS** Functional, light, and airy with a window the width of the wall, the room is as conducive to reading and relaxing as to sleeping. The room is furnished with pieces made from the new materials pioneered by Gropius and his contemporaries: bent and moulded plywood, tubular steel, glass, and laminated wood.

Mondrian's geometric paintings but also a physical statement of what modernism itself was all about.

The undoubted powerhouse of early modernism was the Bauhaus, an art, architecture, and design school founded by the architect Walter Gropius in Weimar, Germany, in 1919. The school initially handcrafted items but became more of a research centre producing machine-made prototypes for industry. Among its most famous products was Marcel Breuer's tubular-steel framed chair and a glass and nickel desk lamp designed by Wilhelm Wagenfeld, which so closely embodied the theories of the school it became known as the Bauhaus lamp.

## MASS MODERNISM

This shift from the individually crafted to the mass-produced product reflected the move away from the theoretical, and from the enclosed world of private exhibitions and small-circulation magazines, towards a practical, industrial mass application. Modernist architects were involved in the vast new housing projects in Germany, Austria, and the Netherlands designed to solve the post-war housing shortage, while modernist ideas influenced everything from typography to tea sets and chairs.

By the 1930s modernism had lost its social and political beliefs and become a recognizable design style, based on abstract, rectilinear geometry using industrial production techniques and materials, notably chrome, steel, and glass. It also became more national, with different styles appearing in Britain, Czechoslovakia, the United States, the Soviet Union, and, despite extreme political differences, in Fascist Italy and Nazi Germany.

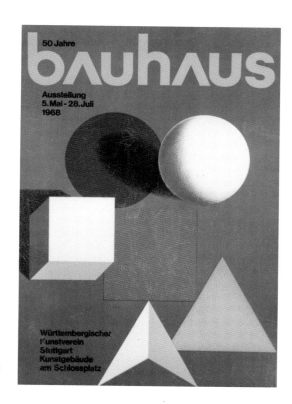

**EXHIBITION POSTER** This poster by Herbert Bayer for a retrospective exhibition captures the spare, geometric spirit of Bauhaus design. *1968. H:66cm (25in).*

# ELEMENTS OF STYLE

The first modernist designers had completely different philosophies from each other but were united by a desire to break new ground. Drawn away from naturalistic representation by the perceived freedom of abstract forms and the possibilities of new materials, they created decorative arts untrammelled by history. There was a conflict between affordability and exclusivity, as well as debate about how far natural forms should be rejected.

KEITH MURRAY VASE
### SIMPLICITY
To break away from decorative tradition, the early modernists rejected 19th-century fussiness and demanded a minimalist approach. In favour of reductionism, they pared down design to its essential elements. Function was more highly regarded than ornament, which was considered regressive.

CHRISTOPHER DRESSER VASE
### NEW SHAPES
Strange new forms were a blend of organic and geometric shapes. The highly stylized "art botany" of Christopher Dresser had a huge influence on modernists, who turned 19th-century naturalism into ever more extreme and abstract forms.

PIET MONDRIAN POSTER
### GRAPHIC DESIGN
Modernists absorbed influences from painting and graphic design. Bolshevist propaganda posters in the Constructivist style helped spread abstraction through Europe. Typographers at the Bauhaus rejected heavy German black letter type in favour of a simpler sans-serif style, free of ornament.

MIES VAN DER ROHE BARCELONA CHAIR
### LUXURY MATERIALS
Modernist designers working on bespoke commissions used animal hides and leather for coverings and upholstery to satisfy their clients' taste for luxury. Designers such as Frank Lloyd Wright and Josef Hoffmann produced grand integrated interiors with the finest materials.

CHARLES RENNIE MACKINTOSH CHAIR
### GEOMETRY
As the influence of abstract art spread, geometric motifs and forms increased. Designers allied to the De Stijl movement attempted to reduce every plane to a straight line. The rigid geometric look of the Glasgow School was admired and emulated in Germany and Austria.

MIES VAN DER ROHE CHAIR
## CANTILEVERED STEEL
The properties of tubular steel – affordable, versatile, durable, and lightweight – were ideally suited to the modernist agenda. The cantilevered design fused form and function, doing away with the need for sprung upholstery and reducing the number of chair legs from four to two.

KASIMIR MALEVICH PLATE
## ABSTRACT DECORATION
Cubism in France, Futurism in Italy, Russian Constructivism, and English Vorticism all dismissed representational art. Instead of nature ruling supreme, designers celebrated the triumph of the machine with abstract shapes and patterns.

MARCEL BREUER CHAIR
## PLYWOOD AND LAMINATED WOOD
Building on the work of Michael Thonet, modernists made the most of bent plywood and laminated wood. Bentwood reduced the components of furniture, which meant fewer joins and a smoother overall design. These were the first steps towards producing furniture from single pieces of material.

BERNARD LEACH BOWL
## HANDCRAFT
The paradox of modernist decorative art was that, in the age of the machine, so much supposedly industrial design was made by hand. Many of the Bauhaus handcrafted prototypes, for instance, were never mass-produced.

CHRISTOPHER DRESSER VASE
## GLAZES
Interest in the raku tradition of Japan led Western ceramicists to experiment with wood-fired climbing (stepped) kilns for the first time. The result was a huge variation in glaze tones and colours. This led to continual creation of new colours and effects. Matte glazes complemented smooth surfaces.

BAUHAUS SOFA BY WALTER GROPIUS
## COLOUR
To modernists, form was more important than ornament, so solid blocks of colour were often used to mask texture and throw shape into sharp relief. Designers tended to favour primary colours and monochrome black and white rather than more subtle and varied tones.

BERNARD LEACH VASE
## JAPANESE INFLUENCE
Frank Lloyd Wright was a great admirer of Japanese woodwork and Christopher Dresser was beguiled by the simplicity of Japanese design. The sparseness of Oriental ceramic design – particularly early Chinese blue-and-white and Japanese Kakiemon porcelain – was a precursor of modernist minimalism.

CHRISTOPHER DRESSER FACSIMILE SIGNATURE ON VASE
## BRANDING
Designers worked with industry to mass-produce attractive, functional homeware for the general public. Christopher Dresser introduced the concept of branding by having his facsimile signature stamped on to the products he designed. Graphic artists experimented with the first logos.

# CHRISTOPHER DRESSER

IN HIS POPULAR *MANUAL OF BOTANY*, CHRISTOPHER DRESSER IMAGINED HIS ERA AS "THE EARLY MORNING OF THE LONG HOPED-FOR DAY". HIS WORK WAS THE ROOT OF A REVOLUTION IN ART AND DESIGN.

**LARGE BRASS EWER** Manufactured by Benham & Froud to a design by Dresser, its bulbous, conical body is raised on a circular foot and tapers to an angled tubular spout also linked by a hooped handle. *1880s. H:5cm (2in).*

**PROPELLER VASE** Designed while Dresser worked with the Ault Pottery, the form is fluid and dynamic, with a shimmering blue and green aventurine glaze. *1890s. H:33.5cm (13in).*

**PAIR OF VASES** Also designed for the Ault Pottery, their form is of Islamic inspiration. The glaze is splashed and streaked in an abstract pattern. *1890s. H:26cm (10¼in).*

Dresser's audacious talents were apparent from a young age and he was enrolled in the Government Design School at Somerset House in London when he was just 13. Born in 1834, he was an exact contemporary of William Morris and had an equal influence on the decorative arts, albeit in a totally different direction. Many of his designs stood radically apart from those of his contemporaries.

Dresser's studies at Somerset House included botany and he continued to specialize in this field, receiving his honorary doctorate from the University of Jena in Germany in 1859. When his application for Chair of Botany at the University of London was rejected, Dresser resolved to forge a career as a designer, setting up his studio in 1860.

## ART BOTANY

In 1857 Dresser had contributed drawings of plants to Owen Jones's *Grammar of Ornament*, the leading sourcebook for Victorian designers. He fused his great skill as a botanical draughtsman with his interest in geometry and pattern to produce a new stylization of nature that he referred to as "art botany". The distinction between representational (imitative) and imagined (ideal) art was important to Dresser. He considered decorative art, as opposed to pictorial art, the more noble pursuit as it was more likely to be ideal. This contention boldly challenged the entrenched interests of the artistic establishment. In voicing it, Dresser played a key role in raising the status of the designer.

**SUGAR BOWL** Manufactured in silver plate by Elkington & Co., the conical body raised on three slender legs is an Egyptian-inspired form which, pared down, has a decidedly modern look. *1885. H:8.25cm (3¼in).*

At his studio Dresser would repeat favourite maxims to his students. One of the most common was "maximum effect with minimum means", instilling an economy of style. A voyage to Japan in 1876 as the representative of the South Kensington Museum – later to become the Victoria and Albert Museum – strengthened Dresser's preference for form over ornament. It reaffirmed his view that "fitness for purpose" was the basis of good design. The European avant-garde later championed these same principles – particularly the Bauhaus, although that organization did not enjoy the same industrial success as Dresser.

## THE DRESSER BRAND

The list of firms that carried the Dresser brand in the late 19th century reads like a roll call of the cream of Victorian industry. Some of Dresser's most radical work was for metalware manufacturers Elkington & Co. – pioneers of the electroplating process. In the 1880s his designs for James Dixon & Sons rivalled even De Stijl's in their geometry. Dresser put his belief that free blowing was the best way of manipulating glass into practice with his Clutha range for Couper and Sons of Glasgow, which featured deliberate imperfections, bubbles, and irregular handles and rims. With John Harrison and Henry Tooth, he founded Linthorpe Pottery in 1879, and experimented with ceramic glaze and form. After the venture failed, Ault Pottery acquired many of the moulds and persuaded Dresser to contribute new designs. Dresser died in 1904 having made his proto-modernist vision available to ordinary people by working with industry to create attractive, functional, and affordable household wares.

## EXOTIC INFLUENCES

Dresser travelled to Japan, the United States, Europe, and the Middle East, constantly adding to his mental inventory of colour, form, and ornament. By refusing to restrict himself to specific design conventions, he fused local exotic flavours into something new. His Egyptian designs included creations for Wedgwood and Minton, a chair which appeared in his book, *Principles of Decorative Design (1873),* and another which retailed through the Art Furnishers' Alliance, as well as a design commission for Bushloe House in Leicester.

**EGYPTIAN REVIVAL SOFA** With its sphinx carvings, this sofa was originally attributed to Dresser, but is now thought to have been bought by him on a trip to Egypt. *W:144cm (56½in).*

**FLOWER STUDY** This plate of colourful drawings for *The Grammar of Ornament* was Christopher Dresser's first published work. Dresser's emphasis on the underlying geometry of the flowers is clearly evident.

Nº 13. OLOSOCOMIA CLEMATIDEA

5. ONION

Nº 3. DAFFODIL

Nº 8. HONEYSUCKLE

Nº 4. NARCISSUS

Nº 11. SPEEDWELL

# FURNITURE

RADICAL DESIGNERS FROM ACROSS EUROPE AND THE UNITED STATES CAME UP WITH STARTLING NEW 20TH-CENTURY FURNITURE DESIGNS THAT WERE SLEEK, GEOMETRIC, AND SOMETIMES SEVERE IN THEIR SIMPLICITY.

## THE GLASGOW SCHOOL

Under the directorship of Francis Newbery from 1885, the Glasgow School of Art expanded quickly, building on its already formidable reputation as one of the foremost government design schools.

It was around this time that a group of four young designers, brought together through their association with the school, formed a loose alliance that would stimulate a creative revolution across Europe. Known as the Glasgow Four, the group was made up of Charles Rennie Mackintosh and James Herbert MacNair, with their respective wives, sisters Margaret and Frances Macdonald.

## THE FAMOUS FOUR

Together they took elements from the Arts and Crafts and Art Nouveau styles that were popular at the time and passed them through the filter of the Celtic Revival to produce something new. Mackintosh himself designed new premises for the Glasgow School of Art in 1896 using the archaic Scottish Baronial style as his base, embellished with restrained and functional decorative details. Although considered his masterpiece today, at the time the building attracted little if any press attention outside Glasgow.

The elongated elements that characterize much of Mackintosh's furniture were a trademark of the Glasgow style, dubbed the Spook School by some commentators in reaction to its exaggeratedly stretched lines and ghostly figures. Mackintosh often obliterated the wooden grain of his furniture by applying glossy black lacquer or coloured painted finishes. His use of white and pale green echoed the palette used by other members of the Glasgow Four in their painting, needlewo rk, and gesso panels. Mackintosh saw his dark colour schemes as masculine, contrasting with his light feminine schemes.

The decorative motif most commonly associated with Mackintosh's work is the Glasgow rose. His representation of the flower is so acutely stylized that it is almost abstract – a series of curved and straight lines within a roughly circular border. Similarly, the pierced motifs cut into the oval top

*The bird-in-flight cut-out* is typical of Mackintosh's stylized organic motifs

*The wide spacing* of the back splats creates a light and airy quality

*The elegant arches* of the seat rails echo the oval top above and an arched apron below

*The front legs* are thin, tapering, and square sectioned to underpin the composition, at once robust and delicate

*The back legs* change from round to oval to square – an extremely complex piece of carpentry

**ARGYLE CHAIR** Designed for the Argyle Street Tea Rooms in Glasgow, this was Mackintosh's first high-back chair, and remains one of his most striking designs. *1897. H:137cm (54in).*

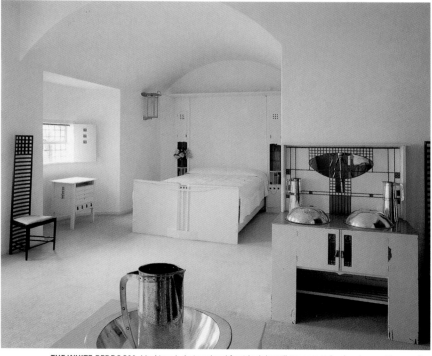

**THE WHITE BEDROOM** Mackintosh designed and furnished the Hill House in Helensburgh, near Glasgow, for the publisher Walter Blackie in 1904. The furniture in the guest room, including a ladder-back chair, is embryonic modern in its predominantly linear and geometric form and decoration.

**DUGOUT SETTLE** This seat was designed by Mackintosh for the Dugout, in the basement of the Willow Tea Rooms in Glasgow. The latticework in the back and sides is a recurring motif in Mackintosh designs, inspired by Cotswold School Arts and Crafts pieces. *1917. W:137cm (54in).*

**MUSIC ROOM CHAIR** Designed by Mackintosh for Miss Cranston's Hous'hill in Glasgow, the vertical back splats instantly convey his rectilinear style. As often in his earlier work, it is softened by gentle curves, here seen in the front seat rail. *1904. H:75.5cm (30in).*

rails of Mackintosh's tall Argyle chairs, designed for Miss Cranston's Tea Rooms in 1897, are just recognizable as birds in flight. This bold move towards abstraction is all the more remarkable for occurring more than a decade before the Cubist movement gained momentum.

The furniture designed by both MacNair and Mackintosh is rigidly geometric, comprising horizontal and vertical members that intersect to produce repeated square spaces. Ovals and arcs complement and temper these perpendicular lines without sacrificing any of their stark simplicity.

Mackintosh's Hill House chair is one of the most striking examples of this style – ostensibly a heavily stylized version of a traditional ladder-back chair, it features more than two dozen horizontal bars, augmented towards the top with vertical members to create a grid section behind the sitter's head.

## FEMININE INPUT

This unconventional approach was the vanguard of a movement that would sweep the European mainland. When Mackintosh collaborated with Frances and Margaret Macdonald to create a room

for the 1900 Vienna Secession Exhibition, key figures of the Secessionist movement such as Gustav Klimt and Josef Hoffmann were so impressed by the exhibit that they began to incorporate the Glasgow School aesthetic into their own work.

So synonymous is the name of Charles Rennie Mackintosh with the Glasgow style that the contribution made by the Macdonald sisters and the many other women who followed in their footsteps is too often overlooked. Francis Newbery actively encouraged women to enrol in the Glasgow School of Art and many of them came to excel in the design and creation of mural panels, screens, and embroidery.

Margaret Macdonald contributed her own designs to Mackintosh's decorative scheme for Miss Cranston's Tea Rooms. Looking back on their work, Mackintosh declared: "I had talent, Margaret had genius." The Glasgow School was diverse and its adherents created an integrated style that was more than the sum of its parts.

*Stylized roses* are a recurring motif in Mackintosh's earlier designs

*The wood* is painted white for one of Mackintosh's feminine colour schemes

*Tapering, pilaster-like* forms soften a rectilinear carcase

**WHITE CABINET** Originally designed by Mackintosh as one of a pair for Kingsborough Gardens, Glasgow, it is painted white with inlaid glass panels. The panels have stylized imagery of a woman holding a rose ball – a feminine touch attributed to the influence of Mackintosh's wife. *1902. H:154.5cm (61in).*

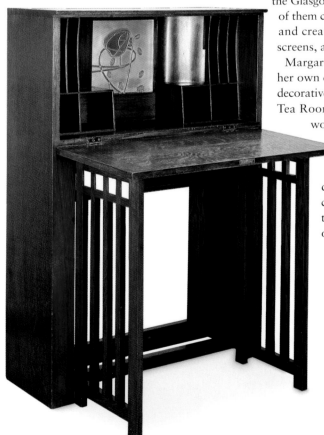

**HOUS'HILL WRITING TABLE** Made of ebonized mahogany inlaid with mother-of-pearl, ceramic, and ivory, and further embellished with leaded glass and metal, this was designed for the blue bedroom at Hous'hill, and is recognized as one of Hous'hill's most accomplished pieces.

## THE WIENER WERKSTÄTTE

Josef Hoffmann and Koloman Moser left the Vienna Secession in the first years of the 20th century, frustrated by their peers within the movement who were in thrall to the florid Art Nouveau style. Together they drew up a manifesto for a pioneering, integrated decorative art idiom relevant to the modern age. Having secured the financial backing of wealthy industrialist and patron of the arts Fritz Wärndorfer, they founded the Wiener Werkstätte in 1903.

Based upon the same medieval model that had inspired C.R. Ashbee's Guild of Handicraft, the Wiener Werkstätte anticipated the Bauhaus in that its members were taught practical crafts alongside the theory of design. In common with many of the groups that reacted against the historical revivals of the 19th century, the Wiener Werkstätte believed that every element of a building's architecture and interior fittings should follow a single theme. Unlike the modernists who followed in their wake, Hoffmann and his disciples made few concessions to the mass market, recognizing that the fruits of their intensive labour would be available only to the wealthy. Among the many maxims Hoffmann instilled at his workshop was "better to work ten days on one product than manufacture ten products in one day" – a sentiment far closer to the values of William Morris than Le Corbusier.

### INTEGRATED DESIGN

Hoffmann took the Wagnerian concept of *Gesamtkunstwerk* (synthesis of the arts) and applied it to the architectural commissions he took on behalf of the Wiener Werkstätte. The first of these was the Purkersdorf Sanatorium, intended as a luxury refuge and spa. The spartan cleanliness

**VIENNESE APARTMENT** Baroness Magda Mautner-Markhof's apartment was furnished by Josef Hoffmann in 1902. It reveals his move away from sinuous Art Nouveau to the elegant linear style promoted by Charles Rennie Mackintosh.

**UPHOLSTERED ARMCHAIR** This beech reclining chair was designed by Josef Hoffmann for J.&J. Kohn. It has openwork decoration and spherical motifs. c.1905. W:50cm (19¾in).

**NEST OF TABLES** Designed in overtly geometric form and detail by Josef Hoffmann at the Wiener Werkstätte, and designated model number 968, the tables (three here from a set of four) were made in mahogany-stained beech by J.&J. Kohn. 1905. Largest: H:75.5cm (29¾in).

demanded by this kind of environment later became a feature of much modernist design. The unified design scheme included dozens of fixtures to provide soft, even lighting.

This first commission was followed by an opportunity in 1905 to develop a grand private residence in Brussels for Baron Stoclet, who gave the workshops extraordinary freedom to appoint the interior with everything from furniture to cutlery. The designer-craftsmen of the Wiener Werkstätte developed and expanded the range of wares made for the Palais Stoclet for their first exhibition, entitled *Der gedeckte Tisch* (The laid table), in 1906.

## SIMPLE LINES

Hoffmann became an admirer of the elongated lines expressed by the Glasgow Four when they exhibited at the Secession House in 1900. The steamed wood pieces are a follow-on from the early bentwood pieces perfected by Michael Thonet. Josef Olbrich – who later designed a number of significant modernist buildings – nd Koloman Moser often made a feature of front risers that ascend from a base rail and curve backwards to form armrests. This geometric simplicity was most eloquently expressed by Hoffmann's Cabaret Fledermaus chair, designed for the café of the same name in Vienna.

Unusually for Wiener Werkstätte products, furniture was usually made by other Vienna workshops rather than carried out on site. Preferred contractors included Thonet and J.&J. Kohn – both venerable firms with expertise in bentwood construction. J.&J. Kohn produced Hoffmann's adjustable reclining chair, model no. 670, from around 1905. With its rectangular openwork decoration and radial bentwood members, the chair is rigidly geometric in form. The round knobs are functional as well as decorative, providing a mechanism that allows the back of the seat to recline. By applying his rigid design aesthetic to the Morris chair developed by Philip Webb in 1866, Hoffmann had created something entirely new.

Moser left the Wiener Werkstätte in 1907. World War I deprived the workshops of talent and resources. When it ended, the defeated Austrian nation was less able to support such a lavish venture. Attempts to open branches in other cities, including New York in 1922, met with some success but Hoffmann had to shut down his project in 1932.

*Geometric forms* in the Hoffman style are evident in the glazed doors

*Decoration* is typically understated and includes annular (ring-shaped) ribbing on the spindle supports

*The marble top* is characteristically both practical and decorative

*The escutcheons* and ring-pull handles are made of brass

**WALNUT-VENEERED SIDEBOARD** Designed in the style of Josef Hoffmann, its marble-topped base with cupboards and a drawer supports a mirror-glass panel and, with a pair of spindles, a raised cupboard. *1902. H:178cm (70in).*

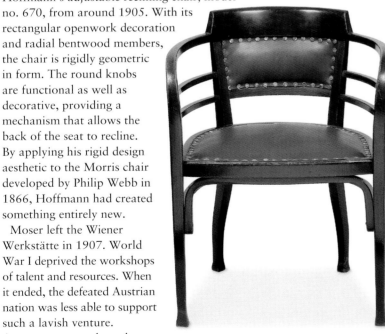

**UPHOLSTERED ARMCHAIR** This chair is one of the many variations of the J.&J. Kohn 714 series. It was inspired by the 19th-century English smoker's chair. The traditional design was supervised by the Kohn design director, Gustav Siegel. *c.1902. H:76cm (30½in).*

**WRITING DESK** Designed by Koloman Moser, and made by J.&J. Kohn in mahogany-stained beech with a mirror and brass hardware, the composition of the desk is rectilinear. Its subtly undulating back acknowledges the existence of a more curvaceous Art Nouveau style. *c.1900. W:113cm (45¼in).*

# THE BAUHAUS

Founded in 1919, the Bauhaus was inevitably shaped by the aftermath of World War I. The Treaty of Versailles had crushed Germany, forcing her to give up valuable tracts of land and imposing restrictions on her economy. In the wake of such a humiliating defeat, the designers at the Bauhaus turned their backs on the past, ignoring tradition and convention, and reassessed the fundamental nature and purpose of good design.

## VISION FOR THE FUTURE

The vision of Walter Gropius, the first Bauhaus director, found expression in the Haus am Horn, the 1923 exhibition home by Georg Muche furnished by Bauhaus students. The inside of the building provides a glimpse of domestic interiors that are true to the Bauhaus ideals of economy, durability, fitness for purpose, and aesthetic merit.

The principle that underpinned all of the work done under Gropius's direction was close collaboration with industry – Bauhaus products were designed as archetypes that could be made cheaply by machine. While the Bauhaus was at Weimar its remit expanded to embrace architecture, stone, metal- and woodworking, pottery, painting, weaving, graphic design, and, of course, furniture. Students were encouraged to learn how to work with confidence in as many design spheres as possible.

## NEW CHAIR DESIGNS

The furniture of the early Bauhaus was often far removed from the sleek chromed steel pieces with which it is most commonly associated. Marcel Breuer started a woodwork apprenticeship there in 1920 and constructed his Slatted Chair, inspired by the angular designs of Gerrit Rietveld, from maplewood and horsehair cloth. The integration between the arts that the Bauhaus strove for found a neat expression in Breuer's African Chair, made from stained oak painted and upholstered in fabric by the weaver Gunta Stölzl.

A year after completing his course, Breuer returned in 1925 as a young master at the second incarnation of the Bauhaus, based at new premises in Dessau designed by Walter Gropius. It was here that he developed the tubular-steel furniture that has become synonymous with the modular International Style. Breuer was attracted to tubular steel as a furnishing material because it was cheap and versatile. It provides recoil without the need for springs and is easy to clean.

His Wassily chair and Thonet shelving unit show how he applied a similar tubular frame to a range of design briefs. Breuer continued to teach at the Bauhaus until 1928, eventually leaving at the same time as Walter Gropius.

**DESSAU BAUHAUS** The concrete monolithic structure has glass curtain walls, which were a complete innovation in the 1920s.

*The upholstery* is made from black leather straps

*The tubular steel* frame was inspired by Breuer's bicycle

**MARCEL BREUER CHAIR** Originally designed for Wassily Kandinsky's quarters at the Dessau Bauhaus, the iconic Wassily B3 was revolutionary in its use of a bent steel frame for residential furniture. *1925–27. W:69.75cm (27½in).*

**SOFA TABLE** Designed by Marcel Breuer, the nickel-plated frame has a crystal glass top. It was reissued by Tecta in 2004. *H:60cm (23½in).*

## MIES VAN DER ROHE

Ludwig Mies van der Rohe is mainly remembered for his work in the United States, yet his early career in Germany produced some of his finest achievements. He believed that chair design was a challenge equal to that of skyscraper architecture because of its "endless possibilities and many problems". His MR10 chair was a close relative of Breuer's Wassily model, although the cantilevered construction was indebted to the S33 chair designed by Mart Stam, another star of the Bauhaus.

While working on a 1929 commission from the German government to design the German pavilion at the Barcelona International Exhibition, Mies van der Rohe devoted as much time to the furnishings as he did to the building itself. Not yet involved with the Bauhaus and certainly not a believer in its iconoclastic manifesto, he based the designs for his Barcelona chair and ottoman on a classical Roman form. They were nonetheless thoroughly modern in conception, although their high construction cost made them unsuitable as models for cheap mass production. Faced with growing opposition from conservatism and the rising Nazi party, the Bauhaus was dissolved in 1933, just a year after it had moved to Berlin under Mies van der Rohe's directorship. In the turbulent years that followed many of the figures associated with the school fled Germany. Gropius and Breuer worked on the modernist Isokon project in London during the 1930s before eventually settling in the United States. Mies van der Rohe crossed the Atlantic in 1937 and forged a successful career designing high-rise buildings and teaching.

**ERICH BRENDEL TABLE** Tecta's 2004 reissue of Brendel's design incorporates the original four-flap octagonal top above a shelf and cupboard, raised on a plinth with casters. *1924. W:147cm (57¾in).*

**The colourway** of ash white is one of several choices: others are black, red, or natural ash

**BARCELONA OTTOMANS** Designed by Mies van der Rohe to accompany his best-known chair, the Barcelona MR90, and originally made by Joseph Müller, their chromed X-frame was derived from the classical *sella curulus* – a Roman magistrate's stool – but given a decidedly modern twist. *1929. W:63.5cm (25in).*

**MR20 CHAIR** Designed by Mies van der Rohe, it has a then-revolutionary cantilevered, chromed tubular steel frame. Here the seat and back are leather, but woven equivalents remain an option. *1926–27. W:53.5cm (21in).*

## DE STIJL IN THE NETHERLANDS

After the end of World War I a small band of artists developed an extremely strict template for utopian design that they spread through the journal *De Stijl*, Dutch for "The Style". The goal of De Stijl was to restrict both colour and form so much that their compositions included only vertical and horizontal lines and primary colours. Diagonal lines were sometimes permissible. Adherents included the painter Piet Mondrian and the architect Gerrit Rietveld, who also produced furniture to De Stijl principles. The most complete realization of De Stijl is the Rietveld Schröder house in Utrecht. Like the philosophy that underpinned the Bauhaus, De Stijl rejected historicism, making a clean break with the past.

**Painted decoration** is restricted to a primary colour, red, on the chair back

**The oblique angle** modifies the tension between vertical and horizontal lines

**ZIGZAG CHAIR** A stark assertion of function and visual simplicity, incorporating the De Stijl movement's desire for oblique diagonal lines, Gerrit Rietveld's cantilevered, modular chair is structurally complex in its use of dovetail joinery, and nuts and bolts through each of the horizontal, vertical, and oblique panels. *1922.*

**RED-BLUE CHAIR** Rietveld's design classic, here reproduced under licence by Cassina, is the three-dimensional equivalent of an abstract painting by Piet Mondrian. *1917.*

# LE CORBUSIER

European avant-garde design was not confined to the Bauhaus. Le Corbusier, probably the most influential modernist figure, was born in Switzerland and spent most of his career in France. Le Corbusier was a phenomenon. Largely self-taught – and self-named – he designed his first house aged just 18, under his real name Charles-Edouard Jeanneret. He laid out his manifesto for furniture in his 1925 publication *L'Art Décoratif d'aujourd-hui* (Decorative Art Today), in which

he argued that furniture designers should create objects that worked like extensions of the human body.

Like Frank Lloyd Wright before him, Le Corbusier was in favour of open-plan living spaces and often designed his housing units with free-standing interior walls that the owner could rearrange at will. Wright, however, was not won over by Le Corbusier's style, describing his Villa Savoye units as "big boxes on sticks". Corbusier's furniture has proved less controversial than his

architecture, providing a model of corporate modernism years ahead of its time. He was influenced by Adolf Loos's polemic *Ornament and Crime*, which linked surface decoration to decadence, dishonesty, and waste.

## MACHINE FOR LIVING

Le Corbusier's first forays into furniture design were made in 1928 after he invited Charlotte Perriand to join his studio. Despite having rejected her initial job application with the remark "We don't embroider cushions here", Le Corbusier relied on Perriand to provide him with furniture designs for almost a decade. Aiming to fulfil three distinct briefs, the pair produced three very different chairs – one for conversation, one for sleeping, and one for relaxation – for the Maison la Roche in Paris. The relaxation model, otherwise known as the LC2 *Grand Confort* armchair, demonstrated

**LA JAOUL, PARIS** Designed by Le Corbusier, the vaulted brick ceiling unites the open-plan living and dining areas, providing a view through to the staircase.

**TABLE 1852** Here in square rather than rectangular form, the Le Corbusier/Paul Jeanneret/Charlotte Perriand design has chromed legs and a linoleum-covered wooden top with aluminium edging. *c.1929. H:78cm (30¾in).*

**Tubular steel** recurs as a functional motif in early modernist furniture

**The leather upholstery** was conceived as black, now produced in other colours including tan and, as here, burgundy

**LC2 LOVESEAT** Also known as the *Petit Confort*, the prototype was designed by Le Corbusier in 1929, but was not put into production until 1959. This example was made by Cassina under licence. *1980s. W:167.5cm (66in).*

# FRANK LLOYD WRIGHT

WRIGHT'S ARCHITECTURAL CAREER SPANNED MORE THAN
60 YEARS. RATHER THAN SEEING THE ROOMS OF A HOUSE AS
A SERIES OF BOXES, HE AIMED TO LET SPACE FLOW, INTEGRATING
FURNITURE, BUILDING, AND LANDSCAPE.

In 1887 Wright left the University of Wisconsin and went to Chicago to find work at Adler & Sullivan, the best architectural practice in the city. Despite his lack of training, he began to develop and promote his own Prairie House style, which was similar to the Craftsman model of Gustav Stickley and Harvey Ellis.

## PRAIRIE HOUSE STYLE

So called because a building should "begin to associate with the ground and become natural to its prairie site", Wright chose materials to make his Praire House style homes blend into the landscape. Robie House was typically arranged around a central hearth with open-plan interiors fully integrated down to the art glass windows, recessed lighting, and fitted cupboards. Wright believed that "every chair must be designed for the building it will be in" – an extension of the Arts and Crafts integrated interior and a precursor of modernism.

Wright based his wooden furniture on Japanese models, having come to the conclusion that, "with the exception of the Japanese, wood has been misused and mishandled everywhere". His Barrel chair, designed in 1937 for the Johnson house, displays Japanese influence in its galleried vertical slats and intersecting horizontals. Wright's many variations of his high-backed chair anticipated the strict geometry of Gerrit Rietveld. Unlike Hoffmann, who clung to circular and rectangular forms, Wright was more flexible, incorporating hexagons and octagons into his furniture design.

## THE TALIESIN FELLOWSHIP

Work was scarce during the Depression and Wright, who had an outspoken personality and a sscandalous private life, found few commissions. But young architects flocked to Wright's home after he published his autobiography in 1932. About 30 apprentices lived and worked with him under the Taliesin Fellowship, reinvigorating his career in the process. In 1936 Wright completed designs for Fallingwater – arguably his most famous work. Built directly over a rocky waterfall, horizontal levels of smooth concrete set at different angles are supported by stone verticals. The luxury house fulfils the ideal of living in nature.

The next year Wright made plans for Taliesin West in Arizona, to be a winter base for the Fellowship. One of Wright's most enduring bequests is the Usonian model, a system for designing and building affordable homes that could be adapted for different families. This organic design, while undoubtedly modern, was a far cry from the strict modular Bauhaus standard.

**BARREL ARMCHAIR** Evolved from a 1904 prototype, it was designed by Frank Lloyd Wright c.1937 with a cherry frame and an upholstered seat, and has been reissued by Cassina since 1986. H:81cm (32in).

**OCCASIONAL TABLE** Fashioned in metal with an octagonal top, this is probably a prototype for tables which Frank Lloyd Wright designed for the Biltmore Hotel in Arizona. c.1926. W:66cm (26in).

**EXECUTIVE CHAIR** Designed by Frank Lloyd Wright for his only skyscraper, the Price Tower, in Oklahoma, it has an aluminium hexagonal seat and back, raised on a faceted aluminium and wood base. c.1952. H:91cm (36in).

**DINING SUITE** Incorporating illuminated corner posts, this suite was designed by Frank Lloyd Wright for the dining room at the Robie House, in Chicago. The high slatted chair backs help to keep the dining and living areas distinct. c.1909. Chair: H:133cm (52¼in).

**ROBIE HOUSE** The living room displays the Prairie House style open floor plan, dramatic overhangs, stretches of glass, and sweeping horizontal lines that revolutionized 20th-century architecture. The furniture echoes the horizontal emphasis. The house was designed in 1908 and completed in 1910.

# CERAMICS

CERAMICS CREATED AT THE FORWARD-LOOKING DESIGN COLLECTIVES OF
EARLY 20TH-CENTURY EUROPE WERE DISTINCT FROM THE STUDIO POTTERY
MOVEMENT, BUT MODERNIST NOVELTY AND FUNCTION PERMEATES THEM ALL.

## EUROPEAN MODERNISM

After the First World War, Dagobert Peche rather
than Josef Hoffmann became the guiding influence
at the Wiener Werkstätte. From around 1915 Peche
introduced a more playful style to the workshops,
with more colour and freer surface decoration.
Ceramics designed by Peche for Wiener Keramik
combine restrained formalism and liberated
experimentation. His colourful use of geometric
decoration coincided with Art
Deco, which was emerging.

The fusion of organic and geometric shapes
happened throughout the early modern period.
The work of Hilda Jesser, who designed ceramics
and glassware for the Wiener Werkstätte, provides
a typical illustration. Her ceramic vase has flared
sides, concave corners, and a fitted lid set beneath
the rim of the vessel, all of which combine to give
a Cubist impression of a ripe fruit on a branch.

Albin Müller, from the Art Nouveau artist's
colony in Darmstadt, came from the same Secession
background as many of the designers allied

*The vase* is handpainted
with a geometric pattern

**WIENER WERKSTÄTTE VASE**
Gudrun Baudisch designed
this vase with a footed ovoid
body, asymmetric handles, and
a trumpet-shaped, flared neck.
*c.1920. H:25cm (10in).*

*The loop handle, applied
twisted and cut, resembles a stalk*

*Naturalistic
decoration contrasts
with the geometric
monochrome base*

**KERAMOS FOOTED VASE** Inspired by
Dagobert Peche, the bell-shaped body is
handpainted with a stylized branch and a
geometric pattern on the foot. *1925.
H:21cm (8¼in).*

**HILDA JESSER BOX**
Designed for the Wiener
Werkstätte, this box is
reminiscent of a piece of fruit,
despite its almost square section and its
abstract imagery. *c.1920. H:19cm (7½in).*

*Highly glazed applications*
mimic droplets of juice

**DAGOBERT PECHE BOWL**
Of squat, bulbous form under
a bell-shaped cover, the bowl
is handpainted with a chequer
pattern and motifs that include
flowers and crowns. *c.1912.
H:10cm (4in).*

**The matching cover** *has a ball finial*

**JUTTA SIKA COFFEE POT** Designed for the Jos. Böck porcelain company in Vienna, the tapering cylindrical body has a circular pattern. The angular handle of both pot and lid is pierced with a hole as a finger grip. *1900–05. H:18cm (7in).*

**ALBIN MÜLLER LIDDED JAR** Made of glazed earthenware by Villeroy & Boch, Müller's design has an octagonal foot. The geometric form is accentuated with vertical bands of blossom and leaves against a white ground. *c.1912. H:46cm (18½in).*

to the Wiener Werkstätte. He created ceramic forms that went well beyond Art Nouveau, highly stylized like the art botany of Christopher Dresser.

## THE BAUHAUS

The pottery workshop at the Bauhaus was separated from the rest of the school both physically and ideologically. The studios were based at Dornburg an der Saale, just outside Weimar, under the direction of Gerhard Marcks. His idea of the school as a forum for free experiment and learning sometimes put him at odds with other Bauhaus masters such as Walter Gropius, who saw the school as a powerhouse of industrial design.

Ceramics students trained under master potter Max Krehan, who instilled in them the local vernacular pottery tradition of Thuringia. Once they were adept at this they could experiment with freely modelled sculptural receptacles. Krehan's star students included Otto Lindig, who became master of the school in 1924, and Theodor Bogler developed a modular system for designing ceramics entirely in tune with avant-garde philosophy. Bogler devised teapots that could be constructed from a series of basic elements.

## GERMAN FACTORIES

Despite these efforts to comply with industrial needs, attempts by Bauhaus ceramicists to forge links with German factories were only moderately successful. Big-name firms such as KPM Berlin and Velten-Vordamm did take on some Bauhaus designs, but they were reluctant to risk investing heavily in anything too new.

The Bauhaus had to leave Weimar in 1925 and the ceramics studios did not survive the move to Dessau, but it continued to influence ceramic design – former pupils of the pottery school took jobs within Germany's mainstream ceramic industry and founded their own studio potteries. Walter Gropius went on to design one of the most famous modernist ceramics – his sleek and functional TAC1 teapot is still made by Rosenthal today.

## RUSSIAN CONSTRUCTIVISM

Taking their lead from abstract, machine-minded European art movements such as Cubism and Futurism, Russian designers began to reject representational art after the Russian Revolution. Constructivism and Suprematism, founded by Vladimir Tatlin and Kasimir Malevich respectively, aimed to reflect the dominance of the machine and its triumph over nature. They were among the first to renounce any depiction of natural form, however stylized. Their compositions relied on precisely arranged geometric shapes, sometimes using mathematical tools and formulae. The Soviet establishment commissioned Constructivist artists to create propaganda for the state.

The Suprematists' aim of making Suprematism part of everyday life for the masses came closest to being realized by Nikolao Suetin, a pupil of Malevich, who worked at the State Porcelain Factory from 1923 to 1924. His geometric designs continued to be made into the 1930s. However, a proportion was sold abroad to bring in much needed foreign currency.

**KASIMIR MALEVICH PLATE** Designed for the Russian State Porcelain Factory, the porcelain body is decorated with an abstract geometric Suprematist pattern. *1923. D:24cm (9½in).*

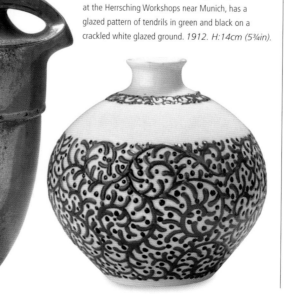

**STONEWARE VASE** This vase, designed by J.K. Liehm at the Herrsching Workshops near Munich, has a glazed pattern of tendrils in green and black on a crackled white glazed ground. *1912. H:14cm (5¾in).*

**R. HANKE VASE** Designed by Henry van de Velde and made in Höhr, the vase has two handles and is decorated with a crystalline glaze. *c.1902. H:17.5cm (7in).*

**ILJA TSCHASCHNIK PLATE** The white-glazed earthenware ground is decorated with Tschaschnik's Constructivist geometric pattern. *1924. D:34cm (13½in).*

## THE BIRTH OF STUDIO POTTERY

One of the most enduring legacies of the Arts and Crafts movement and its veneration of the solitary artisan was the beginning of studio pottery. The pioneering approach taken by figures such as George Ohr and Auguste Delaherche was to merge form and decoration – aspects of the trade that factory ceramicists had traditionally separated.

Often called the father of studio pottery, Bernard Leach was inspired by the raku wares used in the Japanese tea ceremony.

His link with Japan started when he spent part of his childhood with his grandparents, who were teachers in Kyoto. It was while working as a teacher in Japan that Leach became fascinated by traditional raku ceramics. Captivated by the transformations wrought by the heat in the kiln, Leach looked for a tutor and was taken on by the raku master Ogata Kenzan VI. It was only after his mentor's death in 1920 that Leach returned to England, accompanied by his friend Shoji Hamada.

Hamada familiarized himself with aspects of the English ceramic tradition such as slipware by studying exhibits at the British Museum. He settled with Leach in Cornwall, where they founded the St Ives pottery and built the first wood-fired climbing (stepped) kiln in Europe. Burning wood creates fly ash in the kiln, helping produce the delicately textured glazes for which Leach's work is known. As well as Oriental methods, Leach worked with Western techniques such as salt glaze and slip decoration. In *A Potter's Book*, published in 1945, Leach discussed his methods in detail. He set forth his thoughts on proportion, decoration, and function, expressing among other things a very

**BERNARD LEACH BOTTLE** Japanese influence is evident in the shape of Leach's design. A flat-sided vessel with a narrow waisted neck and a spreading oval foot, it is also decorated with Japanese-style calligraphy against a two-tone chequer-pattern ground. *c.1923. H:19.5cm (7¾in).*

**SHOJI HAMADA BOWL** Thrown by Hamada at Bernard Leach's studio in St Ives, the footed stoneware bowl is finished with a traditional Japanese iron temmoku glaze, which runs from black to a rusty hue where it thins. *1920–23. D:15cm (6in).*

*The distinctive glaze* is Leach's emulation of a traditional Japanese rust-black temmoku

**BERNARD LEACH CHARGER**
Made in stoneware, its centre was hand-painted by Leach with impressionistic Zodiac imagery: the Gemini twins rendered in the temmoku glaze also applied as the overall finish. *c.1927. D:38cm (15in).*

modern fondness for minimalism: "Overstatement is worse than understatement".

## LEACH'S DISCIPLES

With Leach's growing reputation as a master of his art, the St Ives pottery attracted an entire generation of studio potters. Michael Cardew, Leach's first student, left to pursue a career crafting traditional slipware. Katharine Pleydell-Bouverie and Norah Braden, both educated at the Central School of Arts and Crafts, met while working for Leach at the St Ives pottery in 1925. Inspired by Leach's methods, Pleydell-Bouverie built a wood-fired kiln on her family's estate at Coleshill. Braden joined her in 1928, and they set about experimenting with the dozens of varieties of wood on the estate, each of which produced subtly different glaze effects when burned in the kiln.

Their partnership, which lasted until 1936, produced a range of simple thrown vessels in a gamut of glazes. As a woman of independent means, Pleydell-Bouverie was able to keep the cost of her pottery low, making it accessible to a wide audience.

## LUCIE RIE

Leach also influenced Lucie Rie's work, persuading her to extend her craft to include stoneware and porcelain as well as earthenware. Rie was born in Vienna and studied at the Kunstgewerbeschule, the art school associated with the Wiener Werkstätte. She settled in London in 1938 and began to make ceramic buttons for the Bimini Glass and Jewellery Workshop.

## KEITH MURRAY

In 1933, the department store John Lewis exhibited a new range of Wedgwood ceramics that thrust their designer, Keith Murray, who was an architect from New Zealand, into the international spotlight. At a time when many leading ceramicists were turning out Art Deco designs – dismissed by Le Corbusier as "the final spasm of a predictable death" – Murray was conspicuous in his restraint. His plain forms were minimally adorned, often with little more than a series of lathe-turned grooves interrupting an otherwise perfectly smooth surface. The matte glazes developed for Murray by Norman Wilson were a perfect match for the uncluttered lines of his pots.

**VASE AND BOWL** With their lathe-turned ribbed and fluted decoration, these pieces are typical of the elegant, machine-like, earthenware forms Keith Murray designed for Wedgwood. *Early 1930s.* Vase: H:19cm (7½in); Bowl: D:35cm (13¾in).

After the war, she resumed her experiments with art pottery, drawing on arenas as diverse as Scandinavian modernism, Oriental ceramics, and the British decorative tradition. Infused with her bold spirit, Rie's work appears less derivative and more modern than Leach's pottery. It is dominated by functional forms such as stem bowls and bottles and has a strong architectural presence. Rie's glaze work is extremely varied, ranging from pitted volcanic glazes to intricate sgraffito filigree.

From the late 1940s she worked with Hans Coper, who became a partner in her studio. Coper would often shape his pots by hand after throwing the basic form on a wheel. His work is more sculptural and less functional than Rie's.

The rise of art pottery to the status of fine art was a slow process, gradually achieved through the work of key figures such as Leach. William Staite Murray, another British studio potter who made large vases with brush-painted decoration, put pottery on a par with sculpture and painting. He began to title his works in 1925 and stage annual exhibitons in conjunction with modern painters. Along with the high prices he charged – sometimes up to 100 guineas a pot – this tactic encouraged the art establishment to take notice of studio pottery.

**RIE AND COPER SALAD BOWL** A stoneware bowl made by Lucie Rie when she worked with Hans Coper, it encapsulates the dynamic sturdy yet frail quality known as the Lucie Rie quiver. *Late 1950s.* H:15cm (6in).

**LUCIE RIE SAUCEBOAT AND BOWL** Both stoneware vessels display a favourite Rie finish: bleeding and dripping bands of manganese or copper oxide glaze contrasted against a white tin glaze ground. *1950s.* Sauceboat: L:20.25cm (8in); Bowl: D:12.75cm (5in).

# GLASS AND LAMPS

GLASSMAKERS IN BOHEMIA TRADITIONALLY FOLLOWED THE LATEST TRENDS FROM THE FASHIONABLE CITY OF VIENNA. THEY WERE QUICK TO ADOPT THE NEW MODERN STYLE IN THE EARLY 20TH CENTURY.

## GLASS AND LAMPS

Once again the Glasgow Four acted as a catalyst. While Josef Hoffmann's 1899 Ariel vase rests in a modern frame, the glass component itself is organic, with languorous curves more a product of the Secessionist Art Nouveau style than anything else. The elongated stems and straight decoration of Otto Prutscher's 1907 wine glasses, by comparison, betray the unmistakable influence of the Glasgow School. Bohemian factories excelled at cutting glass, although they were used to naturalistic or jewel-like designs rather than grids and other geometric structures. Josef Hoffmann continued a long-standing association with Loetz in the years leading up to World War I, but his designs changed dramatically. His experiments with colour led him to combine milky white opaque glass with contrasting red, blue, or pink. In shape, Hoffmann's glass moved towards the formalism of the Constructivists, incorporating discs, cylinders, and rods.

**CHARLES RENNIE MACKINTOSH LIGHTS**
Two of four ceiling lights fashioned in copper with stained glass panels, they are reproduced from the fittings Mackintosh originally designed for his homes in Glasgow. *1900. H:16cm (6¼in).*

**Gadrooning** *with vegetal curves is a recurring motif in Hoffmann's earlier designs*

**The cylindrical bowl** *at the top completes the machine-like symmetry of the composition*

**The Loetz glass** *has a shimmering iridescence similar to Tiffany's Favrile glass*

**The axe-like buttressing** *of the mount predates some of Archibald Knox's Tudric and Cymric designs for Liberty*

**Cut chequer-pattern** *decoration reinforces the geometric form*

**JOSEF HOFFMANN VASE** Designed by Hoffmann for Bakalowits & Söhne of Vienna, this vase was made by Loetz Witwe in Luna pattern glass, shaded pale green to blue, and is raised on a black-painted wooden mount. *1899. H:38.5cm (15½in).*

**OTTO PRUTSCHER GLASS**
Commissioned by Bakalowits & Söhne, Prutscher's design was manufactured by Meyr's Neffe in blue-on-clear overlaid glass with geometrical cut decoration. *1907–12. H:21cm (8½in).*

## BAUHAUS CLASSICS

The Wiener Werkstätte look softened with the arrival of Dagobert Peche after World War I and the modernist cause was championed by avant-garde designers elsewhere, notably at the Bauhaus. Of all its departments, the metal workshop came closest to fulfilling Walter Gropius's original vision by becoming a "laboratory of modernity" through its association with lighting manufacturer Körting and Mathiesen.

One of the first lamp designs produced by the school was the 1924 MT8 table lamp by Wilhelm Wagenfeld and Carl Jucker. It was an instant classic and remains in production to this day. Its form has been pared down to the bare essentials of a disc base, cylindrical shaft, and domed shade. Made from glass and metal, it presages the favoured materials of International Style architects.

The director of the metal workshop at this time was Christian Dell, credited with designing the basic form of the modern desk lamp. Originally trained as a silversmith, Dell went on to design iconic lamps for large German companies throughout the 1930s and 1940s.

Dell left the Bauhaus in 1925, but the metalwork programme continued unabated. After the move to Dessau in 1925, Bauhaus students designed and manufactured all of the light fittings for Gropius's new building in the improved metal shop. In 1928 the start of a working relationship between the Bauhaus and Körting & Mathiesen's Kandem lighting brand represented the pinnacle of the school's cooperation with industry. Tens of thousands of Bauhaus-designed Kandem lighting units had been sold by 1930 and many models are still popular into the 21st century. Marianne

TABLE LAMP Employing a near-hemispherical, multi-rotational shade, this lamp is one of many eminently functional designs by Christian Dell, who was master of the metal workshop at the Bauhaus Weimer from 1922 to 1925. *H:43cm (17in).*

TABLE LAMP Designed by Marianne Brandt and Hin Bredendieck for Kandem, this lamp was made by Körting and Mathiesen with a hemispherical, enamelled shade and a curved steel stem. The foot is pressed glass, but other versions had a steel foot. *c.1928. H:47cm (18½in).*

Brandt and Hin Bredendieck, among others, worked alongside Kandem technicians to ensure that the designs were in keeping with Bauhaus principles and suitable for factories.

## STUDIO GLASS IN FRANCE

Originally a Fauve painter, Maurice Marinot reinvigorated French glass design throughout the 1920s and 1930s. He started by decorating blown glass with enamels. Later he taught himself to blow glass and his interest shifted to bringing out the decorative possibilities of the material itself. He experimented with air bubbles and metals, creating streaks, veins, and trails, crackling and bubbling. He inspired sculptor Henri Navarre to mould vases with internal decoration sandwiched between two layers of glass.

While Marinot's glass was highly acclaimed at the 1925 Paris International Exhibition, it was

Scandinavian glass that starred at the 1937 Paris Exhibition. Inspired by the peasant dress of his native Finland, Alvar Aalto designed the prize-winning Savoy vase for Karhula-Iittala glassworks in 1936. It is still made today.

### MOSER'S LOETZ DESIGNS

Like Josef Hoffmann, Koloman Moser designed glassware for Loetz. His contributions, including a series of ten electric lamps, show the influence of Christopher Dresser in their bulbous organic forms with geometric components.

Moser's original sketches for these lamps suggest more restrained decoration than on the finished article, indicating that Loetz may have altered his submissions to conform to their house style.

MAURICE MARINOT BOTTLE Of flattened oval form, the bottle has a typically imaginative, swirling marble-like pattern in tones of grey, green, and black, with white enamelling to the rim. *1910–20. H:16cm (6¼in).*

ALVAR AALTO SAVOY VASE Made by Karhula-Iittala, Aalto's design is of undulating, slightly flared free-form section. This example is mould-blown in green tinted glass. *c.1936. H:15.25cm (6in).*

KOLOMAN MOSER DESIGN Hanging from a brass mount, this lamp was made by Loetz Witwe from Moser's drawing, in clear and coloured iridescent glass with a mottled and striated pattern. *1900. L:24.5cm (9½in).*

# METALWARE

NATURALLY LINKED TO MACHINES, METAL WAS THE IDEAL VEHICLE FOR MODERNISM. FUNCTIONAL DESIGNS WITH LITTLE DECORATION ENABLED DESIGNERS TO SHOW A RESPECT FOR THEIR RAW MATERIAL.

**C.R. MACKINTOSH CUTLERY** The knife, fork, and spoon are from an 18-piece suite of electroplated cutlery designed for Miss Cranston's Tea Rooms in Glasgow. Their trefoil terminals may echo Gothic ornament, but their overall clean, uncluttered lines pre-empt modernism. c.1905. Knife:H: 22.5cm (8in).

## MAN OR MACHINE

After Christopher Dresser's extraordinary experiments in the late 19th century (*see p.242*), the earliest metalware designers to show modernist tendencies were linked to Charles Rennie Mackintosh in Glasgow and Josef Hoffmann in Vienna. Mackintosh designed flatware to go with his tea room interiors in Glasgow. Plain and simple, his cutlery often has trefoil terminals, slender stems, and elongated tines, blades, or bowls. Hoffmann used the same ball motif on his *Sitzmaschine* chair for his metalware.

Koloman Moser of the Wiener Werkstätte took the length and geometric symmetry of the Glasgow School and fused them with architectural innovations from the United States. The result was polished metal skyscraper vases, inspired by structures such as the Flatiron Building in Manhattan, New York.

Work at the metal studios of the Wiener Werkstätte was handcrafted to look as if it was machine-made – the opposite of what many other firms were seeking to do with the symmetry and simple details of the fashionable Craftsman look. It emphasized balanced

**WIENER WERKSTÄTTE VASE**
Designed in silver by Koloman Moser, its skyscraper-like body, pierced on four sides with bands of square apertures, is typical of Moser's vertical, architectural foms and geometric pattern decoration. *1905. H:20.25cm (8in).*

proportions and indicated how much this new breed of designers venerated the machine.

### MARIANNE BRANDT

The work of Marianne Brandt is similar to that of Christopher Dresser. In 1924 she became the first woman to enrol at the metal workshop of the Bauhaus. Although initially sidelined by her male colleagues, she instantly took to the medium. Items she crafted in her first year are still classics today. She was influenced by her Hungarian tutor László Moholy-Nagy, who was an enthusiast of the Constructivist movement.

Among Brandt's iconic designs is her functional MT49 teapot – so famous that it has appeared on a postage stamp in Germany. Although intended as an archetype for mass production, fewer than ten were ever made. When the Italian designer Alberto Alessi revived selected designs from the Bauhaus archive he reluctantly rejected Brandt's teapot as,

even with contemporary production technology, it presented too many problems. A common misconception among members of the Bauhaus was that simple, geometric shapes were bound to be suited to factory production. Like metalware made at the Wiener Werkstätte, much of the Bauhaus

**MARIANNE BRANDT COASTER HOLDERS**
Made by Ruppelwerk, these are good examples of Brandt's enamelled metal designs – in this case, one of the pair is enamelled in off-white with a red trim, the other in green with a black trim. c.1930. D:13cm (5in).

*Enamelled metal* comes in different colourways

**PEWTER CANDLESTICKS**
Designed by Joseph Maria Olbrich for the German firm Metallwarenfabrik Eduard Hueck, the candlesticks have wide, flared bases and Art Nouveau-style decoration. They are marked with the artist's initials. c.1901. H:36cm (14in).

*The curving decoration* is in low relief

*The flared bases* balance the candle holders at the top

**JAN EISENLOEFFEL TEA SERVICE** Made by Sneltjes of Haarlem, Eisenloeffel's brass, wicker, and glass composition has functional features such as long, non-drip spouts and an insulating handle. The form was inspired by European and Japanese designs. *c.1905. D:30cm (12in).*

*An angled neck gives the composition an organic harmony*

**PETER BEHRENS KETTLE** This hammered-brass electric kettle has a canework handle. Designed for AEG, it is a groundbreaking example of individualized mass production in the burgeoning electrical appliance industry. *1909. H:21.5cm (8½in).*

*The insulator handle is in the more traditional ebony, rather than an early plastic such as Bakelite*

metal shop's output was bespoke craftsmanship masquerading as industrial design. Brandt left the Bauhaus in 1929 and was employed by Ruppelwerk. In her three years with the firm she designed a range of mass-produced functional metalware, including ashtrays and napkin holders.

Some architects in Germany provided competition as well as inspiration. Peter Behrens, a hugely influential planner within the modern movement, designed a range of hammered-metal electric and traditional kettles.

## DUTCH DESIGNERS

The architect H.P. Berlage preached the honest use of materials and inspired a purity of form among modernist Dutch designers, especially Frans Zwollo and Jan Eisenloeffel. Zwollo specialized in furniture mounts with an Oriental slant. Eisenloeffel's sleek and practical tea sets made a major contribution to Dutch modernism and he established a workshop for handcrafted silver services and machine-made copper sets.

## SCANDINAVIAN SILVER

While Norway made a name for itself with *plique-a-jour* enamelwork, Danish silversmiths dominated the modernist Scandinavian scene. Mogens Ballin handmade metalware and jewellery decorated with abstract organic shapes. In 1901 Georg Jensen went to work for him. The sleek silverware produced by Jensen generally owes more to the flowing lines of Art Nouveau than the functional demands of modernism. But from 1906 his colleague Johan Rohde designed silver that helped propel Jensen's workshop into the international spotlight. Some of it was so modernist that it was pulled from production until consumer taste caught up.

**GEORG JENSEN WATER JUG** The smooth, baluster silver body and bow-like handle with an ebony insulator fuse form and function. Design No. 432 by Johan Rohde was far ahead of its time. *c.1925. H:22.5cm (8¾in).*

# TEXTILES

IN THE EARLY 20TH CENTURY FORWARD-THINKING DESIGNERS
CHALLENGED TRADITIONAL NATURALISTIC IMAGERY ON TEXTILES
WITH THEIR STYLIZED MOTIFS AND GEOMETRIC PATTERNS.

## GLASGOW SCHOOL TEXTILES

At the Glasgow School of Art, Jessie Newbery, the wife of the principal, began offering embroidery classes in 1894. Since many of her students were young beginners, intending to become teachers themselves, Newbery favoured inexpensive materials and easier techniques like appliqué. *Educational Needlecraft*, the popular book she co-authored with Margaret Swanson in 1911, demonstrated new ways of teaching embroidery as a means of self-expression.

Newbery's embroideries were characterized by simplified Art Nouveau motifs. Her influence can be seen in several of her ex-students' textile designs including Jessie Marion King and the McDonald sisters, Frances and Margaret. In 1902 Margaret contributed embroidered hangings, with elongated figures and geometric components, to her husband Charles Rennie Mackintosh's booth at the Turin Exhibition and his decoration schemes for the Willow Tea Rooms and Hous'hill in Glasgow.

### WIENER WERKSTÄTTE

The textile division was the most successful part of Austria's Wiener Werkstätte. It exerted a major influence on textile design over the course of a quarter century, on everything from table linens and embroidery to lace and even clothing. Some were made by hand; others were manufactured. More than 80 designers worked on textiles. Best known are Josef Hoffmann, Maria Strauss-Likarz, Mathilde Flögl, Max Snischek, Koloman Moser, Dagobert Peche, Carl Otto Czescheka, Bertold Löffler, and Kitty and Felice Rix.

Early Wiener Werkstätte textiles and rugs feature uniform rows of geometric motifs or linear forms –

**JULIUS ZIMPEL SILK** Designed by Zimpel for the Wiener Werkstätte (and printed WW in the selvage), Zimpel's Bahia pattern comprises polychrome, interlocked rectangular forms, and is characteristic of his machine-like compositions. *1925. L:73.5cm (29in).*

**DAGOBERT PECHE SILK** Peche's Wiener Werkstätte Liszt pattern is a now-iconic combination of stylized organic and geometric imagery, in which formalized flowerheads are compartmentalized within vertical rope-like and plain horizontal borders. *1911–13. L:101.5cm (17¾in).*

**JOSEF HOFFMANN COTTON** The *Luchs* (Lynx) pattern comprises stylized, wreath-like plant forms with triple leaf or petal centres, joined by interlaced scrolling stems to form an overall geometric pattern, and is printed in black against a parchment-coloured ground. *1910–12. L:94cm (37in).*

mostly printed in black on white. They introduced stylized floral patterns inspired by folk art around 1910, and by the 1920s their textiles had become increasingly colourful and capricious.

## OMEGA WORKSHOPS

Captivated by French post-Impressionist art, English art critic Roger Fry and artists Duncan Grant and Vanessa Bell founded the Omega Workshops in 1913, to create home products that reflected this bold new way of painting. They painted plain furniture, pottery, and fabrics by hand, as if they were blank canvases, their work characterized by improvization and spontaneity. Many of their colourful, striking designs feature abstract forms outlined in black for definition.

## EILEEN GRAY

Eileen Gray, an Irish-born designer who worked in Paris, used rugs decorated with striking angular patterns to offset the radical minimalism of her interior designs. Many of Gray's rugs were made for her at a studio directed by Evelyn Wyld. She also produced furnishing fabrics. Originally she designed on commission for clients' homes. However, Gray began creating limited edition rugs for the shop she opened in 1922.

## THE BAUHAUS

Until it was closed by the Nazis in 1933, Germany's revolutionary Bauhaus Art School promoted simple, unadorned designs for mass

**OTTO PRUTSCHER TABLECLOTH** Made in linen by Herrburger & Rhomberg of Austria, and distributed by the Wiener Werkstätte, the repeat geometric motifs recall the ornament on a Classical frieze. *c.1919. Sq:131cm (52½in).*

**GUSTAV KALHAMMER FABRIC** Printed as cotton dress fabric, Kalhammer's Schönau design for the Wiener Werkstätte is a polychrome riot of stylized flowers against an equally abstracted foliate ground. *1910–12. W:117cm (46in).*

manufacturing. Ironically few Bauhaus designs were actually put into production – they were considered too radical at the time. From 1926 to 1931, under the direction of weaver Gunta Stadler-Stölzl, the textile workshop was one of the few Bauhaus departments to take design prototypes through to mass production on a regular basis.

The teaching of abstract artist Paul Klee, a Bauhaus tutor, greatly influenced Bauhaus textile design, which often featured geometric forms and vivid colour contrasts. There was an emphasis on colour, texture, and tactility. Decorative effects were frequently integral to the fabric weave rather than printed on it. The careers of Stadler-Stölzl and other designers associated with the Bauhaus, like weaver Anni Albers, went on to flourish following World War II. The Bauhaus had a marked impact on textile design for the next 30 years.

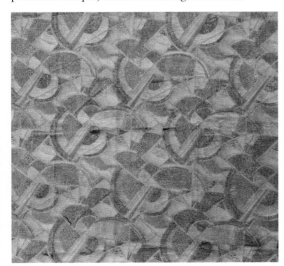

**BAUHAUS FABRIC** Printed on cotton and rayon, the unattributed Bauhaus pattern is abstract-geometric with a pronounced three-dimensional quality. It comprises a diagonal repeat of quadrant forms in shades of gold and brown. *1920s. L:227cm (90¾in).*

**EILEEN GRAY WOOLLEN RUG** The central abstract-figural pattern is entitled Solidadi: Nude/Torso, and is woven in grey, brown, and black on a cream ground, and set within grey, repeat crescent borders. *Late 1920s. L:312.5cm (125in).*

**GLASGOW SCHOOL DESIGN** This watercolour design for a batik is by Jessie M. King. The repeated stylized fuchsia blossoms give a sense of movement. *H:26cm (10½in).*

# ART DECO
## 1920–1940

# STYLISH MODERNITY

FOR A STYLE SO CLOSELY ASSOCIATED WITH THE 1920s AND 1930s, IT IS SURPRISING THAT THE NAME ART DECO WAS USED FOR THE FIRST TIME ONLY IN 1966. IN THAT YEAR, AN EXHIBITION CALLED *LES ANNÉES "25":* *ART DÉCO/BAUHAUS/STIJL/ESPRIT NOUVEAU* WAS HELD IN FRANCE.

**BERGÈRE** This chair by Paul Follot has a ribbed, upholstered, arched back and ebonized, fluted, tapering feet, which are typical of his elegant reinterpretation of 18th-century Classicism. *c.1920.* H:81.5cm (32in). CAL

## THE INTERWAR YEARS

The 1966 exhibition distinguished French decorative arts of the 1910s and 1920s from other modernist styles such as Bauhaus and De Stijl. Two years later, the British design historian Bevis Hillier published *Art Deco of the 20s and 30s*, defining Art Deco as "an assertively modern style, developing in the 1920s and reaching its high point in the 1930s…a Classical style in that, like Neoclassicism but unlike Rococo or Art Nouveau, it ran to symmetry rather than asymmetry, and to the rectilinear rather than the curvilinear; it responds to the demands of the machine and of new materials…[and] the requirements of mass production."

The ending in 1918 of the Great War, as World War I was known at the time, led to profound changes in society. The war had been so lengthy, and so costly in human life and physical, social, and economic destruction, that people were determined the world must never again go to war. There was also a belief that it should be possible to construct a new, better world out of the ruins of the old. So the war and its immediate aftermath represented a break from the failed past and a move into modernity, into the future.

Art Deco neatly spans the end of the Great War in 1918 and the start of World War II in 1939. It began in the tumult of revolution in Russia and defeat in Germany and Austria-Hungary, continued through the rise of fascism in Italy and the worldwide Great Depression of the 1930s, and ended with Nazism in Europe and totalitarianism and militarism in Japan and elsewhere.

But Art Deco also spanned an age of social and economic advance, in which women received the vote in many countries and some of the old political and economic inequalities were removed. For the first time ever, working people had leisure time, and the money to enjoy it, while light industries mass-producing cheap domestic appliances such as telephones, wirelesses, and electric irons transformed daily life. This was the age of the flapper and the Hollywood movie, of the skyscraper and the luxury ocean liner, the cheap car, and, in Germany, the *Autobahn* or purpose-built motorway.

**CHRYSLER BUILDING** Architect William Van Alen designed the New York skyscraper in stainless steel with automobile-derived ornamental details. Completed in 1930, it was the world's tallest man-made structure to date.

**PERFUME BOTTLE** Ancient Egypt was one of the inspirations of Art Deco. This English glass perfume bottle has a silver stopper in the style of an Egyptian sarcophagus head. H:16.5cm (6½in). SF

# THE INFLUENCE OF ART DECO

Art Deco reflected all these changes in society. It was essentially a pragmatic rather than a utopian style: it had no belief in the redemptive value of art, as did the designers of the Arts and Craft movement or Art Nouveau, or indeed the modernists. It was also increasingly democratic and popular, delivering high-quality, often mass-produced artefacts at affordable prices, even if it did have strong associations with high fashion and elite tastes.

Art Deco drew on a range of influences. Historic European styles, the pictorial inventions of contemporary avant-garde art, and the urban imagery of the machine age combined to form the mature style. So too did a romantic fascination with ancient Egypt and pre-Columbian Meso-America, as well as the arts of Africa and Asia and a vogue for the exotic or *l'art nègre*, as personified by the dancer Josephine Baker.

Art Deco's influence on the modern world was immense, affecting the design of skyscrapers and cinemas, trains and cars, furniture and domestic appliances, silverware and jewellery, book design and typography, posters and postage stamps.

**DAILY EXPRESS NEWSPAPER'S ENTRANCE HALL** Designed by Robert Atkinson, the former London offices of the newspaper are modernist on the outside and Art Deco on the inside, with battered gold and silver flowing over exploding geometric shapes.

# AN INTERNATIONAL STYLE

In some parts of the world Art Deco was largely associated with European elites: the princely courts in India; the Anglo-American business community in Shanghai; and the white elite of South Africa. But it reached a mass audience through the 1925 *Exposition Internationale des Arts Décoratifs et Industriels Modernes* in Paris, an international exhibition attended by over 16 million people.

From here it spread to the United States where, later, manufacturers affected by the Depression developed an innovative style known as streamlining. They saved money by producing contoured forms that best lent themselves to mass-production processes using new, cheap materials such as plastics, Bakelite, aluminium, and chrome. The style transformed small towns all over Depression America, reshaped the cities of Latin America, and finally achieved worldwide success through Hollywood movies.

**GLASS VASE** The geometric pattern on this Schneider vase is acid-etched. The contrasting black pedestal base is signed "Le Verre Français". c.1925. H:23cm (9in). DD

# ELEMENTS OF STYLE

MANY PEOPLE CONSIDER Art Deco to be the first truly international design movement – and with good reason. Not only did Art Deco affect design on every continent, it also drew on inspiration and ideas from around the globe. Influences range from Classical antiquity and African sculpture to Aztec ziggurats and new technology. Designers used an eclectic range of exotic materials – from rare ebony to new, inexpensive plastics.

H.G. RICHARDSON VASE
### GEOMETRIC
Many Art Deco designers wanted to create a style stripped of all historic references and naturalistic ornament. A design vocabulary based on non-representational motifs, clean lines, and pure geometric forms is more typical of later Art Deco.

CLUTCH BAG IN THE STYLE OF SONIA DELAUNAY
### CUBISM
The 20th-century abstract art style Cubism was developed in the first decade of the 1900s by artists such as Pablo Picasso and Georges Braque. By the mid-1920s progressive design incorporated characteristics of Cubism such as distortion, faceted forms, and geometric arrangements.

ARGY-ROUSSEAU *PÂTE-DE-VERRE SCARABÉES* VASE
### EGYPT
The 1922 discovery of Tutankhamun's tomb by archaeologist Howard Carter sparked off a taste for Egyptian designs. Ancient Egyptian-style images of pharaohs, eagles, and scarabs, as well as hieroglyphs, appeared on everything from jewellery to cinema walls. The craze had largely died out by the late 1920s.

RAYMOND SUBES CONSOLE TABLE
### JAZZ
In the 1920s and 1930s the fast-paced sound of jazz swept young people around the globe on to the dance floor. Portraits of jazz performers such as Josephine Baker symbolized the good times. Designers took the swinging tempo of the genre and translated it into rhythmic linear motifs and bold colour harmonies.

CLARICE CLIFF CIRCULAR CHARGER
### SUNBURST
From architecture to ceramics, there are countless variations on the sunburst in 1920s and 1930s design. This classic Art Deco motif – especially in bright gold or glowing reds, oranges, and yellows – radiates warmth and energy. The sunburst expresses the excitement of the modern age and optimism for the future.

FIRESCREEN ATTRIBUTED TO EDGAR BRANDT
### FLOWERING DESIGN
Colourful, exuberant, and semi-naturalistic floral imagery is mainly associated with early Art Deco design. Motifs such as garlands, swags, and baskets of blossoms, which harked back to the 18th century, had a stylized twist. Designers were particularly fond of roses, hollyhocks, palms, ferns, and orange trees.

JEAN MAYODON OVOID VASE

## ANCIENT GREEK AND ROMAN ART

The elegant poses and muscular proportions of Classical figures from ancient Greek and Roman art appealed to Art Deco designers, who also freely imitated and applied Classical ornaments such as swags. They revived and reworked sculptural façades of buildings and adapted imagery from Classical mythology.

GOLDSCHEIDER FIGURINE BY STEFAN DAKON

## WOMEN

In Art Deco design, women are more animated than their languid Art Nouveau counterparts, reflecting their growing independence after World War I. They are seen on the go, dancing, and participating in sports – their physiques gamine and supple, their hair and skirts fashionably short.

MAURICE DUFRÊNE MAHOGANY DRESSING TABLE

## INLAYS

The Art Deco love of fine craftsmanship and exotic materials is embodied in inlaid furniture decoration. Designers composed floral, figurative, and geometric patterns in contrasting veneers of rare woods like ebony, mahogany, and satinwood, or materials like mother-of-pearl, ivory, and shagreen, a type of sharkskin.

LÉON JALLOT SECRETAIRE

## SLEEK DESIGN

Clean, uncluttered lines are a common design theme throughout the Art Deco era. By the 1930s the Classicism popular in the previous decade gave way to streamlined, curving forms. Most typical of American Art Deco, streamlining was a feature of industrially produced technology, as well as traditional homeware.

KARL HAGENAUER-DESIGNED MASK

## AFRICAN INFLUENCE

African art had a powerful effect on artists and designers in the early 20th century. The features of tribal masks and ancestral figures influenced the representation of both faces and people, and there was an increase in the use of exotic African materials such as ivory, Macassar ebony, and leopard skin.

DUNHILL ALUMINIUM HUMIDOR

## MACHINE AGE

Art Deco designers drew inspiration from contemporary urban life and modern industry and embraced new materials such as plastic, tubular steel, and plywood. They seized on the dynamism of new technology and streamlined features of the automobile, aeroplane, and ocean liner to produce glamorous motifs.

FRENCH BRASS VASE

## STEPPED OR ARCHITECTURAL FORMS

The stepped forms and solid blocks characteristic of some Art Deco design are derived from the temples and pyramids of the Aztecs, Incas, and other ancient American cultures. Art Deco designers also borrowed imagery such as lightning flashes, sun rays, and zigzags from these ancient sources.

FRENCH PRESSED-AMETHYST GLASS VASE

## STYLIZED ANIMALS

Exotic beasts popular in the Art Deco era included elephants, parrots, zebras, and panthers. Frolicking deer and graceful doves also featured prominently in Art Deco design. In the 1920s and 1930s designers were almost as partial to greyhounds and terriers as 1950s designers were to poodles.

# FURNITURE

THE ART DECO ERA WAS AN INCREDIBLY FRUITFUL PERIOD FOR FURNITURE DESIGN. MANY OF THE 20TH CENTURY'S MOST ENDURING AND INFLUENTIAL SHAPES AND STYLES WERE PRODUCED DURING THIS TIME.

**FOLDING SCREEN** This decorative room divider, or screen, comprises four tall, hinged sections. Both sides of each individual section are faced in light- and dark-wood parquetry – including some fruitwoods – arranged in differing geometric patterns. *1930s. H:185cm (72¾in).*

## A CHANGE IN STYLE

It is now generally accepted that the style known as Art Deco first evolved in Paris before World War I. Its originators wanted to create a type of design that was not only identifiably French, but also capable of launching a new style for a new century.

Many of these early Art Deco designers used 18th- and early 19th-century French furniture as a starting point for their work. They then removed all the curls and whiplashes characteristic of Art Nouveau furniture design and developed a simpler, more disciplined look.

### PREWAR ART DECO FURNITURE

Paul Follot was one designer who created furniture with this new look. He used simple traditional furniture shapes from the 18th century for his exotic-wood pieces. He often embellished his designs with flattened, stylized carvings – usually fruit, flowers, and leaves. Follot was responsible for the basket of flowers, which became a favourite Art Deco motif. His early prewar furniture was more richly decorated than his later work.

The 18th- and 19th-century furniture that fascinated early Art Deco designers such as Follot was derived from ancient Greek and Roman designs and is defined as Neoclassical. Maurice Dufrêne also designed fairly plain furniture based on Neoclassical style before World War I. His furniture was more austere than Follot's, with very little carved detail. Léon Jallot produced Neoclassical-style furniture

*Each side door* is inlaid in ivory with connected spirals of dots; Ruhlmann used this decorative device often

**MAHOGANY ARMCHAIR**
A variant of Ruhlmann's Napoleon design, this mahogany armchair has an oval back above a hexagonal upholstered seat. The slender, tapering legs are to the outside of the seat, rather than beneath it. *1920. W:56cm (22in).*

*Short, fluted, spindle legs* are typical of Ruhlmann

The central drawer front is carved in medium relief with a bowl of flowers

**ROSEWOOD CABINET** Inspired by 18th-century designs, this rosewood cabinet by Ruhlmann is of *demi-lune* form with two curved side doors flanking a central pull-out shelf, a shelved recess, and a drawer. The back of the cabinet bears the coveted "Ruhlmann Atelier A" branding. *c.1920. W:129cm (50¾in).*

**BIRD'S-EYE MAPLE TABLE** Designed by Süe et Mare, this table has a *demi-lune* form and cabriole legs that betray the 18th-century inspiration in much of their work. The piece has a broad cross-banded top above a thumb-moulded edge and a single frieze drawer. *W:122cm (48in).*

with large, flat surfaces, which he veneered, lacquered, or applied shagreen and parchment to. Often he enlivened his pieces with geometric designs. His furniture was influential and inspired the work of leading manufacturers such as De Coene Frères in Belgium.

## THE BALLETS RUSSES

The formative period of Art Deco, before World War I, was greatly influenced by a dance company called the Ballets Russes. Under its spell, designers fell for bright hues, striking geometric patterns, and sumptuous exotic materials. Furniture designers began using colourful and contrasting veneers such as Macassar ebony and palisander. These rare woods had such dramatic grains that they needed hardly any other decoration. Designs were enriched with exotic ivory, shagreen, and lacquer, which were used to create bold patterns such as checks and sun rays.

## SÜE ET MARE

The Art Deco style would have dominated design by 1920, had it not been for the onset of World War I. Designers Louis Süe and André Mare had been designing Art Deco furniture since about 1910. They resumed their work together after the war and formed a business to collaborate with colleagues such as Maurice Marinot, Marie Laurencin, and Jacques Villon on interior design and furnishing projects. The official name of the company was *Compagnie des Arts Français*, but any projects they worked on together were usually dubbed Süe et Mare.

The solid Neoclassical style of the early 19th century inspired their furniture designs. They liked massive pieces with a lot of gilding, shiny lacquers, or extravagant cast-metal fittings, and they created numerous show stoppers for exhibitions.

Süe et Mare worked on a number of important commissions, including decoration for the Parfumerie d'Orsay shop and the French embassies in Washington and Warsaw.

## RUHLMANN

No furniture designer of the 1920s and 1930s was more famous for his fabulously crafted and luxurious furniture than Émile-Jacques Ruhlmann. Ruhlmann openly admitted that most of his work was inspired by 18th- and early 19th-century Neoclassical pieces. However, he passionately believed that "one ought only to find inspiration in them

[and then] adapt them for our time". He created sleek, elegant furniture with minimal detail using exotic veneers and opulent materials such as lacquer and ivory. Until the 1925 Paris International Exhibition brought him global renown, only his wealthy patrons knew his work.

Other major French designers creating similar Art Deco furniture included Jules Leleu and Pierre Legrain, who combined Neoclassicism with an African style, creating incredibly exotic results.

**EBONIZED DINING CHAIR** This hardwood dining chair by Léon and Maurice Jallot has a modernist feel to it. The green-leather-upholstered seat has chrome side rails and is raised on tapering, chrome-mounted legs. *1930. W:61cm (24in).*

**ROSEWOOD COFFEE TABLE** With its tubular chrome uprights, the simple design of this rosewood and walnut-veneered coffee table by De Coene Frères veers towards modernism. *Early 1930s. H:62cm (24½in).*

## EILEEN GRAY

The radical Irish-born designer Eileen Gray lived in Paris for most of her life. In the early 1920s she created entirely modern designs, divorced from all past influences, that anticipated 1930s modernist Art Deco furniture. She based her highly individual style on geometric forms, producing minimalist chairs, couches, stools, and lacquered screens. Interested in new materials for making furniture, Gray was an early convert to tubular steel. Though her pieces were originally created in limited editions for the exclusive use of wealthy patrons, it would have been easy to mass-manufacture her furniture. However, her designs were too avant-garde at the time for such consideration.

**MAHOGANY SECRETAIRE** This elegant secretaire by Jules Leleu is inlaid with rosewood and ivory. The cabinet has a fitted interior behind two doors, and two small drawers flank an arched apron. The whole is raised on tapering, octagonal legs. *c.1930. H:121cm (47¾in).*

**TRANSAT CHAIR** The brown-leather-upholstered sling seat of this chair has an adjustable back rest and is suspended on an unlacquered wooden frame with chrome fittings. *1925–30. L:106.5cm (42in).*

## SIMPLE DESIGN

After the Wall Street crash of 1929, Americans lost their appetite for luxury goods. Apart from a few exceptions like Eugene Schoen and T.H. Robsjohn-Gibbings, America's leading furniture designers were pretty indifferent to specialized craftsmanship and rare materials. Influenced by Germany's Bauhaus art school, they were interested in creating good-quality, practical, mass-manufactured pieces from innovative, industrial materials such as tubular steel. The majority of cutting-edge designers agreed with Paul Frankl, who in 1930 famously said, "Ornament equals crime." They absorbed the Bauhaus passion for design with simple lines, devoid of references to the past or nature. The Depression's onslaught made Bauhaus ideas even more attractive. The production of stylish, affordable goods led to a uniquely American 1930s interpretation of Art Deco.

### SKYSCRAPER FURNITURE

Frankl, a key member of New York's progressive design circles, saw the skyscraper as the United States' greatest expression of modern art. In 1925 he introduced a line of stepped wooden pieces

known as Skyscraper Furniture. Other American Art Deco furniture designers and manufacturers imitated Frankl's distinctive skyscraper style. From 1930 he concentrated on designing metal furniture.

### ROHDE AND MILLER

Gilbert Rohde did much to popularize Bauhaus furniture design in the United States. He combined a sleek look with solid practicality, using wood, glass, and metal details. The majority of his designs were produced for manufacturers such as Heywood-Wakefield and, most notably, Herman Miller. Indeed, it was Rhode who started Herman Miller's association with modern design.

### STREAMLINED FURNITURE

Another uniquely American twist on Art Deco is the so-called streamlined style, popular in designs for furniture from the early 1930s to the late 1940s. Streamlining drew on the machine for inspiration – the power and speed of trains or aeroplanes – and, crucially, it was highly suitable for manufacture by machine. A 1930s streamlined sofa, for example, might have a trim around its base that resembles the speed trim from a 1930s locomotive. The streamlined furniture style is well represented by the metal pieces of industrial designers such as Warren McArthur and Walter Dorwin Teague. However, this look is more widely

The metal maker's tag reads
"Skyscraper Furniture Frankl Galleries
4 East 48th St. New York"

*The semicircular, mirrored back* is simple and frameless

*The chromed-steel trim* and drawer pulls accentuate the table's sleek lines

**SKYSCRAPER DRESSING TABLE** Inspired by the 1920s Manhattan skyline, Paul Frankl designed a range of furniture under the Skyscraper name. The black-lacquered wood and chrome trim of this dressing table, and the considered asymmetry of its design are typical of the Skyscraper range. *c.1925. W:112cm (44in).*

**ROCKEFELLER CENTER NEW YORK** This New York Central Lines poster by Leslie Ragan offers a bird's-eye view of the cityscape that inspired much American furniture of the Art Deco period. *c.1935. H:102.75cm (40½in).*

**RADIO CITY MUSIC HALL SOFA** The use of curvaceous lines and bold colour are typical of Deskey's work. Here the rosewood frame is upholstered in brown vinyl married with a vibrant orange fabric. *c.1930. W:183cm (72in).*

**CLUB CHAIR** The plush, taupe-coloured, fabric-upholstered seat and back of Warren McArthur's Old Point Comfort club chair are encased within a simple, tubular aluminium frame. *H:60cm (23½in).*

**KNEEHOLE DESK** This Widdicomb D-shaped kneehole desk designed by Donald Deskey has a black-lacquered wood top, frieze, and plinth, with rosewood-veneered sides and drawers and chrome-plated banding. *c.1935. W:127cm (50in).*

associated with Donald Deskey, who produced streamlined furniture featuring wood and industrial materials such as plastic and metal. Best known for the Art Deco interiors of New York's Radio City Music Hall, Deskey created a variety of pieces – from one-off luxury suites, to inexpensive designs for mass production by manufacturers such as the Ypsilanti Reed Furniture Company.

## BRITISH ART DECO

During the 1920s and 1930s the Arts and Crafts movement was still a strong force in British design. It promoted simple, solid, handcrafted furniture, which was labour-intensive to produce and expensive to buy. Arts and Crafts designers were more interested in rediscovering traditional furniture-making techniques than in being at the cutting edge: they wanted to show that their furniture was handcrafted.

Also in this period, furniture designers Ambrose Heal and Gordon Russell produced pieces that were a hybrid of Arts and Crafts design and the modern Art Deco look. They both rose to prominence by designing and retailing Arts and Crafts furniture that involved some machine work and was aimed at a wider market.

Furniture designer Betty Joel originally designed Arts and Crafts-style pieces inspired by Regency furniture. In the 1930s, however, she changed direction and began producing Art Deco designs characterized by curvilinear geometric shapes and exotic woods. Joel's Art Deco designs were very popular in wealthy circles.

Two London-based reproduction-furniture specialists – Epstein and Hille – moved progressively into Art Deco style at this time, with light-wood furniture based on Classical forms. Hille's pieces in particular show the influence of French furniture designers such as Paul Follot, while Epstein's capitalized on the very British taste for dining suites, often producing a matching Art Deco table, chairs, sideboard, small server, and bar cabinet.

Manufacturers Isokon and Gerald Summers produced highly innovative and influential plywood furniture in the 1930s. Though British designers produced some experimental tubular-steel furniture at the time, as a rule, the public preferred the warmth of wood – even in an industrially moulded form such as plywood.

**OAK BOOKCASES** Each of these oak bookcases designed by Betty Joel has fluted, square feet and a random arrangement of open shelves and cupboards. The asymmetrical design is reminiscent of Frankl's Skyscraper pieces. *1932. W:92cm (36¼in).*

## EUGENE SCHOEN

Initially an architect, Eugene Schoen switched his focus to furniture and interior design after visiting the 1925 Paris International Exhibition. Unlike many of his American contemporaries, Schoen preferred designing wooden furniture. His clean, classical lines and emphasis on rare woods, exotic veneers, and fine craftsmanship reveal the influence of French Art Deco furniture designers such as Émile-Jacques Ruhlmann. The majority of Schoen's pieces were made by top New York furniture-maker Schmieg & Kotzian (which also traded as Schmieg, Hungate & Kotzian). Featured in numerous magazines of the period, Schoen's Art Deco furniture was both critically acclaimed and popular with well-to-do Americans.

**CHEST-ON-STAND** Designed by Eugene Schoen for Schmieg, Hungate & Kotzian, this three-drawer solid- and veneered-mahogany chest-on-stand has a cross-hatched parquetry front with circular drawer pulls. *c.1935. W:114.5cm (45in).*

*Each drawer* has a fluted wooden handle

**CORNER DESK** This large cherrywood-and-walnut corner desk was designed by Gordon Russell. It has a shaped working area above an arched apron flanked on each side by two drawers. Design no. 705. *W:116cm (45¾in).*

# FURNITURE GALLERY

Art Deco furniture is characterized by bold shapes and forms. Architect-designed pieces became popular in this period, with many well-known architects creating bespoke lines. Advances in engineering were highly influential, and the form of the skyscraper was frequently invoked. Chrome was commonly used, giving furniture a stylish, modern feel. Monochromatic schemes were also popular, with black a particularly fashionable colour.

## KEY

**1.** Wolfgang Hoffmann coffee table. 1934. ④ **2.** American cocktail table with chrome banding. c.1935. W:91.5cm (36in). ④ **3.** Beresford & Hicks standing mirror with stepped feet. 1935. H:53cm (21in). ① **4.** English walnut chest of drawers with black-lacquer banding. 1930s. W:123cm (48½in). ② **5.** Russel Wright/Heywood-Wakefield asymmetric server with black-lacquer finish. H:107cm (42¼in). ③ **6.** Sideboard by M.P. Davis of London, in bleached mahogany. 1929. H:96cm (37¾in). ③ **7.** John Widdicomb commode with stylized inlays. H:111.5cm (44in). ② **8.** Skyscraper vanity with rectangular mirror and black enamelled trim. H:154.5cm (60¾in). ②

1 *Hoffmann coffee table*

2 *American cocktail table*

3 *Standing mirror*

4 *Walnut chest of drawers*

5 *Wright asymmetric server*

6 *Bleached mahogany sideboard*

7 *Widdicomb commode*

8 *Skyscraper vanity*

9 *Kem Weber chair*

10 *Modernage lounge chair*

11 *French armchair*

**9.** Kem Weber American triple-band chair for Lloyd Manufacturing Company. 1937. W:70cm (27½in). ④ **10.** Modernage lounge chair in light grey ultra-suede. H:79cm (31in). ① **11.** French mahogany armchair (one of a pair). H:80cm (31½in). ④ **12.** Norman Bel Geddes vanity with chromium-plated base and trimming. H:182cm (71¾in). ③ **13.** Belgian occasional table with a mahogany-coloured finish. c.1920. H:78.5cm (31in). ③ **14.** Table by Soubrier. c.1930. H:61cm (24in). ④ **15.** Side table by Charles Hardy, for Belmet Products of New York. c.1935. W:51cm (20in). ③ **16.** Robert Winthrop Chanler three-panelled screen painted with two zebras. 1928. H:198cm (78in). ⑤ **17.** Beechwood screen by Bauman. c.1930. W:201cm (79in). ② **18.** Circular walnut veneered display cabinet with twin glazed doors. H:187cm (73½in). ①

13 Belgian occasional table

14 Soubrier table

12 Bel Geddes vanity

15 Charles Hardy side table

16 Three-panelled screen

17 Beechwood screen

18 Walnut display cabinet

# EXOTIC INFLUENCES

FROM THE USE OF RARE MATERIALS LIKE SHAGREEN TO THE DEPICTION OF SERPENTS, EXOTICISM PERMEATED ART DECO STYLE. DESIGNERS TOOK IDEAS FROM THE ORIENT AND THE AZTECS, BUT THE MOST IMPORTANT INFLUENCES WERE TRIBAL AFRICA AND ANCIENT EGYPT.

**FACETED VASE** The stepped sides and partly red-enamelled, metal ziggurat mounts on this Boch Frères vase were inspired by the architecture of the ancient Inca and Aztec civilizations. *H:25.5cm (10in)*.

### JOSEPHINE BAKER

From the moment Josephine Baker first danced on the Parisian stage in 1925, she was a big star. Audiences were entranced by the African-American entertainer's uninhibited movements, dark beauty, and quick wit. In Europe, Baker embodied the energy of American jazz and the mysteries of Africa, and she played up her exoticism both on and off the stage. Sculpted, photographed, and depicted by many leading artists and designers of the day, Baker helped pave the way for a shift in the perception of African-Americans.

***LE TUMULTE NOIR*** The dancer in this stylized drawing by Paul Colin is thought to be Josephine Baker; certainly she was the inspiration. Exotic-looking women had a great impact on American Art Deco design. *1927.*

Western artists and designers discovered Africa at the beginning of the 20th century and began collecting tribal African sculpture, masks, textiles, and other artefacts. They incorporated elements of this tribal art into Art Deco design in the use of simplified, stylized facial features and figures, as well as bold geometric patterns. Art Deco colour combinations such as black/yellow/green and red/cream/black had African connotations, as did the use of contrasting light and dark earth tones.

### TRIBAL AFRICA

Art Deco designers used exotic African materials for their work, including ivory, snakeskin, zebra hide, and leopard skin. Furniture-makers such as Émile-Jacques Ruhlmann adored the striking grains of rare African woods, producing pieces veneered and inlaid with palisander, Macassar ebony, amaranth, and amboyna. This type of furniture proved so desirable that there was even a special pavilion at the 1931 Paris *Exposition Coloniale* dedicated to promoting the use of these exquisite woods.

The shapes of ceremonial chairs and tribal stools inspired the chaise longues and other seating by designers such as Pierre Legrain and Eileen Gray. They liked the simplicity of African furniture, as well as the newness, in the sense that Western designers had not previously referenced African pieces. Other Art Deco designers chose to depict exotic wild animals. Jean Dunand, for example, used big cats and gazelles on his lacquered screens.

African culture and design also had a huge impact on Art Deco jewellery – from angular stone cuts and geometric bracelet links, to tribal masks and elephant motifs. The fashion for wearing big bangles up to the elbow had African roots, as did the taste for big beads.

**CARLTONWARE JAR** This ginger jar is printed and enamelled with hieroglyphs from Tutankhamun's tomb. The Egyptian influence extends to the large gilt-and-black pharaoh finial on the lid. *H:32cm (12½in)*.

**OWL MASK** Art Deco designers were inspired by the primitive designs of African tribal art such as this mask, with its limited use of colour and bold, geometric shapes. *H:57cm (22½in)*.

### ANCIENT EGYPT

Howard Carter's dramatic unearthing of Tutankhamun's tomb on 4 November 1922 was perhaps the biggest media phenomenon of the interwar years. Pictures of the splendid riches found in the young pharaoh's tomb captured the imagination and sparked a craze for all things Egyptian. By February 1923 the *New York Times* was reporting "businessmen all over the world are pleading for Tut-Ankh-Amen designs for gloves, sandals, and fabrics".

Ancient Egyptian-style patterns and motifs such as pharaoh's heads, eagles, cobras, pyramids, sphinxes, and scarabs appeared everywhere. Designers even turned ancient Egyptian writing – hieroglyphs – into decoration. The sheer quantity of golden objects in Tutankhamun's tomb had especially astonished and delighted the public. Designers began splashing gold colouring about with abandon, combining it with white, earth red, turquoise, and ultramarine – colours associated with the pharaohs.

In the 1920s "Tutmania" had an impact on every conceivable form of design – from sculptures and cigarette packaging, to shawls and cinema interiors. Even the innovative designer René Lalique (*see p.286*) adopted ancient Egyptian motifs, personalizing them in his glass designs. The taste for ancient Egyptian style resulted in some outstanding Art Deco jewellery and clocks by top jewellers such as Cartier. Just like the pharaoh's possessions, these were made from precious materials and stones, including mother-of-pearl, coral, diamonds, emeralds, and sapphires.

**CELEBRATING AFRICA'S CONTRIBUTION**
The Salon d'Afrique at the Musée des Arts d'Afrique et d'Océanie in Paris (originally the Musée des Colonies) features murals by Louis Bouquet and furniture by Émile-Jacques Ruhlmann.

# CERAMICS

DURING THE 1920S AND 1930S CLASSIC POTTERY SHAPES AND DECORATION WERE REINTERPRETED IN THE ART DECO STYLE. THE RESULTING CERAMICS LOOKED STARTLINGLY FRESH AND MODERN.

## FRENCH CERAMICS

One of France's premier ceramics manufacturers, Sèvres has been associated with high quality since the 18th century. With one eye on the past and the other on the future, in the interwar years director Georges Lechavallier-Chevignard commissioned leading Art Deco designers to inject some modernity into the firm's traditional product range.

## CELEBRITY COLLABORATIONS

Lechavallier-Chevignard's beliefs were very much in keeping with the design philosophy of Émile-Jacques Ruhlmann. Fanatical about fine craftsmanship, the Parisian furniture-maker and interior decorator collaborated with Sèvres on several successful ornamental ceramic projects. Lechavallier-Chevignard also persuaded animal sculptor François Pompon to re-create his stylized bronzes – including his celebrated polar bear – in earthenware, to much acclaim. Other important figures in Art Deco design employed by Sèvres included Raoul Dufy, Jean Dupas, and Marcel Goupy.

Witnessing the success of these collaborations, other French ceramics firms, including Haviland of Limoges, soon followed suit, commissioning leading designers to revamp their wares.

## JEAN MAYODON

Sèvres's artistic director from 1941 to 1942, Jean Mayodon first worked for the ceramics manufacturer on a freelance basis before World War II. His studio pottery was renowned throughout the 1920s and 1930s. This was due in part to its exciting designs, inspired by traditional Persian, Chinese, and Japanese wares and featuring figurative decoration taken from Greek and Roman mythology. What made Mayodon's ceramics truly distinctive, though, were their earthy, mottled glazes, including lavish amounts of gold.

As well as smaller pieces like vases, bowls, and plates, Mayodon also produced architectural fittings such as tiles, fountains, and panels. He contributed ceramic designs to a number of distinguished steamship decoration schemes including the *Normandie*.

**JEAN MAYODON OVOID VASE** Classical and Biblical imagery was a source of inspiration for Mayodon. This vase, decorated with polychrome enamels and gold, features images of Adam and Eve with three snakes. It has a wooden base. *1930s. H:57cm (22½in).*

**OVOID CERAMIC VASE** Jean Mayodon's footed vase is decorated with Classical- and Renaissance-style nudes and stylized animal figures. The images are rendered in natural colours on a mottled and slightly crazed brown- and gold-enamel ground. *c.1930. H:24.5cm (9¾in).*

*The snake* was a common Art Deco motif, appealing for the texture and patterning of its skin.

*Muted tones* and painterly execution of images are typical of Mayodon's work

**CIGARETTE BOX** Designed by Wilhelm Kåge, this exquisite cigarette box was one of the Argenta line of pottery produced by Gustavsberg. The matte aqua-green pottery has a silver overlay decoration depicting a muscular nude female reclining and enjoying a cigarette. *1930s. W:15cm (6in).*

## ALL-IMPORTANT FINISH

Boch Frères in Belgium and Longwy in France were industrial manufacturers that hand-finished their ceramics to make them look like studio pottery. Both firms produced decorative vases with innovative crackled glazes that gave their ceramics the appearance of ancient pots found in archaeological digs. The stylized animals, floral motifs, and human figures used for decoration came from a variety of sources, including traditional African vessels and Greek and Roman urns. Boch Frères' ceramics often bear a facsimile of the signature of their principal designer, Charles Catteau.

Upmarket shops and department stores sold Boch Frères and Longwy's vases. Longwy's main retailer was Primavera, the stylish homeware section of Le Printemps department store in Paris. Famous for its chic, modern ceramics, Primavera commissioned pieces from leading firms, as well as manufacturing its own designs at its factory outside Tours.

## ITALIAN CLASSICISM

Benito Mussolini's Fascist government gave enthusiastic support to quintessentially Italian design. According to Margherita Sarfatti, organizer of the Italian Pavilion at the 1925 Paris International Exhibition, designers should respond to "the native traditions in each country – which for us means Classicism".

*HEXAGONAL VASE* Made by the Faiencerie de Longwy, this stoneware vase with a stepped neck is decorated in blue, yellow, and red enamels over a glazed *craquelure* ground. It bears the maker's mark. c.1925. H:18cm (7in).

*The richly coloured motifs* betray the influence of ancient Egypt

**SÈVRES BOX AND COVER** The lid is decorated in relief with a geometric gilding design. Along with the additional gilding to the sides of the box, this contrasts well with the vivid blue-green mottled glazed ground. c.1925. W:16.5cm (6½in).

Many designers like Gio Ponti, Angelo Biancini, and Gigi Chessa used Italian heritage, especially Roman antiquity, as a starting point for their ceramics during the 1920s and 1930s.

## SCANDINAVIAN CERAMICS

The simplicity and purity of form of Neoclassicism, a style loosely derived from designs from the ancient, Classical world, had a huge impact on Scandinavian Art Deco. Danish ceramics manufacturers Bing & Grøndahl and Royal Copenhagen added an angular, stylized Art Deco flourish to Neoclassical designs. In Sweden Wilhelm Kåge, the artistic director of ceramics firm Gustavsberg, combined traditional Far Eastern shapes with images from Classical mythology to create a striking range of ceramics called Argenta. Made from mottled-green stoneware with silver-overlay decoration, this popular range featured sculptural figures that were reminiscent of the engraving on Sweden's famous Orrefors glass.

*Typical of Boch Frères*, enamelling in shades of blue and yellow is thickly applied to create pattern in relief

**OVOID FAIENCE VASE** Made by Boch Frères, this vase is decorated with stylized flying pelicans against a blue sky and flanked above and below by similarly stylized clouds on an off-white *craquelure* ground. H:34.5cm (13½in).

**STONEWARE VASE** The striking blue, yellow, and green design of this bottle-shaped vase repeats a segmented pattern of stylized sunburst-like forms. It was designed by Charles Catteau for Boch Frères. c.1925. H:32cm (12½in).

**EARTHENWARE VASE** The linear design features a central frieze of stylized gazelles – a popular Art Deco motif – painted in green over an ivory *craquelure* ground. By Édouard Cazaux for Sèvres. c.1925. H:32cm (12½in).

## FIGURINES

Many ceramic figurines from the Art Deco era resemble three-dimensional illustrations from contemporary fashion magazines such as *Vogue*. Fashion inspired the way figurines posed, often holding out the fabric of their dresses, which tended to be the latest garments: long evening gowns, bias-cut frocks, sweeping fur-collared coats, smart suits, and beach pyjamas. The figurines also wore their hair in short, modern styles, sporting sleek bobs and Marcel waves. From their cloche hats to the tips of their painted fingernails, these figurines were the height of fashion.

### MOULDING A LIFESTYLE

Art Deco fashions and fabrics offered designers the perfect showcase for virtuoso modelling and painting. Incredibly elaborate moulds were required to duplicate wide-brimmed hats, wind-blown scarves, and softly draped fabrics. Ceramic decorators skilfully imitated the bright hues and stylized patterns of contemporary fashions. Even nude figurines frequently carried a swathe of fabric to show off the designer's technical flair. A group of figurines, the greatest test of a ceramicist's talent, often included a dog, usually the designer's favourite breed: greyhound,

borzoi, or terrier. The canines' distinctive outlines and straining energy nicely set off the slim physiques and elegant dress of the human figures. A writer wryly commented in *Vogue* during the 1920s: "Dogs are now so fashionable that one wonders why they are not sold by the couturier."

As well as illustrating fashionable clothing, ceramics figurines also depict the glamorous lifestyle many women aspired to. Most Art Deco figurines portray lively, independent young women. Even the exotic dancers are usually playfully seductive rather than predatory. These figurines dress up as Pierrette or a Spanish dancer for a costume ball, flirt at parties with feathered fans, and sophisticatedly smoke cigarettes. Active and animated, they participate in sports such as golf, tennis, swimming, and horse-back riding.

### GOLDSCHEIDER'S REIGN

Arguably the most popular name in contemporary Art Deco figurines, the Austrian manufacturing firm of Goldscheider was renowned for its attractive designs, high-quality modelling, and

*Modern couture* – including accessories such as hats, gloves, and shoes – was faithfully copied

**LADY WITH BORZOI** This female figure in a flowing blue floral-print dress and broad-rimmed hat is portrayed walking a borzoi hound. Designed by Klara Herczeg for Goldscheider, the figure was also available wearing a red dress. *c.1935. H:43cm (17in).*

*The borzoi hound* was a popular Art Deco motif

**FEMALE GOLFER** Designed by Stefan Dakon, this Goldscheider figurine reflects the Art Deco preoccupation with the modern woman, portrayed here taking part in a predominantly male pastime. *H:27cm (10½in).*

detailed decoration. What set Goldscheider apart from other figurine specialists in the 1920s and 1930s was its unique ability to re-create the latest fashions faithfully, down to the last flower on a colourful fabric. Typical Goldscheider figurines depict dancers in flowing skirts or women stylishly dressed in a naturalistic way. Some are recognizable portraits of celebrities and famous performers of the day such as actress Dolores del Rio.

High-profile sculptor Josef Lorenzl and leading ceramics modeller Stefan Dakon were responsible for many of Goldscheider's more popular figurines. The firm also employed designers associated with the Wiener Werkstätte, such as Michael Powolny and Vally Wieselthier, to produce more experimental ceramics.

## ENGLISH FIGURINES

Between the two World Wars Leslie Harradine was Royal Doulton's most successful and prolific modeller. He is best known for his traditional china ladies in crinoline, which hark back to the 18th and 19th centuries. However, Harradine also designed a number of figurines that reflected contemporary pastimes, such as Harlequinade, a flapper dressed for a costume ball, and Sunshine Girl, a 1920s bathing beauty under a Chinese parasol.

## OTHER NOTABLE MAKERS

Goebel und Hutschenreuther in Germany and Royal Dux in Czechoslovakia also produced a variety of figurines portraying exotic dancers, sailor girls, and other bright young things. Italian ceramic manufacturer Lenci specialized in languid, often-nude female figures. Designed by Helen König Scavini or Sandro

**PORCELAIN FIGURINE** Delicate and exquisitely painted porcelain is characteristic of Rosenthal pieces, as seen in this elegant figurine. *c.1935. H:27.5cm (10¾in).*

**LADY WITH FAN** This model was designed by Paul Scheurich for Meissen. It is polychrome-painted in shades of pink and blue. *1929. H:47cm (18½in).*

Vacchetti, many Lenci figurines have a distinctive doe-eyed sweetness about them.

Apart from a few exceptions, in the 1920s and 1930s, venerable figurine manufacturers such as Meissen, Berlin, and Royal Copenhagen mainly focused on designs inspired by their heritage.

## WALL MASKS

Probably inspired by the way African art collectors hung tribal masks, wall masks reached the height of their popularity in the interwar years, when they were as ubiquitous as that other iconic Art Deco product for the home, the cocktail shaker. Practically every major name in ceramics – from Clarice Cliff and Beswick, to Goldscheider and Lenci – made wall masks. Most portray chic young women in the latest hairstyles and hats, their accessories often highlighted in jazzy colours like jade green, cherry red, and tango orange.

**GOEBEL WALL MASK** This ceramic mask portrays a young lady in profile. She wears contemporary make-up and sports fashionably short blond hair in tight, stylized curls. *L:21.5cm (8½in).*

*Fancy dress* features in several Royal Doulton figururines

*Clowns were popular* theatrical figure and sources of inspiration

**THE MASK** In this Royal Doulton figurine, a young girl in a theatrical pose dressed as a clown or a Pierrot-type figure gazes searchingly into the face of a mask that she is holding.

**MARIETTA** Designed by Leslie Harradine, this Royal Doulton Art Deco figurine is dressed as if for a ball in a devil-style black-and-red fancy dress. *H:21cm (8¼in).*

**ANGELA** This Leslie Harradine Royal Doulton figurine is dressed in a dancer's clothes. She sits on top of a truncated column, holding a large fan behind her head. *1932–45. H:19cm (7½in).*

## FEMALE DESIGNERS

During the 1920s and 1930s a number of creative British women took ceramic production in new directions, setting fashions that put Britain at the forefront of Art Deco ceramic design.

### THE CLIFF FACTOR

For many, Clarice Cliff and Art Deco are synonymous terms. Cliff's bold, distinctive interpretation of traditional themes – landscapes, cottages, and floral borders – in her instantly recognizable palette of reds, oranges, yellows, blues, and greens epitomizes the look of Jazz Age ceramics. She called her range Bizarre Ware and gave her patterns names such as Black Luxor, Fantasque, and Ravel.

Cliff used plain mass-produced pottery in traditional shapes and more daring geometric styles as a base for her patterns. The decoration was handpainted on these so-called "blanks" – sometimes by Cliff herself, but mainly by the decorators at her studio. She encouraged her predominantly female decorators to interpret her designs freely. Clarice Cliff became a celebrity in the 1930s and her Art Deco pottery sold in huge quantities in Britain as well as internationally.

### COOPER'S MASS APPEAL

Another big name in British Art Deco ceramics was Susie Cooper. She worked for A.E. Gray & Company before setting up her own decorating and design business, Susie Cooper Pottery, in 1930.

At the time, much of the tableware available to people with limited resources had staid, traditional decoration. A talented businesswoman as well as a designer, Cooper realized there was a market for reasonably priced ceramics with a fresh, modern look.

The majority of her designs are for practical tableware, though she also produced some decorative items like candlesticks and wall masks. Some of her handpainted geometric designs are similar to Cliff's, while others feature Cooper's distinctive dots, dashes, bands, and shaded crayon lines. According to the *Pottery Gazette* of June 1931, Cooper had "a unique capacity to achieve the maximum degree of effectiveness in pottery decoration by recourse to the simplest modes of expression".

Stylish, well-executed designs were Cooper's priority. It didn't matter to her if her designs were handpainted or transfer-printed. By the mid-1930s she was producing designs for large-scale transfer-printing on tableware. Her most popular transfer designs from the 1930s – Dresden Spray, Patricia Rose, and Nosegay – had stylized flowers in their centres and pastel borders.

Susie Cooper's ceramics were immensely popular. In recognition of her innovative work, she was appointed Royal Designer for Industry in 1940.

### CLIFF AND COOPER'S INFLUENCE

Other British ceramic companies quickly picked up Clarice Cliff and Susie Cooper's jazzy modern look. Some, such as Myott, capitalized on Cliff and Cooper's popularity by imitating their geometric patterns, stylized motifs, and bright colours. Others responded by bringing out their own fresh, modern lines. Shelley Pottery developed a reputation for geometrical tableware with dramatic Cubist decoration, while Wiltshaw and Robinson produced Carlton Ware – a highly successful tableware range resembling green leaves.

**WALL CHARGER** Designed by Clarice Cliff, this Windbells-pattern wall charger comprises a stylized tree with a black trunk and blue leaves against a red, yellow, and green ground. *1933–34. D:25.5cm (10in).*

**CONE-SHAPED SUGAR SIFTER** The design of this sugar sifter is rendered in Clarice Cliff's typically bold colours. Sifters were produced in a number of patterns; this Summerhouse pattern is extremely rare. *H:14cm (5½in).*

**SQUARE STEPPED VASE** The Latona Tree pattern on this Clarice Cliff vase features a tree with a black trunk and stylized blue, orange, red, purple, and green foliage. Design no. 369A, it bears a painted Latona mark. *H:19.5cm (7¾in).*

**JUG AND COFFEE POT** Susie Cooper's tableware often reflects her interest in European design. Pieces are primarily functional, and decoration is usually geometric in form, with simple, banded designs in soft colours, such as in these examples. *Jug: 1930. H:17cm (6¾in); Coffee pot: 1928. H:20.5cm (8in).*

## AMERICAN JAZZ

Many of the best American Art Deco ceramics were inexpensive and mass-produced. By the late 1930s, for example, nearly every American kitchen had a piece of Homer Laughlin China Company's Fiesta ware. Jazzy colours and streamlined shapes make this tableware range among the most iconic of all American Art Deco designs.

However, some factories also produced daring hand-finished limited-edition ceramics. In 1924 Roseville Pottery introduced Futura, a striking range of angular vases with mottled glazes. This was one of the most advanced American Art Deco ceramic ranges of the day. Cowan Pottery produced a variety of products including studio pottery. Owner Reginald Guy Cowan employed cutting-edge designers – Margaret Postgate, Waylande Gregory, A. Drexler Jacobson, and Viktor Schreckengost among them. Now considered one of America's foremost potters, Schreckengost created a number of seminal Art Deco designs while at Cowan, the most famous of which is the spectacular turquoise Jazz Bowl. Decorated with images of New Year's Eve festivities in New York City, it encapsulate the spirit of the Jazz Age perfectly.

## DEVELOPMENTS IN DORSET

Some of the highest awards given out for ceramics at the 1925 Paris International Exhibition went to a pottery in Poole, Dorset – the partnership of Charles Carter, Harold Stabler, and the husband-and-wife team of John and Truda Adams. Today this business is known as Poole Pottery. Poole won acclaim for its striking handmade and hand-decorated Art Deco stoneware, which featured stylized flowers and deer, as well as geometric motifs. The simple shapes of Poole pottery were often inspired by Japanese ceramics and decorated with matte glazes and subdued colours.

Truda Adams (who later married Charles Carter) defined the highly original look of Poole pottery. Stabler's wife, Phoebe, also produced distinctive Art Deco stoneware figures for Poole, as well as for other companies such as Royal Doulton and Ashtead Potters. In the mid-1930s Poole introduced more commercial designs, such as Streamline tableware by John Adams.

**PUNCH BOWL** This limited-edition bowl was designed by Schreckengost for Cowan. It is known as the Jazz Bowl, although its official name is New Year's Eve in New York City. *1931. W:35.5cm (14in).*

**HAND-THROWN VASE** The strong, repeated pattern of this barrel-shaped vase with a short, narrow neck is rendered in blue and yellow against a white ground. It was designed by Ruth Pavely.

**OVOID STONEWARE VASE** From the Poole Pottery, this hand-thrown vase features the Leaping Deer pattern 599/TZ designed by Truda Carter. The decoration is rendered in a polychrome palette beneath a semi-matte glaze. *1934–37. H:21cm (8¼in).*

**ROSEVILLE TANK VASE** The modern, angular form of this vase and the blended orange-to-blue mottled glaze are typical of the Futura range. This rare example still bears a partial paper label. *1920s–30s. H:23.5cm (9½in).*

# CERAMICS GALLERY

Art Deco ceramics are characterized by strong geometric forms that are often asymmetrical. More traditional shapes tend to distinguish themselves for bold geometric patterns and bright colours. Decoration was frequently added by hand-painting. Many of the ceramics pieces of this period convey a sense of cheerfulness and optimism – sunshine was a recurring theme. Other popular motifs were female figures posing in Jazz Age pursuits and Egyptian-influenced patterns.

## KEY

1. Sybille May ceramic of a kneeling female figure holding aloft a gold ball. 1930s. H:20cm (8in). ② 2. Ashtead Pottery Corn Girl figurine by Allan C. Wyon. 1927. H:20cm (8in). ① 3. Czech Goldscheider-style terracotta wall mask. H:29cm (11½in). ① 4. Viktor Schreckengost's Madam Kitty figurine of an acrobat on horseback. 1930s. H:24cm (9½in). ① 5. Primavera figurine of an ermine, thickly glazed in black and white. H:31.5cm (12½in). ③ 6. Elly Strobach's stylized bust of a red-haired woman holding a cigarette. 1930s. H:17.5cm (7in). ② 7. Maling Anzac-pattern part tea service. ③ 8. Czechoslovakian handpainted jug by Ditmar Urbach. H:19cm (7½in). ①

1 Sybille May figurine

2 Corn Girl figurine

3 Czech terracotta wall mask

4 Madam Kitty figurine

5 Figure of an ermine

6 Elly Strobach bust

7 Maling tea service

8 Czechoslovakian jug

9 Charles Catteau vase

**9.** Cylindrical earthenware vase by Charles Catteau. c.1925. H:29cm (11½in). ② **10.** Circular wall plaque of a female dancer. 1930s. D:24cm (9½in). ① **11.** Stefan Dakon's figurine of a young lady in a dancer's pose. 1930s. H:38cm (15in). ③ **12.** Pinecone-range cornucopia-shaped vase. 1931. H:22cm (8¾in). ① **13.** Two-handled blue vase. H:38cm (15in). ② **14.** Chinese Bird vase by R. Guy Cowan. c.1925. H:28.5cm (11¼in). ② **15.** Roseville Futura pink and green rectangular vase. ② **16.** Myott Pottery Pyramid vase with an Orange Flowers pattern. 1930s. H:21.5cm (8¼in). ①

10 *Female dancer plaque*

11 *Dakon figurine*

12 *Cornucopia-shaped vase*

13 *Two-handled vase*

14 *Cowan vase*

15 *Roseville Futura vase*

16 *Myott Pyramid vase*

# LALIQUE

THE NAME RENÉ LALIQUE IS NOW SYNONYMOUS WITH ART DECO GLASS. LIGHT YEARS AHEAD OF THE COMPETITION, LALIQUE PROVED THAT IT WAS POSSIBLE TO USE INDUSTRIAL TECHNIQUES TO MASS-PRODUCE WELL-DESIGNED, INNOVATIVE GOODS. HIS STYLISH GLASSWARE APPEALED TO EVERYONE – FROM MILLIONAIRES TO HOUSEWIVES.

**A MODERNIST AT HEART** René Lalique used modern techniques of mass production – among them hot metal moulds, compressed air, and advanced decoration – to create a wide range of glass products.

**SUZANNE STATUETTE** Mounted on a bronze peacock-pattern illuminated base, this opalescent-glass statuette is moulded as a young female nude with outstretched arms amid flowing drapery. c.1925. H:28cm (11in).

René Lalique originally made a name for himself as a jeweller, creating fantastic sculptural orchids, dragonflies, and maidens from enamel and gold in the Art Nouveau style. As part of his jewellery design, he also started experimenting with glassmaking. His first glassware commission was from perfumer François Coty, who wanted attractive bottles for a scent he was launching. The perfume bottle was a big hit. Intrigued by the versatility of glass and the idea of replicating the same design, Lalique switched from jewellery to glassmaking.

### TECHNIQUES AND INSPIRATION
Lalique breathed new life into industrial glassmaking techniques including moulding and stamp-pressing. Preferring to work in ordinary glass rather than expensive lead crystal, he gave his pieces frosted and opalescent finishes. Sometimes he stained or tinted them in pastel shades, or coloured them in striking gem hues such as aquamarine and garnet.

Lalique once said he wanted to "achieve a new result…to create something never seen before". The singular look of his pieces was achieved by treating glass as a sculptural material, taking his glass moulds – be they for a statuette or a vase – from wax models. His sources of inspiration were plants and animals, but increasingly he turned to Classical nudes and draped figures for imaginative glass designs.

### ECLECTIC PRODUCTION
By the 1920s Lalique had a flourishing glass-manufacturing business. Incredibly prolific, he created a vast array of tableware and decorative objects such as vases, clocks, statuettes, and jewellery. Lalique also made light fittings, panels, doors

**SERPENT PERFUME BOTTLE** The snake, or serpent, was a popular Art Deco motif. Here the head of the serpent forms an elaborate stopper, while the scaly body of the snake is coiled on the surface of the bottle. c.1920. H:9cm (3½in).

for interiors, and even glass furniture. Car mascots were also among his strengths. These quintessentially Art Deco ornaments decorated motorcar hoods in the interwar years, and Lalique created 28 different types, the most famous being the Victoire, a woman's head with swept-back hair.

After his success with Coty, however, perfume bottles became among Lalique's best-known designs. Over the years he produced more than 30 bottles for perfume houses and couturiers, including Houbigant and Worth.

The 1925 Paris International Exhibition was a triumph for Lalique. Not only did he have two pavilions, but he also contributed to other exhibits such as the Hall of Perfume, as well as several displays around the grounds including a magnificent fountain. The exhibition led to more high-profile architectural and interior-design commissions such as the lighting and decorative panels for France's legendary liners: the *Île de France* and *Normandie*.

### A SLEW OF IMITATORS
Lalique's distinctive items had a far-reaching effect on international glass manufacturers. Sabino and Etling were two of the numerous French firms influenced by Lalique. They used his moulded glass and motifs – especially the fish and nudes – as a starting point for their own statuettes. The Belgian glassworks Val Saint-Lambert produced Lalique-style wares called Luxval, while in Britain the Red-Ashay firm specialized in car mascots. Some American manufacturers, including the Consolidated Lamp & Glass Company, replicated Lalique's exquisite vases and lighting.

**PERRUCHES VASE** This ovoid vase is moulded with pairs of wooing budgerigars on branches in electric-blue opalescent glass with an enamel-washed patina. The vase has a moulded "R. LALIQUE" mark. c.1920. H:25cm (10in).

**L'ÉLÉGANCE PERFUME BOTTLE** This square bottle, made for D'Orsay, is moulded with nymphs. The clear frosted glass has been highlighted with a sepia patina. c.1920. H:9cm (3½in).

# GLASS

GLASS WAS INCREDIBLY POPULAR THROUGHOUT THE ART DECO
ERA. GLASSMAKERS EMBRACED NEW STYLES AND USED THE LATEST
TECHNOLOGY TO KEEP UP WITH PUBLIC DEMAND.

**TWIN-HANDLED BOWL** Produced by Daum Frères, this footed bowl is
made from black and brown glass. It is cut with simple sweeping lines in
shallow relief. *c.1925. H:14.5cm (5¾in).*

## DAUM AND FRENCH GLASS

The Nancy-based firm of Daum, one of the best-known manufacturers of Art Nouveau cameo glass, updated its range after World War I. Its cameo glass vases, lamps, and bowls now came in jazzy colours like tango orange, scarlet, pink, and jade green. They featured the latest decoration such as Egyptian motifs, stylized flowers, and animals, as well as plenty of geometric patterns. In the early 1900s the glassmakers at Daum carved many of their cameo glass pieces by hand, but by the 1920s much of the production was mechanized, which resulted in a striking flattened appearance.

By the early 1930s the public taste for cameo glass was dying out and, accordingly, Daum started moving in a different direction. Its new designs were more abstract in concept and relied on contrasting textured finishes or internal decoration such as bubbles, mottling, and striations, as well as tiny flecks of gold and silver. They came in opaque and opalescent shades of colours, including sea green, grey, turquoise, amber, and pale yellow. The glassmakers often blew their new glass into decorative metal mounts made from bronze or wrought iron. Leading manufacturers –

including Majorelle and Edgar Brandt – produced handsome mounts especially for them. Created with the latest technology, Daum glass – like Lalique's – proved that handcrafting was not the only way of achieving high quality and good design. Many Daum pieces were made in limited editions or as one-of-a-kind items.

### SCHNEIDER

Several other French firms, including Muller Frères and Schneider, produced similar glassware to that created at Daum. Schneider specialized in

cameo glass in distinct shades of garnet, bright yellow, orange, and plum, which was developed at the Schneider brothers' factory near Paris. Typical pieces included tall, thin cameo glass vases etched with naturalistic floral, insect, and animal motifs. Schneider also made undecorated vases and bowls from mottled coloured glass, as well as decorative glass items acid-etched with geometric designs. The factory marketed many of its pieces under the name *Le Verre Français*, a range that was sold through major department stores in France and the United States.

*The outer layer* is acid-etched with a stylized pattern

**BELL-SHAPED BOWL** Made by
Daum Frères, this large clear-glass
bowl is overlaid with yellow and
orange enamel and acid-etched
with a stylized leaf-and-berry
design. *1920s. D:32cm
(12½in).*

**DAUM FRÈRES VASE** This squat-shaped vase with pink, white, and blue
mottled-glass overlay is mounted in an openwork wrought-iron armature
of geometric design by Louis Majorelle. *1920s. D:25cm (9¾in).*

## VAL SAINT-LAMBERT'S CUT GLASS

Belgium's biggest glassmaker, Val Saint-Lambert, was renowned for its cut-glass production. In the early 1920s the firm began using traditional glass-cutting techniques to create stylish Art Deco geometric patterns on its crystal. At the time Val Saint-Lambert was one of the few glassmakers outside Bohemia making multicoloured cut-glass vases. These pieces usually had a clear body with ruby, cobalt blue, or amethyst on top. This hand-cut glassware was extremely expensive to produce, and little was made after the American Depression.

## MARCEL GOUPY

As artistic director of Georges Rouard's furnishings gallery in Paris for more than 40 years, Marcel Goupy saw both Art Nouveau and Art Deco come and go. A talented designer, he produced striking designs for ceramics and silverware during the 1920s and 1930s. However, Goupy is most celebrated today for his enamelled glassware with brightly coloured Art Deco decoration. His tableware and decorative pieces were free-blown from clear or slightly tinted glass and were then decorated by hand. Goupy's enamel glassware often featured images that are now considered typically Art Deco, including cypress trees, weeping willows, jazz musicians, stylized flowers, billowing clouds, and cherry blossoms. Glass decorator Auguste Heiligenstein painted many of these striking designs, even though they bear

Goupy's signature. Heiligenstein went on to work alone and won acclaim for his finely detailed enamelled and gilt pieces decorated with figures taken from Classical mythology.

Many glass designers used enamelled decoration during the 1920s and 1930s. Jean Luce produced glassware decorated with stylized enamel floral motifs before moving on to engraving and sandblasting geometric designs.

**CASED PEDESTAL FOOT VASE**
With a blue exterior and a red interior, this Val Saint Lambert vase is cut with geometric forms on both the inside and the outside. It has an undulating rim. *H:40.5cm (16in).*

**VAL SAINT-LAMBERT VASE** Known as a Kipling design, this tapered, cylindrical cased vase stands on a spreading octagonal foot and is cut with a ruby red lozenge pattern over clear glass. *1930s. H:30.5cm (12in).*

## PÂTE-DE-VERRE

At the turn of the 20th century, France saw a revival of the ancient glassmaking technique of *pâte-de-verre* (or *pâte-de-cristal*). Looking like crystalline coloured sugars melting together, *pâte-de-verre* involves placing finely ground glass paste in moulds and firing it to resolidify the glass. During the Art Deco era Victor Almaric Walter, the leading *pâte-de-verre* specialist, continued to produce pieces decorated with the same lizards and nudes that first got him noticed in the Art Nouveau period. François-Émile Décorchemont, who was first acclaimed for *pâte-de-verre* in the early 1900s, embraced a more geometric style before abandoning decoration completely in favour of stark shapes.

**LEGRAS GLASS VASES** Produced by Legras, these two pieces have strong, geometric acid-etched motifs. The cased ball-shaped vase has a clear outer layer and an inner layer with orange-red and brown powdered-enamel inclusions. *Ball-shaped vase: c.1930. H:17.5cm (7in); art-glass vase: 1920s. H:21.5cm (8½in).*

**Ball-shaped vase by Legras**

**Art-glass vase by Legras**

**TALL *LE VERRE FRANÇAIS* VASE** Decorated with stylized berried branches in green, mottled orange, and brown, this vase has an applied "candy cane" signature. *H:49cm (19¼in).*

**PÂTE-DE-VERRE BOWL** The shape of this footed, loop-handled bowl by François-Émile Décorchemont was inspired by ancient Roman forms. The decoration is a Classical geometric pattern. *1920s. D:28cm (11in).*

## CUT AND ENGRAVED GLASS

It would be easy to assume that the finest glass made during the Art Deco era came from France, but important developments were also taking place in other European countries and in the United States during the 1920s and 1930s.

### BRITISH GLASS

Clear cut glass in Neoclassical designs had been a speciality of British glass manufacturers since the late 18th century. Even in the 1920s and 1930s most glass produced in Britain was clear, apart from the odd exception such as the bubbly Monart range from Scotland's Moncrieff Glassworks.

In order to keep up with the times, many firms started commissioning cut-glass designs from leading artists. James Powell asked furniture designer Gordon Russell to produce a tableware range, while Clyne Farquharson worked for glass manufacturers John Walsh Walsh, creating a series of plain, shaped tableware with simple cut decoration such as leaves.

One of the most successful and prolific pairings of traditional glass producer and Art Deco designer was that of the firm of Stevens & Williams and Keith Murray. During the 1930s Murray designed tableware and vases for the firm with simple cut or engraved decoration influenced by Swedish glassmakers Orrefors.

### STEUBEN

Founded in the early 1900s by Frederick Carder and Thomas Hawkes, Steuben was one of the few American glass factories to produce finely handcrafted tableware and limited-edition work. Steuben glass from the 1920s often features Oriental and Classical imagery. Its jade green glass and bubbly Cluthra range were also popular.

In the 1930s Steuben started specializing in clear engraved glass – for which it is now celebrated. Designer Sidney Waugh's glassware incorporated stylized animals and Classical figures, and it was comparable in quality and

style to the best designs from Orrefors. Waugh's delicately engraved Gazelle bowls are among Steuben's best-loved designs. In the 1930s the firm also commissioned simple engraved tableware, including several drinking glass ranges from leading industrial designer Walter Dorwin Teague.

### MURANO GLASS

Renowned since the Renaissance for creating high-quality glass, glassmakers on the Venetian island of Murano specialized in free-blown glass with applied decoration. Paolo Venini, a lawyer interested in cutting-edge design, bought a glass studio in the early 1920s to produce modern pieces featuring bold colours and strong, abstract forms.

**FLUTED VASE** Cut with horizontal bands of fluting in a repeating pattern that matches its form, this inverted conical-shaped vase was designed by Thomas Webb for the Rembrandt Art Guild, England. *c.1935. H:17.5cm (6¾in).*

**ENGRAVED BOWL** Designed by Sidney Waugh for Steuben, this near-spherical lead-crystal bowl with thick walls has a central frieze engraved with leaping gazelles. *1935. H:18cm (7in).*

**BUCKET VASE** This John Walsh Walsh cut-glass bucket vase features a repeating geometric pattern of ovals and flutes beneath a geometric border. It is marked Walsh Birmingham. *1930s. H:16.5cm (6½in).*

The Handkerchief vase was his company's most famous design. Venini employed a number of progressive designers, including Napoleone Martinuzzi, and in the 1930s his studio pioneered many innovative forms of glass and glassmaking techniques.

## BOHEMIAN GLASS

Like France, Bohemia (the modern-day Czech Republic) had a thriving, long-established glassmaking industry. By the early 1900s, apart from a few strongly artisanal firms, handcraftsmanship had largely given way to mechanized production. Throughout the 1920s and 1930s the consumer demand for decorative glass and everyday tableware such as ashtrays was efficiently met by many Bohemian glass manufacturers. If a glass design was successful, they made an inexpensive, mass-produced version. They were responsible for countless perfume bottles, which were sold empty, ready for women to fill with a scent of their choice. Many had fan-shaped stoppers or attached atomizers. Bohemian glassmakers also created decanters and liqueur sets, engraved or decorated with enamel in geometric patterns.

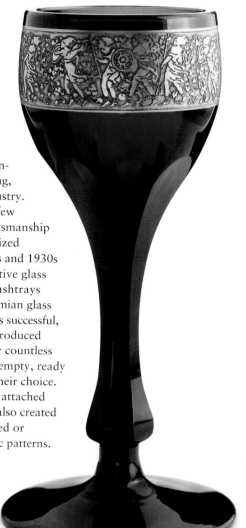

**PURPLE GOBLET** The bowl of this goblet has an etched and gilded frieze depicting an Amazonian scene. The glass has a hexagonal-faceted stem and conical foot. Base engraved "Moser Karlsbad". c.1920. H:19cm (7½in).

## ORREFORS

Responsible for revitalizing the traditional art of glass engraving, Orrefors had a huge impact on glass design of the 1930s. One of Sweden's largest glass manufacturers, in the early 1920s the firm opened a small glass workshop under the direction of Simon Gate and Edvard Hald. Distinctive glassware quite unlike anything else available at the time was produced here, with finely detailed motifs and figures inspired by Greek and Roman mythology wheel-engraved on clear lead-crystal vases and bowls. Neoclassicism played an important role in Scandinavian Art Deco design, and the crisp, sculptural images contrasted nicely with the brilliant sparkle of the glass. Orrefors's display at the 1925 Paris International Exhibition brought the firm international attention and won it rave reviews. In the late 1920s and early 1930s glass designer Vicke Lindstrand introduced new themes to engrave on the firm's glassware, such as underwater scenes. Other innovative and imaginative glass designers employed by Orrefors included Knut Bergqvist and Edvin Öhrström.

**ORREFORS JUG** The engraving of the female dancer and the use of geometric forms on this clear glass jug are characteristic of Simon Gate's Neoclassical Art Deco style. 1927. H:22cm (8¾in).

---

## MASS-PRODUCED AMERICAN GLASS

Apart from limited-edition work by designers such as Victor Durand for Vineland Flint Glasswork, most American Art Deco glass was cheap, even when compared with inexpensive imports from Bohemia.

Moulded and pressed glass dominated production by American glass factories during the 1920s and 1930s. Several firms, such as the Phoenix Glass Company and the Consolidated Lamp & Glass Company, copied Lalique designs using cost-cutting techniques. The Consolidated Lamp & Glass Company also produced a more original pressed glass range called Ruba Rombic. Strikingly angular, and in colours such as Smoky Topaz and Jungle Green, Ruba Rombic glassware was created by Reuben Haley, who was inspired by Cubist art.

Depression glass put Art Deco design within the reach of those with modest incomes. Its production started in the 1920s but really took off in the 1930s, hence its name. This uniquely American form of pressed glass was sold for pennies in "five and dime" stores across the country. Most pieces of Depression glass tended to be functional everyday wares such as butter dishes and plates. They usually came in clear or pale pastel hues and relied on simple geometric shapes for effect. Ice-cream soda glasses and banana split dishes are among the more iconic Depression-glass designs. Some of the best-known Depression glass manufacturers were Hocking Glass, Indiana Glass, and Jeanette Glass.

**DURAND KING TUT VASE** Although this pattern had been used by Tiffany and Loetz since around 1900, this blown-glass vase was inspired by ancient Egyptian decoration following the discovery of Tutankhamun's tomb in 1922. 1924–31. H:16cm (6¼in).

**RUBA ROMBIC VASE** Inspired by Cubism, this pale green glass vase was produced by the Consolidated Lamp & Glass Company. The multi-angular, asymmetrical design is visually striking. H:23cm (9in).

# GLASS GALLERY

The Art Deco period saw a boom in mass-production techniques. In glassware, these were pioneered by Lalique, who used hot metal moulds, giving way to new forms and designs. Bold geometric shapes were fashionable, as was Egyptian-influenced styling following the discovery of Tutankhamun's tomb in 1922. Stylized flora and fauna also remained popular. Polychromatic cased glass and iridescent and opalescent glass became fashionable, while the status of cameo glass gradually declined.

**KEY**

**1.** Czechoslovakian decanter and three glasses with amber overlay. Decanter: H:26.5cm (10½in). ①
**2.** Czechoslovakian clear-glass perfume bottle and stopper. H:11.5cm (4½in). ① **3.** Czechoslovakian clear-glass perfume bottle with black puffer. H:17cm (6¾in). ① **4.** Orrefors glass vase with stylized flowers, by Simon Gate. H:15.5cm (6¼in). ⑤ **5.** Schneider mottled-glass vase. H:26cm (10¼in). ③ **6.** One of a pair of French pressed black-amethyst glass vases. H:15.5cm (6in). ① **7.** Stuttgart School of Applied Art thick glass vase designed by Wilhelm von Eiff. H:20cm (8in). ② **8.** Marcel Goupy vase of faceted emerald cut glass. H:14.5cm (5¾in). ① **9.** Schneider ovoid vase, acid-etched with a broad geometric pattern. H:31.5cm (12¼in). ① **10.** Glass vase with green and gold swirls. H:21cm (8¼in). ② **11.** Stuart yellow blown-glass vase. H:18cm (7in). ① **12.** Jean Sala bowl for Cristalleries

2 *Perfume bottle*

3 *Perfume bottle*

4 *Orrefors vase*

5 *Schneider vase*

1 *Decanter and three glasses*

6 *French vase*

7 *Wilhelm von Eiff vase*

8 *Marcel Goupy vase*

9 *Schneider vase*

10 *Glass vase*

11 *Stuart vase*

12 *Jean Sala bowl*

13 *Saint Louis vase*

de St. Louis. H:16.5cm (6½in). ③ **13.** St. Louis cut-crystal vase, with stylized floral motifs. H:16.5cm (6½in). ① **14.** Marcel Goupy enamelled vase, with gilt details. H:25cm (9¾in). ④ **15.** Venini *pulegoso* vase by Napoleone Martinuzzi. c.1930. H:36cm (14¼in). ⑥ **16.** Vase by Vittorio Zecchin, made by M.V.M. Cappellin. H:24.7cm (9¾in). ② **17.** WMF Ikora flared bowl, with a graduated green rim. c.1930. D:27.5cm (10¾in). ① **18.** Walsh intaglio Gay Ware bowl with floral design. W:25cm (9¾in). ① **19.** Décorchemont glass bowl with stylized flower design. W:28cm (11in). ③ **20.** *Le Verre Français* tall glass vase with stylized Japanese blossoms. H:47.5cm (19in). ③ **21.** Daum Frères acid-etched glass vase. H:30cm (11¾in). ③

14 *Marcel Goupy vase*

15 *Venini vase*

16 *Vittorio Zecchin vase*

17 *WMF Ikora bowl*

18 *Walsh Gay Ware bowl*

19 *Décorchemont bowl*

20 *Le Verre Français vase*

21 *Daum Frères vase*

# LIGHTING

BY THE 1920S ELECTRIC LIGHT WAS WIDELY ESTABLISHED AND NO
LONGER A NOVELTY. HOWEVER, ART DECO DESIGNERS STILL FOUND
THIS TECHNOLOGICAL LEAP AN INSPIRING CHALLENGE.

## FIGURATIVE LAMPS

In the 1920s and 1930s many glass designers followed the lead of their Art Nouveau predecessors by making lamps that blurred the boundaries between ornament and practicality. In particular, figurative lamps were enormously popular. They usually had glass shades, and the bases were made of brass or the cheaper spelter (a zinc alloy). The classic Art Deco figurative lamp features a nude dancing girl holding up a globe of light.

## FRENCH GLASS LIGHTS

France's leading glass manufacturers – including Daum, Müller Frères, and Schneider – had had a reputation for exciting glass lamps and shades since the early 1900s. By the Art Deco era, however, they had moved away from the earth-toned glass fashionable at the turn of the 20th century towards vivid colours such as bright orange. Further visual impact was provided by marbled, mottled, or textured glass surfaces, which were often decorated with stylized flowers, geometric patterns, and Egyptian motifs. Shapes were simple and elegant.

René Lalique produced vast quantities of glass lights – from hanging bowls, to his one-off commissions for the ocean liner *Normandie*. Department stores, hotels, restaurants, cinemas, and public buildings around the world commissioned light fittings from his famous glass company. Usually made from opaque or opalescent glass, Lalique's lights feature his typical shell shapes, cascading blossoms, and female figures.

**BRONZE TABLE LAMP** The stem of this table lamp is in the form of an archetypal Art Deco nude female figure. Her arms are raised to support the glass-ball shade. *1930s.*

*Athletic poses*, like this one, were favoured by many Art Deco designers

*The girl's pose* is reminiscent of an Egyptian dancer's

*Scantily clad women* were a popular subject for Art Deco sculptors

*The chryselephantine (ivory and bronze) figure* is taken from a sculpture by Richard W. Lange of Rosenthal and Maeder

**EGYPTIAN LAMP** This lamp by Raymond Guerbe features a young woman wearing an Egyptian robe. Made from green patinated bronze, she holds an orange, fan-shaped glass shade. *H:52cm (20½in).*

**PARACHUTE LAMP** This lamp has a stitched-vellum shade in the form of a parachute above a bronze-and-ivory base with a fairy-like figure of a female dancer. *1925. H:86cm (34in).*

**AMERICAN TABLE LAMP** The domed chrome shade of this lamp is suspended on a chrome-and-black-enamelled stem with a round, stepped base. H:46cm (18in).

**MACHINE AGE LAMP** This brushed-nickel table lamp has a fluted, tapering base and a shade with similar decoration. The shade clips directly on to the bulb. H:28cm (11in).

**MARC EROL LAMP** Half frosted glass, half metal cone, the shade of this lamp sits atop a slim stem with a metal ball at the top and stands on a circular base. c.1925. H:40cm (15¾in).

**WOOD-AND-METAL LAMP** The rectangular shade sits above a distinctive medallion-shaped section decorated with carved birds and foliage and a rectangular plinth-type base. c.1940. H:59cm (23¼in).

## FLOOR LAMPS

Often found in pairs, floor lamps are reminiscent of torchères, tall, narrow 18th-century candle and lamp stands. Many leading Art Deco metalworkers, including Edgar Brandt, Paul Kiss, and Albert Simonet, produced Art Deco floor lamps. Brandt teamed up with Daum to produce a variety of lighting. His *La Tentation* floor lamp with a cobra coiling up to a Daum marbled-glass bowl is among his best-known designs.

## RUHLMANN'S LIGHTING DESIGNS

By the 1920s and 1930s designers realized that lighting could create a mood or atmosphere. As a result, lighting became an increasingly important element of interior design, whether it was spotlighting, uplighting, directed lighting, or diffused lighting.

Celebrated furniture and interior designer Émile-Jacques Ruhlmann saw electric lights as an integral part of his decorating schemes. As with all his work, the pared-down Classicism of his chandeliers, wall sconces, and lamps is loosely derived from 18th-century forms. Legendary for his high standards of craftsmanship, Ruhlmann allowed the exquisite properties of materials he used for lights – black marble, alabaster, gilt bronze – to shine through.

Other Parisian designers such as Jacques Adnet, Jean-Michel Frank, and Jean Perzel also produced Art Deco lights with a similar minimal, Classical feel. Parisian firm *La Maison Desny* took this idea a step further with its abstract geometric lights.

## AMERICAN LAMPS

The New York-based furniture designer Paul Frankl wrote that "modernity and America have come to mean, in the mind of the world, one and the same thing". It is true that, from the 1930s onwards, American designers produced some of the most exciting modern lighting of the Art Deco era. Their designs were Machine Age-sleek, abstract, and made from the latest materials, including aluminium, chrome, and plastic.

Among the most iconic examples of American Art Deco lighting are Walter Dorwin Teague's daring series of streamlined desk lamps for production by the Polaroid Corporation, which were inspired by motorcars, trains, and science fiction. Donald Deskey's one-off cherrywood, chrome, and black-plastic desk-and-lamp suite, created for impresario Samuel "Roxy" Rothafel's office at the Radio City Music Hall, was also very influential.

**FLOOR LAMP** Wrought iron, a relative newcomer to interior design, has been used for the elegant, partially gilt stand of this floor lamp, designed by Raymond Subes. H:150cm (59in).

**PAIR OF TORCHÈRES** Designed by the American Russel Wright, each of these torchères has a trumpet-shaped shade atop a bamboo shaft with ribbed banding. H:65.25cm (25¾in).

## ANGLEPOISE LAMP

The English automotive engineer George Carwardine, who owned a factory that specialized in vehicle suspension systems, created the Anglepoise lamp in 1932. His highly original lamp had a shade on an articulated spring. It allowed the lamp's beam to move in any direction yet remain rigid when positioned. Carwardine drew inspiration from the "constant-tension principle of human limbs" – the way arms are both flexible and immobile. At first Carwardine thought that his light would be useful in factories, where you might need to focus on a specific area, but he soon realized this could apply to work in offices, too. Carwardine licensed his design to Herbert Terry & Sons. The Anglepoise lamp is still in production today and, much copied, has had a huge impact on lighting design in the second half of the 20th century.

**ANGLEPOISE LAMP** Designed in 1932 by George Carwardine, the black-lacquered Anglepoise lamp is an iconic piece of the Art Deco era. It was reissued by Tecta in 2004. 1932. H:90cm (35½in).

# CHROME AND PLASTIC

ARGUABLY THE MOST INNOVATIVE MATERIALS FROM THE ART DECO ERA, CHROME AND PLASTIC WERE WIDELY USED FOR INEXPENSIVE MASS-PRODUCED ITEMS THAT PUT STYLISH MODERN DESIGN WITHIN THE REACH OF THOSE ON A BUDGET.

**OCCASIONAL TWO-TIER TABLE** The use of chrome to edge laminate table tops is typical of Art Deco design. This piece has an elegant, clean, almost modernist feel. *H:75cm (29½in).*

**BULLET RADIO** Made from butterscotch, blue, and red Catalin, this Fada radio (model 189) achieves a thoroughly modern look. The sleek design includes smooth knobs. *W:26cm (10¼in).*

## AVANT-GARDE MATERIAL

Plastic could be easily – and inexpensively – moulded into the latest streamlined Art Deco shapes, which made it ideal for stylish yet cost-effective accessories. Ashtrays, dressing-table sets, napkin rings, and handbags were all fashioned from the latest plastics. The material could also be made in a range of fashionable colours to suit every taste.

Even luxury liners such as the *Queen Mary* were home to plastic pieces, since few trend-setting venues were without items made from the new wonder material.

**GEOMETRIC ASHTRAY** Created for the luxury cruise liner the *Queen Mary*, this ashtray was made in pink on black urea-formaldehyde plastic by the British Buttner Pipe Company Ltd. *1930s. H:11.5cm (4½in).*

The word "chrome" comes from chromium, a metallic element rarely seen in its pure, solid form but widely used as a plated finish on objects made of other metals. Chrome-plating protects an object from corrosion and gives it a unique mirror shine.

Art Deco designers were quick to spot the potential of chrome-plating. The French sculptors who made motorcar mascots liked its gleaming, weatherproof durability, while the metal-furniture designers influenced by the Bauhaus ethos liked the fact that this striking finish was an innovative and inexpensive mass-production process.

### INEXPENSIVE APPEAL

Chrome-plating was especially popular in the Depression-hit United States, where it was associated with the distinctive machine-styled, streamlined look of American Art Deco. In the 1930s American metalwork manufacturers saw chrome-plated tableware as an attractively priced, low-maintenance, modern option – a substitute for silverware that would appeal to cash-strapped

**DESK FAN** The design of this fan, which looks like a propeller, is influenced by the Machine Age. Produced by Ventaxia, it is made from Bakelite, wood, chrome, and metal. *1940s. H:34cm (13½in).*

**EMPIRE COCKTAIL SHAKER** This Revere shaker by William Archibald Welden combines polished chromium with brass. It is finished with a Catalin trim on the spout, lid, and spire finial. *1938. H:31.75cm (12½in).*

consumers. Companies like Chase and Revere employed leading designers – Peter Müller-Munk and Norman Bel Geddes among them – to create chrome-plated pieces such as pitchers and cocktail sets. The chrome-plated, streamlined look was also used to make domestic appliances such as vacuum cleaners and toasters more enticing to consumers.

### MOULDING THE FUTURE

The term "plastic" describes anything that can be moulded or shaped, whether natural materials such as amber, wood, and ivory, or man-made materials such as phenolic resins and Lucite. Many early 20th-century plastics are now dubbed "bakelite", after the first synthetic plastic invented in 1907.

At the start of the Art Deco era designers used plastics mainly to mimic other materials. They pressed them into imitation ebony knobs and ivory-like boxes. In the late 1920s phenolic resins became available. This combined Bakelite's robustness with a new translucency and unprecedented colours, opening plastic production up to new possibilities.

In the lean 1930s plastics were seen as a Machine Age wonder. These cheap, new materials were simple to cast into streamlined geometric or curvilinear shapes. Plastic products relied on their surface quality and overall form, rather then on decoration, to make them desirable. Müller-Munk recalled that the use of plastic was "the hallmark of modern design…the mysterious and attractive solution for almost any application requiring eye-appeal". Other designers turned plastic into highly original pieces that included jewellery and electrical appliances such as radios. Even everyday 1930s tableware – napkin rings, for example – had an added "jazz" factor when they were made from plastic.

**NICKERBOCKER BAR** Guests on board the steamer *The Empress of Britain* enjoy cocktails en route from Southampton to Quebec. The chrome fittings are archetypal examples of the streamlined Art Deco style.

THE COCKTAIL BIRD

# METALWARE

WHETHER CHARACTERIZED BY LUSH ORNAMENT OR STARK STREAMLINING,

SOME OF THE FINEST SILVER AND METALWORK OF THE 20TH CENTURY WAS

PRODUCED DURING THE ART DECO PERIOD.

**JEAN TÉTARD TEA AND COFFEE SET** The tea and coffee pots, creamer, and covered sugar bowl in this set are of unembellished cylindrical form, with hardwood handles and finials. *c.1930. Creamer: H:10cm (4in).*

## EUROPEAN SILVERSMITHS

One of the most innovative silversmiths of the Art Deco period was Jean Puiforcat, who, in the early 1920s developed the use of unadorned geometric shapes such as cubes, spheres, and cylinders for tea services, flatware, and other silver pieces.

Puiforcat believed that form should follow function. His silverware is indeed characterized by an absence of any superfluous detail; yet it is incredibly sensuous to look at and touch. Many pieces have sumptuous details like handles and knobs made from rock crystal, lapis lazuli, or exotic woods. Renowned for his use of the best-quality materials and high standards of craftsmanship, Puiforcat was the silversmith counterpart to Émile-Jacques Ruhlmann, the cabinet-maker, with whom he collaborated on a display at the 1925 Paris International Exhibition. He also exhibited and worked with other leading designers of the period, including Le Corbusier.

## ABSTRACT ELEMENTS

By the mid-1920s other silversmiths started to take on elements of Puiforcat's geometric style. At the 1925 Paris International Exhibition the Belgian Wolfers Frères exhibited an angular tea and coffee set, the Giaconda service, featuring ten-sided forms and bold ivory handles. It was a big hit, and the firm continued to make silverware based on geometric shapes throughout the late 1920s and 1930s.

French craftsman-designer Jean Tétard was interested in creating pieces stripped of all reference to historic styles. He began exhibiting plain silverware produced at his father's metalworks to critical acclaim in 1930. These striking designs, featuring angular and cylindrical forms, look deceptively simple. In reality, they were complicated to make and are a tribute to Tétard's technical skills.

**SILVER-PLATED COMPOTE** Designed by Luc Lanel for Christofle and produced for the *Normandie* ocean liner, this simple, shallow compote is raised on a modernist sphere base. *c.1935. D:33cm (13in).*

**CHAMPAGNE BUCKET** Christofle produced most of the silverware for the *Normandie*. Here the simple styling, geometric banding, and solid handles are all characteristic of Art Deco style. Designed by Luc Lanel. *c.1935. H:20cm (8in).*

**FLÈCHE (ARROW) CANDLESTICKS** This pair of two-flame, Gallia-metal candlesticks was designed for Christofle by Gio Ponti. The piece takes its name from the arrow between the two intertwined cornucopias. *1930s. H:20cm (8in).*

## BALANCING PAST AND FUTURE

The French firm of Christofle made mainly electroplated silverware, using a process it had introduced to France in the 1840s. During the late 1920s and 1930s Christofle produced traditional pieces alongside contemporary Art Deco vases, trays, tea services, and other items. Designers such as Carl Christian Fjerdingstad, Gio Ponti, Luc Lanel, Paul Follot, and Maurice Dufrêne were responsible for many of these pieces. Some were specially produced for the Compagnie Générale Transatlantique, which owned the famous *Normandie* and other ocean liners.

A number of other major silver manufacturers reacted to the modern Art Deco style. The British firm Mappin & Webb commissioned several designs for tea services and cocktail sets from leading designer Keith Murray, for example. In the United States Tiffany created contemporary pieces like cocktail shakers and table lighters and made a splash with its modern designs for the New York 1939 World Fair.

**NICKEL-PLATED BRASS CANDLESTICK** The candle sockets are raised on a footed, semicircular frame pierced with stylized animal forms. Made by the Hagenauer Werkstätte. *1925. H:23.5cm (9¼in).*

**CAR MASCOT** This large, rare, leaping-lion mascot in heavy, chromed bronze was designed by Casimir Brau. *c.1920. L:21cm (8¼in).*

**HUNGARIAN SILVER SUGAR BOWL** The body and lid of this sugar bowl with a circular foot and a slightly domed lid are chased with a geometric pattern. *1930s. W:11cm (4¼in).*

## WROUGHT IRON IN INTERIORS

Normally associated with garden furniture and gates, in the 1920s wrought iron was put to innovative use indoors. Edgar Brandt, Paul Kiss, and other metalworkers made elevator panels and door frames for grand office and retail schemes. They also created firescreens, radiator grilles, console tables, mirrors, floor and table lamps, and book ends for use in domestic settings. The increased use of wrought iron in homes paved the way for the acceptance of tubular-steel dining-room chairs and other furniture in the 1930s.

**AMERICAN WROUGHT-IRON GATE** Fashioned in the style of Wilhelm Hunt Diederich, this gate (one of a pair) shows leaping hounds and stags in a stylized landscape. *1930s. H:159.5cm (62¾in).*

## GEORG JENSEN

The most famous of all the Art Deco silversmiths is the Danish Georg Jensen, whose machine-made metalware is of exceptionally good quality. Jensen designs are very simple, usually based on curvilinear rather than angular forms. The main focus is on shape and, accordingly, Jensen kept decoration to a minimum, even leaving some pieces completely unadorned. His wide range of silverware includes tea and coffee services, candlesticks, and raised bowls, as well as pieces that were emblematic of the Jazz Age, such as cocktail shakers, cigarette boxes, and brush-and-mirror sets for dressing tables. Jensen also produced inexpensive silver jewellery – brooches, bracelets, and earrings – featuring stylized animals and floral motifs. His flatware – in the Pyramid pattern created by his brother-in-law Harald Nielsen, for example – was especially popular.

The firm employed a number of gifted designers. Pre-eminent among them was Johan Rohde, who designed the bestselling Acorn flatware pattern in 1916 and jug in 1920, which famously anticipated the streamlined designs of the 1930s. Jensen achieved international acclaim and opened shops in Paris, London, New York, and Buenos Aires. His designs were widely imitated by silversmiths throughout Europe, the United States, and Mexico. The Jensen firm is still making many of its celebrated Art Deco designs today.

**SILVER PILLBOX** This simple yet elegant pillbox produced by Georg Jensen features a stepped lid with a series of offset concentric circles – a recurrent Art Deco motif. *c.1930. D:4.5cm (1¾in).*

**JENSEN COCKTAIL SHAKER** The stark, geometric form of this jug-shaped cocktail shaker designed by S. Bernadotte is accentuated by the banding on its lid and handle and the check patterning. *c.1940. H:14.5cm (5¾in).*

## AMERICAN METALWARE

Throughout the 1920s handmade or hand-finished European silver had set trends in metalwork design. Machine-made silver was not highly esteemed, and there was very little on display at the 1925 Paris International Exhibition. However, this situation changed when the Depression set in, in the early 1930s.

### ALTERNATIVES TO SILVER

By the end of World War I most American silver manufacturers used the latest technology to mass-produce silverware. As incomes rose during the Roaring Twenties, people wanted to entertain more lavishly, and American silver manufacturers responded to this by churning out traditional designs alongside watered-down Art Deco designs.

The market for silverware dried almost overnight as a result of the Wall Street stock-market crash of 1929. Already geared up for mass production, American silver manufacturers concentrated on more modestly priced silver-plated pieces, and turned to even cheaper alternatives such as aluminium, pewter, copper, and chrome-plate.

### ART DECO DESIGNS

Many companies also employed leading Art Deco designers to tantalize consumers with daring and affordable new designs in these less expensive materials. The Revere Copper & Brass Company commissioned about 17 designs from Norman Bel Geddes, a highly influential American Art Deco

**SILVER BUD VASE** Of elegant proportions, this Kalo vase rises from a flat bottom to a tapering neck. The slightly flared top has wire applied to the rim. c.1925. H:17cm (6¾in).

designer who helped popularize streamlining. Bel Geddes's linear Manhattan cocktail set stands out among his designs for Revere. It consists of a cylindrical cocktail shaker, matching stemware, and a stepped tray. Bel Geddes also produced metalwork designs for other manufacturers – for example, aluminium candleholders for the Kensington Company.

Perhaps more than any other metalwork manufacturer, the Chase Brass & Copper Company was determined to bring adventurous Art Deco design to those on a budget. Chase's chrome-plated designs were widely available in department stores at prices comparable to Depression glass, an inexpensive substitute for crystal. The firm employed several major industrial designers including Walter von Nessen, whose best-known work for Chase is the Diplomat tea and coffee service, a modern variant on Neoclassical forms.

Another key name employed by chase was industrial designer Russel Wright, who used spherical and cylindrical forms in chrome-plated brass kitchen utensils and tableware manufactured by the American company.

### LEADING THE WAY

Wright also experimented with a new material developed for the aircraft industry: spun aluminium. He turned it into tea services, trays,

**TIFFANY BOWL** With chased bands below the rim and around the foot, this hemispherical bowl combines a satin finish on the outside with a brilliant-finish interior. c.1925. D:14cm (5½in).

plates, and tumblers that he had mass-produced by manufacturers such as West Bend Aluminium. These designs proved so popular that soon other manufacturers – the ALCOA company, for example – were producing similar ranges.

Meanwhile, the United States' largest silver manufacturer, the International Silver Company, commissioned cutting-edge designs from the Finnish-born architect Eliel Saarinen. Her most celebrated design for the company was a spherical

**LIQUEUR SET** This set of six chrome-plated cordial cups on a cobalt-blue glass tray was designed by Russel Wright for the Chase Brass & Copper Company. 1934. Tray: D:15cm (6in).

**PANCAKE AND CORN SET** A Russel Wright design for the Chase Brass & Copper Company, this set comprises a chrome-plated, sphere-shaped pitcher and shakers on a cobalt-blue glass tray. 1934. Tray: D:15cm (6in).

silver-plated coffee urn on a pierced cylindrical base with a matching tray. These futuristic pieces, exhibited at the 1934 Metropolitan Museum of Art's show devoted to industrial design, influenced many other designers, including Walter von Nessen, who created a similar chrome-plated urn for Chase Brass & Copper Company four years later.

## OTHER INDUSTRIAL DESIGN STARS

A few American craftsmen-designers – among them, Peter Müller-Munk – switched successfully from silversmithing to industrial design in order to make a living during the Depression era.

Before opening his own studio in 1927, Müller-Munk had worked for Tiffany. Unlike most handmade American silver from the period, Müller-Munk's studio pieces were not influenced by Danish designs. His studio silver is very angular and geometric. Later, as an industrial designer in the 1930s, Müller-Munk created perhaps the most celebrated of all American Art Deco chrome-plated designs for Revere, the famous *Normandie* pitcher inspired by Cassandre's iconic poster image.

**NEW YORK SPEAKEASY** Streamlined metal featured increasingly in interiors. In fashionable bars and clubs, metal railings might encase the cocktail bar, while chrome or silver cocktail shakers were employed to mix drinks.

## COCKTAIL SHAKERS

Nothing evokes the Art Deco era more than a cocktail shaker. The essential drinks accessory of the 1920s and 1930s was usually made of inexpensive silver-plated or chrome-plated metal, or from glass, with a silver-plated or chrome-plated top. Cocktail shakers inspired leading designers, including Walter Dorwin Teague. Most glass and metalwork manufacturers – from Steuben and Lalique, to Tiffany and Jensen – produced one. The classic form is a graduated cylinder with a bell-shaped top. Other popular designs resemble coffee pots with spouts and handles, or have a sleeve that twists to reveal the ingredients required for a cocktail. Novelty shapes include dumbbells, champagne bottles, penguins, and even aeroplanes.

**MANHATTAN COCKTAIL SHAKER** This Bel Geddes cocktail shaker has raised vertical ribs. The clean lines and use of chrome epitomize Art Deco styling. *1936–40. H:33cm (13in).*

## MARIE ZIMMERMANN

In the 1920s and 1930s acclaimed silversmith and metalworker Marie Zimmermann had a thriving New York workshop: the National Arts Club Studio. Here she made a variety of pieces, including jewellery, vases, candlesticks, and tableware. A keen gardener, Zimmermann also produced garden gates and furniture.

Her designs feature simple, often fluted forms that rely on patination, colour, and texture for effect. She enjoyed working in iron, copper, bronze, brass, and gold, as well as silver, and her pieces often incorporate ivory and cabochon stones such as jade, amethyst, and quartz for an added touch of exoticism.

In her heyday, Zimmermann exhibited across the United States, and institutions such as the Metropolitan Museum of Art collected her pieces. After she closed her workshop in 1944 and moved away from New York's art scene, she slipped into relative obscurity. A 1985 retrospective at the Metropolitan Museum of Art helped rekindle an appreciation of her craftsmanship and stylish designs.

Along with other American metalworkers such as Robert Jarvie, Margaret Craver, and Clara Barck Welles, the founder of the Kalo workshop, Zimmermann remained faithful to Arts and Crafts principles in the interwar years but gave her designs a modern Art Deco twist.

**GOLD-PLATED COPPER VASE** This cornucopia-shaped vase in hammered, gold-plated copper has applied chased leaf forms at the end of a curling tail that terminates in another leaf form. *W:27cm (10¾in).*

**TWO-PIECE CENTREPIECE** Both vase and stand are in hammered, gold-plated copper. The three-lobed vase flares out at the top in stylized leaf form, while the stand features heavy wirework with applied leaves and chased detail. *W:43cm (17in).*

# METALWARE GALLERY

Art Deco metalware is simpler in style than Art Nouveau metalware, with angular and streamlined shapes. Geometric forms were very popular, as was stylized figural imagery. Technological advances at this time brought new materials such as stainless steel, chrome, and aluminium to the fore. There was also a rise in mass production of decorative metalworking. However, fine handcraftsmanship remained prevalent, often used in conjunction with mass-production techniques where pieces were hand-finished.

## KEY

**1.** Chase bud vase in polished chrome. H:23cm (9in). ① **2.** Kalo silver candlesticks in tulip form. H:35.5cm (14in). ⑥ **3.** Georg Jensen silver candelabra. c.1935. H:16.5cm (6½in). ⑥ **4.** Set of Russel Wright box-shaped salt and pepper shakers. 1930. H:3.75cm (1½in). ② **5.** Chase centrepiece box marked The Architex, from a set with a pair of candlesticks. W:15cm (6in). ① **6.** Set of sterling-silver geometric powder boxes by Eliel Saarinen for International Silver. H:10–13cm (4–5in). ③ **7.** One of a pair of chrome Face lamps by the Revere Company. 1930s. H:25.5cm (10in). ① **8.** French silver-plated box with Bakelite handles. 1930s. W:27.5cm (10¾in). ④ **9.** Georg Jensen silver ashtray. 1930s. D:12.5cm (5in). ② **10.** One of a pair of French silver salt dishes. ② **11.** French wrought-iron firescreen attributed to Edgar Brandt. 1920s. H:72.5cm (28½in). ⑥ **12.** French iron

[3] *Jensen silver candelabra*

[1] *Chase chrome bud vase*

[2] *Kalo silver candlesticks*

[4] *Wright salt and pepper shakers*

[5] *Chase Architex box*

[6] *Saarinen powder boxes*

[7] *Revere Face lamp*

[8] *French silver-plated box*

[9] *Jensen silver ashtray*

[10] *French silver salt dish*

radiator cover of angular, modernist design with rosette motif. H:95cm (37½in). ④ **13.** Evans leaping gazelle silver compact with copper accents. 1930s. D:7.5cm (3in). ① **14.** French brass vases of stepped shape decorated with an embossed panel of floral motifs. c.1925. H:16cm (6¼in). ②
**15.** One of a pair of copper and brass book ends by Walter von Nessen for Chase. 1930s. W:13.5cm (5¼in). ① **16.** Georg Jensen cocktail shaker designed by Harald Nielsen. c.1925. H:25.5cm (10in). ④
**17.** French silver Cubist tea and coffee set by Ravinet d'Enfert with Macassar ebony handles. Coffeepot: H:19cm (7½in). ④ **18.** German copper and wicker coffee set. Tray: D:29cm (11½in). ②
**19.** Manning Bowman chrome and Bakelite Connoisseur cocktail shaker. 1936. H:30.5cm (12in). ①
**20.** Silver martini shaker by Mappin & Webb. H:23cm (9in). ②

11 French wrought-iron firescreen

12 French iron radiator cover

13 Leaping gazelle compact

14 French stepped brass vases

15 Copper and brass book end

16 Jensen cocktail shaker

18 German copper coffee set

17 French tea and coffee set

19 Connoisseur cocktail shaker

20 Mappin & Webb martini shaker

# CLOCKS

IN THE 1920S AND 1930S THE POPULARITY OF THE ART DECO STYLE WAS ALSO REFLECTED IN CLOCK-CASE DESIGN – FROM UNIQUE WORKS BY DESIGNER NAMES TO MASS-PRODUCED ITEMS.

## STYLISH TIMEPIECES

People's desire for a coherent "look" for their home or office meant that every object had to fit into their design scheme. Most rooms had a clock, and there was a seemingly endless supply to choose from – from the most expensive examples, like Cartier's, decorated with diamonds, to simple mirror-glass electric wall clocks by Smiths.

## DESIGNERS AND SPECIALISTS

Most Art Deco clocks were made by specialist clockmakers such as ATO, Le Coultre, and Omega. Paris-based ATO made its own designs and also sold movements in cases designed by Lalique. There are more than 20 Art Deco ATO models, all highly stylized and usually made in glass, metal, and plastic, with a battery movement. American mass-produced clocks abound, mostly with electric movements in a streamlined case featuring chrome and Bakelite. They were made by firms such as Manning Bowman and Lawson Time, Inc.

Leading French designers such as Jean Trenchant and Albert Cheuret produced one-off designs or limited editions, and styles ranged from the highly decorated to the most severe and economical of designs. Meanwhile, celebrated decorators Louis Süe and André Mare produced clocks as part of their interior schemes.

Designers often made clocks with the intention of complementing their other work. Furniture designer Maurice Dufrêne, for example, produced a palisander longcase clock in 1925 to match his furniture. Like many of his

**MOULDED GLASS CLOCK** The face of this clock has bronze-painted numerals and stands on a stepped, black base. Designed by René Lalique, the piece is signed on the bottom right of the face. *1930s. H:25cm (10in).*

*The numerals* are in a geometric Art Deco style

**SQUARE-FACED CLOCK** This French Art Deco clock has a carved and frosted-glass square face. It stands on a stepped, black, Bakelite base. *1930s. H:22.25cm (8¾in).*

**TABLE CLOCK** The green-enamelled face of this striking table clock is set within a simple chromed frame. The clock features a Jaeger-Le-Coultre-movement. *1925. H:25cm (10in).*

*The clock* stands on a circular, black, Bakelite and chrome base

**MANTEL CLOCK** The square face of this clock is set within a simple alabaster case with stepped sides. On the top is the spelter figure of a scantily clad female. *W:47cm (18½in).*

**TABLE-TOP CLOCK** This striking clock has a variegated marble case housing a lozenge-shaped clock face. A spelter woman sits on the top balancing a ball. *W:32.5cm (12¾in).*

**VIKING MANTEL CLOCK** The colour combination of this catalin clock makes it a desirable collector's piece. The simple round face is mounted on a black base and is flanked on either side by a decorative scroll. *1930s. H:9cm (3½in).*

*The angular, geometric forms* are typically Art Deco

**TELECHRON ALARM CLOCK** Designed by Paul Frankl, this green catalin clock is architectural in form. A light bulb is set within the silvered ring around the dial. *H:19.5cm (7¾in).*

contemporaries, Dufrêne advocated using technology to produce large numbers of machine-made pieces at moderate prices.

## INFLUENCES ON CLOCK DESIGN

Designers borrowed widely for inspiration. Following Howard Carter's discovery of Tutankhamun's tomb in 1922, Egyptian motifs began appearing on all sorts of objects. The numerals and green sun-ray enamelling on a small mass-produced table clock by Meyrowitz identify it as unmistakably 1920s, but the most striking feature is the pair of scarab wings, one each side of the clock – a sign of the popular Egyptian influence. Paul Frankl's 1928 design of the Skyscraper clock for the Warren Telechron company is made of a combination of polished and textured silver.

## LALIQUE'S CLOCKS

René Lalique produced clock cases in his characteristic moulded glass. In his search for new uses for decorative glass, he designed a clock set in a semicircular slab of glass with a light bulb in its bronze base. When switched on, the bulb illuminated the two nude figures – male and female – surrounding the clock face with a subtle light, giving a mysterious effect. Lalique managed to maintain the unusually high quality of his design and finish in mass-produced versions of his designs.

## HERMAN MILLER

Famous modern furniture manufacturer Herman Miller originally studied clockmaking in Germany. With his son-in-law, D.J. De Pree, he started a subsidiary business, the Herman Miller Clock Company, in 1927, initially to make traditionally designed reproduction wall and mantel clocks. In the early 1930s, looking for a way to save the company's fortunes after the Great Depression, De Pree met Gilbert Rohde, a designer from New York. Rohde convinced De Pree to move away from traditional designs and focus on new products that were more suited to the changing lifestyles of Americans. A Gilbert Rohde design for a clock about 40cm (16in) wide, made by the company in the early 1930s, has a self-starting electric movement. The unusual hour hand is characteristic of Rohde's designs. The case is made from solid wood and has exceptionally clean lines, while the grain of the veneer emphasizes its sleek design.

In 1937 Herman's son, Howard, took over the clock business and changed the company name to the Howard Miller Clock Company. The firm continued to have success with its modern clock designs.

**ROSEWOOD MANTEL CLOCK** This Gilbert Rohde/Herman Miller electric mantle clock has a rosewood case, a circular dial, red-and-black-enamelled metal hands, and chrome details. *W:42.5cm (16¾in).*

**ELECTRIC CLOCK** Attributed to Gilbert Rohde, this streamlined clock has a square face with abstract numerals set within a curving burr-walnut-veneered case with three applied chromed bands. *W:33cm (13in).*

# TEXTILES

DURING THE ART DECO ERA DESIGNERS FROM ALL FIELDS OF THE DECORATIVE ARTS TRIED THEIR HAND AT TEXTILE DESIGN. THEIR INTEREST WAS PARTLY EXPLAINED BY THE DESIRE TO ACHIEVE A UNIFIED LOOK FOR INTERIORS.

**WOOL ART RUG** The design of this rug is based on a work by the French Cubist painter Fernand Léger. The asymmetrical arrangement and geometric shapes are characteristic of Art Deco design. *L:166.5cm (65½in).*

## NEW IDEAS

Designing textiles gave artists the opportunity to express radical ideas and have them picked up by a wider audience, especially since the public has always been far more receptive to ground-breaking ideas when these are presented in the decorative arts than in fine art. In the 1930s women who had rejected or been shocked by the industrial scenes depicted in modern art happily decorated their homes with textiles covered in similar motifs.

### POIRET'S INFLUENCE

The impact of the Ballets Russes' 1909 visit to Paris on the development of Art Deco in France was immediately evident in textiles and clothing design. The celebrated fashion designer Paul Poiret was responsible for popularizing their colourful, exotic look in his extravagant couture garments. Poiret was also an interior decorator. In 1911 he set up the Atelier Martine, a workshop where talented girls – often in their early teens – with no formal training were encouraged to produce naive artworks that he then used as the basis for his textiles and furnishings.

Poiret got the idea for the Atelier Martine from Austria's Wiener Werkstätte, whose Arts and Crafts workshops he visited in 1911. The Wiener Werkstätte was especially renowned in artistic circles for its fabrics, which featured geometric and stylized floral patterns based on folk designs.

### ARTIST'S CREATIONS

It was Poiret who originally encouraged the Fauve painter Raoul Dufy to design textiles. Dufy worked on a number of projects for the Atelier Martine before becoming artistic director at Bianchini-Férier, a Lyon textile manufacturer. With designs featuring abstracted figures and bold colours, Dufy soon developed a reputation as one of the foremost textile designers of the Art Deco era.

The Russian-born but Paris-based painter Sonia Delaunay was also renowned for her textiles. A set designer for the Ballets Russes, Delaunay was interested in Cubism and colour theory; her abstract canvases were dominated by geometric shapes, mainly in primary colours. Delaunay explored the same visual ideas in her textiles and patchwork designs.

### HARMONIOUS VISIONS

The exquisite quality of Émile-Jacques Ruhlmann's creations is legendary. No material was too costly, no detail too small for this French furniture and

**SILK GAUZE PANEL** Like much of the work produced by Sonia Delaunay, this panel betrays a clear Cubist influence in its use of contrasting earthy tones and simple geometric shapes. *c.1925. W:142cm (56in).*

interior designer. Ruhlmann not only produced his own designs for fabrics, he also commissioned one-off designs from other artists for unique textiles to use in his luxurious decoration schemes. A real perfectionist, he had these materials produced by the best names in French textiles, such as Aubusson and Cornille Frères, the Lyon silk weavers.

The Irish designer Eileen Gray is best known today for her lacquered screens and tubular-steel furniture, but she also designed fabrics and rugs. Gray lived in Paris for most her life and was a pioneer of the modernist Art Deco movement. Her textile designs, like her furniture, were based on geometric forms. She used her colourful and boldly patterned rugs as a vital accent in her otherwise radically austere interior schemes.

## TEXTILES GO GLOBAL

The 1925 Paris International Exhibition confirmed France's obvious lead in textile design, but daring, abstract, woven textiles were being produced by the Bauhaus art school in Germany. Until this time, these artists had achieved only limited recognition outside their own country. However, by the 1930s designers all over the western world were catching up and promoting their own versions of the Art Deco style. English designer Marion Dorn developed a name for herself designing luxurious geometric-patterned carpets, while Donald Deskey's famous Swinging Woman carpet in the auditorium of New York's Radio City Music Hall helped popularize Art Deco textiles in the United States.

**PARK LANE HOTEL FOYER** Elegant arches and stylized fern leaves decorate the carpet in the foyer of the Park Lane Hotel in London. These Art Deco shapes are echoed in the curved wall lights and column decorations.

**MOHAIR PANEL** The bold use of colour and the pattern of this French rug, with its overlapping triangles, quadrants, stripes, and squares, make it a classic Art Deco design. *L:300cm (118in).*

**VOIDED VELVET COVERLET** The fountain was a recurring motif in the early Art Deco years. It often appeared in stylized form, as in this design woven in wool and silk. *L:216cm (85in).*

## RUTH REEVES

Ruth Reeves is one of the best-known American textile designers of the 1930s. She produced designs for W. & J. Sloane, a chic New York interiors shop that promoted the latest styles. Her wall hangings and furnishing fabrics depict scenes from contemporary life, such as families listening to the radio, telephonists at a switchboard, or a tennis game among friends. Reeves's use of earth tones and block printing is indicative of her Arts and Crafts roots, which she developed between 1911 and 1913 while at the San Francisco Institute of Art, a hotbed of the American Arts and Crafts movement. She continued her studies with the Cubist painter Fernand Léger when she lived in Paris in the 1920s. Her stylized tubular figures and everyday urban themes demonstrate her familiarity with avant-garde European painting. Reeves moved to India in 1956 and spent her last decade studying and collecting traditional Indian crafts.

**THE AMERICAN SCENE** Commissioned by W. & J. Sloane in New York, this block-printed cotton tapestry is one of several in which Ruth Reeves captured the essence of everyday life. *c.1930. W:211cm (83in).*

# SCULPTURE

IN THE INTERWAR YEARS SCULPTURE WAS AN IMMENSELY POPULAR MEDIUM FOR ARTISTIC EXPRESSION. FROM PREISS'S DANCERS, TO PROST'S SLEEK PANTHERS, SOME OF THE ERA'S MOST ENDURING IMAGES WERE PRODUCED BY SCULPTORS.

## IDEALIZING THE FEMALE FORM

Decorative sculpture was highly popular throughout the Art Deco period, and women were by far the favourite subject. In the 1920s and 1930s women were far more active and independent than their predecessors had been. They danced with abandon, participated in sports, and drove motorcars. Art Deco sculptures of female figures capture this dramatic transformation: slim and fit, the ideal beauty is dressed in short skirts or, even more daringly, in trousers.

## NEW AND TRADITIONAL MATERIALS

Sculptors and foundries met the increasing public demand for sculptures with a plethora of designs in differing materials and of variable quality.

Many portraits of women were produced using a special combination of bronze and carved ivory known as chryselephantine. More affordable, mass-produced pieces were made from bronze, white metal, or spelter, a zinc alloy that was often patinated or painted to resemble bronze or to produce a silvered or gilt finish. Many

of these mass-produced pieces were unsigned. Most Art Deco sculptures sit on marble or onyx bases that are modelled in the stepped style that was fashionable at the time.

## THE LIBERATED WOMAN

Demêtre Chiparus is probably the best known of the Art Deco sculptors. The Paris-based artist was famous for his figures of dancers in elaborate, Oriental-style costumes inspired by the Ballets Russes. His showgirls look as if they have stepped straight off the stage of the Folies Bergère on to the pedestal. Chiparus created more than 100 sculptures, mainly large and impressive figures with tight costumes highlighted with gold paint and gilt.

Another successful Art Deco sculptor, Ferdinand Preiss, was renowned for his charming, naturalistic portraits of newly independent women. Many of his works depict women performing some kind of physical activity – swimming or playing golf or tennis – or dancers and gymnasts in dramatic poses holding torches, hoops, and balls. A number of his finely carved and modelled sculptures were inspired by the female athletes taking part in the

*The ivory face* is intricately carved

*The bronze body* is decorated with gold paint and gilding

*Chiparus used dancers* on the Paris stage as his inspiration

**JANLE SCULPTURE** This chrome figure on a black marble base is signed by Max LeVerrier. The woman's pose is reminiscent of a gymnast's. *H:32cm (12½in).*

**FEMALE EMANCIPATION** Athletic female pursuits were becoming acceptable by the 1920s and 1930s, a liberation celebrated by Art Deco sculptors, who depicted women in numerous sporting poses.

**DANCER OF KAPURTHALA** Dancers in elegant poses are characteristic of Demêtre Chiparus's work. Here the figure wears a headscarf and bodysuit and stands on a stepped brown and green onyx base. *c.1925. H:55cm (21¾in).*

1936 Berlin Olympics. In the ultimate celebration of the liberated woman, Preiss produced a figure of a female pilot based on Amy Johnson, the famous pioneering aviator .

Bruno Zach's sculptures of women are the dark counterpoint to Preiss's wholesome athletes and dancers. The German sculptor specialized in erotically charged portraits of women who were part of the decadent Berlin night scene. His "blue angels" are totally sexually liberated and unabashed about their nakedness.

## AUSTRIAN OUTPUT

Austrian sculptor Josef Lorenzl also concentrated on images of women. He stylized his mainly nude figures in a distinctive way, elongating their limbs and abstracting the facial contours. His sculptures of women are lively and animated, with outstretched legs and arms and thrown-back heads. His most ambitious design is probably a figure of Diana the Huntress flanked by two hounds and holding a bow aloft.

Lorenzl's models were made in various

sizes and from a variety of materials. He also turned his hand to figural clocks, book ends, hood ornaments, and models for the ceramics firm Goldscheider. There, his elegant women were dressed in the latest fashions or exotic costumes.

The Austrian firm of Hagenauer Werkstätte also mass-produced statues in the Art Deco style under the creative guidance of Karl Hagenauer, the son of the company's founder. Hagenauer's figures fall into two main categories: Western-influenced and African-influenced. Made from chrome, brass, or bronze, they were particularly popular in the United States. The highly stylized figures include Masai warriors, nude dancers, bellboys, and athletic tennis players.

**The body is elongated** and slim, highlighting the elegance of the pose

**Lorenzl's figures** often stand on tiptoe

**Aphrodite** is semi-draped in a robe with a jewelled and turquoise belt

**PREISS FIGURE** This patinated-bronze and ivory figure portrays a young contemporary woman in a short-sleeved shirt and slacks, mounted on an onyx base. *H:30.5cm (12in).*

**LORENZL FIGURE** This stylized figure is cast in bronze from a model by Josef Lorenzl and patinated with a silver finish. It stands on a cone-like green onyx base. *H:38cm (15in).*

**APHRODITE** This Preiss bronze and ivory figure of the Greek goddess portrays her with her hands behind her head. She stands on a circular pink marble base. *H:23cm (9in).*

## DEPICTION OF ANIMALS

Along with women, animals were a favourite subject of Art Deco sculptors. Silhouettes were simplified, and their shapes reduced to curvilinear forms and geometric planes. François Pompon was one of the first to move away from realism in the early 1920s. His smooth, stylized polar bears were a great success. Others, such as Gaston Le Bourgeois, Maurice Prost, Edouard-Marcel Sandoz, and Max Le Verrier, soon followed Pompon's lead. Art Deco sculptors portrayed the elegant dynamism of animals such as deer, doves, and horses. Reflecting Art Deco's fascination with exoticism, they were also drawn to African and tropical wildlife – antelopes, monkeys, and angelfish. Panthers in various poses were arguably the most popular of all animal subjects, though sculptors also captured the cool, calculating instincts of other predators, including foxes, eagles, and cobras.

**STAG AND HOUND** An iron sculpture by Wilhelm Hunt Diederich, this rare piece portrays a stag and hound in black patina mounted on a green and (later) white marble base. *H:52cm (20½in).*

**GRECIAN WITH TORCH** Ferdinand Preiss sometimes created figures in Classical robes, as here with this bronze and carved-ivory Grecian female holding a flaming torch. *H:28cm (11in).*

# POSTERS

BY THE 1920S AND 1930S POSTER ADVERTISING REACHED UNPRECEDENTED HEIGHTS OF SOPHISTICATION. AS A RESULT, POSTERS OF THE DAY FEATURED SOME OF ART DECO'S MOST EYE-CATCHING AND COLOURFUL DESIGNS.

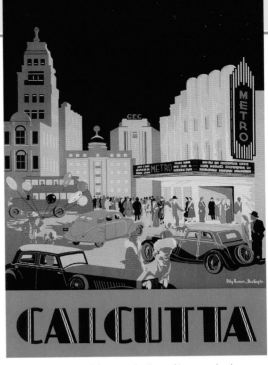

## FRENCH VANGUARD

Since Art Deco began in France, some of the most inventive posters of the period were by French designers. Paul Colin employed a bold, simple figurative style to get his clients' message across. He became renowned for his posters of Parisian performers such as Josephine Baker. Jean Dupas explained that he used "a re-creation of nature according to [his] own temperament" to grab attention for the products that his posters were promoting, such as London Underground and the upmarket department store Saks Fifth Avenue.

The Art Deco period was also known as the Machine Age. During this time, modes of transportation, such as motorcars, aeroplanes, and ocean liners, were celebrated by graphic artists and elevated to new heights in the public's eye. A.M. Cassandre, the master of Art Deco graphics, was responsible for iconic images of locomotives and steamships that transcended the poster world and were readily recognized. Widely admired, he also inspired countless poster designs including Willem Ten Broek's poster for the Holland America Line.

## BRITISH POSTERS

Some of the most enlightened British graphic arts patrons were the London Underground and railway companies such as Great Western, London

**CALCUTTA** Designed by Philip Kumar das Gupta, this poster advertises a fashionable evening out at Kolkata's first MGM cinema with its fabulous Art Deco façade. *1938. H:99cm (39in).*

**HOLLAND-AMERICA LINE** Characteristic of travel posters of the era, this example by Willem Ten Broek features a stylized luxury liner – a powerful, sweeping image. *1936. H:98cm (38½in).*

***NORD EXPRESS*** Strong lines and geometric shapes combine with bold use of colour in this striking image by Cassandre, which captures the modernity and speed of rail travel. *1927. H:105cm (41¼in).*

**AMERICAN AIRLINES** Designed by Edward McKnight Kauffer, this advertising poster evokes the splendid grandeur of New York's skyscrapers from the perspective of the pedestrian. *c.1950. H:98cm (38½in).*

**JAPAN** This design by Munetsugu Satomi depicts the blurred view from a speeding train as it hurtles through the countryside. Subtle features include the Japanese flag and a cherry tree in full blossom. *1937. H:97.5cm (38½in).*

Midland, and Scotland and Southern Railway. They employed leading artists and encouraged imaginative poster designs to advertise events, beauty spots, historic sites, seaside towns, and leisure facilities reached by tube or train. One of the most prolific and best remembered graphic designers to be employed by the Underground was the American-born Cubist, Modernist, and Vorticist designer Edward McKnight Kauffer. He was also commissioned to design work for Shell, American Airlines, and Pan-American Airlines.

## AMERICAN POSTERS

Some of the most creative American posters produced in the interwar years were also travel-related, commissioned by railway companies such as the Pennsylvania Railroad, steamship owners like Matson, and airlines, including Pan American. These posters capture the power of the speeding trains, the awesome skyscrapers of the big cities, and the sizzling nightlife of tropical destinations such as Cuba. Others encourage visitors to come and see the future in science, design, and technology at the World's Fairs in Chicago, New York, and San Francisco.

President Roosevelt's New Deal programme, aimed at economic recovery after the Depression, commissioned poster artists to create a series of campaigns to publicize travel and tourism, health and safety issues, cultural and educational programmes, and community activities. The artists were given a fairly free hand, and the results were more than 2,000 striking silkscreen, lithograph, and woodcut posters.

**LOTERIE NATIONALE**
Designed by Paul Colin, this poster celebrates the Grand Prix de Paris horse race. The horse and rider's streamlined poses suggest a dash to the finishing line. *H:155cm (61in).*

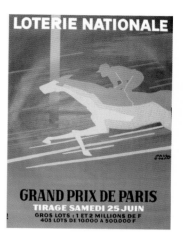

## DECO POSTERS IN OTHER NATIONS

The modernity, fantasy, and glamour of Art Deco also affected poster design outside the West. Despite living relatively traditional lifestyles, people in cities such as Tokyo, Shanghai, and Mumbai were open to the latest technology, design, and fashion trends from abroad. One of Japanese graphic designer Sugiura Hisui's best-known posters, The Only Subway in the East, illustrates this beautifully. He depicted passengers in both kimonos and Western attire in a colourful, stylized manner. Hisui's efforts to promote Art Deco graphic design in Japan included founding *Affiches*, a journal that introduced Japanese audiences to contemporary European and American poster design. Art Deco-flavoured posters and advertising material also appeared in South America and even some African nations.

**1939 WORLD'S FAIR** This poster by Shawl, Nyeland & Seavey shows the Inca-inspired Tower of the Sun flanked by the Golden Gate and San Francisco Bay bridges. *1937. H:87.5cm (34½in).*

**NEW YORK WORLD'S FAIR**
Designed by Nembhard N. Culin, this is a colourful bird's-eye view of the futuristic Perisphere, Trylon, and Helicline buildings. *1937. H:73.5cm (29in).*

# MID-CENTURY MODERN

## 1940–1970

# A NEW OPTIMISM

AS COUNTRIES RECOVERED FROM WORLD WAR II, DESIGNERS SEIZED ON FRESH OPTIMISM AND USED NEW MATERIALS TO CREATE A WORLD UNLIKE ANYTHING THAT HAD GONE BEFORE. THE NEW DESIGNS WERE EASY TO MASS PRODUCE AND SOON BECAME MAINSTREAM.

**FLOOR LAMP** Designed by Gino Sarfatti, this *Triennale* three-arm lamp has enamelled metal shades and handles on a polished brass frame. *1950s. H:157.5cm (62in).*

## THE POST-WAR MOOD

The end of World War II in 1945 brought peace, but it did not restore prewar levels of supply and demand for goods, let alone prosperity. The only nation to emerge richer from the war was the United States, for it alone had escaped invasion, occupation, or bombardment. Elsewhere, recovery took time, in some cases well into the 1950s.

However, as economies started to grow and people began to prosper again, the demand for consumer goods escalated as never before. It was met by a breed of designers excited by the possibilities of mass production and enthusiastic to work with the host of new materials being made available to them. And with the beginnings of youth culture, a new market for modern, fashionable goods – many the result of wartime inventions – was born.

## CHARLES AND RAY EAMES

The war did bring one benefit, however, for many of the techniques pioneered for military purposes were now available for peacetime application. One of the most surprising benefits came from the technique of moulding a piece of plywood in two directions, originally developed by Charles Eames for the US Navy in 1942 to make leg splints for injured servicemen. After the war Charles and his wife, Ray, adapted this technique to produce some of the most striking and innovative furniture of the 20th century.

Charles Eames was an architect and draftsman, and Ray Eames an abstract expressionist painter: in their work, they expressed the modernist aim of combining industry and art for social good. Their mission was "getting the most of the best to the greatest number of people for the least amount of money", which is why they used mass-produced materials such as aluminium, fibreglass, moulded plywood, and plastic, all of them affordable, flexible, and fresh. They also used the latest production techniques such as aluminium casting, new ways of bonding wood, and that dual-direction plywood moulding. But they applied the techniques to a looser, more sculptural style of furniture, owing more to the sinuous curves of a Brancusi sculpture than to the rigorous straight lines of a Le Corbusier or Bauhaus chair.

## SOFT MODERNISM

Charles and Ray Eames, however, were far ahead of most American designers, for the United States had been slow to accept modernism, particularly modernist furniture design, in the interwar years.

**TWA TERMINAL** The simple, sweeping, arching forms of the Trans World Airlines Terminal at John F. Kennedy International Airport in New York are typical of Eero Saarinen's designs. The building was completed in 1962.

**VERNER PANTON CONE CHAIR** The chair is upholstered with fabric-covered foam on a star-shaped chromed-metal base. It was designed in 1958. *H:85cm (33½in).*

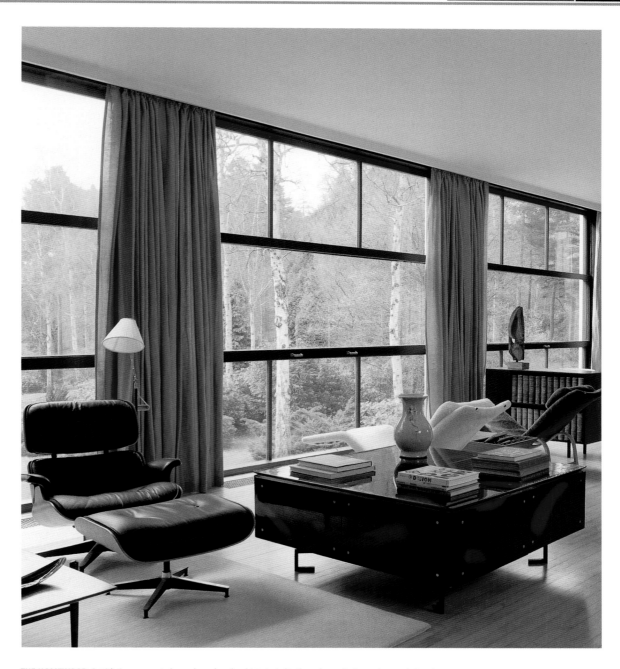

**THE HOMEWOOD** Patrick Gwynne created a modern, clean-lined interior in his Surrey home. An Eames lounge chair and ottoman sit alongside other pieces from the era, including a biomorphic sculpture.

Their work was also far ahead of anything being produced in Europe, but this changed in the late 1940s with the development of new designs in Scandinavia. During the 1930s, Scandinavian designers, notably Alvar Aalto and Bruno Mathsson, had developed a style best described as soft modernism. Inspired by nature, the look was curving and organic. It took a gentler, more ergonomic approach that used wood, with which Scandinavia is abundantly endowed, rather than plastic or steel.

Alvar Aalto, a Finnish designer, had famously remarked that metal furniture was uncomfortable in the cold and was "unsatisfactory from a human point of view". He and others developed a design style that used natural materials and forms and emphasized craftsmanship and traditional rather than hi-tech manufacturing techniques. This softer approach to modernism can also be seen in the work of the Danish designer Arne Jacobson, whose Ant and Egg chairs were sculptural in shape, combining soft lines with strict attention to detail.

## NATIONAL DIFFERENCES
Soft modernism appealed to consumers looking for comfort and reassurance after the war, not just in Scandinavia but in Italy too. Here, Gio Ponti and

Carlo di Carli introduced a sensuousness into furniture design not seen since Art Nouveau. Elements of this new approach can also be seen in Australia, where the influence of Charles and Ray Eames was strong, in Japan, where a hybrid modernism used local styles, and in Germany.

In France, however, designers went in another direction, adding decorative effects to the basic modernist style in order to sell their individually made items at high prices to an affluent elite. In Britain, despite the best endeavours of the 1951 showcase Festival of Britain, consumers by and large rejected the modernist look – however soft or hard – as being too close to the Utility range of

furniture forced on them by rationing during the war.

**OVOID GLASS VASE**
One of the big names in Murano glassmaking of the 1950s, this Seguso Vetri d'Arte vase is designed by Flavio Poli. *c.1960. H:30.5cm (12in).*

# ELEMENTS OF STYLE

The multifarious strands of mid-century design make this a loose and mercurial era. The transition between 1950s formality and 1960s hedonism turned prevailing fashion on its head in a short space of time. A climate of scientific discovery informed many new developments in this period, while the shortage of materials after the war resulted in the need to design functional objects that were simple and easy to manufacture. This gave rise to the idea of "good design", a concept coined by Edgar Kaufman at the Museum of Modern Art in New York.

GEORGE NAKASHIMA TABLE

### WOOD

Early in this period manufacturers working in wood dominated furniture design. Designers such as Finn Juhl and Hans Wegner sowed the seeds of the Scandinavian style with their simple and organic forms. In the United States George Nakashima kept Japanese woodworking traditions at the fore of fashion.

MIDWINTER PLATE

### DOMESTIC TASTE

A new domesticity saw the reinforcement of gender stereotypes after the disruption of war. Young homemakers were enticed by a huge array of labour-saving devices and bright new abstract patterns. The vogue for entertaining led to mass-produced tableware, oven-to-table crockery, and the hostess trolley.

CASED MURRINE GLASS

### REINTERPRETATION OF TECHNIQUES

In this age of innovation even time-honoured techniques were reinvented. Charles and Ray Eames revolutionized Thonet's 19th-century techniques for steam-bending wood, while in Italy the glassmakers of Murano updated traditional decorative methods to infuse glass with new colour and variety.

PSYCHEDELIC FABRIC

### POP

The distinction between high and low art was eroded by a new generation of artists in the 1960s. Popular culture was taken more seriously and in response it threw up outrageous and informal commodities in tune with the outlook of the newly empowered youth movement.

FAIENCE CHARGER

### CRAFTSMANSHIP

Many artisans still practised craft skills, often in tandem with more industrial work. The Studio movement pervaded the decorative arts, from ceramics and glass to furniture and metalware. Many of the styles and techniques developed by artist-craftsmen were adopted in time by industrial designers.

MURANO GLASS VASE

### EXUBERANT COLOUR

From the subtle naturalistic hues of Scandinavian glass to intense day-glo fluorescence, colour was all-important. Designers used it in an unashamed bid to be noticed, discarding all rules regarding proper combinations. Drab colours were seen as old-fashioned and stuffy.

PLASTIC TELEPHONE
## FORM AND FUNCTION
A culture of convenience encouraged the production of highly specialized goods that demonstrated fitness for purpose. Designers questioned traditional design in everything from the chair to the telephone. This telephone was designed to fulfil its purpose, curving to fit neatly from ear to mouth.

FLYING SAUCER FLOOR HEATER
## FUTURISTIC DESIGN
The space race was one manifestation of the Cold War that grabbed the attention of the world. In the period leading up to the first moon landing in 1969, globe shapes and representations of UFOs and satellites proliferated, from Sputnik lighting fixtures to the JVC Videosphere television.

BENT PLYWOOD TABLE
## NEW MATERIALS
The war effort led to great advances in materials technology, which then brought new developments to the consumer market after the Allied victory. Inventive designers incorporated aluminium, stainless steel, improved plywoods, and even a spray-on plastic polymer into their work.

STACKING PLASTIC ASHTRAYS
## FANTASTIC PLASTIC
Injection-moulding technology gave designers new freedom. Manufacturers took to plastics enthusiastically, revelling in their potential to hold more or less any form or colour. As more and more affordable and versatile synthetic materials hit the market, the range of consumer goods available exploded.

IITTALA VASE
## NATURAL INSPIRATION
Designers drew freely from natural forms in this period, though rarely without adding a stylistic twist. Scandinavian glass and ceramic artists were drawn to the colours and textures of their local landscape, while Pop artists enjoyed the juxtaposition of depicting natural forms in unnaturally vivid colours.

VLADIMIR KAGAN TABLE
## CLEAN LINES
The legacy of early modernism meant that the Cubist influence was still at work. As the 1960s progressed this angular geometry waned, replaced by a more organic aesthetic. Many designers eschewed surface decoration, allowing these simple shapes and clean lines to take centre stage.

HENNING KOPPEL BOWL
## BIOMORPHIC FORMS
Biomorphic design – abstract forms fused with shapes found in nature – was first used in the 1930s by Surrealist artists to create ceramics and metalware. Natural forms were stretched and warped to achieve an effect both familiar and alien by adherents of the Scandinavian style, most notably by Henning Koppel.

ATOM BALL CLOCK
## ATOMIC TECHNOLOGY
The dawn of the atomic age saw designers borrow microscopic natural forms such as atomic structures. Introduced at the Festival of Britain in 1951, this style was adopted enthusiastically in the United States. The Atomium, built in Brussels for the 1958 World Expo, represented the peak of atomic design.

# FURNITURE

A TASTE FOR TRADITIONAL-LOOKING FURNITURE WITH A CLEAN, MODERN EDGE IMMEDIATELY AFTER WORLD WAR II LATER GAVE WAY TO A PERIOD OF FRIVOLOUS EXPERIMENTATION.

**ROSEWOOD SIDEBOARD** Designed by Børge Mogensen, this rosewood-veneered sideboard is characteristic of contemporary Danish design in its clean lines and tapering legs. The sliding doors have book-matched veneers and indents for handles. *1958. L:238cm (93¼in).*

## SCANDINAVIAN TRENDS

During the 1950s Scandinavian designers became more prominent than ever before. They impressed the world with a pared-down vision of modernity that paradoxically relied on traditional materials and working practices. The industrialized killing of the war years had exposed a shocked public to the barbarous face of modernism; they no doubt found the cosy familiarity of carefully worked teak furniture reassuring.

The Danish designer and architect Finn Juhl grew up wanting to be an art historian and although he was dissuaded from this career by his father, it was reflected in his respect for tradition. In collaboration with the cabinet-maker Niels Vodder, Juhl created highly sculptural pieces of furniture inspired both by the free form expression of abstract art and by organic, natural forms. He won five gold medals for his exhibits at Milan Triennale shows during the 1950s and his success helped to whet an international appetite for Scandinavian design, paving the way for other talented individuals to make a similar break.

Børge Mogensen, a close contemporary of Juhl and a fellow Dane, was influenced in his early career by Kaare Klint, an architect and designer who combined interests in Classical historicism and ergonomics. During the 1940s Mogensen headed the Danish Cooperative Wholesale Society, a position that put him at the heart of trends in Danish manufacturing and retail. Armed with a detailed knowledge of Danish consumerism, Mogensen set about producing tailored furniture such as his 1954 Boligens Byggeskabe cabinet system. He was trained in the Danish craftsman tradition and worked primarily in wood, crafting his work with smooth, clean lines. This helped him reach a wide audience, even among those who were wary of modern design.

### NEW IDEAS FROM THE OLD WORLD

During the 1930s the United States benefited from a huge influx of fresh talent, as modernist designers fled the growing instability of Europe and forged new lives for themselves across the Atlantic. One reason why they found their adopted homeland to be so receptive to their ideas was the groundwork that had already been done on their behalf by George Nelson. A two-year tenure at the American Academy in Rome offered Nelson the chance to travel around Europe interviewing the stars of

### HANS WEGNER

Another of the high-calibre Scandinavian designers to find success in this period was Hans Wegner, who produced one of the most acclaimed chairs in the modern canon, model JH501. Known simply as The Chair to its many fans, it was born of what Wegner referred to as the "continuous process of purification" that is the kernel of all good modern design. Its status was enhanced further when CBS purchased 12 of them for use in the famous 1960 televised debates between Kennedy and Nixon. Although there is nothing revolutionary in the teak frame and woven seat construction, the design itself has a timeless elegance.

*The chair's seat and back* are detached, the back appearing to be suspended in mid-air

*The front and back legs* are turned

**CHIEFTAIN CHAIR** Finn Juhl's sculptural chair with an exposed teak frame and shaped dark green leather seat and back was designed for Niels Vodder of Denmark. *1949. H:95cm (38in).*

**THE CHAIR** In Wegner's model JH501 the back rail seamlessly becomes the armrests, raised on four tapering, dowel legs. It has been dubbed the ultimate blend of form and function. *1949. H:76cm (30in).*

**GEORGE NELSON CABINET** The white porcelain pulls and tapering, brushed-metal legs of this Herman Miller rosewood-veneered cabinet by George Nelson are typical of his Thin Edge series. *1950s. W:141.5cm (55¾in).*

avant-garde architecture and design. He published these interviews upon his return home, thus introducing the American public to figures such as Walter Gropius, Ludwig Mies van der Rohe, and Gio Ponti.

George Nelson's own career as a furniture designer was launched when D.J. DePree, the president of the Herman Miller manufacturing company, saw his Storagewall modular system featured in the pages of *Life* magazine. DePree

immediately offered Nelson the design directorship at Herman Miller, and the company then quickly rose to a position of prominence, rivalled only by Knoll in its dominance of the American modern furniture industry.

**HOME OFFICE DESK** George Nelson's all-in-one walnut desk on a tubular brushed-metal frame is a clever combination of leather-covered writing surface, a range of storage cabinets, and a mesh file basket. It was designed for Herman Miller. *1948. W:138cm (54¾in).*

## INNOVATIVE DESIGNS

As large American companies such as Knoll and Herman Miller became more established, they were less willing to take the kind of creative risks that had made their names in the first place. Budding designers such as Wendell Castle and Vladimir Kagan were compelled to work with smaller outfits or produce their own furniture. Kagan's sculptural, organic furniture forms, with trademark splayed legs and sinuous frames, look like direct descendants of Finn Juhl's earlier wooden chairs.

However, companies such as Dunbar made the work of the American designer Edward Wormley more widely available. The Italian designer Gio Ponti proved that extraordinary new things could be achieved even with

traditional methods and materials when he unveiled his *Superleggera* (Super-light) chair in 1952. Weighing in at just 1.7kg (3¾lb), it was the lightest mass-produced chair of its time.

The simplicity of Ponti's design was echoed by that of former employee, Franco Albini, and fellow Italians Gino Colombini and Marco Zanuso, as well as Frenchman Jean Prouvé. Ponti's richly embellished collaborations with Piero Fornasetti were the antithesis of modernist minimalism.

***SUPERLEGGERA* CHAIR** This dining chair with two horizontal back slats and a woven seat was Gio Ponti's version of a simple, rustic-looking chair, designed for Cassina of Italy. *1957. H:81cm (32in).*

**CONTOUR CHAIR** Armchairs with matching ottomans were a popular contemporary form. This example, designed by Vladimir Kagan, has a sculpted walnut frame and retains its original dark brown Kagan swirl chenille upholstery. *H:90cm (36in).*

## AMERICAN STUDIO

Modernist design quickly became the status quo in the United States, where prosperous and fashion-conscious consumers were enjoying the boom years in the aftermath of World War II. Unwilling or unable to fit into this prescribed vision of corporate modernity, a number of solitary designer-craftsmen doggedly pursued their own unique visions.

The pioneer of this reclusive approach was Wharton Esherick, known as the "Dean of American Craftsmen", who first took to carpentry in 1924 when it became clear that his career as a painter would never take off. Esherick pursued a solitary existence in the Pennsylvania hills, working against the grain by striving towards the perfection of his handicraft at a time when craftsmanship was considered to be a relic of the past. Despite this he did not work in total isolation from the wider world, absorbing influences from emerging modern art movements into his work. The result was

**MODERN TO CONTEMPORARY** The timeless style of George Nakashima's furniture means it is perfectly at home in the garden room of a house in Osaka, designed by Chitoshi Kihara. *c.2000.*

sculpted, functional forms that blurred the boundaries between furniture and high art.

Esherick chose to settle near Rose Valley in Delaware County, previously the site of a utopian Arts and Crafts experiment. His early work echoes the heavy aspect of much Arts and Crafts furniture, and exhibits a pronounced vernacular streak – he produced a series of chairs for a local theatre fashioned from axe handles, for example. In time he developed his own idiom, a kind of tactile, free form furniture that was much imitated by his spiritual successors.

**SLAB COFFEE TABLE** The free form top of this cherrywood coffee table, complete with fissures, is typical of George Nakashima's work. *1956.* W:154cm (61½in).

### GEORGE NAKASHIMA

Born in Spokane, Washington, George Nakashima took a circuitous route that brought him to the same locale as Esherick. An MIT (Massachusetts Institute of Technology) architecture graduate, Nakashima worked in Paris and Tokyo before undergoing a transcendental experience in an Indian ashram that informed his later work.

On returning to the United States, Nakashima found himself interred with other Japanese Americans after the bombing of Pearl Harbour in 1941. After his release he settled in New Hope, Pennsylvania, where he established a studio and devoted himself to working with wood. Nakashima

was given the Sanskrit name Sundarananda, meaning "one who delights on beauty" by his guru. His struggle to remove the demands and constraints of the designer's ego from his work led him to a deep appreciation of his chosen material, firmly within the Japanese tradition that was so admired by Frank Lloyd Wright.

Nakashima's dramatic designs rely entirely on the qualities inherent in the wood for their effect. He selected his timbers carefully, preferring pieces that had remarkable burls, good colour, and other notable features such as natural "uro", or recessed areas. Many of his pieces have an unworked free edge, with the intention of expressing the form of the wood as much as possible. Nakashima threw the ebullient natural beauty of his timber into sharp relief by combining it with man-made elements, including angular, geometric members and decorative joinery such as butterfly splays.

**THREE-LEGGED STOOL** The flared dowel legs of this stool have been mortised through the seat and are joined by graduated stretchers. Designed by Wharton Esherick, the stool is carved "WE 1966". W:42cm (16½in).

## PAUL EVANS

Another denizen of the New Hope scene, Paul Evans initially trained as a silversmith before establishing his own studio and beginning to accept commissions for pieces of monumental furniture. During the 1960s he designed for Directional Furniture, a progressive company based in North Carolina, and headed their factory for a time before downsizing once more to work from his own studio in the late 1970s.

Paul Evans's Cityscape range has echoes of Paul Frankl's Skyscraper line (*see p.272*) in both name and look, although Evans's work is far more sculptural. His massive doors and room dividers in particular straddle the boundary between functional furniture and art installations. His sinuous, stalagmite-form table bases are, like much of his oeuvre, constructed from bronze and steel. Evans's early training as a metalworker instilled in him a fundamental understanding of these materials.

Bespoke commissions for wealthy clients allowed Evans to fund the opening of a New York showroom in 1979, thus bringing his work to an even wider audience.

**BRONZE DINING TABLE**
The sculpted base of this Paul Evans table is of serpentine stalagmite form. It supports a round-edged plate-glass top. *1960s. W:222cm (87½in).*

## PHILLIP LLOYD POWELL

During the 1950s Evans shared a showroom in New Hope with Phillip Lloyd Powell, another exponent of studio furniture. Powell gained widespread recognition after his work was exhibited at America House, next to the Museum of Modern Art in New York, which had championed the modernist cause. His furniture incorporates diverse materials, from metal and wood to slate and marble, chosen for their tactile qualities and the ways in which they contrast with one another. Powell's work is highly sculptural and each piece is unique – even handles on individual items will seldom match because, in Powell's words, "they don't have to, like people don't match". One of his favoured woods was walnut, as it is particularly soft and can be sculpted with specialist tools such as the spoke shave, a skill at which he was especially adept.

**ROOM DIVIDER** The front of this steel room divider comprises sculpted compartments, treated in reds, greens, and purples with gold-leaf accents. Signed Paul Evans. *1967. W:244cm (96in).*

**NEW HOPE CHAIR AND OTTOMAN** In walnut and black leather, this is Lloyd Powell's most iconic design. *1956. H:82cm (32¼in).*

**COFFEE TABLE** This Phillip Lloyd Powell coffee table has a circular slate top and lower shelf, on three chip-carved plank legs with hammered-metal hardware and casters. *1960s. H:92cm (36¼in).*

**ARABESCO COFFEE TABLE** This beech-veneered plywood coffee table is typical of designer Carlo Mollino's idiosyncratic style. Originally produced by Apelli & Vareso in 1949, this example is a re-edition produced by Zanotta of Italy. *2004. W:129cm (50¾in).*

*The perforated plywood frame* is bent to provide a magazine rack below the plate-glass table top

## BENT PLY

As the modernist movement matured, desire for the shock of the new ebbed and designers became comfortable revisiting established methods and materials, especially if they could find novel ways to use them. The century-old technology of laminated plywood construction provided the basis for a large proportion of the most iconic furniture of the time. The war had resulted in great advances in laminate technology, and one of the biggest draws of the material was that the same design could be finished with any number of different lacquer, paint, or veneer coatings, offering consumers choice – something they were beginning to demand more of.

The versatility of laminated plywood had been comprehensively explored in the mid-19th century. In the United States, John Belter had exploited its suitability for extreme shapes and pierced decoration, while Michael Thonet had pioneered the steam-bending process in Austria. Their influence can be seen in Carlo Mollino's elegant *Arabesco* coffee table, designed in 1949. The plywood frame represents a synthesis of the Art Nouveau stylings of Antonio Gaudí with the free-form surrealism of Salvador Dali. Mollino was an eccentric designer, obsessed with the occult, and much of his work came from private commissions; the most vociferous exponents of plywood furniture were industrial designers who were interested in large-scale production.

### THE SEARCH FOR A PERFECT FORM

The reductionist obsession shared by many mid-20th-century designers prompted them to eliminate every extraneous feature from their furniture; many imagined the perfect form to be one constructed from a single piece of material, without joins or breaks. Charles and Ray Eames struggled with this concept in the 1940s.

While working as an assistant for Arne Jacobsen during the early 1950s, the young Verner Panton contributed to the design of the celebrated 3100 model, better known as the Ant chair. Originally conceived for use in a canteen, this chair was designed with easy stacking in mind and became the most successful mass-produced chair of the 1950s. The seat and back are moulded from a single piece of plywood, and the tubular plastic (later metal) legs are attached to the seat with a single bolt.

### PUSHING THE LIMITS OF PLYWOOD

In 1956 Panton took this reductionism to its logical conclusion with his S chair. The first cantilevered design in plywood, the S chair was manufactured by Thonet, the spiritual home of bentwood furniture. Its distinctive curves have been borrowed and copied dozens of times since its first production.

Others also chose to explore the sculptural possibilities of plywood. George Nelson's Pretzel chair, for example, was named for the manner in which the top rail and arms twist and bend. A company named Plycraft manufactured dozens of furniture designs on behalf of individuals, including company president Paul Goldman, who were interested in pushing plywood to its artistic limits. The Cherner chair, thought to have been

**S-CHAIR** Designed by Verner Panton for Thonet, this was the world's first single-piece cantilevered chair made from moulded plywood. *1965. H:85cm (34in).*

*The chair* is shaped to fit the human frame, with swooping, organic curves

**The seat and back** are made from a single sheet of bent laminated wood

**CHERNER CHAIR** This walnut-veneered, bent-laminated-wood chair with armrests was designed by Paul Goldman in 1957 but attributed to Norman Cherner at the time. It is based on George Nelson's Pretzel chair. *1957. H:78cm (31in).*

**Plywood** with curves that emulate the female form

**The chair** stands on simple, tubular-steel legs

**TEAK-VENEERED CHAIR** This teak-veneered plywood chair was designed by Robin Day for London's Royal Festival Hall in celebration of the 1951 Festival of Britain. Produced by Hille International Co., this example was made in 1956. *H:77.5cm (31in).*

## NOTORIOUS CHAIR

This iconic and much-parodied image of Christine Keeler straddling what looks like an Arne Jacobsen chair was taken by photographer Lewis Morley at the height of the Profumo scandal in 1963. The aperture beneath Keeler's elbows shows that this is not in fact a genuine Series 7 chair but one of the many imitations that found their way onto the market. Nevertheless, the use of the chair for this powerful image demonstrates that Jacobsen's designs were still regarded as being bold and sexy a decade after they first appeared.

**SERIES 7 CHAIR** The seat and back of this chair are made from a single sheet of shaped and moulded plywood. It has a tubular-steel base with rubber-capped feet. *1955. H:76cm (30in).*

designed by Paul Goldman but attributed to the architect and designer Norman Cherner in order to give it more credibility, is remarkable for the precariously slim transition between the one-piece moulded seat and back. Combined with slender applied arms and legs, this chair manages to convey both the great strength and fluid grace of plywood.

The revival of British industry, celebrated at the 1951 Festival of Britain, depended on designers

to supply economic, interesting products for mass production. Ernest Race provided the event with one of its most talked-about designs: the cast-aluminium BA chair. Robin Day, winner of the Museum of Modern Art's Low Cost Furniture competition, became design director of British manufacturer Hille in 1950 and fulfilled exactly that brief. Day's moulded plywood 661 chair, designed for the Royal Festival Hall, was followed by the immensely successful Hillestak model.

## THE EASTERN AESTHETIC

With a venerable tradition of woodworking behind them, Japanese designers took to plywood construction with aplomb, achieving international recognition. More accustomed to sitting on mats than on chairs, they took the Western idea of the seat – one that is alien to their culture – and infused it with a peculiarly Eastern aesthetic. Reiko Tanabe's geometric Murai stool, for example, makes use of a patchwork construction technique known as *yatoizanetsugi*. It is part of the permanent collection at New York's Museum of Modern Art.

Sori Yanagi accompanied French designer Charlotte Perriand on her tour of Japan when she visited the country in 1940. The cultural exchange between the two may have been the inspiration behind Yanagi's foray into chair design. In accordance with his maxim "True beauty is not made; it is born naturally", Yanagi's Butterfly stool takes its form from the natural world. It is constructed from two bent and shaped plywood forms bolted together with a brass stretcher – suitable for mass production and yet sacrificing none of its elegance to the machine-making process. The perfect symmetry of its form, in

particular the upswept seat, is reminiscent of the gateway to a Shinto temple. Both the Murai and the Butterfly stools rely upon the grain of their wooden veneer in lieu of any other surface decoration.

**BUTTERFLY STOOL** Designed by Sori Yanagi, this rosewood-veneered stool is made from two sheets of laminated and moulded beechwood, joined together by a single stretcher. *1956. W:42cm (16½in).*

**The minimal, geometric design** is achieved by bending each piece in three directions

**MURAI STOOL** Reiko Tanabe designed a laminated, moulded beech stool with teak veneer for Tendo Mokko in 1961. The example shown here is a re-edition. *H:36cm (14¼in).*

# CHARLES AND RAY EAMES

CHARLES AND RAY EAMES DEFINED MID-CENTURY AMERICAN MODERNISM. THEIR WORK WITH THE US GOVERNMENT, THE SMITHSONIAN INSTITUTION, AND BLUE-CHIP COMPANIES SUCH AS IBM PLACED THEM AT THE HEART OF 20TH-CENTURY AMERICAN IDENTITY.

**ESU-400 STORAGE UNIT** A multipurpose storage unit with four sliding doors and five drawers designed for Herman Miller, the ESU-400 is supported on a slender steel frame with polychrome side and back panels. *1950. H:122cm (48¼in).*

**RAR CHAIR** The iconic Rocking Armchair Rod chair, shown here in salmon, has wooden rockers, a metal-rod frame, and a fibreglass-reinforced moulded-plastic seat. It was designed for Herman Miller. *1948–50. W:62cm (24½in).*

## EERO SAARINEN

The collaboration between Eero Saarinen and Charles Eames for the Organic Design in Home Furnishings competition left an indelible mark on Saarinen's personal aesthetic. Like Eames, he developed an interest in office furniture systems and his career followed a similar trajectory as he explored new materials. Among Saarinen's most distinctive contributions to furniture design are the spreading columnar bases of his Pedestal group, which he hoped would "clear up the slum of legs" that restricted movement and comfort in the dining room.

**TULIP TABLE** The elliptical laminated top of the Tulip dining table is supported on a pedestal base. Saarinen designed it for Knoll Associates. *1957. W:244cm (96in).*

Charles and Ray Eames were mentored by Eliel Saarinen, father of Eero, at the Cranbrook Academy of Art in Michigan. Charles initially trained as an architect, while Ray came from the avant-garde New York art scene, where she had experimented with moulded and pressed plywood sculpture. Together, their goal was to create furniture that could be mass-produced at an affordable price.

One of their first products was a moulded plywood chair developed from a concept Charles had worked on with Eero Saarinen for the Organic Design in Home Furnishings competition in 1940. During World War II Eames had worked on commissions for the US navy, producing splints, stretchers, and aeroplane nosecones in plywood. Their extensive research into the plastic properties of plywood produced some true classics such as the 1945 LCW (lounge chair wood) and LCM (lounge chair metal), both of which had moulded plywood components.

The Eames' commitment to providing their customers with choice can be seen in the range of materials in which these chairs were offered, from paint to leather and even animal hide. Their influence increased the options offered to consumers, as their contemporaries drew on their experiments to produce a wealth of plywood chairs in many designs.

### NEW MATERIALS

The development of fibreglass-reinforced plastic made it possible to construct a chair seat and back from a single piece of material, representing the culmination of the Eames' earlier trials with plywood. The Plastic Shell Group was the first series of unlined plastic chairs to be mass-produced, the result of work for the International Competition for Low-Cost Furniture Design.

Unveiled in 1950, the line initially included the RAR (rocking armchair rod) and DAR (dining armchair rod) models and was expanded in later years. The "rod" component of these names refers to the metal rod bases that supported the fibreglass shell seats. *La Chaise*, another fibreglass design conceived for the same competition, proved too expensive to put into production at the time.

**CTW TABLE** This CTW (coffee table wood) table has a moulded ash-plywood circular tray-top on bent plywood legs. It was designed for Herman Miller. *1946. H:86.5cm (34in).*

Charles and Ray Eames continued to design chairs throughout the 1950s and 1960s, most of them made and distributed by Herman Miller. The long relationship between the Eames and this venerable company was first forged when they designed the Herman Miller showrooms in Los Angeles.

The 670 lounge chair and 671 ottoman, with their luxury rosewood veneers, represented the Eames' first foray into the high end of the market and were an immediate success. Their willingness to embrace new materials also saw them using steel rods, aluminium, and Naugahyde upholstery.

Later in their careers the Eames shifted the focus of their work from furniture to photography, film, and exhibition design.

**SWIVEL CHAIR** This American Herman Miller Aluminium Group Model No. EA117 swivel chair has the original purple upholstery over an aluminium frame and star-shaped base. *1958. H:86.5cm (34in).*

**DKW-2 CHAIR** The Dining Bikini Wood (DKW) chair has a welded and bent-steel-rod seat and frame and is raised on wooden legs. It was designed for Herman Miller. *1951. H:84cm (33in).*

**LA CHAISE** The moulded fibreglass seat and back are raised on five polished-steel rods, which rise from an oak star-shaped base. The lack of upholstery emphasizes the sculptural shape. Designed in 1948, this version is a 1990s re-edition from Vitra AG of Germany. *W:134.5cm (53in).*

## MODERN MATERIALS

While Scandinavian designers first found fame with their innovative use of wood, many of them turned to more modern materials in the later 1950s. Sheet metal proved more versatile even than plywood, and its relatively cold and unwelcoming surface could be softened with fabric upholstery.

Some of the earliest steps towards this new vision were taken by Eero Saarinen. The son of a Finnish architect but a naturalized citizen of the United States, Saarinen represented the fusion of Scandinavian modernism with American corporate aesthetic. Having already collaborated with Charles Eames to win a competition run by the Museum of Modern Art entitled Organic Design in Home Furnishings, Saarinen unveiled his Model 70 chair in 1947. Constructed from moulded fibreglass with foam cushions and fabric upholstery, it was soon dubbed the Womb chair in recognition of the invitation to curl up that was offered by its soft contours. Saarinen himself described the chair as being "biological". Its influence was far-reaching, inspiring a number of designs with a similar organic abstraction.

This strain of mid-century modernism was eminently suited to ambitious commissions that aimed to create harmonious environments in which even the smallest details contributed to an overall ambience. The undisputed master of this kind of obsessive total design was Arne Jacobsen. The Royal Hotel in Copenhagen, the world's first designer hotel, is one of his architectural masterpieces. Jacobsen produced the Swan and Egg chairs, two of the most recognizable furniture designs in the modern canon, for the hotel lobby. Their soft, enveloping forms and bright upholstery helped to create an interior aesthetic that contrasted with the angular uniformity of the exterior of the building.

## THE CONE CHAIR

A hotel commission also lay behind one of Verner Panton's biggest successes – the Cone chair. Developed for the restaurant his parents owned within the Komigen guesthouse in a provincial Danish town, this chair caused a global sensation. After it was spotted by a local entrepreneur, Panton agreed to put it into production. The racy photoshoot he devised for a magazine article promoting his design featured naked models – quite enough to court controversy in the stuffy 1950s. When the chair made its New York debut, the police demanded it be removed from the shop window

**The organic form** of the Egg and Swan chair is characteristic of Jacobsen's style

**EGG CHAIR** Made of foam upholstered in wool and supported on an aluminium star-shaped base, the high-backed Egg chair was designed by Arne Jacobsen for Fritz Hansen of Denmark. *1957–58. H:106.5cm (42in).*

**SWAN CHAIR** Arne Jacobsen's chair is made of fabric-covered foam on a moulded fibreglass seat, with a swivelling cast-aluminium base. It was designed for Fritz Hansen of Denmark. *1957–58. H:74cm (29¾in).*

**The heart-shaped** back of the chair is constructed from bent sheet metal for stability

**The chair** takes its name from the womb-like design of the seat

**WOMB CHAIR** Eero Saarinen's chair and ottoman, designed for Knoll Associates, are made from fibreglass upholstered in foam-filled fabric over a bent tubular-steel frame. *1948–50. H:102.5cm (40in).*

**HEART CHAIR** Verner Panton's sculptural chair takes inspiration from the work of Arne Jacobsen. The metal frame and foam construction is fully upholstered in a bright red fabric. *1958. H:101.5cm (40in).*

**BUTTERFLY CHAIR** This early model of the chair designed by Antonio Bonet, Jorge Ferrari Hardoy, and Juan Kurchan has a leather seat. *1950s. H:87cm (34¼in).*

**DIAMOND CHAIR, MODEL 421LU** This sculptural chair has a vinyl-coated, bent and welded steel-rod body and frame, and was designed by Harry Bertoia for Knoll Associates. It would have had a thin, upholstered cushion. *1950–52. W:84.5cm (33¼in).*

## SOUND SCULPTURES

The royalties paid by Knoll Associates to Harry Bertoia for his immensely successful furniture line allowed him to concentrate on sculpture for the rest of his career. His oeuvre is instantly recognizable, consisting of serried rows of metal rods. Bertoia experimented with different types of metal, favouring strong, lightweight alloys such as beryllium copper, and with various shapes of rod, some capped with cylinders or discs to accentuate their kinetic qualities. The result was a series of sonorous sculptures that played a kind of music when touched by the wind or a hand. Bertoia even released a soundtrack, entitled *Sonambient,* of the sounds produced by these works of art.

**V SCULPTURE** In this sculpture by Harry Bertoia, two opposing groups of gilded bronze rods are mounted on a circular bronze base. *1960s. H:20cm (8in).*

after crowds stopping to look at it blocked the street. Like the Heart, its sister chair, the Cone was based on a very simple geometric form. In designing it, Panton had deliberately steered away from his preconceived ideas of what a chair should look like.

### ORGANIC SHAPES IN METAL

Emboldened by the phenomenal success of these radical designs, other designers looked back to the tubular-metal furniture of the pre-war European avant-garde and breathed new life into it, bringing it in line with the organic shapes of mid-century modernism. Tubular-metal frames and legs were already staples of the genre, featuring heavily in the work of Charles and Ray Eames, among others.

The Argentinian design collective Grupo Astral, comprising architects Antonio Bonet, Juan Kurchan, and Jorge Ferrari Hardoy, designed the Butterfly chair (Sling chair or A chair) in 1938. A modernization of Joseph Beverly Fenby's 1877 Tripolina chair, the Grupo Astral model was simply an angular bent and welded iron-rod frame slung with shaped leather upholstery. Later models were made with canvas seats rather than leather. The chair was extremely popular and is still produced today.

More remarkable was the Bertoia Collection, designed by Harry Bertoia for Knoll in the early 1950s. The wire construction he used was revolutionary and surprisingly delicate – as Bertoia said, his chairs were "made mainly of air".

Warren Platner took the idea further, drawing on the benefit of his five years' experience under Eero Saarinen. Aiming to produce furniture with the grace of Louis XV pieces, he relied on the beauty of his nickel-plated steel rods for decorative effect. The Platner Collection, issued by Knoll, included his 1725 table and stools, compared in the catalogue to sheaves of wheat. The hundreds of metal rods that make up these pieces all had to be welded by hand.

*The glass table top* seems to float above the elegant, spindle-shaped base

**DINING SET** With a nickel-plated steel-rod construction, the four stools are upholstered with foam and the table has a glass top. It was designed by Warren Platner for Knoll Associates. *1966. Table: H:71cm (28in).*

**PYRAMID CONE CHAIR** Designed by Verner Panton for Plus Linje of Copenhagen, this chair is of sheet metal construction with foam and cotton upholstery. *c.1960. H:95cm (37½in).*

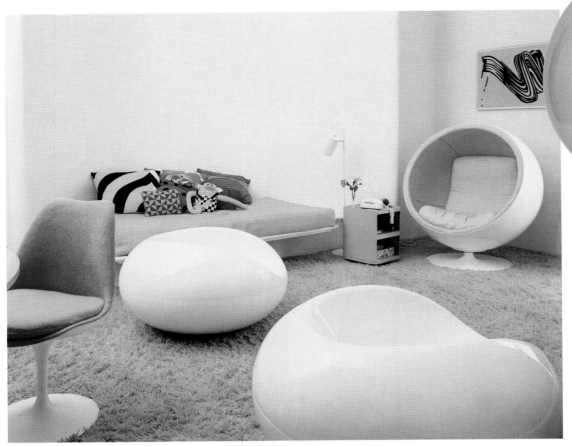

COOL PAD An early 1970s bedroom is furnished with sculpted plastic chairs by Eero Aarnio. The look is completed by cool white walls, a shaggy gold carpet, and a Roy Lichtenstein print.

BALL CHAIR The near-spherical shell of this Eero Aarnio chair is lined with blue fabric-covered foam and is mounted on a painted aluminium base. It was designed for Asko Oy of Finland. *1963–65. H:198cm (78in).*

*The chair* swivels on its own axis over the base

PASTIL CHAIR Designed by Eero Aarnio for Asko Oy of Finland, the fibreglass-reinforced polyester Pastil chair is moulded to fit the shape of the sitter. It can be rocked from side to side. *1967–68. W:92cm (36in).*

# PLASTIC FURNITURE

Good value, durable, colourful, and very versatile, plastic made an impact on the furniture industry during the 1950s and 1960s that was nothing short of sensational. Plastic, and plastic-reinforced fibreglass, allowed designers to realize at a stroke the ambitious forms they had been working towards through their exploratory use of plywood and sheet metal. The advent of injection-moulding technology removed all barriers, making it possible to mass-produce almost any shape quickly and cheaply.

Continuing along the trail-blazing trajectory that had taken him into new territory when most of his contemporaries were busy rediscovering their Scandinavian heritage, Verner Panton conceived his single-piece, cantilevered plastic chair in 1959. Production was delayed for years and the Panton chair finally debuted in 1967. By this time the radical design was in complete harmony with the Pop Art furniture that was then at the height of fashion, exemplified by iconic pieces such as Eero Aarnio's Ball chair.

## THE INFLUENCE OF AARNIO

Like his later Pastil (or Pastilli) chair, Aarnio's Ball was constructed from fibreglass-reinforced plastic. Particularly hardy as well as waterproof, this versatile material allowed consumers to use these products indoors or outdoors – the Pastil could even be floated on water. Consumers were also offered a choice of colours, the Ball originally being produced in black, white, red, and orange.

The premise of the Ball chair could not be more simple; it consisted of a hollowed, sliced sphere raised on a circular swivel base. The scope it presented for customization ensured its longevity – a cocoon insulated from the outside world, the chair was converted by some users into a listening station by the addition of speakers. Others used it as a base from which to make telephone calls.

The shape of the Pastil rocking chair, as suggested by its name, is extrapolated from a lozenge, or a piece of candy – the very epitome of the Pop movement. As Aarnio's most celebrated furniture designs, these two chairs share more than an aesthetic connection. The form of the Pastil is based on the void space of the Ball, and together they form a perfect, solid sphere, although this was not the original intention.

Peter Ghyczy's Garden Egg chair is influenced by Aarnio's Pastil and is again suitable for indoor or outdoor use. In this cult chair the foam upholstery was protected from the elements by the backrest, which folded down to create a watertight seal. The space-age pod design roots this chair firmly in the 1960s. Ghyczy built upon the success of the Garden Egg by founding his own studio and producing exclusive furniture for the top end of the market.

## LUIGI COLANI

Maverick designer Luigi Colani has built his career on plastics and created some extraordinary furniture in the process. His 1971 *Zocker* (Gambler)

STACKING SIDE CHAIR This is an early version of Verner Panton's S-chair. The first cantilevered chair made from injection-moulded plastic, it was produced by Fehlbaum Produktion of Germany. *c.1967–68. H:84cm (33in).*

*Panton's original design* for this chair was as early as 1959–60

*This version* is made from unlacquered Baydur hard foam

**ZOCKER** Made from seamless yellow polyurethane, this Top System *Zocker* designed by Luigi Colani is both a seat and a desk. *1971–72. H:62cm (24½in).*

chair, or *Sitzgerät* (Sitting Apparatus), evolved from a smaller model originally conceived as a piece of child's furniture. Colani is a firm believer in the importance of the ergonomics of good design, and the *Zocker* chair was designed to fit the contours of the human body. As well as functioning as a standard chair, it can be straddled, the backrest forming an integral table.

## THE LURE OF PLASTICS

The Italian designer Joe Colombo was also fascinated by plastics and, like Colani, he was interested in multifunctional designs. His 1969 Tube lounger, composed of four hollow cylinders that can be attached together in any configuration, is a typical example of his functional, versatile design. He pipped Verner Panton to the post in 1967 with his Universale 4860 chair, making it the first full-size injection-moulded chair on the market; the detachable and interchangeable legs made his chair more versatile but sacrificed some purity of design.

While Joe Colombo is well known for his chairs, lamps, and other household designs, he was also obsessed with storage units and trolleys. His greatest achievement in this particular field was the Boby storage trolley, a wheeled unit with rotating drawers that has been a bestseller ever since its inception in 1970.

The first designer to successfully draft a single-piece moulded chair of traditional four-legged design was Vico Magistretti. His Selene chair used S-shaped legs, which gave it the required structural strength.

The lure of plastics was to prove irresistible even to the leading lights of the studio furniture movement. Wendell Castle's Molar Group furniture products, dating from the late 1960s, saw the designer apply his vision to the material that defined the age. One of the biggest attractions for Castle was the possibility of colouring plastic in any shade. "One day it just dawned on me that everything I had been making was brown," he said.

**STORAGE TROLLEY** Designed by Joe Colombo, this trolley has hinged drawers and compartments stacked one above the other. It is made from injection-moulded ABS plastic and was produced by Bieffeplast of Germany. *1970. H:53cm (21in).*

**GARDEN EGG CHAIR** The fibreglass-reinforced polyester shell of this chair is hinged at the back and lifts up to reveal an upholstered interior. When closed, it has a flattened ovoid form. It was designed by Peter Ghyczy for Reuter Produkts of Germany. *1968. L:82cm (32¼in).*

**MOLAR GROUP COFFEE TABLE** As the name suggests, the range was inspired by the shape of molar teeth. This is one of the few designs in plastic by Wendell Castle. *1969. H:58.5cm (23in).*

**The shape of** the table top is mirrored in the base

**The table** has a swivel action at the point where it is at its narrowest

# FURNITURE GALLERY

Post-war modernist furniture explored new, often sculptural forms. This development was aided by the birth of new materials such as laminate and plastic that allowed for greater flexibility in design. Bright primary colours were fashionable and often covered the entire structure, making a bold statement. Wooden furniture remained popular, with the simple, elegant designs produced in Scandinavia influencing designers worldwide.

## KEY

**1**. Coffee table by Isamu Noguchi. 1944. H:37cm (14½in). ③ **2**. Double school bench designed by Jean Prouvé, for Ateliers Prouvé-V.S.A. c.1948. W:120cm (47¼in). ③ **3**. Greta Magnusson Grossman coffee table with three circular tops laminated in primary colours. c.1965. W:58in (145cm). ⑤ **4**. Austrian coffee table, the red synthetic top with swivelling, detachable grey-plastic tray. 1960s. D:62cm (24½in). ① **5**. Ebonized chest-on-stand by Tommi Parzinger, the drawer with silver-leaf front. c.1952. H:90cm (36in). ③ **6**. Pair of low bronze tables by Philip LaVerne, decorated with an Oriental motif. 1960s. H:43cm (17in). ③ **7**. Jean Prouvé wall-hanging cabinet with a single sliding door and enamelled metal compartments. 1950s. H:296cm (116½in). ⑤ **8**. Sideboard by Finn Juhl. c.1950. L:208cm (82in). ③ **9**. Coffee table by Roger Capron, its top with geometrically shaped tiles. 1960s.

1 *Isamu Noguchi coffee table*

2 *Jean Prouvé school bench*

3 *Greta Magnusson Grossman coffee table*

4 *Austrian coffee table*

5 *Tommi Parzinger chest-on-stand*

6 *Philip LaVerne tables*

7 *Jean Prouvé cabinet*

8 *Finn Juhl sideboard*

10 *Paul McCobb credenza*

9 *Roger Capron coffee table*

11 *Tommi Parzinger sideboard*

W:121.5cm (47¾in). ③ 10. Paul McCobb credenza with sliding cloth doors and two adjustable shelves. c.1950. W:152.5cm (60in). ③ 11. Custom-designed sideboard with orange-lacquered finish by Tommi Parzinger. 1950s. W:213.5cm (84in). ⑤ 12. Malitte seat system by Roberto Matta, consisting of five foam elements. 1966. H:157.5cm (62in). ⑤ 13. Oskar Hodosi Fleur seat, made of polyurethane and foam-rubber padding with purple fabric. 1969. H:84cm (33in). ③ 14. Mezzadro stool by Achille and Pier Giacomo Castiglioni. 1957. H:51cm (20in). ① 15. Pair of George Nelson Coconut chairs. 1955. L:101cm (39¾in). ④ 16. Pelican chair by Finn Juhl. 1940. H:71cm (28in). 17. Sessel Karuselli armchair designed by Yrjö Kukkapuro, with fibreglass and leather seat and chrome base. 1965. H:90cm (35½in). ③ 18. Allunaggio outdoor stool, with steel legs and an aluminium alloy seat, by Achille and Pier Giacomo Castiglioni. 1965. H:74cm (29in). ③ 19. Fibreglass Group armchair by Erwine and Estelle Laverne. H:75cm (29¼in). ②

12 *Malitte seat system*

14 *Mezzadro stool*

13 *Oskar Hodosi Fleur seat*

15 *George Nelson Coconut chair*

16 *Finn Juhl Pelican chair*

17 *Sessel Karuselli chair, designed by Yrjö Kukkapuro*

18 *Allunaggio outdoor stool*

19 *Fibreglass Group armchair*

# CERAMICS

MID-CENTURY CERAMICS ENCOMPASSED BOTH MASS-PRODUCED
WARES AND THE STUDIO POTTERY MOVEMENT, WHICH CONTINUED
TO BLUR THE BOUNDARIES BETWEEN CERAMIC CRAFT AND FINE ART.

*Organic, asymmetrical* designs, like this one, are typical of the 1950s

**REPTIL VASE** Designed by Stig Lindberg for Gustavsberg of Sweden, this yellow-glaze vase has a textured surface reminiscent of the reptile skin after which it is named. *1950s. H:18.5cm (7¼in).*

**LARGE BOWL** This is an early and unique example of Bjørn Winblad's studio work. It is handpainted in a design typical of his themes of folklore and fairy tales. *1956. D:47cm (18½in).*

**TEAPOTS** These matte-glazed porcelain teapots, designed by Ulla Procopé for Arabia of Finland, betray Asian influences in the rounded shape of the pots, the flattened lids, and the cane handles. *c.1957. H:15cm (6in).*

## SCANDINAVIAN CERAMICS

Mid-century Scandinavian ceramics occupied a curious middle ground between factory production and art pottery. Some of the larger companies opened public galleries at their premises, both enhancing their image within the community and subtly encouraging competition among their designers. In 1932 the Finnish company Arabia established a studio in which artists could work free from the pressures of the factory environment and production quotas, which proved to be an extremely fruitful venture in terms of generating new design ideas.

During the late 1940s Arabia designer Kaj Franck responded to the austerities of war by producing the aesthetically and financially lean Kilta service. This economy of style became a hallmark of Scandinavian ceramic design, and was instrumental in the success achieved by Finnish factories at a series of Milan Triennale shows throughout the 1950s. Franck gathered a talented team around him at Arabia that included Ulla Procopé, whose well-proportioned table- and ovenware had a sculptural quality that belied its functional role.

Swedish potters enjoyed success on the same scale as their Finnish neighbours. The 1930 *Stockholmsutsällningen* (Stockholm Exhibition), directed by architect Gunnar Asplund, highlighted the extent to which Swedish ceramicists had embraced the modernist ideals of the Bauhaus, and marked the beginning of a golden age that peaked in the 1950s.

The Gustavsberg pottery followed the lead established by Arabia and founded an experimental studio in 1942. Many of the designs that successfully made the migration from the drawing board to the production floor were devised by Stig Lindberg, the dominant figure of Swedish pottery in this period, who took over artistic directorship of Gustavsberg in 1949. His work for the company included a series of hand-painted faience bowls in the 1940s and 1950s, and the Reptil range of textured vases and bowls in various matte and, less frequently, gloss glazes during the 1950s. His work is mostly associated with his plates, dishes, and bowls that mimic natural, organic forms.

## INSPIRATION FROM NATURE

This kind of biomorphic style also prevailed at Rörstrand, another Swedish factory. Both Carl-Harry Stålhane and Gunnar Nylund had a background in sculpture before turning their attentions to ceramic design and this is evident in their pieces. Both worked primarily with stoneware, producing vessels with decorative schemes steeped in the French abstract traditions of the Cubists and other modern art movements.

**RÖRSTRAND BOWL** Biomorphic forms and motifs were not uncommon in Scandinavian design, as in this oblong bowl with a spiral relief pattern designed by Carl-Harry Stålhane for Rörstrand of Sweden. *L:20cm (8in).*

**MARSELIS VASE** The geometric Marselis pattern is seen in a striking green glaze on this Royal Copenhagen Alumina faience vase by Nils Thorsson. *1950s–60s. H:11cm (4¼in).*

The most enduring of the products issued by the Rörstrand factory in the mid-20th century was Louise Adelborg's Grace porcelain dinner service. The repeated relief pattern depicting ears of wheat is typically Scandinavian in its homage to the sustaining bounty of nature.

This love of the Scandinavian countryside can also be seen in the work of Danish polymath Bjørn Winblad. His early slip-decorated ceramic forms, first exhibited in 1944, draw on the woodland and water spirits of Nordic folklore. Winblad used archaic Scandinavian potter's tools such as a cow horn and goose quill to manipulate his slip (clay and water mix), giving it a naive, even crude aspect that makes his subject matter all the more unsettling.

## ROYAL COPENHAGEN

In Denmark potter Gertrud Vasegaard successfully lobbied first Bing & Grøndahl and then Royal Copenhagen to tailor their materials and production methods in order to realize her own artistic vision. This extraordinary flexibility demonstrates both the high esteem in which Vasegaard's stoneware vessels were held and the willingness of Scandinavian industry to accommodate its best designers. This certainly paid dividends for Royal Copenhagen, which found huge sales with Grethe Meyer's simple dinner services and a porcelain service of organic design by Henning Koppel in the early 1960s.

The output of the Alumina factory that produced earthenware ranges for Royal Copenhagen was dominated by designs by Nils Thorsson. His Marselis range of affordable, functional wares was decorated sparingly with ribs and geometric patterns picked out on solid glazes in natural tones.

## STIG LINDBERG

Frederick Sigurd (Stig) Lindberg wanted to forge a career as a painter until he was taken under the wing of Wilhelm Kåge at Gustavsberg in 1937 at the age of 21. His tenure at the firm went on to span almost 50 years, lasting right up until his death in 1982. Lindberg's output was extremely diverse, ranging from wall plaques with applied figural decoration through folk-inspired wares, and his celebrated leaf-decorated dishes to the starkly geometric and monochrome Dominio series of platters. Lindberg remains one of Sweden's favourite cultural figures and his legacy continues to exert an enormous influence on contemporary Scandinavian ceramic design.

**SWEDISH FAIENCE PLATTER** One of Stig Lindberg's popular leaf-decorated ceramics, this platter was designed for Gustavsberg of Sweden. *c.1948. L:31.5cm (12½in).*

**LAMP BASE** Designed by Carl-Harry Stålhane for Rörstrand of Sweden, this porcelain lamp base is square in form and has an abstract design repeated in reverse on alternate sides. *c.1970. H:24.5cm (9¾in).*

**SALAD BOWL** In Lindberg's earthenware salad bowl designed for Gustavsberg, the shape is accentuated with simple stripes that radiate from a "stalk" at one end of the bowl. *c.1950. H:24cm (9½in).*

# THE MASS MARKET

The mid-century notion of the happy home ruled by a dedicated housewife was a powerful driving force behind the rampant consumerism of the age. One of its most enduring legacies is the matching dinner service. While fine porcelain tableware had been the preserve of the wealthy, cheaper ceramic services were more democratic and their use permeated every strata of society.

One of the most remarkably successful lines of mass-produced tableware started life outside a factory. When Russell Wright began to draft the first designs for his American Modern dinner service in 1937, the manufacturers he approached were unwilling to invest in it. He eventually persuaded the Steubenville Pottery of Ohio – a previously bankrupted firm – to resume operations and take up the challenge. The organic style of this new service was informed by Surrealist art; the hard ceramic appears soft and mutable, bringing to mind Dali's melting clocks. Wright was perhaps also paying tribute to his Quaker background by exercising great restraint and keeping the shapes simple and free of extraneous ornament. The progressive colour scheme he developed included a pale pink shade called Coral and a green, named Seafoam.

The Steubenville Pottery's gamble paid off. Wright accompanied the 1940 launch of American Modern tableware with a marketing campaign advertising the service as a starter set, appealing to the home-making instincts of young couples. It flew off the shelves, earning Wright a million dollars in royalties and becoming the biggest-selling dinner service ever.

**STEUBENVILLE TEAPOT**
Russell Wright designed his American Modern range in the late 1930s and Steubenville produced it from 1940 to 1961. The Bean Brown seen here was an early colour. *L:25.5cm (10in).*

Similar organic forms and unusual colours can be seen in the Town and Country service designed by Eva Zeisel for the Red Wing Pottery in the 1940s. The handles of her dishes resemble fish tails and her pitchers have handles and spouts that look as if they have been peeled back from the mouth of the vessel.

## CERAMICS IN THE UK

Imitation of Wright's phenomenally successful dinner service was widespread, and not limited to the United States. Roy Midwinter, sales director of the Midwinter pottery in Staffordshire, was advised by an American buyer to travel to the west coast of the United States to learn from Wright's

**PRIMAVERA PLATE** The Stylecraft shape of this plate is characteristic of Midwinter's embracement of American designs. Primavera was designed by Jessie Tait. *c.1954. D:24.5cm (9½in).*

## FIESTA WARE

Frederick Hurten Rhead, artistic director of the Laughlin China Company in East Virginia, introduced Fiesta ware in 1936. His use of primary colours, geometric forms, and industrial production resulted in a range of ceramics for everyday use that the Bauhaus would have been proud of. The forms consist of little more than plain, circular and globular shapes, decorated simply with concentric circles in relief. Bright glazes in tones of yellow, red, blue, and white complete the minimalist modern aesthetic. Unusual design features include the "cut-out" section of the pitcher with a thin strip of ceramic forming the handle, following the circular outline of the body. Loop handles on the teapot and cups continue this single-minded devotion to the circle. Fiesta ware was particularly popular in the post-war period. It was undoubtedly an important influence on Russell Wright and, through him, on British potteries such as Midwinter.

**FIESTA WARE PITCHER**
Frederick Hurten Rhead's pitcher, here in yellow, exemplifies the Art Deco styling of the range, with its aerodynamic, near-spherical form and concentric-circle decoration. *1930s–50s. H:18cm (7in).*

**TUREEN WITH LID**
The geometric decoration emphasizes the tureen's tapered form. It was designed by Marianne Westmann for Rörstrand in 1956, with production continuing until 1969. *H:22cm (8¾in).*

**FIESTA WARE CRUET SET** Strong, bold colours were, and still are, a hallmark of the Fiesta ware range, as seen here in this pair of cobalt-blue salt and pepper shakers. *1930s–50s. H:6.5cm (2½in).*

**BOHUS BERSA BOWL** This high-fired earthenware bowl, transfer-decorated with a geometric leaf pattern, was designed by Stig Lindberg for Gustavsberg in 1960 and stayed in production until 1974. *D:16cm (6¼in).*

production if he wanted to make the most of the American export market. He did just that, and once British post-war austerity measures were lifted, he had his modellers design an entirely new line of shapes called the Stylecraft range.

After the Stylecraft wares were launched in 1953, the enthusiastic reception they received was due in no small part to the decorative schemes devised by Jessie Tait. Her 1954 Primavera pattern, comprising cartouches of diverse shapes containing a mix of stylized floriform and geometric motifs, was an early success. Another favourite was the Zambesi pattern, made up of handpainted zebra stripes with rims and handles painted in red. Terence Conran also contributed patterns to the Stylecraft line, including Plant Life, Chequers, and Melody, the names evoking the mix of floral, geometric, and symbolic decoration that the range encompassed.

The Homemaker pattern, designed by Enid Seeney for Ridgway in 1956 and sold by Woolworths in Britain, is a quintessentially mid-century design. Among other motifs, the repeating pattern includes a Robin Day armchair and a Sigvard Bernadotte sofa. Ridgway also produced the Barbecue pattern in a similar style, depicting kebabs ready for roasting.

## POOLE AND PORTMEIRION

Mass-produced Scandinavian ceramics such as those made by Rörstrand were a rich mine of inspiration for Alfred Read, head of design at Poole Pottery from 1952 to 1957. The works had been largely rebuilt following the war and Read reinvigorated the pottery's output, introducing a range of contemporary shapes such as the Peanut vase, available in various sizes. These new forms were decorated with either a solid colour glaze or Read's own banded patterns that incorporated stylized ferns and other natural forms as well as more abstract geometric designs.

The textile designer Susan Williams-Ellis

**HOMEMAKER TRIO SET** The transfer-printed design by Enid Seeney for Ridgways features domestic motifs on a striated ground. *c.1957. Cup: H:7cm (2¾in); Saucer: D:14cm (5½in); Plate: D:18cm (7in).*

started production at the Portmeirion Pottery using blanks she obtained from Gray's Pottery. The different diameters and lengths suggested to her a cylindrical coffee set, which is exactly what she produced. The enforced simplicity of her shapes proved an instant hit, encouraging her to experiment with surface decoration. In 1963 Williams-Ellis unveiled her Totem pattern, consisting of embossed geometric shapes and available in blue, amber, and olive.

**PEANUT VASE** This Poole Pottery Peanut vase is decorated with the geometric PKT pattern in alternating strips of blue and red with white. It was designed by Alfred Read and painted by Gwen Haskins in around 1953, and remained in production into the 1960s. *H:34cm (13½in).*

**ZAMBESI COFFEE SET** The striking black-and-white pattern accentuates the slightly angular forms of this Midwinter pottery Zambesi pattern coffee set, comprising coffeepot, sugar bowl, cream jug, and six cups and saucers. It was designed by Jessie Tait. *1956. Coffeepot: H:19cm (7½in).*

# STUDIO POTTERY

The fledgling studio pottery movement went from strength to strength during the mid-20th century, as the seeds of creativity planted by Bernard Leach and Shoji Hamada began to flourish. The new generation at the Leach Pottery in St Ives included David Leach, son of founder Bernard, and Janet, who became Bernard Leach's third wife in the early 1950s. While David Leach's work is mainly functional, with interior glazes and plain outer surfaces, Janet Leach developed a more eclectic idiom, building complex bottles, flasks, and vases from multiple thrown forms accompanied by coiled constructions.

*The volcanic glaze* gives a heavily textured surface, which is characteristic of Beatrice Wood's work

**VESSEL AND VASE** In these two fine sculptural forms by Beatrice Wood, the vessel has a blue-green mottled volcanic glaze and the tapered vase a uranium-red volcanic glaze. Both are signed "Beato". *Vessel: H:15cm (6in); Vase: H:39cm (15½in).*

*The near-spherical vessel* has a short neck and very small opening

The most prolific of Bernard Leach's early pupils was Michael Cardew, who revived a defunct pottery in Gloucestershire and, together with a local potter, rediscovered historical slip-decoration techniques. Then, in 1942 Cardew performed a complete volte-face and swapped the production of traditional English red earthenware with slip-trailed designs for teaching at an art college in the Gold Coast (now Ghana) in West Africa. Opting to stay in the area, he later opened the Volta Pottery and lived between Britain and Africa until 1965. His studies of traditional Nigerian pottery and his own experiments led to his publication of *Pioneer Pottery*, still valued by contemporary potters for its extensive technical notes.

Shoji Hamada's influence was most evident in the work of William Staite Murray, who was involved with Wyndham Lewis and the Vorticist movement in the early 20th century. Already a potter, after meeting Hamada in the 1920s, Murray became interested in Oriental high-fire glazes. He constructed his own kiln at Rotherhithe in London, where he attempted to re-create classical Chinese effects such as the dark temmoko glaze.

## AMERICAN STUDIO POTTERY

Many of the boldest advances in studio pottery at this time were made in the United States by individuals with a background in the fine arts. Beatrice Wood, the daughter of San Francisco socialites, attended the prestigious Académie Julian in Paris before settling in New York and falling in with a group of actors and Dadaists. Her relationship with Marcel Duchamp and Henri-Pierre Roché is supposed to have inspired the novel

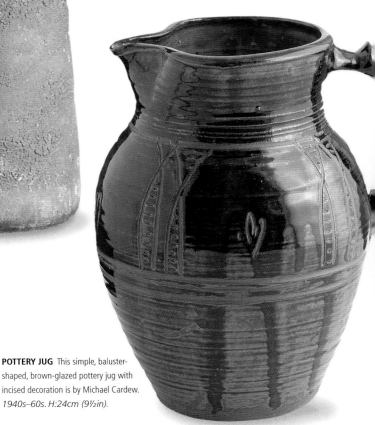

*The bowl* is covered with a typical ash-green glaze

**STONEWARE BOWL** Designed by Katherine Pleydell-Bouverie, this elegant bowl of simple form bears an impressed seal mark and is incised "280". *1940s–60s. D:14.5cm (5¾in).*

**POTTERY JUG** This simple, baluster-shaped, brown-glazed pottery jug with incised decoration is by Michael Cardew. *1940s–60s. H:24cm (9½in).*

and subsequent film, *Jules et Jim*. Wood did not become interested in ceramics until she was in her forties, by which time she had become an adherent of the Theosophical Society. This occasioned her move in 1948 to Ojai, in California, to be close to Jiddu Krishnamurti.

Wood's pottery is primarily sculptural; many of her vessels have tiny apertures that make them unsuitable for any practical use. During this period she developed a range of volcanic glazes in bright colours and earth tones characterized by myriad tiny pits on the surface of her vessels. Other characteristic features of her varied output include the use of applied decoration inspired by India.

## MAIJA GROTELL

A generation of teacher-practitioners in the United States propagated the concept of modern studio pottery and its place in ceramic tradition. One of

## OTTO AND GERTRUD NATZLER

Husband and wife team Otto and Gertrud Natzler were born in Vienna. After winning a silver medal at the 1937 World's Exposition in Paris they settled in southern California. They divided their work between them, according to their own specialities: Gertrud worked the wheel while Otto formulated the glazes and fired the pots. They quickly won respect in their small community of Californian ceramicists by insisting on using the local clay at a time when many of their contemporaries preferred to import it from elsewhere. Gertrud initially concentrated on fashioning bowls because they were more likely to sell but, as her fame spread, she began to produce other vessels including gourds and bottles as well as reproductions of natural forms including seed pods and shells. Otto's porous glazes, at first considered defective by many commentators, included Crater, Pompei and Lava. His experiments with kiln conditions included the introduction of drafts at various stages of the firing and the use of many different reduction agents.

**BOWL AND VASE** The large, hemispheric bowl is covered in a gunmetal and deep-purple crystalline glaze, with oxblood flashes to the exterior, while the monumental bulbous vase is covered in a blue-green striated volcanic glaze. *1960s. Bowl: H:119.5cm (7¾in); Vase: H:44.5cm (17½in).*

**FOOTED BOWL** This fine Maija Grotell stoneware footed bowl has a sheer, flowing, umber lustre glaze to the exterior and a white, crackled interior. The bowl is incised "MG". *1940s–60s. D:23cm (9in).*

the most dedicated was Maija Grotell, who had studied under Alfred William Finch in her native Finland before settling in the United States in 1927. Her most long-lived teaching post was at the Cranbrook Academy of Art between 1938 and 1966, which brought her into contact with leading exponents of American mid-century modernism, including Charles Eames. It was thanks to Grotell's research into glazes that Eero Saarinen was able to include glazed bricks in his design for the General Motors Technical Centre. Among her many innovations were a number of bright turquoise hues made using copper oxides.

Grotell's skill at the wheel was such that she could throw perfect pots of immense weight. She would often repeat the same design, improving it by increments until she finally reproduced exactly the form she had in mind before moving on to her next project.

Among the many pupils that she inspired was Toshiko Takaezu, born in Hawaii. Takaezu was enthused by Grotell's Scandinavian interest in landscape,

combining it with her own Zen Buddhist beliefs. As her career progressed, Takaezu became entranced by Abstract Expressionism, making her wares progressively less functional. This eventually culminated in a series of ceramics built together from numerous component thrown vessels.

**SLAB VASE** Janet Leach's stoneware slab vase is decorated at the front with brushstrokes of brown on a speckled blue, white, and buff ground. The vase bears the impressed mark "JL". *1940s–60s. H:27.5cm (11in).*

*The design* is inspired by Japanese pots

*Celadon glaze* is a traditional Chinese glaze

**LOWERDOWN POTTERY FOOTED VASE** David Leach's vase has curved and fluted decoration and a celadon glaze. It is impressed with the "DL" seal. *1960s. H:13.5cm (5½in).*

## FIGURES AND FORMS

During this mid-century period a growing number of studio ceramicists started to use pottery as a canvas for figural forms and other ideas that had previously been the preserve of fine art. Many of these ceramicists were classically trained artists who had either switched from a career behind the easel or were keen to expand their repertoire in a different medium.

Trained as an artist at Stanford University and in London and Paris, Henry Varnum Poor felt that ceramic art was the only medium to offer him complete control of his work. His oeuvre, mainly dishes and vases with painted and sgraffito figural decoration, was motivated by a mistrust of the march towards conformity and perfection that

characterized corporate modernism in the United States. His priority, he said, was to gain intimate knowledge of his medium: "Clays are like wines – part of the flavour comes from knowing the hillsides and vineyards that grew the grapes."

### FOLK ART TRADITIONS

Edwin and Mary Scheier learned the art of pottery while watching over kilns on behalf of colleagues at the Federal Art project in Tennessee during the late 1930s. Finding that they were increasingly drawn to the medium, the couple embarked on a tour of the southern states, discovering the folk art traditions of the region. They set up a studio in Glade Spring, Virginia, after spotting untapped deposits of red clay there. Their work soon

**FAIENCE CHARGER** This charger by Henry Varnum Poor has sgrafitto decoration and is handpainted in yellow, green, and brown glazes. It is signed "HVP 47". *1947. D:32cm (12¾in).*

*The curving* form contrasts with the geometric, linear pattern, reinforcing its modernity

**FAIENCE FIGURES** These Fantoni faience figures depict a pair of Venetian revellers in the Cubist style. Each is covered in a bright polychrome glaze. *1950s. Tallest: H:38cm (15in).*

*The bright colours* and angular forms are reminiscent of Cubist paintings

*The matte glazed* finish is a typical feature of much of Fantoni's work

**FAIENCE VASE** Guido Gambone's bottle-shaped faience vase is painted with Cubist figures in an indigo and matte-white glaze. *H:28.5cm (11¼in).*

garnered national acclaim, and they were invited to teach at the University of New Hampshire.

In 1946 the Scheiers took a sabbatical to train workers for Puerto Rico's ceramics industry, developing an appreciation of that country's art and its African influence. They believed that ceramic vessels could convey "some aspect of the human spirit" and dealt with basic human themes such as birth and protection. Edwin's simple line drawings, done by combining sgraffito and relief decoration, give their work a naivety reminiscent of tribal art.

## ANCIENT EUROPEAN FORMS

The figural tendency in mid-century Italian studio pottery was expressed most eloquently by two Florentine potters – Guido Gambone and Marcello Fantoni. Gambone's exaggerated stoneware and earthenware vessels often have simple, painted decoration and thick lava glazes. Despite his modern techniques, his work frequently harks back to ancient Etruscan pottery in its simplicity.

Fantoni was a far more prolific practitioner who gathered around him a vast pool of talented students. Like Gambone's work, Fantoni's ceramic sculptures and vessels reference Etruscan forms. His sympathies for modern art and his Italian heritage combined to create something new and unique.

Frenchman Georges Jouve also looked back to ancient European forms, even as he explored modern techniques. He did much to develop the art of ceramic glazing, his use of selenium leading to some extraordinarily vivid colours.

## FRENCH AND SPANISH FORMS

Some of the most individualistic ceramic works of the period were wrought by the titans of modern art. Pablo Picasso worked with potters Georges and Suzanne Ramie at the Madoura pottery in Vallauris, France, from 1947. He would manipulate clay bottles the Ramies had

TERRACOTTA CHARGER Designed by Jean Cocteau, this red terracotta charger is painted with a female profile with a yellow eye on a blue and white striped ground. It is signed and dated with the manufacturer's marks. *Late 1950s. D:35.5cm (14in).*

*MAINS AU POISSON* Picasso's ceramic plate, designed for Madoura, is moulded with two black hands and a fish in terracotta, green, and cobalt. This is 37 from an edition of 250, stamped "*Empreinte Originale de Picasso/Madoura Plein Feu*". *c.1954. D:30.5cm (12in).*

EARLY SCHEIER FOOTED FLOOR VASE Decorated with typical tribal imagery, the vase is covered in a volcanic bronze glaze against a graduated matte-turquoise glaze. *1966. H:56cm (22½in).*

FOOTED VASE An example of Georges Jouve's work, this ceramic vase has an applied high-relief sun with rays and face, with incised compass directions above and below. *c.1948. H:30.5cm (12in).*

left to dry into figural and animal shapes, working against traditional ceramic form. His own designs are decorated with stylized depictions of the body, similar to those in his drawn and painted work.

Joan Miró was equally comfortable with clay and canvas. He worked alongside Spanish ceramicist Josep Llorens Artigas during World War II, painting the potter's vases and plaques. Miró eventually started to mould his own forms based on objects he found around Artigas's farm, indulging his Surrealist's impulse to elevate the accidental to high art.

At the height of his fame in the late 1950s, Jean Cocteau found refuge from public expectation in the workshop of Philippe Madeline in Villefranche-sur-Mer. He developed a method of "drawing" directly onto terracotta, and became so enthused with this new medium that he found it hard to bear the frustration of waiting for his chargers and vessels to cool after the firing process.

# CERAMICS GALLERY

Mid-century modernism saw a dichotomy in the production of ceramics. The simple shapes that were fashionable could be produced cheaply in factories, yet studio ceramics also enjoyed a renaissance. Scandinavian design was highly influential, especially the bold patterns that were handpainted onto studio pieces and transfer-printed onto mass-produced wares.

## KEY

**1**. Villeroy & Boch Acapulco pattern tray, with printed marks. 1960s. L:30cm (12in). ①
**2**. Troika pottery wheel vase, modelled in relief with a face design, painted marks. 1970s. H:19.5cm (7¾in). ① **3**. Midwinter pottery Plant Life pattern plate designed by Terence Conran. 1956. W:30cm (11¾in). ① **4**. Denby Arabesque pattern handpainted coffeepot designed by Gill Pemberton. 1964–70s. H:31cm (12¼in). ① **5**. Swedish Gustavsberg wall plaque by Lisa Larson, with a stylized bird design. 1960s. W:28cm (11in). ① **6**. Tête-à-Tête porcelain tea set by Trude Petri for KPM Berlin. c.1950. Saucer: D:13cm (5in). ② **7**. Portmeirion Tivoli pattern Seraph coffee set designed by Susan Williams-Ellis. c.1964. H:31cm (12¼in). ① **8**. Midwinter pottery Cannes pattern celery vase designed by Terence Conran. 1960. H:17cm (6¾in). ① **9**. Antonio Prieto ovoid vase, decorated in

2 Troika pottery wheel vase

3 Terence Conran plate

5 Gustavsberg wall plaque

1 Villeroy & Boch tray

4 Denby Arabesque coffeepot

6 Trude Petri tea set

7 Portmeirion coffee set

sgraffito. 1950s. H:26cm (10¼in). ③ **10.** Danish Royal Copenhagen Tenera vase by Bert Jessen, with a stylized flower design. 1970s. H:19cm (7½in). ① **11.** Ebb Tide large conch basket by A. Hull, with a stylized fish handle. c.1960. H: 25.5cm (10in). ① **12.** H.J. Wood Piazza ware vase. c.1957. H:24cm (9½in). ① **13.** Richard Batterham cut-sided bowl, with a green-grey glaze. 1960s. H:14.5cm (5¾in). ① **14.** Norwegian Stavangerflint bowl, with handpainted decoration. 1950s. H:11.5cm (4½in). ① **15.** Danish Palshus Torpedo vase by Per Linnermann-Schmidt, in a blue haresfur glaze. 1950s. H:22cm (8¾in). ① **16.** Italian Bistosi Rimini Blu vase decorated with impressed symbols and a blue glaze. c.1960. H:21cm (8¼in). ① **17.** Royal Haeger shell vase with moulded marks. 1950s. H:18cm (7in). ① **18.** Troika St Ives Pottery chimney vase, with a green-blue glazed ground and geometric embossed panels. c.1970. H:20cm (8in). ②

**10** Bert Jessen vase

**9** Antonio Prieto vase

**8** Terence Conran vase

**11** Ebb Tide conch basket

**12** Piazza ware vase

**13** Richard Batterham bowl

**16** Bistosi vase

**14** Stavangerflint bowl

**15** Torpedo vase

**17** Royal Haeger shell vase

**18** Troika St Ives chimney vase

# GLASS

MID-CENTURY GLASS DESIGN WAS LED BY SCANDINAVIAN FACTORIES AND BY
MASTER GLASSMAKERS IN MURANO WHO SUCCESSFULLY REVIVED THE
ANCIENT CRAFT OF THEIR ISLAND.

**APPLE VASE** Ingeborg Lundin's Apple vase, designed for Orrefors of Sweden, has extremely fragile-looking thinly blown walls and a short neck to suggest the stalk of the fruit. *1957. H:37cm (14½in).*

## COLOURED GLASS

The flawless surfaces and soft natural hues of vessels produced by the Orrefors factory in Sweden exemplify Scandinavian glass design of this period. Nils Landberg's delicate *Tulpanglas* was an early, iconic Orrefors shape, manufactured in various permutations of proportion and colour. Its slender, attenuated trumpet stem balances the long, flute-like bowl. He also devised a jug with a distinctive ice-catching lip that remains in production.

Landberg's abstractionist treatment of the tulip found a mirror in Ingeborg Lundin's Apple vase, which has a globular body and a diminutive neck that is reminiscent of an apple's stalk. Both Landberg and Lundin used colour and form in a way that aimed to incorporate the Scandinavian landscape into their work. These references to the natural world are often subtle or oblique, as if seen through mist and rain beneath a darkening sky.

The cool colours and organic forms seen on glass manufactured by the Danish firms Holmegaard and Kastrup represent a veritable celebration of the chromatic possibilities of glass. Both firms are known for the clarity of their glass. Per Lutken succeeded Jacob Bang as staff designer at Holmegaard in 1942 and used splashes and streaks of colour to enliven his clear and opaque white glass forms. The coloured opaline feet of his *Vintergaek* (Snowdrop) range are echoed in the opaline patches that mottle their otherwise clear glass bowls.

Lutken employed similar techniques in his sculptural work. His free-blown Forms dating from the 1970s are made from semi-opaque white glass with streaky brown, red, and blue inclusions.

**TULPANGLAS** A hallmark of Swedish design, this is an elegant form with a tulip-shaped bowl on a tall, slender stem. It was designed by Nils Landberg for Orrefors. *1957. H:51.5cm (21in).*

Lutken's Carnaby glass vases paved the way for the bold plastic forms and colours of Michael Bang's later Palet range. Bang joined Holmegaard in 1968 and helped bring the company into the Pop era. His Palet tableware used a layer of opaque white glass cased with a brighter colour, a combination that made his pieces resemble the plastics that were so crucial in other decorative art of the period. It was the first Holmegaard range to use bright red and yellow cased glass.

### RIIHIMÄEN LASI OY GLASSWARE

A trio of female designers – Helena Tynell, Nanny Still, and Tamara Aladin – was largely responsible for the mid-century success of Riihimäen Lasi Oy. Tynell joined the firm in 1946 and is best remembered for her textured forms such as the Emma vase. This geometric mould-blown vase with patterning is also known for its jewel-like

colours, which include a brilliant ruby red. Tynell's even more complex Pironki vase was manufactured in pale translucent shades, the edges appearing darker and so giving the form more definition.

### KAJ FRANCK

Also in Finland, the multi-talented Kaj Franck turned his attention to glassware on behalf of Nuutajärvi Notsjo. Many of his designs were produced in a range of strong colours in recognition of a public appetite for colourful glassware that grew ever more voracious from the 1950s onwards. Some of Franck's earliest experiments in this direction resulted in his 1952 *Saippuakupla* (Soap Bubble) line of simple and elegant oviform coloured glass vessels.

As Franck became more ambitious, he began to set himself new challenges. Among these was his self-imposed quest to devise a carafe that

**KASTRUP VASE** This vase is typical of Jacob Bang's work with its clean lines, austerity, and lack of surface decoration. It concentrates instead on form and colour. *1950s. H:21cm (8¼in).*

**NAEBVASE VASE** The name of this asymmetrical, heavy-based vase means "beak vase". It was designed by Per Lutken for Holmegaard. *1959. H:16.5cm (6½in).*

**The rims** are pulled out, accentuating the organic, bud-like form. The design was highly influential

**BLUE VASE** Kaj Franck produced a number of minimal designs for Nuutajärvi Notsjo. Here a tall, blue-case vase stands on a thick, clear-glass base. *1960s. H:30cm (12in).*

didn't require a handle and so could be made more quickly and cheaply. His solutions included a waisted design from 1954 that the user could grip around the middle. This was made available in a rainbow of bright translucent colours, accompanied by matching tapering tumblers. He later came up with a decanter form with a handhold neck and an idiosyncratic stopper in the form of a speckled pink, red, and blue cockerel.

Franck's Luna range of functional pressed glass tableware was prompted by Nuutajärvi Notsjo's acquisition of new glass-pressing machinery in the early 1960s. The advent of simpler and more efficient low-cost production meant that these wares could be offered inexpensively in a choice of shades. They were launched in 1968 in clear, amber, and green glass, later to be followed by more colours as sales picked up.

**EMMA VASE** Designed by Helena Tynell for Riihimäen Lasi Oy, this is a mould-blown and cased vase. *c.1976. H:21cm (8¼in).*

**PIRONKI VASE** This mould-blown cased vase of shaped form was designed by Helena Tynell for Riihimäen Lasi Oy. *c.1974. H:21cm (8¼in).*

## THE GRAAL TECHNIQUE

The arresting Graal technique was invented at Orrefors in around 1916 and was extremely popular in the 1950s and 1960s. The process involves engraving the desired motif onto a coloured glass vessel before reheating it and casing it within an outer shell of clear glass, which is then blown into the final form. The internal reflections of the clear glass refract and multiply the original design, producing an interesting optical effect.

Edvin Öhrström, Vicke Lindstrand, and glass master Gustav Bergkvist developed Ariel glass during the late 1930s, naming it after the character in Shakespeare's *Tempest*. It is similar to Graal glass with the addition of trapped air between the cased layers.

**FISH VASE** Designed by Edvard Hald, this is an exceptional example of a Graal vase, with the various layers clearly visible. The fish design is one of several produced by Hald for Orrefors. *1937. H:18.5cm (7¼in).*

## TEXTURED GLASS

The superlative skills of Scandinavian glassmakers were by no means limited to coloured glass. They also excelled in the field of textured and engraved glass, none more so than Timo Sarpaneva and Tapio Wirkkala, who designed for the Finnish firm Iittala. Their careers followed a similar path – both had a background in sculpture and worked with metal, plastic, and wood as well as with glass. Both were also invited to contribute designs to Murano glassmakers. They began their careers at Iittala within a few years of each other, Wirkkala in 1946, and Sarpaneva in 1950.

### GLASS AS SCULPTURAL ART

Sarpaneva in particular played a crucial role in the elevation of Scandinavian glass from functional household necessity to sculptural art. He achieved this through an involvement with Iittala that was prolonged and intense. Even if his Lansetti I and Orkidea designs were, strictly speaking, vessels on account of the inclusion of void space in their interiors, they were completely impractical for use as vases. These decorative cased glass sculptures formed part of Sarpaneva's prize-winning exhibit at the 1954 Milan Triennale.

Sarpaneva's Arkipelago range combines controlled bubble inclusions with a wavy, ridged surface – the small shot glasses juxtapose cast stems decorated in this manner with clear, unblemished blown bowls. However, one of Sarpaneva's most successful designs was his 1967 Festivo candlestick, cast in a charred wood mould in a similar fashion to his signature Finlandia line of 1964.

Tapio Wirkkala used a series of fine cuts, comparable to the Inciso technique used by Murano factories, to produce his *Kantarelli* (Chanterelle) bowl, in which the unpolished vertical lines echo the flutes of the chanterelle mushroom. His *Tuonen Virta* vase, issued in a limited numbered edition,

**LANSETTI II** Timo Sarpaneva's sculptural vase for Iittala is made from colourless glass surrounding a white opaque-glass hollow core. *1952. H:27cm (11in).*

*The sculptural shape* of the vase is reminiscent of a lancet and typical of Sarpaneva's style. It has perfect balance of form

uses the same technique to depict a scene from the *Kalevala*, the Finnish national epic poem. Wirkkala was preoccupied with the degree to which clear glass was visually akin to ice, and his mould-blown *Jäävuori* (Iceberg) glasses are perhaps the most literal manifestation of this in his work. Textural and chunky, they share a similar aesthetic with his *Kanto* (Tree Stump) range. Wirkkala's *Paaderin Jää* sculptures were also designed to resemble cracked and melting ice.

### VICKE LINDSTRAND

The most prominent figure in mid-century Swedish cut glass was Vicke Lindstrand. His cased glass designs for Kosta Boda in the early 1950s use textural ribbed effects and spiralling stripes. Lindstrand's various talents also stretched to book illustration, and this can be seen in the designs he drafted for Kosta Boda's talented engravers, who used cutting, engraving, and acid-etching techniques. Some of the

**THE BATH** A bathing nude is engraved on this vase designed by Vicke Lindstrand for Kosta Boda. *1950s. H:21cm (8¼in).*

**KANTO** The gently rippled form of Tapio Wirkkala's squat, thick-walled vase suggests a tree stump and ice. It was designed for Iittala. *1947. H:11.5cm (4½in).*

most accomplished specimens use a combination of engraving methods. Lindstrand's Bath vase, for example, features a milky delineation of a figure stepping into water represented by sharp, clean-cut concentric circles.

## COPPER-WHEEL ENGRAVING

Lindstrand also produced textural designs for Orrefors, this work being characterized by thick-walled vessels with copper-wheel engraving. The Orrefors stable included a number of talented engravers, the most celebrated of whom was Sven Palmqvist. After studying sculpture at the Académie Ranson in Paris, Palmqvist completed his training at Orrefors's in-house glass-engraving school. He was especially adept at figural representation and also had an interest, like so many of his contemporaries, in natural forms.

Other notable contributors to this rich seam of Scandinavian glass design include Gunnel Nyman, who was among the first to give expression to the region's developing organic style through her work with Nuutajärvi Notsjo in Finland. Much of her best work, including her combinations of heavy crystal glass with trapped bubbles or opaque white glass strands, was done in the late 1940s before her career was cut short by her untimely death in 1948.

In Sweden self-taught glass worker Gerda Strömberg and her husband, Edward, took over the Eda glassworks in 1933. They renamed their new venture Strömbergshyttan and produced chunky decanters, bowls, candlesticks, and other forms with thick walls and austere engraved decoration.

**PEARL BAND VASE** Curving lines of controlled internal air bubbles often appear in Gunnel Nyman's work, such as this vase for Nuutajärvi Notso. *1946. H:17.5cm (7in).*

*A simple,* austere form with heavy walls is characteristic of Strömberg's work

*Trapped bubbles* were a recurring feature of glass in the 1950s and 1960s

**STRÖMBERGSHYTTAN VASE** Gerda Stromberg's designs are typified by chunky forms with engraved decoration. *1950s. H:15cm (6in).*

**TALL VASE** Gunnel Nyman designed this glass vase for Nuutajärvi Notsjo, using rose glass cased in clear glass. The clear casing has a web of internal controlled bubbles. *1947. H:31.5cm (12½in).*

**KOSTA ENGRAVED VASE** Designed by Vicke Lindstrand, the vase has a typical rock-like textured surface cut with primitive figures like a cave painting. *1950s. H:20.5cm (8in).*

## THE INFLUENCE OF LANDSCAPE

Showing the typical Scandinavian identification with landscape, glass designers drew extensively on their surroundings for inspiration. The prevalence of wood and ice in the local terrain, and their domination of everyday life in the frozen north, held a particular fascination for Timo Sarpaneva and Tapio Wirkkala.

In 1961 Wirkkala built a traditional wooden house in Lapland as a refuge where he could observe the landscape and translate it into his work. His turned leaf bowl for Iittala is scored with dozens of thin line cuts – a stylized representation of the infinitesimal veins that are found on real leaves.

Timo Sarpaneva's Finlandia range of textured glass, which was first made in 1963, was cast in carved and fired alderwood moulds. Each piece is unique, as the molten glass charred and reshaped the moulds each time they were used. The resultant effect has been compared to both tree bark and cracked ice, the two most characteristic features of the Scandinavian winter landscape.

**TURNED LEAF BOWL** Tapio Wirkkala designed a wide range of pieces inspired by nature. This bowl, cut with lines that echo a leaf form, was produced by Iittala. *1953. H:18.5cm (7¼in).*

**FINLANDIA VASE** Greyish in colour, this transparent vase with a textured surface resembling bark was designed by Timo Sarpaneva for Iittala. *c.1965. H:17cm (6¾in).*

**ORIENTE VASE** Combed multicoloured bands and silver foil inclusions decorate this rare Barovier & Toso *Oriente* vase of baluster form, designed by Ercole Barovier. *c.1940. H:18cm (7in).*

**FRATELLI TOSO *STELLATO* VASE** Designed by Pollio Perelda, the vase has star-patterned murrines laid onto a clear glass body. The bright colours are typical of the period. *1953. H:28.5cm (11in).*

## TIMELESS MURANO

A combination of new blood and old glassmaking dynasties taking a renewed pride in their work revived the glass industry of the Venetian island of Murano during the 20th century. Since the Middle Ages this region had specialized primarily in hot decorating techniques such as blowing and lampwork, and it was these areas that were reinvigorated by key figures such as Dino Martens, Ercole Barovier, and members of the Toso family.

The Aureliano Toso glassworks, established in 1938, enjoyed enormous critical and commercial success from the mid-1940s, producing vessels designed by Dino Martens. His background in painting prompted him to reinterpret traditional Muranese decorating techniques, often to startling effect. His *Oriente* range combined pinwheel murrines, bright enamel colouring, and inclusions of aventurine metal oxides and powders within the same piece to produce tapestry-like glass vessels with powerful visual impact.

### THE *ZANFIRICO* TECHNIQUE

In tandem with Anzolo Fuga, Martens reworked the traditional Venetian *zanfirico* technique for the AVEM factory. Named after the 19th-century Venetian art dealer Antonio Sanquirico, who revived this ancient process, the *zanfirico* technique consists of heating multicoloured glass rods, twisting them together, and encasing them within a clear glass shell, resulting in an intricate filigree effect. It is just one manifestation of *filigrana* glass, meaning any type of glass that relies on coloured

rods or threads for decorative effect. Murano factories had been practising variations on this basic theme since the island's 15th-century heyday and now they began to infuse it with a new exuberance in the form of bright, bold colours.

### *INTARSIO* GLASS

Ercole Barovier gave up his medical training to join the family glass factory in 1919. Like Dino Martens, he was influenced by abstract painters – his *Oriente* range for Barovier & Toso (not to be confused with the Aureliano Toso product of the same name) uses shining foil inclusions and swirling bands of colour to produce an effect not seen before in glassware. Barovier was wholeheartedly

**TEARDROP JUG** This Aureliano Toso *Oriente* jug is of teardrop form, with a handle and various inclusions, among them zanfirico rods and plates and a large star-shaped murrine. It was designed by Dino Martens. *c.1954. H:32.5cm (13in).*

**INTARSIO VASE** This Barovier & Toso *intarsio* vase has a clear glass body overlaid with an irregular mosaic of diamond-shaped tiles and a stylized floral motif at the base. *1961. H:30.5cm (12¼in).*

*The base* is in the form of a floral pinwheel

*The glass* is designed to look like a stained-glass window

**ATHENS CATHEDRAL VASE** A rare Barovier & Toso Classically-inspired vase designed by Ercole Barovier, this piece is composed of clear glass overlaid with opal-white, blue, and green Athens murrines. *1967. H:33cm (13in).*

## MURRINES

The use of murrines was by no means a novelty in the 20th century, but Ermanno Toso elevated the technique to a previously unattained status. Murrines are made by slicing thin sections from long canes of clear and coloured glass with designs running through them. Flowers, spirals, and abstract designs have featured heavily in 20th-century murrines. Once the cut sections have been laid out in the required formation, molten glass is rolled over them, incorporating them onto the body of the vessel. Certain types of murrine are associated with particular makers or factories. Shown below is a Fratelli Toso factory sample board with various murrines dating from the 1950s to the 1970s.

**KIKU MURRINE VASE** The clear glass body of this Ermanno Toso vase is densely covered with blue, orange, black, and white murrines, some with yellow centres. *1950–58. H:26cm (10¼in).*

engaged in the modernization and reinterpretation of antiquated Muranese techniques, and during the 1960s he used the *intarsio* method to create a series of patterned vases. These were made by laying out mosaic patterns of thin glass patches that were then encased in clear glass. When the gather – the mass of molten glass collected on the end of the glassmaker's pipe – was blown, the *intarsio* sections would morph and distend at different rates, depending on their position on the vessel. The resultant patterns are a fusion of geometric order and organic mayhem.

## PERIPATETIC DESIGNERS

Many key figures working on Murano during this period migrated from factory to factory, often on a freelance basis. Alfredo Barbini, who eventually founded his own company, was no exception. His mid-century work is characterized by a Scandinavian restraint, with a palette limited to one or two colours and very simple forms. His use of the *inciso* technique developed by Venini, where the surface of the glass is scored with intricate series of horizontal bands, is typical of his work. Cold working techniques such as this were unusual in Murano at this time.

The peripatetic way of working that was shared by Barbini and some of his peers was a boon to the glass factories, which could benefit from the diverse skills of many

different designers. The Vistosi factory, founded in 1945, reaped the rewards of associations with many of Europe's most outstanding draughtsmen, including Fulvio Bianconi, Etorre Sottsass, Vico Magistretti, and Peter Pelzel.

Some of the glass produced at Vistosi represented the whimsical side of mid-century Murano. Alessandro Pianon's charming stylized birds, while undoubtedly amusing, nevertheless exhibit a very high degree of skill on the part of the maker. From the murrine eyes to the textured finish, they showcase some of the sophisticated decorative techniques that define this period in Murano's long history.

**OVOID VASE** Alfredo Barbini's ovoid vase with a narrow inverted rim has a double horizontal band of inclusions in ochre. *1968. H:24cm (9¼in).*

**PULCINO** The burnt-orange body of this Vetreria Vistosi chick is cased with textured clear glass, has murrines as eyes, and stands on copper legs. It was designed by Alessandro Pianon. *c.1962. H:22cm (8½in).*

## MODERN ITALIAN GLASS

The 20th-century renaissance of Murano glassmaking was not wholly reliant on updated versions of old techniques. The prevailing climate of creativity threw up many original forms and decorative treatments that peripatetic workers and designers helped to disseminate between competing factories. One of the key ingredients was colour, and vivid hues predominated, most frequently used in crystal-clear transparent glass to catch the light better.

### SOMMERSO GLASS

One of the most prevalent of the new techniques developed in the Murano factories was *sommerso* cased glass, which was perfected by Carlo Scarpa for Venini during the 1930s. The name *sommerso* (which translates as "submerged") is a fair evocation of the decorative effect produced by *sommerso* vessels, which can look remarkably like blocks of glass suspended in a coloured liquid. *Sommerso* glass production is extremely demanding, as it requires the maker to manipulate

globs of molten glass evenly without the glass falling out of its line or developing bubbles.

The Cenedese factory produced a wide range of *sommerso* vases designed by Antonio de Ros, which have a clear outer layer sheathing one or two bands of coloured glass, usually at one side of the vessel. However, Flavio Poli, working for Seguso Vetri d'Arte, became the foremost producer of this type of glass during the mid-20th century. His elliptical *Valva* vases in particular allow the cased colour combinations to come to the fore, untrammelled by decorative embellishments. In his *Siderale* range, the more technically remarkable vessels are made up of concentric circles of cased glass in alternating colours.

**VALVA VASE** A *sommerso* ovoid vase with purple and red glass cased in solid clear glass, designed by Flavio Poli for Seguso Vetri d'Arte. c.1952. H:23.5cm (9½in).

### VENINI

In his capacity as artistic director at Venini between 1934 and 1947, Carlo Scarpa was responsible for many other innovations that helped cement the reputation of Paolo Venini's fledgling company. Among these are an opaque milky white glass known as *Lattimo* and a matte glass with a

**OCCHI VASE** Tobia Scarpa's tall, square-section vase, designed for Venini in 1959, has overlaid red murrines with colourless centres. c.1960. H:32cm (13in).

**D-SHAPED VASE** Cobalt blue is cased in solid clear glass in this *sommerso* vase designed by Antonio da Ros for Vetreria Gino Cendese. c.1962. H:26.5cm (10½in).

**PULEGOSO VASE** Archimede Seguso's elegant vase has a translucent green layer of randomly bubbled *Pulegoso* glass, above which are orange swirls and a clear top casing. c.1948. H:32cm (12½in).

**CANNE VASE** Designed by Gio Ponti for Venini, this vase has the bright colours that are characteristic of much contemporary Italian glass design. The stripes are produced by overlaid coloured canes. 1955. H:28.5cm (11½in).

**TESSUTO VASE** The design of this vase is such that one half has green and black stripes and the other green and white. It was designed by Carlo Scarpa for Venini in 1940 and produced in a limited edition of 100. 1980. H:34cm (13½in).

**FAZZOLETTO BOWL** Designed by Fulvio Bianconi and Paolo Venini for Venini, this handkerchief-shaped bowl was widely copied throughout Europe. Stripes were a more common decoration than the spots seen here. 1949. H:15.5cm (6¼in).

## FULVIO BIANCONI

The extraordinary partnership between graphic designer Fulvio Bianconi and Milanese lawyer-turned-glass-designer Paolo Venini was a driving force behind some of the greatest successes of mid-century Murano glass. As befits a designer who said, "Mistakes are what I like best", Bianconi was a consummate risk-taker who constantly explored and tested the properties and limitations of glass. His trademark flair for caricature informed his series of glass figures based on stock characters from the Italian folk tradition of the *Commedia dell'Arte*. Other figures, dressed in regional costumes, poked fun at the tourist tat hawked by the more derivative Murano factories.

Bianconi's patchwork *Pezzato* vases, created from fused glass panels of different colours, found immediate popularity when they were first introduced in 1950.

**VENINI PEZZATO VASE** The clear glass body of Fulvio Bianconi's vase is overlaid with tesserae (squares of coloured glass) in the Paris colourway. 1950s. H:20.5cm (8¼in).

faint iridescent sheen called *corroso*. Scarpa also developed his own variations of traditional Venetian filigrana decoration, including the spiralling *mezza filigrana* and the complex *tessuto* technique, which resembles woven textile threads. By the time Paolo Venini died in 1959, his factory was regarded as one of the most proficient and sophisticated in Murano.

Carlo Scarpa's son, Tobia, joined the firm that same year and continued in the trailblazing vein that had been established by his father. One of his most distinctive creations are the *Occhi* vases, which have clear glass murrines, or "eyes", set within a coloured body.

## ARCHIMEDE SEGUSO

Master glassblower Archimede Seguso brought the Seguso Vetri d'Arte factory to international prominence from the 1940s. His use of the bubbly *Pulegoso* glass, first devised for Venini by Napoleone Martinuzzi, was a notable success. He was also responsible for realizing Flavio Poli's designs for a range of miniature glass animal sculptures. Seguso's twisted *Polveri* vases combined organic forms with gold powder inclusions and are quite unlike anything else produced by Murano factories during the 1950s.

## THE *FAZZOLETTO* VASE

As Murano factories attracted greater esteem, the market for their wares expanded commensurately. Smaller factories determined to profit from this boom quickly appropriated the most commercially attractive designs.

One of the most widely copied mid-century Muranese forms is the *Fazzoletto* (handkerchief) vase, developed by Paolo Venini in collaboration with Fulvio Bianconi in 1948–49. This eccentric design has become a fixture of the Murano canon, appropriated by innumerable competitors.

The distinctive shape of the *Fazzoletto*, which resembles an inverted draped handkerchief, has been produced in innumerable patterns, shapes, and sizes. Many of the variations continue the handkerchief theme with patterns of spots or stripes. From around 1950 it became a feature on sideboards and coffee tables throughout Italy and further afield.

**BLENKO BOTTLE** Wayne Husted's Persian blue tapering bottle with stopper is made from crackle-effect glass. This colour was produced in 1959 only, but it was available in other colours until 1964. *1959. H:73cm (28¾in).*

*The elaborate stopper* is almost half the height of the finished piece

## STUDIO GLASS

The range of art glass produced by specialist manufacturers during the mid-20th century was extremely diverse. Consumers were in a position to choose between moulded, blown, and cut forms in an enormous array of colours and decorative styles.

The old London firm of Whitefriars – by now relocated to suburban Wealdstone on the outskirts of London – received a shot in the arm in 1951 in the form of an invitation to exhibit at the Festival of Britain. The company built on the momentum this opportunity generated by appointing top Royal College of Art graduate Geoffrey Baxter to the design team in 1954. His early soda glass forms have the uncluttered clarity of the coloured Scandinavian glassware produced by Orrefors or Holmegaard.

### TEXTURED GLASS

The Knobbly vases created by chief designer William Wilson in 1964 signalled a change in direction at Whitefriars, but it was Geoffrey Baxter who made the most wholehearted foray into textured glass with his Textured range in 1967. Baxter created moulds for his glass from natural phenomena such as pieces of tree bark but also used a curious assortment of detritus, including copper wire, nail heads, and bricks to produce his deep relief effects.

The Bark, Drunken Bricklayer, and Banjo vases, all dating from the 1960s, were blown in cast-iron moulds copied from Baxter's prototypes constructed from these bits of flotsam and jetsam. Their appeal was enhanced by the fresh range of Pop colours, including tangerine, kingfisher blue, and meadow green, and a grey tone called pewter.

### BLENKO GLASS

In the United States, Blenko was one of the most innovative glass producers.

**DRUNKEN BRICKLAYER VASE** This kingfisher blue vase designed by Geoffrey Baxter for Whitefriars resembles three bricks stacked awkwardly one on top of the other. *1969. H:33cm (13in).*

**BANJO VASE** The bright colour and geometric form of this tangerine Banjo vase, designed by Geoffrey Baxter for Whitefriars, reflect the influence of Pop culture during the 1960s. *1967. H:32cm (12½in).*

**WHITEFRIARS VASE** This small, bulbous amethyst vase was part of the Blown Soda range designed by Geoffrey Baxter in 1962. *H:10cm (4in).*

**SHERINGHAM CANDLE HOLDERS** Five King's Lynn candleholders of varying heights and colours follow a design by Ronald Stennett-Wilson. Each has a series of discs forming its stem. Wedgwood continued this design after 1969. *1967. Tallest: H:36cm (14in).*

After World War II, William H. Blenko Jr became the third generation to join the family firm and his arrival coincided with that of Winslow Anderson, the first in-house designer employed by the Blenkos. Trained as a ceramicist, Anderson had no experience with glass but was nevertheless given carte blanche to design the new range of vases and tableware produced between 1948 and 1953. His most famous creations include the sculptural Horn vase and the 948 decanter, its bent neck the result of a happy accident on the blowing floor.

When Anderson left Blenko, he was replaced by Wayne Husted, who produced outsized designs with large, sculptural stoppers. These playful, decorative vessels were caricatures of traditional functional forms. The Blenko glass of this period was produced in vibrant colours, a legacy of the firm's origins in the stained-glass industry. Some have famous associations: Rose, for example, was much loved by Jackie Kennedy.

## NEW AND TRADITIONAL CLASSICS

Smaller independent factories also found success. British glass designer Ronald Stennett-Wilson established the King's Lynn glassworks in 1967, employing Swedish makers to assist him. The firm's Sheringham candlesticks with multi-disc stems are a design classic, while the Brancaster glasses and candlesticks have hollow, attenuated stems that are reminiscent of Nils Landberg's

*Tulpanglas*. King's Lynn Glass was acquired by the Wedgwood Group in 1969.

Foremost among mid-20th-century studio practitioners were the British designer Sam Herman, who produced free form shapes with decorative effects including trapped air and iridescence, and the American Dominick Labino, whose delicate Emergence series uses multiple casings.

Following World War II the Czech glass industry was nationalized under the Communist regime and dozens of rival factories were brought into a single government-owned enterprise. However, individual glassmakers continued to flourish and to demonstrate the advanced engraving and cutting skills that have been a feature of Bohemian glass for generations. Many factories also produced pressed and cut glass.

**FREE FORM VASE** Multicoloured swirling streaks with iridescent areas decorate this hand-blown studio glass vase by Sam Herman. *c.1972. H:27cm (10½in).*

**TREE OF LIFE** Designed by Jacob Landau and Donald Pollard for Steuben, this unique sculptural piece is both human and tree-like in form. The surface is engraved with human figures. *1959. H:37cm (14½in).*

**WATERFORD VASE** This clear and cased blue glass vase is of simple symmetrical form and has been engraved with a stylized swordfish motif. *c.1960. H:22cm (8¾in).*

## CUT GLASS

Central European cut glass flourished during this period, despite the oppressive political climate. Work by masters such as Jiri Harcuba show great skill and sophisticated, often abstract, decorative expression. Vessels in Harcuba's oeuvre sometimes have concave lens panels set into one side to magnify the hand-cut decoration. Stylized and abstracted depictions of trees, birds, and animals, often incorporating geometric patterns, feature heavily in the cut glass of this period. Although clear glass predominates, some examples use layers of colour to accentuate the cut designs.

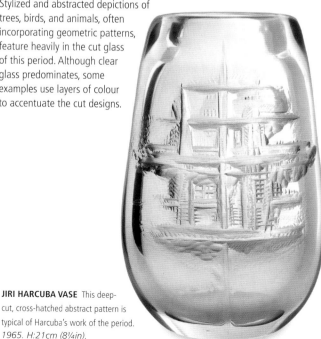

**JIRI HARCUBA VASE** This deep-cut, cross-hatched abstract pattern is typical of Harcuba's work of the period. *1965. H:21cm (8¼in).*

# GLASS GALLERY

Mid-century glassware saw an explosion of modern forms and bright colours. Designers experimented with textures and patterns and the revolutionary studio glass movement began during this period, with beautiful handcrafted and original pieces created. In Scandinavia designers drew their inspiration from nature to make sculptural glassware, while on the island of Murano ancient techniques were reinvigorated and used in new ways.

**1** *Orrefors vase*

**2** *Boda Sun Catcher*

**4** *Stuart barrel vase*

**3** *Fluted Fiesta ware plate*

**5** *Higgins rectangular dish*

**6** *Ravenhead tumbler*

**7** *Viking purple decanter*

**8** *Pilgrim decanter*

**9** *Isle of Wight bottle*

**10** *Fenton crimped bowl*

Wight studio glass bottle. 1974–79. H:38cm (15in). ① **10.** Fenton Coin Dot double crimped bowl.
c.1950s. D: 10½in). ① **11.** Caithness Glass lamp base by Domhnall O'Brion. 1960s. H:9cm (3½in). ①
**12.** Dartington vase by Frank Thrower, with moulded, textured Greek key design. H:9cm (3½in). ①
**13.** Mould-blown glass vase designed by Pavel Hlava. 1959. H:36cm (14in). ①
**14.** Mdina double-cased fish vase by Michael Harris. 1969. H:29cm (11½in). ① **15.** Murano triple-
cased sommerso cut glass ashtray. 1960s. H:10cm (4in). ① **16.** Finnish Riihimäen Lasi Oy mould-
blown vase by Tamara Aladin. c.1970. H:25cm (9¾in). ① **17.** A canne cased vase designed by Anzolo
Fuga. c.1960. H:25cm (9¾in). ③ **18.** Blown and cut crystal glass vase by Monica Morales Schildt for
Kosta Boda. 1957. H:23cm (9in). ①

11 *Caithness glass lamp base*

12 *Dartington Glass Greek key vase*

13 *Pavel Hlava vase*

14 *Mdina fish vase*

15 *Murano ashtray*

16 *Tamara Aladin vase*

17 *Anzolo Fuga vase*

18 *Crystal glass vase*

# LIGHTING

FROM LIQUID PLASTIC POLYMERS AND POLISHED CHROME TO
ARTICHOKES AND GIANT PILLS, MID-CENTURY LIGHTING DESIGNERS
REVELLED IN USING MODERN MATERIALS AND SCULPTURAL FORMS.

*GATTO* **TABLE LAMPS** This pair of lamps, produced by Flos in 1960, consist of a sprayed plastic cover strung over a corseted wire frame. *H:30cm (12in).*

## SCULPTURAL LIGHTING

The same advances in materials technology that gave rise to Pop furniture design also transformed lighting, which was even more experimental and bold. Versatile plastics were the key to this, since the globes, curves, and colours of Pop lighting would have been far more expensive to reproduce in any other medium.

Joe Colombo explored the multifaceted applications of plastic in a table lamp which he designed for Kartell in the 1960s. The opaque plastic shade diffused the light evenly, while the silvered plastic base mimicked the more expensive chromed finish that had been a prominent fixture of earlier modernist light fittings. Each segment was moulded in an organic shape in much the same way as Gae Aulenti's *Pipistrello* (Bat) lamp for Martinelli Luce, which took its name from its folded, organic plastic shade.

The telescopic shaft meant that it could be used as either a table lamp or a floor lamp, according to the owner's wishes.

The longstanding partnership between Achille Castiglioni and Flos – two of the heavyweights of mid-century Italian lighting design – produced some of the most remarkable lamps of the period. Founded in 1960 by Dino Gavina and Cesare Cassina, Flos quickly became a market leader through its associations with a host of leading designers. The company's first products were a series of lamps made from liquid polymer sprayed over a wire frame. Designed by Castiglioni, the Viscontia and *Gatto* lamps were very similar to the Bubble lamp range that was made in the United States by Howard Miller to designs by George Nelson. Nelson had first seen this space-age cocooning material used in New York Harbour to protect shipping in 1947 and was immediately inspired to put it to a more decorative use. Many variations of these lamps were made, from globes to more complicated shapes.

**BULBOUS LAMP** This table lamp with a bulbous, opaque plastic shade on a silvered spreading plastic base was designed by Joe Colombo for Kartell of Italy. *1960s. H:41cm (16in).*

*PIPISTRELLO* **LAMP** Designed by Gae Aulenti for Martinelli Luce, the *Pipistrello* table lamp has a black-enamelled metal base and white, hard plastic shade. The stainless steel shaft is telescopic. *1967. H:91.5cm (36in).*

**DALU TABLE LAMPS** Vico Magistretti's Dalu lamps, influenced by spacemen's helmets, were moulded from hard red plastic in a single piece. They were produced by Artemide. *1969. H:27cm (10½in).*

**BUBBLE LAMP** This George Nelson lamp, designed for wall mounting, has a walnut panel with an adjustable-height tubular-aluminium arm. It was produced by Howard Miller. *1955. H:51cm (20in).*

## COMMERCE VERSUS ART

Flos's rivals within the Italian market also took advantage of the versatility of plastic in order to create sculptural Pop designs. Vico Magistretti, who designed many of Artemide's best-selling

### ISAMU NOGUCHI

The concept of light as sculpture was explored in depth by Isamu Noguchi. Born in Los Angeles, Noguchi grew up in Japan but trained as a sculptor in the United States, where he then spent most of his life.

His Akari design, named after the Japanese word for light, debuted in 1951. Produced in Gifu, Japan, using traditional materials such as paper made from mulberry bark, Noguchi's lamps fuse the Eastern paper lamp aesthetic with Western design concepts, making use of both man-made and natural materials. Noguchi was especially drawn to the ephemeral qualities of the paper lantern form, remarking of his own lamps that "they seem to float, casting their light as in passing".

**AKARI 31P** A tubular, black-enamelled metal structure covered with Japanese paper, Isamu Noguchi's standard lamp pays homage to the monumental Infinite Column sculpture by Brancusi that stands at Tirgu-Jiu in Romania. *c.1960. H:190cm (75in).*

products, produced a range of lighting that was very much in the Pop idiom, using bright colours and geometric shapes. Despite the consistently high quality of his work, Magistretti was under no illusions about the commercial and industrial nature of his job, famously stating that he was in the business of selling products, not creating art.

Other artists rejected this straightforwardly commercial approach and preferred to concentrate on the sculptural quality of their work. Serge Manzon, for example, said of his own creations, "My objects cannot be marketed industrially. They are living aesthetic sculptures." In the 1970s Manzon created a series of "perfect" simple furniture forms. These prototypes for ideal design have ideological and aesthetic roots in the Bauhaus experiment (*see p.248*).

Some of the most iconic work of this period occupies a space between functional lighting and artistic sculpture. The *Pillola* lamps by Cesare Casati and Emanuele Ponzio for Ponteur are a prime example of this. The design is fun, funky, and fresh, and the chosen form is quintessentially Pop – just as Warhol found art in a Campbell's soup can, so Casati and Ponzio found it in a pill. There is also an implicit acknowledgement of the growing culture of drug-taking, both amid youth movements and tranquillizer-using adults.

## DISTORTIONS OF SCALE

The close scrutiny of everyday objects encouraged by enlarging them to ridiculous proportions is another hallmark of the Pop Art movement and the increased interest in product design that it helped to bring about. Gaetano Pesce's 1970 Moloch floor lamp is a particularly witty manifestation of this trend – a giant version of the best-selling Luxo or Anglepoise desk lamp first popularized by the Jac Jacobsen company. Every detail is correct, down to the giant springs, but this room-filling design would never fit on a desk. In what was surely a

**SCULPTURAL LAMP** The square-section stand of this lamp by Serge Manzon is covered with purplewood veneer, while the shade is composed of ivory- and red-lacquered metal semicircles. *c.1975. H:98cm (39¾in).*

mischieviously facetious remark, designed to poke fun at corporate modernism, Pesce said, "Moloch was conceived for a practical need: to illuminate large American skyscraper lobbies."

*PILLOLA* **LIGHTS** In Cesare Casati and Emanuele Ponzio's design for Ponteur, a collection of lights made from ABS hard plastic in the form of oversized pills are set on plastic ring stands. The lamps can be angled into different positions on the floor. *1968. H:55.5cm (22in).*

## RODS AND RAYS

The importance of electric lighting in creating harmonious and coherent interiors had been a continuous theme since the end of the 19th century. However, where their predecessors, particularly in the Arts and Crafts movement, had sought to create unobtrusive lighting that blended into the overall scheme, mid-century modern designers produced fixtures that were features in their own right.

The Danish firm Louis Poulsen laid the ground by means of its collaborations with many of the boldest designers of the day, including Verner Panton. His Moon Visor ceiling lamp, produced by Poulsen from 1960, was composed of concentric plastic bands that could be manipulated around a central metal rod to produce different levels of illlumination. This could range from muted to bright light, giving the same effect as a waxing and waning moon. The Flower Pot hanging fixture, designed later in 1968, was available with single or multiple plastic fittings in deep blue and orange colours, some with psychedelic swirling patterns.

Like Panton's, the lamps of sometime Poulsen collaborator Arne Jacobsen are firmly rooted in the 1960s by their globular forms.

### THE PH ARTICHOKE

Perhaps the most iconic mid-century lamp produced by Poulsen was the PH Artichoke. Designed by Paul Henningson, this complex piece was handcrafted from 72 individual steel leaves mounted on a cage of struts. Arranged in staggered rows to resemble the leaves of an artichoke, they diffuse the light evenly. It was originally commissioned for the Langelinie Pavilion Restaurant in Copenhagen Harbour, but Henningson's design proved so popular that Poulsen put it into production and, despite a high price tag, it was a bestseller.

### ITALIAN DESIGN

A more restrained, often linear, attitude to lighting design was expressed by the trio of companies that dominated post-war Italian lighting design. Arredoluce, Flos, and Arteluce benefited from the regeneration of Italian industry that peaked in the mid-1960s, at the height of the Pop Art craze.

Arredoluce was formed in the 1950s, originally producing chandeliers. Acclaimed designers such as Gino Sarfatti – who went on to found Arteluce – helped cement Arredoluce's reputation for innovation and high style.

The company was responsible for the Milan Triennale, which remains an archetype of the stylish fixtures produced by Italian firms during this

**THE PH ARTICHOKE** Designed in 1958 by Paul Henningson, this pendant ceiling lamp comprises a near-spherical grouping of overlapping, white-finish metal leaves. It was produced by Louis Poulsen of Denmark. *1970s. H:49cm (19¼in).*

*The arrangement* of the metal "leaves" resembles those of a globe artichoke

**FLOWER POT** Designed by Verner Panton for Louis Poulsen, this pendant lampshade has a light and dark blue swirl pattern over its enamelled exterior and a white-enamelled interior. *1971. H:34cm (13½in).*

**MOON** Verner Panton's pendant Moon lampshade consists of nine, revolvable, flexible, white-lacquered rings arranged around a vertical axis. It was produced by Louis Poulsen of Denmark. *1960. D:34cm (13½in).*

**PENDANT LAMP** Arne Jacobsen's elegant aluminium pendant lamp shade has a white-lacquered interior. It was possibly made by Ateljé Lyktan of Sweden. *H:30.5cm (12in).*

**TRIENNALE FLOOR LAMP** Produced by Arteluce, this lamp has three arms in a brass finish with brown leather-covered handles, three enamelled shades, and a circular white-marble base. It is marked "Made in Italy". *H:152.5cm (60in).*

*Each of the enamelled shades* is a different colour: white, teal, and black

material to a supporting role being typical of Achille Castiglioni's irreverent approach to design. The more radical Toio lamp makes features of industrial components – an example of Italian "anti-design".

In the United States, radical mid-century lighting in the Atomic style included the avant-garde T-3-C lamp by James Harvey Crate. Nominally resembling a spacecraft, the cork feet and finials also bring to mind electrons orbiting a nucleus.

period. Versions with coloured shades proved especially popular and could be found in fashionable interiors across Europe. The more abstract strain of Arredoluce's output is exemplified by the Eye (or Cobra) lamp with its Cyclopic magnetic fixture in the centre of a slender chrome shaft.

Arteluce was formed in 1939 in Milan. Gino Sarfatti drafted the majority of his firm's early designs himself and, as it grew in stature, the company attracted the talents of leading designers such as Marco Zanuso and Franco Albino.

### CASTIGLIONI DESIGN

In 1974 Arteluce was taken over by Flos, which achieved dominance thanks to the superlative design skills of the Castiglioni brothers. Their contributions to the Flos catalogue of 1962 included the Arco and Taccia models. They quickly became fixtures of modish interiors and have since achieved classic status within the genre.

The monumental Arco floor lamp in particular is synonymous with mid-century lighting design. The long, bowed steel arm and aluminium reflector are held in place by a block of Carrara marble acting as a counterweight, the relegation of this noble

**T-3-C TABLE LAMP** This rare Heifetz lamp by James Harvey Crate has a spring-mounted reflector over black-enamelled metal and spun aluminium components. The ball finials and feet are cork. *1951. H:61.5cm (24¼in).*

**TOIO FLOOR LAMP** Designed by Achille Castiglioni for Flos, this floor lamp has unusual components such as a transformer and a car headlamp. *1962. H:200cm (78¾in).*

*The shaft* is made of polished chrome

**EYE LAMP** This piece has a black-enamelled metal base and an adjustable fixture on a magnetic socket. Produced by Arredoluce of Italy, the design is attributed to Angelo Lelli in 1964. *H:62cm (24½in).*

### SERGE MOUILLE

Metalworker and sculptor Serge Mouille began to create lighting fixtures in the early 1950s after an approach from Jacques Adnet of La Compagnie des Arts Français. His most famous designs include the *Oeil*, *Flammes*, and Saturn lamps. He viewed the dominant Italian designs as "too complicated", preferring a simpler aesthetic. The "teated" shape of his aluminium shades was designed to disperse light over as wide an area as possible. The development of neon strip lighting prompted Mouille to experiment with lamps that combined both fluorescent and incandescent light sources. He won commissions to design lighting for many large institutions including universities and cathedrals.

**DOUBLE-ARMED LAMP** This Serge Mouille lamp has two aluminium shades, each with black exteriors and white interiors, and black-painted rods and ball joints. *c.1955. H:180cm (70in).*

# LIGHTING GALLERY

Mid-century modern lighting was heavily influenced by the space age, the real possibility of space exploration being a source of contemporary excitement as well as a springboard for the imagination. Many lamps of this period echo the form of flying saucers or satellites. The forms are futuristic, and mix smooth shapes with angular lines. Another trend was the move towards sculptural forms (many influenced by the Surrealists and by artist and sculptor Jean Arp) as well as minimal, linear designs.

## KEY

**1**. Red-lacquered metal book light. 1950s. H:40cm (15¾in). ① **2**. Serge Manzon metal lamp inspired by flying saucers. H:50cm (19¾in). ⑤ **3**. Verner Panton VP-Globe lamp, a plexiglass sphere containing aluminium disks. 1970. D:50cm (19¾in). ③ **4**. Brass desk lamp by Pierre Paulin for Philips. c.1955. W:41cm (17in). ① **5**. Chrome-plated Stilnovo Mini Topo desk lamp by Joe Colombo. 1968. H:35.5cm (14in). ① **6**. Painted and textured plaster table lamp with original parchment shade. 1950s. H:83cm (32½in). ① **7**. Fontana Arte desk lamp in brass and enamelled metal. c.1960. H:46cm (18¼in). ② **8**. Heifetz Company floor lamp with magnetic ball and socket pivoting arm by Gilbert Watrous. 1951.

1 Metal book light

2 Serge Manzon metal lamp

3 Verner Panton VP-Globe lamp

4 Pierre Paulin desk lamp

5 Mini Topo desk lamp

6 Table lamp with parchment shade

7 Fontana Arte desk lamp

8 Heifetz Company floor lamp

9 Kaiser & Co. table lamp

H:134.5cm (53in). ④ **9.** Kaiser & Co. table lamp. 1950s. H:39cm (15½in). ① **10.** Twelve-arm brass chandelier with opaque glass shades by Paavo Tynell for Idman. 1950s. H:138.5cm (54½in). ⑥ **11.** Chrome and glass chandelier. 1960s. W:45cm (18in). ① **12.** Studio Tetrach Pistillino gold-plated wall/table/ceiling light. 1970s. W:30.5cm (12in). ① **13.** Sputnik chandelier and pair of matching wall sconces, with polished chrome frames and radiating spokes. 1970s. Chandelier: H:114.5cm (45in). ③ **14.** Chrome-plated metal chandelier with smoked glass shades. W:45.5cm (18in). ① **15.** Gaetano Sciolari polished brass chandelier with nine sockets and lucite accents. 1960s. W:63cm (25¾in). ② **16.** Vistosi chandelier with discs in orange and clear blown glass suspended from a tiered frame. z1960s. H:55cm (22in). ②

10 *Paavo Tynell chandelier*

11 *Chrome chandelier*

12 *Studio Tetrach Pistillino light*

13 *Sputnik chandelier and sconces*

14 *Chrome-plated chandelier*

15 *Gaetano Sciolari chandelier*

16 *Vistosi chandelier*

# METALWARE

AFTER THE WAR ALUMINIUM AND STAINLESS STEEL ALLOYS

PROVIDED A NEW AND CHEAPER ALTERNATIVE TO THE USE OF

SILVER AND GOLD IN DECORATIVE METALWARE.

## FLUID LINES

During World War II huge advances were made in the industrial application of aluminium and stainless steel alloys. After the war these materials became increasingly available and popular within the decorative arts.

Nevertheless, precious metals such as gold and silver did not lose their appeal. One Scandinavian silverware firm remained peerless during this period: Georg Jensen, for whom Henning Koppel in particular created outstanding functional forms. Characterized by fluid lines and sinuous curves, Koppel's work is a blend of the biomorphic and the sculptural. Tapio Wirkkala produced similarly modest and elegant silverware, often based on his stylized perceptions of natural forms.

### AUSTERITY AND FUNCTIONALITY

In addition to this organic modernism, many designers at Georg Jensen invigorated the company's output with other reinterpretations of modernism. For example, Sigvard Bernadotte's designs are typified by classic geometric shapes

**WATER PITCHER**
Henning Koppel designed this stunning, sculptural silver water pitcher of organic form for Georg Jensen of Denmark. *1950s. H:30cm (12in).*

*Koppel* is renowned for the biomorphic forms he created

*The satiny surface* of the piece was created using a technique developed by Jensen

*The hammered surface* is typical of Devlin's work

*The texture of the body* of the jug is repeated on the handle

**WATER JUG** Stuart Devlin's silver water jug has a flared form with hammered effect and an abstract gilt handle. It bears an impressed "SD" seal and hallmarks for London. *1973. H:28.5cm. (11¼in).*

with a strong element of streamlining, while Jørgen Jensen became known for his sleek, mannered interpretation of modernism.

Austere and functional, Arne Jacobsen's designs also contributed enormously to the dominance of Scandinavian style during this period. They are typified by his AJ range of cutlery, designed in 1957, which featured in Stanley Kubrick's film *2001: A Space Odyssey*, and by the Cylinda line of tableware, designed around 1968. Both retain a futuristic aura.

The Royal College of Art played a crucial role in the drive to revitalize British industry after the war. Professor Robert Goodden was tutor to, among others, the metalworkers Robert Welch and David Mellor. After graduation Mellor returned to Sheffield, the centre of Britain's steel industry, where he worked on behalf of various

manufacturers. His strong belief in mass production saw him collaborate with many of the biggest names in British industry, including Elkington. He also produced a pared-down cutlery set called Thrift for the government's Ministry of Works, designed specifically for use in institutions such as hospitals and prisons, as well as in railway stations.

Similarly, Robert Welch combined a devotion to industrial design with a latent sympathy for the modernist ideal. He subscribed to the Scandinavian philosophy of designing simple, everyday objects that were functional, beautiful, and affordable for most people. His stainless-steel Connaught tea service and Bistro cutlery set became staples in cafés and restaurants across Britain.

In the United States, Russel Wright, famous primarily for his ceramics, also produced metal tableware in a new, streamlined form, and often in aluminium. In Italy Lino Sabbattini – the great Italian master of silver design during this period – produced objects for daily use that combined grand elegance with the modernist aesthetic.

**MEXICAN MARTINI PITCHER** Designed by William Spratling in sterling silver, this pitcher has a distinctly modernist shape with no surface decoration. *1961–67. W:14cm (5½in).*

**SAUCE LADLE** Lino Sabattini's elegant silver-plated sauce ladle with a wooden handle was designed for Christofle & Cie of France. *c.1950. H:26cm (10¼in).*

## A TASTE FOR EMBELLISHMENT

Gerald Benney, who had trained in an Arts and Crafts workshop, studied under Goodden at London's Royal College of Art and travelled extensively in Scandinavia. All these diverse influences appear in his modernist work. Benney developed a textured finish for silver in the late 1950s, which he later used on pewter. This was extensively copied by other designers.

The Australian designer Stuart Devlin, another graduate of the Royal College of Art, produced simple forms with rich, decorative embellishment. In order to find a market for his work, Devlin had to temper the prohibitive cost of his

intricate hand-tooled finishes. The result was striking textured finishes that were far removed from the clean surfaces preferred by adherents of the more austere Scandinavian style.

In the United States, the metalware designs of polymath designer Tommi Parzinger were equally distinctive. Reluctant to subscribe to any particular school, Parzinger fitted his furniture with his own handcrafted metalware, and designed a range of brass accessories for the American manufacturer Dorlyn. Among the designs that became iconic are his classical geometric shapes adorned with banding and accentuated loops.

**SILVER VASE** This silver elongated vase was designed by Tapio Wirkkala for Kultakeskus of Finland. *1955. H:19cm (7½in).*

**COFFEEPOT** Designed by Tommi Parzinger for Dorlyn Silversmiths, this tall brass and stainless-steel coffeepot has horizontal bands adorning a tapering body. *c.1950. H:42cm (16½in).*

**PRIDE TEAPOT** David Mellor designed this silver-plated teapot for Elkington as part of a range of silverware that included cutlery. *1957. L:23cm (9in).*

# METALWARE GALLERY

$\mathbf{M}$id-century modern metalware is characterized by simplicity and elegance. The style is of modern, clean lines where the form itself is the decoration, and there is very little added ornamentation. As this streamlined effect could be achieved by using inexpensive materials, most commonly stainless steel, silversmiths saw a decline in trade. However, they were able to edge back into the market and display their talent by creating handcrafted pieces with interesting textures that appealed to the sensibilities of the time.

## KEY

**1.** Old Hall stainless steel Alveston tea set designed by Robert Welch. c.1962. Teapot: W:24cm (9½in). ① **2.** Stelton Cylinda line coffeepot designed by Arne Jacobsen. c.1970. H:20cm (8in). ①
**3.** Deakin & Francis silver ashtray with textured rim and gold wash. Birmingham hallmarks for 1971. D:10cm (4in). ① **4.** Black wire and raffia wine pourer by Desmond Sawyer. c.1950. H:18cm (7in). ①
**5.** Set of four Danish Krenitware enamelled metal bowls designed by Hebert Krerchel in 1954. Largest: D:16cm (6¼in). ① **6.** Stelton Cylinda line cocktail shaker in stainless steel designed by Arne Jacobson. c.1970. H:23cm (9in). ① **7.** Georg Jensen bowl designed by Henning Koppel, design no. 980. 1950s. D:38cm (15in). ⑥ **8.** Pair of silver vases by Hans Bunde for Carl M. Cohr. 1963. H:18cm (7in). ②
**9.** Silver cruet set by Gordon Hodgson with ivory and black stained hardwood inserts, hallmarked for

1 | Old Hall tea set

2 | Cylinda line coffeepot

3 | Silver ashtray

4 | Wine pourer

5 | Krenitware bowls

6 | Cylinda line cocktail shaker

7 | Georg Jensen bowl

8 | Pair of silver vases

London 1969. H:6.5cm (2½in). ② **10.** Pair of Danish Meka sterling salt and pepper pots in the form of fish with enamel decoration. H:5.5cm (2¼in). ① **11.** Viner's stainless steel candleholder with textured gold-plated stem, designed by Stuart Devlin. H:15.25cm (6in). ① **12.** Candleholder sculpture by Nagel, composed of individual sections that can be assembled into any combination. 1960s. H:28cm (11in). ① **13.** Viner's stainless steel flower holder or bud vase by Stuart Devlin with gold-plated domed top. c.1969. H:8cm (3in). ① **14.** Condiment set by Frantz Hingelberg for Aarhus in silver and black Bakelite. 1950s. Sugar sifter: H:13.5cm (5¼in). ② **15.** Viner's stainless steel wine goblet with textured gold-plated stem by Stuart Devlin. c.1970. H:13.5cm (5½in). ① **16.** Pair of Old Hall stainless-steel triple candlesticks designed by Robert Welch. H:23cm (9in). ① **17.** Set of six silver goblets with textured lower sections, a hollow base, and bowl interiors with gold wash. 1974. H:16cm (6¼in). ②

**9** *Silver cruet set*

**10** *Meka salt and pepper pots*

**12** *Nagel candleholder sculpture*

**11** *Viner's candleholder*

**13** *Flower holder*

**14** *Condiment set*

**15** *Viner's goblet*

**16** *Old Hall candlesticks*

**17** *Silver goblet*

# PRODUCT DESIGN

THE AMERICAN DREAM WAS FULFILLED POST-WAR THROUGH THE CONSTANT
ACQUISITION OF NEW GOODS, WHILE IN BRITAIN HAROLD MACMILLAN TOLD
HIS ELECTORATE THAT THEY HAD "NEVER HAD IT SO GOOD".

## THE CONSUMER DREAM

During the 1950s it was hard to escape the idealized image of the nuclear family living in their perfect suburban home that was propounded by advertising in print and on television. This branded vision of happiness relied upon consumerism to perpetuate itself. Hand-in-hand with the smiling family and the suburban house, came the car in its garage, the fashionable furnishings, the labour-saving appliances, and the state-of-the-art communications equipment. Manufacturers were keen to encourage this insatiable demand for novel products and even designed obsolescence into their goods, thereby conditioning the buying public to covet the latest thing and throw away the old. This fetishizing of consumer goods was driven in part by the designers who made them so attractive in the first place.

Families had begun to gather around the wireless in the 1920s, but since that time its design had changed beyond recognition, new plastics such as bakelite being used to produce stylish, streamlined designs. However, during the 1950s radio began to face increasing competition from television, which soon became the dominant mass media source. The television sets of the 1950s and early 1960s were often designed to be the centrepiece of the living room, representing the high esteem in which this revolutionary new technology was held.

Surely the most ostentatious entertainment centre ever made, the Komet Super Luxus Automatic was an enormous walnut and wenge-wood housing for a television, cassette tape deck, and

**KOMET ENTERTAINMENT SYSTEM** The angled high-varnished case houses a 53cm- (21in-) television set, radio, Telefunken tape deck, Imperial record player, and speakers. It was produced by Kuba of Germany. *1957–62. H:216cm (85in).*

**BOOMERANG** This Philco Model 49-501 Transitone brown bakelite radio was named Boomerang on account of its angular design. *1949. W:29cm (11½in).*

**JVC VIDEOSPHERE** The design of this television set, based on a spaceman's helmet, was influenced by the American lunar landing of 1969. *1969–70. H:33cm (13in).*

**ATOM BALL CLOCK** The atom ball was a popular motif. Here it acts as the numerals of a wall clock, designed by George Nelson for the American Howard Miller Clock Company. *1947. D:33cm (13in).*

**ERICOFON** Designed in the late 1940s, Ericsson's Ericofon telephone went into production in 1954. A model with a dial in the base was released for home use in 1956 in a number of different colours. *H:21cm (8¼in).*

**"JUST WHAT IS IT...?"** The exhibition poster for a retrospective exhibition of the work of Richard Hamilton in 1976 has as its main image a 1956 collage designed by Hamilton. *1976. H:75cm (30in).*

**RADIO NURSE** Designed by Isamu Noguchi for America's Zenith Radio Corporation, this bakelite radio has a typical late 1930s and 1940s streamlined look. *1937. H:21cm (8¼in).*

**TRIMPHONE** An iconic British design from this era, the plastic Trimphone (TRIM for Tone Ringer Illuminated Model) was available in three two-tone colours: blue, green, and ivory. *1964. L:19.5cm (7¾in).*

turntable. The angular, sculptural top section conceals eight speakers as well as the relatively small screen – the technology for larger screens had not yet come into existence. Later in the 1960s less obtrusive but equally distinctive designs began to proliferate. The Videosphere by JVC, based on an astronaut's helmet, made its debut in 1969, the year of the moon landings.

## CATCHING THE CONSUMER'S EYE

Eye-catching design was so vital for attracting consumers that many manufacturers hired famous names to help them. Isamu Noguchi's Radionurse, designed to transmit sounds from a baby's cot to its parents elsewhere in the house, looks like a cross between a robotic nanny and a samurai's kabuto helmet.

Marketing its 1963 turntable cabinet as "a stereo set for individualists", the German manufacturer Wega loudly trumpeted Verner Panton's input. A product of the more understated approach to design that began to take hold in the 1960s, it is sleek, simple, and geometric, the buttons and dials arranged in tidy rows on the top.

Pioneering companies willing to take risks with product design often found the rewards were great. Ericsson's Ericofon telephone handset, first produced in 1954, was a functional but unusual one-piece design with the dial in the base. Available in 18 colours, it became a bestseller and even broke into the notoriously difficult American market. The market leader in Britain was the Trimphone, designed by Martyn Rolands and produced on behalf of the GPO, which operated the national telephone exchange at the time. Thousands of people rented the handsets from the GPO (General Post Office), the more daring among them paying extra for a two-tone model.

Richard Hamilton satirized the ubiquity of such products in his 1956 collage *Just What Is It That Makes Today's Home So Different, So Appealing?* Advertising is represented by the woman vacuuming the stairs, while a black arrow extols the virtues of the brand of appliance she is using.

**3300 STEREO SYSTEM** This 1960s German Wega model 3300 stereo system housed in a moulded white plastic case was designed for the company by Verner Panton. *1963. H:43.5cm (17¼in).*

# POP AND PLASTICS

JUST AS EARLY MODERNISTS WERE INSPIRED BY ABSTRACTIONIST ART MOVEMENTS SUCH AS CUBISM, MID-CENTURY DESIGNERS FOUND NEW STIMULATION IN THE POP ART MOVEMENT THAT BEGAN IN THE LATE 1950S.

Like Cubism, Pop Art was initially a reaction against the art establishment. Young artists like Richard Hamilton, David Hockney and Peter Blake rejected abstract expressionism, which they considered to be too high-minded and cerebral, and turned instead to everyday objects. They aimed to reconnect art with the normal lives of ordinary people. Critic Lawrence Alloway first coined the term Pop Art in 1958 in recognition of the way the movement eliminated the distinction between high art and low art, or popular culture. It is characterized by bright colours, collage, pastiche, convenience and innovation. Leading advocates of the style made their work available in a variety of media, releasing art from the constraints of the gallery. Peter Blake devised the cover art for the Beatles' album, *Sergeant Pepper's Lonely Hearts Club Band*, one of the most frequently reproduced images in the Pop canon.

**THE SOUPER DRESS** Influenced by Andy Warhol's images of Campbell's soup cans, this papery cellulose dress reflects the disposable nature of the Pop culture of the time. 1966–67. L:96.5cm (38in).

**COATHANGER** This elaborate American plastic coathanger is charged with classic 1960s images and design motifs: the mirrored pebble glasses, lurid colours, and psychedelic swirls. H:34cm (13½in).

**PENTAGRAM ASHTRAYS** A group of interlocking Pentagram stacking ashtrays, made from moulded plastic, each in a different bold colour. They are marked "DO Reg No. 954.589 *PENTAGRAM*". Each: H:4.5cm (1¾in).

## FAMOUS FOR 15 MINUTES

The movement surfaced in the United States, where Andy Warhol became its most prolific exponent. His exaltation of the mundane was most famously expressed by his various sculptural and graphic treatments of Campbell's soup packaging. At his Factory studio in Manhattan, Warhol employed teams of workers to assist in the production of his silk-screen prints – in effect turning art into an industrial process. Warhol prophesied that "in the future, everyone will be world famous for 15 minutes", acknowledging the disposable culture that had come to dominate modern life.

This emphasis on transience and intensive production made plastic a natural ally of the Pop movement. Novel, cheap, disposable, and accessible, it had the added benefits that it could take on just about any form or colour. Moulded plastic forms were designed to save space and contribute to a clutter-free lifestyle.

**POP SHAPES** The red-and-white cased glass vase by Holmegaard, named Carnaby, has an opacity, colour and shape mimicking contemporary plastics such as the *La Bomba* plastic picnic set. Vase: 1961. H:22cm (8¾in); Picnic set: c.1975. H:39cm (15½in).

Helen von Boch's *La Bomba* picnic set, for example, slots neatly together to form a portable capsule when not in use.

## THE PREDOMINANCE OF PLASTICS

The deluge of witty, throwaway designs from this period ranges from the sublime to the ridiculous. Some, like the inflatable Blow armchair produced by Zanotta, remain in production today. Like Gruppo DAM's *Libro* chair, it is representative of the new style of furniture demanded by consumers used to more informal living.

Plastic played such a pivotal role that products made from other materials were sometimes designed to look like it. Per Lutken's Carnaby vases – the name itself an allusion to one of the focal points of Swinging London – are glass made to resemble plastic.

**BLOW ARMCHAIR** Designed by Gionatan de Pas for Zanotta of Italy, this armchair was made of radio-frequency welded PVC. It was the archetypal example of disposable Pop Art plastic furniture. 1967. H:47cm (33 in).

**LIBRO CHAIR** Gruppo DAM's lounge chair is designed to resemble an open book. The aluminium frame has polyurethane foam "pages" upholstered in black and white vinyl. W:80cm (31½in).

**FLOWERS** Andy Warhol's *Flowers* is from a portfolio of ten screenprints. It is signed on verso, framed, and published by the American firm Aetna Silkscreen Products, Inc. c.1970. H:91.5cm (36in).

# TEXTILES

REFLECTING EVERYDAY FASHION ON THE STREET AND IN THE HOME, TEXTILE DESIGN IS A BAROMETER OF POPULAR TASTE. MID-CENTURY FABRICS ENCOMPASSED THE RANGE FROM FLORAL TO GEOMETRIC PATTERNS.

## ABSTRACT DESIGNS

Lucienne Day, partner of British designer Robin Day, changed the face of British interiors with her designs for a huge range of textile products. Calyx, her most celebrated pattern, takes its name from the parts of a flower that protect the bud. The highly stylized floral design is made up of vertical stems and roughly delineated, semi-circular buds. Inspired by a trip to Scandinavia, where Lucienne and Robin had seen the subtle allusions to natural forms expressed by designers in that region, Calyx was commissioned for the Festival of Britain in 1951 and originally retailed through Heal & Son.

Day's next design for Heal & Son was Flotilla, which, like Calyx, was made with the screen-printing method. This had been used industrially since World War I, but it was not until the 1950s that more durable screen materials and advances in stencil technology made it viable for mass production. Day's association with Heal & Son continued until 1974 and resulted in dozens of acclaimed designs.

Other prominent British manufacturers of textiles included David Whitehead and the Edinburgh Weavers. Artists such as John Piper and Henry Moore contributed designs to these firms.

The resurgence in the crafts movement saw textile artists such as Richard Landis and Anni Albers hand-weaving colourful fabrics. Albers also designed colourful textiles, as did Alexander Girard, who worked for furniture manufacturer Herman Miller.

***CHIESA DELLA SALUTE*** Produced by Sanderson, this pair of curtains has a screen-printed design by John Piper that features the Venetian church of the same name. The design was commissioned for Sanderson's centenary. *c.1965. H:200cm (78¾in).*

**CALYX FABRIC** One of many fabrics designed by Lucienne Day for Heal & Son, Calyx was screen-printed. *1951.*

FANDANGO **FANDANGO** This length of patterned fabric was designed by Maija Isola for Marimekko of Finland, and is an elegant duotone repeating floral print. *1963. L:210cm (82½in).*

**SWIRL-PATTERN RUG** Produced by Edward Fields, this room-size rug has an overall random swirl pattern in black, white, red, and purple. *W:274cm (108in).*

**SPECTRUM** The bold, geometric shapes in strong colours on this velvet fabric are characteristic of much of Verner Panton's work with patterns. It was produced by Mira-X of Switzerland. *c.1975. W:120cm (47¼in).*

## AREA RUGS

The more transitory lifestyle that many Americans led in the post-war years meant that they frequently moved home and abandoned their carpets. Edward Fields pioneered the concept of the "area rug" in the early 1950s as a solution to this. In partnership with the designer Raymond Loewy, Fields introduced a range of five patterned rugs for the living room. Names such as Infinite Star, Legend, and Stellar highlighted the futuristic nature of his designs. Fields's rugs became a huge success when they went on sale at Lord & Taylor's on Fifth Avenue.

Other interior designers followed suit, including icons of 1960s fashion such as Pierre Cardin. Aiming to create a homogeny between street fashion and interior furnishing, Cardin began to retail a line of rugs and other textiles that echoed the motifs he used in his clothing designs. His output was thus dominated by swirls, concentric circles, and ellipses in purples, reds, and blues. Much of Cardin's work and that of his contemporaries was indebted to key figures from the art world such as Andy Warhol; the optical effects of Bridget Riley's Op-Art were another key influence.

## PANELS AND WALLHANGINGS

Verner Panton's Spectrum textile designs for Mira-X were indebted to Riley's oeuvre. His repeating swirls and geometric blocks were composed of graduated colours chosen to blend with other Panton-designed elements within an interior to create a unified environment. Mira-X produced fabric panels of Spectrum designed for use as wall hangings. This concept quickly became very popular, and throughout the 1970s many companies produced imitations. Finlayson of Finland, for example, retailed a pattern called Soundwaves, made up of bouncing waves of white, cream, brown, and black bands. The name as well as the design were calculated to tap into the consciousness of the youth movement.

**QUARTO FABRIC** Typical of the designs which Lucienne Day produced for Heal & Son during the late 1950s, this framed panel of fabric has blocks of single colour alternating with geometric patterns. *1960. H:91cm (35¾in).*

**DEKOPLUS FABRIC** This length of synthetic fabric was produced by Dekoplus and possibly designed by Pierre Cardin. The pattern comprises large, off-centred circles in various shades of blue. *c.1970. L:7.24m (23¼ft).*

# POSTERS

THE COMMERCIAL ART OF THE MID-20TH CENTURY LIFTS THE LID

ON THE ASPIRATIONS, ANXIETIES, AND ABOVE ALL FASHIONS THAT

PREOCCUPIED PEOPLE DURING THESE TUMULTUOUS YEARS.

## GRAPHIC DESIGN

The early experiments in modern typography by the Constructivists and the Bauhaus, and their overall avant-garde design style, found their way to the United States through the many prominent artists who fled to the United States in the years just prior to World War II. Here they blossomed into a new kind of graphic design. Corporate America flocked to designers such as Paul Rand to commission logos that would embed their name and identity firmly in the public mind. This revolution in information design was spearheaded by Ladislav Sutner and by Charles and Ray Eames, who released their first educational film, *A Communications Primer*, in 1953.

## THE POWER OF PROMOTION

During World War II the Royal Society for the Prevention of Accidents harnessed the power of modernist graphic design to promote worker safety – an impressive and progressive campaign that stood out markedly from the drab and uninventive images normally associated with the style. Many of these posters were designed by Tom Eckersley, who went on to create witty and dynamic

**BOAC** Tom Eckersley created this striking image for the airline BOAC. Coupled with the slogan "It's A Small World By Speedbird", the poster shows the globe being traversed by an abstract bird/plane image. *1947. H:99cm (39in).*

**OLIVETTI TYPEWRITERS** Frederic Henri Kay Henrion's Post-Surrealist image of an eye above a typewriter makes a symbolic link between the eye and the machine, as manifested by the dotted line. *1950s. H:299cm (119½in).*

## PSYCHEDELIC POSTERS

Inspired by the sinuous whiplash curves of Art Nouveau from an earlier era and by the hallucinogenic effects of LSD, psychedelic poster design thrived as a means of advertising the rock gigs, multimedia shows, and assorted happenings that defined the acid wave that spread out from San Francisco in the late 1960s. Promoters including Bill Graham and the Family Dog commissioned this work by approaching underground illustrators such as Chet Helms and Stanley Mouse, who were invariably members of the scene. The style is characterized by inflated lettering, day-glo colours, and surrealistic imagery. It was later commercialized by artists such as Peter Max.

**CINZANO** A reworking of the Cinzano emblem created in 1910, this poster (*far left*) was designed by Jean Carlu. It makes use of the *ligne souple* (supple line) – a green halo on a dark background. *1950. H:160cm (63in).*

**4 GITANES CAPORAL** The four different kinds of Gitane cigarette available are each accompanied by an image of a Romany-type woman in a headscarf. Designed by Jean Colin of France. *1950s. H:160cm (63in).*

**CLEOPATRA** This poster by American Pop artist Peter Max is typical of the psychedelic art of the age and was much copied. *c.1967. H:91cm (36in).*

images for a variety of clients including Shell and London Transport. His work is characterized by subtle flourishes such as the logo of the London Underground appearing in place of the pivot on a pair of scissors in his *Victoria Line* poster. In contrast to this practical approach, the advertising work of Frederic Henri Kay Henrion shows the influence of the Surrealists, his juxtaposition of a giant eye with an Olivetti typewriter being reminiscent of Man Ray's *Indestructible Object*.

## CINEMA POSTERS

The mid-20th century was a golden period in cinema history, and the posters that advertised films such as *Rebel Without A Cause* and *Breathless* are suffused with the glamour and intrigue that kept people flocking to the cinemas despite the advent of television. Artwork for films such as *The Day the Earth Stood Still* highlights a preoccupation with space and science fiction, while the Bond franchise was sold on a steady stream of guns, girls, and gambling.

*Barbarella*, one of the seminal films of the 1960s, is the epitome of Pop. From the big hair to the kinky boots sported by Jane Fonda, the film and the artwork that went with it represent a distillation of the exploitative yet whimsical preoccupation with sex that pervaded the 1960s.

Behind the Iron Curtain, film posters took on a very different countenance. Rather than concentrate

**THE DAY THE EARTH STOOD STILL** An American poster for the sci-fi film bears the hallmarks of contemporary fantasy and sci-fi design: a composite image featuring various scenes from the film and the use of bold, sans-serif type. *1951. H:104cm (41in).*

**BARBARELLA** In this rare Argentinian poster for the sci-fi/fantasy film starring Jane Fonda, the image is of Barbarella superimposed on a psychedelic pink and yellow background. *1968. H:109cm (43in).*

**DR NO** The film poster for the first-ever James Bond film, starring Sean Connery, shows Bond and the various "Bond" women, each in a different single colour. The 007 logo, with gun, also features. *1962. H:104cm (41in). ATM*

on images of the stars, they presented atmospheric and highly individual interpretations of the film's content. Wiktor Górka's artwork in Poland for *Cabaret*, starring Liza Minnelli, features a Nazi swastika composed of stocking-clad dancer's legs – an altogether darker and more intriguing representation than that used on Western posters.

Polish artists such as Lucjan Jagodzinski, Wiktor Górka, and Franciszek Starowieyski worked on behalf of the state film distribution industry. They flourished from the mid-1950s when the government repealed restrictions on graphic representation, allowing more freedom of design, and their work is much sought after today.

**VERTIGO** Featuring artwork by Saul Bass, this Argentinian poster bears the Spanish title for the French novel from which the film is adapted. *1958. H:109cm (43in).*

**KABARET** A Polish film poster for the Bob Fosse film *Cabaret*. The striking image, with Liza Minelli's head at the centre of a swastika made up of four performing legs, is by Wiktor Górka. *1973. H:84cm (33in).*

**THE BIRDS** The Czech poster for the Hitchcock film with artwork by Josef Vyletal has an eerie image featuring a collage of Max Ernst's Surrealist painting *Attirement of the Bride*. *1970. H:84cm (33in).*

# POSTMODERN AND CONTEMPORARY

## 1970 ONWARDS

# ECLECTIC DIVERSITY

AS A REACTION TO THE MODERNIST OBSESSION WITH FORM AND FUNCTION, DESIGNERS EXPERIMENTED WITH WITTY, IRREVERENT, COLOURFUL WORK. THEIR INDIVIDUALISTIC APPROACH CONTINUES TO ENCOMPASS HIGH TECHNOLOGY AND TRADITIONAL CRAFTS.

**IGNITED LUNAR LUNACY**
Updating the ancient technique of murrines, this sculptural vase crosses into the realms of art. c.2003. H:101cm (40in).

## POSTMODERNISM BEGINS

The name itself sits uncomfortably, for we now appear to be living in a follow-on age rather than an age in itself, and there is always the suspicion that, in future years, postmodernism may acquire its own name in its own right, or perhaps be retitled as pre-something or other as yet undefined.

Postmodernism owes its birth to the ending of the modernist dream, that utopian belief that it was possible to create a better world using the power and potential of the machine and of industrial technology. That dream began before World War I, flourished in the interwar years, and managed to survive in a different form after World War II. It ended as the optimism of the 1960s gave way to the reality of a high-inflation and high-unemployment economy in the 1970s. As oil prices soared and petrol was rationed, the previous optimism was replaced by a cynicism that infected all contemporary culture. The *Zeitgeist* of the 20th century was further shaken by the failure of American technological superiority in Vietnam as well as the ephemeral qualities of Pop. Many people now saw that modernist culture had come to a dead end. When the world's economies began to grow again in the 1980s, the main motor was self-interest and personal enrichment at the expense of community. Without any all-embracing culture to make sense of this change, postmodernist thinkers suggested that the only appropriate response was to plunder the past for inspiration. Art, architecture, design, and fashion revived past styles at random, leading to such inspired creations as Philip Johnson's modernist AT&T skyscraper in New York with its Chippendale pediment.

## THE MEMPHIS GROUP

The main feature of postmodernism is wit, the incongruity between what is expected and what something really is. One of the most ironic, and most innovative, of postmodernist design outfits is the Memphis Group, formed in Milan, Italy, in 1980. "Memphis tries to separate the object from the idea of functionalism," said their leader, Ettore Sottsass. "It is an ironic approach to the modern notion of philosophical pureness. In other words, a table may need four legs to function, but no one can tell me that the four legs have to look the same."

Memphis designs are characterized by bold colour and inventiveness. The designers were comfortable taking risks, mixing motifs from different eras and ethnic groups and combining expensive and inexpensive materials. Each item can be viewed as furnishing, art, and fashion accessory and grabs attention in a way that fitted well into the conspicuous consumption of the 1980s.

## A NEW REALISM

By the early 1990s this colourful mix of styles and ideas was losing favour, and designers reacted by looking for more subdued – although not necessarily less colourful – means of expression.

**GUGGENHEIM, BILBAO** Architect Frank Gehry designed this museum, which opened in 1997, to look like a ship, in keeping with its setting in the Spanish Basque port. The reflective titanium panels look like fish scales, continuing the marine theme.

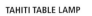

**TAHITI TABLE LAMP**
This design by Ettore Sottsass does away with the traditional lampshade. Instead, a halogen bulb is housed in an enamelled metal structure that sits on a plastic laminate base. 1981. H:65cm (25½in).

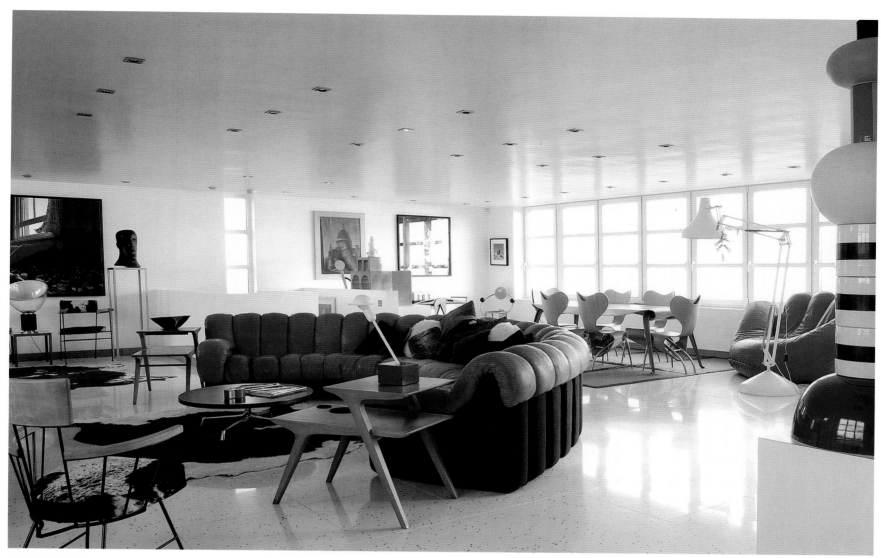

**THE BIG WHITE HOUSE, SUSSEX** The house includes work by postmodern and contemporary designers such as Sottsass, Mendini, and Arad. The interior is truly contemporary in its eclectic mixing of styles from the mid- to late 20th century.

The economic crash of 1987 was the beginning of the end for the culture of greed that had dominated the 1980s. This, combined with political uncertainty following the collapse of communism, a growing environmental awareness, and the threat of terrorism, made the 1990s and early 21st century a more subdued period. Design became simpler and more true to its materials, with wicker and clear acrylic in common use.

## THE DIGITAL AGE

Of crucial importance to the recent development of postmodernist design has been the impact of the digital revolution, driven by the extraordinarily fast growth of the internet, mobile telephones, and the computer industry. Designers now use computers as an essential tool in creating a product, largely doing away with the need to draw up detailed designs and make models. What results

can be smooth and technical in appearance, a look that has long defined electronic consumer goods and now features in the decorative arts as well.

The ease of communication that enables designers to access and share ideas and images at speed also creates an international culture that changes fast and frequently. With materials sourced from all over the world and manufacturing increasingly relocating to low-wage countries, postmodernist design is now the first truly global style.

**THE LANGUAGE OF MICHAEL GRAVES** With a typically postmodern playful element, this exhibition poster uses the designer's name as the material for a typographical picture. *1983. W:45.5cm (18in).*

# ELEMENTS OF STYLE

**P**ostmodernism was an eclectic genre, absorbing a number of radical concepts and trends. Paramount was the rejection of the "form follows function" tenet of modernism: designers felt encouraged, even obliged, to challenge the preconceived ideas of good design. In doing so they were able to re-examine the natural properties of various media – especially glass, plastics, wood, metals, and ceramics – and reinterpret the styles of the past. The results are daring, unconventional, and often ironic.

GAETANO PESCE *OSSO* TABLE LAMP

### INDIVIDUAL DIVERSITY

The economic climate created a prosperous elite to fund one-off creations. This provided a secure environment in which designers could produce the ultimate expressions of their own creativity. They did not confine themselves to one discipline, but chose instead to experiment across the decorative arts.

DANNY PERKINS MALIBU GLASS SCULPTURE

### COLOUR

Colour was key for postmodern designers, sometimes elevated to a status equal to form or function in a piece. Designers often relied on their creative use of colour to provide the visual impact of a piece – especially by combining bright or clashing colours and through the use of extraordinary patterns.

PETER SHIRE SINGLE-PEDESTAL DESK

### ASYMMETRY

Perhaps the clearest expression of anti-modernism was asymmetry. Designers deliberately avoided symmetry, through colour, structure, or materials. The results often challenged the accepted norms of conventional design, making pieces difficult to make sense of, even displeasing to the unaccustomed eye.

BORIS SIPEK PO-LAM WARDROBE

### MIXING MATERIALS

The use of two or more utterly different materials was a common anti-modernist device. Costly materials such as heavy marble, semi-precious metals, and leather were teamed up with cheap and garish plastics or synthetic textiles. Designers also gave cheaper materials an expensive-looking finish, as here, where the marbling is simply a paint effect.

ETTORE SOTTSASS IVORY TABLE

### SURFACE DECORATION

For many postmodern designers, the challenge of visual impact outweighed the importance of form or function. To this end, they experimented with a wide range of materials for surface decoration. Of particular significance was the popularity of plastic laminates imitating anything from wood grains to animal hides and exotic textiles.

ROBERT VENTURI QUEEN ANNE CHAIR

### HISTORICAL APPROPRIATION

As in previous eras, postmodern designers looked to the past for inspiration. Borrowed motifs appeared variously across the decorative arts, sometimes combining several from different eras in one piece. The aim was to challenge the accepted symbolism of archaic forms by presenting them in an unexpected, irreverent way.

FRANTISEK VIZNER SPHERICAL VASE
## SIMPLE FORMS
Early postmodern designers such as those associated with the Memphis group gave their work impact by using simple, conventional shapes in unconventional ways. As the movement waned and a new minimalism emerged, unornamented forms found favour in metalwork, ceramics, and sculpture.

MOI VOLKOV MARILYN SCULPTURE
## POPULAR CULTURE
A theme across all disciplines was an obsession with popular culture and consumerism. Some designers incorporated instantly recognizable images such as cartoon characters, film idols, and punk motifs. Others recycled objects from contemporary living – a nod to anti-consumerist sentiments.

DALE CHIHULY HARRISON RED BASKET SET
## UNIQUE CRAFTS
Tired of the precision manufacturing of the modern age, and of all the new plastics that had emerged since the 1950s, some designers returned to handcrafts as an alternative. They explored the natural properties of wood, glass, metals, and ceramics, producing a host of unique pieces.

ALCHIMIA NEEDLE AND SPOOL TABLE LAMP
## HUMOUR
In moving away from conventional forms, it was not uncommon for designers to incorporate unexpected, often witty, elements in their work. Examples of humour include objects with one function designed to resemble something with another, as here, or outsized versions of everyday objects.

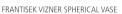

WENDELL CASTLE CALIGARI PIANO
## REINTERPRETATION
Postmodern designers were adept at giving conventional forms a new and humorous lease of life. Here a Steinway piano is painted in the abstract expressionist style. Other reinterpretations include Alessi's micro-architectural style of domestic appliances and the adoption of zoomorphic (animal-like) or anthropomorphic (human) forms.

MARC NEWSON FELT CHAIR
## NEW MINIMALISM
By the end of the 1980s some designers rejected busy, symbolism-charged designs and turned to a new minimalism. Using materials with plain surfaces – glass, brushed metals, clear or single-colour plastics, and untreated woods – designers began to make products where the simplicity of the medium accentuated the form of the work.

ADRIAN OLABUENAGA METAL PHOTOGRAPH FRAME
## ARCHITECTURE
Architecture was one of the first disciplines to adopt the theories of postmodernism, and a number of architects also became involved in the decorative arts. The result was the appearance of architectural forms and motifs across all disciplines, but in particular in the designs of Michael Graves and Robert Venturi.

ALCHIMIA ATROPO TABLE
## GEOMETRIC LINES
Geometric patterns were used to striking effect by postmodern designers, particularly in furniture design, textiles, and ceramics. Geometric lines – whether structural or decorative – might also be reinterpretations of popular stylistic genres such as Art Deco, or of designs specific to different cultures such as the Aztecs.

# FURNITURE

DRAWING ON A DIVERSE RANGE OF SOURCES, AND PAYING LITTLE ATTENTION TO FUNCTION, POSTMODERN FURNITURE DESIGNERS REJECTED THE LESSONS OF MODERNISM IN FAVOUR OF A MORE ECLECTIC APPROACH.

## SEEDS OF POSTMODERNISM

In an essay entitled *The Return of Historicism*, written in 1961, the celebrated British architecture and design critic Nikolaus Pevsner referred to a new trend among architects and designers for borrowing from the past. Since the emergence of the modern era in the early 1920s, architects and designers had steadfastly refused to look back, focusing only on the future, so Pevsner described this new development as postmodern.

### ARCHITECTURAL DESIGN

What Pevsner had spotted was the seeds of a movement in architecture and design that only fully began to flower during the latter half of the 1970s, reaching its zenith a decade later. The appropriation of the past (usually by adopting stylistic conceits from bygone eras) was an important ingredient in the postmodern style, as

Pevsner had pointed out early on, and so too were references to popular culture (such as films and cartoons), the use of unusual materials, and a theatrical use of colour. Low on the list of priorities of the postmodern designer was function, which had been so important to earlier generations.

### AGAINST MODERNISM

The reasons for there being such a strong backlash against the rational, reductivist methods of modernism were numerous. Robert Venturi, the American architect, designer, and theorist was an early spokesman for postmodernism (particularly through writings in his highly influential books, *Complexity and Contradiction in Architecture*, first published in 1966,

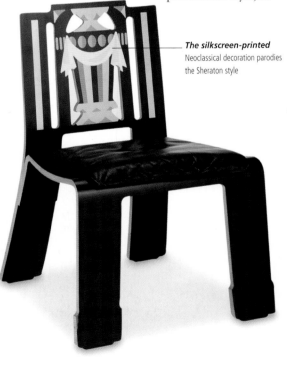

**The silkscreen-printed** Neoclassical decoration parodies the Sheraton style

**KNOLL SHERATON 378 CHAIR** Designed by Robert Venturi, this chair, of moulded plywood with a black leather-upholstered seat pad, playfully recalls the Neoclassical furniture design epitomized by Thomas Sheraton. *1984. H:84.5cm (33¼in).*

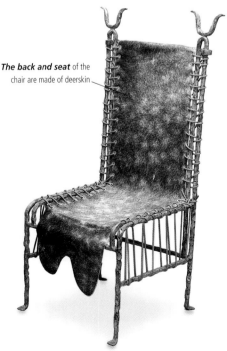

**The back and seat** of the chair are made of deerskin

**BARBARE CHAIR** Elizabeth Garouste and Mattia Bonetti based the design of this chair on an African tribal throne. It has a patinated bronze frame onto which a deerskin is laced. *1981. H:118cm (46½in).*

**FRANKFURT F1 SKYSCRAPER CABINET** Designed by Norbert Berghof, Michael Landes, and Wolfgang Rang, and made by Draenert GmbH, this cabinet is veneered in various exotic woods. The doors open to reveal a detailed interior including two secret compartments. *1985–86. H:230cm (92in).*

**The Mickey Mouse ears** compare with the two-part headrest on Toshiyuki Kita's earlier Wink armchair

**AKABA S.A. GARRIRI CHAIR**
This black leather and metal-framed chair was designed by the Spanish artist, designer, and cartoon enthusiast Javier Mariscal. c.1988. H:96.5cm (38in).

**PLAZA DRESSING TABLE**
Memphis, the Milan-based collective of young postmodern designers, dominated early 1980s design with innovative pieces such as this dressing table in laminate and briar root wood by the architect Michael Graves. c.1981. H:226cm (89in).

**The shape** of the piece is architectural

**LITTLE BEAVER ARMCHAIR AND OTTOMAN**
Designed by Frank Gehry for Vitra, these pieces form part of his Experimental Edges series, which exploited the expressive qualities of corrugated cardboard. The series evolved from Gehry's 1972 mass-produced Easy Edges cardboard furniture line. 1987. Armchair: H:81cm (32in).

**Laminated cardboard** gives the piece a startling, cutting-edge expressivity

## ETHNIC INFLUENCES

Besides the many cursory references made to the past in postmodern furniture, there was also a proliferation of interest in ethnic design styles – most famously and explicitly in Elizabeth Garouste and Mattia Bonetti's controversial *Objets Barbares* and *Objets Primitifs* collections of 1981. By alluding to indigenous design languages, designers asserted their indifference to the drive towards an essential, international style that united designers of the modern era.

The fact that the complex and contradictory style of postmodernism (to paraphrase Robert Venturi) found its full voice during the late 1970s is no coincidence. This was a time of global economic uncertainty and the furniture industry, like many others, was at a low ebb. Without much commercial work to keep them busy, many designers began to pursue more individual, experimental projects and took the time to develop the convoluted design vocabularies common at this time. Even when money began to pour back into the furniture industry during the 1980s, this period of intense intellectual activity shone through – most remarkably in the intriguing work of the Memphis group (*see p.390*).

## CRAFTSMANSHIP

One of the most significant paradoxes of the postmodern movement (a movement that was riddled with them) was the fact that despite the fascination with so-called "low rent" popular culture, the furniture was almost invariably expensive. A chair made out of cardboard would be sold in an upmarket gallery to wealthy collectors, and a chair with Mickey Mouse ears – an image that you could see adorning many cheap, mass-produced products – was only available in limited numbers. Many of the furniture designs that were so indebted to the culture of quick turnover and disposability were lovingly produced by craftsmen in antiquated workshops. It was precisely these sorts of inconsistencies, however, that postmodernism embraced.

and *Learning from Las Vegas*, 1972). He described his fascination with the speed of contemporary culture and its obsession with surface. These, he argued, were just as interesting for architects and designers to explore as the pursuit of pure form and technical expertise. Venturi's furniture designs for Knoll (1978–84) made extensive use of plastic laminates and veneers (very postmodern materials), and played with entirely tongue-in-cheek references to past design styles, thereby commenting on – and indeed celebrating – what he saw as culture's largely superficial interest in history.

**BAMBI CHAIR** With its apparent structural instability and frail form, this brass, maple, organza fabric, and steel limited-edition chair designed by Borek Sipek embodies extravagance and whimsy. 1983. H:75cm (29½in).

**FORREST MYERS ARMCHAIR** This La Farge chair looks like a gravity-defying ball of wool unravelling from a box. Made from tubular black metal and copper panels, it is a variant of Myers's sculptural wire material drawings. (Unmarked). W:79cm (31½in).

**The sculpted metal seat** forms an experimental, irregular structure

**S-CHAIR** Tom Dixon designed his steel-framed S-chair, inspired by Verner Panton, in 1988, and it was adapted by several manufacturers. This straw example by Cappellini is also available in woven cane, felt, and latex. *c.1991. H:100cm (39½in).*

*Woven marsh straw* lends the piece sinuous movement and expression

*The bold structure* rejects the excesses of earlier postmodern design

**MONO SIDE TABLE** One of a set of four, this table by SCP was designed by Konstantin Grcic. German-born Grcic took a democratic approach, advocating accessible and understandable furniture design. *1995. H:75cm (29½in).*

**KNOTTED CHAIR** This chair by Cappellini was designed by Marcel Wanders. Made of carbon fibre and epoxy resin, it is a successor to Forrest Myers's sculptural and eccentric armchair, but has a regular, functional form. *1995.*

## CONTEMPORARY FURNITURE

The 1980s was a decade of excess in all areas of design. This was a reaction to the sobriety of modernism, which had been under attack since the 1960s. But by the end of the 1980s, as stock markets declined and belts were tightened, attitudes began to change. After almost 15 years of overt postmodernism and its rich, complex style, people felt the need for simpler, cleaner designs.

During the later years of the 1980s and into the 90s, the clashing colours drained out of furniture. Clear glass and acrylic were more widely used, as were natural materials such as exposed wood and wicker. When colour was employed, it was used on its own – pattern and surface decoration were considered little more than an unnecessary distraction. The obsession with laminates and mixing materials evaporated too, as designers began to revive the modernist spirit of "truth to materials".

Many of the old modernist values seeped back into furniture design. A love of clean lines, pared-down forms, and an interest in utility were typical of designers in the 1990s. Despite this, however, many of the privileges won for designers by postmodernism lived on. Designers were aware, for instance, that function was not the be-all and end-all of furniture. They knew too that a certain amount of idiosyncrasy was welcome and that humour was an acceptable ingredient of design.

### FREEDOM FROM CONSTRAINTS

Jasper Morrison, the British designer who led the move towards the more streamlined design style of the 1990s, stated in an interview that the most important designers for him were early modernists such as Eileen Gray and Marcel Breuer. Morrison also pointed out how important postmodernism was – particularly the Memphis group – by explaining: "It's not the most practical kind of design but it had the effect of freeing everything up, to show that we don't have to accept all these constraints and ridiculous rules about how one should design – design should be open to different ways of working."

**BIRD ROCKING CHAIR** Designed by Tom Dixon for the Italian firm Cappellini, this wooden-framed, multi-density foam rocking chair shows a contemporary emphasis on functionality. This piece is more suited to industrial production than many of Dixon's more intricate designs. *c.1991. H:89cm (35in).*

*The clean lines* and removeable single-colour cover made the Bird Chair relatively simple to manufacture

**BRICK BOOKSHELVES** This modular storage system consists of a number of honeycomb-shaped lacquered-plywood shelves stacked one on top of the other. Available in a range of colours, it was designed by Ronan and Erwan Bouroullec for Cappellini. *Each module: H:50cm (19¾in).*

**The shelves** are held in place by plywood book ends

## DESIGN AND PERSONALITY

During the 1990s designers felt able to pursue their own personal styles, something that was made easier by advances in technology. The growing sophistication of computer programs and manufacturing techniques meant that mass-produced furniture became increasingly refined. Giving objects a personality, however, was not only about the designer expressing himself, but also something of a marketing ploy. In an increasingly crowded market, furniture needed to stand out from the crowd and appeal to consumers not only from a practical but also an emotional point of view. For this reason, soft, subtly curvaceous shapes were also popular during the 1990s, as was furniture whose forms resembled natural objects, such as birds and trees.

Italy had produced many of the most important designers of the 1950s, 1960s, 1970s, and 1980s, and this continued as the century drew to a close. As the world's most important country for furniture manufacture, Italy went from strength to strength. Companies such as Cappellini, B&B Italia, and

Edra produced some of the most interesting furniture of the decade. Many of the firms employed foreign designers. In fact, this era is notable for a global cross-pollination of ideas.

## CHANGING INFLUENCES

Jasper Morrison, Tom Dixon, Ron Arad, Marc Newson, Konstantin Grcic, and many others all spent formative years in the United Kingdom, most of them attending the highly influential Royal College of Art in London. France, on the other hand, gave the design world Philippe Starck, whose sleek, witty designs dominated the latter years of the 1980s and early years of the 1990s (*see p.392*) and the Bouroullec brothers.

At the beginning of the 21st century Ronan and Erwan Bouroullec were undoubtedly the designers in greatest demand, as companies appreciated the subtle sophistication of their furniture designs. Dutch design at the end of the 20th century was important mainly because of Droog, a loose collective of designers including Richard Hutten, Marcel Wanders, and Hella Jongerius, which reintroduced a political and conceptual element into their designs that had not been seen since the late 1970s.

At the turn of the century, after a rollercoaster ride through the extremes of modernism and postmodernism, design had arrived at a point where the lessons of both had been learned and designers were equipped to follow their own paths and develop their own ideologies.

## GAETANO PESCE

Few designers in history have followed their own instincts with as much conviction as Gaetano Pesce, a designer born in Italy in 1939. Paying little heed to custom, convention, or prevailing design trends, Pesce has said that his only commitment is to "communicating feelings of surprise, discovery, optimism, stimulation, sensuality, generosity, joy, and femininity". A veteran of numerous Italian avant-garde design and architecture movements of the 1960s and 1970s, Pesce moved to New York in 1980 and established a series of companies dedicated to producing his own designs. Taking great pleasure in making what he calls "poorly made" products, his designs at the end of the 20th century were often made from resin in a rainbow of colours, and were idiosyncratic in the extreme.

**NOBODY'S CHAIR** Designer Gaetano Pesce continues to experiment with new forms and materials. This Zero Disegno for Etro limited-edition chair comprises panels of coloured polyurethane-based elastic resin inlaid with silk fragments. *2004. H:88cm (34¾in).*

**BERNINI BROADWAY 6 CHAIR**
This limited-edition chair designed by Gaetano Pesce was available in blue, red, or black, with the colour of the thermochromatic plastic seat changing slightly with the heat of the sitter. The nine sprung feet give a pleasant rocking feeling. *2001. H:75cm (29½in).*

**ETRUSCAN CHAIR** This glass and stainless steel chair was designed by leading glass sculptor Danny Lane. It shows off Lane's particular skill in glass cutting and embraces the salvage movement branch of postmodern style. *1986. H:88cm (34¾in).*

**The seat and back** are made of high-strength 25mm (1in) glass

**The single yellow feather** is subtle yet makes a dramatic impact.

**FEATHER STOOL** Shiro Kuramata's design for Ishimaru & Co. features a translucent acrylic block base with internally cased feathers and an aluminium backrest. It looks more like a piece of sculpture than a chair. *1990. H:54cm (21¼in).*

# WENDELL CASTLE

INVENTIVE AND ADVENTUROUS, WENDELL CASTLE IS A ONE-OFF
WHO HAS FREQUENTLY ENTERED TERRITORY TRADITIONALLY
OCCUPIED BY SCULPTURE. WITH HIS RICH, ECLECTIC STYLE,
CASTLE QUICKLY BECAME THE DARLING OF AFFLUENT AMERICAN
ART AND DESIGN COLLECTORS.

**LOUNGE CHAIRS** This rare and early pair of stacked
oak laminate chairs illustrate Castle's 1960s style of curvy
wooden furniture. Once other designers latched onto it,
Castle's work changed direction. *1967. H:82.5cm (33in).*

The open-minded approach taken by
Wendell Castle to art, design, craft, and
industry has allowed the American-born
designer and artist to operate across the
borders of all four fields since he started
his career in Kansas in the early 1960s.
During this decade,
Castle became well
known for his
organically shaped,

sculptural furniture carved from stacked, laminated
wood. His fame reached greater heights in the 1980s,
when he became known as a leading exponent of
the Studio Craft movement.

Castle's move away from the curvaceous wooden
furniture he made in the 1960s to his more eclectic
output of the 1980s was a gradual process. By the
1970s the stacked, laminated wood process that
he had developed had been adopted by numerous
other American designers, and Castle felt a desire
to move on.

to start a new so-called "fine" style of his own. His
first piece of this period was the Lady's Desk with
Two Chairs (1981), made of English sycamore and
decorated with ebony and plastic dots. The piece,
according to Castle, "picked up where Émile-
Jacques Ruhlmann, the last of the great *ébénistes*,
left off". Castle's plundering of the past, as seen
with the Lady's Desk, has often been described
as a postmodern trait but Castle himself denies
it, referring to his work of the early 1980s as
historical classicist. Indeed, Castle does seem to
treat past styles with a degree of reverence and
attention that was hardly conjured up by the more
cynical, magpie-like designers of postmodernism.

**CALIGARI PIANO** Combining
the jazzy angularity of abstract
expressionism with tradition and
fine craftsmanship, Wendell Castle
teamed up with Steinway & Sons
to create this striking indigo and
white piano and bench. *1990.
W:177.5cm (69¾in).*

## FINE FURNITURE

Around the 1960s and 1970s, Castle was also
impressed by the work of John Makepeace, a
designer based in England who used a team of
highly skilled craftsmen to create extravagant,
one-off pieces of furniture in a diverse range of
exotic materials. On Makepeace's advice, Castle
employed an English craftsman called Stephen
Proctor, putting him in charge of his New York
studio. During this time Castle also took on Silas
Kopf and Donald Sottile, two other highly
competent technicians. Although Castle had never
previously placed much importance on technical
virtuosity (believing it distracted both the maker
and the user/viewer from the overall impression of
the piece), he saw that it would prove essential in
realizing his ideas for what he called his range of
"fine" furniture.

At the end of the 1970s Castle was invited
by the Memorial Art Gallery in Rochester, New
York, to curate an exhibition of historical furniture
borrowed from the Metropolitan Museum
of Art. This curatorship inspired him

## ENERGETIC AND SYMBOLIC

Castle's work from the mid-1980s to the 1990s
can really only be described as postmodern. Paying
only a passing interest to function, his furniture of
this era occupies itself far more with form, colour,
and conceptual content. Having seen the work of
the Italian Memphis group (*see p.*390), Castle
(a designer who always knew a hot trend when
he saw one) allowed his work to become far more
expressive, energetic, and rich in symbols. Surface
pattern became increasingly important too as he
began to paint, stain, and lacquer the wood that
he used. One of Castle's most successful series of
furniture of this type was the 1986 Dr Cagliari
collection. Inspired by the tense, awkward
atmosphere created by the
film sets in the classic 1920s
horror film, *The Cabinet of
Dr Cagliari*, Castle's furniture
is purposefully angular and
patterned with brushstrokes to
make it appear almost camouflaged.
Another decorative device that Castle
often used at this time was forms
resembling pots or plants, adding a
touch of the absurd to his furniture.

**URN CABINET** This typically
postmodern piece combines
a bold, abstract polychrome
composition on the single
door, concealing two drawers
and two shelves, with a
Classical form – the urn
– employed as supports.
*1991. H:179cm (70½in).*

**ANGEL CHAIR** The labour-intensive Angel Chair series is
considered by many to be Castle's finest achievement. This
memorable piece, entitled Night Voyages, is made of wood
and patinated bronze. *1991. W:157.5cm (63in).*

**ANGEL CHAIR DESIGN** This signed and dated pencil and gouache painting
by Wendell Castle shows the geometrical Bolstered Egos Angel Chair and
illustrates a postmodern "form over function" aesthetic. The seat of the real
chair is made of mahogany. *1990.*

# FURNITURE GALLERY

Furniture designers took the freedom of expression granted to their mid-century predecessors and used it to push design as far as they could. An element of historical and cultural reference often leads to playful pieces that defy preconceptions of what a chair or table should be. The result is exuberant extremes.

### KEY

**1.** Metal-framed mirror and lamp by Nanda Vigo. 1986. ④ **2.** Geoffrey Harcourt/Artifort Cleopatra sofa of upholstered foam and tubular steel. 1973. W:185.5cm (74¼in). ② **3.** Armchair by Toshiyuki Kita, 1984, reissued by Tendo Mokko, 2004. H:67.5cm (26½in). ① **4.** Licence to Build sofa/children's game made from high-resilience foam by Matali Crasset of France. 2000. ③ **5.** Bird personal desk made of burr elm, wych elm, and Lebanon cedar by John Makepeace. H:101cm (39¾in). ⑦ **6.** McCain recycled plastic chair by Beata Bär, Gerhard Bär, and Christof Knell. 1994. W:47cm (18½in). ① **7.** Stainless steel armchair with a leather seat cushion by Jonathan Singleton. H:104cm (41in). ④ **8.** Eighteen chest-of-drawers by John Makepeace. H:135cm (53in). ⑧ **9.** High-Heel chair with

**2** Geoffrey Harcourt sofa

**3** Toshiyuki Kita armchair

**4** Matali Crasset sofa

**6** Recycled chair

**1** Nanda Vigo mirror

**5** Bird desk

**7** Stainless steel armchair

**8** John Makepeace chest of drawers

**9** High-Heel chair

**10** Mats Theselius armchair

leopard-print upholstery, attributed to David Bury. c.1980. W:49cm (19¼in). ① **10.** Armchair with an elkskin seat by Mats Theselius for Källemo AB of Sweden. 1991. ④ **11.** Magis Tam Tam rotational moulded polyethelene stool by Matteo Thun. 2002. H:35cm (14in). ① **12.** Side table made from panels of red and clear rubbery plastic by Gaetano Pesce. 2002. H:49cm (19¼in). ① **13.** Pierre Sala notebook table. H:72cm (28¼in). ② **14.** Gary Knox Bennett Table #8, in patinated bronze with an arrow-shaped top and three tapered legs. H:48cm (19in). ③ **15.** Kick Table by Toshiyuki Kita for Cassina. 1983. H:52cm (20½in). ② **16.** Fish Bench by Judy McKie. **17.** Tavolo table, made of cast bronze with a glass top by Sandro Chia. 1989. H:80cm (31½in). ⑤ **18.** Table Table, a centre table with an inset leather surface on printed MDF by Clementine Hope. H:76cm (30in). ① **19.** Sgaboo foam rubber and plastic stool by Markus Benesch for Post Design. 2005. H:44cm (17½in). ①

12 *Gaetano Pesce side table*

11 *Matteo Thun stool*

13 *Notebook table*

14 *Gary Knox Bennett table*

15 *Kick table*

16 *Fish bench*

17 *Tavolo table*

18 *Centre table with leather inset*

19 *Sgaboo stool*

# PRODUCT DESIGN

MANY DESIGNERS WORKED ACROSS A RANGE OF DISCIPLINES, FROM FURNITURE TO CERAMICS AND FROM GLASS TO KITCHEN GADGETS. THE POSTMODERN STYLE BEGAN WITH ALCHIMIA.

## ALCHIMIA

Throughout the 1960s and early 1970s, a number of Italian designers had begun to chip away at the prevailing idea that form must follow function, a concept that was core to the values of modernism. However, it was not until the birth of Studio Alchimia in 1976 that this idea, and all that it entailed, was finally and unceremoniously consigned to the dustbin.

Studio Alchimia was formed when designers Alessandro and Adriana Guerriero invited a number of their friends to design some new work – not for the purposes of putting it into production but to include in an exhibition in a Milan gallery. Free from commercial constraints, the designers – including Alessandro Mendini, Paola Navone, and Michele De Lucchi – didn't hold back and produced a collection of experimental work.

It was the work's eclecticism, however (what Mendini called its "kaleidoscopic beauty"), that came to define the Alchimia style. In 1979, in a clear statement that the rigid rules of modernism – summed up by the architect Mies van der Rohe as "Less is more" – were being purposefully flouted, Alchimia produced a collection of bastardized Bauhaus furniture. Marcel Breuer's concise Wassily chair of 1925, in the hands of Alchimia, became a steel frame smothered in flaps of exuberantly patterned fabric. Echoing the sentiments of fellow rebel Robert Venturi, who retorted "Less is a bore", Alchimia's leader Alessandro Mendini stated: "The act of making signs is what counts today."

**KANDISSA MIRROR** This lacquered-wood framed mirror designed by Alessandro Mendini unites a traditional design with modern influences such as Kandinsky's paintings. Fewer than ten examples of this mirror exist. *1978. H:100cm (39in).*

***FABBRO* CERAMIC VASE** This extremely rare Alchimia limited-edition vase was designed by Alessandro Mendini. It is decorated with transfer-applied dots and geometric ceramic shapes. *1970s. H:30.5cm (12in).*

*The handpainted decoration* exemplifies the postmodern ideal of merging art and furniture design

*The cast metal legs* mimic traditional turned wooden furniture legs

**ATROPO TABLE** This piece designed by Alessandro Mendini has gold-coloured metal legs and a handpainted table top with gold foil highlights. The colourful, abstract design emphasizes surface decoration, and the table blends laminates and metal with traditional furniture styles. *1984. H:71cm (28in).*

*The vase* combines a simple form with seemingly random decoration

**STAZIONE SIDEBOARD** Nothing is what it seems in this piece made of glass and laminated wood, designed by Andrea Branzi for Alchimia. Shelves slide out, the top has a hinged lid, the normal position of a drawer is protruding, and what look like grey drawers are in fact hinged doors. *c.1979. L:150cm (59in).*

*The glass shelves* can slide in and out

## ALESSANDRO MENDINI

Without the input of Alessandro Mendini, the tireless Italian designer and theorist, it would be fair to say that the design world at the end of the 20th century would have been a far duller place. Born in Milan in 1931, Mendini's early career as a partner in the firm Nizzoli Associati was unremarkable but at the beginning of the 1970s he began to find his voice.

As the most prominent member of the radical Alchimia group, he established himself as a designer of great invention and intellect. His clear ability to create products that made people sit up and take notice soon attracted the interest of a number of manufacturing companies, including Swatch (the Swiss watch manufacturer) and Alessi (the homeware manufacturer). As Art Director of Swatch in the late 1980s, he helped make them one of the most popular and prominent brands of the time, and his work for Alessi has similarly done much to establish the identity of the Italian company.

**VENINI MURANO VASE**
Alessandro Mendini designed several series for Venini in the 1980s. This large glass vase is of elongated globular form and is clear cased with vertical lines in turquoise, red, and blue. *c.1980. H:39.5cm (15½in).*

## REDISCOVERING SOUL

The members of Alchimia believed that the success of the production line had sterilized the field of design. The early modernist's dreams of marrying art and industry had, by the 1970s, become all too true and the search for "practical efficiency", as Mendini put it, had meant that design had lost touch with "the object's soul". In an attempt to recover some of the romance of design, the work produced under the Alchimia banner revelled in a riot of clashing colour, pattern, and purposefully awkward forms.

One of the most radical ploys pursued by Alchimia's designers was to produce objects that employed a wide variety of materials. Mendini talked of a "confusion of craft and industry", as "low" materials such as painted metal and plastic laminate were combined with "high" materials such as crystal glass or polished briarwood. The ever-eloquent Mendini described Alchimia's look as "full and violent".

Alchimia's sphere of activity during the late 1970s and throughout the 1980s encompassed not only furniture design but also graphic design, stage sets, and fashion. No design discipline, it seemed, remained unaffected by the Alchimia crusade. In his role as contributor to numerous design publications (some of which he also edited during one time or another), Mendini ceaselessly promoted Alchimia and its message of Banal Design. An intentional echo of Bel Design – a phrase much used during the post-war era to describe design of good taste and honest practicality – Banal Design followed the idea that the discordant, complex nature of life at the end of the 20th century made it pointless to pursue the pure forms with which designers had previously been so obsessed. Embracing contemporary culture, in forms both high and low, became Alchimia's concerted aim.

## FINAL YEARS

The aggression, energy, and strong voice of the Alchimia group meant that their influence spread far and wide. Their essentially anarchic approach to design struck a strong chord with young designers across the globe. Commercially, however, Alchimia was never much of a success. When the Museo Alchimia (a shop dedicated to selling the group's products) opened in Milan in 1988, it was little surprise that it folded shortly afterwards. The fact that the group championed style over substance also condemned them to having a limited lifespan. By the end of the 1980s most of the designers who had worked under the Alchimia banner had moved onto other things. The short life of Alchimia, however, remains one of the most thrilling episodes in recent design history.

**NEEDLE AND SPOOL LAMP** This table lamp designed by Lapo Binazzi consists of a turned wood cotton reel and needle, with the electric cable acting as the thread. *1982. Needle: L:54cm (21in).*

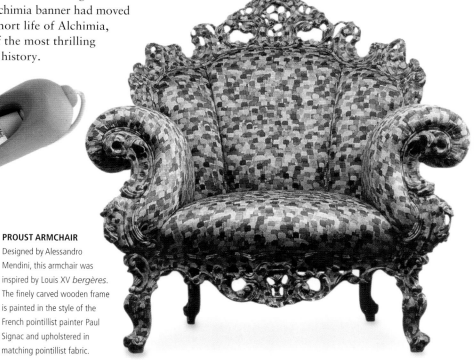

**PROUST ARMCHAIR**
Designed by Alessandro Mendini, this armchair was inspired by Louis XV *bergères*. The finely carved wooden frame is painted in the style of the French pointillist painter Paul Signac and upholstered in matching pointillist fabric.

## ETTORE SOTSASS

Although Ettore Sottsass is best known for his founding of (and subsequent work with) the Memphis design group of the 1980s (*see p.390*), he can still be considered one of the most important designers of every decade that he has worked in from the 1950s to the 2000s. Despite working prolifically across design disciplines, Sottsass's energy and talent always ensures high standards.

### ARCHITECTURAL BACKGROUND

Born in 1917 on the border of Italy and Austria, Sottsass studied architecture in Turin, graduating in 1939. His father, also called Ettore, was an influential Italian architect. Having studied under the proto-modernist architect Otto Wagner in Vienna, Sottsass's father became a key member of the Italian Rationalists, an avant-garde group that took up the cause of modernism at a time when the Fascist regime favoured less radical, more Neoclassical tendencies in design.

Despite (or perhaps because of) his father's adherence to the functionalist creed of modernism, Ettore Sottsass has always espoused a freer, more sensual style. There was an early indication of these leanings when in 1956 he chose to travel to New York to work for the celebrated American designer George Nelson. During the post-war period, American designers had loosened the straitjacket of European modernism by experimenting with organic forms and expressive colours, which attracted the young Sottsass.

**WOLF HOUSE, RIDGEWAY, COLORADO** Designed by Ettore Sottsass and built with project architect Johanna Grawunder from 1987 to 1989, this was the first architectural project to embody themes employed by the Memphis group: the importance of painted colour, choice of materials, and surface finishes, and providing equal attention to the exterior and garden as the interior.

### THE OLIVETTI YEARS

On his return to Italy in 1957, Sottsass began working for Olivetti, the office equipment firm that was then at the forefront of a technological revolution. Entirely new products such as computers and electronic calculators were being developed, and Sottsass soon became the primary

**IVORY TABLE** Designed by Sottsass in his Memphis period, the table of polychrome laminate is made in three parts: one straight, one jagged, and one wavy. It has a circular glass top. *1985. H:100cm (40in).*

**BIEDERMEIER SOFA** Designed by Ettore Sottsass, this sofa is made from coloured plastic-laminated plywood with foam rubber padding. *1983. H:137cm (54in).*

***The sofa legs*** are an irreverent pastiche of Classical columns

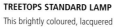

***A moveable metal connector*** makes it possible to tilt the light

**TREETOPS STANDARD LAMP**
This brightly coloured, lacquered metal lamp was designed by Sottsass for the Memphis group. *c.1981. H:180.5cm (71½in).*

**CARLTON BOOKCASE** Sottsass designed this hallmark geometric set of shelves with diagonal bookends for Memphis. The surfaces are made of brightly coloured, laminated wood. *1981. W:190cm (74¾in).*

**SOL FRUIT BOWL** Sottsass reworked the traditional tazza form to create this quirky glass fruit bowl for the Memphis group. *1982. H:26cm (10½in).*

**ASTEROIDE TABLE LAMP** Designed by Sottsass for Poltronova, this fluorescent lamp is reminiscent of neon lighting seen in Las Vegas. *1968. H:72cm (28½in).*

designer responsible for deciding what form these objects took. It was at Olivetti that Sottsass learned how important it was for a product to communicate with its user, a skill that became apparent in all his subsequent work. His early designs for portable typewriters, computers, and electronic calculators (which many buyers would never have handled before) used simple colour coding schemes and tactile forms to ensure that they did not appear too forbidding.

## THE FLAMBOYANT 1960S

Throughout the 1960s, Sottsass continued to develop many technical products for Olivetti as well as working on increasingly flamboyant furniture and lighting designs for the Italian firm Poltronova. During this decade he also began to experiment with glassware and ceramics, something that became a lifelong obsession.

Following travels to Asia and the United States, references to the two diverse cultures of these countries began to crop up in his work, most notably in his Shiva range of ceramics (1964) and his Pop Art-inspired Asteroide light (1968).

## CHANGING CLIMATE

The 1970s were not the most productive years for Sottsass (as was the case for many designers), because the harsh financial climate meant that money for manufacturing new designs was scarce. Despite this, Sottsass remained at the cutting edge by involving himself with the numerous radical design groups that were springing up in Italy, many of whom were more interested in ideologies than actually making products.

In 1973 Sottsass helped to establish Global Tools, a short-lived group dedicated to making design deomocratic by teaching people simple systems of design that used everyday objects.

During the late 1970s Sottsass briefly became part of Alessandro Mendini's Studio Alchimia (*see p.386*). Sottsass, however, has always been an essentially open-minded designer. "For me, design is a way to discuss life, social relationships, politics, food, and design itself," he once wrote. Mendini's dogmatic and, at the time, destructive approach to design meant that they did not work together for long. Despite this, Mendini's meticulous deconstruction of the values of modernism – primarily achieved by creating products that flew in the face of functionalism – paved the way for the acceptance of the Memphis group that was founded by Sottsass in the 1980s (*see p.390*).

The Memphis group (formed in Sottsass's Milan apartment in December, 1980) did not have any specific agenda, unlike many of the design groups that existed during the 1970s. The dilettante nature of Memphis designers was summed up by the name Sottsass chose for the group – as his partner, Barbara Radice, wrote at the time, Memphis meant: "The blues, Tennessee, rock'n'roll, American suburbs, and then Egypt, the Pharaoh's capital, the holy city of Ptah." Sottsass's refusal for his designs to be pinned down was still apparent.

## THE LATER YEARS

Following the phenomenal success of Memphis, Sottsass (who was aged 71 by the time the group dissolved in 1988) became one of the most revered figures in design. Far from resting on his laurels, however, Sottsass worked harder than ever throughout the 1990s – sometimes on his own independent projects and sometimes through his guiding of Sottsass Associati, the company that he had set up in 1981. Working on everything from the design of complete houses to ceramics and minor details such as door handles, Sottsass continued to outshine designers far younger than himself.

***The piece*** is a postmodern play on the tribal totem

**BITOSI TOTEM** This handpainted ceramic sculpture has 11 components bolted together through the middle with an iron rod. *1964–96. H:53.5cm (21in).*

# THE MEMPHIS GROUP

Formed in 1980 and disbanded eight years later, the work of Memphis, a group of primarily Italian designers, has come to symbolize 1980s design. Characterized by loud, brash colour, a playful approach to function and form, and a willingness to employ a broad palette of materials, Memphis's output was wildly ambitious and wilfully idiosyncratic. Crossing a wide range of disciplines (furniture, lighting, ceramics, and even clothing and jewellery), Memphis was also a great commercial success.

Despite its basis in the technology-obsessed and materialistic 1980s, the ideology behind Memphis was quite different in many ways. Firstly, Memphis was a collective – a very 1960s concept – and a seemingly successful one at that.

## EARLY INFLUENCES

Memphis's most influential member, Ettore Sottsass, was a veteran of numerous short-lived design collectives that existed during the 1960s and 1970s. He continued to believe in the idea of a collective consciousness. Indeed, many Memphis designs were produced in the immediate aftermath of long, often wine-fuelled, gatherings at Sottsass's Milan apartment. Secondly, technology was of limited interest to Memphis designers. While they did use some up-to-the-minute materials and manufacturing methods, they relied primarily on Milanese craftsmen to produce their pieces.

Despite these paradoxes, there were many aspects of Memphis that were entirely of their time. Most obviously, there was the international flavour of Memphis designs, reflecting the increasing ease of global travel and communication (the fax machine was a much-employed tool of the Memphis designers). Memphis designers also enjoyed a freedom that was unknown in other design groups of the 1970s. Besides the input of the main Italian members of Memphis (Sottsass, Michele De Lucchi, Marco Zanini, Aldo Cibic, and Barbara Radice), there

**KRISTALL TABLE** This geometric table was designed by Michele De Lucchi for the Memphis group. It is made from patterned, laminated wood and plastic-covered steel. *1981. H:50cm (19¾in).*

**FIRST CHAIR** Made from plastic-coated tubular metal and laminated wood, this "first" chair was designed by Michele De Lucchi for the Memphis group. *1983. H:84cm (33in).*

were also contributions from France (Martine Bedin and Nathalie du Pasquier), Spain (Javier Mariscal), England (George Sowden and Gerard Taylor), Austria (Matteo Thun), Japan (Arata Isozaki and Shiro Kuramata), and the United States (Michael Graves and Peter Shire).

The preference by Memphis group designers for surface pattern rather than form was in keeping with the mood of the times. Many of their products were covered with colourful plastic laminates, giving them a smooth, shallow surface that was entirely different in character from that of metal, wood, or any other natural materials. This use of patterned laminate made Memphis products look two-dimensional, as if they were cut out from the pages of a magazine or comic strip.

## MARKETING FOR SUCCESS

Memphis was one of the first design groups that counted among its key members a non-designer. Barbara Radice (who was Sottsass's partner in their personal as well as professional life) held the title of Art Director, but her skills essentially lay in her ability to write eloquently and effusively about

**The yellow box head** and black and white striped neck are shaped in an abstract animal form

**OCEANIC TABLE LAMP** Made from polychrome enamelled metal, this table lamp was designed by Michele De Lucchi for the Memphis group. *1981. H:99cm (39in).*

**SUPER LAMP** Designed by Martine Bedin, this moulded plastic light stands on four rubber wheels so it can move around. The six naked light bulbs all screw into different coloured sockets. *1981. W:50cm (19¾in).*

**CARROT VASE** This Flavia of Montelupo ceramic vase was designed by Nathalie du Pasquier for the Memphis group. *1985. H:30.5cm (12in).*

**CUCUMBER VASE** This transfer-printed ceramic vase was designed for Memphis by Martine Bedin. Memphis designers often chose unlikely names and inspirations to poke fun at their work. *1985. H:30.5cm (12in).*

**STUDIO TEAPOT** Designed by Peter Shire, this ceramic teapot with a funnel-shaped spout parodies traditional forms and is handpainted. *1996. W:23cm (9in).*

## GIOTTO

Named after the 14th-century Florentine artist who set the Italian Renaissance in motion, the Giotto range of products was intended to have a similar revolutionary effect on the homeware market. Giotto gathered together a number of ex-members of the recently disbanded Memphis group including Ettore Sottsass, Nathalie du Pasquier, and Marco Zanuso Jr, as well as number of younger designers including Johanna Grawunder. The Giotto range of vases, fruit bowls, and other objects was as bold and audacious as much of the Memphis output. Unfortunately, poor publicity and manufacturing problems in China hastened the demise of Giotto. Instead of flooding the market as intended, the products eventually ended up as collector's items in expensive European art galleries.

**GIOTTO JG4 VASE** This blue ceramic vase designed by Johanna Grawunder sits in a sprung steel holder. *1992. H:23cm (9in).*

Memphis and in promoting the group's work to the international media and design cognoscenti. With Radice's help, Memphis became an almost overnight sensation, with pictures of their products reproduced across the world. The first Memphis exhibition in 1981 (at the Arc 74 Gallery in Milan) was an instant hit and by the end of the year a coffee-table book had already been produced about the group, their work, and their history. Such accelerated success was unprecedented.

The fact that the Memphis style was so readily accepted was largely thanks to the ground being prepared during the late 1970s by Alchimia, the radical design studio led by Alessandro Mendini (for which Sottsass and De Lucchi had also, briefly, worked). A riotous affront to the purist ideals of modernism, Alchimia successfully eroded the prevailing idea that design was essentially a practical pursuit. Like Memphis's output, Alchimia products often contained a broad sweep of cultural references. But whereas Alchimia tended to present them in an provocative and cacophonous manner, the Memphis designers preferred to blend them into a more seamless, unified whole.

*The black-laquered top* forms an asymmetrical shape

**BRAZIL SINGLE-PEDESTAL DESK** Peter Shire designed this futuristic desk. It has a trapezoidal black-lacquered top on a pastel enamelled steel base. *1981. W:207cm (81½in).*

A Memphis product, then, may have patterns that faintly echo African tribal designs – or their forms might bear some resemblance to American skyscrapers – but these references always take second place to the overall composition of the piece. In this way, Memphis was not as cerebral or as dogmatic as Alchimia and this is perhaps why Mendini, a tireless theorist, never worked with the more instinctive, emotionally driven designers of the Memphis group.

# REVOLUTIONS IN DESIGN

Towards the end of the 1980s, the backlash against modernism was beginning to subside. Designers were even beginning to show nostalgia for the more simplistic, sensual forms of the 1950s. While they found themselves returning to the pared-down shapes of modernism, however, they chose to ignore the ideals of rational reform that the earlier era promoted. Indeed, many designs which followed in the footsteps of postmodernism pusued form for its own sake, rather than being overtly concerned with function.

Philippe Starck, Ron Arad, and Marc Newson are in many ways typical of designers of this era. They display no allegiances to a particular movement or style, but appear to follow their own interests and ideas. A curiosity about materials allows them to explore different possibilities without committing themselves to one particular look. All three, however, seem to prefer the sinuous to the straight line, perhaps a reaction to the jagged or geometric look of much 1970s and 1980s furniture.

All three designers were influenced by living in several different countries, and their design style communicates itself across cultural borders. Appealing to both the head and heart, it creates a strong visual impact.

**ÉTRANGETÉ 66** This teardrop-shaped glass object can be either a vase or a display piece. A typical Philippe Starck form, it was produced as a limited edition of 75 by the French company Daum. *c.1988. L:56cm (22in).*

**ALEPH SIDE CHAIR** Starck designed this three-legged chair for the Royalton Hotel in New York. *H:86cm (34in).*

## PHILIPPE STARCK

During the late 1980s and 1990s there was no bigger name in the design world than that of Philippe Starck. There appeared to be no household item that the designer had not turned his hand to: door handles, toothbrushes, sofas, telephones, and much more. His designs often involved stripping an archetypal object down to its bones in an essentially modernist manner, then adding a layer of postmodern whimsicality such as giving a chair legs made from different materials or a lamp a shade shaped like a bull's horn. This formula proved incredibly successful and brought Starck a degree of international fame that was unprecedented for a designer.

Born in Paris in 1949, Starck claims he rarely attended classes at the furniture-design course in Paris where he enrolled, and is essentially self-taught. Possessing immense energy and ambition, Starck became the Artistic Director at Pierre Cardin at the age of 20. By the mid-1970s he was designing nightclubs, notably Les Bains-Douches in Paris, but his big break came when he was asked to design Café Costes near the Centre Pompidou. Completed in 1984, the interior was, like much of Starck's subsequent work, simple and coherent with a wealth of mischievous details. An oversized clock loomed over the space and the chairs only had three legs (one less for waiters to trip over).

After his work at Café Costes was published in magazines and newspapers around the world,

Starck was soon being courted by a number of (mostly Italian) manufacturers. His exuberant interiors for the Royalton Hotel (1988) and Paramount Hotel in New York (1990) confirmed his status as the world's most in-demand designer, and the 1990s was a prolific decade for Starck.

Although Starck primarily used wood and metal early in his career, his work during the 1990s was mainly made from plastic. This gave him greater flexibility of form and, crucially, made his furniture more affordable. Starck's furniture was usually slender and curvaceous and frequently had elements of zoomorphism – suggestions of wings, horns, and legs were common – giving it a cuteness that broadened its appeal.

By the mid-1990s Starck was working with companies right around the world. Styling himself as the world's first truly international designer, and a superstar in the mould of a Hollywood actor, his profile in the 21st century is now lower. However, he continues to produce many critically acclaimed products and furniture.

**VITRA WW STOOL** Originally designed by Philippe Starck for Wim Wenders, the film director, this biomorphic-shaped stool is made of sand-cast aluminium with a pale green enamel finish. *1990. H:98.5cm (38in).*

**STARCK MODERNISM** Textured aluminium walls, floor-to-ceiling windows, atmospheric lighting, and bar stools with his trademark curvaceous legs are features of Philippe Starck's 1994 design for the Felix Restaurant in Hong Kong's Peninsula Hotel.

## RON ARAD

Never afraid of making bold statements with his furniture and interiors, Ron Arad has been stamping his mark on international design since the beginning of the 1980s. Born in Tel Aviv in 1951, Arad moved to London in 1974 to study at the Architectural Association and has been in the city ever since, becoming a British citizen in 1994.

Arad studied under Peter Cook and Bernard Tschumi, two radical architects who emphasized that ideas and aesthetics were just as important as practicality when it came to architecture and design. Following these sentiments, Arad set up his own studio, called One-Off, in 1981 and began to produce a series of unique, experimental furniture designs. Arad's Rover chairs (1981), which used salvaged car seats welded to a steel base, were the most successful of a number of early designs that incorporated found objects. In the tradition of the *objets trouvés* beloved of surrealist and conceptual artists such as Marcel Duchamp, the pieces not only had a political, anticonsumerist element, but they also formed comments on the environmental concerns of the age.

Throughout the 1980s Arad continued to produce thought-provoking pieces, often using raw, industrial materials such as concrete and steel. By the end of the decade, however, he had wound down his One-Off studio and formed Ron Arad Associates, which was more commercially driven.

During the 1990s Arad designed numerous pieces of furniture for mass production, often using plastics. Although these pieces were still strident in their design, they had developed from his earlier "found objects" style. By the beginning of the 21st century Arad had proved himself as both a designer who appealed to more artistically minded buyers (indeed, unique Arad pieces in steel were achieving staggering prices at auction of over US$50,000) as well as the mass market. His plastic Bookworm bookshelf for Kartell has been a bestseller since its introduction in the mid-1990s.

**WELL-TEMPERED CHAIR** The back, arms, and seat of this salvage movement chair are made from temper-rolled stainless steel, which is bolted into place with wing nuts. *1987. H:98.5cm (38¾in).*

**ROVER CHAIR** Arad's ready-made design for One-Off Ltd exemplifies the 1980s preoccupation with recycling. It is made of a salvaged Rover car seat mounted on a tubular-steel frame. *1981. H:96cm (37¾in).*

**EMPTY CHAIR** Made by Driade, this Arad chair consists of a bent, laminated plywood seating section on tubular-aluminium legs. *1993. H:99cm (39in).*

## MARC NEWSON

The Australian Marc Newson is one of the most international and prolific designers of the Southern Hemisphere. "Coming from Australia, my design has been self-taught and instinctive," he says.

Born in 1962, Newson studied jewellery design at the Sydney College of the Arts in the early 1980s, but spent much time in the sculpture department. Largely cut off from the latest developments of the postmodern style that were spreading across Europe, Newson acquired an appreciation for Italian furniture of the 1960s and early 1970s. Furniture by designers like Achille Castiglione and Joe Colombo was relatively common in Australia, and Newson responded to the optimism and forward-thinking they displayed.

A love of the futuristic designs of the past has played an important role in the creation of Newson's style, as demonstrated by his Lockheed Lounge (1985), the piece of furniture that launched his career. First shown in a Sydney gallery, the sculptural lounger was made from fibreglass and riveted aluminium and bore many similarities to the 1950s aircraft from which it took its name. Following the global exposure of this audacious piece of furniture, Newson was invited to Tokyo to work with a new company called Idée. Given few financial or aesthetic constraints, he spent the period from 1987 to 1991 producing some of his most remarkable furniture and establishing his style.

Updating the organic forms of furniture that were so popular among American designers of the 1950s, Newson created a look that was both retro yet entirely of its time in its use of advanced materials and manufacturing techniques.

At the beginning of the 1990s Newson moved to Europe where he worked for different furniture-makers in London and Paris. References to the beach culture of Australia continued to crop up in his work, however, in his use of bold shapes inspired by surfboards and eye-catching colours reminiscent of sun and sand.

*This chair* was also manufactured with felt and leather upholstery

**FELT CHAIR** A characteristically sculptural design by Marc Newson for Cappellini, this armchair is made from a reinforced fibreglass body supported on a polished aluminium leg. *1994. H:86cm (34in).*

*The fibreglass* makes it suitable for indoor and outdoor use

**ORGONE CHAISE LONGUE** This fibreglass lounge chair designed by Newson for Cappellini is available in a range of bright colours. It has an organic, flowing form, and stands on three tapering legs. *1992. L:181cm (71in).*

# NEW TECHNOLOGY

As consumers began to enjoy the benefits of increased leisure time, they placed greater importance than ever on the home as a place for rest, relaxation and entertainment. In order to beautify this environment, designers turned their attention to the minutiae of daily life. The kitchen, reinstated as a hub of family life, became the focus of particular attention.

## ALESSI DESIGN

The Italian design company Alessi has scored some of its most notable successes with appliances and gadgets for the kitchen. Philippe Starck's Juicy Salif citrus squeezer has become an icon of Alessi's achievement in this field. Despite its alleged impracticality, the Juicy Salif has sold well since its introduction in 1990. It is loved as a sculptural object first and a functional household item second.

Other Alessi products have married functionality to eccentric design with greater success. Since first working for Alessi on the Tea and Coffee Piazza range, Michael Graves has contributed a steady trickle of designs to the company's catalogue. His Kettle With Bird, first made in 1985, plays on the traditional notion of a whistling kettle

by attributing the noise to a plastic bird attached to the spout. Although most electric kettles automatically switch off once the water boils, Graves revived this time-honoured warning signal as a witty postmodern embellishment.

The kettle is fashioned from moulded stainless steel and the rivets around its base are designed in the same vein – as a reminder of and a throwback to archaic industrial techniques. The success of Graves's kettle design spawned a companion range of complementary products, all with the tubular blue plastic grip flanked by red spheres and the rivet detailing featured on the original.

Alessandro Mendini created a corkscrew called Anna G. for Alessi in 1994. By literally giving a face to Alessi's accessible, companionable design, Mendini created a phenomenon. From the original corkscrew the range has extended to include a cheese grater, a timer, a lighter, and a host of other products.

This personification of the product has been a constant feature of postmodern product design. The reference might be to a fictional character, as is the case with a pepper mill designed for Swid Powell by Robert and Trix Haussmann, which has large circular ears reminiscent of Mickey Mouse. Other products hint at this personification in a more abstract fashion, or in name only, such as Mattheo Thun's Swinging Marilyn teapot.

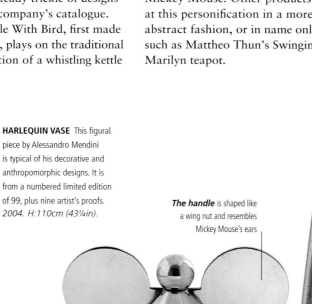

**The juice** runs down the body to be collected in a container placed beneath it

**HARLEQUIN VASE** This figural piece by Alessandro Mendini is typical of his decorative and anthropomorphic designs. It is from a numbered limited edition of 99, plus nine artist's proofs. *2004. H:110cm (43¼in).*

**The handle** is shaped like a wing nut and resembles Mickey Mouse's ears

**Anthropomorphic legs** are a typical Starck motif

**PEPPER GRINDER** This piece was designed by the Swiss architects Robert and Trix Haussmann for the American company Swid Powell. *1986. H:13.5cm (5in).*

**JUICY SALIF JUICER** Philippe Starck designed this long-legged juicer, made of cast aluminium with polyamide feet, for Alessi. A gold-plated limited edition of this popular design was manufactured in 2000. *1990.*

**AMERICAN iMAC POSTER** The iMac was launched in 1998 and was touted as the most original new personal computer since the first Apple Mac in 1984. The design team, led by Jonathan Ive, introduced a new case design with translucent "Bondi blue" plastic. The "Yum – Think Different, Apple Computers (Imac)" poster advertised the introduction of a new iMac model available in five new colours: blueberry, strawberry, lime, tangerine, and grape. *1999. H:91cm (36in).*

**SWINGING MARILYN TEAPOT** Matheo Thun's unusual teapot, designed for Alessi, is made of copper, base metal, and black plastic. The curves are formed from circle and tube segments. *1985. H:22.5cm (9in).*

**ANNA G. CORKSCREW** This corkscrew in plastic and chrome-plated Zamak metal was designed by Alessandro Mendini. It became an Alessi best-seller and spawned a range of objects featuring the Anna icon, such as peppermills, graters, and cigarette lighters. *1994.*

**OLA T1000GD TELEPHONE** This blue plastic telephone is organic in shape and was designed by Philippe Starck for Thomson. *1993. L:28cm (11in).*

*Transparent casing* and brightly coloured motor parts emphasize how the machine works

## APPLE SUCCESS

More recently, large corporations have become more design conscious to win sales in an increasingly competitive marketplace. Through a series of prominent advertising campaigns, Apple Computers has built a brand around creativity and has sought to separate itself from its competition using innovative product design ever since the launch of the Apple II, designed by Jerry Manock in 1977. Apple headhunted British designer Jonathon Ive to lead its design team in 1992. The iMac line, launched in 1998, represented a watershed in computer design. It was one of the first home computers to integrate the monitor and the CPU within a single case. The iMac also had its own quirky circular mouse. The candy colours and transparent case of the iMac have made it an object to display and have been imitated by many other industrial products.

## DYSON

The phenomenal success of James Dyson's 1983 vacuum cleaner must also owe much to its appealing design. It proclaims its "reinvention" with its appearance as much as through its advanced technology. This is another household appliance that consumers are happy to leave out on display rather than hide away in a cupboard.

**DYSON VACUUM CLEANER** This limited-edition Dyson DC02 De Stijl vacuum cleaner was named after the Dutch avant-garde design group's exploration of the relationship between colour, form, and function. *1996. H:50cm (19¾in).*

# CERAMICS

POSTMODERN POTTERY CAME TO OCCUPY A CURIOUS MIDDLE GROUND BETWEEN FUNCTIONAL OBJECT AND SCULPTURE. CERAMICISTS CREATED EXPRESSIVE AND FIGURAL SCULPTURE ALONGSIDE PRACTICAL PIECES.

**PAUL SOLDNER CHARGER** This charger is carved and handcrafted from white clay with glazes over a fossilized image of a fish. Soldner experimented with reduction chambers, used at the end of firing, to try to re-create traditional Japanese raku effects. *D:50cm (19¾in).*

## ABSTRACT EXPRESSIONISM

In 1952 the influential critic Harold Rosenberg, responding to the abstract expressionism of key figures such as Jackson Pollock, famously redefined art as a process rather than a product. Peter Voulkos was the first of a generation of potters to transfer this same idea to the medium of clay. He began to develop the distinctive sculptural idiom that encompassed his stoneware stack, plate, and ice bucket forms in 1954.

## REVOLUTION IN CLAY

Voulkos was at the forefront of the so-called Revolution in Clay that overturned accepted notions of what made good ceramic art. Whereas pottery and porcelain production had previously been linked with a relentless quest for perfection, Voulkos celebrated the raw qualities inherent in unworked clay. Although nominally based on, and named after, functional forms, Voulkos's sculptures are comprehensively torn, twisted, and gouged, and deliberately useless. The violence implicit in Voulkos's work is reminiscent of both Pollock's aggressive brand of Action Painting and the volatile geology of California, the clay of which he uses to create his vessels. Voulkos established the ceramic departments at the Otis Art Institute in Los Angeles and, later, at the University of California at Berkeley. His tenure at Berkeley lasted for more than 25 years from 1959 onwards and gave Voulkos the chance to disseminate his radical ideas on ceramics among many of the most promising young potters of the day.

Paul Soldner was Voulkos's first pupil at the Otis Art Institute. Arriving from the University of Colorado at Boulder, Soldner found that Voulkos's new ceramics department was little more than an empty room, and he set about helping his new teacher to organize the new department. Soldner even devised his own modifications to the pottery wheel they had installed. His interest in the technical side of pottery was so strong that he was compelled to establish a firm to sell his own clay mixers.

## EXPERIMENTING WITH GLAZES

Soldner was unusual among Voulkos's students in that he worked with traditional vessels rather than the abstract and sculptural forms favoured by his mentor. His great legacy is the innovative work he did taking Japanese raku ware as his starting point. Although fascinated by the element of chance involved in the raku glazing process, Soldner felt no natural affinity with the traditional tea wares usually associated with the style. Instead he applied

**STONEWARE CHARGER** The tears, incisions, and random pattern in the iron oxide and brown glazes of this large platter by Maria Woo show the influence of Voulkos. *H:49cm (19¼in).*

**TOTEMIC VESSEL** Made by Peter Voulkos, this tall brown stoneware piece incorporates tears, gouges, and incised lines. *H:68cm (27in).*

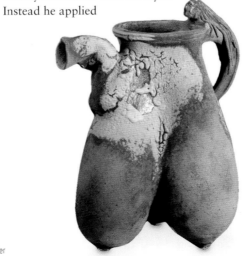

**EARTHENWARE VASE** This sensual vase by Ken Ferguson has three large lobes, a handle in the shape of a mermaid, and a twisted spout. It is covered in a verdigris and grey dead-matte volcanic glaze. *H:19cm (7½in).*

**PETER VOULKOS CHARGER** This large stoneware plate in dark brown glazed clay is typical of Voulkos's work. It is freely formed and features expressive tears and roughly applied pieces. *1995. D:53cm (20¾in).*

raku glazes to modern forms and plunged them into water while the glaze was still molten, cooling them quickly and accelerating the already speedy process of raku glazing. Soldner also developed a low-fire salt fuming technique. Both of these new processes produce a range of unpredictable effects depending on the exact conditions in the kiln.

Ken Ferguson, a former student of Voulkos, also experimented with salt glazes on his high-fired stoneware. Ferguson proved to be an inspirational teacher and many of his charges have since become influential contemporary potters in their own right.

## HOMEWARE AS ART

A band of female potters inculcated the British ceramics scene with a host of new ideas in the 1970s. Carol McNicholl made functional homeware using the slip-casting technique that has long been used to manufacture mass-produced homeware. Her individual pieces are, however, made entirely by hand and are gently subversive of traditional domestic forms. Her aim in this was to re-establish the home as a suitable venue for art.

Alison Britton trained under Hans Coper at London's Royal College of Art. Like Voulkos, Britton creates work that lies between utility and sculpture. She uses a slab-building technique to make vessels from sheets of clay, taking inspiration from sources as varied as ancient Oriental works of art to modern art.

The most prominent American woman working in a similar style is Betty Woodman. Among her most celebrated works are a series of pillow-shaped pitchers with mottled majolica glazes that resemble both Tang dynasty Chinese sancai ware and the poured-paint technique of Jackson Pollock. The elongated necks and gracefully curved handles on these vessels are inspired by Greek and Etruscan forms that Woodman had seen when visiting the Mediterranean.

**DRYSPACE POT** This tall, box-like piece was made by the British potter Alison Britton. It was built from slabs of clay rather than thrown on a wheel. *2003. H:47cm (18in).*

*Striped decoration* creates a dramatic effect

**PATTERNED VESSEL** Entitled New World Order, this piece by Carol McNicholl juxtaposes the expressive and unique nature of handbuilt clay with the repetitive qualities of the printed pattern. *H:22.5cm (9in).*

*Woodman's glazes* and exuberant use of colour are painterly

**PILLOW PITCHER** Just one of the many forms that Betty Woodman employs, this piece, of white clay with an applied handle, is covered in green, magnesium, yellow, and gunmetal majolica glazes. *W:51cm (20in).*

## THE FUNK MOVEMENT

Ceramics in this period moved on from their craft status. Encouraged by the freewheeling spirit of the 1970s, ceramicists made the most of the expressive and sculptural possibilities of their medium and produced a more varied body of work than ever before. Centred around the San Francisco Bay area, the Funk movement borrowed elements from Dadaism and Pop Art and used them to create a new ceramic idiom with a political and social agenda. The work of key figures such as Hui Ka Kwong, who made boldly decorated, symmetrical sculptural forms, is highly individual and characterized by a desire to communicate an emotional response to the world in the tradition of expressionist art.

This individualistic expressionism found a monumental exponent in Viola Frey. Her enormous columns and figures – often more than 3m (10ft) high – are so large that she was forced to chop them into sections to fire them. Frey would then paint the individual sections by hand before re-assembling them to form the finished sculpture. The process of creation was an intuitive one for her – it was only after figures were complete that she would "discover if they are intelligent or not, if they are good or bad, or if they have any sense of humor". In time she would abandon even this limited self-interrogation and work almost compulsively.

Akio Takamori, a Japanese potter who settled in the United States, had a more personal relationship with his

art. He first realized it was possible to create expressionist ceramics when a travelling exhibition of Western works passed through the town where he was apprenticed to a master folk potter. The anti-authoritarian nature of these works was a revelation to Takamori and he travelled to Kansas to embark on a degree in Fine Art. Takamori's

**CRUCIFIXION** This Akio Takamori faience sculpture depicts two naked men flanking a crowd of people watching a crucifixion. It has an outline of a bloodied cross on the reverse. *H:53cm (21in).*

**The four-armed piece** resembles a circus figure

**FUNK POTTERY LAMP** Hui Ka Kwong's piece has five sockets and two rows of arms on a flared base. The colourful trumpet-like form emphasizes the fun in the Funk aesthetic. *H:96.5cm (38in).*

**RED CLAY SCULPTURE** This piece by Beatrice Wood is composed of three wall-like panels with five door-shaped openings. Within them are figures of single women and embracing couples, all mounted on a pine board. *W:152.5cm (60in).*

**The figures** are covered with a cadmium-yellow volcanic glaze

**RAZZ-MA-TAZZ** This large vessel by Rudy Autio is characteristic of his style. In his pieces, which are often American West in theme, Autio blends curved, bulbous clay forms with painted figures. *1998. H:80cm (31in)*.

## DAVID GILHOOLY

Since enrolling in his first pottery class in pursuit of an elusive girl, David Gilhooly has become a leading exponent of the Funk ceramic movement. His work ranges from representations of animals named after old acquaintances to enormous pieces of junk food, replicated in clay in an effort to resolve his eating problems. Gilhooly's extensive FrogWorld series – a trawl through human history with frogs taking the roles of the main protagonists – threatened to take over his work, and he tried repeatedly to kill them off before finally consigning them to space. Gilhooly subsequently developed a distaste for clay, renouncing it forever in 1996. This might be considered something of a handicap for a ceramicist, but Gilhooly has continued his inimitable work in plexiglass.

**FROGS IN BEANS** This sculpture, one of the FrogWorld series, depicts three frogs frolicking in a cast-iron pot full of black-eyed beans. *c.1970. W:14.5cm (5in)*.

*The grotesque faces*, covered in polychrome oxide glazes, capture the Bosch spirit

**BOSCH TEAPOT** Noi Volkov's earthenware teapot alludes to the instantly recognizable work of the Dutch Renaissance painter Hieronymus Bosch. The piece is about form and decoration and pays littlel attention to function. *2005. L:30.5cm (12in)*.

**BASKETFUL FOR JOHN** This painted and transfer-printed piece is by the Funk ceramicist Richard Shaw, who is well known for his trompe l'oeil ceramics. It features items of his everyday life such as a deck of cards, a pack of cigarettes and matches, poker chips, paint, and a small cruise ship in a woven basket. *1992. W:38.5cm (15in)*.

early work was conspicuous for its sexual content, while his later figures draw on memories of his childhood in Japan and depict entire communities in clay. The common theme uniting these strands in his work is his exploration of the relationship between the physical and the emotional.

## ART INSPIRATION

A number of potters who have enjoyed long and varied careers have produced works that fit within the Funk agenda. Beatrice Wood, who died at the age of 105 after attributing her longevity to "chocolate and young men", created a number of obliquely evocative works during her later career.

Rudy Autio trained alongside Peter Voulkos at Montana State University in the late 1940s, aided by financial provisions made by the GI Bill of Rights – legislation to ease servicemen returning from the war back into civilian life. Like many 20th-century studio potters, Autio was influenced by prominent visual artists in his formative years. The impact on Autio of paintings by Henri Matisse and prints by Shiko Munakata is particularly evident in his flowing painted decoration. Autio's handbuilt vessels have a freedom of line and form that echo the sweeping contours of the figures he depicts in his work.

More recently, Noi Volkov has reached further back into art history in his search for inspiration. His postmodern juxtaposition of the contemporary and the historical comes in the form of bizarre, faux-functional forms decorated with startlingly

accurate re-creations of paintings by famous artists, from Hieronymus Bosch to Vincent Van Gogh. Volkov was a citizen of the Ukraine under Soviet rule and his attempts to use his extensive artistic training as a means for self expression attracted the attention of the KGB, who closed down his kiln. In 1989 Voulkov moved to the United States, where he has pursued his individual vision with vigour. Many of his unorthodox ceramic works incorporate everyday objects he has found such as taps and even a pair of jeans.

The Funk ceramicist Richard Shaw also uses everyday objects as a basis for his work, but he re-creates them in clay. His pieces include ceramic representations of objects as diverse as dominoes, cruise liners, cigar boxes, and playing cards.

# VESSELS OF IDEAS

The postmodern reinterpretation of ceramic art did not revolve solely around expressive and figural sculpture. Numerous potters, including many who also explored sculptural representation, chose to work within the constraints imposed by traditional vessel forms.

Potters such as Takeshi Yasuda pursued a new minimalism that was a world apart from the outlandish models being made by Gilhooly and the other Funk ceramicists (see p.398). Yasuda embraced accident and chance, and his intense interest in the process of modelling his pots was rooted firmly in the tradition of Peter Voulkos, even if the eventual results were far more refined. His celebrated Unfolding Vases were the result of a throwing error at the wheel.

In attempting to create tall, tapering vessels with very thin walls, Yasuda overreached himself, and some of the pots collapsed. When he hung the ruined vessels upside down they stretched back into buckled versions of their original shapes.

He created his companion Folding series by allowing plates propped up on stands to collapse in on themselves within the kiln. Both of these concepts highlight the plasticity of clay – a quality that is usually evident only while it is being worked.

## WALTER KEELER

English ceramicist Walter Keeler has been called Britain's leading maker of individual domestic wares. He plays with functional

**THREE UNFOLDING VASES** These warped porcelain vases by Takeshi Yasuda were made by collapsing the pieces on the wheel, then hanging them upside down. H:45cm (17in).

*The folded shapes* are all random and unique

**STONEWARE LIDDED JAR** This jar by Walter Keeler is typical of his angular, often humorous tilting forms and attractive salt-glaze decoration. H:22.5cm (9in).

*The clean shapes* are inspired by many forms, including 18th-century Staffordshire ceramics and oil cans

*Speckled salt* glaze

**PORCELAIN SCULPTURE** This piece by Karl Scheid consists of a series of slab-built vessels that are reminiscent of open books set back to back and side to side. c.2000. H:60cm (23½in).

**STONEWARE BOTTLE** Jim Malone used the Korean *hakeme* technique – applying a white slip glaze in swirls with a stiff brush. c.2000. H:32.5cm (12¾in).

**TAKAEZU STONEWARE VESSEL** This spherical vessel by Toshiko Takaezu is simply decorated with random, leaf-like brushtrokes in earthy colours, reflecting her interest in the natural world. Takaezu has made many vessels like this in a wide range of sizes. H:17cm (6in).

**OCEAN I AND OCEAN 11** These two jugs by Emmanuel Cooper are Western in shape and design, their elegant and simple forms highlighted with his brightly coloured hallmark glazes. *Larger pot: H:20cm (8in).*

*The rich blue glaze* recalls Egyptian faience

*The colour* has been randomly applied by brush and slip trailers

**POPPY TEAPOT** Janice Tchalenko's popular poppy design, along with designs such as Peacock and Tornado, for Dartington Pottery update traditional forms with free, handpainted decoration. They helped to revive primary colours in mainstream ceramics. *1980s. H:22cm (8¾in).*

### GRAYSON PERRY

An artist who works in many media but is best known for his ceramics, Grayson Perry enjoys the conflict between the colourful, naively decorative aspect of his pots and the brutally frank way in which they deal with often disturbing themes. His work mixes the autobiographical, dealing with issues drawn from his own life and that of his alter ego, Claire, with the political. He also uses ceramics to satirize the work of other artists, poking fun at Alexander Calder's mobiles and Jackson Pollock's pouring technique, among other things. Unlike most studio potters, who have tried to elevate the status of pottery, Perry revels in its position as a subordinate medium to painting or sculpture. Perry accepted the 2003 Turner Prize with the words: "It's about time a transvestite potter won the Turner."

forms, for instance, by applying ceramic arms resembling severed tree limbs to his vessels, thus creating "extraordinary objects to do a commonplace job". By forcing the user to negotiate a network of thorny branches in order to brew a pot of tea, Keeler interrupts an everyday action and transforms it into something novel. As his career has progressed, he has experimented with stoneware and earthenware, raku, and reduction firing, adapting his work to new processes and techniques. His work can be seen as part of a move to restore art to the home.

### COLOUR AND PATTERN

Other studio potters have worked towards the same goal through their work with colour and pattern. Elizabeth Fritsch has produced coil-built stoneware vases since training under Hans Coper in the early 1970s. She decorates her vessels with smooth layers of slip in complex geometric patterns. Her palette has ranged from pale colours early on, through bold greens, reds, and blues to monochrome. Julian Stair, on the other hand, has restricted colour to the natural tones of black basalt, white porcelain, and red stoneware. His sparsely decorated work includes functional pieces such as funerary urns,

teapots, and caddies as well as more abstract forms.

From the 1970s the British studio pottery movement gradually grew away from its roots in the Oriental tradition. Emmanuel Cooper experimented with glazes and produced a range of effects including tactile volcanic surfaces. Janice Tchalenko opened her studio in London in 1971, initially working within the boundaries defined by Bernard Leach before becoming enamoured with the English style rendered by his pupil Michael Cardew. As she travelled to exotic locations, she learned from diverse folk traditions. She fused her admiration for the Renaissance French ceramicist Bernard Palissy with Russian and Iranian decorative styles, opening the floodgates for influences other than the Oriental.

Tchalenko's work consists mainly of unpretentious, functional forms that use repeat patterns, stencilled motifs, and trailed glazes for decorative impact. She brought her work to a wide audience through an association with Dart Pottery from 1984. Tchalenko has also produced unique commissions including a range of pieces representing the seven deadly sins. These pieces were designed in collaboration with the team behind the TV programme *Spitting Image* for the Victoria & Albert Museum in London.

**PRECIOUS BOYS** Although traditional in shape, this vase is circled with figures at the top and has a mottled glaze overlaid with outlines of fighter jets below them. *2004. H:53cm (21in).*

# FACTORY CERAMICS

Although the truly mass-produced ceramics of the late 20th century can be inferior in terms of both quality and appearance when compared with mid-century classics such as Russel Wright's American Modern, a middle tier of manufacturers, spanning the gap between the studio potteries and the cheap and cheerful factories, catered to a growing demand for well-designed homeware.

## SWID POWELL

Nan Swid and Addie Powell, a pair of New York designers, exploited this new market with admirable aplomb. In Nan's own words, "I knew that very few people would ever live in houses designed by Richard Meier or Robert Venturi, but I thought they would like to experience that aesthetic level." Swid and Powell gathered a coterie of their talented friends around a table at the Four Seasons Restaurant and unveiled their business plan. They would commission these eminent architects and designers – Robert Venturi and Michael Graves among them – to create tableware and other useful objects for mass production. As leading proponents of the postmodern style in their architectural work, these individuals brought the same ideas to the designs they drafted for Swid Powell.

With his Grandmother mug, for example, Robert Venturi starts with a traditional motif – namely a transfer-printed design of flowers – and gives it a contemporary 1980s twist by adding short pairs of parallel black lines. Venturi also used this underlying chintz motif on his chairs – in both instances the idea, as suggested by the name,

is to poke fun at the notion of taking tea with grandmother, the table spread with a 1930s floral tablecloth. Venturi's Notebook service, also designed for Swid Powell, juxtaposes standard dinner plates and serving dishes with a truly unexpected design based on the covers of school notebooks.

Michael Graves's Big Dripper teapot and Little Dripper creamer and sugar bowl make oblique external references to their intended function. The red cruciform bases symbolize the heat used to warm the vessels, bringing to mind a traditional stove-top kettle, while the blue wavy lines signify the liquid contained inside them.

**GRANDMOTHER MUG AND PLATE**
This Swid Powell ceramic mug and plate, designed by Robert Venturi, are decorated with transfer-printed pastel flowers and pairs of black lines. *1984. H:9.5cm (3¾in).*

**LITTLE DRIPPER TEA SET** Designed by Michael Graves for Swid Powell, this tea set consists of a transfer-printed tea- or coffeepot, a milk jug, a sugar bowl with a spoon, and a coffee filter holder. With typically postmodern appropriation from history, however recent, the set appears to be influenced by Art Deco and even Christopher Dresser. *1987. Teapot: W:23.5cm (9in).*

*The blue waves* obliquely hint at the object's function

**FLASH CHEESE DISH** This angular cheese dish decorated with blocks of geometric patterns was designed by Dorothy Hafner for the Rosenthal Studio Linie. *1985. W:19cm (7½in).*

**ROSENTHAL POLLO STUDIO LINIE PORCELAIN VASE** Tapio Wirkkala designed the Pollo range in three sizes, black or white. They were made in moulds using a slipcast process. *H:12cm (4¾in).*

**FLOWERS PLATE** This plate, designed by Robert Venturi for Swid Powell, is decorated with stylized flowers – a traditional floral chintz updated for the postmodern generation.

## OTHER FACTORY CERAMICISTS

Alessi, that other great democratizer of architectural design, achieved a similar feat to Swid Powell in the field of ceramics and metalware. During the late 1990s Alessi issued a series of mugs and other vessels designed by Andrea Branzi. His *Genetic Tales* motif has adorned a number of products and also formed the subject of a book by the architect. The playful design features cartoon-like heads and symbols taken from mathematical equations to create a dialogue about similarities and differences, both between individuals and between cultures. Branzi has also produced other ceramics, notably the *Tatzine e Tatzone* (a wordplay on the Italian for "little cups" and "big cups"). This collection of objects, made by Tendentze, part of Alessi since 1989, has wilfully perverse yet resolutely functional forms.

Through her work for Rosenthal, Dorothy Hafner has done much to popularize the postmodern aesthetic. Her angular Flash and Spirit shapes have been particularly successful but it is her patterns that are most distinctive. Hafner's palette is diverse – extending to turquoise, orange, purple, and red – and always bright and bold. She plays with contrasts not just between colours but also between patterns, so chequered and striped areas mingle on the same piece with blocks of solid colour. As well as work for Rosenthal's designer-led range Studio Linie, Hafner also creates individual platters and tureens in a similar style.

The Studio Linie range also includes pieces designed by Tapio Wirkkala, better known for his organic glass forms. He brings a similar aesthetic to his tableware for Rosenthal. The variation between the work done by Hafner and Wirkkala for the same brand of ceramics reflects Rosenthal's commissioning policy, and that of Swid Powell and Alessi: to offer the public a smorgasbord of contemporary design, as disparate as it is daring.

**TENDENTZE *TATZINE* TEACUP AND SAUCER** Designed by Andrea Branzi, the conical cup has a stylized face transfer on the handle. The cup can rest only on its saucer, a flat oval plate joined to a short cylinder that holds the bottom of the cone. *1986. H:8.5cm (3½in).*

**MANITOBA CRUET SET** This set of four pieces with a transfer-applied pattern was designed to sit in the corners of a tray by Matteo Thun for the Memphis group. *1982. Tallest: H:10cm (4in).*

## VENTURI'S VILLAGE

With the Village tea set, Robert Venturi took Swid Powell's idea of bringing architecture to the table literally. The set is moulded and decorated in the forms of miniature buildings.

The coffeepot, for example, references a Tuscan tower, while the teapot is based on a temple from the ancient world. Other pieces resemble more prosaic buildings, including one that looks like a child's drawing of a house. Other whimsical touches include the inscription "Amo Amas Amat" along the pediment of the temple-shaped teapot – this conjugation of the Latin verb "to love" is another nod to the ancient history of Italy.

*The motifs* are taken from different architectural and ceramic periods

**VILLAGE TEA SET** Robert Venturi designed this eclectic tea set for Swid Powell. The design recalls Venturi's 1977 Eclectic House series. The set, in form and decoration, plays on the traditional country cottage connotations of taking tea. *1986. Teapot: H:23cm (9in).*

# CERAMICS GALLERY

By their very nature, postmodern ceramics are diverse and confound attempts to draw too many parallels between them. It is, however, possible to see common themes, including cultural commentary, inspiration from historical themes, and ironic humour. Some ceramicists defied function and made art pots which were purely decorative; others embraced mass production and designed tablewares which sold in their thousands.

**KEY**

**1.** Square platter by Vivika and Otto Heino, painted and incised with leafy branches. W:45.5cm (18in). ③ **2.** Peter Max covered pot shaped as a man wearing a hat. H:21cm (8¼in). ① **3.** Ritzenhoff Dinner For Two set of transfer-printed oval dinner plates by Alessandro Guerriero. 1990. W:32cm (12¾in). ① **4.** Swid Powell Volumetric transfer-printed dinner plate by Steven Holl. 1986. D:30.5cm (12in). ① **5.** Swid Powell Beam transfer-printed dinner plate with gold highlights by Zaha Hadid. 1988. D:30.5cm (12in). ① **6.** Swid Powell Notebook transfer-printed dinner plate by Robert Venturi. 1984. D:30.5cm (12in). ① **7.** Rosenthal wall plate by Roy Lichtenstein. D:30.5cm (12in).

1 *Square platter*

2 *Peter Max covered pot*

3 *Alessandro Guerriero dinner plates*

4 *Volumetric dinner plate*

5 *Zaha Hadid dinner plate*

6 *Robert Venturi dinner plate*

7 *Roy Lichtenstein wall plate*

8 *Robert and Trix Haussmann mug*

9 *Studio pottery abstract*

10 *Spirit of Art tea service*

11 *Marco Zanini cups on stand*

① **8.** Swid Powell Black Stripes pattern transfer-printed mug by Robert and Trix Haussmann. 1984. H:10cm (4in). ① **9.** Gordon Baldwin abstract piece. 1971. ① **10.** Spirit of Art tea service, after Keith Haring. 1992. Plates: D:33cm (13in). ③ **11.** Pair of cups on a stand by Marco Zanini. c.1990. ① **12.** Covered pot by Ursula Scheid. **13.** Bitosso E-vasi double vase, the central urn-shaped vase sliding out of the main vase, by P. Pallma and C. Vannicola. 1990. H:24.5cm (9¾in). ① **14.** Wood-fired vase by Paul Soldner, with random painted and incised decoration. H:21.5cm (8½in). ② **15.** Win Ng squat vase, covered in volcanic glaze. 1960s. W:16.5cm (6½in). ① **16.** Pair of cornucopia vases on organic stands by Nancy Jurs. H:32cm (12½in). ① **17.** Ron Nagle bud vase with a four-sided structure attached to an angled one. W:17cm (6¾in). ④ **18.** Red clay wood-fired pot by Paul Chaleff. 1984. D:30.5cm (12in). ③ **19.** Sculptural vessel by Rudy Autio. H:52cm (20½in). ⑥

**12** Ursula Scheid pot

**13** Double vase

**14** Paul Soldner vase

**15** Win Ng vase

**16** Cornucopia vases

**17** Bud vase

**18** Paul Chaleff pot

**19** Rudy Autio vessel

# GLASS

THE REVERBERATIONS OF THE "REVOLUTION IN CLAY" WERE FELT THROUGHOUT THE ART WORLD, AS DESIGNERS IN OTHER FIELDS WOKE UP TO A NEW WORLD OF POSSIBILITIES.

## COLOURFUL FORMS

The birth of the American studio glass movement can be traced back to a glassblowing workshop held at the Toledo Museum of Art in 1962. It was here that ceramicist Harvey K. Littleton and research scientist Dominick Labino perfected a miniature furnace and glass formula that finally made it possible for solitary artists to manipulate hot glass. Their collaboration led to the establishment of the first Fine Art programme in glassworking, at the University of Wisconsin.

One of the first and most prolific students of this programme has been Marvin Lipofsky. His relationship with glass has fluctuated – in his early California Loop Series he sought to bury the glass beneath flocking and paint. He also used mirroring and electroplating to coat his glass before finally coming to an acceptance of the inherent beauty of his chosen material, emphasizing its extraordinary propensity for colour in particular.

Early in his career, Richard Marquis deliberately manipulated glass to make it resemble clay – he rarely produced clear pieces and frequently chose forms traditionally associated with pottery, such as teapots. Many of his techniques are drawn directly from the Viennese glassmaking tradition: a legacy of the time he spent in Murano. Marquis's enthusiastic use of murrines has even extended to the presentation of sample boards of these slices of transparent or opaque glass as complete pieces in

their own right. His Marquiscarpa vessels, decorated with murrines and based on ancient forms, take their name from a combination of Marquis and Scarpa in honour of Venetian architect Carlo Scarpa. The complicated construction of these pieces is made up of blown, fused, slumped, and carved elements.

Other studio artists such as Pauline Solven resisted this temptation to produce convoluted pieces and instead focused on simple blown forms.

It is testament to the wilfully perverse attitude of many postmodern designers that Dan Dailey developed a passion for working with Vitrolite plate glass at a time when it was out of fashion. The opaque plate glass had been a popular structural material during the 1930s but was no longer manufactured when Dailey began working,

making it necessary for him to scavenge for it wherever he could. His Vitrolite, *pâte-de-verre*, and bronze decorative additions provide, in his own words, an "element of deluxe" to his colourful blown forms.

## COLLABORATIONS IN PRODUCTION

A recent trend in the studio glass community has led to solitary craftsmen surrounding themselves with assistants and dividing the process of manufacture between them, each specializing in a specific skill. Dailey's glass forms can be the product of up to a dozen individuals working on his original vision. As the artist explains, "I couldn't do what I do alone physically. My skills are not at the level of all my friends."

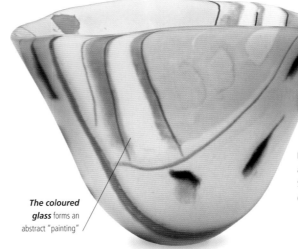

*The coloured glass* forms an abstract "painting"

**EMERGING SUN** This piece by Pauline Solven is made from blown and cased elements, with a sandblasted finish creating a matte texture. The individual segments were welded together with ultraviolet bonding. *2000. H:35.5cm (14in).*

**MARINE LIGHT III** Colour and tone, rather than form, inspired this abstract blown and cased coloured-glass piece by Pauline Solven. Shaped like a limpet shell, it was inspired by the changing light at different times of the day on a beach. *2003. H:15cm (6in).*

**CRAZY QUILT TEAPOT** This colourful and humorous piece by Richard Marquis is made of free-blown colourless glass overlaid with multicoloured murrines. *1988. H:18cm (7in).*

*The murrines* have different designs such as hearts and stars

*The colours* resemble the plumage of an exotic bird

**THREAD VASE** Mary Ann (Toots) Zynsky's richly coloured vase was made by layering many fine, coloured glass threads, then fusing them together in a kiln using a mould. *c.1990. H:19.5cm (7in).*

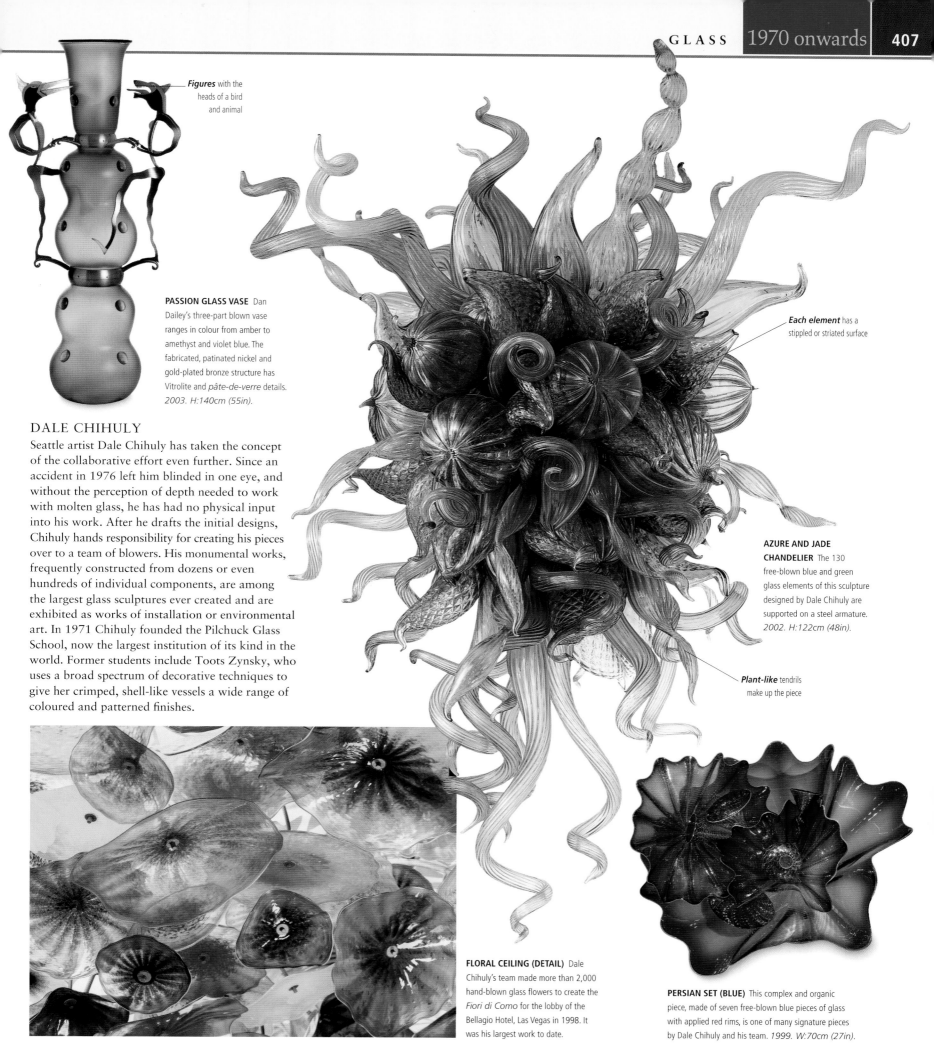

**Figures** with the heads of a bird and animal

**PASSION GLASS VASE** Dan Dailey's three-part blown vase ranges in colour from amber to amethyst and violet blue. The fabricated, patinated nickel and gold-plated bronze structure has Vitrolite and *pâte-de-verre* details. *2003. H:140cm (55in).*

## DALE CHIHULY

Seattle artist Dale Chihuly has taken the concept of the collaborative effort even further. Since an accident in 1976 left him blinded in one eye, and without the perception of depth needed to work with molten glass, he has had no physical input into his work. After he drafts the initial designs, Chihuly hands responsibility for creating his pieces over to a team of blowers. His monumental works, frequently constructed from dozens or even hundreds of individual components, are among the largest glass sculptures ever created and are exhibited as works of installation or environmental art. In 1971 Chihuly founded the Pilchuck Glass School, now the largest institution of its kind in the world. Former students include Toots Zynsky, who uses a broad spectrum of decorative techniques to give her crimped, shell-like vessels a wide range of coloured and patterned finishes.

**Each element** has a stippled or striated surface

**AZURE AND JADE CHANDELIER** The 130 free-blown blue and green glass elements of this sculpture designed by Dale Chihuly are supported on a steel armature. *2002. H:122cm (48in).*

**Plant-like** tendrils make up the piece

**FLORAL CEILING (DETAIL)** Dale Chihuly's team made more than 2,000 hand-blown glass flowers to create the *Fiori di Como* for the lobby of the Bellagio Hotel, Las Vegas in 1998. It was his largest work to date.

**PERSIAN SET (BLUE)** This complex and organic piece, made of seven free-blown blue pieces of glass with applied red rims, is one of many signature pieces by Dale Chihuly and his team. *1999. W:70cm (27in).*

## CLEARLY OPTICAL

Optical glass, first available on a large scale from the 1940s, is a flawless glass used in the manufacture of lenses and prisms. Its fundamental quality is that it allows as much light as possible to pass into and through it. This has made it attractive to glass artists wanting to explore the intrinsic clarity of glass, or its reflective and refractive properties. Other makers have found alternative, but equally novel, ways in which to explore the properties of their medium.

Sidney Hutter has investigated the vase form more thoroughly than most contemporary glassmakers and studies his works from a decorative rather than a functional perspective. His compositions are built up of dozens of thin, transparent glass plates, cut and stacked to resemble a vase in silhouette

but in fact they are completely solid. To extend the boundaries of his chosen form, Hutter often removes sections from groups of plates in order to create impossibly top-heavy loads. Although the glass from which Hutter constructs these pieces is perfectly clear, he often uses pigmented glues. When viewed on a plane parallel with the surfaces of the plates, light passes directly through the clear glass without picking up any colour. When viewed from any other direction, however, the dyed glues flood the vases with colour, yielding a wide range of unexpected optical effects.

Hutter's choice of the vase shape represents a postmodern acknowledgment of the importance this form has assumed in the history of glassmaking. At the same time, however, he asserts its irrelevance in contemporary creative developments by making it completely nonfunctional.

## TECHNICAL CHALLENGES

Many artists working with high-performance glass seem to revel in the technical challenges it presents. Colin Reid combines casting, cutting, and polishing to mimic natural forms such as rock, wood, and sand. His monumental Cipher Stone, cast to resemble Cotswold stone, has a magnifying lens set into one of its facets through which the viewer can make out chunks of text inscribed in English, Morse code, and binary. This stone is a reference to the Rosetta stone, updated for the digital age.

**VASIFORM SCULPTURE** This piece by Sidney Hutter is entitled *90 Degrees of 4 Colorwheel: Jerry Vision Vase #195*. It is made of clear glass plates stuck together with brightly coloured glues. *2003. H:42cm (16in)*.

**The cut-out plate sections** draw attention to the unusual construction of the piece

**The lens** emphasizes the optical effects of the glass

**R999 GLASS PIECE** In this sculpture by Colin Reid, optical glass was cast into a mould where it picked up copper powder. The piece was then removed and the flat surfaces ground and polished on a machine. *2003*.

**BLUE GLASS SCULPTURE** This three-layered piece by Tom Patti entitled *Compacted Solarized Blue with Dual Ring* has an unusual convex base as a stand. *W:15cm (6in)*.

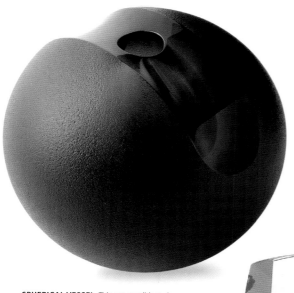

**SPHERICAL VESSEL** This cut, sandblasted, and polished dark green glass piece by the Czech glass artist Frantisek Vizner demonstrates his love of simple, geometric shapes and rich opaque colour. *1970s. D:14.5cm (5in).*

Tom Patti's work, meanwhile, straddles a boundary between art and engineering. He has developed a number of unique laminating and fusing techniques, transferring breakthroughs made in his architectural work to his glassmaking. Other innovations build on ancient techniques. Ronald Pennell, for example, uses a copper wheel to draw freehand sketches directly onto the surface of his glass vessels.

## CZECH TRADITION

Glassmakers in the Czech Republic and Hungary have continued to build on their Bohemian heritage. Husband and wife team Stanislav Libensky and Jaraslava Brychtová first worked together in the 1950s. Their work is characterized by smooth surfaces and carefully modelled interior voids. As a professor at the Prague Academy

from 1963, Libensky influenced the cream of Czech glass artists. Frantsiek Vizner's solid blocks of coloured glass, cast in subtly modified geometric shapes, clearly owe a debt to Libensky's work. Vizner's flawlessly smooth polished finishes stand in marked contrast to the textural edges of work by Hungarian sculptor Maria Lugossy. Yan Zoritchak, another Czech glassmaker of this period, settled in France in 1970 after studying under Libensky. Since the 1980s Zoritchak has produced smooth, clean-lined forms with plain outer surfaces and complex internal decoration, as in his *Messenger de l'Espace* (Messenger from Space) series.

Czech glass was exhibited at various International Exhibitions, including Osaka in 1970, where it influenced glassmakers from around the world. Studios such as Studio Lhotsky – which specializes in cast glass – are widely known today.

*Natural elements* within the glass create an imaginary landscape

**MESSAGER DE L'ESPACE**
This piece by Yan Zoritchak demonstrates the artist's preoccupation with the transparent and distorting qualities of glass. *2003. H:46cm (18in).*

*A man and his dog* are confronted by three figures, one of whom is holding a sunburst

**GREEN GLASS SCULPTURE** This piece by Maria Lugossy is typical of her cast glass, which is characterized by muted colours, layering, and lenses. *1988. H:25cm (9¾in).*

**DOG DAYS A SUN FETISH** Made by Karl Nordbruch and engraved by Ronald Pennell, this vessel is made from amethyst glass. Pennell's engravings are often concerned with past civilizations and cultures. *2003. H:20.5cm (8in).*

## ENGRAVED GLASS

As precision tools have become more accurate, glass artists have been able to achieve a wider range of effects using engraving and cutting techniques. Czech engraver Jiri Harcuba is the foremost exponent of glass portraiture. His extensive work includes three-dimensional depictions of artists and writers in blocks of clear glass. The features of the subjects are cut into the back of the glass block so that, when they are viewed from the front, they cast shadows on the perfectly flat surface.

In Scotland Alison Kinnaird engraves figures on glass panels and solid blocks. Her more complex pieces combine Celtic knotwork with human figures, through which she passes light with optical fibres. Her use of dichroic glass produces intense colours while eliminating glare.

**FRANZ KAFKA'S PORTRAIT** Jiri Harcuba's uses techniques such as diamond, stone, and copper wheel cutting for his engraved glass portraits. *1991. W:21.5cm (8½in).*

**ECLIPSE** Alison Kinnaird's engraved, sandblasted, and cased glass panel explores tone. It is adorned with figures and is mounted on a metal stand. *2001. Panel: H:29.5cm (11in).*

# FIGURES AND MATERIALS

As the studio glass movement has matured, practitioners have begun to tackle more evocative themes. Human history, politics, and the relationship between people and their environment have all come under the scrutiny of glass artists with the confidence to explore such profound topics.

## KILN FORMING AND CASTING

Describing himself as a "constructivist", Keith Cummings combines his cast- and built-glass forms with metals. Like many contemporary studio glassmakers attempting to reach beyond traditional vessel shapes, Cummings prefers to mould his forms in a kiln rather than blow them. His observational work draws on the landscape and ancient heritage of his native England. Alfred's Mirror, inspired by a 9th-century jewel owned by King Alfred, demonstrates how the intricate work required of the contemporary glassmaker compares with that of a jeweller. During his tenure at the University of Wolverhampton (previously Stourbridge College of Art), Cummings has helped nurture some of the finest talent on the contemporary glass scene.

David Reekie trained at Stourbridge during the late 1960s, where Cummings instilled in him the historical traditions of glass casting. Despite its status as a pre-eminent technique in the contemporary studio movement, glass casting was known in ancient Rome and has a longer history even than blowing. Reekie uses lost-wax casting – another Roman innovation – to produce his moulds. The process of pouring, setting, and cooling the glass is both time-consuming and inherently risky; a single trapped air bubble can be enough to destroy hours of work.

*The polished glass ovoid* surmounting the opaque section resembles a winter sun

**ALFRED'S MIRROR** Keith Cummings's piece combines kiln-formed opaque glass, which looks almost like jade, with inlaid copper wire and bands. *2003. L:37cm (14in).*

*The piece is inlaid* with glass faux pearls

**SEASON** For this piece, Keith Cummings used cast kiln-formed opaque glass with metal additions, with cast and polished glass. *2003. W:13cm (5in).*

The new significance of glass as art has been explored by a number of artists. Dutch glassmaker Dick van Wijk combines geometric and figural forms in glass with more traditional sculptural materials such as marble, bronze, and steel. In France Georges and Monique Stahl work together, juxtaposing ethereal glass formations that represent figures, water, and air with hunks of metal, representing earth.

In the United States William Morris uses glass to scrutinize the widening temporal rift that separates humanity from its pagan roots. Since working as the gaffer on Dale Chihuly's blowing team in the

early 1980s, Morris has produced glass in eerily archaic forms, many of them based on ritual vessels such as the rhyton and shamanic rattles. His decorative techniques include acid-washing, etching, and the application of powdered glass and other minerals to give his work the semblance of great age. An important secondary theme in Morris's work is the repudiation of modern man's relationship with nature, and a desire to return to a more innocent age. To this end, Morris practises traditional bow-hunting skills in pursuit of a "pure" confrontation between man and beast. These sentiments manifest

**GLASS AND PEWTER HEAD** Created by David Reekie in 1986 as part of a series of four, the head was made from cast glass using the lost wax process. *H:16.5cm (6½in).*

*Stahl pieces* often feature marine themes, with dramatic glass wave forms

**ZONNEWIND (SOLARWIND)** This sailboat-like sculpture is by the Dutch artist Dick van Wijk. The glass was made by Jan Willen van Zijst. *L:110cm (43in).*

**DÉSIR D'AILES (DESIRE FOR WINGS)** This evocative piece by Georges and Monique Stahl is made of polished concrete and *pâte-de-verre. H:50cm (19¾in).*

**Thin canes** of coloured glass are melted and shaped by an oxyacetylene torch to produce a botanical picture

**PAUL STANKARD ORB** This unique paperweight from the Whitman Botanical series has an internal cased lampwork design of a honeycomb, two bees, moss, flowers, and lilies. *2004. D:11cm (4in).*

themselves in Morris's glass in the form of detailed depictions of birds and deer heads. The antediluvian aspect of Morris's work is made all the more jarring by his use of glass – an inherently fragile material that ancient cultures would have found impossible to manipulate into the forms that Morris achieves.

Fellow American artist Paul Stankard also relies on nature as his muse but, whereas Morris presents natural forms in the context of human interference, Stankard isolates them in clear glass cases and spheres, as if exhibiting natural beauty as an artwork in its own right. Stankard's expertise in the lampworking technique, where rods of coloured glass are heated and engineered into precise shapes, is unsurpassed. His detailed flowers, leaves, and tendrils are complemented by equally complex root systems, which demonstrate an appreciation of natural complexity that would be the envy of any Victorian botanist. Stankard introduces a spiritual element by adding tiny figures to represent the elemental forces of nature. The magnifying effect of Stankard's glass crystal cases accentuates the virtuosity of his lampwork forms.

**Prehistoric sources** such as cave paintings inform Morris's work

## GLASS COMBINATIONS

In the 1980s and 1990s glassmaking started to lose its status as a craft and was increasingly seen as an art form. Museums added contemporary glass to their collections and glassmakers began to experiment as they realized that, if something made from glass could be seen as a sculpture, there was no reason why glass could not be combined with other materials.

Designers such as Gernot Schlufer and Georges and Monique Stahl began combining concrete, petrified wood, metal, and marble with glass to create sculptures that sometimes do not appear to be made from glass at all. The new trend has been taken further by Jorg Zimmerman, who blows glass through netting to create inventive shapes.

**The rough texture** of the wood contrasts with the smooth glass

**LILAC-BREASTED-ROLLER BIRD** The work of Austrian Gernot Schlufer celebrates the unspoilt natural beauty and diverse animal and bird life of the Alps. *c.2000. H:21cm (8in).*

# GLASS GALLERY

Postmodern glass is brightly coloured, playful, and often witty. Studio art glass in particular displays freedom of form and technical experiment. As such pieces are purely decorative, they do not need to conform to any traditional functional shape. The United States and Italy lead the way in innovation.

## KEY

**1.** Luigi Camozzo blown glass vase, with vertical canes. H:18cm (7in). ② **2.** Sculpture with hand-painted decoration by Ulrica Hydman-Vallien for Kosta Boda. 1999. H:37cm (15in). ② **3.** No. 8801 by Jörg Zimmerman of Germany. D:34cm (13½in). ③ **4.** Murrine cased vase by Vittorio Ferro at Fratelli Pagnin of Murano. 2004. H:24cm (9½in). ② **5.** Orange opaque half-globe and quarter-globe in clear glass by Milos Balgavy. D:25cm (9¾in). ⑤ **6.** Keith Brocklehurst pâte-de-verre bowl, legs cast with the piece. 1980s. D:19.5cm (7¾in). ③ **7.** Multicoloured vase by Bertil Vallien for Kosta Boda. c.1985. H:20cm (8in). ③ **8.** Zip bowl by Kjell Engman. ① **9.** Bowl by Bertil Vallien for Kosta Boda. c.1980. H:12cm (4¾in). ① **10.** Vase by Philip Baldwin and Monica Guggisberg. H:47cm

2 Handpainted sculpture

3 Jörg Zimmerman sculpture

4 Murrine vase

1 Luigi Camozzo vase

6 Keith Brocklehurst bowl

5 Globe sections

7 Bertil Vallien vase

8 Zip bowl

9 Bertil Vallien bowl

10 Philip Baldwin and Monica Guggisberg vase

11 Dale Chihuly piece

12 Danny Perkins sculpture

(18½in). ④ **11.** A five-piece Harrison Red Basket Set by Dale Chihuly. 2003. H:28cm (11in). ⑥
**12.** Malibu, blown glass sculpture with painted decoration by Danny Perkins. 2005. H:119.5cm
(47in). ⑤ **13.** Flaring bowl by Kjell Engman for Kosta Boda. W:25.5cm (10¼in). ① **14.** Vase by
Alberto Donà, the clear glass encased with multicoloured threads and strings. 2000. H:38.5cm (15in).
② **15.** Handmade vase by Licata. H:41cm (16in). ② **16.** Simon Moore jug with fins. 1986. H:34cm
(13½in). ② **17.** One of Dante Marioni Green Trio of blown forms. 2001. H:73.5cm (29in). ⑥
**18.** Dinosaur by Lino Tagliapietra. 2003. H:38cm (15in). ⑦ **19.** Borek Sipek vase with ceramic bowl
and glass stem. 1980s. H:60cm (24in). ② **20.** Vase by Gianni Versace for Venini. 1988. H:25cm
(9¾in). ① **21.** Thick-walled three-sided vase with multicoloured bands cased in clear glass by Fulvio
Bianconi for Venini. 1992. H:25cm (10in). ⑤

13 *Kjell Engman bowl*

14 *Alberto Donà vase*

16 *Fin jug*

15 *Licata vase*

17 *Dante Marioni form*

18 *Dinosaur*

19 *Borek Sipek vase*

20 *Gianni Versace vase*

21 *Fulvio Bianconi vase*

# LIGHTING

DURING THE LATTER HALF OF THE 20TH CENTURY, LIGHTING BECAME AN INCREASINGLY IMPORTANT AND EXCITING FIELD OF DESIGN. IT STARTED AS A VEHICLE FOR INNOVATION BUT BECAME A QUEST FOR QUALITY OF LIGHT.

**85 LAMPS CHANDELIER**
Designed by Rody Graumans for the Dutch The Product Matters Company, the chandelier is made of 85 15-watt light bulbs. The individual parts of this lamp are completely plain but the combination makes an opulent chandelier. *1993. H:110cm (43½in).*

## EXPERIMENTAL IDEAS

While tables, chairs, vases, and other objects had been designed and made for centuries, electric lights were still a relative novelty at the beginning of the 20th century. The fact that designers were free from the weight of history in this respect seems to have encouraged them to express many of their most creative ideas through the medium of lighting design.

It was the designers of the 1960s who really opened up the world of lighting design, as the widespread use of plastic gave them a wonderfully malleable material to work with. Bright colours and bold shapes were used to create designs where the actual light emitted from the bulb was of secondary importance to the object itself.

## SOBRIETY AND INDUSTRY

The Middle East oil crisis of the early 1970s pushed the price of plastic up to prohibitive levels, however, and the levity that ran through earlier lighting design soon disappeared. A new, more staid approach dominated the early years of the 1970s as designers returned to a more rigorous, rational style of design (one that was eventually to be labelled High-Tech). This reflected a new

**Lamps with chips** are touch sensitive. When lightly touched, they create a small symphony of sounds

**ALDA LAMP** Of multicoloured polyurethane resin, this lamp was designed by Gaetano Pesce and named after his mother. The brightly coloured resin lamp is made in large or small forms, with bells that jingle to the touch or electronic chips. There is also a wall sconce. *2004. H:71cm (24in).*

sobriety that had swept through Western society following the fall in financial markets and the uncertainty that surrounded the future of the world's energy supplies.

By the late 1970s, however, this cautious and considered approach to design – one that gave us numerous lamps of geometric form produced in muted colours – was submerged as a new generation of designers developed a more abrasive and energetic style. This attitude, particularly apparent in Italy, was a clear sign of the frustration that was felt by young people throughout the West whose prospects, as the 1970s wore on, did not appear to be improving.

Designers such as Gaetano Pesce, Alessandro Mendini, and Michele De Lucchi produced lights that defied convention by using a motley collection of materials and loud, discordant colour. Lamps no longer looked like mathematicians' diagrams but like artists' sketches. The Memphis group, led by Ettore Sottsass, took this look into the 1980s, although their work was a little more light-hearted and less confrontational than the lighting designs of a few years earlier.

As the 1980s developed, and consumer confidence returned, lighting design became more playful once again. However, in contrast to the straightforward, fun-loving products of the Sixties, the lights of the 1980s were a little more cerebral in their design. Many lights took on an anthropomorphic element as sophisticated technologies made it possible to create more complex forms.

Not all designers during the 1980s were infatuated with new technologies, however. Indeed, many made a conscious effort to avoid the cutting edge and return to the virtues of craft. This movement, variously known as the studio movement, the craft revival, or (later on in the decade) neo-brutalism or

## INGO MAURER

When discussing lighting design of the later decades of the 20th century, one name stands out above all others – that of the German designer, Ingo Maurer. Having dedicated his career solely to lighting design since he set up Studio M in 1966, Maurer has created many of the most innovative and enduring designs of recent years.

As comfortable operating at the cutting edge of technology as producing sculptural pieces from primitive materials, Maurer is a designer of remarkable dexterity and invention. In reference to his monogamous relationship with lighting design, Maurer has said that "I have always been fascinated by the light bulb because it is the perfect meeting of industry and poetry".

**BɪBɪBɪ TABLE LAMP** Designed for Design M, this table lamp is constructed of porcelain, metal, and plastic. The styles of Ingo Maurer lamps are part art and part lighting. *1982. H:55cm (21¾).*

**LIGHT STRUCTURE** Ingo Maurer and Peter Hamburger's punning floor lamp design straddles modernism and postmodernism. The delicate-looking structure comprises tubular bulbs, acrylic, and electric cable. *1983. W:45.5cm (18in).*

**FIVE LIGHT FIXTURES** These elongated brushed-steel forms, complete with purple nylon cords, were designed by Philippe Starck for the Paramount Hotel in New York. *H:120.5cm (47½in).*

the salvage movement, was a rebellion against the rampant consumerism that so defined the 1980s. Often using recycled objects or materials, designers pursuing this style worked independently and their output was on a very small scale. Lights that fall into this category often resemble sculptures that just happen to have a bulb or two attached.

### MOOD LIGHTING

These whimsical and often wild designs were little seen during the 1990s, as lighting design became a subject that was approached with increasing gravity. Research began to show that lighting could seriously affect people's mood, productivity, and eyesight. The increased awareness of the psychological and physical impact of artificial lighting led designers to concentrate more on the quality of light from the lamps than on the objects themselves. A strand of wit pervaded the 1990s (notably in the inventive, amusing lighting of Droog, the Dutch design collective), but the fantastical designs that flourished in the 1970s and 1980s soon died out.

*The reused materials* are part of the salvage look

**A NITE ON LINDQUIST RIDGE TABLE LAMP** Designed by Gary Knox Bennett of California, the lamp is constructed with stovepipe housing with five flexible black and white shaft fixtures. It is inscribed with the title and the mark "In Oakland/GKB/Anno 90". *H:56cm (22in).*

*The shade* is made of multicoloured polyurethane plastic with unique colouring

**OSSO TABLE LAMP** Gaetano Pesce designed this American limited production lamp. The base is of shaped and textured faceted cast metal and supports the plastic shade. The lamp is one of a series of ten different examples, each with random colouring. *1989. H:95cm (37½in).*

*The metal frame* has a lightly textured finish

**NR 607 HALOGEN LAMP** Designed by Gino Sarfatti for Arteluce, this pioneering table lamp is typical of the High-Tech movement and was the first to use halogen bulbs. *c.1971. H:31cm (12¼in).*

**ITALIAN WIRELESS WL01C TABLE LAMP** Designed by Andrea Branzi and distributed by Design Gallery Milan, the lamp is battery powered, creating a modern effect without the use of cords, cables, or wires. The main body is open revealing the rice-paper shade. *1996. H:41cm (16¼in).*

# METALWARE

FROM SOLIDLY ARCHITECTURAL FORMS TO GOSSAMER WEBS, POSTMODERN
METALWARE TAKES ON DIVERSE FORMS. IT IS A BLEND OF HISTORICALLY
INFORMED DESIGN AND NEW IDEAS.

## SCULPTURAL DESIGNS

What Peter Voulkos achieved for ceramic artists,
Albert Paley has done for the humble blacksmith.
In 1995 he became the first metal sculptor to
receive the Institute Honors Award, the highest
accolade awarded to non-architects by the
American Institute of Architects. Working
primarily in milled steel, Paley produces
monumental sculpture, architectural furniture
such as door handles, and smaller pieces like
paperweights and candlesticks. He has completed
many prestigious public commissions, including
the Portal Gates at the Renwick Gallery of the
Smithsonian Institution and Synergy, a ceremonial
archway in Philadelphia. Paley's work is not
mass-produced and tends to be site-specific,
incorporating decorative elements designed
to complement their immediate environment.

Designers with architectural backgrounds
have dominated postmodern and contemporary
metalware design, often working to commissions
from influential design houses such as Alessi and
Swid Powell.

## SCALED-DOWN ARCHITECTURE

The prolific architect Robert Venturi, active in
so many spheres, produced a pair of candlesticks
for Swid Powell based on cut-out silhouette designs
in a similar vein to his archly ironic series of chairs
for Knoll. Although based on conventional
columnar forms, Venturi's candlesticks confound
expectation by existing solely along two
perpendicular planes rather than as solid
tubes. In effect, Venturi turns the traditional
candlestick inside out.

Husband and wife team Robert and Trix
Haussmann designed several metal objects,
including an abstract aluminium chandelier for
the Swiss Pavilion at the Osaka International
Exhibition in 1970. The tiny candlesticks they
produced for Swid Powell during the 1980s
exhibit a stylized geometry that is reminiscent
of Art Deco. Steven Holl's 1986 candlesticks
for the same company have a verdigris-style finish
suggestive of age and wear. A flex-like strand of
metal snakes down from the sconce to
the base, giving the impression that
the candle is powered by electricity.

**SILVER-PLATED CANDLESTICKS** Robert Venturi
designed this pair of candlesticks in two flat planes
at right angles to one another, blurring the distinction
between two and three dimensions. They were
produced by Swid Powell. *1986.*

**SWID POWELL CANDLESTICKS** Designed by Robert
and Trix Haussmann, these small silver-plated candlesticks
are stepped and have a small base tapering upwards to a
wider top. *1980s. H:7cm (2¾in).*

*The brass insert* is
shaped at the top and
flows down to the base

**SUNRISE TALL CANDLESTICKS** Designed by Albert Paley
for the American Ballet Theatre, the candlesticks are made
of forged and fabricated steel with brass inserts. *1993.
H:52cm (20½in).*

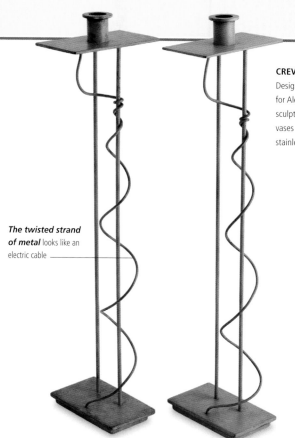

**The twisted strand of metal** looks like an electric cable

**PAIR OF CANDLESTICKS** Designed by Steven Holl and produced by Swid Powell, the candlesticks have a metal verdigris-style finish. The underside of the bases have a stamped facsimile signature. *1986. H:51cm (20¾in).*

**CREVASSE VASES** Designed by Zaha Hadid for Alessi, this pair of sculptural, undecorated vases is made of polished stainless steel. *2005.*

**The design** is influenced by Hadid's architectural training

**BLOW UP CITRUS BASKET** Designed by Fernando and Humberto Campana for Alessi, this is part of a set of tableware. The lengths of stainless steel wires create a unique holder. *2004.*

**The flip design** of the lid turns the ashtray into a clean, beautiful object

**RAY HOLLIS ASHTRAY** Designed by Philippe Starck for the French company XO, this polished aluminium ashtray has a curved flip lid to hide and seal in the ash and cigarette butts. *1986. H:10cm (4in).*

The Italian design giant Alessi has been behind many of the most iconic pieces of mass-produced metalware of recent years. Through collaborations with the most innovative designers, the firm has developed a range of individualistic products. Iraqi-born architect Zaha Hadid, now settled in Britain, unveiled her Crevasse vase in 2005. Its sheer sides defer to the decorative properties of the stainless steel from which it is constructed. There is no concession to surface decoration – the involvement of the designer is evident only in the twisted, tapered form that resembles an awkward skyscraper.

The São Paolo-based Campana Brothers – lawyer Humberto and architect Fernando – designed the Blow Up series of products for Alessi in 2004. The range comprises a citrus bowl, trivet, basket, and centrepiece bowl that defy the concept of form. Constructed from a series of steel rods that appear to be suspended in space or bound by magnetism, the effect is every bit as striking as the exploded shed Cornelia Parker exhibited under the title *Cold Dark Matter* in 1991.

Many recent innovations in metalwork have come from improved materials and techniques. Others have been occasioned by changing social mores. The aluminium Ray Hollis ashtray, designed by Philippe Starck for XO, is a product of the increasing controversy surrounding smoky environments. A simple click of the lid seals any lit butts within the bowl, starving them of oxygen and so extinguishing them. It also prevents smoke and ash smells from escaping into the room. This is an

ashtray with non-smokers in mind – a design oxymoron. After working as an interior designer during the 1970s, Starck became interested in product design, founding Starck Product in 1979. His irreverently playful approach has won commissions from many of the biggest names in modern manufacturing.

## ALESSI'S TEA & COFFEE PIAZZA SERVICES

Alessi became one of the first companies to produce architect-designed homeware when Alessandro Mendini commissioned the Tea and Coffee Piazza services in 1979. Robert Venturi contributed subtly engraved and gilded forms on a tray with a pattern based on Michelangelo's pavement at the Piazza Campidoglio in Rome. Japanese architect Kazumasa Yamashita came up with stark geometric forms with spindly spouts and knops in the shapes of letters representing the contents of each vessel. Charles Jencks, an American architect who has done much to clarify postmodern architecture through his

extensive writing on the subject, looked back to ancient Greek columns for his service. The four component pieces of Jencks's set, presented on a stepped tray, each exhibit subtly different fluting techniques. He also uses volutes and capitals based on the Greek Doric order. Despite these authentic touches, Jencks distorts his columnar forms by tapering, pinching, breaking, or otherwise manipulating them in an amiable parody. The Tea and Coffee Piazza services were exhibited in Milan in 1983 and a follow-up range called Tea and Coffee Towers, comprising 22 distinct services, was released in 2002.

**The fluting** recalls the shafts of Classical columns

**TEA AND COFFEE PIAZZA SERVICE** Designed by Charles Jencks, this set is an Alessi limited edition of 99 copies. It comprises coffeepot, teapot, milk jug, sugar bowl, and tray. *1983.*

# USEFUL ADDRESSES

## MUSEUMS AND GALLERIES

### Australia
**Powerhouse Museum**
500 Harris Street Ultimo
PO Box: K346 Haymarket
Sydney NSW 1238
Tel: 00 61 2 92170111
www.phm.gov.au

### Austria
**Museen der Stadt Wien**
Karlsplatz
A-1040 Vienna
Tel: 00 43 1 50587470
www.museum-vienna.at

**Österreichisches Museum**
für Angewandte Kunst
Stubenring 5
A-1010 Vienna
Tel: 00 43 1 711360
www.mak.at

### Belgium
**Musée Horta**
Amerikaans Straate/rue Américaine
23–35, 1060 Brussels
Tel: 00 32 2 543 04 90
www.hortamuseum.be

### Canada
**Art Gallery of Greater Victoria**
1040 Moss Street
Victoria
British Columbia V8V 4P1
Tel: 00 1 250 384 4101
www.aggv.bc.ca

**Glenbow Museum**
130 9th Avenue SE
Calgary, Alberta T2G OP3
Tel: 00 1 403 268 4100
www.glenbow.org

**Ross Memorial Museum**
188 Montague Street
St Andrews, New Brunswick E5B 1J2
Tel: 00 1 506 529 5124

**Royal Ontario Museum**
100 Queen's Park
Toronto
Ontario M5S 2C6
Tel: 00 1 416 586 8000
www.rom.on.ca

### Denmark
**The National Museum of Denmark**
Frederiksholms Kanal 12
1220 Copenhagen K
Tel: 00 45 3313 4411
www.natmus.dk

### Egypt
**Egyptian Museum**
Tahrir Square, Cairo
Tel: 00 20 202 5782448
www.egyptianmuseum.gov.eg

### Finland
**Alvar Aalto Museum**
Alvar Aallon katu 7, Jyväskylä
Tel: 00 358 14 624809
www.alvaraalto.fi/museum

**Designmuseo**
Korkeavuorenkatu 23, 00130 Helsinki
Tel: 00 358 9 6220540
www.designmuseum.fi

**National Museum of Finland**
Mannerheimintie 34, Helsinki
Tel: 00 358 09 40 501
www.nba.fi

### France
**Musée des Arts Décoratifs**
Palais du Louvre
107 rue de Rivoli, 75001 Paris
Tel: 00 33 1 44 55 57 50
www.paris.org

**Musée de L'École de Nancy**
36–38 rue de Sergent Blandan
54000 Nancy
Tel: 00 33 3 83 40 14 8
www.nancy.fr

**Musée du Louvre**
Pyramide-Cour Napoléon, A.P. 34
36 quai du Louvre, 75058 Paris
Tel: 00 33 1 40 20 55 55
www.louvre.fr

**Musée des Tissus**
34 rue de la Charité, Lyon
Tel: 00 33 78 38 42 00
www.musee-des-tissus.com

### Germany
**Bauhaus**
Gropiusallee 38, 06846 Dessau
Tel: 00 49 340 65 08 0
www.bauhaus-dessau.de

**Germanisches Nationalmuseum**
Kartäusergasse 1, D - 90402 Nürnberg
Tel: 00 49 911 13310
www.gnm.de

**Staatliche Kunstsammlungen Dresden**
Dresdner Residenzschloss
Taschenberg 2, 01067 Dresden
Tel: 00 49 3 51 49 14 20 00
www.skd-dresden.de

**Vitra Design Museum**
Charles-Eames-str. 1
D-79576 Weil-am-Rhein
Tel: 00 49 7621 702 3200
www.design-museum.de

### Italy
**Museo di Palazzo Davanzati**
Via di Porta Rossa 13, 50122 Florence
Tel: 00 39 552 388 610
www.polomuseale.firenze.it/davanzati

### Japan
**Tokyo National Museum**
13-9 Ueno Park, Taito-ku, Tokyo 110-8712
Tel: 00 81 3 3822 1111
www. tnm.jp

### Netherlands
**Rijksmuseum**
Jan Luijkenstraat 1, Amsterdam
Tel: 00 31 20 6747000
www.rijksmuseum.nl

### Norway
**Kunstindustrimuseet**
St Olavs gate 1, Oslo
Tel: 00 47 22 036540
www.nasjonalmuseet.no

**Museet for samtidskunst**
Bankplassen 4, Oslo
Tel: 00 47 22 862210
www.nasjonalmuseet.no

### Russia
**State Hermitage Museum**
Palace Embankment
38 Dvortsovaya Naberezhnaya
St Petersburg
Tel: 00 7 812 1109625
www.hermitagemuseum.org

### South Africa
**Stellenbosch Museum**
Ryneveld Street, Stellenbosch, 7599
Tel: 00 27 21 887 2948
www.museums.org.za/stellmus

### Spain
**Museo Art Nouveau y Art Deco**
Calle Gibralta 14, 37008 Salamanca
Tel: 00 34 92 3121425
www.museocasalis.org

### Sweden
**National Museum**
Södra Blasieholmshamnen, Stockholm
Tel: 00 46 8 51954300
www.nationalmuseum.se

### United Kingdom
**American Museum**
Claverton Manor, Bath BA2 7BD
Tel: 01225 460503
www.americanmuseum.org

**Cheltenham Art Gallery and Museum**
Clarence Street, Cheltenham GL50 3JT
Tel: 01242 237431
www.cheltenhammuseum.org.uk

**Design Museum**
Shad Thames, London SE1 2YD
Tel: 0870 909 9009
www.designmuseum.org

**Geffrye Museum**
Kingsland Road, London E2 8EA
Tel: 020 7739 9893
www.geffrye-museum.org.uk

**Hunterian Museum and Art Gallery and Mackintosh House Gallery**
82 Hillhead Street
University of Glasgow, Glasgow G12 8QQ
Tel: 0141 330 4221
www.hunterian.gla.ac.uk

**Victoria and Albert Museum**
Cromwell Road, London SW7 2RL
Tel: 020 7942 2000
www.vam.ac.uk

**The Wallace Collection**
Hertford House, Manchester Square
London W1U 3BN
Tel: 020 7563 9500
www.wallacecollection.org

**William Morris Gallery**
Walter House, Lloyd Park, Forest Road
London E17 4PP
Tel: 020 8527 3782
www.walthamforest.gov.uk/wmg

### United States
**American Folk Art Museum**
45 West 53rd Street
New York, NY 10019
Tel: 00 1 212 265 1040
www.folkartmuseum.org

**Delaware Art Museum**
2301 Kentmere Parkway
Wilmington, DE 19806
Tel: 00 1 302 571 9590
www.delart.org

**The DeWitt Wallace Decorative Arts Museum**
The Colonial Williamsburg Foundation,
P.O. Box 1776
Williamsburg, VA 23187
Tel: 00 1 757 229 1000
www.colonialwilliamsburg.org

**Elbert Hubbard Roycroft Museum**
PO Box 472, 363 Oakwood Avenue
East Aurora, NY 14052
Tel: 00 1 716 652 4735
www.roycrofter.com/museum.htm

**High Museum of Art**
1280 Peachtree Street, N.E.
Atlanta
GA 30309
Tel: 00 1 404 703 4444
www.high.org

**Isabella Gardner Museum**
280 The Fenway
Boston, MA 02115
Tel: 00 1 617 566 1401
www.gardnermuseum.org

**John Paul Getty Museum**
Getty Center
Los Angeles, CA 90049-1687
Tel: 00 1 310 440 7300
www.getty.edu

The Metropolitan Museum of Art
1000 Fifth Avenue
New York, NY 10028-0198
Tel: 00 1 212 535 7710
www.metmuseum.org

The Museum of Modern Art
11 West 53rd Street
New York, NY 10019 5497
Tel: 00 1 212 708 9400
www.moma.org

National Ceramic Museum
7327 Ceramic Road N. E.
Roseville, Ohio 43777
Tel: 00 1 740 697 7021
www.ceramiccenter.org

Philadelphia Museum of Art
26th Street & Benjamin Franklin Parkway
Philadelphia, PA 19130
Tel: 00 1 215 763 8100
www.philamuseum.org

Smithsonian Museums
Washington, D.C. 20013-7012
Tel: 00 1 202 633 1000
www.si.edu

Stickley Museum
at Craftsman Farms, 2352 Rt. 10-West, #5
Morris Plains, NJ 07950
Tel: 00 1 973 540 1165
www.stickleymuseum.org

Winterthur Museum
Winterthur, DE  19735
Tel: 00 1 302 888 4907
www.winterthur.org

The Wolfsonian Museum of Modern Art
and Design
1001 Washington Avenue
Miami Beach, FL 33139
Tel: 00 1 305 531 1001
www.wolfsonian.org

# HISTORIC BUILDINGS

## Austria
Schönbrunn Palace
Schönbrunner Schlossstrasse 47, Vienna
00 43 1 81113 239
www.schoenbrunn.at

## Belgium
Hôtel Solvay
224 avenue Louise, 1050 Brussels
00 32 2 647 3733

## Denmark
Rosenborg Castle
Øster Voldgade 4, 1350 Copenhagen K
Tel: 00 45 3315 3286
www.rosenborg-slot.dk

## France
Château de Fontainebleau
77300 Fontainebleau
Tel: 00 33 1 60 71 50 70
www.musee-chateau-fontainebleau.fr

Château de Groussay
Rue de Versailles
78490 Montfort l'Amaury
Tel: 00 33 1 34 86 94 79

Château de Malmaison
Avenue du château
92 500 Rueil-Malmaison
Tel: 00 33 1 41 29 05 55
www.chateau-malmaison.fr

Château de Versailles
834-78008 Versailles
www.chateauversailles.fr

Hôtel de Soubise
60 Rue des Francs-Bourgeois
75003 Paris
Tel: 00 33 1 40 27 60 97

## Germany
Neue Rezidenz, Bamberg
Domplatz 8
96049 Bamberg
Tel: 00 49 89 179 080
www.schloesser.bayern.de

Charlottenhof
Sansoucci Park
Potsdam
Tel: 00 49 331 9694223

Schloss Charlottenburg
Spandauer Damm 20
Luisenplatz Berlin 14059
Tel: 00 49 331 9694202
www.schlosscharlottenburg.de

Schloss Neuschwanstein
Neuschwansteinstrasse 20
87645 Schwangau
Tel: 00 49 8362 939 88-0
www.schloesser.bayern.de

Schloss Nymphenburg
Eingang 19, 80638 München
Tel: 00 49 89 1 79 080
www.schloesser.bayern.de

## Italy
Pitti Palace
Piazza Pitti 1, 50125 Florence
Tel: 00 39 552 388 610
www.polomuseale.firenze.it

Reale Palace
Piazza Castello, Turin
Tel: 00 39 114 361 455
www.piemonte-emozioni.it/cultura/eng/
residenze_sabaude/pal_reale

## Netherlands
Schröder House
Prins Hendriklaan 50
Utrecht
Tel: 00 31 030 2362 310

## Portugal
Palacio Nacional de Queluz
Queluz, Lisbon
Tel: 00 351 214 343 860
www.ippar.pt/monumentos/palacio_queluz

## Russia
Summer Palace
Letny Sad, 191186 St Petersburg
Tel: 00 7 812 314-0374
www.saint-petersburg.com

Pavlovsk Palace
Pavlovsk, St Petersburg
Tel: 00 7 812 4702155
www.pavlovskart.spb.ru

## Spain
Palacio Nacional Madrid
Calle Bailén, 28071 Madrid
Tel: 00 34 91 4548800
www.patrimonionacional.es

## Sweden
Drottningholm Palace
178 02 Drottningholm
Tel: 00 46 8 4026280
www.royalcourt.se

Gripsholm Castle
647 31 Mariefred
Tel: 00 46 159 10194
www.royalcourt.se

The Royal Palace
Slottsbacken 1, Gamla Stan
Stockholm
Tel: 00 46 8 4026130
www.royalcourt.se

## United Kingdom
Castle Howard
York, North Yorkshire Y060 7DA
Tel: 01653 648444
www.castlehoward.co.uk

Georgian House
7 Charlotte Square
Edinburgh EH2 4DR
Tel: 0131 226 3318
www.nts.org.uk

Harewood House
Moor House
Harewood Estate
Harewood
Leeds LS17 9LQ
Tel: 0113 218 1010
www.harewood.org

Hill House (The)
Upper Colquhoun Street
Helensburgh
Glasgow G84 9AJ
Tel: 01436 673900
www.nts.org.uk

Lotherton Hall
Lotherton Lane, Aberford
Leeds LS25 3EB
Tel: 0113 2813259
www.leedsgov.co.uk

Osterley Park House
Isleworth
Middlesex TW7 4RB
Tel: 020 8232 5050
www.osterleypark.org.uk

The Red House
Red House Lane
Bexleyheath DA6 8JF
Tel: 020 8304 9878
www.nationaltrust.org.uk

Rodmarton Manor
Cirencester
Gloucestershire GL7 6PF
Tel: 01285 841253
www.rodmarton-manor.co.uk

The Royal Pavilion
Brighton
East Sussex
BN1 1EE
Tel: 01273 292820
www.royalpavilion.org.uk

Standen
West Hoathly Road
East Grinstead
West Sussex
RH19 4NE
Tel: 0 1342 323029
www.nationaltrust.org.uk

Strawberry Hill
St Mary's College
Waldegrave Road
Twickenham TW1 4SX
Tel: 0871 560 9489

Temple Newsam House
Temple Newsam
Leeds LS15 0AD
Tel: 0113 2645535
www.leedsgov.uk

## United States
The Gamble House
4 Westmoreland Place
Pasadena, CA  91103
Tel: 00 1 626 793 3334
www.gamblehouse.org

Marston House
3525 Seventh Avenue
San Diego, CA  92103
Tel: 00 1 619 298 3142
www.sandiegohistory.org/mainpages/
locate3.htm

Nathaniel Russell House
51 Meeting Street
Charleston, SC  29402
Tel: 00 1 843 723 1159
www.historiccharleston.org

Robie House
5757 S. Woodlawn Avenue
University of Chicago
Chicago, IL
Tel: 00 1 708 848 1976
www.wrightplus.org/robiehouse

The Stickley Museum
at Craftsman Farms
2352 Rt. 10-West, #5
Morris Plains, NJ 07950
Tel: 00 1 973 540 1165
www.stickleymuseum.org

# FURTHER READING

Alessi, Alberto, *The Dream Factory: Alessi Since 1921* Electa/Alessi, Milan, 2001.

Andrews, John, *Arts and Crafts Furniture* Antique Collectors' Club Woodbridge, 2005.

Anscombe, Isabelle, *Arts & Crafts Style* Phaidon Press Ltd, London and New York, 1991.

Arwas, Victor, *Art Deco Sculpture* Academy Editions, London, 1995.

Arwas, Victor, *Art Deco* Academy Editions, London, 1992.

Aslin, Elizabeth, *19th Century English Furniture* Faber and Faber, London, 1962.

Baker, Fiona & Keith, *20th Century Furniture* Carlton Books, London, 2000.

Bangert, Albrecht and Karl Michael Armer, *80s Style* Thames & Hudson, London, 1990.

Battersby, Martin, *The Decorative Thirties* The Herbert Press, London, 1988.

Battersby, Martin, *The Decorative Twenties* The Herbert Press, London, 1988.

Benton, Charlotte, Tim Benton & Ghislaine Wood (eds), *Art Deco 1910 to 1939* V&A Publications, London, 2003.

Casey, Andrew, *20th Century Ceramic Designers in Britain* Antique Collectors' Club, Woodbridge, 2001.

Duncan, Alastair (ed), *Encyclopedia of Art Deco* Headline Books, London, 1988.

Duncan, Alastair, *Modernism* Norwest Corporation, Minneapolis, 1998.

Fahr-Becker, Gabriele, *Wiener Werkstatte* Benedikt Taschen Verlag, Köln, 1995.

Fiell, Charlotte and Peter, *1000 Chairs* Benedikt Taschen Verlag, Cologne, London, Paris etc, 1997.

Fiell, Charlotte and Peter, *Design of the 20th Century* Benedikt Taschen Verlag, Cologne, London, New York etc., 1999.

Fiell, Charlotte and Peter, *Modern Furniture Classics* Thames & Hudson, London, 1991 & 2001.

Fisher, Volker (ed), *Design Now* Prestel Verlag, Munich, 1989.

Fleming, John and Hugh Honour, *Penguin Dictionary of Decorative Arts* Viking, London, 1989.

Forrest, Tim *The Marshall Guide to Antique China & Silver* Marshall Editions Ltd, London, 1998.

Frantz, Susanne K., *Contemporary Glass* Harry N. Abrams, Inc., Publishers, New York, 1989.

Gallagher, Fiona, Michael Jeffery & Nicolette White, *Christie's Art Deco* Watson-Guptill Publications, London, 2000

Giovanni et al, *Furniture by Wendell Castle* Founders Society, Detroit Institute of Arts, 1989.

Gleeson, Janet *The Arcanum* Warner Books, New York, 1998.

Greenhalgh, Paul (ed), *Art Nouveau 1890–1914* V&A Publications, London, 2000.

Hamerton, Ian (ed), *W.A.S. Benson* Antique Collectors' Club Woodbridge, 2005.

Hawkins Opie, Jennifer, *Scandinavia: Ceramics & Glass in the Twentieth Century* V&A Publications, London, 1989.

Jackson, Lesley, *20th Century Factory Glass* Mitchell Beazley, London, 2000.

Lesieutre, Alain, *The Spirit and the Splendour of Art Deco* Secaucus, New Jersey, 1978.

Levin, Elaine, *The History of American Ceramics 1607 to the Present* Harry N. Abrams, Inc., Publishers, New York, 1988.

Lewis, Philippa & Gillian Darley, *Dictionary of Ornament* Cameron & Hollis/David & Charles, 1990.

Livingstone, Karen, and Linda Parry (eds), *International Arts and Crafts* V&A Publications, London, 2005.

Mendes, Valerie, *The Victoria & Albert Museum's Textiles Collection* V&A Publications, London, 1992.

Miller, Judith, *20th Century Glass* Dorling Kindersley, London, 2004.

Miller, Judith, *Art Deco* Dorling Kindersley, London, 2005.

Miller, Judith, *Art Nouveau* Dorling Kindersley, London, 2004.

Miller, Judith, *Arts & Crafts* Dorling Kindersley, London, 2005.

Miller, Judith, *Furniture* Dorling Kindersley, London, 2005.

Morrison, Jasper, *Everything but the walls* Lars Muller (Princeton Architectural Press), 2002.

Pile, John, *A History of Interior Design* Laurence King Publishing, London, 2005.

Radice, Barbara, *Memphis* Rizzoli, New York, 1985.

Raizman, David, *History of Modern Design* Laurence King Publishing, London, 2003.

Ramsey, L.L.G., (ed), *The Complete Encyclopaedia of Antiques* The Connoisseur, London, 1962.

Ricke, Helmut, *Glass Art* Düsseldorf, Prestel, Munich, Berlin, London and New York, 2002.

Riley, Noël (Ed) *The Elements of Design* Mitchell Beazley, London, 2003.

Taylor, David A. and Jason W. Laskey, *Georg Jensen Holloware* The Silver Fund Plc, London and New York, 2003.

Thornton, Peter, *Authentic Décor: The Domestic Interior 1620–1920* Seven Dials, London, 1993.

Todd, Pamela, *The Arts & Crafts Companion* Thames & Hudson, London, 2004.

Venable, Charles L. et al, *China and Glass in America 1880–1980*, Dallas Museum of Art, 2000.

Venturi, Robert, Steven Izenour and Denise Scott Brown, *Learning from Las Vegas* MIT Press, Cambridge, MA, 1972.

Volpe, Tod M. and Beth Cathers, *Treasures of the American Arts and Crafts Movement* Thames & Hudson, London, 2003.

Whiteway, Michael (ed), *Christopher Dresser* V&A Publications with Cooper-Hewitt, London, 2004.

Wilk, Christopher (ed), *Modernism 1914–1939* V&A Publications, London, 2006.

Wood, Ghislaine, *Essential Art Deco*, V&A Publications, London, 2003.

Young, Robert, *Folk Art* Mitchell Beazley, London, 1999.

# GLOSSARY

**Acanthus leaf** The fleshy, scalloped leaf of a Mediterranean plant that was a popular motif for furniture and metalwork.

**Acid etching** The technique of engraving a design into glass using hydrochloric acid. The longer the vessel is exposed to the acid, the deeper the relief.

**Agate glass** An opaque, marbled glass used to imitate vessels made from semi-precious stones such as agate, chalcedony, and jasper.

**Albarello** An Italian word for a waisted tin-glazed earthenware container made for drug storage from the 15th century in Italy, Spain, and the Netherlands.

**Andirons (fire dogs)** Two large iron rests placed in a hearth to hold logs, their fronts often made in reflective material, such as silver, brass, or polished steel.

**Anthemion** A fan-like decorative motif resembling the honeysuckle leaf and flower that was used as a repeat pattern on, among other items, Neoclassical friezes.

**Appliqué** A decorative technique in which pieces of one fabric are laid onto another fabric and stitched in place.

**Apron** The frieze rail of a table, the base of the framework of a piece of case furniture, or a shaped piece of wood beneath the seat rail of a chair.

**Arabesque** Stylized foliage arranged in a swirling, interlaced pattern and combining flowers and tendrils with spirals and zigzags.

**Arita** *See* Kakiemon.

**Art pottery** Handmade and/or hand-decorated ceramics dating from the late 19th century onwards.

**Bakelite** A robust, non-flammable synthetic plastic invented by L.H. Baekeland in 1909.

**Baluster** A short bulbous post or pillar, such as a table leg, or one in a series supporting a rail and forming a balustrade.

**Basalt ware (basaltes ware)** A black, unglazed earthenware developed by Wedgwood in the 1760s.

**Batik** Method of producing patterned fabric by protecting parts of the cloth from dye with wax.

**Beading** A decorative Neoclassical border, often used on furniture, which consists of a single row of applied or embossed beads.

**Bentwood** A technique perfected in Austria by Michael Thonet in the mid-19th century that involves bending solid or laminated wood over steam to make curved sections for table and chair frames.

**Bergère** A French term for an informal, deep-seated chair of generous proportions. It usually has a caned or upholstered back and sides and a squab cushion.

**Berlin wool work** Embroidery worked in coloured wools on a canvas background with published patterns and wools that were originally imported from Berlin.

**Blackamoor** A life-sized carved figure of a black slave in brightly coloured clothes, originating in Venice, and used as a pedestal support for *torchères* from the 18th century.

**Blanc-de-chine** A type of translucent white Chinese porcelain that was widely copied in Europe. Wares include crisply modelled figures, cups, and bowls.

**Bombé** A French term used to describe a bulbous, curving form.

**Bonheur-du-jour** A French term for a small, delicate lady's writing desk that has a flat writing surface with tiered drawers and compartments at the back.

**Bonnet** An American term used to describe the domed or arched top found on clocks and highboys.

**Boullework** A technique named after the French cabinet-maker André-Charles Boulle which involves the elaborate inlay of brass into tortoiseshell or ebony and vice versa. Other precious materials may also be used.

**Bracket clock** A spring-driven clock first made after the invention of the pendulum in the mid-17th century. The clock was designed to stand on a wall bracket.

**Bright-cut engraving** A form of engraving on metal, primarily used from 1770 to 1800, in which the metal was cut at an angle to create facets that reflected the light and glittered.

**Brilliant cut** The ideal form of cutting for diamonds, consisting of 58 facets.

**Buffet** A French term for a large, heavy display cupboard with open shelves that was used for displaying silverware from the 16th century onwards.

**Bureau** A French term for a desk. A *bureau plat* is a flat-topped writing table. A *bureau à cylindre* is a roll-top desk. The sliding cover, made of slats of wood, hides the writing surface and pigeonholes. The most elaborate also contained candlesticks, clocks, and drawers.

**Cabochon** A French term for a smooth domed gem.

**Cabriole leg** A furniture leg with two curves forming an attenuated S-shape, like an animal leg. On chairs it often terminated in a claw-and-ball or stylized paw foot.

**Cameo glass** Glass made up of two or more separate layers of coloured glass. The top layers are carved or acid-etched to produce a relief image and reveal the different-coloured layers beneath.

**Cantilever chair** A chair with no back legs, in which the weight of the seat is supported by the front legs and base of the chair alone.

**Carcase** The shell of a piece of case furniture before the drawers, doors, shelves, or feet have been added.

**Carriage clock** A small spring-driven clock designed for travelling, developed in early 19th-century France. The case, usually plain or gilt brass, is rectangular with a carrying handle and often set with glass panels.

**Cartel clock** An ornate spring-driven wall clock made in France and Sweden in the 18th and 19th centuries, usually featuring a white enamelled dial set in a carved and gilded wood or gilt-bronze frame.

**Cartouche** A panel or tablet in the form of a scroll with curled edges, sometimes bearing an inscription, monogram, or coat of arms, and used as a decorative feature.

**Caryatid** A full-length female figure of Greek origin that is used as a support for a piece of furniture.

**Cased glass** A type of glass that consists of two or more layers of different colours – the first, inner layer is blown and the second and any subsequent layers added on top. The layers fuse when reheated.

**Cast iron** Metal produced by casting iron with a high carbon content in moulds of compressed sand. It is used for grilles, fireplace furnishings, furniture, and railings.

**Caudle cup** Two-handled silver or pottery cup with a lift-off cover to take caudle – a medicinal wine and gruel drink.

**Celadon glaze** A semi-opaque, distinctively coloured olive green glaze that imitated jade, used in China, Japan, and South Korea.

**Chaise longue** A French term for an upholstered day bed that has a high support at one end.

**Chalkware** Ornaments made from plaster of Paris and decorated with bright colours, popular from the 18th to the mid-20th centuries in the United States and Britain.

**Charger** A large, often ornate, dish, principally for display but also for serving at the table.

**Chasing** A surface decoration on metals, especially silver, often used with embossing, made by hammering with a blunt ball-point chisel or punch to add fine details and texture to the metal's surface.

**Chiffonier** From the French term, *chiffonière*, a small side cabinet with drawers. A *table en chiffonière* has longer legs and a shelf below the drawers.

**Chinoiserie** A decorative style in which fanciful, exotic motifs derived from Chinese originals were applied to European furniture, textiles, wallpaper, and ceramics.

**Chrome** A silvery metal usually plated on a base metal such as steel.

**Chryselephantine** A combination of ivory and metal, usually bronze.

**Claw-and-ball foot** A termination for furniture legs said to be based on Chinese examples of a dragon claw clasping a pearl.

**Classical orders** A column in Classical architecture, usually with a base, and always a shaft, capital (head), and entablature (upper part made up of an architrave, frieze, and cornice) decorated and proportioned as set out in Doric, Ionic, or Corinthian mode. The forms and motifs were borrowed extensively in the decorative arts from the Renaissance onwards.

**Cloisonné** A method of enamelling in which thin strips of metal are soldered onto the surface of an object to form decorative cells. These are filled with powdered enamel and then fired in a kiln.

**Commode** A French term for a chest of drawers; and also a small cupboard concealing a chamber pot.

**Compote** A dish with a long-stemmed base or foot, usually ceramic, used to hold fruit or sweetmeats.

**Cornice** An architectural term for a decorative, moulded projection that crowns a piece of furniture, particularly tall cupboards or display cabinets.

**Court cupboard** A two- or three-tiered structure with open tiers to display plates.

**Crackle glass (*craquelure*)** A type of glass, also known as ice glass, which has a crackled surface produced by plunging hot molten glass into cold water.

**Creamware** A refined cream-coloured earthenware developed in Staffordshire in around 1740 to rival imported porcelain.

***Cristallo*** An Italian name for colourless soda glass, developed in Venice in the mid-15th century.

**Crossbanding** A decorative strip of veneer in contrasting wood that runs at right angles to the main veneer.

**Crystalline glaze** A glaze with crystals of zinc or calcium suspended in it, creating attractively patchy colour, an effect produced by cooling the firing kiln extremely slowly.

**C-scroll** A carved or applied decoration in the shape of a C.

***Cuerda seca*** A decorative technique used on pottery, in which the pattern outlines are drawn in wax or grease to prevent different coloured enamels from running into each other.

**Cut glass** Glassware decorated with grooves and facets cut by hand or a wheel.

**Damask** A rich woven silk, linen, or cotton fabric with a satin weave.

**Day bed** *See* Chaise longue.

**Decanter** A decorative, usually handle-less, glass container with matching stopper, used for serving wine, sherry, and spirits that have been emptied (decanted) from the bottle.

**Delft ware** Tin-glazed earthenware inspired by Oriental blue-and-white porcelain, which was made mainly in the town of Delft in Holland from the 16th century. Similar wares made in Britain are called delftware with a lower-case "d".

***Demi-lune*** A French term for a half-moon shape.

**Dovetail** A joint in which two pieces of wood are joined together at right angles. Each piece of wood has a row of fan-shaped teeth, which interlock at the joint.

**Dowel** A small headless wooden pin used to join two pieces of wood.

**Earthenware** Pottery made from a porous clay body, which has to be waterproofed with a glaze.

***Ébéniste*** The French term for a cabinet-maker, derived from the word ebony. *Ébénistes* specialized in making veneered furniture.

**Ebonized wood** Wood stained black in imitation of ebony.

**Electroplating** A method of chemically depositing by electrolysis a layer of metal (usually gold or silver) onto any object (usually base metal) that will conduct electricity. It was used from around 1840.

**Embossing** The decoration of metals (or leather) using hammers to punch the material to produce a raised (relief) or impressed pattern. The details of the pattern are usually enhanced by chasing.

**Enamel** Coloured glass fused by heating in a furnace to create a design or decorative finish on a metallic surface. Enamel can be produced in a broad spectrum of translucent or opaque colours.

**Enamel colours** A vitreous onglaze ceramic pigment that fuses when fired at a relatively low temperature, called *petit feu* (literally "little fire") in French. A full palette of colours was in use by the end of the 17th century.

**Engraving** A process for decorating glass and metal in which the design is cut with a sharp instrument such as a diamond point or wheel to create an image in small dots or intaglio or relief. Also a print made by cutting a picture into wood or metal, inking it, and pressing paper onto it.

***Entrelac*** An interlaced tendril of Celtic origin, primarily used in jewellery making.

**Escutcheon** A protective and usually ornamental keyhole plate, sometimes in the shape of a shield, on a piece of furniture.

***Étui*** A pocket-sized case to hold small useful articles such as sewing accessories or writing sets, dating from the 18th to the 19th centuries and made of silver, gold, enamel, gilt metal, tortoiseshell, or lacquer.

***Façon de Venise*** A type of grey-toned soda glass with elaborate *filigrana* or applied decoration, made in Europe from around 1550 to 1700, often by emigrant Venetian glassmakers.

**Faience** A French term for tin-glazed earthenware popular in Europe from the 16th and 17th centuries, corresponding to maiolica in Italy and Spain and Delft ware in Holland and England. Lightly baked and of a buff or pale red colour, it was covered with white glaze to imitate porcelain.

***Famille jaune, noire, rose, verte*** Terms used to classify Chinese porcelain by its colour palette. In *famille verte*, green and iron-red predominate. *Famille jaune* used *famille verte* colours on a yellow ground and *famille noire* used a black ground. *Famille rose* used mainly pink or purple.

***Fasces*** A decorative motif of a bound bundle of rods, often incorporating the head of an axe, the emblem of authority of the magistrates in ancient Rome.

***Fauteuil*** A French term for a large, upholstered open armchair, first used at the Court of Louis XIV.

***Fazzoletto*** An Italian word for a handkerchief vase – a vase that takes the form of a falling handkerchief.

**Feather or herringbone banding** A banding of veneer formed of two narrow strips laid together, with the grain of each running diagonally to produce a herringbone or feather effect.

***Femme-fleur*** A sensual Art Nouveau motif, a hybrid of a female form and a flower.

**Festoon** A Classical decorative motif in the form of a garland of fruit and flowers tied with ribbons.

**Fibreglass** A strong, lightweight, and versatile material made from matted glass fibres bonded with a synthetic resin.

***Filigrana*** A technique in which decorative threads of coloured glass or rods are incorporated into a piece of glass.

**Finial** A decorative ornament on top of a household item, often in the form of an urn, an acorn, or a pinecone.

**Flambé glaze** A high-fired deep crimson glaze, which may flow in the kiln, creating flame-like streaks of purple or blue.

**Flashed glass** A thick layer of clear glass covered with a thinner layer of coloured glass. This might be acid-etched, cut, or sandblasted to reveal the layer of clear glass underneath.

**Flatware** All flat table articles such as plates, spoons, and forks, but excluding those with a cutting edge (cutlery). It is also the collective name for all tableware, such as plates or salvers, as opposed to other wares, such as vases, which are termed hollow wares.

**Flint glass** An archaic term for English lead glass. It refers to glass made in the mid-17th century in which ground flint was the source of the silica.

**Flute** A tall drinking glass with an extremely narrow inverted conical bowl resting on a very short stem.

**Fluting** Parallel lines of shallow, concave moulding (as opposed to reeding, which is convex) running from the top to the bottom of a column or column-shaped object such as a table leg.

**Folk art** Items such as painted furniture and treen, toleware, and pottery that are made by people with little or no formal training and reflect the traditional crafts and social values of their community.

***Fraktur*** A form of folk art from Germanic Europe exported to colonial America with the settlers. Originally a style of broken lettering, it has come to describe a variety of illustrated texts including birth records, writing samplers, and rewards of merit.

**Fretwork** Originally Chinese, carved decoration consisting of intersecting lines with perforated spaces between them.

**Frieze** A Classical term used to describe the horizontal strip that supports a table top or the cornice on a piece of case furniture.

**Fumed** A term used to describe a technique in which a chemical was used to darken the natural colour of a wood, usually oak, to make it look older.

**Gadrooning** A row of concave or convex flutes used along the edge of a surface.

**Gesso** A mixture of gypsum (plaster of Paris) and size, and sometimes linseed oil and glue. It was used as a base for carved and gilded decoration on furniture.

**Gilding** A decorative finish in which gold leaf or powdered gold is applied to wood, leather, silver, ceramics, or glass.

**Giltwood** Wood that has been gilded.

**Glaze** A layer of glass fused onto a ceramic body to make it watertight and stronger.

**Goût grec** A French term describing the renewed interest in ancient Greece and Rome that resulted in the Neoclassical style of the late 18th and early 19th centuries.

**Grand feu** See High temperature colours.

**Greek key** A decorative band of interlocking, geometric, hook-shaped forms.

**Grisaille** Decorative patterns painted on wood, glass, ceramics, plaster, or stone in a neutral palette of grey, black, or white to imitate marble or stone figure sculptures or relief ornament.

**Grotesque** A type of ornament in which real and mythical beasts, human figures, flowers, scrolls, and candelabra were linked, often in vertical panels.

**Guéridon** A French term for a small stand or table, first seen in the 17th century, that was usually ornately carved and embellished.

**Guilloche** A decorative motif that takes the form of a continuous band of strands twisted or plaited together.

**Highboy** An American term for a chest-on-chest, often made with a matching lowboy – a low dressing table.

**High temperature colours** The colours green (copper oxide), blue (cobalt), purple (manganese), yellow (antimony), and orange (iron) used to decorate tin-glazed earthenware until the 18th century, after which *petit feu*, or enamel colours, were more common. They are known in French as *grand feu* due to the high temperature used to unite them with the tin glaze.

**Hyalith** An opaque, jet-black or sealing-wax red glass made around 1819 in Bohemia.

**Ice glass** See Crackle glass.

**Inciso** The Italian term for incised glass. The technique creates many shallow, horizontal cuts across the surface of the glass.

**Inlay** A decorative technique in which different-coloured woods, stones, or exotic materials are inserted into the solid wood surface or veneer of furniture.

**Intarsia** An Italian term for pictorial marquetry. It was often used for decorative panelling on furniture in Renaissance Italy and 16th-century Germany.

**Intercalaire** Cased glass where decoration can be applied on different layers.

**Iridescence** A lustrous, rainbow-like surface that changes colour depending on how the light hits it.

**Ironstone** A hard white earthenware containing ironstone slag, patented by C.J. Mason in 1813.

**Islamic wares** Ceramics, glass, metalware, and furniture decorated with designs taken from Islamic art, especially flat, dense, repeating abstract patterns, pierced fretwork, interlacing, and calligraphic kufic script.

**Istoriato** Painted decoration found on Italian maiolica that depicts a story of historical, mythological, allegorical, genre, or Biblical origin.

**Japanning** A decorative technique in which furniture was coated with coloured varnish to look like Chinese or Japanese lacquer.

**Jardinière** A French term for a large ornamental vessel, usually ceramic, for holding cut flowers or growing plants.

**Jasper ware** A fine-grained, unglazed stoneware introduced by Josiah Wedgwood in 1775. It could be white or stained with metallic oxides, producing coloured bodies, including the well-known blue, and was often decorated with white relief Classical-style figures.

**Kakiemon** A term for porcelain produced at Arita in Japan using a distinctive palette of red, yellow, blue, and turquoise. Well-balanced, the decoration is usually high quality, delicate, and asymmetric, sparsely applied to emphasize the white porcelain. The style was much copied in Europe.

**Klismos chair** A chair with a broad, curved top rail and concave sabre legs that originated in ancient Greece.

**Knop** The decorative knob on lids and covers, or the cast finial at the end of a spoon handle. Also the decorative bulge halfway up the stem of a drinking glass, goblet, or candlestick.

**Lacca povera** An Italian term meaning "poor man's lacquer" that describes a form of decoration in which cut-out sheets of engravings were pasted onto furniture and varnished to look like lacquer.

**Lacquer** A resin produced from the sap of the *Rhus* tree that, once processed and dried, forms a hard, impermeable, smooth, and lustrous surface. Used from the 6th century, it was popular in Asia and particularly Japan, where lacquered objects were highly prized. The lacquer is brushed onto a wood or composition base in very thin layers that are dried and polished.

**Ladder-back chair** A country chair with a back made up of horizontal rails, like the rungs of a ladder, between the uprights.

**Lambrequin** A decorative fringe, originally based on the scarf worn across a knight's helmet and its heraldic representation, found on drapery, furniture, silver, or ceramics.

**Lamination** The technique in which thin layers (laminates) of wood are sandwiched together with the grain at right angles for strength and glued.

**Lampas** A patterned textile similar to damask but heavier, and often referred to as damask.

**Lampwork** A delicate ornamental glass technique in which thin rods are shaped, bent, and heated to attach them to each other. The resulting designs are often embedded in paperweights and spheres.

**Lattimo** (milk glass) An Italian term for opaque white glass that resembles porcelain. Developed in Venice in the 15th century, in the 17th and 18th centuries it was made in France (called *blanc-de-lait*), Germany (*milchglas*), and Britain, and was often decorated with enamelling and gilding.

**Lava glass** Iridescent gold art glass, known also as volcanic glass, developed and patented by Tiffany in the late 19th century, with an irregular form, and "dripping" decoration that resembles the flow of molten lava.

**Lead crystal glass** Glass with a high lead content, ideally suited to cut decoration. Perfected by George Ravenscroft in 1676, it is also popularly known as crystal or quartz crystal because of its brightness and light-reflecting quality.

**Lead glaze** A translucent glaze made from lead oxide and applied to pottery that has already been fired.

**Leaded glass** A technique of assembling pieces of cut glass (into windows, panels, or lamps) using small strips of lead known as "cames".

**Lithography** A printing process that was initially used on paper, but was also used for decorating ceramics from the late 1840s.

**Lithyalin** Opaque marbled glass designed to resemble hardstones. Invented by Friedrich Egermann and patented in 1828, it was used for beakers and scent bottles, often with cut and gilded decoration.

**Longcase clock** A tall, narrow, free-standing weight-driven clock, introduced around 1660. It is called a tall case clock in the United States.

**Lustre glaze** A shiny, iridescent glaze for ceramics, created by painting on a mixture of metallic oxides, such as gold, silver, and copper suspended in oil, before firing.

**Lyre motif** A decorative motif based on the ancient Greek musical instrument.

**Maiolica** In Italy, tin-glazed earthenware was known as maiolica because of the importance in the trading network of the island of Majorca, then called Maiolica. The term was first applied to Hispano-Moresque lustrewares from Spain, then to lustrewares made in Italy.

**Majolica** A corrupted form of the word "maiolica", this term was used in the 19th century for an elaborately modelled type of earthenware covered with thick colourful glazes in lead blue, purple-pink, turquoise, and yellow.

**Mantel clock** A type of clock designed to stand on a shelf or mantelpiece. The term is used to refer to bracket clocks, and also to describe some late 18th- and early 19th-century French clocks, often featuring gilt-bronze or marble cases embellished with figures, porcelain plaques, and a variety of Neoclassical motifs.

**Marquetry** A decorative veneer made from shaped pieces of wood in different colours placed together to form a pattern or picture.

**Mauchlineware** Wooden souvenir ware, including boxes and small household goods, which are usually made from sycamore and are decorated with printed transfers, frequently depicting a view.

**Mica** A shiny silica material that was combined with shellac by Arts and Crafts designers to create lampshades.

**Micromosaic** Miniature mosaics formed from elongated rather than square tesserae, popular in the 19th century.

***Millefiori*** From the Italian for a thousand flowers, a glass technique often used in paperweights in which tile-like cross sections of brightly coloured canes are arranged in patterns and embedded in clear glass.

**Mocha ware** An inexpensive type of pottery derived from "mocha stone", a variety of moss agate with feathery markings. The decoration was achieved by dripping an acid colourant onto an aklaline ground: the chemical reaction formed tree-like striations.

**Mortise and tenon** An early type of joint in which one piece of wood has a projecting piece (tenon) that fits into a hole (mortise) in the second piece of wood.

**Mould blown** A technique in which glass is blown into a mould to create a uniform shape, either by hand or as part of a mechanized process.

**Mount** A term for brass, ormolu, or bronze decorative details that were applied to furniture in the late 17th and 18th centuries.

**Murrine** A slice, usually patterned, of a coloured glass cane.

***Nécessaire*** A small item of silver, leather-covered wood, porcelain, or enamel, which carries everything necessary to accomplish a task. A *nécessaire à coudre*, for example, contains the needles, bodkin, thread, thimble, and scissors necessary for sewing.

**Needlepoint** A form of lace created by embroidering stitches using a single thread and needle on paper that was cut away when the design was complete. Also embroidery on canvas using simple, even stitches over counted threads.

**Objet de vertu** A small accessory such as a snuff box, pomander, *étui*, or *nécessaire* made of luxury materials, including porcelain, gold, silver, gemstones, or enamel, and valued more for beauty than function.

**Opalescence** A glass effect that is created when phosphates are added to the batch, it has a milky-blue appearance in reflected light and an amber tint in transmitted light.

**Opaline glass** A semi-opaque glass, developed in France in around 1825 by adding bone ash to the glass mix. This results in the "fire", whereby the colour of the glass changes when held to the light.

**Ormolu** Based on the French term *or moulu*, meaning "ground gold", a process of gilding bronze for decorative mounts.

**Overglaze** A technique in which enamels are painted onto fired and glazed porcelain, which is then fired again.

**Palladian** A restrained Classical style of architecture and decorative features that was derived from the works of the Italian architect Andrea Palladio.

**Palmette** A Classical decorative motif based on the shape of a palm leaf.

**Papier-mâché** A lightweight material made from paper and paste, which can be moulded into any shape. Pieces were often gilded, painted, japanned, and then varnished for decorative effect.

**Parian ware** A type of porcelain first made in England in the mid-19th century and named after the Greek island of Paros, which was famous for its white marble.

**Parquetry** A decorative veneer made up of a mosaic of small pieces of wood in contrasting colours pieced together to form a geometric pattern.

***Pâte-de-verre*** From the French for "glass paste", ground glass is mixed with a liquid to form a paste, pressed into a mould and slowly heated to form the required shape.

**Patera** An oval or circular ornament on a flat surface, which is often decorated with a floral design, a rosette, or fluting.

***Pâte-sur-pâte*** A ceramic term from the French for paste-on-paste, in which white slip is built up in layers to give a striking effect of depth on a dark background.

**Patina** A sheen on the surface of metal and furniture, the result of years of handling and a gradual build-up of dirt and polish.

**Pearl ware** A type of English creamware evolved by Wedgwood, in which the cream colour is counteracted by a blue-tinted glaze, and often printed or painted.

**Pedestal** The base that supports a column in Classical architecture. Since the Renaissance, decorative pedestals have been used as bases for vases, candelabra, lamps, and sculpture.

**Pediment** An architectural term for the triangular gable found above the portico of a Greek temple; a similar feature applied to the tops of large pieces of case furniture.

**Pembroke table** A small table, often with an elaborately inlaid top, with two frieze drawers, two drop leaves, and usually on legs with casters.

**Pendulum** A device controlling the timekeeping of a clock. A brass, steel, or wooden rod is made to swing in a regular arc by a flat or bulbous metal weight (bob) at the end.

**Penwork** A technique in which the entire surface of a piece of furniture is japanned black before being worked with an intricate decorative pattern of white japanning.

***Petit feu*** See Enamel colours.

**Pilaster** An architectural term for a flattened column attached to the surface of a building or piece of case furniture as a form of decoration, rather than for support.

**Planishing** A technique in which a sheet of metal is given a smooth or flat surface, either with rollers or, more usually, by supporting it on a stake then beating it with a planishing hammer, which has a broad, smooth, polished head.

***Plique-à-jour* enamel** A technique by which a translucent enamel is held in an unbacked framework to produce an effect similar to that of a stained-glass window when light is shone through it.

**Plywood** A flexible, composite wood made of several layers of laminated wood laid at right angles to each other.

**Polyurethane foam** A synthetic substance used to fill seat cushions and backs.

**Porcelain** A hard, dense, usually white ceramic first made in China in the late 6th century CE. It is translucent, watertight, and usually glazed. Soft-paste porcelain was developed in Europe in the 16th century as a substitute for the highly prized hard-paste porcelain being imported from China. It was made from a variety of ingredients, mainly white clay and ground glass, and was fired at low temperatures. A type of hard-paste porcelain was not made in Europe until 1709, when a formula was developed at Meissen. Made from kaolin and china stone, it was fired at higher temperatures.

**Pratt ware** A type of pottery made in Staffordshire, similar to pearl ware but characterized by a strong high-temperature palette of blue, green, and yellow.

**Pressed glass** Glass that has been shaped by being pressed in a mould.

**Prunt** A blob of molten glass applied to a piece of glass as decoration, particularly associated with drinking vessels.

***Putto*** An Italian term for "cherub" or "boy", which denotes a motif used during the Renaissance and the 17th century.

**Quatrefoil** A Gothic decorative motif, often used in tracery, of four asymmetrical leaves resembling a four-leafed clover. Similar motifs with three leaves (trefoil) and five leaves (cinquefoil) are also common.

***Raku* ware** A kind of lead-glazed Japanese earthenware, typically irregular in shape and used especially for the tea ceremony.

**Red ware** An American term used to describe stoneware and, generally, provincial pottery with a porous red body, typically decorated with coloured lead glaze and trailed slip or sgraffito work.

**Repoussé** A French term for the relief decoration on malleable metals that have been embossed and chased.

**Reverse painting** An image that has been painted in reverse on the inner surface of glass, especially lamps.

***Rocaille*** A French term meaning "rockwork", which denotes the asymmetrical rock and shell forms characteristic of the Rococo style.

**Rock crystal** The commonest mineral in existence, composed of pure silica. Found worldwide, it has been used in the decorative arts for centuries.

**Rosso antico** The name used by Josiah Wedgwood for an unglazed red stoneware he developed in the 1770s. Decorations were based on ancient Greek and Roman designs – hence the term "antico".

**Rummer** A 19th-century English drinking glass in the form of a goblet with a short stem. It sometimes has a domed or a square foot.

**Salt glaze** A hard translucent glaze, produced by adding salt to the kiln during firing at high temperature.

**Sampler** Originally a record of stitches and patterns made as a reference tool by professional and amateur needleworkers. By the 17th century samplers were used to show the skill of the embroiderer – often a young girl – and alphabets, inscriptions, and pictorial elements became ubiquitous on 18th-century samplers.

**Sancai ware** Three-coloured wares from China decorated with green, amber, and cream lead glazes, and used for burial figures and boxes.

**Sang-de-boeuf** From the French for ox blood, a brilliant red or plum-coloured glaze originally used for Chinese monochrome wares from the Kangxi period.

**Schwarzlot** From the German for black lead, a type of monochrome handpainted decoration in black or brown enamels applied to glass and ceramics and especially popular on bowls and beakers from around 1650 to 1750.

**Sconce** A candleholder designed to be mounted on a wall.

**Screenprinting** A printing technique in which ink is forced over a stencil supported on a mesh or screen (originally made of silk). The image can be built up by applying a succession of different colours over a series of carefully aligned stencils.

**Secretaire** A French term for a large writing cabinet in two sections. The lower section has a fall front that drops down to provide a writing surface and reveals a number of pigeonholes and drawers. Above this there is a bookcase or glazed cabinet.

**Serpentine** Wavy or undulating. A commode with a serpentine front has a protruding central section flanked by concave ends. Serpentine stretchers are curved cross-stretchers.

**Settle** A wooden bench that has a high back and open arms.

**Sgraffito** From the Italian for little scratch, a form of decoration made by scratching through a surface to reveal a lower layer of a contrasting colour, typically done in plaster or stucco on walls, or in slip on ceramics before firing.

**Shagreen** Shark or ray skin, used by some furniture designers as an inlay. It is also known by the French term *galuchat*.

**Slip** A homogeneous mixture of clay and water, usually finer and richer than the clay body it covers. Slips are used for coating, to provide colour and a smooth surface.

**Slipware** Pottery with one or more coatings of more refined clay, which is then decorated with designs trailed on in different coloured slips. The name of the potter and the date may be added. The lead glaze finish gives a characteristic yellowish colouring.

**Soda glass** The earliest form of glass, made from soda and lime. The glass is light and often tinged with yellow or brown.

**Sommerso** From the Italian for submerged, a glass technique that involves casing one or more layers of transparent coloured glass within a layer of thick, colourless glass.

**Spatter ware** Cheaply decorated pottery, common in Staffordshire, in which the colour was applied with a sponge, creating a blurred effect.

**Spelter** A term for zinc or an alloy of zinc and lead or aluminium, used as a substitute for bronze for mass-produced cast items, such as candlesticks and figures.

**Splat** The flat, vertical, central part of a chair back.

**S-scroll** A decorative carved or applied ornament in the shape of an S, developed during the Rococo period.

**Stained glass** A term for coloured, stained, or enamelled glass, often used with lead strips in an abstract or figurative design, set in an iron framework and used in an architectural context, usually a window, or as a decorative panel.

**Stoneware** A type of ceramic that shares characteristics of earthenware and porcelain. The body is made of clay mixed with a fusible stone that makes it watertight, although salt glaze or lead glaze are also added for decorative effect.

**Streamlining** A term borrowed from engineering and used to describe American Art Deco furniture with smooth, clean-lined shapes in the 1920s and 1930s.

**Stretcher** A rod or bar extending between two legs of a chair or table.

**Stringing** Narrow lines of inlay on a piece of furniture, used to create a simple, decorative border around drawer fronts or table tops.

**Studio pottery** The work of independent artist potters working in individual studios or with other like-minded potters wishing to express their own artistry without commercial pressures.

**Style rayonnant** A style of painting on ceramics that resembles lacy embroidery. The patterns on plates and dishes radiate inwards from richly decorated borders. It was first used on blue-and-white faience in the late 17th century at Rouen in France.

**Swag** A Classical decorative motif of a hanging garland of fruit, husks, flowers, or laurel leaves.

**Tall case clock** *See* Longcase clock.

**Tapestry** A weaving technique in which coloured weft threads are woven into an undyed warp thread to form a decorative or pictorial design. The different coloured weft threads are wound on bobbins and woven as far as the warp thread that marks the edge of a particular area of colour. Thus each part of the design is built up independently. The term also applies to wall hangings and furnishings made by this method.

**Temmoku glaze** A Japanese term, used originally to describe Chinese stoneware cups with a streaky black/brown glaze, favoured by the Japanese as tea ceremony wares. Named after the Tianmu mountains in China, the term is now used to describe almost any pottery or stoneware with a thick black/brown glaze.

**Tenon** *See* Mortise and tenon.

**Tesserae** The small pieces of glass used to make mosaics.

**Tessuto** A design in glass that looks as if threads or strips of glass have been woven together over the body.

**Tin glaze** A glaze technique used to make the opaque white coating on maiolica, faience, and Delft ware. After a first firing, the pottery was dipped into a glaze of oxides of lead and tin, which produced a porous white surface. It was then decorated and fired again, possibly with the addition of a lead glaze.

**Toleware** A term for *tôle peinte*, the French name for painted tinware, used for lampshades and hollow wares.

**Transfer printing** A process for decorating ceramics in which an engraved copper plate is covered with ink, prepared with metallic oxides. The engraved design is then transferred to paper, which while wet with pigment is pressed onto the surface of the object. The design is then fixed by firing.

**Treen** A term for carved or turned wooden household items made in rural communities in Europe and North America.

**Trefoil** *See* Quatrefoil.

**Tubular steel** Lightweight and strong hollow steel tubes, which can be bent into any shape.

**Tunbridgeware** Small wooden domestic objects and also, rarely, work tables. The surfaces are decorated with patterns created from an intricate mosaic of coloured woods, often as souvenirs of the spa town of Tunbridge Wells in south-east England where it was made.

**Tureen** A deep ceramic or silver bowl with a lid, two handles, and oval or circular in shape. Large tureens were for soup; small for sauce. They were made in sets or pairs.

**Underglaze** Decoration painted onto a biscuit (unglazed) ceramic body. As the colours have to withstand the full heat of the kiln, the palette is restricted.

**Vellum** A fine-grained, unsplit animal skin that has been prepared for writing on or for book-binding. Also used by Carlo Bugatti to decorate and cover furniture in the late 19th and early 20th centuries.

**Veneer** A thin layer of fine wood that is applied to the surface of a furniture carcase made of a coarser, cheaper wood, for decorative effect.

**Verdure** A tapestry featuring leafy plants and/or wooded landscapes, sometimes with birds and animals.

**Vermeil** A French term for silver gilt: silver that is covered with a thin film of gold.

**Vernis Martin** A generic name to describe an 18th-century French japanning method on wood, named after the Martin brothers. Although less durable than the Oriental lacquering that inspired it, the attractive brilliancy and depth of *vernis Martin* made it a fashionable varnish for indoor panelling, furniture, small boxes, and even carriages.

**Vitrine** A cupboard with large glazed panels, originally designed as a bookcase but later used to display ornaments. From the mid-19th century vitrines often had mirror backs, which made it possible to view both sides of the displayed objects.

**Vitruvian scroll** A wave-like series of scrolls used as a decorative motif – carved, painted, or gilded – on friezes.

**Volute** A Classical motif, consisting of a spiralling scroll, thought to resemble the horns of a ram.

**Wucai** Meaning five-coloured, a type of decoration on Chinese porcelain with washes of underglaze blue and overglaze coloured enamel. Outlines are usually in red or black.

# DEALER ADDRESSES

Many of the items shown in this book were photographed at dealers or auction houses that are either selling or have sold the piece. Inclusion in this book does not constitute or imply a contract or a binding offer on the part of any contributing dealer or auction house to supply or sell the pieces illustrated, or similar items, at the price band, where stated.

**BETH ADAMS**
Unit GO43/4, Alfie's Antiques Market
13 Church Street, London NW8 8DT
Tel: 020 7723 5613

**BEVERLEY ADAMS**
30 Church Street, London NW8 8EP
Tel: 020 7262 1576

**NORMAN ADAMS LTD**
8–10 Hans Road, London SW3 1RX
Tel: 020 7589 5266
www.normanadams.com

**ALESSI**
www.alessi.com

**ALL OUR YESTERDAYS**
6 Park Road, Kelvin Bridge
Glasgow G4 9JG
Tel: 0141 3347788
Email: antiques@allouryesterdays.fsnet.
co.uk

**ALTERMANN GALLERIES**
Santa Fe Galleries, 225 Canyon Road
Santa Fe, New Mexico 87501, USA
Tel: 00 1 505 983 1590
www.altermann.com

**ALBERT AMOR**
37 Bury Street, London SW1Y 6AU
Tel: 020 7930 2444
Email: info@albertamor.co.uk

**ANTIQUE TEXTILES AND LIGHTING**
34 Belvedere, Landsdowne Road
Bath BA1 5HR
Tel: 01225 310795
www.antiquetextilesandlighting.co.uk

**ARK ANTIQUES**
PO Box 3133, New Haven
CT 06515, USA
Tel: 00 1 203 498 8572
www.ark-antiques.com

**ART DECO ETC**
73 Upper Gloucester Road
Brighton, East Sussex BN1 3LQ
Tel: 01273 329268
Email: johnclark@artdecoetc.co.uk

**AT THE MOVIES**
17 Fouberts Place, London W1F 7QD
Tel: 020 7439 6336
www.atthemovies.co.uk

**AUX TROIS CLEFS**
117 boulevard Stalingrad
69100 Villeurbanne, France
Tel: 00 33 4 72 44 22 02

**BARRETT MARSDEN GALLERY**
17–18 Great Sutton Street
London EC1V 0DN
Tel: 020 7336 6396
www.bmgallery.co.uk

**BEAUSSANT LEFÈVRE**
32 rue Drouot, 7500 9 Paris, France
Tel: 00 33 1 47 70 40 00
www.beaussant-lefevre.auction.fr

**BELHORN AUCTION SERVICES**
PO Box 20211, Columbus
OH 43220, USA
Tel: 00 1 614 921 9441
www.belhorn.com

**PIERRE BERGÉ & ASSOCIÉS**
12 rue Drouot, 7500 9 Paris, France
Tel: 00 33 1 49 49 90 00
www.pba-auctions.com

**AUKTIONSHAUS BERGMANN**
Möhrendorfestraße 4
91056 Erlangen, Germany
Tel: 00 49 9 131 450 666
www.auction-bergmann.de

**THE BIG WHITE HOUSE**
www.thebigwhitehouse.com

**BLANCHARD**
86/88 Pimlico Road, London SW1W 8PL
Tel: 020 7823 6310

**BLANCHET ET ASSOCIÉS**
3 rue Geoffroy Marie
75009 Paris, France
Tel: 00 33 1 53 34 14 44

**BLOCK GLASS LTD.**
60 Ridgeview Avenue
Trumbull, CT 06611, USA
Tel: 00 1 203 556 0905
www.blockglass.com

**DELORME ET COLLIN DU BOCAGE**
11 rue de Miromesnil
75008 Paris, France
Tel: 00 33 1 58 18 39 05

**BONHAMS, BAYSWATER**
10 Salem Road, London W2 4DL
Tel: 020 7313 2727
www.bonhams.com

**BONHAMS, BOND STREET**
101 New Bond Street, London W1S 1SR
Tel: 020 7629 6602

**BONHAMS, EDINBURGH**
65 George Street, Edinburgh EH2 2JL
Tel: 0131 2252266

**BONHAMS, KNOWLE**
The Old House, Station Road
Knowle, Solihull B93 0HT
Tel: 01564 776151

**ROGER BRADBURY**
11 Church Street, Coltishall
Norwich, Norfolk NR12 7DJ
Tel: 01603 737444

**T.C.S. BROOKE**
The Grange, Wroxham
Norfolk NR12 8RX
Tel: 01603 782644

**BROOKSIDE ANTIQUES**
44 North Water Street, New Bedford
MA 02740, USA
Tel: 00 1 508 993 4944
www.brooksideartglass.com

**BRUNK AUCTIONS**
PO Box 2135, Ashville, NC 28802, USA
Tel: 00 1 828 254 6846
www.brunkauctions.com

**JOE DE BUCK**
43 Rue des Minimes
B-100 0 Brussels, Belgium
Tel: 00 32 2 512 5516
Email: jdb-tribalart@belgacom.net

**BUCKS COUNTY ANTIQUE CENTER**
Route 202, 8 Skyline Drive
Lahaska, PA 18914, USA
Tel: 00 1 215 794 9180

**BUKOWSKIS**
Arsenalsgatan 4, Box 1754
111 87 Stockholm, Sweden
www.bukowskis.se

**JOHN BULL (ANTIQUES) LTD**
JB Silverware, 139A New Bond Street
London W1S 2TN
Tel: 020 7629 1251
www.antique-silver.co.uk

**BURSTOW & HEWETT**
Lower Lake, Battle, East Sussex TN33 0AT
Tel: 01424 772374
www.burstowandhewett.co.uk

**CALDERWOOD GALLERY**
1622 Spruce Street, Philadelphia,
PA 19103-6719, USA
Tel: 00 1 215 546 5357
www.calderwoodgallery.com

**CAPPELLINI**
Sede Legale via A., Massena 12/7
20145 Milan, Italy
Tel: 00 39 031 759224
www.cappellini.it

**CASSINA SPA**
Via Busnelli 1, Meda, MI 200 36, Italy
www.cassina.it

**CATALIN RADIOS**
5443 Schultz Drive, Sylvania
OH 43560, USA
Tel: 00 1 419 824 2469
www.catalinradio.com

**LENNOX CATO**
1 The Square, Church Street
Edenbridge, Kent TN8 5BD
Tel: 01732 865988
www.lennoxcato.com

**CHEFFINS**
Clifton House, 1 & 2 Clifton Road
Cambridge CB1 7EA
Tel: 01223 213343
www.cheffins.co.uk

**CHENU SCRIVE BERARD**
Hôtel des Ventes, Lyon
Presqu'île Groupe Ivoire
6 rue Marcel Rivière
69002 Lyon, France
Tel: 00 33 4 72 77 78 01
www.chenu-scrive.com

**CHEZ BURNETTE**
615 South 6th Street
Philadelphia
PA 19147-2128, USA
Tel: 00 1 215 592 0256

**CHICAGO SILVER**
www.chicagosilver.com

**CHINA SEARCH**
PO Box 1202, Kenilworth
Warwickshire CV8 2WW
Tel: 01926 512402
www.chinasearch.co.uk

**CHISHOLM LARSSON**
145 8th Avenue
New York, NY 100 11, USA
Tel: 00 1 212 741 1703
www.chisholm-poster.com

**CHISWICK AUCTIONS**
1–5 Colville Road, London W3 8BL
Tel: 020 8992 4442
www.chiswickauctions.co.uk

**CLEVEDON SALEROOMS**
The Auction Centre, Kenn Road
Kenn, Clevedon
Bristol BS21 6TT
Tel: 01934 830111
www.clevedon-salerooms.com

**THE COEUR D'ALENE ART AUCTION**
PO Box 310, Hayden, ID 83835, USA
Tel: 00 1 208 772 900 9
www.cdaartauction.com

**CONTEMPORARY CERAMICS**
William Blake House
7 Marshall Street, London W1V 1LP
Tel: 020 7437 7605

**GRAHAM COOLEY**
Email: graham.cooley@metalysis.com

**COTTEES**
The Market, East Street, Wareham
Dorset BH20 4NR
Tel: 01929 552826/01929 554915
www.auctionsatcottees.co.uk

**COWDY GALLERY**
31 Culver Street, Newent, Glos GL18 1DB
Tel: 01531 821173
www.cowdygallery.co.uk

**MATALI CRASSET PRODUCTIONS**
26 rue du Buisson, Saint Louis
F-75010 Paris, France
Tel: 00 33 1 42 40 99 89
www.matalicrasset.com

**CUVREAU EXPERTISES ENCHÈRES**
6 boulevard Saint-Vincent-de-Paul
40990 Saint-Paul-Les-Dax, France
Tel: 00 33  558 35 42 49

**DAVIES ANTIQUES**
Tel: 020 8947 1902
www.antique-meissen.com

**DECO ETC**
122 West 25th Street
New York, NY 100 01 USA
Tel: 00 1 212 675 3326
www.decoetc.net

**DECODAME.COM**
853 Vanderbilt Beach Road
PMB 8 Naples, FL 34108, USA
Tel: 00 1 239 514 6797
www.decodame.com

**DELORENZO GALLERY**
956 Madison Avenue, NY, USA
Tel: 00 1 212 249 7575

**THE DESIGN GALLERY**
5 The Green, Westerham, Kent TN16 1AS
Tel: 01959 561234
www.designgallery.co.uk

**DESIGN20C**
www.design20c.com

**GEOFFREY DINER GALLERY**
1730 21st Street NW
Washington DC 20009 USA
Tel: 00 1 202 483 500 5
www.dinergallery.com

**GALERIE MARISKA DIRKX**
Wilhelminasingel 67
NL-6041 CH Roermond
The Netherlands
Tel: 00 31 475 317137
www.galeriemariskadirkx.nl

**PALAIS DOROTHEUM**
Dorotheergaße 17
A-1010 Vienna, Austria
www.dorotheum.com

**DREWEATT NEATE**
Donnington Priory Salerooms
Donnington, Newbury RG14 2JE
Tel: 01635 553 553
www.dnfa.com

**DREWEATT NEATE**
The Nottingham Salerooms
192 Mansfield Road, Notts NG1 3HU
Tel: 0115 9624141
www.dnfa.com

**DREWEATT NEATE**
Auction Hall, The Pantiles
Tunbridge Wells, Kent TN2 5QL
Tel: 01892 544500
www.dnfa.com

**DROOG DESIGN**
Staalstraat 7a–7b
1011 JJ Amsterdam, The Netherlands
Tel: 00 31 20 523 50 50
www.droogdesign.nl

**DYSON**
www.dyson.com

**THE END OF HISTORY**
548½ Hudson Street
New York, NY 10014, USA
Tel: 00 1 212 647 7598

**ETIENNE & VAN DEN DOEL**
Anna Pauwlonastraat 105a
2518 BD, Den Haag, The Netherlands
Tel: 00 31 703646239
www.etiennevandendoel.com

**JILL FENICHELL INC**
Brooklyn, NY 11238, USA
Tel: 00 1 718 237 2490
Email: jfenichell@yahoo.com

**FESTIVAL**
136 South Ealing Road, London W5 4QJ
Tel: 020 8840 9333

**THE FINE ART SOCIETY**
148 New Bond Street, London W1S 2JT
Tel: 020 7629 5116
www.faslondon.com

**FINESSE FINE ART**
Empool Cottage, West Knighton
Dorset DT2 8PE
Tel: 01305 854286
www.finesse-fine-art.com

**AUKTIONHAUS DR FISCHER**
Trappensee-Schößchen
D-74074 Heilbronn, Germany
Tel: 00 49 71 31 15 55 70
www.auctions-fischer.de

**GALLERY 532**
142 Duane Street , New York
NY 10013, USA
Tel: 00 1 212 964 1282
www.gallery532.com/

**GALERIE HÉLÈNE FOURNIER GUÉRIN**
18 rue des Saints-Pères
75007 Paris, France
Tel: 00 33 1 42 60 21 81

**FRAGILE DESIGN**
14/15 The Custard Factory
Digbeth, Birmingham B9 4AA
Tel: 0121 224 7378
www.fragiledesign.com

**FREEMAN'S**
1808 Chestnut Street
Philadelphia, PA 19103, USA
Tel: 00 1 215 563 9275
www.freemansauction.com

**RICHARD GARDNER ANTIQUES**
Swan House, Market Square
Petworth, West Sussex GU28 0AH
Tel: 01798 343411
www.richardgardenerantiques.co.uk

**GALLERY YVES GASTOU**
12 rue Bonaparte, 75006 Paris, France
Tel: 00 33 1 53 73 00  10

**THOS. WM. GAZE & SON**
Diss Auction Rooms
Roydon Road, Diss, Norfolk IP22 4LN
Tel: 01379 650306
www.twgaze.com

**SIDNEY GECKER**
226 West 21st Street
New York, NY 10011, USA
Tel: 00 1 212 929 8789

**THE GLASS MERCHANT**
Tel: 07775 683 961
Email: as@titan98.freeserve.co.uk

**LEAH GORDON ANTIQUES**
Gallery 18
Manhattan Art and Antiques Center
1050 Second Avenue, New York
NY 100 22, USA
Tel: 00 1 212 872 1422
www.the-maac.com/leahgordon

**GORRINGES, BEXHILL**
Terminus Road, Bexhill-on-Sea
East Sussex TN39 3LR
Tel: 01424 212994
www.gorringes.co.uk

**GORRINGES, LEWES**
15 North Street, Lewes
East Sussex BN7 2PD
Tel: 01273 472503
www.gorringes.co.uk

**GARY GRANT**
18 Arlington Way, London EC1R 1UY
Tel: 020 7713 1122

**HALCYON DAYS**
14 Brook Street, London W1S 1BD
Tel: 020 7629 8811
www.halcyondays.co.uk

**HALL-BAKKER @ HERITAGE**
Heritage, 6 Market Place
Woodstock, Oxon OX20 1TA
Tel: 01993 811332

**JEANETTE HAYHURST FINE GLASS**
32A Kensington Church Street
London W8 4HA
Tel: 020 7938 1539
www.antiqueglass-london.com

**GALERIE MARIANNE HELLER**
Friedrich-Ebert-Anlage 2
69117 Heidelberg, Germany
Tel: 00 49 6221 619090
www.galerie-heller.de

**HERMANN HISTORICA OHG**
Linprunstraße 16
80335 Munich, Germany
Tel: 00 49 895 237 296
www.hermann-historica.com

**HERR AUCTIONS**
W.G. Herr Art & Auction House
Friesenwall 35, 50672 Cologne, Germany
Tel: 00 49 221 25 45 48
www.herr-auktionen.de

**HIGH STYLE DECO**
224 West 18th Street
New York, NY 10011, USA
Tel: 00 1 212 647 00 35
www.highstyledeco.com

**HOLSTEN GALLERIES**
Elm Street, Stockbridge
Massachusetts 01262, USA
Tel: 00 1 413 298 3044
www.holstengalleries.com

**HOPE AND GLORY**
131A Kensington Church Street
London W8 7LP
Tel: 020 7727 8424

**JONATHAN HORNE**
Sampson & Horne Antiques
120 Mount Street, London W1K 3NN
Tel: 020 7409 1799
www.jonathanhorne.co.uk

**JOHN HOWARD @ HERITAGE**
Heritage, 6 Market Place
Woodstock, Oxon OX20 1TA
Tel: 0870 4440678
www.antiquepottery.co.uk

**RICK HUBBARD ART DECO**
3 Tee Court, Bell Street, Romsey
Hampshire SO51 8GY
Tel: 07767 267 607
www.rickhubbard-artdeco.co.uk

**IMPERIAL HALF BUSHEL**
831 N Howard Street
Baltimore, MD 21201, USA
Tel: 00 1 410 462 1192
www.imperialhalfbushel.com

**INGRAM ANTIQUES**
669 Mt Pleasant Road
Toronto, Canada M4S 2N2
Tel: 00 1 416 484 4601

**IVEY SELKIRK AUCTIONEERS**
7447 Forsyth Boulevard
Saint Louis, Missouri 63105, USA
Tel: 00 1 314 726 5515
www.iveyselkirk.com

**JACOBS AND HUNT FINE ART AUCTIONEERS LIMITED**
26 Lavant Street, Petersfield
Hampshire GU32 3EF
Tel: 01730 233933
www.jacobsandhunt.co.uk

**JAZZY**
34 Church Street, London NW8 8EP
Tel: 020 7724 0837
www.jazzyartdeco.com

**JOHN JESSE ANTIQUES**
Tel: 07767 497 880
E-mail: jj@johnjesse.com

**JAMES D JULIA INC**
PO Box 830, Fairfield, Maine 04937, USA
Tel: 00 1 207 453 7125
www.juliaauctions.com

**LEO KAPLAN MODERN**
41 East 57th Street, 7th Floor
New York, NY 100 21, USA
Tel: 00 1 212 872 1616
www.lkmodern.com

**AUKTIONHAUS KAUPP**
Schloss Sulzburg, Hauptstraße 62
79295 Sulzburg, Germany
Tel: 00 49 7634 5038 0
www.kaupp.de

**KELLER & ROSS**
PO Box 783, Melrose, MA 02716, USA
Tel: 00 1 978 988 2070
www.members.aol.com/kellerross

**JOHN KING**
74 Pimlico Road, London SW1W 8LS
Tel: 020 7730 0427
Email: kingj896@aol.com

**ANTIQUES BY JOYCE KNUTSEN**
Email: knutsenglass@aol.com

**GALLERIE KOLLER**
Hardturmstraße 102
Postfach 8031, Zürich
Switzerland
Tel: 00 41 1445 6363
www.galeriekoller.ch

**AUCTION TEAM KÖLN**
Postfach 50 11 19,
Bonner Str. 528-530
D-50971 Cologne, Germany
Tel: 00 49 221 38 70 49
www.breker.com

**DANNY LANE**
www.dannylane.co.uk

**LAW FINE ART LTD.**
Ash Cottage, Ashmore Green
Newbury, Berkshire RG18 9ER
Tel: 01635 860033
www.lawfineart.co.uk

**LAWRENCES' AUCTIONEERS**
The Linen Yard, South Street
Crewkerne, Somerset TA18 8AB
Tel: 01460 73041
www.lawrences.co.uk

**LIBERTY**
Regent Street, London W1
Tel: 020 7734 1234
www.liberty.co.uk

**ANDREW LINEHAM FINE GLASS**
Saturdays only or by appointment
101 Portobello Road, London W11 2QB
Tel: 01243 576 241
www.antiquecolouredglass.com

**LOST CITY ARTS**
18 Cooper Square, New York
NY 100 03, USA
Tel: 00 1 212 375 0500
www.lostcityarts.com

**LOTHERTON HALL**
Lotherton Hall, Lotherton Lane
Aberford, Leeds LS25 3EB
Tel: 0113 2813259
www.leeds.gov.uk/lothertonhall

**DAVID LOVE**
10 Royal Parade, Harrogate HG1 2SZ
Tel: 01423 565797

**FREDERIC LOZADA EXPERTISES**
10 rue de Pomereu, 75116 Paris, France
Tel: 00 33 1 53 70 23 70
www.fredericlozada.com

**LUNA**
23 George Street, Nottingham NG1 3BH
Tel: 0115 9243267
www.luna-online.co.uk

**LYON & TURNBULL**
33 Broughton Place, Edinburgh EH1 3RR
Tel: 0131 557 8844
www.lyonandturnbull.com

**MACKLOWE GALLERY**
667 Madison Avenue, New York
NY 10021, USA
Tel: 00 1 212 644 6400
www.macklowegallery.com

**JOHN MAKEPEACE**
Designers and Furniture-makers
Farrs Beaminster, Dorset DT8 3NB
Tel: 01308 862204
www.johnmakepeace.com

**MALLETT**
141 New Bond Street, London W1S 2BS
Tel: 020 7499 7411
www.mallett.co.uk

**LILI MARLEEN**
52 White Street, New York
NY 10013, USA
Tel: 00 1 212 219 00 06
www.lilimarleen.net

**FRANCESCA MARTIRE**
F131–137 Alfie's Antiques Market
13 Church Street, London NW8 8DT
Tel: 020 7724 4802

**GALERIE MAURER**
Kurfurstenstraße 17,
D-80799 Munich, Germany
Tel: 00 49 89 271 13 45
www.galerie-objekte-maurer.de

**INGO MAURER**
Kaiserstraße 47
80801 Munich, Germany
Tel: 00 49 89 381 60 60
www.ingo-maurer.com

**MEMPHIS AND POST**
Via Olivetti 9
200 10 Pregnan Milanese, Italy
Tel: 00 39 293 290 663
www.memphis-milano.it

**AUKTIONSHAUS METZ**
Friedrich-Eber-Anlage 5
69117 Heidelberg, Germany
Tel: 00 49 6221 23571
www.Metz-Auktion.de

**ARTHUR MILLNER**
Tel: 07900 248 390
www.arthurmillner.com

**MODERNE GALLERY**
111 North 3rd Street
Philadelphia,
PA 19106, USA
Tel: 00 1 215 923 8536
www.modernegallery.com

**MODERNISM GALLERY**
1622 Ponce de Leon Boulevard
Coral Gables, FL 33134, USA
Tel: 00 1 305 442 8743
www.modernism.com

**MOOD INDIGO**
181 Prince Street
New York, NY 10012, USA
Tel: 00 1 212 254 1176
www.moodindigonewyork.com

**MOSTLY BOXES**
93 High Street, Eton,
Berkshire SL4 6AF
Tel: 01753 858470

**THE MULTICOLOURED TIME SLIP**
Alfie's Antiques Market, Unit S00 2
13–25 Church Street
London NW8 8DT
Email: d_a_cameron@hotmail.com

**MUM HAD THAT**
www.mumhadthat.com

**NAGEL**
Neckarstraße 189-191
70190 Stuttgart, Germany
Tel: 00 49 711 649 690
www.auction.de

**LILLIAN NASSAU LTD**
220 East 57th Street, New York
NY 100 22, USA
Tel: 00 1 212 759 6062
www.lilliannassau.com

**JOHN NICHOLSON**
The Auction Rooms, Longfield
Midhurst Road,
Fernhurst, Haslemere
Surrey GU27 3HA
Tel: 01428 653727
www.johnnicholsons.com

**GALLERY 1930 SUSIE COOPER**
18 Church Street, London NW8 8EP
Tel: 020 7723 1555
www.susiecooperceramics.com

**NO PINK CARPET**
Tel: 01785 249 802
www.nopinkcarpet.com

**NORTHEAST AUCTIONS**
93 Pleasant Street
Portsmouth, NH 03801, USA
Tel: 00 1 603 433 8400
www.northeastauctions.com

**GALERIE OLIVIA ET EMMANUEL**
Village Suisse Galeries 24 et 58
78 avenue de Suffren
75015 Paris, France
Tel: 00 33 1 43 06 85 30
www.artface.com/olivia

**R.A. O'NEIL ANTIQUES**
100 Avenue Road
Toronto, Canada
Tel: 00 1 416 968 2806

**ONSLOWS**
The Coach House, Manor Road
Stourpaine, Dorset DT11 8TQ
Tel: 01258 488838
www.onslows.co.uk

**OTFORD ANTIQUES AND COLLECTORS CENTRE**
26-28 High Street, Otford
Kent TN14 5PQ
Tel: 01959 522025
www.otfordantiques.co.uk

**PARTRIDGE FINE ARTS PLC**
144-146 New Bond Street
London W1S 2PF
Tel: 020 7629 0834
www.partridgeplc.com

**GAETANO PESCE**
543 Broadway
New York, NY 10012, USA
Tel: 00 1 212 334 7134
www.gaetanopesce.com

**DAVID PICKUP**
115 High St, Burford
Oxon OX18 4RG
Tel: 01993 822555

**SALLE DES VENTES PILLET**
1 rue de la Libération B.P. 23
27480 Lyons la Forêt, France
Tel: 00 33 2 32 49 60 64
www.pillet.auction.fr

**POOK AND POOK**
463 East Lancaster Avenue
Downingtown, PA 19335, USA
Tel: 00 1 610 269 4040
www.pookandpook.com

**PORT ANTIQUES CENTER**
289 Main Street, Port Washington
NY 11050, USA
Tel: 00 1 516 767 3313
E-mail: visualedge2@aol.com

**POSTERITATI**
239 Centre Street
New York, NY 10013, USA
Tel: 00 1 212 2226 2207
www.posteritati.com

**PRITAM & EAMES**
29 Race Lane, East Hampton,
NY 11937, USA
Email: PritamEame@aol.com

**PURITAN VALUES**
The Dome, St Edmund's Road
Southwold, Suffolk IP18 6BZ
Tel: 01502 722211

**QUITTENBAUM**
Hohenstaufenstraße 1
D-80801 Munich, Germany
Tel: 00 49 859 33 00 75 6
E-mail: dialog@quittenbaum.de

**DAVID RAGO AUCTIONS**
333 North Main Street
Lambertville, NJ 08530, USA
Tel: 00 1 609 397 9374
www.ragoarts.com

**DAVID RAGO/NICHOLAS DAWES
LALIQUE AUCTIONS**
333 North Main Street
Lambertville, NJ 08530, USA
Tel: 00 1 609 397 9374
www.ragoarts.com

**R. DUANE REED GALLERY**
7th Floor, 529 West 20th Street
New York, NY 100 11, USA
Tel: 00 1 212 462 2600
www.rduanereedgallerynyc.com

**DEREK ROBERTS FINE ANTIQUE
CLOCKS & BAROMETERS**
25 Shipbourne Road
Tonbridge, Kent TN10 3DN
Tel: 01732 358986
www.qualityantiqueclocks.com

**ROGERS DE RIN**
76 Royal Hospital Road, Paradise Walk
London SW3 4HN
Tel: 020 7352 9007
www.rogersderin.co.uk

**ROSEBERY**
74–76 Knight's Hill, London SE27 0JD
Tel: 020 8761 2522
www.roseberys.co.uk

**ROSSINI SA**
7 rue Drouot 75009, Paris, France
Tel: 00 33 1 53 34 55 00
www.rossini.fr

**RITCHES AUCTIONEERS & APPRAISERS**
288 King Street East
Toronto, Ontario, Canada M5A 1KA
Tel: 00 1 416 364 1864
www.ritchies.com

**R20TH CENTURY**
82 Franklin Street
New York, NY 10013, USA
Tel: 00 1 212 343 7979
www.r20thcentury.com

**HUGO RUEF**
Gabelsbergerstraße 28
80333 Munich, Germany
Tel: 00 49 89 52 40 84
www.ruef-auktionen.de

**SCP LIMITED**
135–139 Curtain Road
London EC2A 3BX
Tel: 020 7739 1869
www.scp.co.uk

**SENIOR & CARMICHAEL**
Church Street, Betchworth
Surrey RH3 7DN
Tel: 01737 844316
www.seniorandcarmichael.co.uk

**THE SILVER FUND**
1 Duke of York Street
London SW1Y 6JP
Tel: 020 7839 7664
www.thesilverfund.com

**PAUL SIMONS**
Admiral Vernon Antiques Center
141–149 Portobello Road, London W11
Tel: 07733 326 574

**BOREK SIPEK**
www.sipek.com

**SKINNER**
63 Park Plaza, Boston, MA 02116, USA
Tel: 00 1 617 350 5400
www.skinnerinc.com

**SLOANS & KENYON**
4605 Bradley Boulevard
Bethesda, Maryland 20815, USA
Tel: 00 1 301 634 2330
www.sloansandkenyon.com

**SOLLO:RAGO MODERN AUCTIONS**
333 North Main Street
Lambertville, NJ 08530, USA
Tel: 00 1 609 397 9374
www.ragoarts.com

**HANSEN SØRENSEN**
Vesterled 19
DK-6950 Ringkøbing, Denmark
Tel: 00 45 97 32 45 08
www.hansensorensen.com

**STARCK NETWORK**
18/20 rue du Faubourg du Temple
75011 Paris, France
Tel: 00 33 1 48 07 54 54

**STOCKSPRING ANTIQUES**
114 Kensington Church Street
London W8 4BH
Tel: 020 7727 7995
www.antique-porcelain.co.uk

**STYLE GALLERY**
10 Camden Passage, London N1 8ED
Tel: 020 7359 7867

**SPENCER SWAFFER ANTIQUES**
30 High Street, Arundel
West Sussex BN18 9AB
Tel: 01903 882132
www.spencerswaffer.com

**SWANN GALLERIES**
104 East 25th Street
New York, NY 10010, USA
Tel: 00 1 212 254 4710
www.swanngalleries.com

**SWORDERS**
14 Cambridge Road, Stansted
Mountfitchet, Essex CM24 8BZ
Tel: 01279 817778
www.sworder.co.uk

**TAKE-A-BOO EMPORIUM**
1927 Avenue Road, Toronto
Ontario M5M 4A2, Canada
Tel: 00 1 416 785 4555
www.takeaboo.com

**TECTA**
D-37697 Lauenförde, Germany
Tel: 00 49 5273 378 90
www.tecta.de

**TELKAMP**
Galerie Telkamp, Maximilianstraße 6
80539 Munich, Germany
Tel: 00 49 89 226 283

**TENDO MOKKO**
1-3-10 Midaregawa
Tendo, Yamagata, Japan
Tel: 023 653 3121
www.tendo-mokko.co.jp

**TITUS OMEGA**
Cross Street, Islington, London N1
Tel: 020 7688 1295
www.titusomega.com

**TRIO**
L24 Grays Antique Market
58 Davies Mews
London W1K 5AB
Tel: 020 7493 2736
www.trio-london.fsnet.co.uk

**TWENTIETH CENTURY MARKS**
Whitegates, Rectory Road
Little Burstead
Essex CM12 9TR
Tel: 01268 411000
www.20thcenturymarks.co.uk/

**VAN DEN BOSCH**
Shop 1, Georgian Village
Camden Passage
London N1 8DU
Tel: 020 7226 4550
www.vandenbosch.co.uk

**GALERIE VANDERMEERSCH**
Voltaire Antiquités-Vandermeersch SA
21 quai Voltaire
7500 7 Paris, France
Tel: 00 33 1 42 61 23 10

**ROBERT VENTURI**
www.vsba.com

**VETRO & ARTE GALLERY**
Calle del Capeler 3212
Dorsoduro, 30123 Venice, Italy
Tel: 00 39 041 522 8525
www.venicewebgallery.com

**JOHANNES VOGT AUKTIONEN**
Antonienstraße 3
80802 Munich, Germany
Tel: 00 49 89 33079139
www.vogt-auctions.de

**VON SPAETH**
Willhelm-Diess-Weg 13
81927 Munich, Germany
Tel: 00 49 89 2809132
www.glasvonspaeth.com

**VON ZEZSCHWITZ**
Friedrichstraße 1a
80801 Munich, Germany
Tel: 00 49 89 38 98 930
www.von-zezschwitz.de

**JONATHAN WADSWORTH**
Wadsworth's, Marehill, Pulborough
West Sussex RH20 2DY
Tel: 01798 873555
www.wadsworthsrugs.com

**RICHARD WALLIS ANTIKS**
Tel: 020 8529 1749
www.richardwallisantiks.com

**MIKE WEEDON**
7 Camden Passage, London N1 8EA
Tel: 020 7226 5319
www.mikeweedonantiques.com

**WILFRIED WEGIEL**
Cité des Antiquaires
117 boulevard Stalingrad
69100 Lyon-Villeurbane, France
Email: wilfriedwegiel@aol.com

**WIENER KUNST AUKTIONEN**
Palais Kinsky
Freyung 4, 1010 Vienna, Austria
Tel: 00 43 15 32 42 00
www.palais-kinsky.com

**MARY WISE AND GROSVENOR
ANTIQUES**
58 Kensington Church Street
London W8 4DB
Tel: 020 7937 8649
www.wiseantiques.com

**WOOLLEY & WALLIS**
51-61 Castle Street, Salisbury SP1 3SU
Tel: 01722 424500
www.woolleyandwallis.co.uk

**WRIGHT**
1440 West Hubbard, Chicago
IL 60622, USA
Tel: 312 563 00 20
www.wright20.com

**JUNNAA & THOMI WROBLEWSKI**
78 Marylebone High Street, Box 39
London W1U 5AP
Tel: 020 7499 7793
E-mail: junnaa@wroblewski.eu.com

**ZANOTTA**
Via Vittorio Veneto 57
200 54 Nova Milanese, Italy
Tel: 00 39 0362 4981
www.zanotta.it

# INDEX

# ACKNOWLEDGMENTS

## AUTHOR'S ACKNOWLEDGMENTS

The authors would like to thank the following people for their substantial contributions to the production of this book:

Photographer Graham Rae for his patience, humour and wonderful photography as well as John McKenzie, Andy Johnson, Byron Slater, Ellen MacDermott, and Adam Gault for additional photography.

All of the dealers, auction houses, and private collectors for kindly allowing us to photograph their collections, and for taking the time to provide a wealth of information about the pieces.

The team at DK, especially Angela Wilkes and Mandy Earey for all their skill and dedication to the project, and Anna Fischel for her invaluable support.

We would also like to thank the following for their help in the execution of this book: Anthony Barnes, Rago Arts and Auction Center, Lambertville; Pierre Bergé et Associés, Paris; Maison de Ventes Chenu Scrive Bérard, Lyon; Martina Franke; Julie Killam, James D. Julia, Inc., Fairfield; John Mackie, Lyon and Turnbull, Edinburgh; Ron and Debra Pook, Pook and Pook Inc, Lancaster, PA; Paul Roberts, Lyon and Turnbull, Edinburgh; Rossini, Paris; Bernadette Rubbo, Sollo: Rago Modern Auctions, Lambertville; Nicolas Tricaud de Montonnière; Lee Young, Samuel T. Freeman and Co, Philadelphia.

## PUBLISHER'S ACKNOWLEDGMENTS

Dorling Kindersley would like to thank Anna Amari-Parker and Janet Mohun for their editorial help, Sarah Rock, Katie Eke, Adam Walker, Lucy Claxton, and Romaine Werblow for their help with design, Caroline Hunt for proofreading, and Pamela Ellis for compiling the index.

## PICTURE CREDITS

The publisher would like to thank the following for their kind permission to reproduce their photographs:

(Key: A-above; B-below/bottom; C-centre; L-left; R-right; T-top)

akg-images 308 BL. Alamy Images AAD Worldwide Travel Images 374 BL; Bildarchiv Monheim GmBh 16 BL, 238 BL, 248 TR; Michael Jenner 144 L. Alan Moss 307 BR. Albert Amor 11 BR, 37 CC, BL, BC & BR, 211 TR. Alessi 394 BL, 395 TC, 417 TC, TR, BR. All Our Yesterdays 118 TC. Altermann Galleries 140 BC. Andrew Lineham 48 C, 74 TR & BL, 83 BC, 114 BC & BR, 117 BC, 119 TC, 120 BC, 133 BR, 121 TC, 216 no.2 & 3. Antique Textiles and Lighting 47 BL, 135 BC & CR. Antiques by Joyce Knutsen 119 BR. Ark Antiques 179 TL. The Art Archive Musee de l'Ecole de Nancy / Dagli Orti 189 T; Musée Historique Lorraine Nancy / Dagli Orti 207. Art Deco Etc 283 BL.

Arthur Millner 273 BR. At The Movies 371 TR. Auction Team Koln 364 TR. Auktionhaus Bergmann 60 TC, 62 no.15, 69 BL, 70 no.6, 9, 16, 75 BL, 77 no.12, 79 TL, 93 BC, 112 BL, 115 CR, 299 CCR. Auktionhaus Dr Fischer 2 C, 9 CL, 21 BR, 38 TR, BL & BC, 39 TC, TR, BL, BC & BR, 67 TC, 74 BR, 75 TC, TR & BR, 76 no.9, 77 no.14, 117 BL, 120 CC & BR, 121 CR, 156 no.6, 8 & 9, 206 BR, 215 no.10, 291 CC, 316 BL, 346 TL & TC, 347 TL & TC, 349 BR, 353 no.17, 385 no.13, 409 CR. Auktionhaus Kaupp 20 TR, 34 BL, 45 BR, 69 TC, 70 no.8, 94 C, 107 CR, 114 BR, 115 CC & BC, 122 BR, 126 no.10, 127 no.12 & 18, 131 BL. Auktionhaus Metz 34 TR & BR, 37 TL, 114 BL. Aux Trois Clefs 292 no.13. Barrett Marsden Gallery 397 TR. Beaussant Lefevre 24 BR, 25 CR, 42 TR, BR, 42 BR, 50 BC, 62 no.4, 63 no.11, 70 no.4, 72 BR, 93 TC, 278 TR. Belhorn Auction Services 341 no.11. Beth Adams 284 no.8. Beverley Adams 285 no.11. Blanchard 242 BC. Blanchet et Associés 47 TL. Block Glass Ltd 411 BR. Bonhams, Edinburgh 249 BC, 323 CR. Bonhams, Bayswater 249 BR, 250 BR, 259 BC, 260 BL, 323 TC, 345 TR & BCR, 368 CR. Bonhams, Bond Street 104 no.1, 130 TR, 366 CR. Bonhams, Knowle 91 TL, CR, BL & BR. Borek Sipek 378 CL. Bridgeman Art Library: 17 BL, 17 TL, 85. Brookside Antiques 118 CR, 121 TR, 209 BR, 211 BC. Brunk Auctions 101 BR, 136 BR. Bucks County Antiques Center 86 TR, 127 no.15. Bukowskis 59 TL, 62 no.2, 63 no.14, 292 no.4, 318 BR, 342 CR & BL, 344 CC, 392 BL, 393 BC, 413 no.2. Burstow & Hewett 341 no.18. Calderwood Gallery 194 TR, 204 no.7, 224 no.5, 230 BC, 266 TR, 270 CL, 271 TL & CR. Cappellini 380 TR. Cassina SPA 252 TR. Catalin Radios 296 CL, 305 TL. Cheffins 67 TR, 70 no.5 & 7, 105 no.12, 107 CL, 164 TL, 242 CC. Chenu Scrive Berard 66 BR, 194 TC, 270 TR. Cheryl Grandfield Collection 220 BC. Chéz Burnette 305 TR, 364 BR. Chicago Silver 179 BL & BR, 300 TC, 302 no.2. China Search 285 no.10, 340 no.1, 341 no.14. Chisholm Larsson 239 BR, 370 BC & BR, 371 BR, 395 TL. Chiswick Auctions 106 TR, 281 CR, 284 no.3. Christie's Images Ltd.: 227 L. Claudia Capelletti, Cappellini Design SPA 387 BR. Clevedon Salerooms 14 TR. Contemporary Ceramics 397 CR, 400 TL, BC & BL, 401 TL. Corbis: Peter Aprahamian 51 B, 169, 267 T, 307 TR; Condé Nast Archive 328 TL; Dean Conger 15 BR; Owen Franken 213; Michael Freeman 320 TR; Robert Harding 20 BL; Thomas A. Heinz 252 TL, 253; Historical Picture Archive 162 BL, 185 TR; Angelo Hornak 312 B; Robert Levin 325; Museum of the City of New York 301 TL; Gregor M. Schmid 50 BL; Setboun 392 BR; Herbert Spichtinger/zefa 98 BL; Adam Woolfitt 12 BL. Corning Musum of Glass 73 TR & BR. Cottees 283 BC. Cowdy Gallery 406 TR & TC, 408 CC, 409 BC, BR, 410 TC & TR. Cuvreau Expertises Enchères 278 BR. Danny Lane 318 BL. David Love 54 TL, 62 no.3. David Pickup 157 no.14. David Rago Auctions 111 CR & BC, 142 C, 144 BR, TR, 146 CL, 150 TR, 153 CC & CR, 154 BL & BR, 155 CL, CC, CR & BR, 158 BL & BR, 159 TL, TC, B Row (all), 160, TR, BL & BR, 161 TR, CR, BL, BC & BR, 162 BC & BR, 166 no.1, 2, 3 & 9, 167 no.12, 15, 16, 18 & 19, 171 TL, 172 TR & BL, 173 TL & BR, 178 BR, 179 TC, 180 no.1 & 10, 184 TC, 202 CR, BL, BC & BR, 203 TL, TR, CC & BL, 204 no.1, 8 & 10, 205 no.11, 13, 14, 15, 16 & 17, 210 BL, 211 BR, 216 BL, 214 no.5 & 7, 215 no.14, 15 & 16, 263 TL, TC, TR, CL, BL, BC & BR, 283 CR & BR, 285 no.14 & 15, 286 CL & BL, 287 CC, 289 BCR, 291 BR, 293 no.20, 301 BC & BR, 323

BR, 324 TR, CR & BL, 330 no.1, 3, 5 & 11, 337 CL, 338 TL, 339 BL, 358 no.6 & 7, 359 no.13, 15 & 16, 361 TR & BC, 394 BC & BR, 398 CR, 399 TR & CR, 405 no.17, 413 no.13 & 21, 495 no.15. David Rago/Nicholas Dawes Lalique Auctions 286 CC. Davies Antiques 281 TL. Deco Etc 8 C, 295 TL & TCL, 302 no.7, 358 no.6. Decodame.com 267 BR, 278 BL, 289 BCL, 298 CR, 300 BL & BC, 302 no1, 4 & 6, 303 no.11, 12, 13, 17 & 20, 304 TR & BL. DeLorenzo Gallery 270 BR, 272 BR. Delorme et Collin du Bocage 106 BL, 355 BL, 365 BR. Derek Roberts Fine Antique Clocks & Barometers 81 BR, 153 BC & BR. Design20C 353 no.15, 354 BR, 359 no.12, 364 BL. DK Images: British Museum, London 10l, 10 R, 14 R; Musee Carnavalet 25 TR. Dreweatt Neate, Donnington 9 C, 20 CL, 32 BR, 40 TR, 62 no.9, 65 BR, 67 BR, 71 no.19 & 20, 72 TR, 73 TL, 76 no.2, 4 & 8, 77 no.15, 16, 17 & 18, 101 TR, 103 BL, 105 no.16, 108, 115 BR, TL & BC, 117 TL, BR, 123 BR, 128 BL, 132 BR, 137 BL, 167 no.17, 175 BR, 180 no.7 & 9, 181 no.12, 18 & 21, 200 BR, 201 BR, 205 no.18 & 20, 281 BR, 292 no.9, 305 BC, 345 BL, 351 TC. Dreweatt Neate, Not tingham 224 no.7.  Dreweatt Neate, Tunbridge Wells 133 TL & CL, 221 CL, 224 no.8. Droog Design 414 TR. Dyson 395 BR. Etienne & van den Doel 3 R, 7 L, 407 BR, 409 CL, BL, 412 no.5 & 10. Festival 334 CR & CBR, 335 TC, 340 no.4. Finesse Fine Art 299 CCL. Fragile Design 333 BR, 343 TC, 359 no.11 & 14, 366 TR, 369 BR. Francesca Martire 413 no.15. Frederic Lozada Enterprises 311 TR. Freeman's 27 BR, 50 TR, 57 BC, 62 no.8, 63 no.20, 86 BL, 90 BL, 92 BC, 97 BR, 104 no.2, 112 BR, 122 BL, 124 CL, CC & BR, 125 BL, 126 no.2 & 7, 130 BR, 131 TL, 135 CC, CL & BL, 137 CL, 141 CC, 157 no.16, 171 TR, 250 BL, 261 TL, 291 BC, 310 no.6, 331 no.15, 353 no.18, 354 BC, 367 CC, 385 no.13, 389 TC. Gaetano Pesce 414 BL. Galerie Helene Fournier Guerin 32 CC, 66 BL, 71 no.13. Galerie Marianne Heller 400 CR, 405 no.12. Galerie Mariska Dirkx 410 BC & BR, 411 CR, 412 no.3. Galerie Maurer 376 BL, 381 TR, CR, 384 no.1, 385 no.12, 17 & 19, 386 TR, BL, 387 BC, 398 CR, BR, 390 TC, 391 CC, CR, 394 BC, 402 TR, BC, 403 CR, 404 no.3, 4, 5, 6 & 8, 405 no.13, 415 BL, BC, BR, 416 BL, 417 TL. Galerie Olivia et Emmanuel 78 BL, 123 BC, 126 no.1, 127 no.11 & 17, 298 TR, 302 no.10. Galerie Vandermeersch 32 BL, 36 TR, 37 TR. Galerie Yves Gastou 271 BL, 295 BL. Gallerie Koller 2 L, 25 BR, 42 BL, 44 TR & BC, 45 BL, 59 BR. Gallery 1930 Susie Cooper 283 TC. Gallery 532 152 TR, BL, 156 no.7, 172 BC, 173 BL, 178 TR. Gary Grant 333 BL, 335, CR & BL, 340 no.3 & 7, 341 no.8. Geoffrey Diner Gallery 153 BL, 155 BL, 156 no.5, 157 no.10, 162 BL, 173 BC, 176 BR, 178 BL, 180 no.5, 186 C. Georg Jensen AS, Denmark: 222 BL. Getty Images/Hugh Sitton 13 TR. Gilbert Collection: 28 TC. Gorringes, Bexhill 105 no.13 & 15.  Gorringes, Lewes 83 BL, 84 CR, 105 no.14, 130 BL, 131 CC & BR, 166 no.4, 5 & 8, 167 no.20, 215 no.9, 309 CR.  Graham Cooley 341 no.16, 343 TL, 350 CC & BR, 351 BL & BC, 352 no.6, 353 no.11 & 14. Halcyon Days 84 TR & CL. Hall-Bakker @ Heritage 179 TR, 217 no.11. Hansen Sorensen 331 no.16. Hermann Historica OHG 100 BL. Herr Auctions 189 BR, 294 BL, 329 CR, 331 no.17, 340 no.6, 352 no.1, 361 CR, 378 BC, 388 CL. High Style Deco 273 TR, 274 no.2, 275 no.15, 302 no.5, 303 no.15. Holsten Galleries 372 C, 374 TR, 407 TR, 409 BL, 411 CL, 412 no.11, 413 no.17 & 18. Hope and Glory 93 TR. Hugo Ruef 30 BR. Imperial Half Bushel 123 BL.  Ingo Maurer 415 TR. Ingram Antiques 341 BL. The Interior Archive: Tim Beddow 315 TR; James Mortimer 150 BR, 250 CL; Fritz von der Schulenburg 55, 59 TR, 60 BL, 97 B, 195 TL, 239 TL, 244 BL; Ivey Selkirk Auctioneers 219 CR. Jacobs and Hunt Fine Art Auctioneers Limited 204 no.9. James D Julia Inc 118 BL, 121 BR,

183 TL, 208 BC, 209 TC, 210 BC & BR, 211 BR, 212 TR, 216 BR, 217 TL, TR & BR, 214 no.8. Jazzy 274 no.3 & 6.  Jeanette Hayhurst Fine Glass 73 BL & BC, 76 no.1, 5 & 6, 119 TR, 268 BL, 290 CR & BR, 292 no.11, 293 no.18. 343 TR & BR, 344 BR, 351 BR, 352 no.4, 412 no.6, 413 no.16. Jill Fenichell 111 BL & BR. Joe De Buck 276 TR. Johannes Vogt Auktionen 30 CC, 32 TR. John Bull (Antiques) Ltd 78 TC, 79 BC, 96 BR, 123 TR, 126 no.5, 6, 8 & 9, 127 no.13. John Howard @ Heritage 64 BR, 109 CR & BR, 181 no.19. John Jesse Antoques 254 BL, 271 BR, 281 TC, 294 BC, 296 BL. John King 296 TL. John Makepeace 384 no.5 & 8. MGM Mirage/Bellagio Hotel p.407 BL. John Nicholson 165 TR, 209 BCR, 257 BR, 328 TR, 312, 404 no.7. Sollo:Rago Modern Auctions 3 C, 7 CR, 249 TR, 252 CR & BR, 255 CR & BR, 256 CL, 273 TC, 274 no.5 & 10, 275 no.16, 276 TL, 284 no.4, 295 BC, 299 CR, 305 CR, 306 TR, 308 BC, 309 BR, 314 TR, 318 BL, 319 TL, TR, BL & BR, 320 CR & BL, 321 TR, CR, BL & BR, 324 TL, 326 TC & BC, 327 CR, 330 no.9, 331 no.19, 336 CL, 337 TR, 338 BR, 339 TR & CR, 355 TR,  355 TL, 357 TL, CC & BR, 358 no.8, 359 no.10, 366 TL & BR, 368 TR, 369 TL, 374 BR, 378 BL, 379 TR & BR, 382 TR, CL, BL & BR, 383 C, 384 no.2 & 7, 385 no.14, 390 BC, 391 BR, 392 TR, 393 CR, 396 TR, CR, BL & BR, 397 BC, 398 BL & BR, 400 BR, 404 no.1 & 2, 405 no.14, 16, 18 & 19, 409 TL, 415 TL & CC, 416 BR. Jonathan Horne 31 TL, 33 BC. Jonathan Wadsworth 47 TR, 134 TR & BR.  Junnaa & Thomi Wroblewski 228 BR, 229 CL, CR & BR, 262 TR, BL & BR, 263 TR, 307 CC & CR. Keller & Ross 334 BL & BC. Law Fine Art 32 CR, 54 TR, 64 TR, 68 CL & BL, 69 TL, 70 no.10, 71 no.11, 12, 14 & 15, 151 CR & BR, 156 no.3, 157 no.13. Lawrences Fine Art Auctioneers 113 CR. Leah Gordon Antiques 199 BR. Lennox Cato 105 no.10. Leo Kaplan Modern 407 TL. Liberty plc (liberty.co.uk) 157 no.15. Lili Marleen 259 TC, 271 CC, 274 no.11, 275 no.13. Lillian Nassau Ltd 259 BL, 290 BL, 291 CR, 293 no.14, 351 TR. Liz Moore (liz@lizm. eclipse.co.uk): 28 R. Lost City Arts 324 BR, 327 TL, 330 no.10, 313 TL. Luna 365 TC & CR, 395 TC. Lyon & Turnbull 27 TC, 42 TC & TR, 45 TC & TR, 46 BL, 54 BC, 62 no.5, 7, 63 no.12, 16 & 18, 93 BR, 98 BL, 101 CL & BL, 104 no.3, 4, 5 & 8, 105 no.11, 126 no.4, 145 BR, 151 BL, 157 no.11, 166 6 & 7, 175 BL, 176 BL, 180 no.4, 181 no.15 & 20, 182 BL, 184 BL & BC, 185 CC & BR, 195 BC, 197 BR, 204 no.2, 215 no.17, 226 TR & BR, 227 BR, 228 TR, 236 C, 238 BR, 242 TR, 248 BR, 251 TC & TR, 257 BR, 258 TR, 260 TR, 263 BR, 264 BC, 273 CC & BL, 282 BL, 284 no.5 & 7, 308 BR, 309 CC & BR, 329 BL, 354 BL, 368 BL, 385 no.18. Macklowe Gallery 1 C, 2 R, 7 CL, 171 BR, 177 BR, 188 BR, 192 TR & BL, 193 TL, TC BC & BR, 195 BR, 198 BL, 190 BL, 199 TR & BL, 200 TR & BL, 201 TR & BL, 201 TL & TC, 204 no.5, 208 BR, 212 BL & BC, 214 no.1, 215 no.12, 218 TR, BR & BL, 219 TR, CL & BR, 230 BR, 231 TL, BC & BR, 289 BR, 293 no.19. Mallett 40 BC, 61 BC. 62 no.10, 289 TC & TR. Manx National Heritage: 177 TR. Mary Evans Picture Library: 114 BL, 440. Mary Wise & Grosvenor Antiques 113 BL. Matali Crasset Productions 384 no.4. Meissen.de: 35. Memphis and Post 379 CL, 391 TL. Mike Weedon 168 CR, 206 BL, 214 no.4, 217 no.13. Moderne Gallery 275 no.14, 279 BC & BR, 284 no.9. 285 no.13, 292 no.10, 295 TCR & TR, 300 TR, 301 TR, 303 no.14 & 18, 331 no.12, 341 no.9, 357 CR. Modernism Gallery 273 TL, 274 no.1 & 9, 275 no.12. Mood Indigo 296 TR, 303 no.19, 334 TR. Mostly Boxes 82 CR. Mum Had That 332 CR, 334 BR, 343 BL & BC, 344 BL, 352 no.2 & 3, 353 no.16, 353 no.16, 361 BR. Nagel 59 BL, 92 CC, 168 CL. National Portrait Gallery, London: Lewis Morley 323 CRA. National Trust Photographic